The Migration Conference 2017
Programme and Abstracts Book

Compiled by Fethiye Tilbe, Ibrahim Sirkeci, Mehtap Erdogan

TRANSNATIONAL PRESS LONDON
2017

The Migration Conference 2017 - Programme and Abstracts Book
Compiled by Fethiye Tilbe, Ibrahim Sirkeci, Mehtap Erdogan

First Published in 2017 by TRANSNATIONAL PRESS LONDON in the United Kingdom, 12 Ridgeway Gardens, London, N6 5XR, UK.
www.tplondon.com

Transnational Press London® and the logo and its affiliated brands are registered trademarks.

Paperback

ISBN: 978-1-910781-68-5

Cover Design: Nihal Yazgan @nihalidea.com

Conference website: www.migrationcenter.org

CONTENT: SESSIONS AND TIMETABLE

The Migration Conference 2017
Programme & Abstract Book
23rd– 26th August
Harokopio University, Athens, Greece

Welcome by the chairs

We're pleased to welcome you to Harokopio University, Athens in August for the Migration Conference. The 5th conference in our series, the 2017 Conference is probably the largest scholarly gathering on migration with a global scope. Human mobility, border management, integration and security, diversity and minorities as well as spatial patterns, identity and economic implications have dominated the public agenda and gave an extra impetus for the study of movers and non-movers over the last decade or so.

Throughout the program of the Migration Conference you will find various key thematic areas are covered in about 400 presentations by about 400 colleagues coming from all around the world from Australia to Canada, China to Mexico, South Africa to Finland.

We are also proud to bring you opportunities to meet with some of the leading scholars in the field. Our line of keynote speakers include Saskia Sassen, Oded Stark, Giuseppe Sciortino, Neli Esipova, and Yüksel Pazarkaya.

The Migration Conference also offers training and development opportunities and participants are encouraged to register for workshops. Dilek Cindoğlu will be running a workshop on grounded theory while Jeffrey H. Cohen and Ibrahim Sirkeci will be leading the meet the editors session.

As usual we allow significant time to focus on the host country migration debates. Apostolos Papadopoulos, co-chair of the Conference will moderate the roundtable debate on Migration / Refugee Crisis and its Aftermath: Challenges for migration policy in Greece in the evening of the opening day.

We have maintained over the years, a frank and friendly environment where constructive criticism foster scholarship while being nice improves networks and quality of the event. We hope to continue with this tradition and you will enjoy the Conference and Athens during your stay. On the website, we have provided some key information about travel and tourism in Athens too.

Finally we welcome any comments and questions. Please do not hesitate to get in touch with us through the conference email (migrationscholar@gmail.com).

Ibrahim Sirkeci, Apostolos Papadopoulos and Jeffrey Cohen
The Migration Conference Chairs

Contact:
migrationscholar@gmail.com
@migration2017

Main Speakers:

Professor Saskia Sassen is a Dutch-American sociologist noted for her analyses of globalization and international human migration. She is Robert S. Lynd Professor of Sociology and Co-Chairs The Committee on Global Thought, Columbia University. Sassen coined the term global city. Her recent books are Territory, Authority, Rights: From Medieval to Global Assemblages (Princeton University Press 2008), A Sociology of Globalization (W.W.Norton 2007), and the 4th fully updated edition of Cities in a World Economy (Sage 2011). The Global City came out in a new fully updated edition in 2001. Her books are translated into twenty-one languages. She is currently working on When Territory Exits Existing Frameworks(Under contract with Harvard University Press). She contributes regularly to www.OpenDemocracy. net and www. HuffingtonPost. com

Professor Oded Stark is Distinguished Fellow at the Center for Development Research, University of Bonn, Distinguished Professor at the University of Warsaw, Adjunct Professor at the University of Tuebingen, and Distinguished Research Scholar at Georgetown University. He served as University Professor (Chair in Economic and Regional Policy) at the University of Klagenfurt and as Honorary University Professor of Economics at the University of Vienna, and prior to that as Professor of Economics (Chair in Development Economics) at the University of Oslo, and as Professor of Population and Economics and as the Director of the Migration and Development Program at Harvard University. He has written on applied microeconomic theory, development economics, population economics, the economics of migration, labor economics, evolutionary economics, urban economics, regional economics, welfare economics, and the theory of the firm. He is the author of the critically acclaimed books The Migration of Labor (Oxford and Cambridge, MA: Blackwell 1991 and 1993), andAltruism and Beyond, An Economic Analysis of Transfers and Exchanges Within Families and Groups (Cambridge: Cambridge University Press 1995 and 1999), and is the co-editor of the Handbook of Population and Family Economics (in Handbooks in Economics; Amsterdam: North-Holland 1997, and Beijing: Economic Science Press 2004). Oded Stark is Doctor honoris causa (University of Warsaw), a Humboldt Awardee, and a Presidential Professor of Economics (Poland).

Professor Giuseppe Sciortino teaches sociology at the University di Trento, Italy. He is the Chair of SMMS, the migration research center of Trento University. He has been visiting professor at Haverford College, Royal University of Phnom Penh, Yale University and Malmö högskola. He is the past chair of the Research committee 16 'Sociological Theory' of the International Sociological Association. Among its works, Great Minds. Encounters with Social Theory (with Gianfranco Poggi, Stanford UP) and Solidarity, Justice and Incorporation (with Peter Kivisto, Oxford UP). Professor Sciortino serves on the editorial board of Migration Letters and edited a special issue on "Survival Strategies of Irregular Immigrants" including selected papers from the 2010 World Congress of the International Sociological Association in Goteborg, Sweden. His research covers international migration, ethnic relations, social theory, and cultural Sociology.

Prof Jeffrey H. Cohen is Professor of Anthropology at Ohio State University, Columbus, OH, United States. His research focuses on three areas: migration, development and nutrition. Since the early 1990s he as studied the impact, structure and outcome of migration from indigenous communities in Oaxaca, Mexico to the US with support from the National Science Foundation. He has also conducted comparative research on Mexican, Dominican and Turkish migration. His work on traditional foods, nutrition and migration was supported by the National Geographic Society. In addition to ongoing work in Oaxaca, he is currently studying the migration of Mexicans to Columbus. Professor Cohen is authored and edited several books including Eating Soup without a Spoon: Anthropological Theory and Method in the Real World (2015), The Cultures of Migration: The Global Nature of Contemporary Mobility (2011), The Culture of Migration in Southern Mexico (2004), Conflict, Insecurity and Mobility (2016), Global Remittance Practices and Migration during the Economic Crisis and Beyond (2012). He is also co-editor of Migration Letters and Remittances Review journals while also serving on editorial boards of several others. He has co-chaired Turkish Migration Conferences and The Migration Conference since 2012.

Neli Esipova is the Director of Research for Global Migration and Regional Director for Gallup's World Poll for 29 Eastern European and former Soviet states. Esipova leads Gallup's research on global migration and global women's studies, and has managed more than 250 studies on various topics in Europe and Asia. She frequently shares insights from her research with international audiences and has presented at numerous well-being, gender, migration, positive psychology and leadership conferences. Esipova offers her clients extensive knowledge of former Soviet Union countries and migration, gender and experience in survey methodology. She has consulted with The World Economic Forum on survey implementation. Her clients have included the World Bank, the International Labour Organization (ILO), the International Organization for Migration (IOM), the Organisation for Economic Co-operation and Development (OECD), the Broadcasting Board of Governors, Office of International and Refugee Health, the Internal Revenue Service, TNK-BP, IRS and the Belgian Contact Point of the European Migration Network. Esipova is the coauthor of more than 100 published articles. As Director of Global Migration Research, Neli has been published in Migration Letters, the IOM migration research series, and she led the team that wrote the main chapter of IOM 2013 annual World Migration Report and IOM-Gallup report, How the World Views Migration, in 2015. She also led the team that wrote the 2017 ILO-Gallup report, Towards a better future for women and work: Voices of women and men."

Yüksel Pazarkaya is renowned Turkish novelist from Germany. Pazarkaya, born in Izmir in 1940, and moved to Germany to study at Stuttgart University, where he also worked as an assistant and lecturer between 1966 and 1979. He was a director of Turkish broadcasts at WDR Cologne Radio from 1986 to 2003. Pazarkaya won several literary awards in Germany and Turkey. He is considered as one of the most famous first-generation writers of the gastarbeiterliteratur. "Pazarkaya, who writes in Turkish and German and publishes in both countries, is seen as one of the pioneers of Turkish Deutschlandliteratur. His volume of poems Irrwege (Wrong Tracks, published in 1968) is one of the first literary explorations of the problems of foreign workers. The author went to Germany as a student in 1957 and witnessed the Turkish labour migration that started on a large scale in the 1960s. Confrontation with the extreme discrimination experienced by Turkish people motivated him to analyse his own image of Germany." (Sabine Fischer, in Encyclopaedia of Contemporary German Culture edited by John Sandford).

ORGANISING TEAM
Conference Chairs

❖ Prof Ibrahim Sirkeci, Regent's Centre for Transnational Studies, Regent's University London, United Kingdom
❖ Prof Apostolos G Papadopoulos, Department of Geography Harokopio University of Athens, Greece
❖ Prof Jeffrey H. Cohen, Department of Anthropology, Ohio State University, United States
❖ Prof Philip L Martin, University of California Davis, United States
❖ Prof Dr Gudrun Biffl, Danube University Krems, Austria

Conference Advisory Committee

❖ Prof Deborah Anker, Harvard Law School, Harvard University, United States
❖ Prof Petra Bendel, Friedrich-Alexander University of Erlangen-Nuremberg, Germany
❖ Prof Dr Gudrun Biffl, Danube University Krems, Austria
❖ Prof Jeffrey H. Cohen, Ohio State University, United States
❖ Prof Dr Ali Çağlar, Hacettepe University, Turkey
❖ Prof Elli Heikkila, Migration Institute of Finland, Finland
❖ Prof Liliana Jubilut, Universidade Católica de Santos, Brazil
❖ Prof Beatrice Knerr, University of Kassel, Germany
❖ Prof Sokratis Koniordos, University of Crete, Greece
❖ Prof Philip L Martin, University of California Davis, United States
❖ Prof Antonis Moissidis, Panteion University, Athens, Greece
❖ Prof Apostolos G Papadopoulos, Harokopio University, Athens, Greece
❖ Prof João Peixoto, ISEG, Universidade de Lisboa, Portugal
❖ Prof Nicholas Procter, University of South Australia, Australia
❖ Prof Andre de Carvalho Ramos, University of Sao Paolo, Brazil
❖ Prof Ibrahim Sirkeci, Regent's University London, United Kingdom

Transnational Organising Committee

❖ Prof Ibrahim Sirkeci, Regent's Centre for Transnational Studies, Regent's University London, United Kingdom
❖ Prof Apostolos G Papadopoulos, Department of Geography Harokopio University of Athens, Greece
❖ Prof Jeffrey H. Cohen, Department of Anthropology, Ohio State University, United States
❖ Prof Philip L Martin, University of California Davis, United States
❖ Dr Nirmala Devi Arunasalam, University of Plymouth, United Kingdom
❖ Dr Dionysis Balourdos, National Centre of Social Research (EKKE), Greece
❖ Dr Bharati Basu, Central Michigan University, United States
❖ Prof Dr Gudrun Biffl, Danube University Krems, Austria
❖ Dr Paolo Boccagni, University of Trento, Italy
❖ Prof Rajagopal Dhar Chakraborti, Calcutta University, India
❖ Dr Christos Chalkias, Department of Geography, Harokopio University, Greece

- Dr Martina Cvajner, Department of Cognitive Psychology, University of Trento, Italy
- Dr Deniz Eroglu-Utku, Trakya University, Turkey
- Dr Olga R. Gulina, RUSMPI- Institute on Migration Policy, Russian Federation
- Prof Liliana Jubilut, Universidade Católica de Santos, Brazil
- Prof Sokratis Koniordos, Department of Sociology, University of Crete, Greece
- Dr Amanda Klekowski von Koppenfels, University of Kent, Brussels School of International Studies, Belgium
- Dr George Kritikos, Harokopio University, Athens,, Greece
- Dr Vildan Mahmutoğlu, Galatasaray University, Turkey
- Dr Robert Douglas Manning, Prince Mohammad bin Fahd University, Saudi Arabia
- Dr Laoura Maratou-Alipranti, National Centre of Social Research (EKKE), Greece
- Dr George Mavrommatis, Harokopio University, Athens, Greece
- Dr Stefania Giada Meda, Università Cattolica del Sacro Cuore, Milan, Italy
- Dr Christos Michalakelis, Harokopio University, Greece
- Prof Antonis Moissidis, Panteion University, Athens, Greece
- Dr Despina Papadopoulou, Panteion University, Athens, Greece
- Prof João Peixoto, ISEG, Universidade de Lisboa, Portugal
- Dr Marjan Petreski, American College Skopje, School of Business Economics and Management, Macedonia
- Prof Nicholas Procter, School of Nursing and Midwifery, University of South Australia, Australia
- Dr Md Mizanur Rahman, University Brunei Darussalam, Brunei Darussalam
- Dr Muhammed Ali Al Ramadhan, Kuwait Institute for Scientific Research, Kuwait
- Prof Theodoros Sakellaropoulos, Panteion University, Athens, Greece
- Dr Bradley Saunders, Prince Mohammad bin Fahd University, Saudi Arabia
- Dr Paulette K. Schuster, Hebrew University Jerusalem, Israel
- Prof Giuseppe Sciortino, Department of Sociology, University of Trento, Italy
- Assoc Prof Dr Ali Tilbe, Namik Kemal University, Turkey
- Dr Fethiye Tilbe, Namik Kemal University, Turkey
- Dr Carla de Tona, Independent Researcher, Italy
- Dr Alexandra Tragaki, Harokopio University, Athens, Greece
- Dr Joanna Tsiganou, National Centre of Social Research (EKKE), Greece
- Dr Ahsan Ullah, University Brunei Darussalam, Brunei Darussalam
- Dr K. Onur Unutulmaz, Social Sciences University of Ankara, Turkey
- Prof Östen Wahlbeck, University of Helsinki, Finland & University College of Southeast Norway, Finland
- Dr Piyasiri Wickramasekara, Former Senior Specialist at ILO, Sri Lanka
- Dr Pınar Yazgan, Sakarya University, Department of Sosyology, Turkey
- Dr Mustafa Murat Yüceşahin, Ankara University, Department of Geography, Turkey
- Dr Welat Zeydanlioglu, Managing editor Kurdish Studies, Sweden
- Dr Sinan Zeyneloğlu, International Organisation for Migration, KRG, Iraq
- Dr Stavros Zografakis, Department of Rural Development and Economics, Agricultural University of Athens, Greece
- Dr Ayman Zohry, Egyptian Society for Migration Studies (EGYMIG), Egypt
- Ms Loukia - Maria Fratsea, Researcher, Department of Geography Harokopio University of Athens, Greece
- Ms Ülkü Sezgi Sözen, Albrecht Mendelssohn Bartholdy Graduate School of Law, Germany

- ❖ Ms Emilia Lana de Freitas Castro, University of Hamburg, Germany
- ❖ Gul Ince Beqo, UNIVERSITA' CATTOLICA DEL SACRO CUORE DI MILANO (ITALY), Italy
- ❖ Mr Froilan Tuccat Malit Jr, American University of Sharjah and Cornell University, United Arab Emirates
- ❖ Ms Mehtap Erdoğan, Deparment of Public Administration, Karadeniz Technical Universty, Turkey
- ❖ Mr Tove Lager, University of Kent, Brussels School of International Studies, Belgium
- ❖ Ms Çağla Azizoğlu, Volunteer, Turkey

Supporting Organisations
- ❖ Harokopio University, Athens, Greece
- ❖ University of California Gifford Center for Population Studies, USA
- ❖ Universität Hamburg, Germany
- ❖ Ohio State University Global Mobility Project, USA
- ❖ Danube University Krems, Austria
- ❖ Albrecht Mendelssohn Bartholdy Graduate School of Law, Germany
- ❖ Institut de Recherche, Formation et Action sur les Migrations, Belgium
- ❖ Migration Institute of Finland
- ❖ Regent's University Centre for Transnational Studies, UK
- ❖ EKKE - The National Center of Social Research, Greece
- ❖ Migration Center
- ❖ Hellenic Sociological Society
- ❖ Ria Money Transfers
- ❖ Remittances Review
- ❖ Migration Letters
- ❖ Göç Dergisi
- ❖ Kurdish Studies
- ❖ Journal of Gypsy Studies
- ❖ Border Crossing
- ❖ Social Cohesion and Development
- ❖ Transnational Press London, UK

Summary Programme

Conference Gala Dinner:

TMC 2017 GALA DINNER 20:30
Venue: To Parko Eleftherias
Address: Park Eleftherias, Vasilisis Sofias, Athens 115 21, Greece Website: http://www.toparko.gr

Conference Venue: Harokopio University, Eleftheriou Venizelou 70, Kallithea 176 71, Athens, Greece

The Migration Conference 2017 is hosted by Harokopio University Athens, Greece. The conference venue is Kallithea campus of Harokopio University Athens which is a very special place for several reasons. Harokopio University of Athens is a public university dedicated to promoting research and learning in a small, well focused set of intellectual areas. The university, situated in the centre of Athens and close to the Unesco World Heritage Centre of the Acropolis, originates from an educational institution that was first established in 1929 and gained the status of University in 1990. It takes its name from the national benefactor Panagis Harokopos.

The University's excellent campus facilities houses four academic departments, the central administration, the library, the IT centre and student advisory services. Harokopio University of Athens is located close to many important cultural sites of interest such as the Acropolis Museum, Thissio, Panathenaic Stadium (Kallimarmaron), Keramikos and the Benaki Museum.

The meeting will take place in Harokopio University campus in Kallithea. In the campus there are a library with reading rooms, lecture halls, computer training rooms, seminar rooms, IT research laboratories and training rooms for camera work and film editing.Registration, exhibition and poster sessions will be located next to the session halls/rooms.

Harokopio University, Eleftheriou Venizelou 70, Kallithea 176 76, Athens, Greece

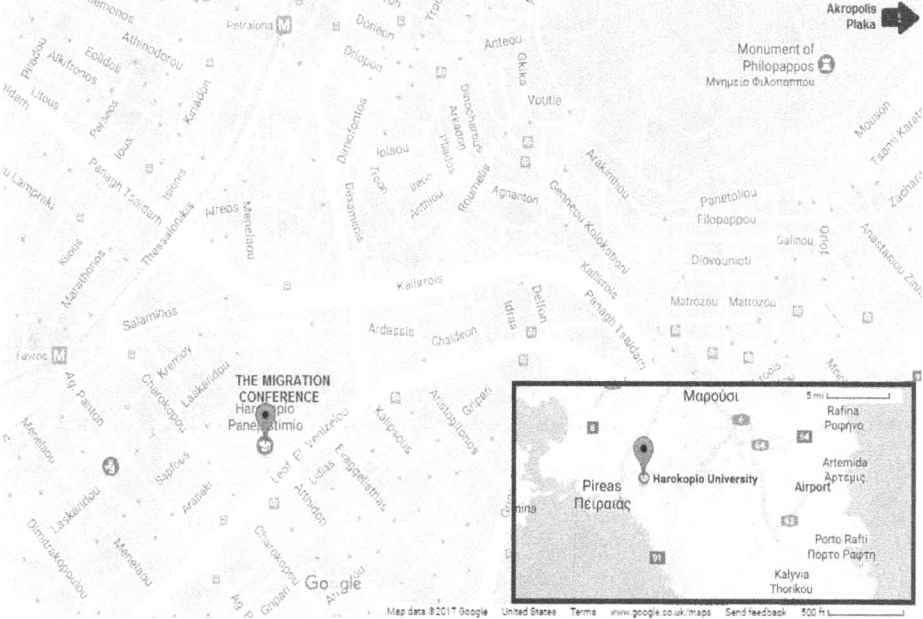

12:30-18:00	REGISTRATION DESK OPEN

14:00-17:00   **OPENING PLENARY SESSION I[Main Auditorium] WELCOMING SPEECHES**

Ibrahim **Sirkeci**, Regent's University London, UK
Mara N**ikolaidou**, Rector of Harokopio University, Greece
Apostolos **Papadopoulos,** Harokopio University, Greece
Invited Speeches
-   "Gallup World Poll Migrant Acceptance Index"
Neli **Esipova**, Gallup World Poll, USA

-   "The Other Side of Transnationalism. A Sociology of Disaffiliation"
Giuseppe **Sciortino**, University of Trento, Italy

-   "Migration when social preferences are ordinal: Steady state population distribution, and social welfare"
Oded **Stark**, University of Bonn, Germany

17:00-17:15	BREAK

17:15-19:00   PLENARY SESSION II **[Main Auditorium]**

Roundtable: Migration / Refugee Crisis and its
Aftermath: Challenges for migration policy in Greece
– Chaired by Apostolos **Papadopoulos**, Harokopio
University, Greece
-   Angelos Syrigos, Associate Professor of International Law and Foreign Policy, Panteion University, former Secretary General of Population and Social Cohesion.
-   Vassilis Papadopoulos, Lawyer, former Secretary General of Migration Policy.
-   Stathis Poularakis, Lawyer, Doctors of the World Greece.
-   George Tsiakalos, Professor of Education, Aristotelian University of Thessaloniki / Activist.
-   Ahmet Moavia, President of the Greek Forum of Migrants

SESSION 1A – Movers and Identities

	Room: A1
Chair	**Jeffrey H. Cohen, Ohio State University, US**
1123	'Where Are You From?' Negotiating Identities and Belonging among Second Generation African-Canadians. - **Gillian Creese**
1351	Cross-National and Transnational Lives of Refugees: "Bounded Mobility" of Syrians and Eritreans in Europe - **Irene Tuzi**
1022	Heterogeneous Ethnic Identities in a Diasporic Community - **Georgia Charpantidou**
1160	Transnational Living of Migrants with Dementia – **Hürrem Tezcan-Güntekin, Yudit Namer**

'Where Are You From?' Negotiating Identities and Belonging among Second Generation African-Canadians

(1123) Gillian Creese (University of British Columbia)

This paper explores the multiple meanings attributed to the query, 'where are you from', and its centrality to mediating identities and belonging among second-generation adults of diverse sub-Saharan African origins living in Vancouver Canada. Many people face questions when they are away from their home communities and differences of language, accents, or lack of familiarity with local conventions might lead to such conversations. For those who are racialized as Black in Vancouver, however, strangers asking 'where are you from' is an almost daily occurrence that signals they are not perceived to be at home even when they are home. This paper is based on interviews with young women and men whose parents migrated from countries in sub-Saharan Africa. For those who are born in or largely raised in Canada, queries about 'where are you from' signify that some bodies are out of place and need to account for their presence by recounting origins from somewhere else. I argue that the selective interrogation of origins routinely experienced by second generation African-Canadians is a discursive strategy that prevents many from claiming a Canadian identity, including people who have no memory of ever living anywhere else.

***

Cross-National and Transnational Lives of Refugees: "Bounded Mobility" of Syrians and Eritreans in Europe

(1351) Irene Tuzi (Sapienza University of Rome)

Today's forced migration flows arriving to Europe are utterly nonlinear, multi-directional and unsteady. Forced migrants do not move through a one-directional path from a sending country to a receiving country. Rather, they move across several international borders and are forced to stop in different geographic areas before reaching their final destination. Even once people arrive to Europe, their journey is not completed. The EU immigration laws, reception policies and system of distribution of asylum seekers among member States, force people to redesign their migration path along the way and to experience a multiple displacement. Within this context, this study examines two inter-related aspects of today's forced migration, which are worth to be studied in correlation – cross-national (im)mobility of refugees and transnational mechanisms arising among forcibly displaced people. The literature on transnationalism has largely neglected and understudied refugees, or it has only focused on their political activities (Al-Ali et al., 2001) as a diaspora. Starting from the assumption that migrants approaching Europe today are involved in what we call mixed flows, I assume that forcibly displaced people, just as economic migrants, undertake transnational activities which are able to affect those left behind. Mobilisation of transnational information and social remittances, such as

2

transmission of knowledge, skills and values can also contribute to later reconstruction (Ragab et al., 2017) and reconciliation. Cross-national displacement and "bounded mobilities" (Gutekunst et al., 2016) of refugees are contrived by EU hospitality, protection and border control policies. In this sense, the article gives an interpretation of means of allocation provided by Europe for forced migrants. In particular, it focuses on the schemes of resettlement (the transfer of displaced persons in need of international protection from a third country to a member State), relocation (the transfer of persons in need of international protection among member States), and humanitarian corridors (promoted by private and public institutions as an alternative measure of allowing safe transit of persons in need of protection). Tracing the experience and migration path of two of the largest refugee groups forcibly approaching Europe today – Eritreans and Syrians, I will develop my analysis by exploring how cross-border (im)mobility entails transnational mechanisms. Eritreans and Syrians are two very different communities, as for migration path, type and causes of migration. Yet, they have something in common – a nationality with a EU-wide average asylum recognition rate of 75% or higher and a bounded mobility in which they exist. These two communities move across several international borders and experience an intra-regional migration before undertaking an extremely risky international journey to Europe. The high rate of recognition gives them favoured access to asylum in many European countries. Though, the "regime of mobility" (Glick-Schiller et al. 2012) in which they live, limit their possibilities to cross borders and entails further challenges and displacements. This paper is the result of an analysis of literature on mobility and transnationalism as well as a qualitative study conducted in 2017 through semi-structured interviews with migrants, social workers and experts, in Italy, France and Germany. It lies on the idea that when people's mobility is bounded, they move their ideas, values and cultural heritage instead.
***

Heterogeneous Ethnic Identities in a Diasporic Community
(1022) Georgia Charpantidou (Panteion University)

Literatures on Greek diaspora have implied or supported that Community is the archetypal pattern of organization with common characteristics unchangeable through time and space. This approach, connected with the ideology of the homogeneity of Greek ethnicity, limits our understanding on the diversity of diasporic institutions and their internal and external evolving. This paper focus on the Greek Orthodox Community of Melbourne particularly in its foundation period at the end of the 19th century and the beginning of the 20th. It is based on research on primary archival resources of all involving state and ecclesiastical institutions which reveal the unmentioned so far, heterogeneous regional and ethnic identities of the immigrant Greeks in Australia. The antagonism over church administration issues and its property brought out differential ethnic identities between citizens of the Greek State and the Greeks subjects of the Ottoman Empire and divided them. Predominance of the first group resulted in the exclusion of any member of not Greek origin and the pursuit of protection of their church by the Greek State and Church. This study is part of a growing body of PhD project which concerns the evolvement and transformation of the Greek Community of Melbourne over its 116 years of existence aiming to contribute to the unexamined issue of Greek diaspora organization in the 20th century.
***

Transnational Living of Migrants with Dementia
(1160) Hürrem Tezcan-Güntekin (Bielefeld University), Yudit Namer (Bielefeld University)

Guest workers of Turkish origin who came to Germany as a result of binational recruitment agreements with the expectation to eventually return to their home country. Most labor migrants of Turkish origin decided to chose to lead a transnational lifestyle, however between Turkey Germany (Krumme 2003; Strumpen 2012). As the care needs of the first-generation migrants increase and mobility-competencies decrease with their age, they have to negotiate staying in the host country or returning to their country of origin (Sparacio 2016). The study asks how Turkish migrants with dementia and their families negotiate a transnational lifestyle and how the decision is reached regarding which country the person with dementia will continue living in as the disease progresses and travelling becomes more difficult. With a qualitative approach, interviews with seven family caregivers of Turkish people with dementia who pursued/pursues a transnational life are conducted. The interviews are analyzed with the hermeneutic method of Documentary Method (Bohnsack 2003). The analysis process explores the arrangement of the living environment in the home and the host countries and the constitution of the sense of home and allegiance by Turkish migrants with dementia and their families. Interlocking mechanisms of denial, changing levels of status between the two countries, persistence of gender and generational roles, anxiety regarding keeping up appearances appear to be recurring themes in migrants' families living a transnational lifestyle and facing the progression of dementia.

***

SESSION 1B – Migration in Frames

	Room: A2
Chair	**Deniz Ozalpman, University of Vienna, Austria**
1187	Language Differences and Home Visits in Accented Cinema -**Sandor Klapcsik**
773	'Good' versus 'Bad': Constructing Binary Oppositions in Yesilcam Cinema about Turkish Migration to Germany –**Deniz Güneş Yardımcı**
1118	Immigrant Female Killers in TV series: A Psychosocial Perceptive - **Anna Zaptsi**
1352	Representation of Migration in Science Fiction Movies: "District 9" - **Vildan Mahmutoglu**

Language Differences and Home Visits in Accented Cinema
(1187) Sandor Klapcsik (Technical University of Liberec)

This paper analyzes migrant and diasporic films which foreground the problematics of varying cultural skills, especially the different levels of language proficiency, in the immigrant families. Socio-psychological studies indicate that both the host country citizens and immigrants find the question of language fluency important (Scott, Scott & Stumpf 1989, 78-94). Studies confirm that first generation immigrants usually prioritize the culture and language of origin, while the second generation feels closer to the host society's culture and language (Anwar 1988). The varying degree of multilingual proficiency is observable not only in the different generations, but significant differences are also noticeable between siblings or spouses. These can easily result in family conflicts, as it becomes noticeable in several semi-autobiographical films, such as British Pakistani writer Ayub Khan Din's East is East (1999) and French North African Fatima Elayoubi's Fatima (2015). However, as Khan Din's West is West (2010), American Indian director Mira Nair's The Namesake (2006) and German Turkish Yasemin Şamdereli's Almanya – Willkommen in Deutchland (2011) indicate, the return migration of certain family members or a short visit to the home country may bridge the gaps between the different language levels and cultural skills, creating a more unified value system for the family. Thus, the major intra- and intergenerational conflicts are resolved or at least become alleviated.

***

Good' versus 'Bad': Constructing Binary Oppositions in Yesilcam Cinema about Turkish Migration to Germany
(773) Deniz Güneş Yardımcı (Royal Holloway University of London)

The representation of former Turkish guestworkers and the present Turkish diaspora in Germany in Turkish German cinema since the 1990s has attracted strong academic interest. Scholars such as Göktürk (1999), Burns (2006), and Berghahn (2012) have explored these films produced by second and third generation Turkish German directors like Fatih Akin, Thomas Arslan, and Ayse Polat in a broader context of European diasporic cinema and transnational cinema. The majority of scholars in the field of Turkish German cinema agree on a shift in the representation from a victimizing social worker perspective that puts emphasis on the hardship of being a guestworker in a foreign country in German cinema in the 1970s and 1980s, towards cinematic perspective that appreciates the heterogeneity of the Turkish diaspora and their cultural hybridity in Turkish German cinema since the 1990s. However, the perspective of Turkish cinema about Turkish external migration is so far a neglected academic field. Ömer Alkin (2015, 2016, 2017) and Ersel Kayaoglu (2011, 2012) are two of the few scholars, who have recently started to identify the relevant corpus of films and in particular approach thematic tendencies. This paper contributes to the newly emerging scholarship about Turkish external migration cinema by exploring how specific Yesilcam cinema conventions have influenced the representation of Turkish migration to Germany in Turkish cinema between the 1960s and 1980s. In doing so, I argue that Yesilcam's characteristic of constructing diverse binary oppositions, which are related to the prime conflict of good versus bad, have a vast impact on films about external migration and lead to a pessimistic depiction of Turkish emigration to Germany.

***

Immigrant Female Killers in TV series: A Psychosocial Perceptive
(1118) Anna Zaptsi (University of Seville)

The aim of this paper is to investigate immigrant female killers on five American television series, from a psychosocial perspective, broadcasted in Spain from 2000 to 2015. On the one hand, in light of contrasting the evolution and the increase of real female annihilators as an equalization matter between females and males in order to reveal the bias in fictional female characters, whenever they commit death crimes voluntarily, and, on the other hand, to raise awareness of the most common personality disorder that they tend to have. The selection of the research topic, responds to the striking impacts of the combination of media and psychology in human kinds and in society, and its power in establishing stereotypes of female gender, whenever female protagonists appear on the small screen. Whenever the television programs were focused on immigrants, it has been observed a massive employment of negative stereotypes assigned to the image of the immigrant in all series and a correlation between reality and fiction.

***

Representation of Migration in Science Fiction Movies: "District 9"
(1352) Vildan Mahmutoglu (Galatasaray University)

Genre films are commercial films that tell similar stories in similar conditions with similar characters. Genre films have common features and films are produced around these features. The analyze of science fiction cinema by splitting into periods enables us to understand the background of each period more clearly and establish a connection with the emergence conditions of films. In this study, the characteristics of science fiction cinema will be discussed by analyzing "District 9". Because, the science fiction cinema looks the future while it indicates today's world problems. "District 9" film differentiating from other science fiction films in terms of theme. As a science fiction film, "District 9" film brings a different perspective to the migration issue.

***

SESSION 1C – Migration and Security

	Room: SR 5
Chair	**Ibrahim Sirkeci, Regent's University London, UK**
1247	Establishing Feeling of Security for the People - **Süleyman Özmen**
936	Securitization of the "Migration Crisis" at the EU Level: Investigating Internal-External Security Nexus in the EU Policy Frames – **Maciej Stepka**
1254	Migration and National Security: a Multidisciplinary Conceptual Framework - **K. Onur Unutulmaz**
1025	The Expulsion of Greeks from Turkey in the early 1960s: Deportation as an Instrument of International Relations and National Formation - **Ibrahim Soysüren, Ali Haydar Soysüren, Ali Soysüren**

Establishing Feeling of Security for the People
(1247) Süleyman Özmen (Rumeli University)

Life is an illusion that shaped by our perception. This perception can be influenced by different factors and influence our behavior a human being. For example, social media can be used to create the illusion of fear or security in our modern world. Media could lead social developments and also clash similarly as we have seen in the Arap spring. Is security significant for human beings? According to Abraham Maslow's hierarchy of needs theory, security lies at the very basic level. Security is essential for human development. In this article, I will discuss the parameters of risk for security and human perception of security. As a conclusion, many people still suffer and can not fulfill their basic needs in regions of the world. We would constantly on associated with one another and answerable for one another. We need to be concerned and take an action to ensure the security of our world for the dignity of human being. Earth is like a human body. The conflict area is something like a cancerous region of the human body. As cancer spreads to the whole body, conflicts do too. The thing that unites us ought further to bolster a chance to be more excellent over what isolates us.

***

Securitization of the "Migration Crisis" at the EU Level: Investigating Internal-External Security Nexus in the EU Policy Frames
(936) Maciej Stepka (Jagiellonian University)

The "migration crisis" has profoundly tested the European Union's (EU) ability to cope with rapid and large-scale humanitarian crises. The dramatic events of 2015 and deaths of hundreds of migrants have put substantial pressure on the EU institutions and European governments to develop comprehensive policy responses and stabilize the situation on and beyond the EU borders (Carrera et al. 2015). Ever since, migration and asylum issues have become one of the highest priorities in the EU, engaging not only politicians but also experts, practitioners and academics. The so-called "migration crisis" has generated quite a momentum for research on topics related to migration, asylum, border control and humanitarism, to name a few (See: Cohen and Sirkeci 2016; Jeandesboz and Pallister-Wilkins 2016; Skleparis 2015). Nonetheless, it is security that has become one of the key concepts and points of reference while debating the crisis. It is not surprising as migration had already been (in)securitizied and commonly incorporated into security policies either at the EU or member state level (Huysmans and Squire 2010; van Munster 2009). In this paper securitization is understood as a process of integrating discursively and institutionally an issue into security frameworks that emphasize policing, control, and defense (Bourbeau 2015:395). In this regard, migration occupies a very specific place in the security realm, linking both internal (policing-based) and external (military-based) aspects and logics of security (Bigo 2000). This peculiar merger of the external and internal dimensions not only creates a very specific field of security but also generates certain conceptual tensions within it. While internal security focuses on risk-based logic, which relies on preventive actions and monitoring of internal vulnerabilities, external security utilizes more threat-based logic based on reactive-emergency measures and focuses on enemies and threats "from outside" (Bourbeau 2015:396). Such a situation affects problematization of the crisis and development of suitable and comprehensive policy responses that could address its root causes and alleviate its consequences. While many researchers observe that this cross-fertilization of domains occurs mainly in the field of practice (e.g. military vessels patrolling EU external border), internal-external security nexus can be also observed at the discursive level (Bourbeau 2014). This paper builds on this assumption and investigates tensions generated by internal-external security nexus in the process of securitization of the "migration crisis" at the EU political level. In doing so, it integrates frame-critical policy analysis and securitization theory in order to identify specific "storylines/sub-frames", which contain elements of external and internal security (Rein and Schön 1996; Watson 2012). In this way, it analyses how the EU institutions frame the crisis in terms of its main characteristics, root causes, moral evaluations and, finally, possible treatment. It also shows how specific elements and characteristics of the two domains are marginalized and/or empowered in the securitization process. The analysis is based on discourse analysis of the

EU political and strategic documents produced in response to the "migration crisis" as well as series of semi-structured interviews conducted with representatives of institutions involved in the development of EU policy responses. The fieldwork was funded by the National Science Centre, Poland – PRELUDIUM Young Talent Grant.

***

Migration and National Security: a Multidisciplinary Conceptual Framework
(1254) K. Onur Unutulmaz (Social Sciences University of Ankara)

While there has been a significant process in which issues of migration are increasingly considered to be matters related to security, i.e. 'securitization of migration', a comprehensive conceptual framework has yet to be created which addresses various relations and interactions of international human mobility and the ensuing ethnic, religious, and cultural diversity, on the one hand; and the transforming notions of national security, on the other. Moreover, existing literature is marked with a form of disciplinary exclusivity, which means that they focus their attention on a specific aspect of the migration/security nexus using the methods, theories, and terminologies of a single discipline. Lastly, the existing literature tends to have 'security-bias' as most of studies investigating the intersection of migration and security appears to prioritize security studies. This paper aims to contribute in the literature by attempting to bridge these three gaps. Firstly, it aims to provide a more general and comprehensive analytical and conceptual framework in which to discuss migration and security. In other words, instead of narrowly identifying its subject matter, it aims to provide a larger framework of discussion concerning migration/security nexus which include these and other points of relation. To briefly introduce, this framework involves such main headings as 'migration and terror', 'failure of integration and radicalization', 'failure of integration and marginalization', 'social polarization with growing racism and xenophobia', 'demographic trends', 'diaspora politics and transnationalism', and 'links with organized crime'. Secondly, instead of adopting the perspective and employing the tools of one discipline, it aims to benefit from a multidisciplinary gaze making use of literatures, theories, and methods of political science, sociology, anthropology, international relations, and psychology. And lastly, it attempts to make up for the security-bias in the field by equally emphasizing the migration-studies aspect.

***

The Expulsion of Greeks from Turkey in the early 1960s: Deportation as an Instrument of International Relations and National Formation
(1025) Ibrahim Soysüren (University of Neuchâtel), Ali Haydar Soysüren (University of Ardahan), Ali Soysüren (University of Marmara)

In order to understand better the deportation of foreigners, a constitutive element of migration policies, it is necessary to historicize and denaturalize (Walters, 2002) the uses of this practice (Soysüren, 2016). According to Cornelisse (2010), different forms of deportation have been used in the past to construct states, to protect and regulate wealth or to spread national ideology. For Anderson, Gibney and Paoletti (2011, 544), "Throughout history, expulsion and deportation have helped constitute societies and define as well as challenge norms of belonging". In his seminal work analysing the historical development of the deportation of foreigners in the United States, Kanstoom (2007: 6) affirms that "The current deportation system is best understood within a long historical frame". In the case of the United Kingdom, Cohen (1997) shows that deportation has constituted a tool against "others", even though the people included in this category have considerably changed throughout history. In his article on Germany, F. P. Weber (1996) shows how the use of deportation was gradually restricted to comprise only foreigners.

Until the 8th Century, German states had deported vagabonds and beggars regardless of their nationality. They gradually renounced the deportation of their "nationals" and agreed to readmit them during the first half of the 19th Century. The role of the distinction between foreigners and Germans, which has become clearer over time, must also be taken into account in this regard. However, the deportation of German nationals was still legally possible until 1934. Germany was obviously not the only state to deport nationals during the first decades of the 20th Century, as Arendt (1962) mentions Turkey amongst several other countries. Our paper will begin with a scientific literature review on different uses of deportation throughout history. Then, we will explain why and how Greek nationals, called établis, were deported, on the basis of articles collected in Cumhuriyet and Milliyet, two leading dailies, in addition to historical and social sciences studies. In the last part of the paper, we will analyse the context (the Cyprus question, the Cold War, the Greek minority in Turkey, nationalism and so on) in which this mass deportation took place. We will show that the expulsion of Greek nationals from Turkey in the mid-1960s corresponds to two different uses of deportation. The first, which is clearly displayed in the analysed materials, is its use as an instrument of international relations. The annulment of the Agreement on Residence, Trade and Movement between Turkey and Greece in 1964 and the mass deportation of Greek nationals were conceived as retaliation measures. They followed the Cypriot President Archbishop Makarios III's constitutional amendments, which the Turkish government considered to be contrary to the interest and legal status of the Turkish Cypriot minority. As for the second use of deportation, a historical analysis reveals that theses mass expulsions are the most recent use of deportation as an instrument for the creation of a homogeneous nation (Soysüren, Soysüren and Soysüren, 2016). However, they were certainly not the most notable examples. The Lausanne Convention of 30 January 1923 on population exchange forced more than 1.2 million Christians to leave Turkey for Greece and about 400,000 Muslims to Greece for Turkey. The Lausanne Treaty of 24 July 1923 aimed to secure their rights of minorities. However, from the beginning, it was clear that these minorities were not part of the homogenous nation project. The state implemented several measures which could push minorities to leave Turkey. Amongst these measures is the Law of 1932 on Arts and Services Allocated to the Turkish Citizens in Turkey, banning foreigners from occupying certain professions. The government also established forced labour camps for 18- to 45-year-old non-Muslim males and introduced the property tax in 1942. The Riots against the Non-Muslims of Turkey on 6-7 September 1955 pushed many of Greeks into leaving Turkey (Güven, 2011 and Soysüren, 2002). The annulment of Agreement mentioned above in 1964 is one of these measures against non-Muslim minorities. Following this, the Turkish government did not extend the residence permits of approximatively 12,000 Greek nationals and forced them to leave Turkey. Together with their family members, who had Turkish nationality, they were estimated to number 40,000. The conclusion of the paper will restate the outcomes of our analysis and briefly point out the changes in the uses of deportation in Turkey since the period considered, that is, the 1960s.

***

SESSION 1D – Gender and Migration in Turkey - 1

	Room: A5
Chair	**Lucy Williams, University of Kent, UK**
1173	Bitter Lives of Syrian Women Workers in Adana's Fertile Land: Gendering Syrian Migration in Turkey - **Saniye Dedeoğlu**
1099	How to Take Gender as an Analytical Category in Migration Research? Some Initial Reflections of the Turkish Experience – **Selmin Kaşka**

Bitter Lives of Syrian Women Workers in Adana's Fertile Land: Gendering Syrian Migration in Turkey
(1173) Saniye Dedeoğlu (Muğla Sıtkı Koçman University)

Turkey stands at the centre of migratory waves and has a long experience of migration as sending and receiving country. After the collapse of Soviet Union in the mid-1990s Turkey faced with increasing number of women migrants not as dependent on male migrants but as solo independent migrants playing an active role in international movements and labour migration. The profile of Turkey as a migrant receiving country has dramatically changed with the beginning of the Syrian crisis and Turkey now hosts the largest Syrian refugee community in the world. This also means that Turkey is hosting a large number of women and children from Syria. However, there is little information on women Syrian migrants in Turkey and how migration process affects the ways in which gender roles and ideologies played out in the Syrian community living in Turkey. This paper assesses Syrian women's work in the seasonal agricultural production in the province of Adana and how in return this affects the ways in which migration and women's agricultural work affect gender roles and relations in Syrian migrant community in Adana's fertile lands. By focusing on research findings collected in the summer of 2016 in Adana[1], the paper provides an overview of working and living conditions of women Syrian agricultural workers and their families. The migration patterns, the operation of the seasonal farm labour market, and the relationships between labour intermediaries and workers and living conditions endured in tent areas of Adana will be the topics covered. There will be also a discussion of women's experience of migration and its implications for changes in gender roles and relations.
***

How to Take Gender as an Analytical Category in Migration Research? Some Initial Reflections of the Turkish Experience
(1099) Selmin Kaşka (Marmara University)

As migration scholars, predominantly feminists, argue, migration has become feminised in the global migration era. Turkey has been experiencing the same trend since the beginning of 1990s. Since then Turkey has become a migration receiving country, but at the same time has become a host country for women migrants from different countries. This tendency has been immediately reflected in migration research in Turkey. Different scholars from different disciplines, and with different methodologies, have examined "gender" dimension of migration in Turkey, particularly with a reference to the migration experience of women migrants from the former socialist countries. However, as Erder and Yükseker argue, existing studies tend to focus on migrant women "rather than incorporating gender into the design and theorization of migration research". In this paper, I will first try to evaluate existing research on women migrants; asking to what extend they contribute to analyse "gender" in migration research. When doing this I will limit myself with the studies on the field of labour market. This evaluation will be drawn on a critical assessment of the existing studies asking, particularly, to what extent they look at the

---

[1] The study involved a questioner applied to the representatives of 266 Syrian migrant households living in tents areas in Adana which yielded information on 1662 individuals and in-depth interviews with employers, labour intermediaries, NGOs and public institutions and other related organisations.

migration regime of Turkey with a gender perspective. Following the same path, secondly, I will ask the peculiarity of migration flows of Syrians, in other words, why, after almost 5 years of migration experience, movements of Syrian women have not been reflected adequately in gender and migration research in Turkey.

***

Gendered Effects of Turkey's Asylum/Refugee Regime
(1097) Emel Coşkun (Duzce University)

Previous research shows that gender is a determining factor in asylum seeker/refugee women's experiences and women face different difficulties than men during their asylum application process and afterwards. The number of women asylum seekers and refuges has increased in the recent years. The number of Syrian refugees crossed the borders of Turkey to seek asylum has reached over 2,7 million in the mid of 2016 and half of them are women. The number of asylum seeker and refugee women aged between 18 and 59 is around 57,000 in Turkey according to UNHCR Turkey Office. Either in temporary protection or as asylum seekers refugee women might face similar difficulties in their stay in Turkey. They are given some conditional rights to live in Turkey such as limited access to health, education and social benefits for those who are registered and living in satellite cities or refugee camps in border cities as asylum seekers and refugees. This paper explores how the refugee regime in Turkey is gendered and how it affects women's experiences both during and after the asylum application process. Founded on empirical research with a qualitative methodology approach, I will focus on the experiences of individual asylum seeker women from different nationalities including Syria. I will seek answers for some questions as follows: In which circumstances women seek and access protection? Is the application process itself an accessible for women? What kind of difficulties women face during and after application process? What kind of protection women get from the refugee system in Turkey? Their experiences show that both the application process itself and keeping the asylum status is very difficult and involve in gendered risks for those individual asylum seeker women. Based on my preliminary interviews, I will argue that the restricted rules on refuges, gender neutral asylum processes and no support mechanisms for refugees structurally produce vulnerabilities for asylum seeker/refugee women in Turkey.

***

"So Far Too Close", Accounts of Social Workers in Working with Syrian Women in Turkey
(1014) Reyhan Atasü – Topçuoğlu (Hacettepe University)

The war in Syria has entered its seventh year. 4,812,993 refugees have left Syria to seek asylum in various countries. According to the March 2016 statistics of the UNHCR, 120,00 Syrian refugees are in Egypt, 256,000 in Iraq, 636,000 in Jordan, 1 million in Lebanon and 2,700,000 in Turkey. More than 890,000 Syrians have applied for asylum in Europe. The refugee influx has challenged neighboring states as well as European countries at the junction point of the protection of human rights, costs and the politics of identity. Within this context the relation between the welfare state of the host countries and refugees is very challenging for both sides. It is challenging for the welfare states, which are generally structured to serve to citizens according to different conditionalities mostly depending on work. Moreover, the interaction between people and welfare regimes consists of trickly political aspects including citizenship, gender regimes, kinship regimes, work orientation, family orientation, and also patriachal or democratic approaches of the states. Migration possesses challenges in all these areas. On the other hand, getting in touch with the welfare system - meaning access to shelter, safety, health, education and social aid – is, all in all, a matter of survival for most of the Syrian refugees, who had to flee from their homes and hence have very limited financial and social resources. Whether they are working in public social services and/or NGOs, social workers are the very people who are enabling and also practicing this critical relation. Hence their attitude towards Syrians is very important in the provision of social services and in relating them with the welfare regimes. This paper will analyze the above-mentioned welfare systems and the migration challenge with the example of Syrians in Turkey, and will review the governmental response to the 'Syrian refugee crisis' in terms of the welfare state and social services in theory. It will then provide some insight into the actual practice via analysing the accounts of social workers dealing with Syrian women in Turkey. The study is qualitative research, based on in-depth interviews with social workers actively working with Syrians in different organizations in Ankara. Interviews are analysed in the following categories: difficulties in working with Syrians, due to limitatiosn of policy and infrastructure; due to cultural dirrerence, social workers' perceptions of Syrians, attributed meanings to femininity in the context of migration and need, different interests in promoting gender equality, identifying needs and trust relations between social workers and women.

***

SESSION 1E – International Migration Law and Policy

	Room: B1
Chair	**Ülkü Sezgi Sözen, University of Hamburg, Germany**
811	A Review of Labour Rights Protection for Migrant Fishermen in Distant Water: Case of Taiwan - **Lichuan Liuhuang**
807	EU's Responses to Refugee Crises from early 1990s to mid-2010s: Evolution of the Temporary Protection Regime - **H Deniz Genç, N Aslı Şirin-Öner**
1353	Discussions and Researches on the Legal Nature of Migration Law: A Common Taxonomy Given by Brazilian, German and the European Union Law? - **Emilia Castro**
1270	Implications of the European Union-Turkish Migration Agreement for the Slovak Domestic and Foreign Policy – **Barbora Olejárová**

A Review of Labour Rights Protection for Migrant Fishermen in Distant Water: Case of Taiwan

(811) Lichuan Liuhuang (National Chung Cheng University)

"Leave home happily and return home safely!" is a traffic slogan; but it also expresses the basic hope of migrant workers working abroad. There are two recruitment forms for foreign fishermen employment in Taiwan; one is inshore hiring in accordance with the Employment Services Act while the other one is offshore hiring; meaning that the foreign crew shall be "hired onto and dismissed from fishing vessels in foreign ports". The fishermen who opt to use the offshore hiring system are excluded from any fundamental legal protection while working conditions on board are based on labour contract. This fragile administrative framework has become Taiwan's national policy, which opened the legal access for fishing vessels in distant waters to hire migrant workers. Such a contract is merely a piece of document, which cannot be monitored or enforced by law and with nowhere for the worker to file a complaint. In recent years, there have been numerous cases including maritime violence, ship owner abandoning crewmen in a foreign port after being accused of engaged in IUU fishing (illegal, unregulated, unreported), foreign fishers falling overboard, missing or dead due to violence and abuses on board, bloodshed events at sea, and so forth. Factors behind the "racing-to-the-bottom" fishing business model are as the following; 1.   The hierarchical operations using migrant fishermen as the main labour force and nationality based wage frequently induce class conflict and violence on board; 2. The high cost of coming to Taiwan may subject them to become debt- bonded slave labourers; 3. False reporting of catch records, illegal catching, and unregulation of IUU fishing (illegal, unreported and unregulated fishing) conspires with unfair working conditions; 4. Non-skilled migrant fishermen lack occupational safety and health facilities, standard operating procedures and educational training leading to falling overboard or missing; 5. Forced labor and maritime violence to seek profit maximisation or cost savings. Recommendations to the parties of government, transnational seafood trader and international society are listed as follows; 1. Taiwan has long been excluded from the supervision of the International Labour Standards since 1971. However, being an economic, social and fishing entity, Taiwan government should bear her own international responsibility in respect of international legal instruments. Taiwan is a major power of distant water fishing, and the government shall not ignore migrant workers' fundamental right to life being unprotected in the territory of Taiwan. International, regional and bilateral cooperation should go beyond political boundary and put social sustainability as the core. 2. The Executive Yuan (the Cabinet) should provide a concrete response to the implementation measures of relevant labour laws and regulations for offshore hired migrant fishermen, such as augmenting a labour chapter for fishing workers with referring to the ILO Convention Work in Fishing, C188, in the Labor Standards Act, to ensure the rights and interests of local and migrant fishermen. 3. How to transform the fishing supply chain into value chain will rely on multi-stakeholders keeping dialogue and making fishing workers organized and voice heard.

***

EU's Responses to Refugee Crises from early 1990s to mid-2010s: Evolution of the Temporary Protection Regime

(807) H Deniz Genç (Istanbul Medipol University), N Aslı Şirin-Öner (Marmara University)

Faced with large number of displaced persons, the international community has been making use of temporary protection more and more as a remedy in order to act rapidly and provide protection to these people. Temporary protection appears to be an important option when a country faces a mass influx of asylum-seekers. It may be considered as an intermediate step in the process of finding a durable solution for the displaced persons. Being far from a conflict-free area, Europe has been facing refugee crises from time to time and the European states have been providing temporary protection to those people in need. Temporary protection is, at the same time, a crucial element of the EU's response to the refugee crises. The crises in the 1990s, particularly the Bosnian and Kosovar ones, showed the need for special procedures to tackle with mass influxes of displaced persons. Based on this need, the EU mapped out the basics of temporary protection, which culminated in the adoption of the Temporary Protection Directive in 2001. In other words, the 2001 Directive was the Union's concrete response to this need. This paper examines the EU's response to refugee crises in the last two decades with a particular focus on the practice of temporary protection. After elaborating on the eulogies and criticisms about the temporary protection, the paper scrutinizes the Union's practice in five refugee crises, namely Bosnia (1992-95), Libya (2011), Tunisia (2011), Ukraine (2014) and Syria (2011 – ongoing). As it examines the theoretical and the historical context of the temporary protection as well as the EU's application of it in five major refugee crises, the paper presents the genealogy of the EU's Temporary Regime and it provides a fertile ground to discuss its future in providing protection.

***

Discussions and Researches on the Legal Nature of Migration Law: A Common Taxonomy Given by Brazilian, German and the European Union Law?

(1353) Emilia Castro (Universität Hamburg)

In this work, it will be conducted an analysis explaining how Migration Law is seen both under Brazilian Law and German Law, this last one analyzed under the context of the European Union Law. The goals of this paper are to (i) identify – through Comparative Law - the differences of treatments given to Migration Law in these abovementioned juridical orders, as well as to, with the help of Transnational Law and cosmopolitanism theories, (ii) try to give Migration Law a new taxonomy. After all, depending on the juridical order in which Migration Law is inserted, several names and different treatments can be attributed to the same social phenomenon, namely migration. This paper tries to prove that, depending on the classification given to Migration Law, the phenomenon of migration can be seen under a perspective which – not always – fits to the necessities of migrants, but to the necessities of the host States. In Brazil, Migration Law is classified and studied under the name of "the legal status of the aliens", which corresponds to (1) the entrance of the foreigner in the Brazilian territory; (2) the rights of the foreigners inside the Brazilian territory; and (3) the compulsory departure of a foreigner from the Brazilian territory. According to Brazil's legal tradition, the scope of Private International Law includes the following subjects: (1) nationality; (2) legal status of foreigners; (3) conflict of laws; (4) and conflict of jurisdictions. Migration Law in the European Union may be classified in accordance with the legal nature of the European Union. The European Union´s peculiarity relies on its supranationality. Under this context, in Germany, Migration Law is part of national public law, from which Administrative Law is a specific field of study, and Migration Law belongs to the special part of Administrative Law. Administrative Law in Germany can have many subdivisions and Migration Law (Ausländerrecht) is related to one of them. Migration Law could be then classified under a specific field of Administrative Law, namely Public Order Law and Inspection Administrative Law, which are responsible for the organization of the State and for the protection of the citizens, as for example Police Law. After analyzing the legal based explanations for several classifications attributed to Migration Law, it could be possible to conclude in this paper that classifying Migration Law as a Private International Law object does not seem to be as obsolete as it is normally proclaimed. In this context, it could be stated that Migration Law consists of a melting pot, classified either as Private International Law, Public International Law, Administrative Law, Refugee Law, Supranational Law, or as many as other possible classifications, depending on the case law in which a migrant is inserted. Under this perspective, the article proposes to build a new concept, classifying again Migration Law and giving it the name of Transnational Law of Human Mobility, where human beings are the main characters, who are entitled to all legal protection needed. This new classification can be reached not only by analyzing the taxonomy of Migration Law under Brazilian and German law, but also by discussing migration under the perspective of cosmopolitanism.
    ***

Implications of the European Union-Turkish Migration Agreement for the Slovak Domestic and Foreign Policy

(1270) Barbora Olejárová (Matej Bel University)

The Slovak Republic is not located on the main migratory routes of people from the third-countries on their way to Western Europe and the state itself has never become final destination for irregular migrants or asylum seekers. Despite this fact, the crisis of migrants coming from the Middle East and sub-Saharan Africa significantly influenced both Slovak domestic and foreign policy and created unprecedented dichotomies between Slovak internal and international stance towards the issue, generating impression that Slovakia is playing both ends. Main aim of the paper is to provide evidence of how intensively can migration waves affect even those countries that are neither source countries nor transit or final destination countries for the migrants. The paper presents position of the Slovak Republic on the ongoing migration crisis and the EU solutions including the deal with Turkey and explains the dichotomy among the opinion of the general public and political leaders on one hand and the official stance country presented as the presiding country of the Council of the EU on the other hand, providing evidence that the argumentation lines of both sites were not as diverse as presented and proved to be right from the long-term perspective.

***

SESSION 1F – Göç ve Politika

	Room: B2
Chair	**Pınar Yazgan, Sakarya University, Turkey**
760	Almanya'da Aşırı Sağ Hareketler ve Medyanın Suçlu Göçmen Söyleminin Resmi Belgeler Işığında İncelenmesi-**Soner Tauscher**
1004	Diasporadan Alevilerle İşçi Sınıfını "Musahip" Yapma Çabası: Kavga/Kervan Dergilerinde Alevilik -**Tuncay Bilecen**
1080	Kıbrıslı Türklerin Göçmen Algısı – **Fikret Topal, Bünyamin Bezci, Soner Tauscher**
1292	Kapitalizmin Yeni Evresinde Göç Politikaları ve Aşırı Sağın Yükselişi - **Bünyamin Bezci**

Almanya'da Aşırı Sağ Hareketler ve Medyanın Suçlu Göçmen Söyleminin Resmi Belgeler Işığında İncelenmesi
(760) Soner Tauscher (Sakarya University)

Avrupa ülkelerinin alışık olduğu düzenli işçi göçü ve kontrollü sığınmacı alımı Suriye iç savaşının üst düzeye ulaştığı 2013/2014 yılından itibaren önemli bir değişim göstermektedir. Avrupa Birliği, kuruluşundan bu yana en yoğun mülteci göçüyle karşılaşmaktadır. Yaşanan bu kontrolsüz ve zorunlu göçe Avrupa toplumları ve devletleri hazırlıksız yakalanmıştır. Mülteci krizini ekonomik olarak fırsata çevirmek isteyen Almanya ise göçmenler için 2015 yazından itibaren açık kapı politikası uygulamaya başlamıştır. Ancak uygulanan açık kapı politikası Alman toplumunun azımsanmayacak bir kesiminde mültecilere ve Müslümanlara yönelik ağır ve şiddetli bir karşı kampanya ortaya çıkardı. Mülteciler ve Müslümanlar aşırı sağ toplumsal hareketlerin gösterilerinde "tecavüzcü", "işgalci", "kriminal dolandırıcılar" vb. sıfatlar ile birlikte anılmakta, medya da bu söylemlerin taşıyıcılığını yaparak kamusallaşmasını sağlamaktadır. Böylece aşırı sağı desteklemeyen, apolitik, ya da sığınmacılara karşı hoşgörülü davranan toplum kesimlerinde kamuoyu oluşturularak sığınmacı ve göçmenlere karşı olumsuz algı gündemde tutulmakta, politik olanın merkezine yerleştirilmektedir. Bu çalışmada öncelikle göçmenlere karşı aşırı sağ toplumsal hareketlerin oluşturduğu olumsuz söylemin McCombs ve Shaw'un gündem belirleme kuramı (Agenda Setting Function) bağlamında medya tarafından siyasetin merkezine nasıl oturtulduğu tartışılacaktır. Ayrıca gündemde tutulan mültecilere yönelik olumsuz söylemin gerçeği yansıtıp yansıtmadığı, göçmenlerin ve sığınmacıların biyolojik Almanlardan daha çok suça meyilli olup olmadığı oluşturulan soyut söylemlerden ziyade Almanya İçişleri Bakanlığı'nın yıllık olarak yayınladığı Emniyet Suç İstatistikleri temel alınarak incelenecektir.
***

15

Diasporadan Alevilerle İşçi Sınıfını "Musahip" Yapma Çabası: Kavga/Kervan Dergilerinde Alevilik

(1004) Tuncay Bilecen (Kocaeli University)

Kavga/ Kervan dergileri, (Yayın hayatına Kavga olarak başlayan dergi 22. sayıdan itibaren Kervan ismiyle çıkıyor) Türkiye Komünist Partisi'nin (TKP) Londra kanadı tarafından Mart 1991 – Aralık 1998 tarihleri arasında 71 sayı yayımlanmıştır. Derginin düşünsel yapısının oluşmasında 1970'li yıllarda politik sebeplerle Türkiye'yi terk etmek zorunda kalan Rıza Yürükoğlu'nun (Nihat Akseymen) katkısı büyüktür. Kavga/ Kervan dergileri Alevilik meselesini çeşitli boyutlarıyla tartışmaya açarken, Alevilikle sosyalizm arasında tarihsel, sınıfsal ve diyalektik ilişkiler kurmuş, Alevi kimliğinin tanınması ve Alevilerin sosyalist mücadele saflarına çekilmesi için mücadele vermiştir. Bu çalışmada, söylem analizi yöntemi kullanılarak Kavga/ Kervan dergilerinin Alevilik ve sosyalizm arasında kurduğu ilişki irdelenecek, derginin diasporada Alevi kimliğinin oluşmasındaki etkisi üzerinde durulacaktır. Bildirinin iddiası, derginin gerek 1990'lı yıllarda Türkiye gündemini yorumlarken gerekse Alevilerin sorunlarını tartışırken Türkiye ve diasporada Alevi kimliğinin oluşmasına katkı sağladığı yönündedir.

***

Kıbrıslı Türklerin Göçmen Algısı

(1080) Fikret Topal (Sakarya University), Bünyamin Bezci (Sakarya University), Soner Tauscher (Sakarya University)

1950'lerden bu yana Kıbrıs içerisinde Türkler ve Rumlar arasında yaşanan çatışmaların artması ile Türkiye'nin adaya müdahalesi gerçekleşmiş ve "1974 Kıbrıs Harekâtı" ile adadaki siyasi yapı değişerek 1983 yılında "Kuzey Kıbrıs Türk Cumhuriyeti" adıyla nihayete eren bir sürece evrilmiştir. Bu bağlamda 1974 yılındaki müdahaleden sonra sadece siyasi yapı değil toplumsal yapı da değişmiştir. Öncelikle adanın bölünmesiyle karşılıklı nüfus mübadeleleri gerçekleştirilmiş, ardından Kuzey Kıbrıs'a Türkiye'den göç gerçekleşmiştir. Oluşan bu sosyoloji ile Kuzey Kıbrıs'ta Kıbrıslı Türk (Yerli Türk), Türkiyeli Türk, Rum ve Kıbrıslı gibi farklı tanımlamalar ortaya çıkmıştır. Tüm farklı gruplara ilaveten son yıllarda sayıları gittikçe artan üniversite öğrencileri de eklenince Kıbrıs'taki toplumsallık karmaşık bir yapı oluşturmaktadır. Bu yapı özellikle siyasetin 90'lı yıllardan itibaren kimlik eksenli tanımlanması ile beraber, "Kıbrıs sorununda" toprağa dayalı federasyon fikrinin kimliğe dayalı bir federasyon fikrine evrilmesine de yol açmıştır. Bu karmaşık yapı içerisinde, Kıbrıs'ın toplumsallığı açısından Kıbrıslı Türklerin kendilerini ve diğer grupları nasıl tanımladıkları önem arz etmektedir. Bu kapsamda yapılan bu çalışmada da Kıbrıslı Türklerin, Türkiyeli Türk, Rum ve Öğrenciler gibi göçmen gruplar üzerindeki algısı ölçülmeye çalışılmıştır. Bunun için bir nicel araştırma hazırlanmıştır. Basit rastlantısal yöntemle seçilen örneklem üzerinden yapılan nicel araştırmada sosyo-demografik değişkenlere ek olarak kültürel, ekonomik, güvenlik içerikli sorular da sorulmuştur. Araştırmada Kıbrıslı Türklerin göçmen algısının yaş, eğitim durumu ve gelir durumu gibi değişkenler üzerinden farklılaştığı görülmektedir.

***

Kapitalizmin Yeni Evresinde Göç Politikaları ve Aşırı Sağın Yükselişi

(1292) Bünyamin Bezci (Sakarya University)

Dünya tarihinde Devletin yanında toplum ve piyasa entiteleri modern dönemlerde ayrı anlamlar kazanmıştı. Kojin Karatani kendi bağlamında dünya tarihinin üretimin örgütlenmesiyle değil mübalenin örgütlenme biçiminin değişimiyle anlaşılması gerektiğini iddia etmektedir. Karşılıklık esasına dayalı mübadele, yönetene iteata dayalı mübadeleye ve o da karşılıklı rızaya dayalı mübadeleye dönüşerek dünya tarihi ilerlemektedir. Devlet, toplum ve piyasa bu mübadele seyrinin somut karşılıklarıdır. Ona göre son zamanlarda karşılıklılığa dayalı mübadeleye yeniden dönüş yaşanmaktadır. Karatani hiç kastetmemiş olsa da son yıllarda yaşanan aşırı sağın yükselişi bu tarihsel gelişimin izdüşümü olarak okunabilir. Şöyle ki Devletlerin tek siyasal varlık biçimi olduğu antik çağlarda yağmaya dayalı mübadele tek topluluklar arası ilişki biçimiydi. Bu anlamda sömürgeciliğin ilk dönemleri de farklı değildir. Fakat Toplum adını verdiğimiz entite societas juristus karşısına sociatas civilis olarak çıktığı Roma'dan Uluslar çağına kadar geçen sürede Devletten özerkliğini kazanmıştır. Bugün aşırı sağda gördüğümüz eğiliminlerin çoğu toplulukların kutsanması dönemine aittir. Oysa Adam Smith'den bu yana Piyasa olgusu hem özgürlükler alanını güçlendirmişti hem de küreselleşmeyi tetiklemişti. Neoliberalizm toplum ve piyasayı güçlendirip devleti sınırlarken göç politikalarını da insani ve ekonomik bağlama oturtmuştu. Bugün ise olan piyasaların yeniden topluma doğru kapanmasıdır. Bu kapanmanın sonucunda özgürlükler alanı doğal olarak daralmakta ve toplumsal kutsalın dar milliyetçi ve faşist kalıpları tekrar anlam kazanmaktadır. Bu kapanma süreci ekonomik gerekçeler bağlamında ve piyasanın güçleri tarafından durdurulamazsa yağmanın mübadele biçimi olduğu Devlete geri dönüş yaşanacak gibi görünmektedir. Bu sunumda Karatani'den mülhem bir göç ve aşırı sağ politikaları okuması yapılacaktır. Fakat Karatani'nin sorun alanı değil, aşırı sağın yükseleşi ve göç politikalarındaki insani değerlerin askıya alınışı eleştirel olarak ele alınacaktır.

***

SESSION 1G – Göç ve Edebiyat - 1

	Room: B3
Chair	**Hanife Nalan Genç, 19 Mayıs University, Turkey**
1065	Bir Sanal Göç Kuramı Denemesi: Dijital Oyuncu Göçleri - **Sait Gülsoy**
1236	'Göç Kültürü ve Çatışma Modeli' Yötembilimi Bağlamında Bir Göç Romanı İncelemesi: Mathias Enard'ın Hırsızlar Sokağı - **Ali Tilbe**
1064	Kemaliye(Eğin) Türküleri ve Manilerinde Gurbet Teması: "İstanbul Dedikleri, Şekerdir Yedikleri"– **Hülya Doğan**

Bir Sanal Göç Kuramı Denemesi: Dijital Oyuncu Göçleri
(1065) Sait Gülsoy (Ataturk University)

Basit ifadesiyle çevre değişimi olarak tanımlanabilecek göç olgusu hem hayvanların hem de insan topluluklarının bir bakıma tarihsel bir bakıma da biyolojik kaderidir. Ekonomik, toplumsal, siyasi sebeplerle bireylerin veya toplulukların ülke içerisinde bir yerleşim yerinden başka bir yerleşim yerine veya bir ülkeden başka bir ülkeye, gitme edimi olarak özetlenebilecek göç olgusu, sosyal bilimlerin statik ve dinamik kavrayışlarını aşkın bir olgudur. Göç, pek çok yaşamsal dinamik tarafından bazen mecbur kalınan bir yerinden edilme durumu bazen de yaşam cazibesi olarak tercihen yeni bir çevreye taşınma durumu olarak biçimlendirilir. Göçe sebep olan mevcut yerleşim yerinden iten, hedef yerleşim yerine çeken sebeplerden söz etmek mümkündür ancak göç ediminden temel beklenti her halükarda 'daha iyi bir yaşam' isteği ya da umudu olmaktadır. Sosyal gerçeklikle biçimlenen ve tarihsel bağlamda sosyal yapıları biçimlendiren göç olgusu, teknolojinin gelişimi ile sanal zaman mekânda, sanal mecralarda da gerçekleşmektedir. Tercih edilen bir sanal mecranın terki ya ondan uzaklaşmakla ya da bir alternatif sanal mecraya geçmekle sonuçlanmaktadır. Kullanılan bir programın arayüzünün, oynanan bir oyunun haritasının değişmesi de bir bakıma sanal mekânın değişmesi anlamına gelmektedir. Bu çalışmada, sanal zaman mekânda göç kavramı merkeze alınarak, kültür yapıcı olan oyun oynamanın sanal zaman mekânda, göç kavramını dijital oyun oyuncuları üzerinden nasıl kurguladığı, örneklerle, kavramsal ve kuramsal olarak tartışılacaktır.

***

'Göç Kültürü ve Çatışma Modeli' Yötembilimi Bağlamında Bir Göç Romanı İncelemesi: Mathias Enard'ın Hırsızlar Sokağı[2]
(1236) Ali Tilbe (Namık Kemal University)

Günümüz dünyasında göç olgusu her geçen gün daha fazla gündemde yer almakta, siyasal, toplumsal ya da daha çeşitli düzeylerde gerçekleşen gerilim ve çatışmaların sonucunda bireysel, ailesel ya da kitlesel yer değiştirmeler gerçekleşmektedir. Bu devinimler çeşitli ekinsel ve toplumsal alanlarda her yönüyle tartışılmakta, bu tartışmanın yapıldığı en etkili alanlardan birisini de, çağına tanıklık eden çağcıl yazarların kurmaca anlatıları oluşturmaktadır. Buna karşın yazın alanında göç araştırmaları istene düzeyde gerçekleşmemektedir. Biz bu çalışmada daha önceki kongrelerde, İbrahim Sirkeci ve Jeffrey H. Cohen'in Çatışma ve Göç Kültürü Modeli'nden devinimle geliştirdiğimiz ve ilk incelemelerini Göç Üzerine Yazın ve Kültür İncelemeleri adlı ortak yapıtta yayımladığımız çatışma temelli göç yazını inceleme yöntembilimimizle çağdaş Fransız yazarlardan Mathias Enard'ın, Faslı bir genç olan Lackhtar'ın Tanca'dan başlayan ve karşı kıyıda İspanya-Barselona'da süren göç serüvenini öyküleyen Hırsızlar Sokağı adlı romanını incelemeyi erek ediniyoruz.

***

Kemaliye(Eğin) Türküleri ve Manilerinde Gurbet Teması: "İstanbul Dedikleri, Şekerdir Yedikleri"
(1064) Hülya Doğan (Atatürk University)

En yalın ifadeyle; ekonomik, toplumsal, siyasi sebeplerle bireylerin veya toplulukların bir ülkeden başka bir ülkeye, bir yerleşim yerinden başka bir yerleşim yerine gitme işi olarak tanımlanan göçün tarihi insanlık tarihi kadar eskidir. Göç, yaşanılan yerden kaynaklanan itici nedenlerle gerçekleşebileceği gibi, gidilecek yerden kaynaklanan çekici nedenlerle de gerçekleşebilir. Göç hangi nedenle gerçekleşirse gerçekleşsin gidenlerin ve kalanların yaşamlarında izler bırakır. Erzincan ili sınırları içerisinde yer alan, Yukarı Fırat'ın dar vadisi üzerinde kurulmuş olan Kemaliye(Eğin)'den göçün tarihi resmi kayıtlarda 18. yüzyıla kadar götürülebilmektedir. Suyu bol olmasına rağmen, Eğin arazisinin kayalık olması nedeniyle tarım ve hayvancılığa elverişli olmamasından kaynaklanan ekonomik sıkıntılara; isyanlar, eşkıyalık ve yağmalar sonucu bölgenin güvensiz hale gelmesi de eklenince, Eğin'den İstanbul'a göç başlamıştır. Ailenin tamamının göç ettiği örneklere rastlansa da, göçler ağırlıklı olarak erkeklerin gurbete gitmesi, kadınların ise sılada kalması şeklinde gerçekleşmiştir. Gurbet ve sıla arasında yaşanan hasretlik duygusu türkülerde ve manilerde de yoğun bir şekilde ortaya çıkmıştır. Aşk, gurbet, ayrılık temaları arkasında sosyal ve ekonomik zorlukların izlerinin okunduğu Eğin türküleri ve manilerinden toplumsal yapıya dair bilgiler de elde etmek mümkündür. Bu çalışma kapsamında Pertev Naili Boratav'ın "Eğinli bir kadının, bir Türk zevce-i metrukesinin figan-ı hasretidir" dediği Eğin türküleri ve manilerinden seçilen örneklere içerik analizi uygulanacaktır.

***

SESSION 2A – Economics of Migration - 1

Room: A1

---

[2] Bu çalışma Namık Kemal Üniversitesi Bilimsel Etkinliklere Katılım Destek Programı kapsamında desteklenmiştir.

Chair	Şule Akkoyunlu, Rimini Centre, Wilfrid Laurier University, Canada
719	Football Player Migration in Greece: Wage Differences and Crowding-out Effects -**Panagiotis Dimitropoulos**
706	The Impact of Social Assistance Programs on the Spending Patterns of Remittance-Receiving Households in Mexico - **Ana Isabel López García**
849	Who Remits and Why? Determinants and Motivations of Internal Migrant Remittances - **Rasadhika Sharma, Ulrike Grote**
1354	Migrants' Remittance and Growth in MENA Labor Exporting Countries - **Sufian Eltayeb Mohamed Abdel- Gadir**

Football Player Migration in Greece: Wage Differences and Crowding-out Effects
(719) Panagiotis Dimitropoulos (University of Peloponnese)

Athlete migration has been on the forefront of academic research for more than twenty years since the migration flows of footballers has increased significantly in Europe. Greece is among the top receiving countries of migrant football players in Europe despite the fact that the Greek championship is not highly competitive as other European leagues. The scope of this paper is to provide some initial evidence regarding the flow of foreign football players in the Greek league. The study analyzed a database of all migrant and local athletes that participated in the professional Greek football championship over the period 2001-2013 and performed descriptive analyses. Descriptive evidence suggests that football player migration has increased significantly from 2001 until 2013 yet the relative numbers of foreign athletes are lower than their natives' counterparts. However, foreign athletes are utilized more by their coaches since they have more actual minutes of participation on clubs' official matches and earn higher income than the native football players. These findings provide support to several voices echoing on the crowding out effect of native athletes by migrants.
***

The Impact of Social Assistance Programs on the Spending Patterns of Remittance-Receiving Households in Mexico
(706) Ana Isabel López García (El Colegio de la Frontera Norte (COLEF))

This paper aims to contribute to the literature by examining the ways in which the delivery of state assistance programs affects the spending patterns of remittance-receiving households in Mexico. The analysis is based on a series of regression models using survey data from the 2016 Survey of Migration at Mexico's Northern Border.
***

Who Remits and Why? Determinants and Motivations of Internal Migrant Remittances
(849) Rasadhika Sharma (Leibniz University Hannover), Ulrike Grote (Leibniz University Hannover)

Given that there are two migrants with the same income, what makes one of them send a bigger proportion of his or her income back home? To explain this heterogeneity, an analysis of both determinants of remittances and motivations behind the remittances needs to be undertaken. Determinants are factors that decide 'who is more likely to remit' and 'who remits more'. These can be analyzed by examining the impact of microeconomic variables on remittances. Motivations in contrast provide a reason for 'why does the migrant remit' or 'why the migrant remits more'; proposed types of motivation are altruism, self-interest, enlightened self-interest and tempered altruism (Stark 1985). To ascertain the motivation, the relationship of migrant and household characteristics with remittances needs to be analyzed. Most existing studies either deal with determinants (Dustmann & Mestres, 2010) or with motivations (Agarwal & Horowitz, 2002), with a few exceptions that look at determinants and casually touch upon the motivations (Phan & Coxhead, 2016). However, an answer to both these questions is required for an all-encompassing study of internal migrant remittances that can ease liquidity constraints and smoothen rural household consumption (Orozco, 2006). We use a unique data set from the DFG-funded TVSEP project that contains information on socio-economic variables for migrants that moved within their respective countries and their rural household for 2010. A household survey from three provinces in Vietnam and Thailand is combined with a migrant tracer survey that was conducted in Ho Chi Minh City and the Greater Bangkok area to obtain a sample of 592 migrants. Using an FIML Heckman model, we find that an increase in human capital, stronger family ties and better living conditions positively influence the migrant's decision to remit. In terms of the amount remitted, migrants engaged in the service sector remit lower shares of their income. Additionally, remittances decrease as the household wealth increases, while private and weather shocks experienced by the household, positively affect the remittance decision. Furthermore, we explore the behavioral side of remittances by constructing proxy groups that represent each strand of motivation. We examine the relationship of these proxy groups and remittances to conclude that exchange or loan repayment motive unpinned by altruism is the strongest motivation in our case.

***

Migrants' Remittance and Growth in MENA Labor Exporting Countries
(1354) Sufian Eltayeb Mohamed Abdel- Gadir (Sultan Qaboos University)

This paper presents an empirical examination of the macroeconomic effects of remittances on remittance-receiving MENA economies. In order to empirically analyze the impact of remittances we estimate growth equations using a set of 7 MENA labor exporting countries during the period 1975-2006. A standard growth models are estimated using both fixed-effects and random effects models. The empirical results show the support of the fixed –effects method as the random effects model is rejected in statistical tests. The results show the support for the view that remittances have a positive impact on growth both directly and indirectly through their interactions with financial and institutional channels.

***

SESSION 2B – Movement and Movers

	Room: A2
Chair	**Christos Michalakelis, Harokopio University, Greece**
1030	Mobile Application for Asylum Seekers - **Antonis Makris, Eleni Petraki, Xronis Dimitropoulos, Styliani Liberopoulou, Konstantinos Tserpes, Christos Michalakelis**
935	Massive Displacement Meets Cyberspace: How Information and Communication Technologies are Helping Refugees and Migrants and How We Can Do Better - **Joseph G. Bock, Kevin McMahon, Ziaul Haque**
1036	Reflections of Human (In)security Concept within Twitter: #EuropeanUnion Hashtag - **Pelin Sönmez, Sinan Aşcı**
1229	Mapping the Refugee Crisis Discourse Online: The Case of Idomeni on Instagram – **Dennis Nguyen, Ioanna Ferra, Radmila Radjoevic**

Mobile Application for Asylum Seekers

(1030) Antonis Makris (Harokopio University of Athens), Eleni Petraki (Greek Asylum Service), Xronis Dimitropoulos (Harokopio University of Athens), Styliani Liberopoulou (Harokopio University of Athens), Konstantinos Tserpes (Harokopio University of Athens), Christos Michalakelis (Harokopio University of Athens)

The Greek Asylum Service has been operational for four years, in an environment characterized by rapid developments. The movement of refugees and migrants to Europe, was probably the defining development for our continent in the last two years. In 2015, the great unforeseen refugee influx led to the expansion of the Asylum Service. Our country is legally and morally obliged to inform and offer protection to refugees, irrespective of their numbers and whether they have entered Greece in a regular or irregular fashion. Towards this direction, the Asylum Service, together with the Harokopio University of Athens worked for a jointly funded action of the Asylum, Migration and Integration Fund (AMIF) 2014-2020. The purpose of this action is the design, development and maintenance of a mobile application and the target group would be the asylum seekers who move or are transferred from the country's external borders, and especially the individuals with a refugee profile.

***

Massive Displacement Meets Cyberspace: How Information and Communication Technologies are Helping Refugees and Migrants and How We Can Do Better

(935) Joseph G. Bock (Kennesaw State University), Kevin McMahon (Kennesaw State University), Ziaul Haque (Kennesaw State University)

Since the global response to the earthquake in Haiti in 2010, the use of Information and Communication Technologies (ICTs) for humanitarian assistance has grown dramatically. Employing these technologies—which involve mobile phones, applications ("apps") and internet-based platforms—has the potential to improve efforts to assist displaced people, or to liberate them in being more able to help each other, or both. This shift is viewed by some humanitarian professionals as a quantum leap both in what outsiders can do in global solidarity and in what insiders can do for each other. Other experts, in contrast, view these technologies as being a distraction, taking away scarce resources from the more difficult work on the ground with displaced people. The magnitude and visibility of the current refugee and migrant crisis has yielded a rich harvest of new platforms. In this paper, we survey some of the main ones, as well as some that are in their infancy. Similar to the acronym ICT4D, commonly used to denote the use of ICTs for development, we refer to the applications in this paper collectively as ICTs for refugees and migrants, or simply ICT4RM. And while platform development has resulted in a patchwork of initiatives—an electronic version of "letting a thousand flowers bloom"—there are patterns emerging as to which flowers grow and have "staying power" as compared to ones that wilt and die. In hopes of providing guidance to would-be developers, we offer explanations for what leads to a successful ICT4RM initiative.

***

Reflections of Human (In)security Concept within Twitter: #EuropeanUnion Hashtag

(1036) Pelin Sönmez (Nişantaşı University), Sinan Aşçı (Nişantaşı University)

Security means the state of being free from danger or threat. In social sciences, human security is an emerging paradigm shift concerning a person-centered, multi-disciplinary understanding of security involving a number of studies and human rights. According to Amartya Sen (2000), the concept "human security" is a keyword to comprehensively seizing all of the menaces that threaten the survival, daily life, and dignity of human beings and to strengthening the efforts to confront these threats. On the other hand, "human insecurity" as a term stands for defining various situations where conflicts lead to perception of deprivation of some-kind, among certain people, in a given context (Sirkeci, 2009). Human insecurity affects migration movements in a way with the connection of 3Ds: namely democratic, development and demographic deficits (Sirkeci, 2017). Accordingly, recent developments, attempted coup on July 15 as an example, have made Turkey as a seemingly possible insecure country when discussed with these 3Ds to define the migration movements in and/or outside the country. According to the reports of Eurostat published in 2016, asylum request demanded by people in Turkey to European countries reached at 3779 in the third quarter comparing to the same quarter of 2015 at 985. After the attempted coup, this tendency seems on the rise, which actually shows us the fact that human insecurity perceptions among citizens. To evaluate this hypothesis, Twitter, as a public social media platform, based on the hashtags used by Turkish people, such as #avrupabirligi and #avrupabirliği (in English "european union") will be evaluated within the methodology content and discourse analysis.

***

Mapping the Refugee Crisis Discourse Online: The Case of Idomeni on Instagram
(1229) Dennis Nguyen (University of Applied Sciences Utrecht), Ioanna Ferra (University of Leicester), Radmila Radjoevic (University of Applied Sciences)

The refugee crisis triggered a controversial and extremely volatile transnational discourse about practical challenges, ethical concerns, causalities, responsibilities and strategies on a European level. The lines of conflict separated stakeholders along political-ideological lines, while the discourse revealed an obvious lack of coordination and consensus among European Union member-states (The Lancet 2016; Grigonis 2017). The discourse was heavily mediatized, as related events and developments dominated the news media landscape; the refugee crisis basically took turns with the Eurozone crisis as the primary topic on the transnational public agenda between 2011 and 2016 (Nguyen 2016) Political communicators across the continent created and distributed their perceptions of the refugee crisis through specific framings that often excluded and ignored refugee perspectives or partly resorted to plain racism (Nail 2015, Mig@Net 2016). The resulting conflicts spanned across off- and online media and raised fundamental questions about European solidarity in times of crisis. Social media expanded the arenas for the contest of frames (Entman 1993); as alternative spaces for public communication about political issues of transnational relevance, they transform the structure of the public sphere (Karatzogianni 2006; Castells 2009; Hepp et al. 2016). Digital public discourses emerge as 'web spheres' (Schneider and Foot 2007; Nguyen 2016) that consist of online communication related to a common topic and form distinguishable communicative contexts; the refugee crisis served as a connecting factor for online content and triggered the formation of refugee crisis web sphere in digital networks (Karatzogianni et al. 2016). Social media provided direct access to these online discourses, which can be scanned for tendencies and trends with content- and network analyses (Nguyen 2016). Digital methods for large-scale data collection facilitate empirical investigations (Rogers 2015). The present paper applies a complementary research design to Instagram as an platform for political online communication. It explores how participants framed the refugee crisis though the discursive practice of 'hashtagging' and what narratives they constructed via visual content. This enables the identification of associations and co-occurring themes related as well as to determine framing strategies. To further refine the research lens, the analysis focuses on the usage of Instagram within the vicinity of the refugee camp in Idomeni, Greece, in March

2016. The case study is guided by two research questions: 1.   What   hashtags   did Instagram users in Idomeni choose during the height of the refugee crisis in 2016? 2. What narrative(s) of the refugee crisis did participants create (visual and in text) in the same Instagram discourse? Though mainly descriptive in nature, answers to both open the way for critical reflections on discursive practices in social media and how they can serve as spaces for alternative framings of the refugee crisis that are not always covered in mainstream media. The now de-functional Instagram Hashtag Explorer (Digital Methods Initiative 2016) was used to collect Instagram posts within a 5-kilometer radius of Idomeni that were uploaded between the 7th and 15th of March 2016. The tool allowed to collect relevant data for specific locations by entering longitudinal and latitudinal data into an application programming interface (API). During the selected timespan, the refugee camp in Idomeni repeatedly made it into the news due to an influx of arrivals from the Middle East, especially Syria (BBC 2016), which informed the sampling strategy. The data include 369 images paired with over 400 hashtags that were shared by 189 user accounts. The image data were processed in a quantitative-qualitative content analysis to identify central themes, while the hashtag- and user data were analysed and visualized with Gephi, an open-source tool for network analysis (http://gephi.org). The findings of the empirical-descriptive analysis are contextualized and critically commented on against the background of theories on transnational public discursivity, crisis communication, and counter-publics (Karatzogianni 2016; 2006; Nguyen 2016; Ferra 2016). The results show how non-mainstream communicators take the discourse on the refugee crisis to alternative public spaces in social media networks and what associations they communicate (e.g. the Syrian Civil War, EU politics, racism etc.). This facilitates a mapping of the refugee crisis debate on Instagram. The analysis of visual content further reveals how the refugee crisis is being documented but also instrumentalised by different political agencies on the left and right. It seems that refugees themselves are to a large part still excluded from the digital discourse, though limited evidence exist for more direct forms of participation. The paper closes with some recommendations for social media strategies with NGOs and other organisations dedicated to refugees as addressees in mind.
***

SESSION 2C – Discourse and Representation

	Room: A4
Chair	**Vildan Mahmutoglu, Galatasaray University, Turkey**
718	British Press Coverage of Immigration into Britain from 2004 to 2010: The Case of Eastern Europeans – **Fathi Bourmeche**
956	The Discriminatory Discourse Against Syrian Refugees in Turkish Print Media: The Case of Sözcü – **Selçuk Çetin, Recep Volkan Öner**
1000	Media, Politics & Migration: Reporting on Syrian "guests" in Turkey - **Sergül Taşdemir**
869	The Depictions of the Refugee Crisis on the Public Arena: An Analysis of the News Frames Promoted by Spanish Digital Media – **Sergio Álvarez, Alfredo Arceo**
764	Immigrant and Refugee Representation in Political Cartoons - **Arda Umut Saygın**

British Press Coverage of Immigration into Britain from 2004 to 2010: The Case of Eastern Europeans
(718) Fathi Bourmeche (University of Sfax)

The study is focused on the way British press covered the influx of Eastern Europeans from 2004 to 2010. A corpus selected from three tabloids and three broadsheets is qualitatively analysed using McCombs' model of agenda-setting and framing. The corpus is also juxtaposed with opinion polls and surveys dealing with the same issues. The fifth EU enlargement resulted in a large influx of Eastern Europeans, considered by John Salt, a geographer at University College London, and Ian Fitzgerald, from Northumbria University, as the biggest influx in British history which surprised everybody, raising controversy over the existence of foreigners. It is argued that media frames and agendas have had a major impact on the British socio-political landscape, representing Eastern European immigrants as new 'Others' that threaten the British national identity, despite their being part of the EU and holding EU citizenship, a status similar to that of Britons. Such a portrayal has also had repercussions on British general elections, contributing to immigration being seen as one of the most important issues facing the country and thus affecting the results of two general elections (2005 and 2010).

***

The Discriminatory Discourse Against Syrian Refugees in Turkish Print Media: The Case of Sözcü

(956) Selçuk Çetin (Gazi University), Recep Volkan Öner (Gazi Universitiy)

Since the beginning of the Syrian civil war in 2011, more than 5 million people had to leave their country. According to the Directorate General for Migration Management, the number of refugees in Turkey has reached over 2.8 million people. This makes Turkey the host country with the largest Syrian refugee population. These refugees face many problems such as social rejection, poverty, segregation etc. The underlying reason of these problems is discrimination. Within the scope of the study, our subject is the discriminatory discourse against Syrian refugees in Turkish print media.

We have used Balibar's "racism without races" conceptualisation as a theoretical framework. According to Balibar, "racism without races is a racism whose dominant theme is not biological heredity but the insurmountability of cultural differences, it does not postulate the superiority of certain groups or peoples in relation to others but 'only' the harmfulness of abolishing frontiers, the incompatibility of life-styles and traditions" (Balibar, 1991:21). In this passage, we can see that Balibar defines racism, not discrimination. However, it is not possible to dissociate the terms such as hate speech, racism and discrimination clearly from each other. They have interal relations, and intersect at many points. Therefore, we take discirimination as a meta category.The discrimination against Syrian refugees is produced by different ideological groups. This paper aims to explore how and in what ways secular nationalist group in Turkey produce and reproduce the discriminatory discourse against Syrian refugees in print media. Thus, we have focused on the daily Sözcü which is one of the main instrument to develop and maintain the common sense of the secular nationalist group in Turkey. We have examined the columns written by 23 columnists that are characterised as "secular nationalist organic intellectuals." The research is limited with a period between 01.12.2016 - 28.02.2017. We have used Van Dijk's critical discourse analysis as a method. As the result of the study, we have detected that the discriminatory discourse covers four fields related with each other. The first field is militarism and masculanity. The columnists ignore the fact that Syrian refugees are civilians and war victims. On the contrary, they promote militarist narratives with patriarchal values and stigmatise the subordinated Syrian men as "cowards." For exemple, in 11.02.2017 a columnist writes as following: "400 thousands of Syrians at an eligible age for military service in our country live off the fat of the land. Then again, we are spending hundreds of millions of dollars for those cowards and scammers." The second field is the

objectification of the female body. The columnists ignore the fact that some of the subordinated Syrian women have to work as sex workers to survive during and after the migration process. On the contrary, they are accused of "giving birth too much." For exemple, in 13.02.2017 a columnist writes as following: "You can be sure that if they had sex this much in their country, the population of Syria would be 50 million and not 20 million!" The third field is the rights and facilities provided by the state. The columnists ignore the living conditions of the Syrian refugees which are incompatible with human dignity. On the contrary, they emphasise that the refugees have high standarts of living. For example, in 17.02.2017 a columnist writes as follwing: "The hospitals are free for the Syrians, but let the Turkish crowl in there. The public transport is free for Syrians, but let the Turkish give their lunch money for it." The fourth field is the unemployment problem in Turkey. The columnists ignore the fact that the refugees are in economic insecurity and exploitation. On the contrary, they emphasise that the refugees are the underlying reason of Turkish "citizens" unemployment problem. For example, in 19.02.2017 a columnist writes as following: "Since April 2010 in Turkey, the refugees can get a jop, but the unemployement rate of the citizens is at its highest level." We know that in Turkey, the secular nationalist group see itself as the defender of the democratic values and human rights. However, the results of the study show that the secular nationalist organic intellectuals producing and reproducing a discriminatory discourse against Syrian refugees. This discourse can be characterized in terms of "racism without races" and it is clearly against the democratic values and human rights. We believe that this "confrontation" - which makes our study important- will be in favor of every individual living in Turkey.
***

Media, Politics & Migration: Reporting on Syrian "guests" in Turkey
(1000) Sergul Taşdemir (Galatasaray University)

The so-called "refugee crisis" in Europe, possibly the biggest story of the last few years attracts little media attention and minimum coverage usually takes place in particular instances; a political deal or a shocking image. In Turkey, host to the largest community of Syrians displaced by the ongoing conflict, public opinion is partly shaped by media and partly by everyday experience. While political discourse is proudly centered around "our Syrian guests" who are actually deprived of refugee rights, journalists' major challenge in covering migration is to go beyond repeating political statements (Chauzy & Appave, 2014) and investigate the issue in depth. This article aims at mapping the coverage of Syrian refugee crisis in Turkish mainstream media through content analysis guided by a framing paradigm. The coverage of the Syrian "refugee crisis" has been analyzed in three majors' private 24/7 TV news channels' websites and social media accounts in Turkey; CNN Turk, NTV and Haber Turk following the death of Alan Kurdi, a Syrian child whose body was washed up on a Turkish beach in September 2015. It has been revealed that all three news channels' online platforms used the photo at first, then its usage and news on the "refugee crisis" has remained rather limited.
***

The Depictions of the Refugee Crisis on the Public Arena: An Analysis of the News Frames Promoted by Spanish Digital Media
(869) Sergio Álvarez (Universidad Complutense de Madrid (UCM)), Alfredo Arceo (Universidad Complutense de Madrid)

As it has been the case throughout Europe, the so-called 'refugee crisis' became a prominent topic on the agenda setting of Spanish media. However, each publication approached the phenomenon in its own way, creating a wide range of narrations about the same conflict. Media outlets adopt journalistic frames to structure those stories and define them for the public. A journalistic frame indicates the aspects of a broad reality on which the journalistic article focuses on. The framing notions suggested by Robert Entman (1993) about how journalists structure and organize meaning in their pieces are a good start, and his 'cascading activation model' (Entman, 2003) is helpful to understand how media influence people and are influenced by other establishments of society. This theory becomes enrichened by the framing contributions from the studies about Social Movements (Snow & Benford, 1992; Gamson, 1992). The later stated that collective action frames can sometimes be promoted from certain spaces allowed by media. Van Gorp (2005) and Veloso Leão (2013) continued the tradition of analyzing specific issue frames started by Nelson & Willey (2001), and excelled among the researchers that decided to apply the framing theory to contents related to migration and refugees. What is more, Van Gorp (2007) opened the door to the construction of a methodology based on the identification of 'reasoning devices', a number of elements not made evident in the text but which, when linked in the mind of the recipient, allow him to decipher the frame and share the suggested definition for the situation. Regarding media effects, a study by Tversky & Kahneman (1981) highlighted how the way that issues are framed can shape the decisions of the recipients and how they perceive their own experiences. Druckman (2001) called this approach the 'equivalency framing effect', which results practical for assessing how a set of elements that articulate the news frame, end up exerting an influence over the reader. If journalistic framing theories are to be followed, it could be argued that media play a big part in the perception of refugees as threats, a very common opinion according to Weiner (1993) and Rudolph (2003). The present research attempts to to identify, describe and establish the frecuency of use of the main news frames that journalists employed during the analysed period; and to analyze the evolution of the frames adopted about the refugee crisis by the top four Spanish digital diaries. The succession of events between September 2015 and March 2016 (EU Refugees Summit, electoral processes, Turkey agreement...) allows thinking on hypothetical shifts. Another aim is to find out the degree of frame sharing among the examined diaries: did they reach a consensus about the depiction of the problem? Finally, the results referred in this paper must provide a starting point for new investigations about the effects that news framing about refugees has on the audiences. From the journalistic informative perspective, seeking the reasoning devices requires a content analysis. The conducted analysis focused on the headlines' zone of each item. A group of four coders was trained in order to successfully detect a series of units comparable to the reasoning devices of news frames. The chosen units of interest comprehend factors such as the section where the news was allocated; the appearance of relevant countries; mentions to ethnical groups or religions; the presence of certain people in the news (from well-known political charges to policemen and children); the selection of images with a certain size and content, or the space conceded to institutional, political and non-governmental organizations. The coding guide also contemplated the presence of topics such as war, terrorism, poverty and displacements, and provided the coders with objective instructions to detect them. The revised literature leads the research team to expect a shift in the depictions of refugees at key dates. Refugees as victims would emerge as the framing trend, as opposed to refugees as intruders (Van Gorp, 2007). However, this would not translate into an overwhelming preference of digital diaries for one frame over the other. Media-sponsored frames should tend to coincide with those of the majority of their respective readers. Additional research could be conducted on how the readers negotiate the meanings proposed by digital journals, and what impact does it have on their opinions about asylum policies. The present investigation should end up providing specific guidelines for that purpose.

***

Immigrant and Refugee Representation in Political Cartoons
(764) Arda Umut Saygın (Gazi University)

Millions of Middle Eastern and African people are forced to leave from their homelands because of the civil wars. While some of them have became refugees or asylum seekers in other countries, thousand of immigrants lost their lives trying to migrate. However, immigrants, refugees or asylum seekers are mostly seen as a problem on global and continues to occupy the agenda as a hot topic. Nevertheless, politicians and world public opinion remains unconcerned with this issue and does not take concrete steps to solve the problem. Political cartoons are illustrations, drawings or comic strips containing political or social messages that usually relates to current events, situations or personalities. They give political messages to the readers by expressing political thought through creative use of art that includes only few words or just lines. In recent years, the refugee issue and the immigration process has been inevitably discussed and represented in political cartoons. The purpose of this study is to show how the refugee case is handled in political cartoons which are woven with messages based on drawings. Besides this, another aim of the study is to describe relationship between semiology and political cartoons. Therefore, poststructuralist semiotic analysis will be used as a method in the study. In the study, the political cartoons are selected from The Aydın Doğan International Cartoon Competition which has been organized since 1993 and globally known as the "Academy Award of Cartoons". Among the cartoons that participated in The Aydın Doğan International Cartoon Competition, those concerning the themes such as immigration, immigrant and refugees will be selected and semiotically evaluated to understand how much place this issue take place and in which context it is discussed.
***

SESSION 2D – Gender and Migration in Turkey - 2

	Room: A5
Chair	**Reyhan Atasü-Topçuoğlu, Hacettepe University, Turkey**
1093	Vulnerable Boys and Dangerous Men: Independent Young Male Refugees – **Lucy Williams**
1098	Gender Matters: Toward a Gender-Sensitive European Asylum System – **Yasemin Bekyol**
1050	'Motherhood' and the Entrepreneurial Migrant Domestics in Hong Kong – **Joy Tadios-Arenas**
726	Forced to Flee: A Case Study Analysis of Sexual Violence During the Syrian Civil War- **Emma Rose von der Lieth**

Vulnerable Boys and Dangerous Men: Independent Young Male Refugees
(1093) Lucy Williams (University of Kent)

The majority of child refugees travelling without parents are boys. As children (i.e. aged under 18) they are protected and given special levels of support in many countries they travel through. Once they reach 18 however many lose any special protection and face the same threats of destitution, detention and deportation experienced by adult migrants and unrecognised asylum seekers. As they move towards 18 and adulthood, boys move from being children who are looked after, albeit reluctantly, to unwanted men who the State refuses responsibility for. Attitudes to young refugees are contradictory and move between narratives of risk and resilience (Chase 2013, Kanics 2010). They are seen as 'at risk' as children alone and without family and 'resilient' as young people who have already survived great danger and negotiated a long and difficult journey. They are also perceived as a risk in themselves as young people with unknown motivations and experiences who may be capable of violence or anti-social behaviour. Another stream of academic work with young people has focused on the infantilising narratives that govern the care of refugee children, mostly boys, arguing that denying the agency of children makes their transition into adulthood ever more difficult (Mai 2009, 2010). Assumptions about the capacities of young men – that they are risk takers and self-reliant - allow policy makers to withdraw support as they assume that young men are resilient and that their migration history demonstrates their capacity to travel and fend for themselves. Young foreign men are blamed for sexual harassment and violence across many countries but rarely receive support in coming to terms with displacement and the heavy burdens they often carry as young people sent out to support their families from abroad. In countries of Western Europe that receive many independent young refugees these stereotypical assumptions about manhood are also mixed with the assumed threat of their Muslim identity which magnifies both their threat as individuals, to women and to the State (Freedman 2016). This paper asks firstly, how the care young asylum seekers receive as children prepares them for life as adults in countries of resettlement. Secondly, it asks how assumptions made by policy makers and care providers about their gender affects their life chances. Thirdly, it asks what are the effects on the communities that these young men are received into in the countries where they seek asylum, countries they transit through and countries they are returned or deported back to. It draws on research with young men in the UK, who arrived as unaccompanied children and who have been refused asylum and are now threatened with deportation and on a small number of interviews with young men in Istanbul who had been deported from EU countries who were trying to transit, or make a life in Turkey.

Gender Matters: Toward a Gender-Sensitive European Asylum System
(1098) Yasemin Bekyol (Friedrich-Alexander-University Erlangen-Nuremberg)

In contrast to previous years, the number of applicants seeking international protection in Europe has risen exponentially to over one million asylum claims in 2015 and 2016. The lack of secure and legal channels for refugees to arrive in the EU and the lack of efficient relocation within the EU has led to a loss of trust and solidarity between Member States and a lack of adequate human rights standards for asylum seekers. The latter is especially true for female asylum seekers since "vulnerable migrants are still falling through the cracks of the protection system." (Eva Cossé in Marsi, 2015) International law and European law do, in principle, guarantee protection of persecution, adequate reception as well as integration measures. However, mainstream migration discourses have been particularly focused on men claiming to be gender-neutral (Wessels, 2017). Nonetheless, gender research, which has come to mean not only gender but also racial, economic and social justice, has caused migration research and practice to evolve. One of the main examples to prove this is that only in the 1980s, after feminist research offered the insight that "the personal is political" (Enloe, 2000: p. 195) did the understanding of the Geneva Convention shift to include refugees who were not solely persecuted in the public sphere by, for instance, being politically active, but also included 'private' actors of all genders who could also be persecuted by their families, neighbors and their own community, such as victims of domestic violence, genital mutilation, forced marriage or forced recruitment (Wessels, 2017). Therefore, in including gender research a different perspective was introduced which enhanced mainstream discourses and offered a better protection and human rights standards. Female asylum seekers are often more exposed to gender-based discriminatory experiences and it is more difficult for them to exercise their human rights at every stage of flight: root causes, transit routes, conditions of admission and accommodation, asylum procedures and, finally, integration opportunities (Bekyol and Bendel, 2016). In 1990, the UNHCR established a policy on female refugees and highlighted the fact that the experiences of female refugees differed from those of men. Even today, the need for statistical data to tailor programs has not been emphasized strongly enough (Edwards, 2006) and there is a misrepresentation of female refugees and all genders in the Common European Asylum System (CEAS). Although gender research has come to understand that the situation of women cannot be assessed without assessing the relationship to men, focusing on women refugees is a first step towards shedding light onto structural shortcomings of the CEAS. Thus, I aim to analyze the representation of gender in the Common European Asylum System. Further, I wish to focus mainly but not exclusively on female refugees and thus include achievements of the Istanbul Convention, which addresses gender-based violence, particularly violence against women, and names a broad range of instruments to protect victims and to persecute perpetrators but has not yet been ratified by all member states, in my analysis. In building on the previously published study "Reception of Female Refugees in Europe – Case Study Germany and Belgium" by Prof. Bendel and me, I will take a step back and offer a broader analysis of the legal European framework and how it incorporates gender in further consulting gender theory. I will illustrate why gender is important and how it could be incorporated into and improve the Common European Asylum System. In addition, I wish to include best practice examples of member states and offer a bottom-up approach towards a gender-sensitive European Asylum System that offers protection to all genders.

***

'Motherhood' and the Entrepreneurial Migrant Domestics in Hong Kong
(1050) Joy Tadios-Arenas (City University of Hong Kong)

The international labour migration has long been glorified because of the huge remittances contributed by migrants to the economies of sending countries. In the context of a migrant household, the contribution of a migrant member has significantly changed and strengthened their positions in the family. This is particularly salient in households where women – mothers or daughters – migrate and work abroad. Various migration studies reveal how mobility have changed women's status and roles in the family and this phenomenon of women migrating for work has raised substantial debate on the implication of labour migration to gender relations back home. Are the new roles taken by women migrants are contained within the common notions of filial duty and motherhood or these are transformed roles that has now changed gender relations? This paper is presenting cases that reveal the former - women migrant domestic workers in Hong Kong has successfully re-shaped their mothering roles to that of an active managers and decision makers. When women are pulled outside the confines of the homes and as they assume the role of main income earners, 'motherhood' as a role is being reworked and manifested in many different ways. While sending gifts and regular communication are the known ways to ensure mothering is continuously practiced, it is sending remittances that has sustained familial relationship back home (Yeoh et al, 2013: 454) and in many instances, mothering is best manifested through remittances (Fresnoza-Flot, 2009). Failure to remit would label migrants as 'ingrates' (as in Cape Verdan families in Åkesson, 2011: 336). Money transfers between migrants and their family members as argued by Castañeda (2012) are socially constructed acts situated and influenced by one's norms or social milieu and this research shows why migrant's gender says a lot about the frequency and quantity of remittances. Women are believed to be the natural 'carers' of the family and as such, they would do their best to ensure immediate family members or kin are well taken care of, properly fed and are sent to good schools. Rhacel Parreñas (in many articles and books published in 2001,

2005, 2008, 2010) argues that women's migration has reinforced traditional gender relations because they have continuously ascribed to gender-based expectations – either self-imposed expectations or those of their family – by doing emotional labour or all 'mothering' acts that maintain the well-being of the family. For Parreñas, women's migration has failed to reconstitute gender relations because women failed to extricate themselves from doing emotional labour. Mothers act as and are assumed to be the only proper carers and take great pains in carrying out this role transnationally. She argued that the only way to change the unequal gender relations is when fathers do care work and/or another female member of the family is not charged with carework when the mother leaves. However, too much emphasis on the ideological constructions of gender roles tends to overlook the fact that as women acquire a 'breadwinning' role, they re-work motherhood into something that is not akin to traditional mothering itself. I reference here the argument made by Lan (2006) that explains how women paid domestic labour could simultaneously encourage women's emancipation and subservience, as it 'provides means for women to exercise agency by shifting across multiple positions embedded in the organization of domestic labour' (2006:14). It is in this light that I look at the transformative potential of emotional labour in the way migrant domestic workers in Hong Kong are performing active transnational household management. This research, through snowball sampling, focuses on case studies of migrant workers with parallel interviews conducted with family members in the Philippines. The case studies reveal the two financial resources of migrants – taking loans and sending remittances – provided mechanisms for migrants to exercise entrepreneurial agency that eventually debunks their subservient role within the family and positions them as respected heads and decision-makers. The data gathered show that migrant workers are active managers of the resources they generate and that they 'transnationally manage' family relationships as well as material resources that are committed to productive investment and reciprocal obligation. Women migrant domestics administer loans and remittances, weigh and calculate risks, decide on recipients and earmarks as well as manages the repercussions of decisions made on personal relationships. The paper concludes that while women migrants fulfill their roles as mothers or daughters abroad, labour migration provided them with the means and resources to develop and demonstrate entrepreneurial agency that has not been recognised before.

***

Forced to Flee: A Case Study Analysis of Sexual Violence During the Syrian Civil War

(726) Emma Rose von der Lieth (Roanoke College)

Since the start of the Syrian Civil War, sexual violence has been rampant, causing most Syrians to cite rape as the primary reason for fleeing their home country. This paper explores the relationship between type of perpetrator and the use of sexual violence during armed conflict in the Syrian Arab Republic. This case study investigates pro-government, opposition, Kurdish, and jihadist groups and analyzes which groups utilize sexual violence and their motivations for doing so. The pro-government group includes the Syrian Arab Armed forces and the shabbiha militia. The jihadist group examined is ISIS, the opposition group is the Free Syrian Army (FSA), and the Kurdish group includes both the People's Protection Units (YPG) and the Women's Protection Units (YPJ). Sources for this research include various reports from non-profit and non-governmental organizations such as the Human Rights Watch, as well as reports from the Syrian Network for Human Rights, United States Department of State, and articles from various news outlets including the BBC. Throughout this case study, various subjects are discussed, including the importance of Syria's history, the use of female combatants, the effects of masculinity and patriarchy on the prevalence of sexual violence, and the use of women as spoils of war. All of these phenomena play an important role in explaining how and why perpetrators use sexual violence. This research shows that sexual violence is used purposefully by jihadist and pro-government groups in Syria, but for differing reasons. Pro-government groups use sexual violence against any whom they perceive to be the enemy, which they believe is any Syrian against the Alawite (Shia) Assad regime. On the other hand, ISIS is more likely than pro-government groups to use women as spoils of war. This is because of the group's emphasis on sexual jihad, and their need to recruit members. With the use of women as spoils of war, ISIS promises members that they can do as they please with these women. The fear of becoming a sex slave for ISIS also helps the group to enforce discipline on the regions they capture. While there is extensive literature regarding the subject of violence against women in conflict, this research is unique in its examination of different types of perpetrators with a narrow focus on Syria. Most importantly, this research provides insight for policy makers around the world regarding the creation of sustainable policy solutions to eliminate sexual violence during conflict.

***

SESSION 2E – Historic Perspectives on Migration

	Room: B1
Chair	**Anastasia Christou, Middlesex University, UK**
852	The "Profound Transnational Character" of State Apparatuses and Policies Regulating Human Mobility: Two Examples from Greece (1952-2017)– **Lina Venturas**
759	The Unexpected Signs of Continuity: Muslim Migration from Monarchist and Socialist Yugoslavia to Turkey – **Vladan Jovanovic**
865	Immigration, Appreciation and Expulsion – The Drastic Fate of 19th Century German Immigrants in Great Britain - **Karl-Heinz Wüstner**
1189	First Nations, Founding Nations & Fleeing from Nations. How Canada's Colonial Projects Inform the Immigrant Experience. – **Marianne Vardalos, Anas Karzai**

The "profound transnational character" of state apparatuses and policies regulating human mobility: two examples from Greece (1952-2017)
(852) Lina Venturas (Panteion University Athens)

This paper aims to explore the role of international or supranational agencies in diffusing hegemonic Western political, social, economic and cultural patterns in addressing human mobility in the postwar world. By examining how the governance of international migration and the assistance to refugees was articulated and practiced through the synergy of the Greek state apparatus with supranational and international agencies, the paper seeks to investigate the "profound transnational character" (Gupta-Ferguson 2002) of state apparatuses and policies regulating human mobility and the asymmetries in their construction. It will investigate international and supra-national agencies' role in shaping peripheral countries' migration apparatuses and their policies on refugee issues using two different examples from Greek post-war history: 1. the relations during the 1950s between, on the one hand, the Intergovernmental Committee for European Migration (named IOM today), a US-led organization created to regulate international migration, and, on the other hand, Greece, a sending state which, although considered part of the Western world, was relegated to its periphery, being relatively poor and powerless in the international sphere. 2. the interplay between the European Union, various international humanitarian agencies and Greece during their current seemingly joint attempt to address the needs of the refugees stranded in the country after the closure of the borders in 2016. Greece is a state which, although it is a member of the European Union, has been relegated to its periphery during the last decade due to its huge depts. In both of these historical conjunctures Greece was largely depended either on the globally-hegemonic US or on the regionally dominant European Union in political and economic terms and adopted many of the mechanisms and policies they instigated in order to address human mobility.

***

The Unexpected Signs of Continuity: Muslim Migration from Monarchist and Socialist Yugoslavia to Turkey
(759) Vladan Jovanovic (Institute for Recent History of Serbia)

My presentation points out some (unexpected) similarities in migration of Yugoslav Muslims to Turkey during the two ideologically opposed regimes: the monarchist (1918-1941) and the early-socialist Yugoslavia (1945-1955). In both cases such a migration was the state-facilitated process, as Yugoslav primary sources have shown. Despite a kind of international benevolence towards the de-Ottomanization of the Balkans, the Yugoslav Kingdom attempts in demographic engineering sharpened its ethnic and religious boundaries, compromising its own minority policy at the same time. Although the uncontrolled emigration was legalized after the Yugoslav-Turkish Convention was signed in 1938, many manipulative factors have survived. Treating Kosovo Albanians as "people of Turkish culture and language" enabled their legal expatriation and "relocation" to Asia Minor during the both interwar and postwar years. Furthermore, the expected improvement in social status was why many ethnic Albanians declared their nationality or even mother tongue differently, depending on current propositions for emigration. These variations and interweaving of identity boundaries indicate a sort of pragmatism, demystifying stereotypes on 'ethnicity obsession' in the name of which the Muslims would sacrifice their own prosperity. This circumstance was sistematically abused by both Yugoslav states in a very similar manner, which I intend to show: restricting the civil and religious rights, cultural and educational marginalization, state repression preceding the expatriation of Muslims, colonization of their land by Serbian settlers, etc. Such measures resulted in growing waves of Turks and Albanians migrants moving towards Turkey within the two decades after the Second World War.

***

Immigration, appreciation and expulsion – the drastic fate of 19th century German immigrants in Great Britain
(865) Karl-Heinz Wüstner (Historical Society for Wuerttemberg Franconia)

My paper will explore a recently discovered migration movement of pork butchers, who throughout the 19th century emigrated from a small rural area, situated in today's north-eastern part of Baden-Württemberg, to the welcoming land of Great Britain. The paper will discuss how the evolving British steel and textile industries of the time created a pathway to success for these enterprising and resourceful butchers in transforming wholesale and retail pork businesses to national prominence. It will also highlight how the large-scale influx of manual labourers, both male and female, into the industrial areas of Northern England and into London led to a change in the way food was processed, prepared and consumed. The working class and industrial society not only required but willingly adopted the new methods of food supply the immigrants could offer. A full-scale integration of the immigrants into their new society as well as a substantial appropriation of their products was extremely hampered after the outbreak of WW I. It is well known that throughout the 19th century many Germans left their homes to seek their fortunes in the New World. Less

well known, however, is the fact that many emigrants chose the new world of Great Britain and not North America as their newfound land of opportunity. At home, these people were confronted with serious economic hardships but in Britain the immense industrial boom offered these German immigrants many employment opportunities in sugar refining, confectionary, and general services. It was, however, in one key trade that the Germans were to excel in the fast-growing industrial towns of Northern England and in the country's capital, London, as well. As pork butchers, the German emigrants achieved a high level of status and craftsmanship using their considerable home-grown expertise. Their unique opportunities became apparent at the end of the 18th century when a small number of young men from Hohenlohe, an agricultural area located in north-eastern Baden-Württemberg, found their way across the Channel and settled in the cities of London, Bath and Sheffield. At home, their families were long established as butchers and innkeepers. As livestock traders, they also made good profit with oxen that they drove as far as Strasbourg and from there to Paris and other big cities abroad. Once in England, the pork products and sausage specialities of these young men became highly accepted and a classic chain migration movement between Hohenlohe and England took its roots. In the times of widespread industrialisation their chances to prosper were exceptionally good as many women in Great Britain were employed in manufacturing processes and had little time for cooking at home. They soon found that the German pork butchers could provide a wholesome and satisfactory meal with little or no preparation. Moreover, "the kind and variety of pork products these pork butchers could make for sale far exceeded anything on show in the conservative English shops." The German butchers became innovators and leaders providing take-away food and fashioning new eating habits in these industrial areas. This extraordinary migration movement was steadily fostered as recognition of the prosperity of these German butchers was regularly communicated to friends and relatives back home. In the course of the 19th century the success and hardworking ethic of these butchers was acknowledged and much admired and they became respected citizens in their new society. They were on the path to full integration. The outbreak of World War I was, however, to become a major turning point. These once highly respected men, and their families, were suddenly considered enemies in their newly adopted country. Most of the butchers were confronted with hatred and rejection, shop attacks, persecution and repatriation. Many men were interned in war camps and women and children were sent back to Germany. After the war, these circumstances caused many of them to emigrate a second time. This time they went to the USA, Canada, Australia or New Zealand, just countries where their newly acquired language was spoken. In today's politically and socially troubled times we should learn our lesson from their fate. Considering social and economic progress, my outline will give an overview on how German pork butchers, throughout the 19th century, rose to prominence in the heartlands of Britain's industrial society by introducing new meals and new marketing strategies, and thus highly influenced food consumption habits, only to abruptly fade into oblivion during and after World War I.
    ***

First Nations, Founding Nations & Fleeing from Nations. How Canada's colonial projects inform the immigrant experience
(1189) Marianne Vardalos (Laurentian University), Anas Karzai (Laurentian University)

Studies on the integration of immigrants into Canadian society have almost exclusively focused on the relationship between new immigrants and the dominant group, namely cultural descendants of the Founding Nations – Great Britain and France. There is little research done on the relationship between older diasporic communities and newer immigrants who are often refugees fleeing war-torn nations. There is even less scholarship on the relationship between new immigrants and Canada's indigenous people, known as the First Nations. In celebration of Canada's diverse make-up, the Government projects what social theorist Anthony Wilden terms, The Imaginary Canadian narrative. This narrative presumes the First Nations are extinct or, like the diasporic immigrant groups arriving over the last 200 years, suspended in time, having had no evolution since leaving the homeland. Both impressions permit Canada to brand itself in a manner which leaves it's colonial past unchallenged. History informs what it means to be from a First, Founding or Diasporic nation as well as what it means to be fleeing from war-torn nations. However, this presentation will show how history is contested through the various points of view of social stakeholders, government, researchers, Aboriginals, immigrants, refugees and NGOs. In 2017, as Ottawa is poised to receive 300,000 refugees who are themselves, fleeing countries the very countries targeted by Canada`s neocolonial invasions, the nation's diverse identity becomes more complicated. In the award-winning documentary, between: Living in the Hyphen, seven individuals disclose their firsthand experiences as "hyphenated" citizens, that is, people whose identities comprise two or more racialized groups. While Canada's official policy promotes multiculturalism, in theory, those who do not resemble the dominant Caucasian phenotype of the Founding Nations, as well as those who do but choose not to self-identify with it exclusively, still encounter racism and discrimination, explicit or implicit. Indigenous scholar, Anne Marie Nakagawa engages subjects whose immigrant experience is deeply impacted when they identify with both the colonizer and the colonized. This presentation brings together the scholarship of Nakagawa and Wilden to show how these identities form what, in 1965, John Porter called a vertical mosaic, in which colonial ancestry concentrates power and confers benefits into the hands of the few.

***

SESSION 2F – Göç ve Tercihler

	Room: B2
Chair	**Tuncay Bilecen, Kocaeli University, Turkey**
1214	Emirdağ Sosyal Sermayesinin Belçika'ya göçe etkisi – **Rukiye Tınas, Zeki Kartal, Özcan Dağdemir, Hüseyin Gürbüz**
838	Türkiye'deki İç Göç Hareketinde Beşeri Sermayenin Etkisi -**Selahattin Güriş, İrem Saçaklı Saçıldı, Mustafa Saygın Araz**
1253	Enformel Göçmen Dövizi Transfer Yönteminin Tercihine İlişkin İtici Etmenler - **Fethiye Tilbe, Selmin Kaşka**
1103	Kentten Kıra Göç Nedenleri Üzerine Bir Alan Araştırması: Tokat İli Örneği - **Emine Çetiner**

Emirdags' Social Capital Impact on Immigration to Belgium

(1214) Rukiye Tınas (Eskisehir Osmangazi University), Zeki Kartal (Eskisehir Osmangazi University), Özcan Dağdemir (Eskisehir Osmangazi University), Hüseyin Gürbüz (Eskisehir Osmangazi University)

Since the 1950s, the Emirdag district located in the province of Afyonkarahisar has been constantly exposed to migration attacks due to the low level of socio-economic development. This situation is continuing today, and it is likely to continue in the future. External migration in the context of Emirdag has gained a different appearance and character since the 1960s (within the framework of Turkey's labor export policy) by influencing the socio-economic level and cultural-sociological processes of the district. Following bilateral labor agreements signed between Turkey and different European countries in this decade, the main receiving country of Emirdag immigrants was Belgium, notably the cities of Brussels, Gent and Antwerp. As part of an ongoing research project realized in Eskisehir Osmangazi University, we are trying to identify the economic and socio-cultural changes of the province within immigration relations, and to reveal the socio-economic development potential and specialization areas of the province in the framework of local development. Furthermore, knowing that the sociological characteristics of Emirdag immigrants and residents of the dictrict have been changed with internal and external migrations, Emirdags' cultural-sociological-economic development is examined in a way to cover different periods with different immigration features. The possible contribution of the cultural and sociological processes of change of people staying behind and emigrating upon the socio-economic development of Emirdag is analyzed through the concept of "social capital". Statistical methods, in-depth interviews, and surveys are used to this end. A SWOT analysis was also carried out with social actors living in Emirdag and Belgium, to take advantage of their suggestions for the future of their district. In the light of the foregoing analysis and survey data, we would like to know whether there is an interaction between "bonding social capital" of Emirdag and immigration from this district to Belgium. "Does the existing social capital in Emirdag - considered as an element increasing the efficiency of other factors affecting migration and population movements (unemployment, poverty, etc.) - have an impact on the migration to Belgium?", constitutes the main question of this study.

***

Türkiye'deki İç Göç Hareketinde Beşeri Sermayenin Etkisi

(838) Selahattin Güriş (Marmara University), İrem Saçaklı Saçıldı (Marmara University), Mustafa Saygın Araz (Marmara University)

Göç, bireyin çeşitli nedenlerle yer değiştirmesi sonucu ortaya çıkmaktadır. Bu yer değiştirmede bireyin sahip olduğu bilgi, beceri yetenek ve niteliklerin toplamı olarak tanımlanan beşeri sermaye kavramının önemli olduğu düşünülmektedir. Bu çalışmanın amacı Türkiye'de iç göç sürecine katılmış göçmenlerin beşeri sermaye özelliklerinin göç etme olasılığı üzerindeki etkisini araştırmaktır. Çalışmada Türkiye İstatistik Kurumu TÜİK'in "2011 yılı Nüfus ve Konut Araştırması" mikro verisinden yararlanılmıştır. Beşeri sermayenin belirlenmesinde Mincer tipi kazanç denklemi kullanılmış, denklemin tahmininde parametrik logit modelden faydalanılmıştır. Araştırma sonucuna göre eğitim ve tecrübenin bireyin göç etme olasılığı üzerinde pozitif etkiye sahip olduğu görülmüştür. Bunun yanı sıra araştırmada erkeklerin kadınlara, evli olanların bekârlara ve gençlerin yaşlılara kıyasla daha fazla göç etme eğiliminde olduğu sonucuna ulaşılmıştır.

***

Enformel Göçmen Dövizi Transfer Yönteminin Tercihine İlişkin İtici Etmenler[3]

(1253) Fethiye Tilbe (Namık Kemal University), Selmin Kaşka (Marmara University)

Göçmenler pek çok farklı gerekçelerle göçmen dövizi gönderiminde enformel para transfer yöntemlerini tercih ederler ve sıklıkla da bu yöntemlere başvururlar. İlgili alanyazın para transferinde düzensizlik olgusunun her göçmen topluluğu arasında dikkate değer biçimde görünürlük sergilediğini göstermektedir. Ancak kullanılan yöntemler ve başvurma sıklığı her göçmen grubu arasında farklılaşabilmektedir. Bu ise, düzenleyici boyut, talep boyutu ve arz boyutu olmak üzere üç açıdan ele alınabilir. Bunlardan birincisi, ülkede kalmak için geçerli izni olmayan düzensiz göçmenler ile düzenli göçmenlerin karşılaştıkları engelleri içeren düzenleyici boyuttur. İkincisi, farkındalık, tercihler, güven, algı ve rahatlığı içeren talep boyutu iken üçüncüsü ise göçmen piyasası için para transfer araçlarının varlığı,

[3]Bu çalışma, TUBİTAK 2214/A Doktora Sırası Araştırma Bursu kapsamında desteklenen doktora çalışmasının saha araştırması bulgularına dayanmaktadır.

özellikleri ve uygunluğunu içeren arz boyutudur (Bester, Hougaard ve Chamberlain, 2010, s.11). Enformel para transfer yöntemlerinin tercihinde hem döviz kuru dalgalanmaları ve göç veren ülkedeki denetimler gibi harici faktörler etkili olurken hem de göçmenler açısından, çalışanları kendi dilini konuşan veya kendi kültürel değerlerini paylaşan bir hizmeti tercih etmek gibi öznel etkenler de belirleyici olabilmektedir. Bu çalışmada, Türkiye'den İngiltere'ye göç etmiş ve bu çalışma kapsamında incelenen olguyu uzunca bir süre deneyimlemiş 27 göçmen ve 7 anahtar görüşmeci ile gerçekleştirilen derinlemesine görüşmelerden elde edilen veriler nitel araştırma yaklaşımı kapsamında analiz edilecektir. Elde edilen sonuçlar, enformel göçmen dövizi transfer yöntemlerinin tercihinde göçmenlik statüsünün, gönderilen göçmen dövizi miktarının, geleneksel ilişki ağlarına olan güvenin, sosyal yardım alıcısı olma durumunun ve göçmenlerin işgücü piyasasındaki çalışma biçimlerinin oldukça etkili olduğunu ortaya koymaktadır. Ancak, ilgili alanyazında enformel transfer yöntemlerinin tercihinde öne çıkan maliyet ve güven unsurunun, bizim çalışmamız kapsamında ele alınan göçmen grubu açısından anlamlı sayılabilecek bir sonuç ortaya koymadığını ifade etmek gerekmektedir.

***

Kentten Kıra Göç Nedenleri Üzerine Bir Alan Araştırması: Tokat İli Örneği
(1103) Emine Çetiner (Atatürk University)

On dokuzuncu ve yirminci yüzyıllar yaşanan endüstriyel gelişmeler sonucu köylerden kentlere doğru büyük bir göç akışına sahne olmuştur. Kente yapılan göçün temel sebepleri arasında sanayileşme sürecinin yarattığı işgücüne olan ihtiyaç ile kentlerin sosyal ve ekonomik yönden köylerden daha gelişmiş durumda olması bulunur. Kırdan kente göçün sebepleri değerlendirilirken genellikle kentin sahip olduğu imkanlar çekici faktörler, kırın ihtiyaçlara yeterli cevap veremiyor olması da itici faktörler olarak nitelendirilir. Türkiye 'de 1950 'li yıllar sanayileşmesinin artmasına paralel olarak kırdan kente göçün başladığı dönem olarak kabul edilir. İlk etapta sorun olarak görülmeyen ve teşvik edilen göç daha sonraki yıllarda özellikle kentsel bölgelerde yaşanan işsizlik, kültür çatışması, gecekondulaşma gibi problemlerle karşı karşıya kalır. Bu nedenle artık kentler cazibe merkezi özelliğini yavaş yavaş kaybetmeye ve çekici faktörler itici faktörlere dönüşmeye başlar. Tersine göç olarak da adlandırılan kentten kıra göç hareketi başlar. Tersine göç hareketinde kentlerin ekonomik özellikteki itici faktörlerinin yanı sıra kentli yaşamın getirdiği stres ve kaygı gibi etkenler de psikolojik itici faktörler olarak karşımıza çıkmaktadır. Kırsal alandaki değişimler de göç olgusunu tetiklemiş ve bu bölgeleri daha cazip hale getirmiştir. Tersine göç hareketi belediye çalışmalarıyla da bir projeye dönüştürülmüştür. Tokat ili Karadeniz Bölgesinde tersine göç alan illerden biridir. Bu çalışmada büyük şehirlerden Tokat'ın ilçelerine geri göç yapan kişilerle yüz yüze görüşme yapılarak nitel veriler elde edilmeye çalışılacaktır. Çalışmanın amacı tersine göçü etkileyen itici ve çekici faktörleri Tokat ili üzerinden ortaya koymaktır.

***

SESSION 2G – Göç ve Edebiyat - 2

	Room: B3
Chair	**Ali Tilbe, Namık Kemal University, Turkey**
914	Sinema ve Göç: Avrupa Ülkelerine Yasa Dışı Yollardan Göçen Birinci ve Üçüncü Kuşak Türk İşçilerinin Türk Sinemasında Temsili: Otobüs (1977) ve Umut Adası (2007) Filmlerinin Karşılaştırmalı Analizi – **Levent Yaylagul, Nilüfer Korkmaz Yaylagül**
770	70'li Yıllardan 2010'lu Yıllara Almanya'ya Dış Göçün Türk Sinemasındaki Yansımaları -**Hanife Nalan Genç**

Sinema ve Göç: Avrupa Ülkelerine Yasa Dişi Yollardan Göçen Birinci ve Üçüncü Kuşak Türk İşçilerinin Türk Sinemasında Temsili: Otobüs (1977) ve Umut Adası (2007) Filmlerinin Karşılaştırmalı Analizi

(914) Levent Yaylagul (Akdeniz University), Nilüfer Korkmaz Yaylagül (Akdeniz University)

1960'lı yıllarda yapılan anlaşmalar çerçevesinde, II. Dünya Savaşı sonrasında yaşanan işgücü açığını kapatmak üzere Türkiye'den Avrupa ülkelerine işçi göçü gerçekleşmiştir. 1973 yılında yaşanan petrol krizi sonrasında işçi alımı durmuş, bunun üzerine işçi adayı Türkler kaçak yollardan Avrupa ülkelerine göçmeye devam etmişlerdir. Yaşanan bu toplumsal gelişmeler 1970'li yıllardan itibaren Türk sinemasında da yansımasını bulmuş ve yurt dışı göç temalı filmler yapılmıştır. Bu süreçte ortaya çıkan gelişmelerden birisi de yasa dişi göç olgusunu ele alan filmlerdir. Bu türün ilk örneklerinden sayılacak Otobüs filmi, yönetmenTunç Okan'ın 1975 yılında çekimlerine başlamasına rağmen 1977 yılında gösterime girebilen filmidir. Bu filmden 30 yıl sonra 2007 yılında yönetmen Mustafa Kara tarafından çekilen Umut Adası filmi de yine kaçak işçi göçünün anlatıldığı bir başka filmdir. Bu anlamda 30 yıl arayla çekilen iki film örneğinden hareketle birinci ve üçüncü kuşak kaçak göçmenlerin Türk sinemasında nasıl temsil edildiği sorusu bağlamında bu süreçte ne gibi değişikliklerin olduğunu ortaya koyabilmek için filmler nitel içerik analizi tekniği ile incelenmiştir. Filmlerde analiz birimi olarak görüntüsel göstergeler ve diyaloglar belirlenmiştir. Film içeriklerine yönelik oluşturulan araştırma sorularında kimlerin, hangi beklentilerle, hangi yollarla, hangi Avrupa ülkesine nasıl gittikleri, burada ne gibi sorunlarla karşılaştıkları, gittikleri ülkeye ilişkin istek, özlem ve beklentilerinin gerçekleşip gerçekleşmediği ve kendilerini nasıl bir sonun beklediği soruları çerçevesinde film içerikleri analiz edilmiştir. Bu bağlamda filmlerin öyküleri, göç edenlerin etnik, dinsel, cinsel kimlikleri, sosyo ekonomik kimlikleri eğitim durumları, meslekleri, kişisel özellikleri, hayattan ve göçten beklentileri, varsa kimlik ve kişiliklerini ortaya çıkaracak davranış ve diyalogları çerçevesinde filmlerin temel ve varsa yan mesajlarını ortaya çıkarmak amaçlanmıştır. Buna göre, Otobüs filminin temsil ettiği ilk kuşak göçmenler sadece erkek, kırsal kökenli, sünni İslam inancına mensup, vasıfsız erkek tarım işçilerinden oluşmaktadır ve göçün nedeni tamamen ekonomiktir. Karşılaşılan en önemli sorunlar, oturum ve çalışma izni olmaması nedeniyle iş bulamama, dil bilmeme, farklı kültürden gelmeleri nedeniyle kültürel adaptasyon zorlukları, cinsel istismar ve ırkçılıktır. Üçüncü kuşak göçmenlerin temsil edildiği Umut Adası filminde ise sadece erkekler değil, kadınlar ve hatta evli çiftler ve hamileler bile birlikte kaçak yollardan göç etmektedir. Burada da yine temel amaç ekonomik neden iken, göç edenler sadece kırsal kökenli vasıfsız, eğitimsiz kişiler değildir. Bunun yanında İstanbul gibi büyük şehirlerde yaşayan, eğitimli bir kesim de dil öğrenmek, mesleki tecrübe kazanmak, macera aramak, suç örgütlerinin elinden kaçmak, istemeden de olsa karışılan kriminal faaliyetlerin sonucunda ceza almaktan kaçmak gibi başka nedenlerle de göç etmektedirler. Bu üçüncü kuşak göçmenlerin sahip oldukları en önemli avantaj, daha önce göç eden Türklerin sağladığı dayanışma ağlarıdır. Bu ağlar, ahlâk ve kanun dışı yollara sapıldığında aynı zamanda dışlama ve cezalandırma ağlarına da dönüşebilmektedir. İlk kuşak kaçak göçmenler için Avrupa imgesi ölüm, işsizlik, sınır dışı edilme, cinsel istismara maruz kalma, özlem hasret, korku ile ifade edilen tamamen bir hayal kırıklığı iken üçüncü kuşak göçmenlerden hayal kırıklıkları ve benzeri sorunları yaşayanlara rağmen, Avrupa ülkelerinde iş bulup tutunanlar, hayallerini gerçekleştirebilenler için yaşanabilecek bir yer olmaktadır.

Gerek birinci kuşak gerekse de üçüncü kuşak göçmenlerden tutunamayanları ölüm, alkol, uyuşturucu, fuhuş gibi sonlar beklerken Türkiye'ye geri gönderilme de en yaygın seçenektir.
***

70'li Yıllardan 2010'lu Yıllara Almanya'ya Dış Göçün Türk Sinemasındaki Yansımaları

(770) Hanife Nalan Genç (Ondokuz Mayıs University)

Dış göç Türkiye'den Avrupa'ya, özellikle de Almanya'ya işçi olarak giden insanlarla ağırlık kazanmış bir olgu olmuştur. 1960'lı yıllarda başlayan süreçle birlikte Türk sinemasında iç göçü konu alan filmler yerlerini yavaş yavaş dışı göçü ele alan filmlere bırakmış ve böylece bir geçiş süreci başlamıştır. İç ve dış göçü konu alan filmler dikkate alındığında bu göçlerin belirme süreçlerinin toplumsal yaşamdaki etki ve yansılarının birbirlerinden farklılıklar taşıdığı görülmektedir. Bu durum iç göçten sonraki bir zaman diliminde ağırlık kazanan ve dış göçü konu alan filmlerin etkilerinin daha geç duyumsanması sonucunu beraberinde getirmiştir. Türk sinemasında yurt dışına yöneliş dış göç olgusunu ele alan filmlerle başlamıştır. Bu çalışmada, 70'li yıllarda başlayıp 2010'lu yıllara kadar devam eden 40 yıllık süreçte çekilen filmler onar yıllık dönemler halinde ele alınmıştır. Bu dört aşamalı süreç kapsamında Almanya'ya göç olgusuna değinen Dönüş (1972), Almanyalı Yârim (1974), Almanya Acı Vatan (1979), Polizei (1985), 40 m² Almanya (1986), Sahte Cennete Elveda (1989), Berlin in Berlin (1993), Duvara Karşı (2004) ve Ayrılık (2010) filmleri incelenmiştir. Almanya'ya dış göçün başlangıcından itibaren yaklaşık kırk yıllık bir süreçte bu filmlerde birinci, ikinci ve üçüncü kuşakların yaşamış olduğu ekonomik, toplumsal ve kültürel sorunlar ve bu sorunlardaki değişim adı geçen filmler temel alınarak ortaya konulmaya çalışılmıştır.
***

Görselin Gör Dediği: Görüntünün Tahakkümünden Göçün Güçsüzlüğü

(1226) Bahar Yalın (Karadeniz Technical University)

Görme, zihindeki imgelemin, gerçek ile düşsel olan arasındaki ilişkisini belirleyen zihinsel bir tasarım sunar. Bu sebeple görüntü, insan üzerinde tahakküm kurar. Fotoğraf, görüntüyü, "an" üzerinden, deneyimlenmemiş olan, anlamı ya da anlaşmayı mümkün kılan bir ortak referans çevresi, ortak bir dil olarak inşa eder. Böylece özünü empati kültürünün oluşmasına olanak sağlayacak duygunun yaratımı ve insan deneyimlerini belgeleyerek tarihsel tasarımın hafızasını oluşturacak "haber"/bilgi boyutu oluşturur. İnsan hareketliliği vurgusuyla yeni çağın en önemli gerçek ve sorunlarından biri haline dönüşen göç; siyasi, ekonomik, güvenlik gibi unsurların çok daha ötesinde sadecemekanın değil, kültürün taşınması bir başka ifade ile kültürel değ/iş/medir. Bu çalışmada göçün çerçevesini, haber/bilgi ve duygu/empati boyutu ile deneyimlemeye olanak sağlayan fotoğrafı, "anlamın aktarımı, anlamın göçüdür aslında" temeline koyarak ele almak amaçlanmaktadır. Bu doğrultuda Uluslararası Fotoğraf Sanatı Federasyonu (FIAP) ve Türkiye Fotoğraf Sanatı Federasyonu (TFSF) onaylı Gölcük Belediyesi ile Gölcük Fotoğraf ve Sinema Sanatı Derneği (GFSD) tarafından düzenlenen 2. Uluslararası Göç konulu fotoğraf yarışmasında ödül kazanan 9 fotoğraf üzerinden göçün nasıl temsil edildiği göstergebilimsel yöntemle incelenecektir.
***

Dil Sınırları Geçmek: Tony Gatlif'in Sürgündekiler Filminde Sürgün Bedenler Üzerine

(1355) Sibel Kaba (Istanbul University)

Savaşların, soykırımların ve böylece büyük ölçüde göçler ve sürgünlerin yoğun olarak yaşandığı modern dönem, belli bir dilde, kültürde, mekanda ve zamanda yerleşik olamama hali ve bunun yarattığı bir kaygı durumunu ortaya çıkarır. Tony Gatlif'in yönettiği Sürgündekiler (Exils, 2004) filmi, bu yerinden edilmişliği, hiçbir yere ait olamamanın bedenlerinde ve ruhlarında açılmış derin bir yaraya dönüştüğü sürgünün bedeni üzerinden bir yol hikayesi olarak takip eder. Film, sürgün olma halini, Paris'ten Cezayir'e, kendi köklerine doğru bir yolculuğa çıkan Cezayir asıllı Fransız bir çiftin, çingeneler, mülteciler, yasadışı çalışan işçiler gibi marjinalleştirilmiş özneler ve sınırdaki mekanlarla bedenleri aracılığıyla bir karşılaşma, birbirlerini keşfetme ya da birbirlerinden kaçma üzerinden ele alır. Duyguları bedenin hareketliliği üzerinden anlamlandıran bu bakış aynı zamanda, duyumsal bir estetiğin benimsendiği bir ifadeye dönüşür. Bu çalışma da Sürgündekiler filmi aracılığıyla, öznellik ve kendi-öteki ilişkilerinin, duyumsallık düzeyinde nasıl deneyimlendiği ve böylece sürgün edilmiş bedenlerin, duygularla olan ilişkisi aracılığıyla ne türden anlamlar ortaya çıkardı sorularına yanıt bulmayı amaçlamaktadır. Bu tartışmaya imkan tanıyan içerisi ve dışarısı, özne ve nesne, madde ve anlam arasında, dünyayı kavrayışımızı şekillendiren en önemli sınırların işareti olarak beden, bedenin kırılganlığı ve anlam verme kapasitesi ile ilişkili tartışmalar ışığında film çözümlemesi yapılmıştır.

***

SESSION 3A – Resources and Movers

	Room: A1
Chair	**Elli Heikkilä, Migration Institute of Finland**
1356	Why Focus on Nutrition and Health Status of Newcomers – **Hassanali Vatanparast**
1228	Right to Health: Provision of Healthcare Services to Syrian Refugees in Turkey - **Tuba Bircan, Seda Güven**
1184	Access to Health Services for Asylum Seekers and Refugees In Turkey: Comparison between Metropol and a Satellite City – **Faize Deniz Mardin, Nuray Özgülnar**
1155	Healthcare Practices of Migrants in Transnational Social Spaces: Retired Circular Migrants Living between Germany and Turkey – **Hürrem Tezcan-Güntekin, Basak Bilecen**
1157	Resources and Burden of Turkish Family Caregivers of People with Dementia – Empowerment of Self-Management Competencies – **Hürrem Tezcan-Güntekin**

Why Focus on Nutrition and Health Status of Newcomers
(1356) Hassanali Vatanparast (University of Saskatchewan)

Refugees are one of the highest at-risk groups for food insecurity. With the increasing rates of immigration to the various countries around the world, particularly the recent influx of Syrian refugees, concerns emerge regarding their basic needs, particularly access to culturally appropriate, affordable andnutritious food. This workshop will provide a comprehensive overview of the food security status ofrefugees, and challenges faced by refugees and the organizations providing refugee resettlement services, to achieve food security among refugees. Various countries in Europe, Middle East, North America and Australia are accommodating Syrianrefugees on a humanitarian basis. Refugees are at higher risk of food insecurity as a basic need, which inturn predisposes them to communicable and non-communicable diseases and other public healthconcerns. Although the wave of refugees has slowed down in the past decade, the Syrian crisis led toadmitting over 5 million Syrian refugees within the past 5 years. These raises concerns regarding ourreadiness for providing nutrition services to them in the light of potential challenges we face due to the language, culture, beliefs and practice barriers. Further, it justifies the need for revisiting our policies andpractices targeting nutrition and food security among refugees.

***

Right to Health: Provision of Healthcare Services to Syrian Refugees in Turkey
(1228) Tuba Bircan (University of Leuven), Seda Güven (Istanbul University)

The conflict in Syrian Arab Republic has resulted a large refugee crisis in the world. Now millions of Syrians, almost half the Syrian population, have been displaced either internally or as refugees in neighboring countries and beyond. A growing number of Syrian nationals have arrived Turkey for seeking international protection since 2011. Now Turkey is the host country with the largest refugee population in the world, including Syrians and other nationalities. Currently Syrian refugees have reached 3.1 million people in Turkey and the number of refugees is increasing. Refugee waves would almost certainly put pressure on the existing resources available to the refugees in Turkey. Growing number of urban refugees is creating a set of tough challenges for Turkey. Because these refugees arrive with a number of humanitarian and economic needs. One of them is about health. Increase of immigrant population makes huge effect in Turkey's health care system. There are significant problems in the access of refugees to the available health services. Despite of being a universal human right, healthcare is provided to all people in a country not based on need but according to their residency status. In Turkey refugees in long-term camp-based settings are often provided health services through health systems parallel to national health systems. However, the health services for refugees outside the camps are more complicated. All registered refugees in Turkey are entitled to receive free healthcare services in the towns that they are registered. But accessing health services and medication is a big problem for Syrian refugees who are living outside the camps. Syrian refugees experience difficulty in accessing health services due to their financial situation, official procedure, cultural and language barriers. The aim of our research is to investigate the international and national legal context on right to health and to discuses the access of Syrian refugees health care delivery for in Turkey.

***

Access to Health Services for Asylum Seekers and Refugees in Turkey: Comparison between Metropol and a Satellite City
(1184) Faize Deniz Mardin (İstanbul University), Nuray Özgülnar (İstanbul University)

During the last decades Turkey became a country of immigration after a long emigration history. In Turkey by January 2017, there were 295.401 refugees and asylum seekers registered by United Nations High Commissionaire of Refugees and up to that 2.910.281 Syrian refugees registered by the Prime Ministry Disaster and Emergency Management Authority . The new law which has been published in April 2013, titled "The Law for Foreigners and International Protection" provides national health insurance also to asylum seekers while previously it was only available for refugees.

This study aims to define the barriers to access to healthcare for refugees and asylum seekers in a metropolis as Istanbul and in a satellite city as Eskişehir after the establishment of the new law. Differences on access to health services between this two cities can be explained thanks to the description of rights in Migration and Health in Nowhereland report. Istanbul is a metropol where it is difficult to have a residency permit except some health conditions. This make Istanbul a "minimum rights" for access to healthcare compared to Eskişehir where almost everyone has a residency permit which defines Eskişehir as a "more than minimum rights" regarding to access to healthcare for refugees and asylum seekers. This is a descriptive study based on semi-structured interviews with refugees and asylum seekers in Istanbul and in Eskişehir at the Human Resources Development Foundation. This foundation has been working with refugees and asylum seekers since 2001 and gives legal consultations and psycho-social support. Interviews with refugees and asylum seekers took place at the Human Resources Development Foundation in Istanbul's office between 06.11.2015 and 08.01.2016 and in Eskişehir's office between 22.09.2016 and 14.10.2016. These interviews include questions about demographic data, UNCHR status, health problems and their experiences related to access to health services followed by their suggestions on how to improve the access to healthcare in Turkey. There has been 30 refugees and asylum seekers interviewed both in Istanbul and Eskişehir. Interviews were conducted with the help of translators of the Human Resources Development Foundation and participants' consents were taken. Among 30 people interviewed in Istanbul 14 (46,67%) were from Iraq, 12 (40,00%) from Iran, others were from Somali, Sudan, Central African Republic and Ethiopia. Regarding their UNHCR status 11 (36,67%) among them got the "Refugee" status and mean time was 24,18 ± 9,96 months to get this status. In Eskişehir among the people interviewed 12 (40.00%) were from Iraq, 7 (23,33%) from Iran, 5 (16,66%) from Democratic Republic of Congo, 4 (13,33%) from Afghanistan and others from Cameroon and Jordan. Regarding the UNHCR status 15 (% 50) of them got the "Refugee" status and mean time to get the status was 27,73 ± 22,18 months. Access to health services is analyzed on organizational, professional and community based barriers. The most common barrier in both cities was not knowing the rights to access to health services. In Istanbul one of the important barriers was difficulty to get residence permit and consequently to access to health services which is not a common barrier in Eskişehir. In Turkey, there has been done big steps regarding access to health services and health insurance coverage but still most of the refugees and asylum seekers do not know their rights. The society in Turkey is changing and the health problems are going to be much more diversified, therefore health services has to attune to this evolution.

***

Healthcare Practices of Migrants in Transnational Social Spaces: Retired Circular Migrants Living between Germany and Turkey

(1155) Hürrem Tezcan-Güntekin (Bielefeld University), Basak Bilecen (Bielefeld University)

Studies on healthcare of migrants usually focus on problems including mental health and psychosomatic complaints, and assume that migrants only use the healthcare services of the host country (Gideon, 2012; Menjivar, 2002; Faist et al., 2013). Criticizing previous research which rather portray confined and deficit-oriented perspectives, this study proposes a dynamic perspective arguing that migrants have simultaneous attachments not only to different nation-states, and thus, healthcare systems, but also to different healthcare practices (Sekercan, 2014). The transnational living is accepted as a lifestyle by older Turkish migrants in Germany and they organize their medical practices in a "welfare-mix" (Krumme, 2003; Strumpen, 2012). As migrants may also use healthcare services in their home countries, we empirically examine the influence of being subject to different healthcare services on migrants' consumption of medicine. This study specifically explores the healthcare practices of migrants from Turkey living in Germany and organized transnationally. A special focus of the study is on medication prescription and use. This study draws on 10 qualitative interviews conducted with older migrants from Turkey living in both Germany and Turkey and analyzed by content analysis (Mayring 2006). The participants choose to go primarily to their family doctors in Germany, get their prescriptions and operated on there because of their formal healthcare entitlements in Germany. Only during emergency cases they also use formal healthcare services in Turkey. The analysis shows that participants use a high number of different medicines and have complaints about this situation. Because they live simultaneously in two countries, irregularities in medication prescription and intake occurs. While they sometimes discontinue some of their prescribed medicine, they also rely on their informal ties to receive their medicine from Germany when living in Turkey.

***

Resources and burden of Turkish family caregivers of people with dementia – Empowerment of self-management competencies
(1157) Hürrem Tezcan-Güntekin (Bielefeld University)

Migrants from Turkey who came during the recruitment of workers in the 1960s/1970s to Europe have now reached the age when their need of nursing care is increasing. Research shows that in the next ten years the care need of older Turkish migrants in Germany will increase substantially (BMFSFJ 2000). Elderly migrants are often being cared for by their family members and they do not take up offers of professional support (Dibelius 2016; Okken et al. 2008; Tezcan-Güntekin et al. 2015). In order to enable family caregivers to continue to take care of their relatives and get access to supporting nursing care services, empowerment is needed (LLanque et al. 2012; Montoro-Rodriguez et al. 2009). The empirical aim of this project is to analyze the psychosocial burden and the needs of Turkish family caregivers of persons with dementia, and to develop concepts to empower the caregivers' self-management competencies. Twelve semi-structured interviews with experts and ten semi-structured interviews with Turkish family caregivers of people with dementia were conducted and analyzed using content analysis (Mayring 2006). The quality of home care is often insufficient because many family caregivers experience health problems and have a lack of knowledge regarding nursing care. Family caregivers are often affected by mental health problems, in particular by depression. The combination of the roles of husband/wife/children and the role of the caregiver represents a hurdle. They seek help at a very late stage because they perceive the dementia of their relative as a taboo in the Turkish community in Germany. Family caregivers suffer from helplessness, only some of them can change their attitude in a paradigm shift to an attitude of constructive action. Turkish family caregivers of people with dementia have a great burden, so that different instruments have to be developed to empower the self-management competencies of this group. The turn from the attitude of helplessness to an attitude of constructive action has to be supported through different instruments. One of them is an innovative self-help-structure, where the participants contact each other by instant-messenger-services and decide autonomously when and where they want to meet each other. Another approach is mother-tongue consultancy, with continuous monthly visits to the family with a person with dementia to model caring techniques, answer the questions of the family caregivers and offer them help possibilities in the changing phases of the disease with different challenges. These instruments are in development in two projects. A third instrument – interprofessional outreach care teams – is in development to give care for both, the person with dementia and the family caregiver. Turkish family caregivers are strongly affected mentally but have difficulty reaching for help. User oriented outreach support instruments have to be established to strengthen their self-help competencies.

***

SESSION 3B – Spatial Patterns in Human Mobility - 1
Room: A2

Chair	**Tahire Erman, Bilkent University, Turkey**
853	Sport in Creating Spaces of Meaningful Multicultural Social Interaction and the Fight Against Marginalisation of Youth – **K. Onur Unutulmaz**
882	As a Local Policy Problematic; Integration-Disintegration Process of Urban Refugees in Turkey – **Erhan Kurtarır, Elif Balı Kurtarır**
921	Linking Life through Time and Space: A Study on Bangladeshi Immigrants in Some Blocks of Indian Sundarbans - **Utpal Roy, Soumen Mondal, Saurav Chakraborty**
894	Futures Diverging: Mapping Japanese-Filipinos' Transnational Identities, Life Course and Aspirations – **Jocelyn Omandam Celero**

Sport in Creating Spaces of Meaningful Multicultural Social Interaction and the Fight Against Marginalisation of Youth
(853) K. Onur Unutulmaz (Social Sciences University)

A significant challenge facing the governments of countries with ethnically and culturally diverse societies is to create channels and mediums through which different segments of society meaningfully interact and communicate with one another. While this issue has mostly been considered in the context of integration policies and programmes targeting the youth of immigrant and minority communities, there is ample evidence for the need to go beyond this approach. It is true that the so-called second and further generation immigrants tend to be more vulnerable to become marginalised and even radicalised. However, it is also evident that the youth of host societies are also under the risk of social marginalisation in their increasingly super-diverse societies where multiculturalism is becoming a defining feature quickly replacing the older cultural norms of their parents. The current rise of populist, nationalist, and xenophobic political currents in the Western world further confirm this need for creating spaces of multicultural social interaction between young people of all backgrounds for sustainable cohabitation. This study investigates sport as one promising medium around which such spaces could be created. In fact, sport has become a consistent element of integration policies and programmes which could benefit the youth of immigrant and minority communities as well as that of host societies. Using the findings of an on-going research project funded by the Social Sciences University of Ankara, a comprehensive review and analysis of existing policies and programmes using various sports for this purpose will be presented. The data collected through rigorous review of secondary sources is complemented with in-depth interviews with coordinators and members of such programmes to understand the common elements of successful initiatives. The review investigates long-term and one-off policies and programmes initiated by the national and local governments as well as those carried out by the civil society organisations including sport clubs and covers countries as diverse as Canada, Australia, Turkey and European countries. Most of the in-depth interviews will be conducted face-to-face in the framework of two international fieldworks covering several countries. The first fieldwork will include the UK and the Netherlands and is planned to take place in June 2017. Therefore, the findings from this fieldwork will be presented at TMC in August.
***

As a Local Policy Problematic; Integration-Disintegration Process of Urban Refugees in Turkey
(882) Erhan Kurtarır (Yıldız Technical University), Elif Balı Kurtarır (Yıldız Technical University)

The majority of migrants and displaced populations move to urban areas. According to UNHCR data and The World Migration Report 2015 of IOM; 60% of refugees and 80% of IDPs are thought to live in urban areas as a result of conflict and other drivers. This massively urbanized problematic, needs local politics, local plan and local responses in order to reach a successful integration process. As becoming a local problem, social integration process of urban refugees is one of the key issues in host countries. Nevertheless, security oriented measures, international/large-scale policy measures and temporary measures for the existing problems of refugees delay the successful integration steps. For example, the key actors of the integration process, municipalities have been disabled in the face of the urban refugee crisis by the central authority of Turkey until now. This paper will compare Turkey's and other host country's urban policy perspectives. In order to clarify the problematic condition of refugees in Istanbul, different local experiences will be evaluated in prominent refugee destinations of Istanbul. Local responses of municipalities to these groups and identity construction process of these refugee groups on public space will be evaluated from international politics, local politics and urban planning perspectives. Finally, the paper aims to address a social debate, which has been very popular in Turkey in recent years; "Are urban refugees nurturing the cultural diversity and productivity or increasing the social and economic problems in the host society?".

***

Linking Life through Time and Space: A Study on Bangladeshi Immigrants in Some Blocks of Indian Sundarbans

(921) Utpal Roy (University of Calcutta), Soumen Mondal (Vidyasagar University), Saurav Chakraborty (Vidyasagar University)

Migration from Bangladesh to India became well-known phenomenon a decade after the partition of India in 1947. Primarily it was likely restricted to the West Bengal, the eastern part of undivided Bihar and the North-East India. Now almost every part of the country is within their reach. British colonial power at the time of leaving Indian right, divided India into two major nations India and Pakistan but a significant portion of territory of Pakistan was located far away from main land. Far away territory designated as Bangladesh since 1971 was known as East-Bengal till 1956, and as East-Pakistan from 1956 to 1971. From 1947 to 1971, migration used to take place due to different reasons than that of migration process after independence of Bangladesh in 1971. After becoming a sovereign and independent country, Bangladesh started dependence on its neighbour country India specially on West Bengal for many purposes mainly its close proximity, porous border, presence of relative or kin, favourable working environment, local political support and so on. This present study is an attempt to address the unfolded reasons of immigration from mainly southern districts of Bangladesh to over the selected part of four blocks of North and South 24 Parganas, West Bengal, India and to understand the livelihood strategy of immigrants' family at the place of destination, a place of new set up with respect to socio-cultural environment, economies, and regional politics. Principally, primary data from immigrants' family over study area have been collected using stratified and snowball sampling methods. Main findings are Hindu immigrants are still coming from Bangladesh to Indian Sundarbas that was started from 1905, main reasons of immigration are religious violence, poverty and insecurity, immigrants prefer to stay near relative house at present place of living, most of the immigrants never stay at a place for long again they migrate in another place in India. The results of it may be helpful to figure out the population dynamics across the study area.

***

Futures Diverging: Mapping Japanese-Filipinos' Transnational Identities, Life Course and Aspirations
(894) Jocelyn Omandam Celero (Waseda University)

Japanese-Filipinos constitute one of the largest groups of second and 1.5 generation born to Japanese and Filipino intermarriages, an outcome of Filipino women's migration to Japan which peaked in the 1980s. As children who are reared in a transnational family, Japanese-Filipinos' their birth and socialization may be characterized by sporadic movements between Japan and the Philippines. Thus, migration functions in their various life stages, inevitably orienting them toward the Philippines and Japan. Existing literature has focused on the instrumentality of Japan-bound migration, and its greatest value in the lives of the first-generation Filipino migrants. Consequently, Japan has been the dominant destination for fulfilling the educational and economic aspirations of most Japanese-Filipinos. Missing in the analysis is whether migration is a strategy of migration or an outcome of transnational practices of their Filipino migrant parents. The current study documents second and 1.5 Japanese-Filipinos' transnational migration experiences. It analyzes how the intersection between class, citizenship, ethnicity and generation may help explain the diverse life aspirations that Japanese-Filipinos build on Japan, the Philippines, and another country of migration. This ethnographic research is based on the author's doctoral dissertation on the transnational life trajectories of Japanese-Filipinos. It builds on the life narratives of (70) Japanese-Filipinos, aged 16-25 and are living in Manila and Tokyo. Fieldwork was conducted in both cities from 2010 to 2015 which involved individual semi-structured interviews, focus-group discussions and participant observations in various activities with more than (100) Japanese-Filipino families. This paper explains how structural inequalities between Japan and the Philippines, and family's transnationality determine their migration and other life aspirations. It aims to show that Japanese-Filipino youth's economic migration to and from the Philippines and Japan contains overlapping motives of realizing family (re)unification, interdependence and individual autonomy. Compared to other children of immigrants whose mobility projects are contingent upon their economic resources and social capital, Japanese-Filipinos' modes of transnational migration include actively seeking blood, historical and cultural affinities to Japanese and Filipino societies. This paper argues that Japanese-Filipinos' aspirations to become migrant workers, dual-nationals and cosmopolitans are both an outcome of their Filipino migrant parents attained social mobility and their own capacity to rationalize their own life course. Beyond meritocratic success that both societies prescribe, social mobility for Japanese-Filipinos means restoring the dignity of their Filipino mothers who likewise suffered from transnational injuries. Japanese-Filipinos' transnationality is their means to gain social acceptance both in Japan and the Philippines. Their cosmopolitan, dual-national, and worker-citizen patterns of transnationalism indicate that the first-generation has reproduced migrant life possibilities for the second-and 1.5-generation Japanese-Filipinos. Their life trajectories have enduring implications on Japan-Philippine relations, as well as the ever-shifting function of migration in the lives of children of transnational families.
***

SESSION 3C – Migration and Insecurity

	Room: A4
Chair	**Seda Taş, Trakya University, Turkey**
907	Legal and Circular Migration in the EU Mobility Partnerships – **Katarzyna Anna Morawska**
1070	Migration and Crisis in Europe: Swiss Migration initiatives as a result of national identity crisis – **Hüseyin Çelik**

Legal and Circular Migration in the EU Mobility Partnershipa

(907) Katarzyna Anna Morawska (Emigration Museum in Gdynia)

Immigration policy is one of the competence that the European Union (EU) shares with Member States. Its main objective is to ensure the balanced approach to legal and illegal migration. In accordance with the art. 79 and 80 of the Treaty on the Functioning of the European Union EU has the right to take action aimed at the management of legal migration, whereby it is for Member States to decide on numbers of admitted migrant workers to their territory. One of the elements of EU immigration policy are mobility partnerships – special agreements between Member States and third countries concerning the management of population flows. These declarations are to promote legal migration to the EU, including circular migration (temporary, repeated migration of foreigners). This article examines already signed declarations and also tries to answer the question to what extent mobility partnerships support legal migration.

***

Migration and Crisis in Europe: Swiss Migration initiatives as a result of national identity crisis

(1070) Hüseyin Çelik (University of Zurich)

This paper will examine Swiss immigration and citizenship policies that aim at fostering certain forms of collective identities. First, it will focus on the bilateral relations between the European Union (EU) and Switzerland, then analyse the interrelation of EU jurisdiction and the notion of sovereignty and constitutional identity of Switzerland. Furthermore, it will deal with the question, how should Switzerland govern immigration in light of the challenge to states' identity and self-determination on the one hand, and the protection of refugees/migrant on the other. The tested cases are initiatives regarding minority rights and aliens law (refugee and immigration). Finally, the paper will analyse the effects of the Swiss federal popular initiatives "against mass immigration" and the "Minaret Initiative" on Swiss-EU relations and ask the question: Is it justified for Switzerland to impose restriction on immigration and freedom of religion in order to protect its constitutional identity?

***

Some Results of Irregular Migration in Turkey

(961) Melek Zubaroğlu Yanardağ (Mehmet Akif Ersoy University), Umut Yanardağ (Hacettepe University)

The issue of irregular migration in Turkey is gaining an increasingly important dimension. In the context of irregular migration, it is known that many foreigners use Turkey as a target or transit country for economic and political reasons. Only in 2016, 174,466 irregular migrants were apprehended in various regions of Turkey. This number has been increasing, especially in recent years. The current irregular migration movements in Turkey affect not only Turkey but also the European countries around it. In 2014, 280 thousand people illegally reached Europe by sea and land. In 2015, this number increased to 1,046,600. It is known that irregular migration concentrates on the Aegean, Mediterranean, and Marmara coasts. According to the Turkish Coast Guard Command, a total of 490 irregular migrants lost their lives while illegally trying to cross into European countries in 2015, 2016, and the first months of 2017. This picture makes it necessary to

address the human dimension of irregular migration from a broader perspective. While coping with irregular migration, policies should be developed by keeping the human dimension of the subject in mind through investigating the causes that drive migrants to irregular migration. In parallel with this, fighting against human smugglers is indispensable. At this point, social work profession, which has to take an active role in the field of migration, must be maintained by improving its practices on the basis of human rights. While working with irregular migrants, social workers must stay away from stigmatizing and judicial attitudes and advocate for the protection of the human rights of these migrants.
***

Ottoman Armenians' Migration to the Balkans in the late 19th century: The case of the 1896 Ottoman Bank Raid in Istanbul
(1047) Hülya Eraslan

The objective of this paper is to analyze how Ottoman Armenians living in Istanbul and Anatolia territory were influenced of the Ottoman Bank Raid, carried out by Armenian Committees on 26th August 1896 in Istanbul, within the context of the migration phenomenon through the Armenian and Ottoman periodicals and Ottoman archive materials. In the 19th century, immigration has become a significant part of the agenda of the states and people. Ottoman Armenians living both in Asia Minor and Istanbul started to immigrate to mainly America, the Balkans, and Europe for a variety of reasons most of which involved socio-economic, political, religious, educational and security problems since 1830s. Particularly towards to the end of the 19th century, the main causes of mobility for Ottoman Armenians can be explained by escaping from the violence and absence of sustainable living conditions. The proclamations of the Hatt-i Sharif of Gülhane (1839) and the Reform Edict (1856), providing many opportunities for non-Muslim citizens, have particularly affected not only Rums and the Jewish but also Ottoman Armenians in a positive way. Concepts such as modernity, citizenship, and identity were begun to be discussed by the young Armenians educated in Europe. The 19th century was the era in which the Ottoman Armenian society experienced a class, sectarian, cultural, social, political and economic transformation. In addition to the gap between İstanbul Armenians and Anatolian Armenians, which is the primary class difference among the Ottoman Armenians, there exist denominational classes, namely Gregorian, Protestant, and Catholic, and class differences, namely the upper class (bureaucrats and Amiras), the middle class (tradespeople, artisans, journalists and authors) and the lower class (hamals). Being affected by the chaotic atmosphere caused by the Ottoman Bank Raid, the community living in Istanbul at that time started to seek new places to live. The Ottoman state had been dealing with separatist movements and rebellions since the beginning of the century and the last actor of the nationalism movement starting with the Serbian uprising in the Ottoman land was the Ottoman Armenians. Great powers of the period always wanted to intervene in the Ottoman's managing style of the crisis with the Armenian community which was defined as the loyal nation and regarded as trustworthy. England, Russia, France and Germany contributed to the reproduction of the Armenian question in different aspects again and again in accordance with their changing and conflicting imperialist interests. Therefore, since the Ottoman State think that the Armenians who immigrated to America started to pose threat, she enforced strict immigration policies both domestic and abroad. The main aim of the Ottoman Bank attack conducted by Armenian Committees was to draw attention to the Armenian question by capturing the financial center of the Ottoman Empire under the leadership of Armenian Revolutionary group. This event was the biggest and the most sensational of nearly 40 actions performed by the Armenian Committee in Ottoman land from the beginning of the 1890's. This incident brought in wide range of short and long-term consequences on the Ottoman Armenian society. Many Armenians and Muslims were killed due to fatalities in Istanbul during and afterwards of this raid. Many Armenians left the capital after the events and started to seek new places to live in the Balkans, Europe, and Anatolia. In this study, the immigration stories of the Armenians who went to the Balkans' cities were tried to be depicted using the Armenian and Ottoman newspapers issued in Istanbul and Varna at the time. The significance of this paper is because it is the first time that these reports and comments on immigration were used in this context. The documents regarding this issue in the Ottoman archive helped us to understand the atmosphere of the time.

***

SESSION 3D – Representation of Migrants

	Room: A5
Chair	**Deniz Ozalpman, University of Vienna, Austria**
1293	Material Culture of Migration: Representation of Migration through Toy Design - **Gökhan Mura**
895	Online News Coverage of the EU and Turkey Refugee Deal – **Nurhan Kavaklı**
1100	World's Reluctant Guests: Comparison of Syrian Refugee Coverage in Turkish and Norwegian Media - **Huriye Toker**
1257	Giving Voice and Dignity to Those in the Shadows: Testimonies of Latin American Immigrants in the United States - **Olga Mariella Bonilla**

Material Culture of Migration: Representation of Migration through Toy Design
(1293) Gökhan Mura (Izmir University of Economics)

This paper is about a toy. Toys as designed commercial objects for the entertainment or education of a certain group of users or as objects for collection and display purposes constitute a unique part of the material culture of societies. This paper discusses a plastic toy as a physical representation of the effect of Turkish migration on material culture in Germany and in Europe. Material culture studies have the potential to provide an invaluable perspective for immigration studies both for delving deeper into the culture of immigration and for expanding the boundaries of immigration studies by including -sometimes mundane- daily objects in the subject matter. There is growing interest in the convergence of the point of views of material culture and immigration studies in the recent years. The material world of the immigrant, the objects and the designed material environment the immigrants build around them presents a fertile domain to discuss especially the cultural questions and opportunities raised due to migration. The material culture research on migration usually embraces the objects and the material environment of immigrants as the focus of their inquiry. What the immigrants bring with them provide insight into how the immigrants' culture is transferred with the objects to their new environment. There is also newly emerging research on the transfer of material culture from the host country to home countries in the case of return migration. In both approaches the research is on the material objects and environments of the immigrant. However, it should also be considered that the material cultures of the receiving societies are also affected by migration. Cultural forms reproduced; created or invented by the immigrants either as daily practices or rituals transform the visual and material culture of the host society as well. It can be said that the integration of the immigrants is not a one-way activity but it is a result of an interaction that creates transformation both in the immigrant and at the receiving societies. This paper aims to discuss the effect of migration to the material culture of the society receiving immigration. It aims to present an initial framework for this discussion through analysis of artefacts produced in an immigration receiving country. The paper argues that a Playmobil toy from Germany can be considered as a physical manifestation of the influence of the Turkish migration to this country. Playmobil is a toy manufacturer founded and based in Germany that produces plastic figurines and accompanying accessories in various themes. This paper is going to focus on one item of Playmobil toys. "Kebab-Grill", a new figurine released in 2016 is a single toy figure of a "döner kebab" seller with his grill stand. The male figurine is black-haired and depicted as preparing take-away kebab in front of a döner grill stand. Playmobil figures and themes represent different cultures from different countries and from different ages of history. So, the figurines clearly resemble figures from that particular culture when wished to express it visually. This particular figurine however does not bare a visual symbol that can be associated with any particular culture. It is only the food that can be interpreted as a sign from an immigrant culture. It can be argued that food is a medium for immigrant groups to express their culture as well as contributing to and participating in the construction of their new society. Appropriation of the food culture of the immigrant groups enriches the collective identity of the whole society. From this point of view, we can consider the pervasiveness of döner kebab as the visible result of the Turkish migration to Germany. "Döner Kebab" becomes an element of the urban texture and a part of the daily routine for the cosmopolitan city dwellers in Germany, and in other European countries as well. This paper proposes to read this particular Playmobil toy as material manifestation of the migration culture. The author argues that the black-haired toy figure, a representation of a döner kebab seller is not representing an eastern looking male immigrant as the materialised form of migration, it does not represent the immigrant himself but it represents the collective urban culture cultivated by the immigrants. In other words, the toy figure represents the culture of migration in a cultural form that belongs to the whole society. This toy facilitates a discussion on how immigration in general and Turkish immigration in particular impacts the material culture of an immigration receiving society and aims to present a novel point of view for analysing the culture of migration in Europe and in Germany in particular.

***

Online News Coverage of the EU and Turkey Refugee Deal
(895) Nurhan Kavaklı (Uskudar University)

On March 18, 2016, Turkey to which Syrians escape from war by either taking refuge in or using as a bridge on their way to Europe, signed the EU-Turkey Migration Deal with the European Union. At its core, the agreement aims to stem migration and refugee flows to Greece which has become a back door to the EU for illegal immigrants. According to the agreement Turkey would accept the return of all "new irregular migrants" who arrived after March by travelling through Turkey. In exchange, EU Member States would increase resettlement of Syrian refugees in Turkey, accelerate visa liberalization for Turkish nationals, and boost existing financial support for Turkey's refugee population. It also would provide for the resettlement of one Syrian refugee from Turkey for each Syrian refugee returned to Turkey. However, the EU-Turkey Deal has raised concerns in Turkey about that the deal is fair for asylum seekers, refugees since it could have an important and dramatic impact on the lives of them and also on the way how Turkish society view them. This brings about the question of how the deal has covered in the Turkish press and also how migrants and asylum seekers are represented in the news, since the news media is considered as playing an important role in shaping public opinion so that in policy implementation. Another question related to the representation of them is whether the perspectives of refugees are reflected in the news. To investigate these questions, this article examines three online Turkish newspapers' coverage of the EU and Turkey Migration Deal

during a three-month period. For the analysis, Hürriyet, Milliyet and Cumhuriyet newspapers'online news are chosen for being influential papers in terms of reaching out to more people with a large variety of social backgrounds. The article uses both content analysis and discourse analysis to trace the way in which the refugees and asylum seekers are portrayed, and to see if the point of view of refugees is given in the news.
***

World's Reluctant Guests: Comparison of Syrian Refugee Coverage in Turkish and Norwegian Media

(1100) Huriye Toker (Yasar University)

In the contemporary world, our lives are persistently being bombarded by news about wars, economic crisis, domestic and international politics. Knowledge about the world has become important and necessary in an increasingly globalized and complicated world (Besova and Cooley, 2009: 220; Lippmann, 1922:9-18). News is the most vital element of mass media and a channel for disseminating the mediated communication. Therefore, it is the critical intermediaries for translating important international politics into forms easily distributed to and understood by the public. Relying on news, people discuss with each other, have opinions and make judgments about the world and relate them to the domestic politics. The vast majority of agenda-setting researches have found support for the idea that the public learns the relative importance of issues from the amount of coverage given to the issues in the news media. According to the related theory, by making some issues more salient in people's mind mass media can also shape the ideas that people take into account when making judgments about events or issues that will affect their opinions, which might cause "change in the standards that people use to make their evaluations" (Iyengar and Kinder 1987: 63). As the theory stated that news selection is at the heart of the agenda-setting process since the issues that fail to pass through the gatekeepers of the news also fail to give salience cues regarding the relative importance of the issues. Agenda-setting effects vary depending on the public's familiarity with an issue. As the flow of migrants and refugees continues to rise worldwide, so do anti-immigrant and anti-refugee rhetoric and examples of harsh treatment of these communities. There has been a sharp, global increase in incidents of both governments and individuals using hate speech against migrants and refugees, blaming them for their nations' struggles. The media play a crucial role in influencing public perception of migrant and refugee populations and their integration by providing accurate, well researched and objective reporting and analysis. However, both deliberate and unintentional negative portrayals of immigrants and refugees are often found in the media, thus negatively impacting people's views of these communities. This article aims to analyze and evaluate the media language and discourse on refugees/asylum seekers through the perspective of democratization and human rights. Two different countries in the Syrian refugee crises, Norway and Turkey, were deliberately selected in order to track the differences and similarities of the media coverage and its retoric. Two newspapers Hürriyet, and Aftenposten were chosen with reference to the level of circulation, ideological stance. Hürriyet is a typical mainstream, quality broadsheet with a high level of circulation in Turkey, Aftenposten is another mainstream newspaper of Norway which has highest readership level. The analysis unit is the front-page news content of the selected dailies which contain refugee/ Syrians related news between 2016-2017. According to the content analysis of Hürriyet 52.390 news included the word Syria and 8.403 of them also included the word refugee. In Aftenposten 7941 Syria and 3315 refugee related news content was found. The main findings of the analysis stated that refugees were mostly depicted in streotypical news framing in both countries. More than half of the news were covered the Syrian refugees as threat for social security in Turkey. However, the percentage is not high the Norwegain newspaper is also depicted Syrian refugees mostly "poor" people "in need of help" as well as "threats" for social security of Europe. These frequently repeated representations and ambivalence show that the representation of Syrian refugees in Turkish newspapers reproduces the stereotypical representation of refugees as defined in international studies. The analysis also reveals that the negative depiction is not a sole problem of Turkey, the other European countries have the similar streotypical coverage regarding the Syrian refugees which resulted the negative attitude of society in Europe.

***

Giving Voice and Dignity to Those in the Shadows: Testimonies of Latin American Immigrants in the United States
(1257) Olga Mariella Bonilla (Stony Brook University)

This paper analyzes the narrative of Latin American immigrants who, in search of the American dream, end up becoming victims of human trafficking. The experiences of these individuals encapsulate the identity crisis many immigrants face after fleeing their homelands looking for a new life in a foreign land that often reveals itself to be an antagonistic place. First, these immigrants' testimonies bear witness to the cruel and dehumanizing hardship endured during forced captivity and servitude at the hands of human traffickers. Using Homi Bhabha's theories as a framework, this paper examines the aspects of forced (non-sexual) labor and human rights violations in immigrants, and shows the numerous factors of human trafficking in the United States. Second, these immigrants' narratives show outstanding levels of low self-esteem and social devaluation. From Julia Kristeva's perspective, this paper examines the constant contradictory struggle immigrants face when trying to find a place in their new home: the erasure of their past (in their individual experiences) and the overemphasis of their past (in their collective experiences).

SESSION 3E – Migration Policy

	Room: B1
Chair	**Petra Bendel, University of Erlangen, Germany**
934	Who Talks about Human Rights? The Effects of ECtHR Case-Law within the German Debate on Asylum and Refugee Policies – **Johanna Caroline Günther**
952	Germany: West Balkan States Regulation – A New Model for Managing Migration? – **Carola Burkert, Marianne Haase**
896	Restriction, Pragmatic Liberalization, Modernization: Germany's Multifaceted Response to the Asylum Crisis – **Axel Kreienbrink**
950	Reflections of the European Union-Turkey Readmission Agreement on Turkey – **Rukiye Deniz**

Who Talks about Human Rights? The Effects of ECtHR Case-Law within the German Debate on Asylum and Refugee Policies

(934) Johanna Caroline Günther (Friedrich-Alexander-Universität Erlangen Nürnberg)

Developed for the special session on "Germany's refugee policy: Lessons learnt and to be learnt", this contribution will analyse the resonance of judgments of the European Court of Human Rights (ECtHR) within German government, media and civil society debates. As point of departure, the author will present the multi-fold responses caused by the ECtHR judgment "MSS v. Belgium and Greece" in German political and policy debates, moving on to other watershed judgments such as "Hirsi Jamaa and others v. Italy" and "Tarakhel v. Switzerland". The purpose of this approach is to assess the discourses preceding the climax of the so-called Flüchtlingskrise in 2015 and 2016. This perspective is however crucial when attempting to understand the development of the German refugee and migration policy – from the Willkommenskultur to increasing restrictiveness. The effects of ECtHR case-law have proven to reach far beyond the states involved in the court proceedings (Alter 2011: 6; Alter 2014: 184; Helfer/Voeten 2014: 80ff). Yet, the characteristics and markedness of these effects largely depend on the one hand on a pool of diverse actors that enable or hamper a judgment's power. On the other hand, norms established in and through ECtHR judgments compete with other "hot topics" for a top position on the public, political and media agenda. In this regard, an analysis taking into account the differing contexts of the pre- and the post migration crisis contexts inflicts itself. Legal studies, political studies and sociology offer various theoretical approaches and concepts helping to explain the effects and impact of ECtHR judgments on EU member states. In order to grasp the complexity of the European Union (EU) environment as well as the multi-fold normative framework of the European Convention on Human Rights (ECHR) the author selected approaches from norm diffusion theory as the main theoretical basis (Börzel/Risse 2009; Checkel 1998; Finnemore/Sikkink 1998; Gilardi/Meseguer 2008; March/Olsen 2009; Shipan/Volden 2008). Methodologically, this contribution is based on a combination of media analysis and discourse analysis – both methodological concepts are rooted in cultural studies but are easily applicable to and very insightful for political science analyses. They provide expressly promising tools for a thorough description of norms manifesting in governmental, media or civil society debates. A preliminary analysis of the responses to the MSS judgment has shown that German policy-makers closely monitor ECtHR case-law. Government, opposition, media and civil society alike engage in the analysis of its impact and meaning for German political practice – although to varying extent and with different foci (Günther 2014: 28ff). The assumption stands to reason that the impact of ECtHR case-law varies according to the policy field concerned, and based on a judgment's specific applicability and implications for the German context. Hence, an assessment of the effects of a greater number of judgments in the area of asylum policy – also to allow for generalisation – suggests itself. In a nutshell, it is yet safe to assume that ECtHR case-law can have a strong impact on political and policy debates; it may even reach beyond debate, thus contributing to policy change or reform.

***

Germany: West Balkan States Regulation – a new model for managing migration?
(952) Carola Burkert (Institute for Employment Research, Germany), Marianne Haase

German migration policies have evolved by introducing an innovative but also pragmatic approach of simultaneously restricting and liberalizing migration from the Wester Balkans to Germany as a consequence of the 2015 refugee crisis. In order to limit the asylum migration from the West Balkan states access to the German labor market for persons from these countries was facilitated in 2015 – parallel to the existing regulations of qualified labor migration. By extending the list of safe countries of origin as a part of a so called „asylum package "in autumn 2015, the legislator has, on the one hand, introduced a restrictive approach, and on the other hand created an unprecedented open and new model of migration. The introduced „West Balkan States Regulation" is quite without presuppositions compared to other labor migration regulations – just a job offer is needed in Germany. Our presentation analyzes the development of this regulation and its objectives and shows first quantitative employment developments on the German labor market. Furthermore, our presentation aims at assessing the regulations' potential to serve as a role model for managing migration and better regulating mixed migration flows.

***

Restriction, pragmatic liberalization, modernization: Germany's multifaceted response to the asylum crisis
(896) Axel Kreienbrink (Harokopio University Athens)

The massive inflow of asylum seekers to Germany in 2015 and 2016 put the country under pressure and challenged all responsible levels of the state. Looking back from today more or less all problems seem to be solved and the situation is fully under control. But this is a result of manifold improvisations and impressive policy developments under high pressure. This intense activity was necessary because the then existing rules and administrative regulations revealed several weaknesses. One may say that Germany chose the way asylum policy has gone many times: restriction. But such a view falls short regarding the variety of changes that were implemented. The paper does not give a simple account of the regulatory changes but analyzes how parallel developments of increasing restriction, pragmatic liberalization (especially in the field of integration policy) and enormous (ongoing) administrative modernization efforts took place at the same time.

***

Reflections of the European Union-Turkey Readmission Agreement on Turkey
(950) Rukiye Deniz (Istanbul Medeniyet University)

The European Union (EU) employs readmission agreements to secure its borders and protect the Member States from an influx of irregular immigrants and also to enable the externalisation of European borders. Turkey and the EU initiated the meetings for the conclusion of a readmission agreement in 2005 and signed the agreement on 16 December 2013. When Turkey's geographical position is considered, the agreement conflicts with the interests of Turkey. The instability in the neighbouring countries compels people to leave their countries and struggle to reach a safe country. These people use Turkey as a transit country towards Europe. In the case of full implementation of the readmission agreement,

Turkey, with a great possibility, will face social, economic, health, and security problems and also encounter hardships in managing returned persons. The paper argues that the readmission agreement has not been a success although it is advertised so in the media and by the politicians and that Turkey will terminate the agreement.

***

SESSION 3F – Kültür, Kimlik ve Uyum

	Room: B2
Chair	**Hasan Boynukara, Namik Kemal University, Turkey**
1217	Bulgaristan Türk Göçmenlerinin Uyum Sürecinin Dilsel Boyutuna Düzenek Kaydırımı/Karışımı Açısından Yaklaşmak - **Zehra Şafak, Sonel Bosnalı**
1067	19. yy Ortalarında Osmanlı Devletinde Romanların Sosyal ve İktisadi Yapısı; Edirne Şehri Örneği - **Muhammed Tağ**
1357	Suriyeli Mültecilerin Ekonomiye ve Istihdama Etkileri: Gaziantep Bölgesi Üzerine Gözlemler – **F. Serkan Öngel**
1114	Köyden Kente Göçün Geride Kalanlara Yansımaları: Kuşçu Köyü Örneği – **Pınar Laloğlu**

Bulgaristan Türk Göçmenlerinin Uyum Sürecinin Dilsel Boyutuna Düzenek Kaydırımı/Karışımı Açısından Yaklaşmak

(1217) Zehra Şafak (Ministry of National Education), Sonel Bosnalı (Namık Kemal University)

1989 yılından sonra Bulgaristan'dan zorunlu göçe tabi tutulan Türkler, Türkiye'ye gelişleriyle kendilerini farklı bir dilsel ortamda bulmuşlardır. Türkiye Türkçesi, Bulgaristan Türkçesi ve Bulgarcadan oluşan çok dilli özellikleriyle yaşadıkları bölgede farklı bir dil topluluğu oluşturmuşlardır. Bununla birlikte, dil kullanımlarına bakıldığında, Bulgaristan Türk göçmen topluluğunun dil değinimi durumunun "değiştirim" (shifting) türüne girdiği görülmektedir. Gerçekten, iki dilli bir yapıdan (BT+B), göç sonrası, önce üç dilli bir yapıya (BT-B-TT) dönüşen topluluk, bir sonraki aşamada Türkiye Türkçesinin daha baskın olduğu, Bulgaristan Türkçesinin işlevlerinin önemli ölçüde daraldığı ve Bulgarcanın neredeyse işlevsiz kaldığı bir yapıya (bt+b+TT) bürünmüştür. Bu sürecin aynı yönde ilerlemesi durumunda, topluluğun yakın gelecekte tek dilli bir yapıya (TT) evrileceği öngörülmektedir (Bosnalı & Şafak 2016). Bu dönüşümü, Berry'nin kültür(süz)leşme türlerinden biri olan asimilasyon olarak değerlendirmek mümkündür. Gerçekten göç olgusunda kültürleşme, genel olarak, yeni kültüre uyumun baskın olduğu asimilasyon, her iki kültüre de uyumun söz konusu olduğu çoklu entegrasyon, etnik kültüre uyumun baskın olduğu ayrışma ve her iki kültürün de reddedildiği marjinalleşme olmak üzere dört farklı türe ayrılır Berry (2003: 23). Bu çalışmada, söz konusu kültür(süz)leşme sürecinin kullanılan dilin yapısı açısından gözlemlenmesinin mümkün olup olmadığı sorgulanmaktadır. Bunun için, katılımcı gözlemleme tekniği ile göçmen ailelerin evlerinde yapılan konuşmaların kayıtlarından oluşturulan bütünce üzerinde kullanılan dilin özellikleri incelenmiştir. Yapılan çözümleme sonucu elde edilen veriler, evlerde aile bireyleri ve arkadaşlar arasında kullanılan dilin genel olarak Türkiye Türkçesi olduğunu ortaya çıkarmaktadır. Bununla birlikte, bazı bağlamlarda, düzenek kaydırımı ve düzenek karışımı yapıldığı anlaşılmaktadır. Düzenek kaydırımı ve karışımın sadece T. Türkçesi ve B. Türkçesi arasında yapıldığı; Bulgarcanın ise sadece, ve çok nadir olarak yapılan, ödünçleme düzeyinde varlığı söz konudur. Sonuç olarak, aile içi dil kullanımında tercih edilen dilin hedef dil (T. Türkçesi) olması, kültürleşme biçiminin asimilasyon yönünde olduğunu göstermektedir denilebilir. Bunla birlikte, bazı bağlamlarda, T. Türkçesinden B. Türkçesine yapılan kaydırım ve T. Türkçesi ile B. Türkçesine ait öğelerin eş zamanlı varlığı çoklu entegrasyonu da andırmaktadır.

***

19. yy Ortalarında Osmanlı Devletinde Romanların Sosyal ve İktisadi Yapısı; Edirne Şehri Örneği
(1067) Muhammed Tağ (Trakya University)

Osmanlı Devleti, Tanzimat dönemi ile birlikte iktisadi olarak köklü değişiklikler yapmayı amaçlamıştır. Bu iktisadi değişimin sosyal ve iktisadi hayata olan yansımalarını anlamak açısından Temettuât defterleri ayrı bir önem arz etmektedir. Defterlerin tutuluş biçimi itibari ile hane reisleri, hane reislerinin fiziki aksaklıkları (kolu çolak, âmâ vs.), vergileri, meslekleri ve meslek gelirleri, yıllık toplam kazançları, mülkleri, sahip oldukları hayvanlar ve bunlardan elde edilen gelirleri, tarımla uğraşanların tarla, bağ ve bahçeleri ve bunlara ait gelirleri ayrıca gelir getiren getirmeyen kişiye ait bütün bilgiler kaydedilmiştir. Bu bilgiler, dönemin toplumsal yapısını hem sosyal hem de iktisadi açıdan inceleme imkânı sağlamaktadır. Bu kaynaklardan elde edilen sosyal ve iktisadi veriler çalışma sahasının belirlenmesinde öncelikli etken olmuştur. Sosyal devlet anlayışının en güzel örneklerini göstermiş olan Osmanlı Devleti, toplumun yapısına binaen yapması gerekeni insan ayırımı yapmaksızın yerine getirmiştir. Bu çalışmada Balkan coğrafyasında önemli bir yere sahip olan Romanların Osmanlı Devleti içerisinde nasıl bir sisteme dâhil edilerek toplumla uyum sağlamış olduğuna değinilecektir. Genel olarak Osmanlı Romanları hakkında bilgi verilecek, daha özelde ise Temettuât Defterleri temel alınarak Edirne'de yaşamış olan Romanlara değinilecektir. Osmanlı Devleti'ne doksan iki yıl başkentlik yapmış olan Edirne'nin kozmopolit yapısında Romanların önemli bir yer teşkil ediyor olması bu çalışmanın inceleme alanının belirlenmesinde önemli rol oynamıştır. Romanların, Edirne açısından değerlendirilmesinde Temettuât Defterlerinin sağlamış olduğu veriler toplum içerisindeki durumlarına ışık tutacaktır. Bahsi geçen defterlerden hareketle Edirne merkezde yaşamış olan Romanların sosyal açıdan nüfusu, şahıs isimleri, lakapları ve meslekleri incelenmiş, iktisadi açıdan ise meslek gelirleri, bağ, bahçe, tarla gelirleri, hayvancılıktan elde edilen gelirler ve ödemiş oldukları vergiler değerlendirilmiştir. Elde edilen verilerde Romanların Osmanlı toplumu içerisinde üretken ve aktif bir rol aldığı aktarılmaya çalışılacaktır.
***

Suriyeli Mültecilerin Ekonomiye ve Istihdama Etkileri: Gaziantep Bölgesi Üzerine Gözlemler
(1357) F. Serkan Öngel (Gaziantep University)

UNHCR verilerine göre Gaziantep'te kampların dışında 280 bin 749 mülteci yaşamaktadır. 38 bin 649 kişi ise ikisi Nizip, ikisi İslahiye, biri Karkamış'ta olmak üzere kamplarda yaşamaktadır. Gaziantep'in hiterlandında yer alan ve Gaziantep ile birlikte Türkiye'nin 26 NUTS2 bölgesinden biri olan Gaziantep alt bölgesini oluşturan Kilis ve Adıyaman ilave edildiğinde kamp dışında yaşayanların sayısı 385 bine, kamplarda yaşayanların sayısı 64 bine ulaşmaktadır. Toplamda bölgedeki mülteci sayısı 449 binin üzerindedir. TÜİK verilerine göre bu üç ilin toplam nüfusu, yaklaşık 2 milyonu Gaziantep'te olmak üzere, 2 milyon 700 bindir. Bu da mülteci nüfusunun bölge nüfusunun % 20'sine yaklaştığını ortaya koymaktadır. Suriye savaşı ile birlikte göçmenlerin ülke nüfusuna göre oranının en fazla olduğu yer, her ne kadar göçmen nüfusunun en kalabalık olduğu ülke Türkiye olsa da, Lübnan'dır. Lübnan'da her 6 kişiden biri, Ürdün'de her 11 kişiden biri ve Türkiye'de her 28 kişiden biri göçmendir. Lübnan'ın nüfusu 5,8 milyon, mülteci sayısı yaklaşık 1 milyondur. Bu veriler Gaziantep ve Gaziantep alt bölgesinin Suriye savaşının etkisini Lübnan ve Ürdün gibi kimi sosyal sorunlarla birlikte ağır biçimde yaşadığını ortaya koymaktadır. Bununla birlikte Gaziantep ve Gaziantep alt bölgesi 2012-2014 döneminde sanayideki katma değerin Türkiye genelinde en çok arttığı bölgedir. Bu sıralamaya göre Kilis

3., Adıyaman 4. ve Gaziantep 6. sıradadır. Gaziantep 2016 dış ticaret istatistiklerine göre Türkiye'de en fazla dış ticaret fazlası veren il konumundadır. Bu çalışmada bu veriler ışığında Suriye savaşı ile birlikte yaşanan göç dalgasının, üretimi emek yoğun sektörlere dayalı olan, Gaziantep bölgesindeki etkileri ekonomi ve istihdamdaki dönüşüm üzerinden irdelenmeye çalışılacaktır. Araştırmanın olgusal dayanakları resmi istatistiklere dayandırılacaktır. Bunun yanında Ürdün ve Lübnan özelinde göçün istihdam üzerindeki etkilerini inceleyen çalışmalar ve Türkiye'de gerçekleştirilmiş kimi saha çalışmaları üzerinden kimi varsayımlarla çalışmanın verileri desteklenecektir.

***

Köyden Kente Göçün Geride Kalanlara Yansımaları: Kuşçu Köyü Örneği
(1114) Pınar Laloğlu (Ataturk University)

Modernleşme bağlamında ele alınan kentleşmeyle beraber ülkemizde özellikle kırdan kente göç daha yoğun olarak gerçekleşmektedir. Şehrin cazibesi, hayat standardı, iş olanakları, eğitim, sağlık vs. gibi pek çok neden kırsal göçü çekici kılmaktadır. Bu noktada göçün en çok tartışılan kısmı göçün şehirdeki yansımaları ve göç edenler üzerinedir. Ancak göçten geriye kalanlar da göç eden insanlar ya da göç edilen şehirler gibi olumlu veya olumsuz olarak etkilenmektedirler. Köyden kente göçün köye bıraktığı en önemli yansıma köylerin nüfuslarındaki azalma veya nüfus baskısının azalmasıdır. Buna bağlı olarak köyden kente göçün köyün fiziksel görünümünü de etkilediğini söyleyebiliriz. Hane sayısının azaldığı köylerde boşalan evler ve bu evlerin yıkık görüntüsü köyde bir terk edilmişlik hissi yaratmaktadır. Bu durum köylerde geride kalanları sosyal ve psikolojik olarak etkileyerek onların yalnızlık hissine kapılmalarına neden olabilmektedir. Tıpkı köyden kente göç edenlerin şehirde yaşadığı yalnızlık hissi gibi. Kuşçu Erzurum'a 18 km uzaklıkta olan; Erzurum Merkez, Aziziye Merkez ve diğer büyük şehirlere göç vermiş ve yakın zamanda da göç vermeye devam eden bir köydür. Göç edenlerin büyük çoğunluğu köyde yeterli düzeyde tarımsal geliri olmayanlardır. Köyde kalanlar ise arazisi olan ve hayvancılıkla uğraşan çiftçilerdir. Bu bağlamda çalışmanın amacı köyden kente göçün köyde kalanlara yansıyan sosyal ve psikolojik etkilerini araştırmaktır. Çalışmanın verileri ise Kuşçu köyünde 13 hanede yüz yüze gerçekleştirilecek nitel görüşmeler aracılığıyla sağlanacaktır.

SESSION 3G – Education and Migration - I

	Room: B3
Chair	**Yaşar Şenler, Namık Kemal University, Turkey**
789	Mevlânâ'nın "Göç Kervanı": "Beyin Göçü" nü Mevlânâ Üzerinden Okumak – **Betül Saylan**
1060	Hidayet Romanlarında Göç ve Kimlik Olgusu – **Cumhur Aslan**
1287	Ebedi Göçer: Medea –**Yıldız Aydın, Özlem Ağvan**
1295	Türk Şiirinde Göç Ekseninde İki Tema: Kaçış ve Hasret – **Yakup Çelik**

Mevlânâ'nın "Göç Kervanı": "Beyin Göçü" nü Mevlânâ Üzerinden Okumak
(789) Betül Saylan (Karadeniz Technical University)

Mevlânâ, kaleme aldığı Mesnevî isimli eseriyle çağlar ötesinden günümüze seslenen, yeri doldurulamamış ve fikirleri aşılamamış bir isimdir. İnsana insanı anlatan, bir endam aynası olan bu isim ve eserin teşekkül sürecinde birçok faktörün rol oynadığı şüphesizdir. Afganistan'ın Belh şehrinde dünyaya gelen Mevlânâ'nın babası Muhammed Bahâeddin Veled, dönemin çeşitli şartları sebebiyle ailesi ve talebeleriyle birlikte Belh'ten göç etmek durumunda kaldıklarında Mevlânâ 5 yaşındadır. Anadolu'ya, Karaman'a geldiklerinde ise, Mevlânâ 18 yaşında bulunmaktadır.13 yıl gibi bir süreyi konar-göçer olarak geçiren bu kervan, bu süre zarfında dönemin çeşitli ve önemli isimleri ile biraraya gelmiş ve fikir alışverişinde bulunmuştur. Mevlânâ'nın zihin yapısının şekillenmesinde babasından aldığı eğitim kadar bu göç esnasında temas halinde olduğu ve rahle-i tedrisinden geçtiği isimlerin de etkisi vardır. Bu seyahat süresince görüşülen isimler, küresel barışın muhtaç olduğu ilâhi mesajı barındıran Mesnevî'nin mayasını ve Mevlânâ'nın düşünce sistemini oluşturmuşlardır.

Bu çalışmada, tasavvuf tarihinde birçok sufinin tecrübe ettiği "göç" kavramı çerçevesinde, Mevlânâ ve âilesinin göç yolculuğunun mercek altına alınması ve bu sürecin Mevlânâ'nın zihin yapısının oluşumuna katkıları tesbit edilmeye çalışılması hedeflenmektedir.

***

Hidayet Romanlarında Göç ve Kimlik Olgusu
(1060) Cumhur Aslan (Çanakkale Onsekiz Mart Unversity)

Bu sunum çerçevesinde 1980'li yıllarda etkili olan Hidayet romanlarında "göç" olgusu ele alınarak, Türkiye'de muhafazakârlığın ve İslamcılığın güçlenmesindeki temel kodlar saptanmaya çalışılacaktır. Türkiye'de 1970'li yıllardan başlayarak, 1980'lerde yükselişe geçen ve bugün iktidara yerleşen İslamcı-muhafazakâr gelenek, tarihsel süreç içerisinde kendi "kimlik" alanını çeşitli "araçlar" yoluyla dile getirmeye çalışmıştır. İslami gelenek tarikatlar, vakıflar, cemaatler, hem şehri gruplar aracılığıyla, hem de gazete, dergi, sinema ve edebiyat aracılığıyla da kendini ifade etme, kimlik ve ideoloji üretimini gerçekleştirmişlerdir. 1970'ler ve 1980'li yıllarda İslami muhafazakâr temalı romanlara "hidayet" romanları adı verilmektedir. 1980'lerden itibaren İslamcılar Türk siyasal ve toplumsal hayatında artan biçimlerde hakim olmaya, kamusal alanı ve özel alanı kontrol etmeye başlamışlardır. Kamusal alanda özellikle 1990'larda belediyeler aracılığıyla güç kazanmaya başlayan İslamcılık, Refah Partisi, Fazilet Partisi ve Akparti örnekleriyle birlikte Türkiye'de temel belirleyici konuma ulaşmış, siyasetten ekonomiye, sanattan kültüre, medyadan edebiyata kadar her alanda etkin konuma ulaşmışlardır. Şerif Mardin'in "merkez-çevre" ikiliğine dayalı toplumsal analiz, 1923-1980 dönemi arasında "merkez" olarak var olan yapıların güç yitirdiğini, bu dönemde "çevre" olarak adlandırılan kesimlerin güç kazandığını göstermektedir (Mardin, 2013:35-79). Sermaye biçimlerini kontrol ederek, iktisadi gücü eline geçirmeye başlayan İslamcı gelenek, Refaf Partisi/AKP ile siyasal alanı da kontrol etmeye başlayınca, söylem, ideoloji ve kültürel açıdan önemli değişimler yaşamıştır. Bu bağlamda edebiyat ve roman geleneği de değişmiş, medya, popüler kültür ve ideoloji önemli oranda dönüşmeye başlamıştır. "Hidayet Romanları" 1980'li yıllarda yazılan İslami nitelikli eserlerin büyük bölümüne verilen isimdir. Bu romanlar 1980'lerde çokça yazılan, popüler nitelikli romanlardır. Hidayet romanları, İslami dünya görüşü doğrultusunda yazılmış "tezli romanlardır" (Çayır, 2008:8) Hidayet romanları "mesaj" verme kaygısı taşıyan, insanları "hidayet" e ulaştırmak için onlara doğru yolu gösteren şematik eserlerdir. Bu yönüyle "hidayet romanları" toplumsal alanın dışında yer alan kesimlerin "kimlik" lerini ifade etmelerinin bir aracı olmuştur. Bu çerçevede özellikle popüler romanlar ve filmler İslami kimliğin oluşmasında, benlik algılarının şekillenmesinde önemli katkılar sunmuşlardır. İslamcılığı toplumsal alanda kolaylıkla mobilize olması ve insanların "benlik" algılarını tamamlamaları açısından İslami romanlar ve filmler ciddi birer ideolojik araç işlevi görmüşlerdir. Hidayet romanları 1960'lardan sonra Türk toplumunda "taşra", "çevre" nin kendini anlatma ve ideolojik olarak kendine yer bulma arayışının bir ifadesi olarak yayınlanmaya başlamış, kısa sürede popülerleşerek geniş kitlelere ulaşmıştır. Hidayet romanlarının en fazla basıldığı, 'Yeşil yayıncılık' alanının da en büyüğü olarak kabul edilen Timaş Yayınları'nın sıralamasına göre en çok satan isimler sırayla şunlar: 1. Ahmet Günbay Yıldız; 2. Şule Yüksel Şenler; 3. Hekimoğlu İsmail; 4. Sevim Asımgil; 5. Halit Ertuğrul (http://hamzaaktan.blogspot.com.tr/2010/07/islami-romanlar-devri-kapanyor.html) Bu çerçevede "ilk dikkat çeken isim, Hekimoğlu İsmail'dir. İlk İslami roman olarak adlandırılabilecek eseri Minyeli Abdullah (1967), yayımlandığında geniş kitlelere ulaşır. Bir diğer önemli roman, Şule Yüksel Şenler'in Huzur Sokağı romanıdır. 1969 yılında ilk olarak bir gazetede tefrika şeklinde yayımlanan roman, daha sonra kitap olarak basılmış ve çok satılan kitaplar arasına girmiştir. Ahmet Günbay Yıldız da dönemin en çok tanınan hidayet romanı yazarları arasındadır. Kitapları defalarca basılan Günbay Yıldız, çok eser veren bir yazar olarak da dikkat çeker. Bu isimlere Emine Şenlikoğlu, Ahmet Talat Uzunyaylalı, Halit Ertuğrul, Şerife Katırcı Turhal, Sevim Asımgil, Mehmet Zeren, Hüseyin Karatay, Ahmet Lütfü Kazancı, Mecbure İnal da eklenebilir (Türkmenoğlu, 2015: 264-265). Hidayet romanları "ideal toplum" ve "ideal insan" anlayışının ne olması gerektiğine dair bir temel çerçeveye dayanır. Toplumun nasıl yaşaması gerektiğine dair "model" sunmayı amaçlayan hidayet romanlarında "göç" önemli bir toplumsal referans kaynağı olarak olarak işlev görür. Hidayet romanlarında "göç" hidayete ermenin, ötekilerle karşılaşmanın ve iyi/makbul vatandaş olmanın açıklanmasında önemli bir kavşak noktasına tekabül etmektedir. "İdeolojik" bir içeriğe sahip olan bu metinler, insanların hidayete ermelerinde "mekan/kültür" bağlamına da ayrıca önem vermektedir. Burada Anadolu/taşra, batı/şehir vurgusu İslamcılığın tarihsel soy kütüğünde kimlik kurucu bir işlev üstlenmiştir. Bu anlamda Anadolu/taşra ile karakterize edilen İslamcı yaşayışın karşısına, Batı/Şehir ikilemi çıkarılmıştır. Temel perspektifi "karşıtlıklar" üzerine dayanan hidayet romanlarında "göç" olgusu, bu karşıtlıkları "mekânsal deneyim" üzerinden kurmakta, dinsel yaşayışa uygun "muhit" ler ile dinsel yaşayışa ters "muhit" ler karşıtlığı üzerinden mekanı politize etmekte, İslamcı yaşayışın yaygınlaşması, bir anlamda kamusallaşması için de örtük mesajlar vermektedir. Bu çalışmada İslamcı söylem ve ideolojide yaygın bir eğilim olarak var olan "biz/onlar" ayrımının kristalize olduğu "mekânsal üretim"in açık biçimde dile getirldiği "hidayet romanları" aracılığıyla "göç", "mekanın üretimi" ve "kimliğin kurulması" süreçlerini ele alıp inceleyeceğiz. Bu çerçevede Hidayet romanları içerisinde yaygın biçimde irdelenmiş olan "kurucu metinler" olarak adlandıracağımız "Minyeli Abdullah" ve "Huzur Sokağı" gibi metinler dışında daha "basit" düzeyde ve "kamusal popülaritesi" düşük fakat bireylerin gündelik davranışlarında daha fazla etkili olan "ideolojik" metinlere odaklanacağız. Bu anlamda hidayet romanlarındaki "vulger" metinler üzerinden mekan/kimlik oluşumunun ip uçlarını yakalamaya çalışacağız. Bu çerçevede Raif Cilasun'un (1906-1998) "Beklenen Sabah", "Oğlum Osman", "Bir Annenin Feryadı ve "Gafiller" romanı üzerinde duracağız. Bunun yanında doğrudan "göç" olgusu üzerine eğilmiş diğer "hidayet romanları" üzerinde de konu ve benzerlik/farklılıklar kapsamında değinilmeye çalışılacaktır.

***

Ebedi Göçer: Medea
(1287) Yıldız Aydın (Namık Kemal University), Özlem Ağvan (İstanbul Aydın University)

Söylencelerde sıra dışı karakterlerden biri olan Medea ilk olarak M.Ö. 431 yılında Euripides tarafından kaleme alınmıştır. Yaklaşık 2500 yıldır yazından resme, tiyatrodan operaya ve sinemaya kadar hakkında yüzlerce yapıt üretilmiş olan bu trajik figür, doğaüstü güçlere sahip güçlü, diğer taraftan ürkütücü kaderiyle yalnız başına kalmış yabancı bir kadın olarak günümüzde hala pek çok yazara ve sanatçıya esin kaynağı olmaktadır. Euripides'in ilk olarak ele aldığı ve dünya yazınına kazandırdığı Medea ağlatısına yakından bakıldığında göç izleğinin önemli bir sorunsal olarak kurgulandığı söylenebilir, çünkü Medea ilkin altın postu almak için Argonot gemisiyle memleketi Kolkis'e gelen Yunan kahramanı Jason ile birlikte batıya kaçar; Jason'un ihanetinden sonra büyücü yetilerinden korktuğu gerekçesiyle Korint kralı tarafından sürgün edilir, son olarak kocasından intikam almak için iki çocuğunu öldürdükten sonra sığınma talebinde bulunarak başka bir yere göç eder. Medea bu üç ulamlı devinim dikkate alındığında dünya yazınında ebedi göçer olarak bilinen ve bir yerde huzur bulamayan Ahasver figürüne de yakınlık göstermektedir. Bir kalıp olarak kullanılan Euripides'in yapıtı hemen hemen bütün Medea çalışmalarında sözü edilen üç ulamlı devinimi görmek mümkündür. Medea alımlamalarında göç, sürgün ve sığınma izlekleri farklı ekinsel ve ulusal öğeleriyle yoğrularak ve her dönemde tekrar edilerek yeniden canlandırılmıştır. Söylencelerde ebedi tekerrür (M. Eliade) diye sözü edilen olgu, Medea söylencesinin güncelliğinin korunmasını sağlamıştır. Sonsuz bir tekrardan beslenen söylenceler üzerine çalışma yapmak bir açıdan ekinsel gerçeklik üzerine çalışma yapmak (H. Blumenberg) bağlamında da ele alınmaktadır. O nedenle Medea söylencesi üzerine çalışma yapan yazar ve sanatçılar bu söylencede bulunan yoruma açık noktalardan hareketle kendi ekinsel gerçekliklerini yapıtlarına katmışlardır. Yaşadığı dönemde toplumsal ve ekinsel olayları oyunlarına entegre ettiği bilinen Euripides'in Medea karakterini oluştururken göç ile birlikte sürgün, sığınma, yabancı ve öteki gibi sorunları bu denli yoğun olarak ağlatısında işlemesi bir rastlantıdan ibaret değildir. Burada gerçeklik ile kurgu ustalıkla bir araya getirilirken, yaşamı boyunca vatan edinme çabası içinde olan yabancı bir kadın kahramanı aracılığı ile dünya yazınına önemli bir malzeme sunulmuştur. Bu çalışmada ilk aşamada yazıntarihsel, yazıntoplumsal ve ekinsel kaynaklardan hareketle Euripides'in dünya yazınına kazandırdığı Medea yapıtında neden yabancı ve barbar bir kadın sorunsalını ele aldığı ve üç ulamlı göçer izleğini nasıl yansıttığı incelenecek; ikinci aşamada dünya yazınında bilinen birkaç Medea alımlamalarını Euripides'in yapıtıyla karşılaştırarak göçer izleği açısından ne ölçüde benzerliklerin bulunduğu analiz edilecektir.

Türk Şiirinde Göç Ekseninde İki Tema: Kaçış ve Hasret
(1295) Yakup Çelik (Yıldız Technical University)

Türk şiirinde göç, daha doğrusu ait olduğu toplumdan ve yaşayış tarzından uzaklaşma; kaçış, arayış ve hasret temaları çevresinde gelişir. Cumhuriyet dönemi Türk şiirinde arayışın ve ruh fırtınalarının vardığı nokta kaçıştır. Bazen toplum dışına itilmiş bazen ruhsal sarsıntılar geçiren bazen de beklentilerine cevap bulamayan bireyin başvuru kaynağıdır kaçış. Bu tema, maceralara yönelme veya zorunlu göç kapsamında da okuyucunun karşısına çıkar. Çünkü bulunduğu mekandan uzaklaşmak; aşktan, sevgiden, şefkatten yoksunluktur. Kaçışın veya yetiştiği değerlerden uzaklaşmanın beraberinde getirdiği bir başka duygu hali hasrettir. Şiirlerdeki duygu haline ve düşünce noktasına mutlaka göç merkezli bakmamak gerekir. Bireyin kendinden, alışkanlıklarından, yetişme tarzından, inançlarından uzaklaşması. Peşinden bütün bunlara duyduğu hasret de bu çerçevededir. Bildirimizde Cumhuriyet dönemi Türk edebiyatında kaçış ve hasret temalarının şiirdeki yansımaları Nazım Hikmet, Attila İlhan, Necip Fazıl Kısakürek, Edip Cansever ve Bahaeddin Karakoç merkeze alınarak değerlendirilecektir.
***

SESSION 4A– Economics of Migration – 2

	Room: A1
Chair	**Şule Akkoyunlu, Rimini Centre, Wilfrid Laurier University, Canada**
814	Dutch Dilemma: Sustainable Economic Growth, Migration, Culture and Integration - **Mustafa Güleç**
1281	International Remittances and Private Healthcare: Evidence from Kerala, India - **Mohd Imran Khan**
1055	Credit constraints and Rural Migration: Evidence from six villages in Uttar Pradesh - **Ruchi Singh**
1288	Main money transfer operators failed to reduce cost of remittances to 10 developing countries - **Andrej Privara, Ibrahim Sirkeci**

Dutch Dilemma: Sustainable Economic Growth, Migration, Culture and Integration
(814) Mustafa Güleç (Ankara University)

In the post-war era, industrialized Western European Countries began to attract cheap labour force from the Mediterranean region. Similarly, Dutch governments recruited less educated temporary workers (hence the term gastarbeider: guest worker) firstly from Italy, Spain, the Balkan region and then mainly from Turkey and Morocco (because Turkish and Moroccon workers were cheaper than, for instance, Italians) upon the request of the Dutch industry. However, when it turned out that social costs of the less educated labour force are too much for the Dutch society, the Dutch government went for a policy shift as of late 1990s and adopted more or less an Anglosaxon-model: in order to make the Netherlands (and the EU at large) the most competitive and dynamic knowledge economy of the world, needs-based and skill-based migratory flows (it can also be named brain-drain) were allowed towards the Netherlands from countries such as Turkey (Kulu-Glasgow, 2015: 69). Interestingly, however, a return migration of even highly educated Turkish employees from the Netherlands can be observed in the recent past as a result of better employment opportunities in Turkey, increasingly hardening Dutch political climate and growing intolerance for non-western migrants. Highly educated Turkish migrants tend to return to their homeland due to the hardened tone of the Dutch public debate on integration of non-western migrants (Kulu-Glasgow, 2015: 80). Consequently, migrants of late 90s stay less at destination countries. More educated Moroccan and Turkish employees tend to reduce their length of stay compared to less educated migrants in the Netherlands (Kahn & Billfeld, 2015: 34). There is thus obviously a necessity for a more encompassing model referring to identified differences of return experiences from migration experience (Şeker, 2015; Künüroğlu, 2015: 136). This paper will focus mainly on the Dutch migration dilemma, which includes an inevitable economic growth and global competitiveness on the one hand; migration, multiculturalism debate and its social consequences on the other. It will show that economic and demographic factors have a compelling function over emotional factors, if one plans a sustainable growth.

***

International Remittances and Private Healthcare: Evidence from Kerala, India
(1281) Mohd Imran Khan (Centre for Development Studies, Kerala)

The inflow of international remittances to Kerala has been increasing for the last three decades. It had increased households' income and enabled them to spend more on human capital investments. Using data from Kerala Migration Survey 2010, this study analyses the impact of remittances receipt on access to private hospitals in Kerala. This study employs instrumental variable (IV-Probit) approach to account for the endogeneity of remittances receipt. The empirical results show that remittances income has a positive and significant impact on access to private healthcare services. After disaggregating the sample into different heterogeneous groups, this study found that remittances have a greater effect on lower income households and Other Backward Class (OBC) households but not Schedule Caste (SC) and Schedule Tribes (ST) as they remain excluded from reaping the benefit of international migration and remittances.

***

Credit constraints and Rural Migration: Evidence from six villages in Uttar Pradesh
(1055) Ruchi Singh (Central University of Hyderabad)

Rural economies in developing countries are often characterized by credit constraints. Various studies confirm that rural labor migration in developing countries is an outcome

of capital market imperfections. Lack of easy accessibility to credit followed by exorbitant rate of interest charged by informal sources of credit worsens the condition of poor households. Uttar Pradesh is among few most backward states of India and exhibits highest rate of male out-migration among all states (NSSO). Although few attempt have been made to understand trends and patterns of male out-migration from Uttar Pradesh (UP), there is dearth of literature on linkage between credit accessibility and male migration in rural Uttar Pradesh. The current study tries to fill this void. Objective of the study is to assess the role of credit accessibility in determining rural male migration. To meet the objective and to have better understanding of the role played by credit constraints in migration decisions, the study undertake primary survey of 370 households in six villages of Jaunpur district in UP. Simple statistical tools and binary logistic regression model have been used. The result of empirical analysis shows that accessibility and various sources of credit play very important role in male migration in rural UP. Study also found that relationship between credit constraints and migration varies across various social groups in UP. Thus, more financial inclusion shall be encouraged in rural Uttar Pradesh and an attempt shall be made to ensure easy access of credit to rural households. Various ongoing schemes on financial inclusion shall be more properly implemented and encouraged among rural households to prevent them from various kinds of exploitation by local moneylender.
***

Main money transfer operators failed to reduce cost of remittances to 10 developing countries

(1288) Andrej Privara (University of Economics in Bratislava), Ibrahim Sirkeci (Regent's University London)

Sending remittances home is still an expensive affair for many migrants. Since the global financial crisis, remittances costs/prices remained relatively high in many corridors. In this study, we have looked at prices for sending remittances from the UK to 10 developing countries with known sizeable receipts of remittances. Despite all positive discourses and political will prices remained high. Variation can be explained by policies, barriers as well as volume of remittances transferred between countries.
***

SESSION 4B – Identity and Migration - 1

	Room: A2
Chair	**Elli Heikkilä, Migration Institute of Finland**
1007	Intersectionality and Migration Studies - **Laís Saleh**
724	The 2011 riots in London: The Response of Kurdish and Turkish Communities – **Olgu Karan**
968	Between high-skilled and low-skilled migration – young Kurds in Istanbul as middling migrants – **Karol Pawel Kaczorowski**
1066	Migration from Dersim to Europe - **Hüseyin Çelik**

Intersectionality and Migration Studies
(1007) Laís Saleh (University of Lisbon)

Engendering migration studies has been an ongoing work from the 1980s until today, and this paper aims to discuss this trajectory. In parallel with changes within feminist literature and debate, migration studies have attempted to incorporate a gender sensitive approach. Surpassing the male bias and the pretense neutrality behind this area of study was the first challenge and the most successful, as gender is no longer seen as a less important category when studying migration. Gender is assumed to be one of the most important social divisions when shaping migratory projects. Yet, this burgeoning field has had difficulties in incorporating more to the mainstream analysis and kept itself in feminist journals and publications. This is the case with intersectionality, which is today one of the most debated contribution from feminist studies to the social sciences. This article will discuss the trajectory of feminism in the construction of the concept of intersectionality and the process of intersectionalising migration.

***

The 2011 riots in London: The Response of Kurdish and Turkish Communities
(724) Olgu Karan (Başkent University)

While there has been a considerable research study into the causes and consequences of the 2011 riots and rioters' composition in terms of their class, ethnic origin and gender, there is much less on the shop-keeper's perspectives on the August 2011 riots in London. One of the consequence of this under-research area is little is known about how riots affect relationships between communities in multi-ethnic London. The paper argues that Kurdish and Turkish (KT) shopkeepers, community organisations and rioters managed to generate a shared working-class consciousness during face-to-face encounters on the streets. The conscious efforts of shopkeepers and rioters constructed an interest alignment against government policy for cutting social programmes, economic deprivation, and police misconduct. To this end, members of ethnic groups prevented inter-ethnic conflict. Shop keepers instead of blaming rioters for the destruction of the stores, they mostly focused on British institutions, such as the media, police, and the government – for inciting tensions, reinforcing economic and political inequalities, and indirectly instigating urban violence. Disputes were generally elaborated as a product of the larger society's structure of opportunity, not of racial, cultural, or ethnic conflicts between communities per se.

***

Between high-skilled and low-skilled migration – young Kurds in Istanbul as middling migrants[4]

(968) Karol Pawel Kaczorowski (Emigration Museum in Gdynia)

This paper aims at examining experiences connected to the processes of migration and acculturation among young Kurdish migrants in Istanbul, of whom majority have migrated to the city in the 21st century with a new, relatively less insecurity driven migration wave. During the fieldwork conducted were 52 in-depth interviews with migrants originating from different parts of Turkey's Southeast. Respondents were chosen basing on chain-referral (snow-ball) sampling method, used often in cases of minorities whose numbers are hard to estimate and who are difficult to access. Findings of my study indicate that despite the fact that majority of interviewed migrants had a middle-class background, all of participants had to struggle with difficulties connected to migrating on their own and experienced periods of economic deprivation. This differs them from high-skilled migration, benefitting often from organizational ties (e.g. corporate networks in different locations). Having not necessarily pure materialistic reasons (e.g. education, self-fulfilment, self-development) for migration and aspiring for middle-class positions contrasts them also with typical low-skilled migrants. These characteristics are described in contemporary migration studies as the phenomenon of middling migrants. Middling migration is a phenomenon analyzed in contemporary migration studies (see: Luthra et al. 2014; Luthra and Platt 2016; Rutten and Verstappen 2012). It describes migrants of middle class background (or the ones aspiring to the middle-class) who experience various challenges connected with their spatial mobility. These challenges concern among others: getting to know the changing laws connected to migration in a destination area, access to social services, facilities and potential employment. Middling migrants face such difficulties on their own, while these problems are unknown to high-skilled migrants who benefit from the assistance of institutional networks (e.g. international corporations). The group, so far, most frequently described by this term are international students. Such terminology may be useful in analysis of new, more voluntary wave of migration in Turkey and particularly experiences of my respondents. It can be argued that the Iintroduction of this terminology is important because in most studies of Kurdish migration, Kurds are regarded solely as low-skilled migrants. It can be argued that, relatively more voluntary migrants (who came to Istanbul and other cities in Turkey with the new wave of migration) are not necessarily the low-skilled ones. In fact, most of my respondents do not fit such a description. At the beginning of my presentation I will propose a typology of internal migration waves in Turkey basing on existing literature on the subject (e.g.: Gedik 1997; İçduygu et al. 1999; Sirkeci 2006) and my research. After explaining the specificity of new, relatively more voluntary migration wave taking place between years 2002 and 2015, presented will be results of my research concerning experiences connected to migrations (e.g. their multi-step character, and reasons for moving), initial situation after arrival to Istanbul and perceptions of acculturation processes affecting Kurds in the city. Spheres of acculturation outlined in Relative Acculturation Extended Model (RAEM) developed by Marisol Navas and her associates (2005) will serve as additional general theoretical framework. Majority of respondents adhering to the new wave of migration could have made use of relations with people who came earlier – relatives, friends or migrants from the same province, such social contacts were usually unavailable for forced migrants (see: Çelik 2005). Knowing a person who already lives in Istanbul (e.g. sibling or friend) was also a factor helping the respondents to make the decision for migration. Social bonds stemming from solidarity of people

[4] The research was funded by a project financed by the Polish National Science Centre, decision number DEC-2013/09/N/HS3/02014.

originating from the same home-region were also important for Kurdish migrants who searched for assistance in the first days after their migration – either in hometown organizations or (more frequently) among known people from the same area. After arrival respondents experienced much better conditions than low-skilled migrants of the previous wave. They however usually had to cope by themselves with finding accommodation, meeting new people and covering expenses in a city which is much more expensive than their previous place of residence. The paper argues that analyzing migrations of Kurds in 21st century in the context of the phenomenon of middling migrants can shed a new light on contemporary spatial mobility of this ethnic group.

***

Migration from Dersim to Europe
(1066) Hüseyin Çelik (University of Zurich)

The following paper will deal with the migration movement from the Dersim region (mainly) to Europe and it is divided in two parts. The first part delivers a short historical and geographical overview, while the second part, focuses on the solidarity networks and association established by migrants from Dersim in Europe. Until the 20th century, Dersim was a region, which hosted an incoming population from other parts of the old Ottoman Empire. According to the last census of January 2017, Dersim is the province with the lowest population of Turkey. Between 1990 and 2000 the population decreased 30% from 133,584 inhabitants to 93,584. It is documented that the first migration from Dersim occurred in the late 19th century. This labour migration wave followed the route from Harput to the USA through the Black Sea ports. The first mass migration from Dersim took place after the 1915 Armenian deportation. The largest internal migration was characterised by Dersimi sent to exile to the western part of Turkey after the Dersim Massacre (Tertele), in the scope of the Compulsory Settlement Law of 1938. The first mass migration from Dersim to Europe happened during the Republic era as a result of the "Turkey-Germany Labour Force Agreement" of 1961. The latest wave of migration was an outcome of forced displacement during the internal conflict in the 90's and due to the eviction of the villagers.This paper shows, that the main reason for migration waves from Dersim is not economic but political. The examples of the Armenian deportation and Dersim Massacre as well as the forced displacements in the 1990's illustrate the negative social effects on the population, which could even amount to serious violations of human rights. The Data used is based on statistical surveys and field research.

***

SESSION 4C – Language and migration

	Room: A4
Chair	**Marie Godin, University of Oxford, UK**
1013	Migration and Linguistic Diversity: Reconversion Strategies of Cultural and Social Capital among Bulgarian Migrants living in Spain – **Monica Ibáñez-Angulo**
932	Language for Resilience for Language Learners on the Move – **Dionysios Gouvias, Vasilia Kourtis-Kazoullis, Marianthi Oikonomakou, Eleni Skourtou**
851	The Effect of Migration on Lexical Aspects of the Movers' Mother Tongues: The Example of Pomak in Turkey – **Hasan Boynukara, Uğur Altıntaş**

Migration and Linguistic Diversity: Reconversion Strategies of Cultural and Social Capital among Bulgarian Migrants living in Spain

(1013) Monica Ibáñez-Angulo (Sociology University of Burgos)

Human societies have always been linguistically diverse despite the multiplicity of linguistic policies that have been developed towards linguistic homogeneization. Current globalizing processes and exchanges through Internet and transnational migration have contributed to such linguistic diversity in, at least, two ways. One contribution refers to the presence of foreign languages in the everyday contexts of Western societies; and the second and most important contribution refers to how these foreign forms of diversity have opened a debate on issues of cultural and linguistic identity, and hence, on the place of so-called mother tongue languages in mainstream cultural and educational policies. In this paper, I will address the strategies developed by Bulgarian immigrants living in Spain in order to promote the learning of Bulgarian language and culture among their children. Starting from the incorporated cultural capital brought by immigrants in the form of habitus (Bulgarian language and culture), I will analyse how this devaluated cultural capital in the migratory context is effectively be reconverted in other forms of cultural capital (objectified and institutionalized) through the development of non-formal and formal courses on Bulgarian language and culture. In this analysis, I will show the articulation between the contexts where these informal, non-formal and formal courses takes place and the reconversion of different forms of social and cultural capital: the initial bonding social capital between family members and close group of compatriots is effectively reconverted into bridging and linking social capital as the organization of these courses requires and contributes to the diversification of social networks. The analysis has also a gender dimension given that in most cases, and certainly in the case of Burgos, women are the main social actors and makers of these strategies (e.g. opening after school programmes, searching for teachers, lobbying in Bulgaria for the official recognition of these courses and in Burgos when looking for classrooms). The main aim of the paper is to contribute to academic literature on migration by showing, first, the relevance of social interaction among (Bulgarian) women who have migrated (to Spain) in the development of reconversion strategies of different forms of social and cultural capital. The paper also expects to raise more awareness towards the relevance of mother-tongue learning in the migratory context.

***

Language for Resilience for Language Learners on the Move

(932) Dionysios Gouvias (University of the Aegean), Vasilia Kourtis-Kazoullis (University of the Aegean), Marianthi Oikonomakou (University of the Aegean), Eleni Skourtou (University of the Aegean)

Resilience can be defined as the ability of individuals, communities and institutions to withstand and recover from shocks and crises (3RP 2015-2016:17). The term Language for Resilience is a term used in the field of language teaching/learning and is based on recognizing the value of offering vulnerable people the language tools they need in order to help them withstand and recover from the effects of conflict and displacement (Capstick and Delaney, 2017). A large number of case studies around the world have focused on how language learning has provided valuable tools for refugees and people on the move. This paper will present a case study of Greek language lessons that were held from December 2016 to June 2017 for refugees at the Linguistics Laboratory of the Department of Primary Education, University of the Aegean in Rhodes, Greece. Although the organizers and teachers had previous experience with teaching Greek as a second language to specific groups such as immigrants, repatriates, Roma, minorities and diaspora, as well as experience with adult education, this particular group posed a great challenge. The language and cultural diversity of the group, the age differences, the mobility of the members as well as the unstable present, past and future of the language learners demanded a learning environment based on resilience. The issues of human mobility and survival led to new types of language learning/teaching practices, e.g.: (1) teaching language as an emergency survival skill, (2) adapting language learning classes to language learners on the move, (3) creating a community of learning and empowerment and (4) utilizing the language and cultural diversity of the classroom.

***

The Effect of Migration on Lexical Aspects of the Movers' Mother Tongues: The Example of Pomak in Turkey
(851) Hasan Boynukara (Namık Kemal University), Uğur Altıntaş (Kırklareli University)

After their migration throughout the decade of 1920s, Pomak people underwent numerous cultural changes, especially in their languages. Being an endangered minority language, Pomak is a Slavic language which demonstrates a reciprocal effect with Turkish language in western parts of Turkey. Upon considering the current danger that Pomak is facing extinction, it would be beneficial to analyze the lexical and morphological differences in the Pomak language amongst the areas where Pomak minorities live. So as to gain necessary data three villages –Tayfur, Çanakkale; Toybelen, Balıkesir; Armağan, Kırklareli– in the Northwestern part of Turkey have been visited and Pomak people are firstly asked to translate fifty basic sentences, and later they are interviewed about the current status of Pomak in the area. Obtained translations have been recorded, and their morphological and vocal similarities and differences have been identified and analyzed. Collecting the data, the effect of Turkish on Pomak is analyzed from a perspective of language ecology. This study is intended to supply linguistic information on Pomak and to help create ways to avoid an undesired extinction of such a colorful language.

***

SESSION 4D – Transnational Living

	Room: A5
Chair	**Nirmala Devi Arunasalam, University of Plymouth, UK**
931	Transnational Lives and the Meaning of the Russian Travel Ban for Migrants from Tajikistan – **Natalia Zotova, Jeffrey H. Cohen**
927	Transcultural Capital as Transnational Artistic Practices in Portuguese Visual Artists Migration – **Leandro Gabriel**
909	Diversity and Creativity in the Center of Athens: Co-Existence or Implicit Conflicts? – **Aggeliki Demertzi, Eva Papatzani**
1199	The European Roma: The Unlikely Indian Diaspora -**Cristina Ioana Dragomir**

Transnational Lives and the Meaning of the Russian Travel Ban for Migrants from Tajikistan
(931) Natalia Zotova (Ohio State University), Jeffrey H. Cohen (Ohio State University)

This paper addresses transnational experiences of Tajik labor migrants and their families and the meaning of the new travel restrictions for them. Over the course of two decades Russia's migration policies have gradually become more restrictive with implementation of new laws and regulations. In January 2015, the Russian government implemented a new law. As a result of this new legislation hundreds of thousands of people were denied entry to the Russian Federation for overstay of the time in the country or other minor civil offenses. More than 330 thousand Tajik citizens found themselves in the "stop-list", being denied entry to Russia for 3-5 years. The paper discusses how new restrictions shape lives of Tajik migrants, who traveled to Russia for a number of years. The paper aims to better understand how being on "stop-list" changes people's expectations around migration and plans for the future, and conceptualizes their experiences through the framework of transnationalism, governmentality and exclusion. The framework of governmentality relies on political economy and policing technologies, and helps to conceptualize "biopolitics of otherness" thorough the politics of border and boundaries. While Russia migration legislation became more restrictive in 2014-2016, the number of apprehensions and deportations has risen significantly. How does governmentality in action shape the lives of transnational migrants and their families in Tajikistan? This paper aims to provide insight into the meaning of travel ban for people whose practices of migration create and sustain transnational connections with Russia; and builds upon ethnographic research among transnational migrants and their family members in Dushanbe, Tajikistan in the summer 2016.

***

Transcultural Capital as Transnational Artistic Practices in Portuguese Visual Artists Migration

(927) Leandro Gabriel (University of Lisbon)

The research presented below is at the crossroad between geography and art, since "art has much to contribute to the development of geographical knowledge and to the formation of geographical subjects" (Hawkins, 2011). It is guided by the need to bridging the scarce scientific production on the mobility of artists – whose subjects, according to Markusen (2013), present many differences compared to other migrant professionals – and in particular their migratory dynamics, as pointed by several authors. Indeed, increased mobility and the emergence of new international migration flows have contributed to a redesign of the social and cultural geography of the art world – popularized by Becker (1982). For many artists, moving, residing and working outside their origin is increasingly an option of life and an integral part of their work. This nomadism allows them to share values and stimulate creativity by expanding their public and the distribution channels of cultural goods and services, far from the point of production and beyond national borders. In fact, "the nomadism of artists is naturally a concerted action of moving and settling in order to discover and to create, in order to renew one's awareness and one's formal responses's" (Haerdter, 2005). Among other reasons, this migration is also due to the ability that some cities in the world – and their cultural scenes (Straw, 2004) – have to stimulate and attract young artists, fueling complex migratory webs between events, cultural institutions and art schools, thus constituting one of the most polarized sociocultural networks of the global migratory system. Among these cities there are those called creative cities that according to the work of Landry (2000) and explored by Gabriel (2013), combine key factors to attract and retain artists and other creative professionals. Additionally, it is well known that transnational artists tend to develop active forms of participation in economic, political, civic and cultural processes simultaneously in their places of origin and destination, boosting the symbolic dimensions of their artistic ability to emotionally connect different individuals to different places. For that reason, it is also highlighted the creation of what Faist (2013) refers by transnational social spaces, related to the artistic networks that have become important in order to capture the multiple and complex flows within the art market and across boundaries. Hence, from the idea of artist mobility and the ramifications it has on the concept of migration, this paper of an ongoing PhD research intends to deepen the relations between the visual arts world and the migration of Portuguese artists and the way they mobilize, interconnect and reinforce their transcultural capital – term adapted from Bourdieu's work as a combination and shared interdependence of social, cultural and economic forms of capital (Bourdieu, 1986) – which represent a whole series of interlinking crucial features in our migrant artists. Like Meinhof & Triandafyllidou (2016) it is crucial in this research to explore several issues related to the art world made possible by migratory flows and the confluence of diverse populations, as well as their coexistence in geographic social spaces. Thus, the concept of transnational capital, aimed at understanding the complex nature of the artistic creativity of transnational artists and their professional networks, concerns a certain mix of that three forms of capital expressed in the transnational practices of the artists who make possible the connection between their migratory destinations and some Portuguese cities. This is based in the strategic use of knowledge, skills and networks imbricated in Portugal and in Portuguese culture which are activated at their new places of residence. Therefore, through the exploration of an online survey results made to Portuguese artists residing outside Portugal, this research besides questioning about why artists move and what they seek in their migration paths, also intends to look at the importance of transcultural capital both in encouraging their departure from Portugal and their adjustment in the new host society. Specially, it is sought here to know what is called as transnational artistic practices – complementary to the activities listed by Portes et al. (1999) – reflecting the capacity that art – from its creation and production to its dissemination – and the artist as a migrant subject, have in traveling through artistic networks, (re)producing transnational and, to some extent, translocal geographies.

***

Diversity and Creativity in the Center of Athens: Co-Existence or Implicit Conflicts?
(909) Aggeliki Demertzi (National Technical University of Athens), Eva Papatzani (National Technical University of Athens)

As Greece is plagued by the multidimensional crisis combined with the recent refugee flows, the center of Athens becomes once more the focus of public discourse's attention. A range of European policies on migration have been launched during the last decades regarding not only the macro-scale of the migrants' legal status but also their (permanent and/or temporary) settlement in central Athens. In parallel, many policies and practices - both by public and private initiatives - are being emerged regarding the creative activities, creative groups, cultural policies etc. In general, a turn to the importance of culture and creativity and its socio-economic impact is being observed. Inevitably, these trends form some of the aspects of the urban policy making. This paper aims to unfold the ongoing discussion on the creative activities, as a part of the proposed socio-spatial policies as well as their impact on the everyday diversity at the center of Athens. In the last few decades Greece constitutes one of the main gateways of migration flows into Europe, and particularly Athens is the main city of reception of new populations. Despite the fact that social networks and informal activities of everyday life have spread immigrants' settlement across Attica region, the historical center of Athens remains the fundamental pole of attraction for diverse ethnic groups, either as a transit place or as a place of permanent settlement. The socio-economic and spatial transformations of the center in the last decades have allowed the development of a variety of small businesses, hangouts and immigrant communities which until now are benchmarks for a wide range of migrant groups affecting migrants' everyday life, creating also a vital laboratory of the everyday negotiation of multiculturalism and diversity. Even before the outburst of the crisis, the center of Athens was placed at the core of the so-called "crisis of Athens' center", a narrative portraying central Athens' diversity as the cause of social contradictions. Both the official policy institutions and the predominant discourse have convicted Athens' center as a ghetto, have lunched repressive policies in order to eliminate immigrants' presence and have proposed measures in order to facilitate native residents' return to the area. Creative and Cultural Industries (CCI) increasingly accumulate the interest in many socio-economic and spatial levels of policies or everyday practices. It is calculated that the total product of CCIs is approx. 3% of Greek GDP presenting an impressive growth (~70%) during the last years and simultaneously, despite the deep economic crisis, the demand for creative and/or cultural products and services have remained in the same levels while the corresponding demand for clothing and footwear presented a remarkable drop. This emerging trend tends to create new balances and transformations in the spatial and socio-economic level becoming more and more influential factor of policies and practices both in public and private degree. According to many recent studies, the historic center of Athens constitutes the main place of accumulation of CCIs based on a series of historical, social and spatial reasons. After a decade of different approaches regarding the center of Athens, it seems that new types of policies are being emerged by the part of the municipality of Athens, putting the CCIs as well as the cultural and creative activities at the epicenter of the urban policies planned. The current policies range from a new upgrading program of the historical center of Athens to the formation of an initiative including "active citizens" and various "creative" practices. This paper aims to explore and define: a. the historically formatted multiethnic and multicultural everyday reality, b. the boundaries and opportunities of CCIs as well as c. their historicity in Athens, d. the ways that public policies and practices could promote the co-existence or the observable results are overlapping. The methodology of research combines the theoretical part of literature review and the part of policies and public discourse focusing on desk research. For the response of the research questions and their evaluation, fieldwork has been conducted. At last, the unfolding of a broader issue is attempted regarding the constantly negotiable meaning of "belonging" and the crucially timely demand to the "right to the city".

***

The European Roma: The Unlikely Indian Diaspora
(1199) Cristina Ioana Dragomir (Center for Advanced Study of India, University of Pennsylvania and State University of New York at Oswego)

Different from the many recognized diasporic communities, there is a group that while spread around the world is not recognized by any nation state: the "Gypsy," or the Roma. Romani people are often marginalized and thought to be different, "not like us," whoever "us" is. Their origin was wrapped in the mystery of history, as for centuries they were thought to come from Egypt, Middle or Far East. But recent linguistic (Matsar, 2014), genetic (Moorjani et al., 2013) and historic work (Dragomir, 2016) sheds light on the ties between the European "Gypsy" and India. This work is mirrored in the political engagements of the Indian government, who in the beginning of 2016 launched a campaign for the possible recognition of the Roma community as a part of the historic Indian diaspora. Minister of External Affairs, Govt. of India, Smt. Sushma Swaraj said in February 2016 addressing the Roma delegates: "You are the children of India who migrated and lived in challenging circumstances in foreign lands for centuries. (...) We in India are proud of you." While many Roma embrace the formal act of recognition, a myriad of political, social and economic implications may spur out of it. Aiming to understand the possibility of recognizing the Roma as a part of the Indian diaspora, this paper takes a look at the political implications of such as act. It analysis the Indian legislation regarding persons of Indian origin living tide of the state borders, and places it in the context of the contemporary India and global politics.

***

SESSION 4E– Dealing with Migration "Crisis"

Room: B1	
Chair	**Kim Kwok, Caritas Institute of Higher Education, Hong Kong**
744	The Syrian Refugee Crisis: To Act Together or Not? An Assessment of Turkey- The EU Relations - **Gül Oral**
1262	Dealing with Refugee Crises in the Postwar Period: Cold War Priorities and the Activity of ICEM - **Yannis G. S. Papadopoulos**
1225	Beneficiary for Whom? The Role of International Organizations and Ngos in the Refugee Crisis in Europe: Insights from Greece –**Ifigeneia Kokkali**
868	The Brazilian Political Answers to a Purported "International Migration Crisis"– **Charles Pontes Gomes**

The Syrian Refugee Crisis: To Act Together or Not? An Assessment of Turkey- The EU Relations
(744) Gül Oral (Kadir Has University)

The ongoing civil war in Syria since 2011 which initially started as peaceful protests has turned into a civil war as violence has increased rapidly and displaced people within and outside the country. The civil war has mainly influenced neighboring countries such as Turkey, Lebanon, Jordan, and even Iraq hosting a significant number of refugees which illustrates how dangerous the circumstances in the country. Especially, Turkey as the largest host country has been received refugees from the beginning of the war by pursuing different types of policies regarding the acceptance of refugees while spending a significant amount of funds and resources in order to sustain assistance for refugees. Even though Turkey has been maintaining the geographic limitation related to the 1951 Geneva Convention which means the country only admits asylum seekers from Europe as refugees, the country has granted temporary protection status to refugees and made some changes in policies and accepted the new law in 2014. These changes display how the country has intended to modify its political and legal framework while handling issues concerning refugees and asylum-seekers. In addition to transformation in the legal and political sphere, it is also substantial to assess how this crisis has influenced the EU, and accordingly its relations with Turkey as the crisis has turned into a global one since summer 2015 due to the growing number of refugees reaching Europe in order to seek international protection. Since the crisis has become an international issue, it has necessitated a common approach requiring advance cooperation and coordination among various actors depending on international law for the protection of asylum-seekers and refugees while dealing with the issue from a humanitarian perspective. Though this expectation seems essential, but though at the same time, the agreement signed between Turkey and the EU could be evaluated as an instance of a collective action with a limited prospect.

***

Dealing with Refugee Crises in the Postwar Period: Cold War Priorities and the Activity of ICEM
(1262) Yannis G. S. Papadopoulos (University of Peloponnese)

During the period after the end of WWII the winning powers had to deal with the fate of millions of uprooted persons in Europe. This number continued to grow in the following years since more people were fleeing the countries under the orbit of the Soviet Union. Initially UNRRA was responsible for the care of refugees in both Europe and Asia. With the dissolution of UNRRA and the emerging Cold War however, the United States, hegemonic power in the post-war world, focused on the situation in Europe; thus, the

international organizations created after 1946 to care for refugees saw their mandate limited to European populations. Although the number of refugees in Asia was equally large in 1945 and grew over the following years, as a result of war and decolonization processes, the Western World and the international organizations it led ignored their fate. The Eurocentrism of the dominant postwar refugee regime resulted in the exclusion of all non-Europeans from internationally assisted mobility. In 1946, the UNRRA was replaced by the International Organization Refugee - IRO (International Refugee Organization - IRO) that took in charge the relief and the transfer of refugees to overseas countries. IRO introduced a "global system of humanitarian-based population transfer" to relieve western European countries from the burden of displaced persons and avert the economic, social and political unrest from the continuous presence of those who were considered idle people. In December 1951, the United States took the initiative for the creation of a new intergovernmental body, outside the United Nations framework that began operations in February 1952 and was initially named the Provisional Intergovernmental Committee for the Movement of Migrants from Europe (PICMME). After a few months, the organization was renamed the Intergovernmental Committee for European Migration (ICEM) and as a result of the Cold War priorities of the United States its life was extended. ICEM's mandate covered refugees and displaced persons, as well as persons who wanted to emigrate from Europe. The ICEM was given responsibility over transporting refugees and migrants, but also it had to assist with health examinations, vocational courses and language training, streamlining of procedures before and after the journey, information services, guidance etc. Refugees comprised 40% of the individuals transported by the ICEM in the 1950s. Immediately after commencing operations the Committee had to deal with the Displaced Persons remaining in Germany and Italy after the dissolution of the IRO. During the following years, the refugee wave from communist countries of Eastern Europe continued to grow, culminating in the exodus after the Hungarian Uprising in 1956. The ICEM was also accredited to deal with the issue of European refugees in Egypt and China. My paper will present the ways ICEM handled the refugee crises during the first decade of its functioning and the ways humanitarian needs were mingled with foreign policy goals of the US government.
***

Beneficiary for Whom? The Role of International Organizations and Ngos in the Refugee Crisis in Europe: Insights from Greece
(1225) Ifigeneia Kokkali (Panteion University)

The paper analyses the role played by International Organizations (IOs) and NGOs in the management of the refugee crisis in Greece through the lens of the education of the refugee children. In 2016, and while a great number of International Organizations were already implementing various activities with/for refugees in Greece, the Greek Ministry of Education (MoE) set-up a programme for the education of the refugee children to start in October 2016. Organizations and national and international NGOs have been willing to second the Greek MoE with the implementation of this programme, mainly through material support and various education activities for children and adult refugees. Trying to assess the educational activities performed by International Organizations and NGOs in Greece in 2016-2017, the paper (i) investigates the distribution of the benefits gained by the implementation of these activities across various target groups (refugee children and their families, Greek nationals, international mobile youth and highly qualified officials working in the humanitarian and NGO sector, etc.), and (ii) analyses the role played by IOs-NGOs in the education sector, focusing particularly on issues of state sovereignty.
***

The Brazilian Political Answers to a Purported "International Migration Crisis"

(868) Charles Pontes Gomes (Center for the Study on the Rights and Politics of Immigration and Refuge)

In big part of the world, States can perform their sovereign act of controlling the influx of foreigners in their territory in absolute terms. But in liberal democracies this control should be tempered with the norms of Human Rights and Refugee Law. This paper affirm that an international migration crisis exist when countries facing huge influx of mixed international migration cannot equally balance the sovereign will with the respect of human rights and the protection of refugees. In this growing International Migration reality, Brazil is not an exception and had the number of asylum seekers and international migrants growing in more than 1200% in the last three years. Considering the delicate balance between Sovereignty and Human Rights/Refugee Law, this paper will analyze this challenging growth of international migrants in the country and evaluate the solutions presented by the two main agencies of the Federal Executive power: the CONARE (National Council for Refugees) and the CNIg (National Council of Immigration).

***

SESSION 4F– Dinsel Gruplar ve Göç - 1

	Room: B2
Chair	**Mehmet Evkuran, Hitit University, Turkey**
779	Müslümanların Avrupa'da Var Olabilme Sorunları – **Erkan Persembe**
780	Göç Olgusunun Dinsel ve Mezhepsel Kimlikler Üzerindeki Etkisi – **Sıddık Korkmaz**
775	European Islam and the Integration of Muslims to European Culture -**Ismail Demirezen**
778	The Role of Religious Groups on the Daily Religious Lives of European Turks - **Yakup Çoştu, Feyza Ceyhan Çoştu**

Müslümanların Avrupa'da Var Olabilme Sorunları

(779) Erkan Persembe (Ondokuz Mayıs University)

Avrupa'da Müslümanların kimliksel var oluşları, son yarım yüzyıl içinde giderek daha çok görünürlük kazanıyor. Bir arada yaşama alışkanlıklarının sınanması, entegrasyon deneyimlerindeki başarısızlık nedeniyle göçmenler ve özellikle de Müslümanlar üzerinden yapılıyor. Müslümanların doğum oranı yüksekliği ve son dönemin sığınmacı akını, Avrupa'nın geleceği konusunda endişeleri artırıyor. 11 Eylül ve sonrasında gerçekleşen terör eylemleri nedeniyle Müslümanlar, terörizmin potansiyel zemini olarak görülüyor ve büyüteç altına alınıyorlar. Bu gelişmeler son yıllarda bir çok Avrupa ülkesinde aşırı sağ hareketlere güç kazandırırken, Müslümanların Avrupa'nın geleceğindeki yeri konusunda tartışmalar yoğunlaşmaktadır. Bu çalışmamızda Avrupa'da Müslümanların günümüzdeki var oluş sorunlarını, son gelişmeler (Sığınmacılar ve İslami terör tartışmaları) odağında değerlendirerek muhtemel geçiş sancılarını tartışmak istiyoruz. Avrupa'daki Müslüman göçmenlerle ilgili literatür, araştırmacının bugüne kadar gerçekleştirdiği çalışmaların sağladığı katkılarla birlikte ele alınarak içerik analizi tekniği ile çözümlenecektir. Günümüzde 15 milyonu aşan Avrupalı Müslümanın büyük bölümü ekonomik yönden dezavantajlı ve topluma çok az entegre olmuş durumdadır. Müslüman göçmenler, genellikle zayıf ekonomileri olan ülkelerin en alt ekonomik tabanından Avrupa'ya göç etmişlerdi. Avrupa'da gözlemlenen parçalı ve çok yönlü kimliksel varoluşlarıyla Müslümanların çok-kültürlü yaşam deneyimlerine katılmaları genellikle mümkün olamamaktadır. Onların kendi aralarında sağlayamadığı uyum, Avrupa toplumunun normları ve değerlerine karşı da olumsuz tutumların geliştirilmesine neden olmaktadır. Batılı değerler ile uyumlu bir İslam yorumu eksikliği, işsizlik sorununu kalıcı olarak yaşayan genç Müslümanlar arasında radikal İslamcı yönelişlere güç kazandırmaktadır. Göle, İslam ile aynı zaman ve mekânı paylaşmanın, dünyanın diğer tüm bölgelerinden daha fazla Avrupa'da can alıcı bir problem olarak gündeme geldiğini dile getiriyor: "Hem Müslümanlar hem de Avrupalılar "öteki" nin karşısında hissettikleri yitirme duygusunu, araya kimlik sınırları çizerek, yeni bir duvar çekerek aşmaya çalışıyorlar." Avrupa, İslâm adına ortaya çıkan çeşitli Müslümanlık yorumları ve bunun farklı yansımalarının tedirginliğini yaşamaktadır. Son dönemde sivil halka yönelik radikal İslamcı gruplarca gerçekleştirilen eylemlerin yarattığı travma, Müslümanlara karşı güvensizliği güçlendirmektedir. Müslümanların kendi ülkelerinden kaçarcasına sığınmaya çalıştığı bu ülkelerde, toplumsal yaşama uyumsuz bir yaşantıyı seçmeleri, çelişkili bir psikolojiyi barındırıyor. Günlük yaşamla ilgili son derece basit bir konu, dini grup ve cemaatler tarafından önemli bir sorun haline getirilerek, onları bir arada yaşama kültürüne uyumsuz bir görünüme mahkum etmektedir. Sorunun temelinde, İslam'ın hoşgörü, barış, dürüstlük adalet ve sevgi gibi değerlerinin yeterince temsil edilememesi yatmaktadır. Buna karşılık radikal grupların gerçekleştirdiği terör eylemlerinin gölgesinde yükselen göçmen karşıtı hareketler, Müslümanların, kıtanın geleceğindeki varlığını ciddi anlamda tehdit etmektedir.

***

Göç Olgusunun Dinsel ve Mezhepsel Kimlikler Üzerindeki Etkisi
(780) Sıddık Korkmaz (Necmettin Erbakan University)

Göç olgusu tarih boyunca insanlığın yüzleşmek zorunda kaldığı bir realitedir. Hayatta kalma, barınma, inançlarını yaşayabilme, tehlikeden uzaklaşma, güvenliğe erişme, ailesini, çocuklarını koruyabilme, neslini devam ettirme, hayat standartlarını yükseltme ya da başka sebepler yüzünden bir yerden başka yerlere intikaller yaşanmıştır. Çoğu zaman zorluk ve meşakkat içinde gerçekleşen yolculuklar hesapta olmayan ürünler ya da sonuçlar doğurabilmektedir. Bunun olumsuz sonuçları olduğu gibi bazen de olumlu sonuçları olabilmektedir. Hz. Peygamber'in kendisini tasdik etmeyen Mekkeli müşrikler tarafından yaşatılan baskı ve eziyetleri sonucu öz yurdunu terk etmek zorunda kaldığı hicret göçü, ilahi mesajı insanlara duyurma görevi olan peygamberlik görevini tamamlayabilmesi gibi olumlu bir sonuçla neticelenmiştir. Medine'de bulduğu rahat ve güven dolu ortam, kendisine inananların oluşturduğu bir toplum oluşturma zaferi vermiştir. Yeni oluşan bu toplumda son ilahi din olan İslam ortadan kaldırılma tehlikesinden kurtulduğu gibi inananlar tarafından bir devlete dönüşme tecrübesini de yaşamıştır. Uzun süre boyunca Medinelilerin üstesinden gelemediği kabile çatışma ya da savaşları şehre gelmiş olan muhacirlerin olumlu katkısı sebebiyle ortadan kalkmıştır. Toplum yeni bir heyecan ve dayanışma duygusu ile tanışmış eski tortularından kurtulmuş ve dünya tarihine adını altın harflerle yazdırmıştır. Daha önceden sıradan bir badiye/çöl şehri olan Yesrib, yeni adıyla "Medine"ye dönüşmüş ve medeniyetin beşiği haline gelmiştir. Şehre yeni gelen peygamber ve onun çevresindeki muhacir kitlesinin desteği ile birlikte ilkel kabile dinlerinden, puta tapıcılıktan ve barbarlıktan kurtulup, İslam dini sayesinde büyük bir aydınlanmaya merkezlik etmiştir. Kültürlerin taşınması açısından önemli bir faktör olan göç olgusu dinî kimlikleri etkilediği gibi, mezhebî değişim ve etkileşimlere yardımcı olabilmektedir. Anadolu ve Balkanlarda yer alan Sünnî İslam anlayışı çoğunlukla bu bölgelere göçler vasıtasıyla gelen Horasan erenlerinin katkılarıyla yerleşmiştir. Öte yandan İran'da yaşanan Şiîlik, özellikle Safevîlerin ülkede gerçekleştirdiği yönetim değişiminden sonra Lübnan bölgesinde yaşayan mezhep alimlerinin yeni coğrafyaya davet edilmesi sonucu taşınmıştır. Mezhepsel düşünceleri taşıyan kişi ya da kesimlerin geldikleri yeri etkilediği gibi, gittikleri bölgelerde karşılarına çıkan kültürlerden etkilenmeleri de söz konusudur. Eskiden beri kültür ve medeniyet merkezi olan Roma ve Bizans toprakları üzerinde inşa edilen Hanefiliğin şehirleşmeyi öncelemesi bunun örneği olarak kabul edilebilir. Aynı şekilde eskiden beri kendine özgü kültür ve medeniyeti bulunan Sasanî coğrafyası üzerinde şekillenen Şiîliğin, Irak Şiîliğine kıyasla daha hırçın ve ötekileştirici olması bu realitenin başka bir örneği olarak kabul edilebilir. Tebliğimizde göç olgusunun dinî ve mezhepsel kimlikler üzerindeki etkilerine değinilecek, bu gerçekten yola çıkarak bazı tarihsel örnekleri verilmeye çalışılacaktır. Buna ilave olarak tarihsel bir realite olan göç olgusunun iyi tahlil edilebilmesinin imkanları sorgulanacaktır.

***

European Islam and the Integration of Muslims to European Culture
(775) Ismail Demirezen (İstanbul University)

Muslim immigration to Europa leads our attention to the discussion of the status of Muslims living in the Europa. Religious identity and religious non-government organizations are two important factors for immigrants to integrate to the culture of the host countries. European Islam as religious identity and European Islamic non-government organizations for European Muslims may be important possibilities for their integration to the European culture. The European Islam emerges as a religious identity in the context of the non-government Islamic organizations embedded in the European culture. It recognizes Muslim identity and also impedes alienation of Muslims and Europeans. Since European Islam is produced by European Muslims who live according to European social and cultural norms, it is most probably compatible with European culture. As Talal Asad argues "if religious symbols are understood, on the analogy with words, as vehicles for meaning, can such meanings be established independently of the form of life in which they are used (1993, 53)?" These meanings are established dependently of the form of life embedded in the European culture. According to Ramadan Tariq (2005) and Bassam Tibi (2000), European Islam is possible. According to Tibi, Euro-Islam "address the effort of devising a liberal variety of Islam acceptable both to Muslim migrants and to European societies, thus an Islam that can accommodate the ideas of Europe, ideas including secularism and individual citizenship along the lines of a modern secular democracy (2014, 206)." Tariq Ramadan has tried to immerse himself in reading Qur'an and Sunna in the light of the new Western context (2004, 3-4). By comparing and contrasting Tariq's approach to the European Islam with Tibi's one, this paper will discuss about the characteristics of the European Islam and its possibility for the integration of Muslims to the European culture. First, the history of Muslim immigration into Europe will be analyzed to establish a ground for our further discussions. Second, we will explore the discussion of integration, assimilation and marginalization of Muslims living in the Europe. Thirdly, it will be discussed about the European Islam by comparing and contrasting Tariq's approach with Tibi's one. Finally, we will explore the possibilities of European Islam for the integration of European Muslims into European culture.

***

The Role of Religious Groups on the Daily Religious Lives of European Turks
(778) Yakup Çoştu (Hitit University), Feyza Ceyhan Çoştu (Hitit University)

Referring the Turks that migrated Europe's several countries as "temporary workers" in 1960, it is obvious that neither Turks nor receiving countries had no policy about migration with the thought that they would "come back". Since late 1970s, the receiving countries' point of view has changed in the way that Turks wouldn't be temporary but permanent. So, they developed some strategies and policies such as social security laws, repentance law for illegal or tourist-worker, family reunification law, foreigner laws etc. The purpose of these new laws was to take the immigration wave under control and supporting immigrant integration in Europe. Turkey as an emigration country, during those days, started to take some serious steps about preventing its own citizens from assimilation and helping them to integrate successfully. European Turks' first attempts to be organized in Europe came about in the middle of 1960s and the very beginning of 1970s, during those years, the religious life of Turkish immigrants had no sign of well-structured organization but some personal efforts. The religious life of the first generations was limited just practising some basic rituals. For that purpose, small flats were rent or purchased. When there was no possibility of returning to their homelands, more than that the second and the third generation raised there in time so those small places because insufficient. Besides, expectations increased and became different so they opened a way for more organized and institutional structure. During the migration process, from the early 1960s to the middle of 1980s, there was no official religious services for Turkish immigrants living in Europe. For 20 years or about, those people had been destined to be on their own in that period of time. Within that period also religious services had been carried out mostly with the hand of some religious groups and communities in Turkey. Those activities, on one hand, had an important mission about protecting and carrying out immigrants Turks' religious and cultural existence, however, on the other hand, the religious groups and communities' different religious discourses, ideological and politic activities made it so difficult to live in unity but rather deepen the competition and disintegration. After the last 20 years, from the middle of 1980s, Religious Affair Administration become organized in European countries, embraced immigrant citizens of Turkey and carried out religious services via the government. That is also meant that fulfilling unity, eliminating differences and disagreements in the religious field. In this paper, from the first years till today, Turkey-connected religious groups and communities' influence on immigrants' daily religious life will be evaluated with a macro-sociological point of view. Besides, the influences and reflections of their religious discourse and practice on their daily religious life will also be analysed.

***

SESSION 5A – Migration and Wellbeing

	Room: A1
Chair	**Pınar Yazgan, Sakarya University, Turkey**
929	Post-Trauma, and Perspectives of Growth Among Young Syrian Refugees in Sweden – **Mayssa Rekhis**
702	The Role of Loneliness in the Process of Addiction Development Among FSU Immigrant Drug Users in Israel – **Liat Yakhnich, Keren Michael**
729	The Impact of Internal Migration on the General and Reproductive Health Status of Immigrant Women in Aydın, Turkey - **Hilmiye Aksu, Hande Dağ, Safiye Özvurmaz, Mevlüt Türe**
1106	Well-being of Law Enforcement Officers at the Spanish Southern border: A requirement for a humanitarian migration management - **Rocío Garrido, García-Ramírez Manuel, María-Jesús Albar, Marta Escobar, Virginia Paloma**

Post-Trauma, and Perspectives of Growth Among Young Syrian Refugees in Sweden

(929) Mayssa Rekhis (Linköping University)

The refugee status is a legal designation granted to individuals who have fled their home country because of persecution as defined in the first article of the United Nations Convention on the status of refugees (UN General Assembly, 1951). Thus, by definition, refugees have experienced traumatizing experiences, which is confirmed by many studies. The trauma literature has been mainly framed around pathology and negative mental health impacts of trauma, with the post-traumatic stress disorder as a central focus. Though, it is more and more clear that even if a lot of refugees suffer long-lasting negative impacts from their experiences of trauma, more survive and go on to lead productive and fulfilling lives (Shakespeare-Finch, 2011). In fact, more than resilience, it is today clear that as a result of struggling with highly challenging circumstances, a number of people experience positive changes, defined as post-traumatic growth (PTG) (Rodgers, 2014). In the case of refugees, it is a survival experience, and even back to Jacques Derrida's definition, survival is 'not more on the side of the death and the past than of life and the future', he has defined it as 'the most intense life possible' in his last interview (Fassin, 2010). The way we perceive the refugees' lives and experiences, either as precarious and ill, or as intense and strong, influences how the services and responses targeting them are designed and implemented. Perceived as vulnerable, the response is based on the model of 'care', which is 'the process of maintaining the thread of the ordinary life' (Laugier, 2015), a model with an unequal power structure but also eventually limiting the possibilities of growth as it only aims to getting back to 'ordinary life'. With this shift in considering the post-traumatic experiences, and the literature tackling the positive trajectories and possibilities that become possible after traumas, we can find more and more studies measuring PTG with different types of quantitative scales among wounded populations and individuals, and exploring correlations either with demography, type of trauma or countries of origin. Though, very little research can be found that is analyzing the process of post-traumatic growth and the personal experiences of individuals in accessing self-perceived positive changes, which leads to a lack of understanding of post-traumatic growth, from the human experience point of view. Thus, this is the question this study aims to explore: how do young refugees experience the post-traumas related to torture, war and flight, how do they perceive positive changes, and how do they see and reach the opportunities of growth? This question is explored through an ethnographic study combining observation and semi-directive interviews with young refugees, conducted in a psychosocial/ mental health support service in Stockholm,

Sweden. It specifically targets Syrian young refugees as Syria is currently the first country of origin of refugees (UNHCR, 2015), and as young people (from 18 to 30 years old) is the most represented age range. The choice of working with a population from the same age group and from the same country of origin is to give the possibility to explore the specificities of being young, and of a common culture and background in addressing the experience of trauma and asylum, to explore the eventual community support, and to tackle the perspective of collective trauma. The study aims to provide a better understanding of the individual experiences of trauma and post-trauma among young Syrian refugees in Sweden, and the perceived positive changes based on interviews and narratives. Through the in depth-analysis of the qualitative data, it will define the main factors and mechanisms of self-perceived post traumatic growth and elucidate the (current and needed) role of the psychosocial and health support services. In a closed, yet globalized, world, the right to asylum is a unique situation where borders dissolve to save human lives. Though, the experiences of war, torture and persecution, the journey, and the resettlement can be highly traumatizing. Even though people reach safety in host countries, the impact of these experiences continues and may impede their health, quality of life and possibilities of inclusion. At the same time, trauma can also lead to positive trajectories and growth, for the young refugees, and in consequence, for the communities. This study will explore the post-traumatic experience by young refugees, the factors and mechanisms that lead to post traumatic growth, in order to elucidate how can social and health services contribute in shifting (not only the paradigms but) the realities of post-trauma from pathology to growth.
***

The Role of Loneliness in the Process of Addiction Development Among FSU Immigrant Drug Users in Israel
(702) Liat Yakhnich (Beit Berl College), Keren Michael (The Max Stern Yezreel Valley College)

Immigrants from the former Soviet Union (FSU) account for approximately 13% of the Israeli population. This group has a comparatively high rate of drug abuse, with about 25-50% of the Israeli treatment services' patients having FSU origins (Isralowitz, Reznik, Spear, Brecht, & Rawson, 2007; Ranz, Dekel, & Izhaky, 2012). This high incidence of drug dependence may be mainly attributed to high rates of substance abuse in immigrants' countries of origin (Isralowitz et al., 2007) as well as to the stress associated with immigration (Kagan & Shaefer, 2001). Immigration is a potentially stressful and challenging experience that involves coping with multiple sources of distress, e.g. language and cultural barriers; family stress; social exclusion and marginalization. Separated from their families and friends, some immigrants cope with these hardships by turning to alcohol and drugs (Cervantes, Cordova, Fisher, & Kilp, 2008; Kagan & Shaefer, 2001). Social exclusion, loss of social relations and acculturation-related challenges may enhance immigrants' sense of loneliness, that is often closely related to emotional problems and drug abuse (Olmstead, Guy, O'Mally, & Bentler, 1991). This paper aims to illustrate the trajectories of development of drug addiction among FSU immigrants, and to stress immigrant users' sense of loneliness as the core issue that characterizes these trajectories. The paper is based on a qualitative phenomenological study that explored the characteristics of drug abuse among FSU immigrant drug addicts in Israel. The information was gathered by interviewing 19 Russian-speaking recovering addict counselors employed in Israeli addiction treatment centers. Criterion sampling was used to select participants with a predetermined potential to provide information relevant to the study questions (Patton, 1990). The study was approved by the Unit for Excellence in Research and Study of Addiction in the University of Haifa. During the data analysis "significant statements" were identified, using a "horizontalization" process (Moustakas, 1994). These statements were grouped into clusters of meaning, that were reorganized in the process of identifying the central themes that emerged from the interviews (Creswell, 2007). After completing the data analysis, eight of the participants were contacted and asked to review the results, a process referred to by Lincoln and Guba (1985) as "member checks." The interview analysis yielded two main trajectories of addiction development among FSU immigrants. The most common one is characteristic of older users who immigrate with already- existing drug problems which almost always become aggravated after immigration. The second trajectory is typical of younger users who immigrate in late childhood and early adolescence, and start using drugs after immigration (and usually in proximity to it). The core issue that characterizes both trajectories is the immigrant users' sense of loneliness. Older and younger immigrant drug users' experiences of loneliness have certain common features as well as substantial differences. It appears that older users often perceive immigration as a chance to change their lives. However, very soon after their arrival, they sink back into abuse and find solace in the immigrant users' social network. Lack of familial support and social isolation increase their distress and the sense of loneliness, thus leading them toward relapse and aggravated drug abuse. The trajectory of loneliness and drug-taking develops somewhat differently among younger users. Many are subjects to peer exclusion and rejection, that result in these youngsters forming social networks that sustain and exacerbate their aggressive behavior patterns. Many immigrant adolescents have no adult figures (parents and teachers) on whom they can rely during this difficult phase in their lives. The sense of loneliness that is created by peer rejection, parental unavailability and ineffective involvement by the educational staff prompts them to seek the company of other young immigrants in a similar situation. In this context, delinquent groups provide marginalized immigrant adolescents with a yearned-for sense of belonging and acceptance. Drug use in these groups serves as a shared ritual that enhances this sense of belonging and facilitates bonding. It appears that sense of loneliness and drug abuse create a snowball effect in both younger and older immigrant user populations. The initial sense of loneliness that originates in the immigration experience prompts drug-taking as a way of self-medicating and enhancing a sense of belonging. However, this same behavior further magnifies the sense of loneliness by undermining the user's hope for recovery, heightening social withdrawal, and escalating coercive social interactions. Implications for prevention and treatment based on the interviewees' reflections, as well as on extant literature, are discussed (e.g. alleviating the immigrant youths' sense of loneliness, strengthening their original cultural identity, education toward multicultural awareness and acceptance at school and empowering immigrant families).

***

The Impact of Internal Migration on the General and Reproductive Health Status of Immigrant Women in Aydın, Turkey

(729) Hilmiye Aksu (Adnan Menderes University), Hande Dağ (Dokuz Eylül University), Safiye Özvurmaz (Adnan Menderes University), Mevlüt Türe (Adnan Menderes University)

The study aim is to determine the general and reproductive health status of the women who migrated from The Eastern and South-eastern Anatolian regions of Turkey to Kadıköy, Ovaeymir and Tepecik where the most migrated regions of Aydın Province are. There are few studies about this subject in our country. In TURKSTAT results, the net migration rate of Aydın between 2012-2013 years was found 2.3 points and the number of immigrants was determined as 34688. This study was designed as a descriptive and cross-sectional type. It was performed with 331 immigrant women who were in the 15-49 age group and volunteering to participate the survey, and identified by stratified random

sampling method, between 21 April and 21 October 2016. The sample of the research was determined from Efeler, Çeştepe and Ovaeymir FHC (Family Health Center) which belong to the regions of Kadıköy (99 women), Ovaeymir (118 women) and Tepecik (114 women). The sample size calculated at least 288 with %80 G power by using bi-directional hypothesis and taking α= 0.05, odds ratio 1.65 (Esteban et al., 2012). The data was collected by using the face-to-face interview technique by the researchers at home visits. The data collection tools are The General Health Questionnaire (GHQ), which consists of 12 questions developed by Goldberg and Williams in 1988 and adapted to Turkish by Cengiz Kılıç in 1996 and The Immigrant Women's General and Reproductive Health Status Questionnaire (IWGRHQ), which consist of 44 questions and developed by the researchers in accordance with the literature. The ethical permissions were taken from Adnan Menderes University Ethical Committee (Protocol No: 2016/813) and Directorate of The FHC and Aydın Provincial Health. In the study, immigrant women's 97% were married, 44.7% were relatives with their spouse, and 89.1% were willingly married. Their 33.5% are illiterate, 94.6% are housewife, 18.4% are quit up their job due to migration, and 81.3% have health insurance. Moreover, 36.3% of them have less income and 38.4% of them live as a large family. The places where they migrated from are 29.9% Ağrı, 14.8% Bitlis and 10.6% Muş. Their migration reasons are 47.7% individual (education, marriage etc.), 36.3% economic and 10.3% family reasons (accompanied by spouse or parent). In addition, 71.3% of these women were very satisfied with their migration and 63.4% stated that they would migrate again if they had a chance. Migration affected the women's economic situation 14.5% and housing conditions 6% negatively and this caused the health problems (21.1%). These health problems are 13.3% menstrual cycle disorder, 12.7% mental depression and 5.1% nervousness and unhappiness. These women's 78.9% have planned pregnancies, 59.8% using the family planning methods, 63.3% had prenatal care in their past-pregnancies before the migration, gave birth 80.3% in the hospital and 17.9% at home. After the migration, 97% had prenatal care in their pregnancies and gave birth 93% in the hospital and 5.7% at home. They had Pap smear control 23.6%, the rate of going to a gynaecologist was 90.3% and 78.9% performed the write perineum cleaning, and 30.2% complained of vaginal discharge. Between the GHQ total score and women's migration period (r:.105, p=0.05), stillbirths (r:.191, p≤0.00), economic impact of migration (r:.141, p=0.10) and health status (r:.317, p=0.00) were found a meaningful relationship in the positive direction. Also there was found a significant negative correlation between the GHQ total score and with the age of the women (r:-.127, p=0.02), their relationship with their partners (r:-354, p=0.10) and children (r:-346, p=0.10) after the migration. The GHQ total score was found three and above which shows 26.7% of the women's general health status was considered to be at risk. The women who married without consent, have unplanned pregnancies, didn't went to prenatal health visits before migration, gave birth at home, have vaginal discharge, menstrual cycle disorder, wrong perineal cleaning habit, negative economic impact of migration, were not satisfied with migration, smoking or using alcohol were significantly determined in the risk group of health (p <0.05). It has been determined that the vast majority of women who have migrated to the province of Aydın from Southeast and East Anatolia have a good general health status. Women whose health status is identified as risky; should be educated by nurses about family planning methods, harms and quitting methods cigarettes and alcohol use and genital hygiene habit, provide psychological support, more frequently health care and control by providing them as priority groups and created job opportunities and support their economic status by the government.
***

Well-being of Law Enforcement Officers at the Spanish Southern border: A requirement for a humanitarian migration management

(1106) Rocío Garrido (University of Seville), García-Ramírez Manuel (University of Seville), María-Jesús Albar (University of Seville), Marta Escobar (University of Seville), Virginia Paloma (University of Seville)

The increasing migration flows is challenging the Europe's Mediterranean borders situation and is highlighting the difficulty of Europe to protect the healthcare system—not only of migrant people, but also of professionals who receive them. This situation is causing a humanitarian crisis without precedent at borders' countries, unable to meet commitments and international agreements. This study analyzed the occupational well-being (OWB) of "guardias civiles" (GC), the law enforcement officers on the Spanish borders, who have the responsibility of controlling migration flows across Melilla's borders. This city is one of the two Spanish enclaves in Morocco (Africa) and, consequently, a focal point of irregular migratory pressure towards Europe (Carling 2007). Melilla epitomizes the challenges that are currently faced by Mediterranean countries regarding refugees. The OWB of the law enforcement officers has become an important issue for public health in the European agendas and policies (IOM, 2015). Literature showed that exposition to highly stressful situations at workplaces can affect health and job performance in the officers (Head, Kivimäki, Martikainen et al. 2006; Juniper, White and Bellamy 2010; Yuan et al. 2011). Then, we considered OWB as a fundamental aspect for ensuring the effective work of GC in a humanitarian way. This study aimed to identify the determinants of the OWB of GC working in Melilla, and more specifically, (1) to describe contextual factors that threaten the OWB of border guards at different levels (i.e. policy, social and organizational); (2) to describe risks and protective factors that affect border guards' OWB. Twenty-two CGs were selected from different operating units, using a convenient sample. All the interviewees were men who served between 9 and 26 years. Their participation was anonymous and confidential. The data collection process was carried out through deep-interviews based on the interview guide of the Equi-Health (http://equi-health.eea.iom.int/) that explores: (a) the reception process of migrants and coordination; (b) the working conditions and perceived health; (c) health training; and (d) knowledge about the regulation of migration. This study was founded by IOM /EC DG SANTE, within the action of Equi-Health: Migrant health at Southern EU border. A content analysis was conducted by two independent researchers (using the ATLAS.ti software) has revealed dimensions with an impact on the OWB of theGCs, which were divided into two blocks: (1) the perceived threats and (2) the strengths with which they can face up to the challenges. Firstly, as perceived threats appeared that they are not exactly aware of which procedures they have to follow or whether these comply with the law. Secondly, they do not feel sufficiently recognised or rewarded by their superiors and their institution. Thirdly, CGs showed their negative public image, provided from NGOs and the media. Finally, they experience physical and psychological vulnerability, because they do not know the diseases and injuries that they have may be exposed to. They often suffer from sleep disorders, guilt and fear of death, and some present symptoms of burnout. Nevertheless, they rarely visit the doctor regarding their mental health, because they worry it may cause a problem to their professional trajectory. Secondly, this study discovered the strengths that CGs have to confront these risks. They highlighted their commitment to the public welfare, their social support (especially, from their families and colleagues), and their spirituality. Additionally, some of them have also developed intercultural competency and empathy. Borders have become contexts of risks where basic needs and rights are frustrated by circumstances that spiral out of control, and this situation affects not only migrant people, but also professionals that receive them. This study has explored the situation of CGs at Melilla, describing the contextual threats perceived at policy, social, and organizational levels that reinforce the GCs' legal, professional, social, physical and psychological vulnerability. Also, it has explored the strengths they have deal with. This study reveals the need to respect national and international laws at European borders and protecting migrants' health and, also, services providers' health. Wellbeing of law enforcement officers represents a requirement to guarantee that they are able to perform their duties humanely, benefiting simultaneously officers, migrants and society at large.

***

SESSION 5B – Identity and Migration - 2

	Room: A2
Chair	**Sokratis Koniordos, University of Crete, Greece**
976	Intergenerational Voices on Identity in Migration: Greek Islanders Speak – **Melissa Afentoulis**
1117	Re-Discovery and Autonomization of the Cretan Identity in Turkey in 2010s - **Ali Gençoğlu**
732	An Examination of White Privilege in Migratory Processes and the Racialized and Gendered Hierarchies in Migration- A Focus on Sao Paulo, Brazil -**Tara Mcguinness**
1088	Transfers of Asylum Seekers to the Peninsula from the Migrant Temporary Detention Center (CETI) in Melilla (Spain): Legal and Psychological Analysis of Qualitative Interviews - **Nuria Ferré, Ángela Ordóñez**

Intergenerational Voices on Identity in Migration: Greek Islanders Speak
(976) Melissa Afentoulis (Harokopio University Athens)

The island of Limnos (known as Lemnos in the English-speaking world) like many other parts of Greece has experienced successive and long periods of foreign domination, wars and economic devastation. During the decades of 1950's - 1970's, a large number of Limnian islanders arrived as young immigrants to Australia to establish a viable and 'normal' life and future after the traumas of war, compounded by the country's social and economic instability. They experienced loss, grief, guilt and dislocation in a foreign land (xeniteia). In this paper, questions of how first and subsequent generations of migrants engage with concepts of home and belonging, the reconstruction and redefinition of identity in contemporary diaspora and the role of ethno-regionalism in identity will be examined. In this research, I examine the context that facilitates identity formation and reformation, the role of 'return visits' to the ancestral home and rediscovered regional identity that shapes the next generation's sense of self. The paper draws on oral history - the voices and stories of the first generation - foundational immigrants and their descendants living in Australia, as a case study of a larger PhD project. Many scholars have noted the relationship between diasporic communities and the homeland is of critical importance. In the case of the Limnian diaspora, the issue is more specific than a generalised consciousness of Greekness (Ellinismos). This 'history from below' is not only about the potential loss of Australian migration historiography, but importantly it is about the legacy of the oral narrative which links the past with the lives and memories of the present and future descendants of this community. I argue that ethno-regional identity is an area that has received comparatively little academic attention but, it remains durable as it reforms on foreign soil.

***

Re-Discovery and Autonomization of the Cretan Identity in Turkey in 2010s
(1117) Ali Gençoğlu (Gazi University)

This study aims to investigate how Cretan Turkish citizens have been building the autonomous Cretan identity from Turkish national identity in the last decade by focusing on western Anatolian-centered Cretan associations' works, and a monthly-newspaper, called Cretans (Giritliler), which has been published by one of these organizations. Cretan Muslim community continuously migrated from Crete to other Ottoman territories (particularly villages and towns which have been located on the Aegean and Mediterranean coasts of Anatolia, the twelve islands; Kos and Rhodes in particular, and today's Syria and Lebanon) from 1820s to the end of the WW II, for approximately 120 years. This process started with the foundation of modern Greece as a nation-state in 1820s, reached its climax in the last period of the 19th century, when the tension between Muslims/Christians (then Turks/Greek) increased and the island was annexed by the Greece in 1897, the population of the Muslim community on the island was totally disappeared with the Greco-Turkish War of 1919-1922, and then the exchange of the population between Turkey and Greece in 1924. The final Cretan Muslim-Turk migration happened after the annexation of the twelve islands by Greece by the end of the WW II, particularly from Kos and Rhodes to the Aegean side of Anatolia. Today, a considerable number of Cretan Turks have been living in Anatolian coastal territories of Aegean and Mediterranean Seas. Cretan Turks actively participated in Greco-Turkish War of 1919-1922, almost all of them fought Greek troops and became influential figures during the establishment of Turkey as a nation-state. They rapidly and enthusiastically adopted strong nationalist policies of the new-born state, started in 1930s. They were molten, were Turkified with the second and third generation. To be Cretan meant to only a territorial belonging for a long time. However, with the rise of the communication technologies in 1990s, firstly, Greek cultural legacy in the Aegean side of Anatolia (cuisine, music, dance, etc.) was re-discovered and it became popular among particularly secular Turks. Recently, Cretan culture has become much more distinctive. Cretan Turks tightened their relations with the people of Crete who migrated from Anatolia, organized reciprocal visits and symposiums. Additionally, they published a monthly-newspaper, called "Cretans (Giritliler)". Inferred from these organizational activities, columns and reports in the newspaper, It is suggested that Cretan immigrants, having Turkish citizenship, have been elaborating and adopting the Cretan identity, autonomous from Turkish national identity, with the help of the establishment of the contact with Cretans of the other countries and the people of Crete, who have Anatolian ancestors. In this study, the activities organized by associations, and particularly the reports and the columns in the newspapers have been focused on for investigating which elements and cultural characteristics are used by Cretan Turks for defining and elaborating the autonomous Cretan identity.
***

An Examination of White Privilege in Migratory Processes and the Racialized and Gendered Hierarchies in Migration- A Focus on Sao Paulo, Brazil
(732) Tara McGuinness (University College Dublin)

The central question of why migration is predominantly a non-white phenomenon and why white people are not categorised as migrants in dominant discourses has only been partially addressed. Scholarship in migration studies has had a tendency to 'study down' and focus on non-white migrants, categorised as economic migrants, asylum seekers and refugees. This research will aim to 'study up' and explore the phenomenon of white migration and contribute to remedying this gap by analysing gendered white migrants as racialized bodies in a country racially structured. This allows the dominant narrative to be challenged that characterises non-white groups as migrants and renders whites exempt from examination. Some scholars of white studies argue that whiteness is an unmarked racial identity (Frankenberg 1993; Dyer, 1997), other scholarship has noted the duality of white identity as both visible and invisible (Garner 1997, Frankenberg, 2001) and some recent texts have noted the racialisation of white identities (Alcoff, 2015). This study aims to explore the centrality of white identities and how these impacts dominant discourses in migration. The Brazilian economy is a good example of an economy of the global south that has made the availability of skilled work open to the well-educated sectors of the global north's workforce. According to the 2010 census, the highest earning group is made up of 82.2% whites and only 17.7% black Brazilian meaning that an intersection of race, class and gender is especially significant in this geo-cultural setting. This research takes an intersectional approach to examining how the supremacy of whiteness impacts on the differing experiences of privileged white male and female migrants and their relationship to non-white Brazilians. Focusing on Brazil, this research provides an example of a specific globalised location which has been viewed as one of the newly advanced developing economies but which is currently in severe economic crisis. During 2013-16, Brazil has been in economic recession and this is set to continue against a background of political uncertainty. This study aims to explore white migration flows against this socio-economic and political geo-cultural setting. Brazil has the second largest black population in the world (after Nigeria) which makes the study of changing racial formation a particularly interesting objective. Historically, whiteness in Brazil, it is argued, is an indicator of status and prestige, Brazil did not outlaw miscegenation due to an elitist belief in 'the whitening ideal' (Degler 1971; and Skidmore 1993). The gender dimension to this project is particularly important as it explores the privileged position of migrant white women in relation to native non-white domestic workers. Drawing on Sassen (2002), this project focuses on the expansion of white bodies into cities in the global south and the white migrant's household tendency to outsource gendered domestic duties (Sassen, 2002; Parrenas, 2002; Hochschild, 2003, 2012). While there is a body of research done on women of colour, white women are rarely researched as a raced group (Dyer 1997; Lipsitz 2006; Garner 2007; Crenshaw 2010). This study adopts a qualitative methodology– based on ethnographic methods and autoethnographic self-reflection. An analysis of how my positionality influences this study is based on the assumption that as a white, western and middle-class woman, researching white privilege, I am myself at the centre of the critique that I am researching. I also explore how scholarship on "reflexivity" and "feminist interviewing" (Oakley, 1981; Riessman, 1987; Cotterill 1992; Campbell 2003) will be used to inform the interview process. Using a feminist perspective on research the idea of a "neutral" knowledge is rejected, as social categories are considered as "historically specific, socially constructed hierarchies of domination" (Weber, 2004). This project "redirects the academic gaze upwards" (Aguiar and Schneider 2012) and aims to study the culture of power and affluence rather than the culture of powerless and poverty (Nader 1969). It has been argued by Chase (2005) that autoethnography is a narrative inquiry in which researchers turn the lens on themselves. Doloriert and Sambrook's (2009) research has shown that through autoethnography, the researcher is researched, which makes her the intellectual idea and her voice the cultural framework. Through her experiences and interpretations, 'her personal' is linked to 'her cultural'. In conclusion, the current political and economic landscape requires scholarship which examines our willingness to racialize some groups and our reluctance to do so with dominant, normative identities.

***

Transfers of Asylum Seekers to the Peninsula from the Migrant Temporary Detention Center (CETI) in Melilla (Spain): Legal and Psychological Analysis of Qualitative Interviews

(1088) Nuria Ferré Trad (Universidad Pontificia Comillas), Ángela Ordóñez Carabaño (Universidad Pontificia Comillas)

Foreigners who cross the border in order to reach Europe and arrive in Melilla, reside at the CETI (Migrant Temporary Detention Center). It is an open center where illegal migrants stay with asylum seekers. The Center lacks public rules governing its operation, and, more relevant, lacks public criteria of transfers to the Peninsula. That means residents do not know when they will be able to leave Melilla which, in the case of asylum seekers, is a break of their right of freedom of movement (Manzanedo, Ferré, Castaño, Buades & Iglesias, 2016). When asylum application is admitted to process, applicants receive a red card "only valid in Melilla", limiting their freedom of movement without any legal basis. International, European and national legislation should be taken into account as it admits the freedom of movement (Amnesty International, 2015). Thus, regarding the international context, there is article 13.1 of the Universal Declaration of Human Rights (UDHR) and article 12.1 of the International Covenant on Civil and Political Rights (ICCPR). At the European context, 4th Protocol of the European Convention of Human Rights (ECHR) gathers the freedom of movement and residence of persons who legally reside in a State member of the EU, in its article 2.1. On the other hand, the Charter of Fundamental Rights of the European Union (CDFUE), in its article 45.2 establishes freedom of movement and residence of citizens of third countries. In terms of the specific legal basis for asylum, the Reception Directive must be mentioned, in its article 7 acknowledges the freedom of movement of asylum-seekers. Regarding the Spanish legal framework, it should be taken into account some precepts of the Constitution, the law on foreigners and asylum law. In addition, several court rulings have condemned the General Administration of the State by limiting the freedom of movement of asylum seekers in the cities of Ceuta and Melilla (SSTJ, 2010). The CETI is not an appropriate location for asylum-seekers or for vulnerable people, which further justifies the need to move them all to the Peninsula. Agencies such as UNHCR or the Ombudsman, have stated on multiple occasions that the Center does not meet minimum reception conditions for all these people and that they should be transferred as soon as possible (Defensor del Pueblo, 2016). For this research, we firstly reviewed the literature in order to contextualize the situation in the Spanish southern border: legislation, reports, doctrine, jurisprudence, etc. From that review, we developed a list of questions that where used as a semi-structured script for the interviews. Altogether 35 interviews with migrants and asylum seekers and 34 to privileged informants (public administrations, social organizations...) were done, on both sides of the border between Spain and Morocco. From the information collected in the interviews and the notes in the journal of field during the four months of participant observation, it became necessary to expand further the analysis of the situation and study it from a psychological perspective, in addition to the legal view. Mental health negative consequences of involuntary institutionalization have already been widely studied in other groups such as prisoners, elderly, children... (Haney, 2003; Leite & Schmid, 2004; McCall, 2013). The scientific literature verifies what was observed in the interviews (Robjant, Hassan & Katona, 2009): migrants and asylum seekers as vulnerable population suffer by the arbitrariness of the transfers to the peninsula, the absence of public regulations and prolonged stays (Fazel & Silove, 2006), triggering many feelings of despair, injustice and degrading treatment, which are often associated with poorer mental health outcomes, as depressive and anxious symptoms. Frequently CETI residents refer that what causes most distress to them is ignoring when they will be able to get out of Melilla. If we take into account that these are

people who have already suffered for several reasons such as armed conflicts, migration route risks, violence, the situation of arbitrary detention is increasing the risk of re-victimization, causing a more complex long-term social integration of all of them.
***

SESSION 5C – Faith Groups and Migration

	Room: A4
Chair	**Marja Tiilikainen, University of Helsinki, Finland**
1035	The Role of Ethnic and Religious Associations in Promoting and Supporting Muslim/Non-Muslim Dialogue. The Case of Milano, Italy – **Stefania Giada Meda, Cristina Giuliani**
802	Not Integration But "Inter-Creation": How Do Turkish Imams and Qur'an Teachers Define Integration in the Netherlands? – **Semiha Sözeri**
1272	A Multi-Faith Response to the Migrant Crisis in Europe: An Initial Examination of the Cooperation between Different Faiths on the Welcoming and Integration of Migrants and Refugees. - **Majbritt Lyck-Bowen, Mark Owen**
1062	Refuge for the Rohingya in Southeast Asia? - **Jera Lego**

The Role of Ethnic and Religious Associations in Promoting and Supporting Muslim/Non-Muslim Dialogue. The Case of Milano, Italy
(1035) Stefania Giada Meda (Università Cattolica del Sacro Cuore di Milano), Cristina Giuliani (Università Cattolica del Sacro Cuore di Milano)

Milano, is a large multiethnic and multicultural city in northern Italy, but is it also a mixed, hybrid place, where to see the result of combining the qualities of people of different ethnic, cultural and religious background? Our contribution falls under the conceptual framework of hybridization (mixité in French, meticciato in Italian. Cf. Gomarasca 2009; 2013; Meda 2016). This is a concept derived from biology and of strong metaphorical impact, applied controversially to the understanding of the exchanges between people and community belonging to different cultures and religions. The concept of hydridization (meticciato/mixité) refers to a transformative process, the birth of a new identity, which exceeds the original characteristics of the individual subjects (Kapchan, Turner Strong, 1999). The concept of hydridization (meticciato/mixité) is investigated with respect to the no-profit associations operating in Milano for the intercultural and interreligious dialogue, especially between Muslims and non-Muslims, a topical issue in the contemporary scenario of European cities (Giuliani, Meda 2016; Meda 2016). We decided to focus on associations composed of migrants because of the importance that they have for their members and for the society that promotes and hosts them (Marini 2013). Three aspects distinguishing Italy from other European countries in which the issue of the intercultural and interreligious dialogue between Muslims and non-Muslims was investigated. First, the specific and weak nature of Italian secularism in comparison with others European countries like France or the Netherlands (Diotallevi 1999; Kosmin & Keysar 2009; Roy 2007): in Italy Catholic Church, activism of ecclesiastical organizations in many sectors (school, sport, social assistance, education, health...), and religious values remain strong and exert influence on public and political spheres. Religiosity and role of religion on social and political domains could be perceived as an element of proximity between Muslims and Catholics. Second, the Muslim migration history is more recent in Italy than in other European countries, and their density is lower. Third, Italy has been less directly affected by terroristic threat, at least until now, keeping antagonism between autochthone and Muslim community lower than in other part of Europe. The idea that we explore is that, vis-à-vis the Otherness brought by Islam, the associations of migrants can play an important function of encounter and mediation, generating potential well-being for individuals, communities and society as a whole, and paving the way for forms still in progress of hybridization (meticciato/mixité). Methodologically, we have identified and analyzed from the ISMU/Orim database of ethnic associations, those operating in Milano for interfaith dialogue and integration, and whose members come mostly from the Muslim world. In addition, we conducted individual and group in-depth interviews with representatives of nine Muslim, four Catholic and one secular associations of immigrants. We found that Milan is "plural" and characterized by quite a number of migrant ethnic associations, whose members and promoters include women and young people, attentive to the needs of their affiliates in what concerns the facilitation of the immigrants' integration, and the research and progressive establishment of a common ground for peaceful coexistence with other members of society. The associations that we studied do not allow us to talk yet about hybridization outcomes in Milano. The research results, on the contrary, question the desirability of hybridization as outcome of the combination of people with different cultural and religious background. The analysis of the interviews rather suggests a more nuanced way of blending cultures and religions for a peaceful co-existence on the public sphere: a sort of "generative" encounter with diversity. This is a form of social relation that does not "replicate" old patterns (morphogenesis/morphostasis), but it gives the social community a new way of being, in a logic of care and reciprocity over time, involving different generations (i.e. a long-term perspective on the future), where everybody is called to be socially responsible over it in order to build a caring, prosper, and peaceful society. Our research shows the conditions that may make the "generative" encounter possible: they are freedom, justice and the opportunity to participate in the building of a shared public space, which is no longer just mine or yours alone, but something "new and beautiful". In this regard, the role of the associations of immigrants in Milano is to ensure the ethnic and religious pluralism.

    ***

Not Integration But "Inter-Creation": How Do Turkish Imams and Qur'an Teachers Define Integration in the Netherlands?

(802) Semiha Sözeri (University of Amsterdam)

Recently the Dutch celebrated 50 years of Turkish migration to the Netherlands. Today the children of the first Turkish immigrants who came with the temporary guest worker agreements in the 60's are called 'nieuwe Nederlanders' or 'the new Dutch', subtly implying that the new citizens are still different than the natives. One major difference is their religion. With a total population of 397, 471 (Statistics Netherlands 2016), the Turks form the largest Muslim community in the Netherlands. When compared to the Moroccans, who are the second numerous Muslim minority, the Turks have stronger communal ties, greater number of communal organizations and higher levels of political participation (Van Heelsum, 2005). Moreover, recent studies point out to their high-levels of second-generation religiosity (Fleischmann & Phalet, 2012), not declining even among highly educated Turks (Maliepaard, Lubbers & Gijsberts, 2010), accompanied by persistent isolationist tendencies (Huijnk & Dagevos, 2012) and socio-economic disadvantages (Gijsberts & Dagevos, 2010). In the light of findings like these, in 2014 the Dutch Minister of Social Affairs and Employment, Lodewijk Asscher has commissioned a research about the four major Turkish Islamic organizations in the Netherlands: the Süleymancı movement, Milli Görüş, Diyanet and the Gülenist Hizmet movement, and their effect on the integration of the Dutch Turks (Asscher, 2014). The results of the report indicate that very little is known about the activities of the mosques governed by these organizations, and that the lack of transparency in terms of their organization, practices and agenda calls for a more comprehensive research on the influence they have in the life of young Turkish

Dutch Muslims (Sunier & Landman, 2014). In this study, I aim to provide perspectives on integration from the key figures of the Turkish Islamic communities in the Netherlands. The integration of Muslim immigrants is usually discussed as an institutionally defined regulation imposed top-down by the host countries rather than a process generated by the immigrants themselves. Often, the imams and the Qur'an teachers in the mosques are viewed as authority figures and role models who can have either aiding or frustrating role on the integration processes within the migrant community they belong to. Particularly the influence of the imams imported from Turkey without knowledge of the Dutch language and society is viewed as problematic (Boender, 2012). To what extent are imams' and Qur'an teachers' definitions of integration different than the official definition of integration of the Dutch authorities? This is the main question I address in this study. The study is based on qualitative content analysis of semi-structured expert interviews (N=37) conducted between July 2016 and January 2017. The respondents come from the four largest Islamic Turkish communities in the Netherlands, namely members of the Diyanet mosques, Milli Görüs mosques, the Süleymanci community and the Hizmet movement. In terms of expertise, the sample consists of stake-holders such as academics teaching in the Dutch Islamic theology programs, Turkish imams, Qur'an teachers, chairs of the Turkish religious organizations, and Dutch ministry and municipality officials. The analysis of the interviews shows that the Turkish imams' and Qur'an teachers' vision on integration shares a number of key issues with the institutional definition of the Dutch state. Most actors agree about the importance of linguistic proficiency, social participation and abiding the laws of the host country for successful integration trajectories. Differently than the Dutch state, however, the imams and the Qur'an teachers see integration as a reciprocal relation through which both the minority and the majority members adapt to each other's culture and as a result, a new society is created out of the interaction of the different cultural and religious elements.

***

A Multi-Faith Response to the Migrant Crisis in Europe: An Initial Examination of the Cooperation between Different Faiths on the Welcoming and Integration of Migrants and Refugees
(1272) Majbritt Lyck-Bowen (University of Winchester), Mark Owen (Winchester Centre for Religion, Reconciliation and Peace)

In 2015, Europe experienced a considerable increase in the number of refugees and migrants trying to enter the continent. More than a million of the refugees and migrants arrived to Europe by sea in overcrowded boats leading to at least 3770 people drowning, though the exact number is unknown and could be higher. From the outset, European countries struggled to cope with the significant rise in people needing immediate help. The countries, Greece, Italy and Hungary where the migrants and refugees first arrived, struggled the most and the significant differences in other European countries' willingness to offer assistance led to tensions in the EU. While government officials at the state level argued over who should help all the new arrivals in Europe, a wide array of non-governmental volunteer groups and organisations stepped up and provided initial assistance to the refugees and migrants. Groups of volunteers such as the Greek Kos Solidarity Group, the Turkish İmece in Çeşme and Help Refugees in Calais were set up to help feed and shelter the many migrants and refugees. In many countries, faith groups and organisations, many of them with longstanding experience in this area, have also been involved in welcoming and looking after the many new arrivals. Some faith organisations like Islamic Relief and Christian Aid are providing direct help to refugees and migrants whereas others such as the Churches' Commission for Migrants in Europe have advocated for the implementation of a more humane asylum and migration policy across Europe. The involvement of faith groups and organisations in helping welcoming and integrating migrants and refugees has already been discussed in the literature. However, the exploration of multi-faith cooperation on common issues such as the welcoming and integration of migrants and refugees has only just been initiated. This important but mainly unexplored area is the focus of this paper that is reporting on the findings of the research project: Faith Organisations and the Migrant Crisis in Europe. Based on the examination of four case studies the paper identifies and discusses possible benefits of a multi-faith approach to welcoming and integrating refugees and migrants.

***

Refuge for the Rohingya in Southeast Asia?

(1062) Jera Beah H. Lego (Asian Development Bank Institute)

As countries, all over the world are increasingly closing their doors to outsiders, refugees and the institution of refuge are in a more precarious situation than ever. This is no different in Southeast Asia where few countries have acceded to the United Nations (UN) refugee conventions despite the region having witnessed massive refugee movements: first, during the so-called Indochinese refugee crisis in the aftermath of US' departure from Vietnam in the 1970s, and second, of the various ethnic minorities fleeing conflict and persecution in Myanmar since the 1980s. Of the latter group, the situation seems bleakest for the Rohingya, a Muslim minority group disowned and oppressed by the government of Myanmar. Since the first large-scale migration of some 200,000 Rohingyas into the Cox's Bazaar region in Bangladesh in 1978, hundreds of thousands more have fled into Bangladesh, across the border into Thailand, and on perilous boat journeys to Malaysia and other destinations, earning for themselves the title "Asia's new boat people" (Lewa, 2008). Some progress is being made in developing frameworks for refugee protection in the region, such as with the adoption of presidential and cabinet decrees in Thailand and Indonesia. Still, human rights advocates are critical of the human rights violations and neglect of refugees and asylum seekers in the region with a number of human rights organizations believing the Rohingyas to be the object of genocidal policies by the Burmese government. This paper builds on previous research to examine the prospects for refuge and protection of Rohingya refugees and asylum seekers in three nearby Southeast Asian countries: Thailand, Malaysia, and Indonesia. Using reports and other secondary sources by various nongovernment organizations (NGOs), the paper traces government and nongovernment responses to the Burmese government's policies towards the Rohingya and to arrivals of Rohingyas both by land and sea, assesses the motivations and impetus for these responses, and teases out possibilities for solutions amidst limited protection space. Possibilities are to be found in interventions made by the Office of the UN High Commissioner for Refugees (UNHCR), local NGOs, and networks of NGOs, working closely with local communities, operating ironically with the acquiescence of and in opposition to the state.

***

SESSION 5D – Migration through Narratives

	Room: A5
Chair	**Giuseppe Sciortino, University of Trento, Italy**
1271	My Name Is Miracle and This Is My Story. Memoirs of (Extra)Ordinary Migration for a New Socio-Political Tale – **Alessia Belli**
1188	Following My Israeli Husband: Narratives of Aliyah – **Paulette K. Schuster**

My Name Is Miracle and This Is My Story. Memoirs of (Extra)Ordinary Migration for a New Socio-Political Tale

(1271) Alessia Belli (Sant'Anna School of Advanced Studies Italy)

This contribution wants to analyse, by capitalizing on my experience as a researcher in political philosophy and as a legal consultant, the complex role played by the momoirs of asylum seekers. In this sense, the reconstruction of their biographical experience, from the country of origin to Italy, not only represents the tool through which they can access the refugee status, but also a fundamental opportunity to rethink the politics of immigration-management tout court. This is as much more urgent in a country, Italy, that still struggles to identify a specific pattern and course of action on the matter (Allievi). Putting at the center the memoirs of the subjects means, more specifically, to introduce a crucial element to challenge the logic of securitization (Bauman), of reduction of asylum seekers to mere numerical data, of de-humanization of the Different. In other words, the emersion and the centrality of the momoirs can represent a critical-deconstructive instrument vis a vis the climate of closure and of refusal that is visible, not only in Europe, in the construction of defensive walls and in political and media campaigns of demonization of the Other. The practice of bringing the individual's life experience to the surface, has two advantages: on the one hand, it guarantees the recognition of the other, meant as a vital human need (Taylor). As such, it enables the subject to re-build, exactly through his/her narration, a sense of self that the migration dynamics have profoundly challenged, provoking identity lacerations or breaks that are hardly treatable. The act of taking care, inscribed in the emersion of the past, is then directly connected to the re-construction of individual agency which is behind every practice of active citizenship. On the other hand, it enables to transfer the momoir from the private to the public-political space and as such, to cross the border of the self to contaminate and challenge the public, media and political debate that is profoundly affected by ignorance and shaped by stereotypes. In this sense, the emersion and visibility of the memoir urgently introduce in that same debate the issue of the responsibility toward other human beings who represent the extreme symbol of vulnerability and marginality, and exactly for this reason perceived as troublesome, unacceptable and therefore isolated. The feminist methodology of 'giving voice', that informs the overall approach of this contribution, putting at the very center the stories and the experiences of women asylum seekers, meant as minorities within minorities, plays a fundamental role in challenging the mainstream rhetoric and some premises of the ongoing immigration policies. Gender, as a category, becomes then a crucial lens to demonstrate how migration and integration policies that fail to recognize and accept the centrality of the most vulnerable subjects' past experiences, and the specific burden of violence and discrimination that they bring with them, can hardly identify sustainable solutions able to guarantee the coexistence of diversities within complex contexts. The act of giving voice, within an empathic listening, becomes the first and unavoidable condition of empowerment, of activation and of participation of the person in the social, economic and political life of a context. The memoir of the most marginal subjects, exactly of women asylum seekers, becomes the lens through which our societies can be analyzed and re-defined within a framework of higher sustainability exactly because they prove to be more people-oriented. This aspect is intrinsically linked to the capacity of accommodating, besides autonomy, also vulnerability and dependency conceived as fundamental conditions of any existence. Thinking the act of giving voice as a tile in an 'ethics of the care' that becomes a general attitude, means giving to the relational dimension of life an important role as an antidote against the ongoing de-humanization and commodification processes. The aim of the present contribution is exactly to analyse the supposed 'perspectival advantage' of a politics of giving voice that works through the memoirs of some women asylum seekers who live in a specific area in Tuscany (Italy), different for age, country of origin, language, religion, ethnicity etc. (Intersectionalism). It wants to argue how this choice represents a crucial condition to tackle the challenges posed by global migrations and by the increasing multiculturalism of our societies, and to re-configure them in the name of a higher justice and equality for all men and women.

***

Following My Israeli Husband: Narratives of Aliyah
(1188) Paulette K. Schuster (Hebrew University Jerusalem)

Extensive literature exists recounting the experiences of Jewish immigrants to Israel and their integration into their new adopted homeland. However, there is much less information about non-Jewish tales. I am interested in exploring in this paper, the narratives of non-Jewish women from Latin America who made Aliyah (immigration to Israel) after marrying their Israeli husbands. Most of these new immigrants, had little or no knowledge of Judaism, did not speak Hebrew and had no historical or emotional ties to this ancestral land. I am also interested in examining different notions of belonging, integration and socialization. How did these women adapt? Did they acquire Hebrew as a second language? Was their acculturation difficult? Did their religion influence their integration in any way? Were they accepted by their husbands' families? Do they feel like they belong? This will be an interesting case study where gender and religious differences are the main variables. Interviews will be held with 15-20 non-Jewish women from Latin America living in Israel for at least a year. Participant Observation will also be conducted.

***

"How Are They Managing Life in Scotland?" A Reflection from a Subjective Wellbeing Study of the Chinese Asylum Seekers and Refugees in Scotland
(1240) Caroline Cheng (Queen Margaret University)

This paper presents the core constructs of subjective wellbeing from the perspectives of the Chinese asylum seekers and refugees in Scotland, in a wellbeing study collaborated with the British Red Cross, the Scottish Refugee Council and the local Chinese Community Development Partnership. The implications for policy practice are discussed, and initial recommendations based on the study are presented. According to UNHCR, the number of refugees worldwide stood at 19.5 million in 2014. At the end of 2014, there were 117,161 refugees, and 36,383 pending asylum cases in the UK (UNHCR 2016). Amongst asylum seekers in Scotland, China registered as the top country of origin from the year 2013 to 2015 with 21% and 25% respectively, and one of the top 3 countries in 2012 besides Eritrea and Iran (Mulvey 2015). The composition of the Black and Minority Ethnic population found that the largest ethnic groups in Scotland were Pakistanis and Chinese (Netto 2006). Nonetheless, most research on Scottish refugee integration has provided limited information on this group. In addition, there was no Chinese refugee present at the workshop organized by the Scottish Refugee Council (SRC) in Glasgow in Oct 2015 when the primary researcher was present as a facilitator. The Chinese interpreter present also mentioned that the Chinese asylum seekers and refugees seldom participate in local workshop or activities possibility due to lack of information and time. Are they managing well or just lost in the new place? The answer is unknown to researchers, policymakers or professionals working with the refugee population in the host community. Remarkably little research has been carried out on the UK Chinese refugee community in the literature, and this study proposed to fill the gap of finding out the subjective wellbeing of this population. Most wellbeing research projects adopt a quantitative approach, and this study aimed to explore the subjective experiences of Chinese refugees and how social connections serve as a mean to achieve wellbeing in a qualitative manner. The researchers have had the privilege to investigate the factors contributing to a good life for 30 Chinese asylum seekers and refugees in the Greater Glasgow area as the first stage of a wellbeing study. Semi-structured interviews were conducted to find out the core constructs of wellbeing from the Chinese people's perspectives and thematic analysis was employed in the data analysis process. Nvivo software package was used to code the data and develop a typology of different themes. The top five themes that emerged were children's education and learning opportunities, living environments, transportation, good health and access to healthcare, and human rights issues such as freedom to pursue one's interests and beliefs. Other constructs that were mentioned include having one's own house, good and affordable transportation, acquire the English language skills, having close friends, being close to family members and having fresh and affordable food produce. Findings also revealed men's isolation, prolonged asylum process, discrimination, limited English skills, communication between Chinese parents and school and difficult transition from asylum to refugee status as barriers to wellbeing. The data gathered would enhance the knowledgebase on the Chinese asylum seekers and refugees for both the British Red Cross and the Scottish Refugee Council. It will provide empirical data for the Chinese Community Development Partnership to apply grants to specific needs of this population.

***

"We are not creating at every new place a new identity for ourselves, you know…": An ethnographic reading of the recreation of 'home' in the case of expat women in Istanbul

(1318) Didem Kılıçkıran (Kadir Has University)

The self-assured remark above in the title is made by Binge, a 55-year-old German woman who lives in Üsküdar, Istanbul, during my first interview with her in the living room of her spacious flat overlooking the Bosphorus. In the last thirty years, Binge has accompanied her husband who works in a global company on his international assignments in different countries, committing herself to the recreation of the home at each stop of their journeys. The sense of the continuity of identities that she refers to owes to the pieces of furniture and objects that travelled long distances with them – some of which have been witnesses of their lives ever since they left Germany. For Binge, these things mend the discontinuities engendered by her movements and make every new space a familiar one. When I ask her where she thinks 'home' is, she says "it is here; this very space is my only home", with a quick warning that she is not talking about the flat in which we are conversing. Then she goes on telling me that 'home', for her, is not Germany either, nor any other country or city where she lived in in the last thirty years, but the space in which she dwells with her own things. In other words, it is the private / domestic space per-se – the space that encloses the life and belongings of her family and becomes a familiar inside wherever they go – that she calls 'home'. This inside with no fixed coordinates acts like an anchor that travels with her and ties her up to a new geography every time she stops. It is also the anchor of her identity. Home, as a place and a set of feelings and personal and social meanings associated with it, lies at the heart of everyday life. Yet, only conditions such as those generated by international migration bring it to the fore as a unique source of attachments, desires and needs (Boccagni, 2016). The central tenet of this paper is that the domestic home-space is both a window on migrants' capacities to appropriate the contexts of their everyday lives and the most notable place to investigate the negotiation of identities in the context of international migration. As Ganguly (1992: 31) writes, although the representation and negotiation of identities is performed on various levels and in different practices and sites of experience, "it is a domesticated concern" since "it is actively played out only [...] within a social context in which the demarcations between an insider and outsider are clear".3 Based on this, I try to uncover how 'home' is perceived and recreated and how identities are renegotiated within the bounds of domestic spaces in conditions of extended mobility – under the influence of a lengthy separation from what used to be 'home'. To do this, I refer to vignettes from my ethnographic research with expat women who live in Istanbul and discuss the meanings these women attach to the home-spaces they inhabit with reference to the ways they perceive their experiences of mobility and their new lives in Istanbul, the changes of lifestyle they have been through, the memories of the places they left behind, the habits and aspects of material culture they have carried with them in the course of their journeys, and the practices through which they construct the boundaries of their private milieus. I show that while for some like Binge, the 'home' is a space that is to be reconstructed on the basis of a sense of continuity regardless of the material geography, for others it is still an achievement to be accomplished. All in all, I conclude that 'home' is an evolving, open-ended experience for these women, the meanings of which is closely related to the meanings they attach to their experience of mobility in their own biographic trajectories.

***

SESSION 5E – Migration and Culture

	Room: B1
Chair	**Vildan Mahmutoglu, Galatasaray University, Turkey**
1072	Musical Habitus of the Turkish Migrants in Germany: The case of Metin Türköz and Yüksel Özkasap Songs – **Mehmet Mutlu, Esin Gülsen**
1303	Immigration Theme in Elif Shafak's Novels - **Reyhana Agali Jafarova**
1358	The Ionians in Anatolia and The Mother Goddess Cybele Cult – **Seher Selin Özmen**

Musical Habitus of the Turkish Migrants in Germany: The case of Metin Türköz and Yüksel Özkasap Songs

(1072) Mehmet Mutlu (Middle East Technical University), Esin Gülsen (Middle East Technical University)

In parallel to the labour migration from Turkey to Germany since 1960's, a unique experience of intercultural encounter has occurred. This study attempts to search this intercultural encounter by focusing on the 'musical habitus' of the Turkish migrants in Germany, through their musical narratives between 1960 and 1980, in the case of Metin Türköz and Yüksel Özkasap songs. Therefore, answers to the relevant questions will be sought. How do the migrants represent their social position by their musical narratives? What are the prominent themes in their songs? Do the lyrics represent the migrant's everyday and working life? What are the forms of representation of self and the German? Is there a hegemonic meaning of being migrant in their songs? Do the musical narratives of the migrants articulated to dominant political and cultural discourses and how? What kind of denotations, connotations, metaphors and metonymies do the songs include? Do the songs include symbolic reversals? Can the musical narratives be taken as a way of hidden resistance? In this context, songs of Metin Türköz and Yüksel Özkasap, two Turkish migrant singers who sang the songs telling the migrants stories since 1960's, are analysed by the methodology of discourse analysis.

***

Immigration Theme in Elif Shafak's Novels
(1303) Reyhana Agali Jafarova (Baku State University)

Immigration factor played a certain role in the formation of the world public social idea. At all times, societies had to leave places they lived for other places. Immigration can be designated as people's leaving their places for other areas or countries, temporarily or permanently on social, political and economic reasons. Therefore, immigration influenced social factors such as policy, economy, geography and culture. This manifested itself particularly, in the literature which is an integral part of the culture. Immigration literature is a distinct example of this effect. Contemporary American immigration literature is the result of people's mass flow to the United States of America. This literature is comprised by the works of immigrant writers representing different ethnic groups. The purpose of this paper is to examine immigration theme based on the novels by Elif Shafak. She is one of the authors who played a great role in the formation and development of Turkish American literature, which is a comparatively young branch of American immigration literature. The cases in her novels are based on different nationalities, cultures and countries. Belonging to a certain nation is of less importance in her novels. She tries to reveal her heroes' identity from multicultural perspective.

***

The Ionians in Anatolia and The Mother Goddess Cybele Cult
(1358) Seher Selin Özmen (Namık Kemal University)

"Migration" has been an important concept for explaining social and cultural change throughout the history of archaeology. Religion, on the other hand, as an important medium for the interaction of different societies and cultures, has been one of the main results of migrations. In antiquity cults spread through different geographical areas by trade, wars and migration. The immigrants brought their beliefs to the new lands and also they adopted the local cults. During the 12th and 11th century BC, a large-scale immigration called "Aegean Migrations" occured from Eastern Europe and Balkans to Anatolia. While the first wave of the Aegean Migrations was a movement of discovery the second peak period caused radical changes with the Ionian, Aeolian and Phrygian settlement in Anatolia. The Phrygians who came from the Balkans to Anatolia destroyed the Hittite State and settled in the Kızılırmak River basin. While The Aeol tribes settled between today's Çanakkale-İzmir shores, the Ionians established a union of twelve city-states between 900-700 BC. These cities were Miletos, Myus, Priene, Ephesos, Kolophon, Lebedos, Teos, Klazomenae, Phocaea, Samos, Khios, and Erythrai. An Aiol city, Smyrna, later joined the union. Ionia had the most glorious period between 650 and 494 BC. Ionian Golden Age came to an end when Miletos, the leader of the union, was occupied by the Persians in 494 BC. However, it is proven in the inscriptions that the union continiued its life till the 1st century BC. When the Ionians came to Anatolia they met the Mother Goddess Cult who had been prayed for thousands of years. The Goddess was given the title of "Mater / Mother" and her characteristic features were created in Phrygia. The recognition of the Mother Goddess Cult in Ionia can be explained by the relations with Phrygia. The purpose of this presentation is to reveal with the archaeological finds that the Ionians, who came to Anatolia with the Aegean Migrations adopted the Mother Goddess Cult Cybele and they added their own cultural characteristics to her.

***
SESSION 5F– Göç ve Edebiyat - 4

	Room: B2
Chair	Yakup Çelik, Yıldız Teknik University, Turkey
960	Yaşar Kemal'in Romanlarında Göç - **Serap Aslan Cobutoglu**
771	Bir Sürgünün Suçu Yücelten Öyküsü: Hırsızın Günlüğü – **Hanife Nalan Genç**
1350	Doğu Alman Yazınında Cumhuriyet Kaçağı İzleği Üzerine: Jürek Becker, Reiner Kunze, Stefan Heym - **Yıldız Aydın, Hayriye Bacaksız, Seher Sevindik**
996	Tahar Ben Jelloun'nun Ülkemde Adlı Yapıtına Göç Olgusunun Yansımaları – **Umran Turkyılmaz**

Yaşar Kemal'in Romanlarında Göç
(960) Serap Aslan Cobutoglu (Çankırı Karatekin University)

Çukurova'nın büyülü atmosferinde okuru düş kurmaya davet eden Yaşar Kemal'in yaşamında ve edebi söyleminde göç olgusu bu çalışmanın konusunu teşkil etmektedir. Çalışmada yazarın birçok eserinde görülen göç, sürgün, yer değiştirme/yerinden edilme meselesi özellikle ana konusunu "göç" kavramının oluşturduğu dört ciltlik Bir Ada Hikâyesi (Fırat Suyu Kan Akıyor Baksana 1998; Karıncanın Su İçtiği 2002; Tanyeri Horozları 2002; Çıplak Deniz Çıplak Ada 2012) serisi, Binboğalar Efsanesi (1971) ve Deniz Küstü (1978) romanları üzerinden incelenecektir. Yazarın Bir Ada Hikâyesi adlı serisi Lozan Antlaşması'ndan (1923) sonra mübadele gereği Yunanistan'a gönderilen/sürülen Rumların boşalttığı Ege'deki bir adada savaşlarda yerini yurdunu yitiren ve yurt edinemeyen diğer sürgünlerin yaşam kurma mücadelelerini konu alır. Bu seride sürgün ve göç hadisesi yersiz-yurtsuzluk, kimlik-aidiyet ve mekân-insan ilişkisi etrafında incelenecektir. Göçebe Türkmenlerin romanı olan Binboğalar Efsanesi ise göç olgusunun kültür yitimindeki çarpıcı etkisini gözler önüne sermektedir. Romanda yerleşik düzene geçememek ve kültür yitiminin beraberinde getirdiği/götürdüğü bellek yitimi önemli konular olarak belirir. Romanda var olmak için mücadele edenlerin yok oluş öyküleri göç hadisesi ışığında incelenecektir. Deniz Küstü adlı romanda göç olgusu yozlaşma ve çürümenin yaşandığı İstanbul kentinin bozulan doğasına paralel işlenmektedir. Romandaki bütün karakterlerin İstanbul'a göç yoluyla gelmeleri romanı ilginç kılar. Gurbete çıkarken hayallerini de beraberlerinde getiren insanların karşısında büyük kentin katı gerçekleri vardır. Bu çerçevede romanda göç olgusu umut-umutsuzluk, var olma-yok olma/bozulma/çürüme kavramları etrafında incelenecektir. Bu çerçevede çalışmada, Yaşar Kemal'in romanlarındaki sürgün/sürgünlük/göç olguları ya da göç hareketleri neden-sonuç ilişkisi içerisinde yer değiştirme/yerinden edilme, yersiz/yurtsuzluk, uyum/uyumsuzluk, kimlik/aidiyet, yurt edinme/yaşam alanı oluşturma, kültür yitimi/bellek kaybı, yozlaşma/bozulma/çürüme kavramları etrafında ele alınırken çalışma, yazarın farklı dönemlerde yazdığı eserlerindeki göç olgusuna da çeşitli bağlamlarda, değişik açılardan bakabilmeyi mümkün kılmaktadır. Ayrıca Yaşar Kemal'in romanlarındaki göç konusu yazarın biyografisinde yer alan göç macerası ile beraber okunduğunda çalışmanın ilgi çekici veriler sunacağı kanaatindeyiz.
***

Bir Sürgünün Suçu Yücelten Öyküsü: Hırsızın Günlüğü
(771) Hanife Nalan Genç (Ondokuz Mayıs University)

Çok yönlü bir yazın insanı olan Jean Genet gerek yazarlığı gerekse yaşam biçimiyle ayrıcalıklı, özgün ya da sıradışıdır. Seçimleri, karşıtlığı onu ayrık bir yaşamın kahramanı yapar. Yazarın romanları özellikle de tiyatrosunda sergilediği sıradışı biçeminin

94

özyaşamından beslendiği açıktır. Bunda yazarın politika aktivisti ve düşünürlüğü önemli bir etkendir. Hırsızın Günlüğü'nde evlilik dışı doğan ve henüz bebekken terk edildiği yaşamını ve onu etkileyen insan ve olayları çekincesizce okurla paylaşan yazar, bir bakıma onu suç dünyasına itenleri ve farklı farklı Avrupa kentlerinde sürgün yaşamaya zorlayan yazgısını yargılar. Genet'nin yerleşik ahlâk kurallarının işlemediği evreninde suç yüceltilen bir olgu olur. Bu evrende başta hırsızlar olmak üzere, kaçakçılar, katiller, fahişeler ve eşcinseller suça bulaşmış yaşamının onurlu simgeleri olurlar. Bu insanların içinden biri olan Jean Genet, 1948 yılında yayımlanan Hırsızın Günlüğü'nde (Journal du Voleur) sakınımsızca kendi yaşamını, ilişkilerini, eylemlerini kendisi gibileri yargılayan topluma ve yaşama bakışını, onları eleştirerek anlatır. Yersiz yurtsuzluğu ve suç dünyasını şiirsel bir dille betimleyen özyaşamöyküsel niteliği olan bu yapıt yazarın yazın alanındaki sıradışılığının da örneği olur.
***

Doğu Alman Yazınında Cumhuriyet Kaçağı İzleği Üzerine: Jürek Becker, Reiner Kunze, Stefan Heym

(1350) Yıldız Aydın (Namık Kemal University), Hayriye Bacaksız (Namık Kemal University), Seher Sevindik (Namık Kemal University)

İkinci Dünya Savaşı'ndan sonra ikiye bölünen Almanya doğuda Demokratik Alman Cumhuriyeti ve batıda Almanya Federal Cumhuriyeti olarak yaklaşık kırk yıl boyunca varlığını sürdürmüştür. Siyasal, ekonomik, ekinsel ve yazınsal alanda birbirinden farklı evrelerden geçen Alman toplumu esasen bilhassa düşüngü sistemlerindeki farklılığından ötürü birbirinden daha da uzaklaştırılmıştır, çünkü Rusya'nın etkisiyle toplumcu bir çizgide ilerleyen Doğu'nun karşısında Amerika'nın etkisiyle anamalcı bir çizgide gelişen Batı Almanya söz konusuydu. İki ayrı devlet, ancak tek toplum olarak Doğu ve Batı Almanya arasındaki uçurumlar gelişim evreleri birbirine koşut olarak tamamlanmadığından giderek artmıştır. Doğu Almanya'da işsizliğin artması, birtakım özgürlüklerin ve bilhassa seyahat özgürlüğünün kısıtlanması, bunun yanı sıra baskıların artmasıyla 50'li yılların sonlarına doğru 260.000 kişi batıya göç eder. Bu göçü durdurmak için önce yasadışı sınır ihlallerini gerçekleştirenlere, başka bir deyişle Cumhuriyet Kaçaklarına, cezai yaptırımlar uygulanır, 1961 yılında ise Berlin kentini ikiye bölen Berlin Duvarı inşa edilir. Doğu Almanyalılar ve özellikle doğudaki hakim siyasi görüşe göre "koruma duvarı" olarak da adlandırılan bu duvar, anamalcı düşüngü sistemine karşı doğuyu batıdan korumalıydı. Ancak sınırdan yasadışı yollarla öteki tarafa geçmek isteyen pek çok kişi öldürülmüştür, bunların içerisinde genç yaşta çocuklar da bulunmaktaydı. Yaklaşık 139 insanın sadece Berlin Duvarı'ndan batıya kaçmak isterken öldürüldüğü tahmin edilmektedir. DAC'nin Cumhuriyet Kaçaklarına karşı bu denli katı uygulamaları yazın dünyasında elbette yansımalar bulacaktı. Doğu Almanya yazarlarından Jurek Becker "Schlaflose Tage" (Uykusuz Geceler), Reiner Kunze "Friedenskinder" (Barışın Çocukları) ve Stefan Heym "Mein Richard" (Benim Oğlum Richard) yapıtlarında sansür edilme risklerine karşı Cumhuriyet Kaçağı izleğini kendilerine özgü bir dille ele almış ve kimi yerde açık kimi yerde şifreli bir dille duvar kurbanlarına gönderme yapmışlardır. Bu karşılaştırmalı çalışmada yazın-tarihsel, ekin siyasal ve özyaşamsal kaynaklardan hareketle Jurek Becker, Reiner Kunze ve Stefan Heym'in yapıtlarında Cumhuriyet Kaçağı izleğini nasıl ele aldıkları incelenecektir. Benzer ve farklı yönler analiz edildikten sonra, yazarların bu izleği ele alırken ortak bir erekten hareket edip etmedikleri tespit edilecektir.
***

Tahar Ben Jelloun'nun Ülkemde Adlı Yapıtına Göç Olgusunun Yansımaları

(996) Umran Turkyılmaz (Gazi Universit)

1971 yılında göç ettiği Fransa'da saygın edebiyat ödülü Prix Goncourt'a layık görülen Fas asıllı Tahar Ben Jelloun, Ülkemde adlı yapıtında aidiyet duygusuyla bağlı olduğu Fas'tan ve alıştığı yaşam biçiminden uzaklaşarak dilini ve kültürünü bilmediği Fransa'ya "öteki" dünyanın insanları olarak göç eden Muhammed Limmigri'nin, emekliliğinin başlaması ile yaşadığı uzamdan ayrılarak köyüne dönme süreci açımlanır. Jelloun, Ülkemde ile sözü Avrupa'ya çalışmaya giden göçmen işçilerden Limmigri'ye verir. Göç eden bir ailenin farklı kuşaklarının yaşadığı değişim sancıları üzerine temellenen yapıt aracılığıyla Fransız ve Arap toplumlarına ayna tutan yazar, dışlanmışlık ve yabancı olmanın sınırlarının ne denli genişleyebileceğini serimler. Küreselleşen dünyada yaşanan krizlere, çatışmalara ya da savaşlara bağlı olarak zorunlu ya da gönüllü olarak gerçekleşen göç olgusu sonuncunda, koşullar ve bu koşullar karşısındaki farklı insan tutumları irdelenir. Çoğu kez kopuş ve kayboluşun hüküm sürdüğü uzamlarda kesintili bir varolma durumunu yaşayan göçmenlerin, kendi kültür ve kimlikleri ile yaşadıkları ülkenin değerleri arasında kalışları ortaya konulur. Çalışmamızda, Jelloun'un Ülkemde adlı yapıtında, günümüz toplumlarının başat sorunsallarından olan göç ve bu döngüyü besleyen göçmenler, göç kuramcıları arasında yerini alan, itici ve çekici güçler yaklaşımının öncülerinden E.G. Ravenstein ve E.S.Lee'nin "itme-çekme" modeli çerçevesinde irdelenecektir.

***

SESSION 6A – Identity and Migration - 3

	Room: A1
Chair	**Besim Can Zirh, Middle East Technical University, Turkey**
735	Options about Democratization of the Alevi Society through Self-Empowerment of the Alevi Women in the European Diaspora – **Zeynep Arslan**
955	The Alevi Youth in German Diaspora – **Deniz Coşan Eke**
879	Construction of Immigrant Identity: Alevi Cultural Centers – **Seher Şen**
829	Language and Identity Problems – **Neriman Hocaoğlu Bahadır**

Options about Democratization of the Alevi Society through Self-Empowerment of the Alevi Women in the European Diaspora
(735) Zeynep Arslan (University of Vienna)

The Alevi faith is propagating the principle of gender equality. While the Alevi women are visible in the community they do not have much decision-making power to shape policy. This contribution makes the suggestion of the development of difference feminism to break with the socio-historically construction of equality of sex within the Alevi society. Six expert interviews show the inexistence of any particular consciousness about demand of equality yet. Through content and discourse analyses of literature, current social and geo-political developments in Turkey, Middle East and Europe and participatory observation within the Alevi associations, the strategic essentialism is discussed as a possible option to enable a development for real gender equality within the Alevi society. After the establishment of difference feminism to force consciousness about the real situation of Alevi women, the strategic essentialism is suggested as an instrument to enable gender equality within the Alevi society in three levels. Accompanied with different Gender Theories, the main argument of the contribution is the empowerment of the Alevi women as the most disadvantaged ones with a perspective from the bottom-up to the complex power and hierarchy structures to enable democratization processes within the Alevi society. In that way, an organized Alevi society that manages to re-discover its principals of humanism, pluralism and pacifism, could be able to (co-)initiate democratization establishment or stabilization processes within the societies they live. The contribution closes with the discussion that in the European Diaspora the Alevis do have better conditions to facilitate an Alevi re-construction process to develop consciousness about its main principals and its political role about dialogue maker in the societies they are part of. The minimum of a common denominator for pluralistic societies of the modern times today is to develop a pluralistic and empowered democracy, while this needs to be realized within the own rows first.

***

The Alevi Youth in German Diaspora

(955) Deniz Coşan Eke (University of Munich)

The migrant's identity construction is a salient theme in the public and political integration debate in Germany as well as in other European countries. The Alevi community faces a variety of specific challenges in transnational space in terms of protecting its identity and the recognition of its cultural and religious differences. The prospect of Alevis recognition both as a religious and cultural group and an immigrant group in Germany has created a growing social and political movement and a diaspora in Germany. Consequently, after more than 50 years, the children of Alevis migrants in Germany, especially third generation, start to grow up in a transnational context and with a diasporic consciousness. With this article, the data on the construction of Alevi youth identity is examined and informed by related literature on diaspora and identity. The article focuses on Alevi young selected from the members of the largest Alevi youth organization (BDAJ) in Germany. By this discussion, the article aims to offer a meaningful and practical contribution to Alevi studies.

***

Construction of Immigrant Identity: Alevi Cultural Centers

(879) Seher Şen (İzmir University of Economics)

It is possible to talk about an Alevi revival since 1990s both in Turkey and in certain European Countries such as Germany, Netherlands, Denmark, France and Austria. The urbanization process in Turkey and urbanization with migration to European cities have broken traditionally structured Alevi community ties that gave rise to redefinition of the community with its own institutions in urban space. Within this context Alevi Cultural Centers and Cemevis emerged as the new spaces of the Alevi identity in the contemporary world. These places have become major institutions of urban Alevis that are both outcomes and mediums of new conditions. In other words, while they were brought by the process of transformation, they have given new shapes to Alevi collective organizations and practices. Moreover, Alevi Cultural Centers and Cemevis have played an important role in the organization of immigrant Alevis throughout the world. This paper aims to understand this process of redefinition of Alevi collective identity in the case study of Alevi immigrants within the context of Alevi Cultural Centers and Cemevis in the Netherlands. The study is based on the evaluation of the in-dept interviews that are conducted with the heads and members of Alevi Cultural Centers and Cemevis in the Netherlands.

***

Language and Identity Problems

(829) Neriman Hocaoğlu Bahadır (Kırklareli University)

Migration, language and identity are three interrelated concepts. These concepts have important effects on the lives of moving families, as their lives are social realities. In this

research, it is aimed to focus on the 1989 migration from Bulgaria to Turkey in order to determine the problems, which people who immigrated in 1989 and afterwards to Turkey came across. To be able to find proper results qualitative method is used in this study. In-depth interviews are planned to conduct to understand the difficulties in relation to language inabilities, identity crisis, adaptation problems, perceptions, acceptance or exclusion by the community, changes in time and differences according to generations. So the research questions are: What were the problems of immigrants who moved from Bulgaria to Turkey? How did these problems change in time? and How did the immigrants solve their problems? The novelty of this research is that it is focused on not only to people who emigrated but also their children who were born either in Bulgaria or in Turkey. So it will be possible to make comparison among the people who lived the act of moving and their children who may also have lived or just felt it in their lives which started in a new country. This will also make it possible to determine changes in time.
***

SESSION 6B – Integration - 1

	Room: A2
Chair	**Apostolos Papadopoulos, Harokopio University, Greece**
1145	System of Hybrid But Limited in Practices for Uams: Turkey As a Case Study -**Cansu Güçlü**
1104	Contextual Cultural Competence in public service providers to promote Well-being and Equity in cultural diverse communities for a humanitarian migration management – **Rocío Garrido, Manuel García-Ramírez, Noelia Muñoz-Fernández**
1218	Tripartite Partners? UNHCR-Government-NGO Cooperation in the South American Solidarity Resettlement Programme – **Mariana Nardone**
710	Assessing National Reintegration Center for Overseas Filipino Workers' Programs for Returning Overseas Filipino Workers - **Jerome Catig Jogno**

System of Hybrid But Limited in Practices for Uams: Turkey As a Case Study
(1145) Cansu Güçlü (University of Szeged)

Ensuring 'best interests' of unaccompanied minors varying from accommodation, access to health services and education as well as legal assistance is shadowed by discrepancies between laws and practices in Turkey. As a signatory of the Geneva Convention of 1951 and the 1989 UN Convention on the Rights of the Child (CRC), Turkey is bound to protect and assist unaccompanied minor refugees. Besides national laws, it needs to be in compliance with recommendations of the European Union institutions, the Council of Europe and international organizations. Under controversial practices, minors are presently living with uncertainty for their future. This empirical study examines non-alignments among the Police and social institutions regarding reception of UAMS and determination of their age, which can result in exploitation of care and psycho-social deterioration of the children. Desperate and fear of being sent back to the zones they escaped from, unaccompanied minors are on hold in child-care facilities or live under heavy work conditions in illegal work places. Referring to improvements regarding detention procedures in recent year (Boček, 2016: 18), the study mainly focuses on still discussed problems that migrant children travelling without parents or relatives face in Turkey: Bureaucratic obstacles for access to facilities, health services or education, foreign identification number, legal guardianship and psycho- social support. Based on reports of national authorities and international organisations, it concludes with recommendations for improvements in the protection of these vulnerable migrants and comparative examples from European Union members.

***

Contextual Cultural Competence in public service providers to promote Well-being and Equity in cultural diverse communities for a humanitarian migration management

(1104) Rocío Garrido (University of Seville), Manuel García-Ramírez (University of Seville), Noelia Muñoz-Fernández (University of Seville)

The recent massive migration flows from war-torn countries in the Middle East and Africa are transforming Europe, which has become in a cultural diverse society. In host communities, public services play a significant role in the integration and wellbeing of migrants (Mladovsky, Ingleby, & Rechel, 2012; Virginia Paloma, García-Ramírez, & Camacho, 2014). Therefore, the cultural competence of service providers has been one of the most studied and promoted topics in the last decades (Balcazar, Suarez-Balcazar, & Taylor-Ritzler, 2009). The goal was to provide knowledge, skills and abilities that enable providers to work effectively in contexts with cultural diversity (Campinha-Bacote, 2002; Sue, Arredondo, & McDavis, 1992). Nevertheless, the explanatory models of cultural competence have not been very effective in reaching some real changes in professional practices, organizations and communities (Beach et al., 2005; Dana & Allen, 2008). Also, in Europe there have been social and political changes that make it unavoidable to review the concept of cultural competence from a perspective that emphasizes human rights and social justice (Rechel, Mladovsky, Ingleby, Mackenbach, & McKee, 2013). In this study, we have proposed the Model of Contextual Cultural Competence (CCC) from a perspective of the community psychology. This perspective has allowed the expand of the CCC's components and the incorporation of its contextual dimension. Therefore, CCC is defined as a process of personal development that takes place at different levels and implies a critical thinking (that leads providers to decode their own cultural background and social determinants of migrant health), skills to manage diversity (communication, etnocultural empathy, flexibility), capacity to act within the organization (constructing new roles and promoting support and changes within the organization) and capacity to act within the community (embedding the community and mobilizing its resources). The CCC is related with the empowerment of providers and results in promoting the wellbeing and social justice in contexts of cultural diversity. The aim of this study was to provide empirical evidence in order to support the validity of the proposed model of CCC. Consequently, we tested the structure of the construct of CCC and the relationships between CCC and three related constructs. In this way, we hypothesized that: (1) CCC is formed by four dimensions: critical thinking, skills to manage diversity, capacity to act within the organization and capacity to act within the community. (2) CCC promotes social justice's beliefs. (3) CCC protects providers from suffering emotional exhaustion –as part of their occupational well-being. This study was conducted in Southern Spain with 526 public service providers from different territorial areas that epitomize the types of multicultural communities regarding migration processes (i.e. a reception community in a border area, a transition community in a rural area, and a long-term-hosting community in an urban area). Participants belonged to law and enforcement (n=163), education (n=124), social and citizens organizations (n=117), healthcare (n=75), and recreation or religious entities (n=43). Data collection was based on the Contextual Cultural Competence Assessment Instrument (CCCAI), created ad hoc. Additionally, for the measurement of occupational well-being we used the four items of the emotional exhaustion dimension of the Maslach Burnout Inventory (Maslach, Jackson, & Leiter, 1996). Finally, for the measurement of social justice beliefs, we used items from Rasinsky (1987). A paper questionnaire with an attached letter of informed consent was applied to. An individual within each organization, collaborated with the research team and assisted in the data collection in order to maximize the response rate. This study was supported by the Coalition for the Study of Health, Power and Diversity, CESPYD (www.cespyd.es) and was founded by the Spanish Government (PROCOMDI. Competencia Cultural Comunitaria: Profesionales Competentes para Comunidades Diversas, PSI2011-25554). A structural equation model revealed that CCC is a multidimensional construct composed by the four proposed dimensions: critical thinking, skills to manage diversity, capacity to act within the organization and capacity to act within community. Also, the model predicted a positive impact of the CCC on social justice beliefs and the occupational well-being of service recipients. The CCC model and the CCCAI offer theoretical and practical contributions to migrant health and professional training. It incorporates a multilevel perspective of cultural competence to achieve equitable practices in public services at multiple levels (providers, organizations and communities). Through the development of critical thinking, skills to manage diversity and capacity to act within the organization and within the community, providers not only address more effectively their users' needs, but also, it allows them to protect their own health and develop social justice beliefs.

***

Tripartite Partners? UNHCR-Government-NGO Cooperation in the South American Solidarity Resettlement Programme
(1218) Mariana Nardone (Universidad del Salvador, Universität Duisburg-Essen)

This field-level empirical study explores the dynamics of inter-organizational cooperation between governments, international organizations and non-governmental organizations (NGOs) for the implementation of resettlement programmes. The focus is on the specific context of the Solidarity Resettlement Programme (SRP), which was adopted by some emerging resettlement countries from the Southern Cone of Latin America to receive resettled refugees coming from countries of first asylum in the region. Despite the SRP being an instrument of great potential in refugee protection, and South-South cooperation between States, international, and civil society organizations (Brazil Declaration, 2014), the Programme has been recently put on hold. This study offers a new perspective to understand how inter-organizational cooperation works in the joint implementation of "non-traditional" resettlement countries (Argentina, Chile, and Uruguay), considering the viewpoint of the three main entities involved: the Governments, the United Nations High Commissioner for Refugees (UNHCR), and UNHCR's partner agencies. This work contributes to the scarce literature on resettlement in Latin America, as well as to the understanding of complex inter-organizational cooperation involving partnerships between local, national and international entities in resettlement programmes. The findings show that despite the SRP is a "tripartite enterprise" (Guglielmelli White, 2012), in practice a lack of concerted effort of UNHCR, governments and NGOs limited broader integration achievements in these emerging resettlement countries. An improved understanding of inter-organizational relations could provide a better understanding of the level of cooperation needed during the joint implementation of resettlement programmes.

***

Assessing National Reintegration Center for Overseas Filipino Workers' Programs for Returning Overseas Filipino Workers
(710) Jerome Catig Jogno (De La Salle University)

What started as a temporary measure to stabilize the country's balance of payment crisis because of oil price shock and high rates of unemployment during the 1970s, the Philippine government is now the world's top sending labor country when it comes to overseas employment. However, with the political and economic uncertainties that surrounds some countries where presence of overseas Filipino workers (OFWs) are found, their employment is at stake and untimely repatriation is on the horizon. The government laid out plans in this kind of scenario to economically reintegrate them back into the society, through cash assistance and livelihood programs readily available for them. This research will focus on the programs offered by National Reintegration Center for OFWs to returning OFWs and assess how effective the program is in fulfilling its mandate. At the end of the paper, the author will discuss factors, specifically savings and investments, and channeling remittances through these financial products, that will also be helpful in determining the success not only of the program but in the temporary stint of Filipinos' employment overseas and their future when they get back to their home country.
***

SESSION 6C – Migration and (In)security

	Room: A4
Chair	**Ibrahim Sirkeci, Regent is University London, UK**
1264	Anti-immigration vs Anti-EU: Analysis of Brexit Decision of the UK - **Nergiz Özkural Köroğlu, Deniz Eroglu Utku**
1019	The Certainty of Uncertainty; The Critical Tool of Certainty in a Migrant's Journey to Effectively Control Issues in Human Security, Fraud and Integration for the Benefit of the Migrant and the Receiving Country - **Sherene Ozyurek**
1181	Perceived Discrimination, Identity Dimensions and Well-Being among Immigrant Muslims Living in Italy - **Cristina Giuliani, Stefania Giada Meda, Semira Tagliabue**
978	The Impact of War on Securitization of Refugees in Postwar Countries - **Ivana Katic**

Anti-immigration vs Anti-EU: Analysis of Brexit Decision of the UK

(1264) Nergiz Özkural Köroğlu (Trakya Universitesi), Deniz Eroglu Utku(Trakya University)

Britain's relation with the European Union has been always distant. The UK has never been a full participant of certain policy areas; particularly in the area of 'justice and home affair' the UK showed limited enthusiasm to cooperate (Carrera et. al. 2016). Nevertheless, Britain's decision to leave the European Union, so called the Brexit decision, has been one of the shocking development happening in 2016. Prima facia the referendum result shows the electorate's historic decision to break away from the EU, however it is actually product of a populist political discourse, which has been shaped by increasing anti-immigrant and Islamophobia sentiments in the UK. The process of Brexit started with the David Cameron's, meantime the prime minister of the country, decision to hold an in/out referendum vote on Britain's EU membership by the end of 2017. Actually, the main reason behind his will for his attempt on holding a referendum was to force EU to make reforms and use this referendum discourse to have an effect on voters. The UK targeted to have "special status" in the EU and to have a braking system for the social aid given to immigrants. Throughout the European integration history, UK always has been in a confederalist camp and became a pro-American polar against pro-European Franco-German axis. Therefore, the UK chose to use opt-out option for being out of Eurozone and Schengen Area. At that point, it is wrong to claim that the UK had been a fully attached to the EU and adopting all union regulations to its domestic policies, it was still momentous decision to asking public choice for the future of membership. After the decision of referendum, all political parties in the country declared their position towards referendum and the EU. Among others, the UK Independence Party (UKIP) Leader Nigel Farage had been the main figure of Leave Campaign. He established his discourse on the grounds of anti-immigration and Islamphobia. During his campaign, he and his party did not refrain from using posters, which have racist propaganda. They claimed that the EU has failed them because could not avoid refugees and immigrants coming into the union countries. What is more although empirical studies argue the opposite (Dhingra et al. 2016), immigrants are targeted as threat to welfare of the country. Although the campaigns against the EU membership continued with anti-immigration, mainly anti-refugee campaign, the first attack after the Brexit decision targeted to all migrants living in the UK. In fact, after the referendum, EU member state citizens have been faced with certain brutal attacks. Polish migrants living in the UK have been mostly faced with these attacks, even some lost their lives as a result of these attacks. According to police report, there has been %41 increase in the hate crime records compared to the records of pre-Brexit (13, October 2016, Independent). In other words, pre-Brexit discourse against to that accuses the EU not to avoid refugee and migration flows turned into actions that are against all immigrants. In this, paper we argue that anti-Muslim and anti-refugee discourses behind Brexit campaign actually is a part of larger anti-immigrant/foreigner attitudes. Therefore, we also argue that Brexit process is not just a threat for refugees coming from outside the continent; it also has potential to harm European identity idea. In other words, we argue that Brexit idea that was boosted with anti-immigration discourse during the campaigns, was a UK version of Euroscepticism which is now increasing all over the EU in parallel to populist political discourses of far-right parties and governments. While European integration was a peace project and European identity is based on the European values which are democracy, multiculturalism, minority rights, freedom, and human rights, Euroscepticsm has potential to open Pandora's box which is full of Xenophobic and Islamaphobic attitudes. In this paper, we examine the process of UK referendum on EU membership by relying on process- tracing. First, we will give some brief historical information on EU-UK relations background. In this part, we will focus on federalist and confederalist challenges and the position of UK in the EU as a Eurosceptic. Then we will analyze the course of the referendum and anti refugee discourses during the campaigns. Later, we will indicate the evolution of these discourses into brutal attacks to all migrants in the country. Finally, by exploring the nonconcurence of anti-refugee discourse with attacks to European citizens in the UK, we show how Brexit decision is actually a part of increasing Euroecepticism in the Europe.

***

The Certainty of Uncertainty; The Critical Tool of Certainty in a Migrant's Journey to Effectively Control Issues in Human Security, Fraud and Integration for the Benefit of the Migrant and the Receiving Country
(1019) Sherene Ozyurek (Monash University, Victoria University)

From an Australian perspective, which can be extended to other countries' migration framework, this study raises the notion that uncertainty negatively modulates systemic issues in ever-important recurring themes of human security, fraud and integration. Such understanding could lead to previously unexplored insights into the migrants' decision-making processes leading to subsequent use of unintended pathways. A sociological and empirical approach was undertaken to determine the impact of uncertainty on migrants in

Australia's migration program as a receiving country. Literature and case study reviews were undertaken, coupled with a quantitative approach analysing retrospective data from Department of Immigration and Border Protection to determine the ineffectiveness of current legislative tools that do not take certainty into account. Practical recommendations are presented for consideration by policy-makers to ensure certainty for the migrant including; to combat human security violations, the provision of a visa pathway for the applicant to remain after lodging a complaint will ensure that both employment and human securities can co-exist; to effectively control fraud, removal of discretion will ensure certainty in pathways of decision-making processes to combat unintended pathways; finally, the permeation of certainty throughout the migration program will ensure that steps to attain citizenship is not out of necessity thus ensuring successful integration. We contend that the use of certainty as a tool in migration policies will result in the shift from migrants' view of regarding the receiving country as a short-term gain and ensure consequential benefits for the receiving country's migration program are attained.

***

Perceived Discrimination, Identity Dimensions and Well-Being among Immigrant Muslims Living in Italy
(1181) Cristina Giuliani (Università Cattolica di Milano), Stefania Giada Meda (Università Cattolica di Milano), Semira Tagliabue (Università Cattolica di Milano)

With the increasing number of Muslim immigrants and their descendants living in Europe, the issue of their psychological well-being has become a very pivotal social and political agenda question in many Western countries. This issue is crucial not only for the first generation of Muslim immigrants, who directly have experienced migration, but also for second generation youth, who was born and/or is growing in the Western countries, so that they are longer exposed to the host culture in their formative years (Khuwaja, Selwyn, Kapadia, McCurdy, Khuwaja, 2006; Stevens, Pels, Bengi-Arslan, Verhulst, Vollenbergh, & Crijnen, 2002; Gonneke, Stevens, Vollenberghm, Pels, & Crijnen, 2005). Discrimination that immigrants perceive in country of settlement constitutes one of the major acculturative stressors that negatively impact on acculturation and psychological adjustment of immigrants, as widely recognized in the literature. In a climate marked by growing fears related to Islam radicalization and terroristic phenomena (Alba, 2005; Allen & Nielsen, 2002;), ethnic and religious discrimination towards Muslim communities represents a serious obstacle to their adjustment. Many studies confirmed the link between perceived discrimination and poorer psychological well-being among first-generation (Heim, Hunter, & Jones, 2011) and second-generation Muslims living in the West (Berry & Sabatier, 2009; Berry e Sabatier, 2010; Vedder, Sam & Liebkind, 2007). Additionally, numerous studies support a relationship between perceived discrimination and different dimensions of identity. For Muslims living in the Western Europe, acculturation process implies not only the question to negotiate competing heritage culture and mainstream host culture orientations, but also their religious diversity within European societies that are historically Christian, highly secularized and increasingly hostile to the presence of Muslims in Western societies (Alba, 2005; Arendt-Toth & van de Vijver, 2004; Duderija, 2008; Phalet & Gungor, 2004; Vertukien, 2007; Vertukien, Thijs, & Stevens, 2012; Britto, 2008 US). The present study investigated the mediator role of multiple identity dimensions (ethnic, national, and religious) in the association between discrimination and psychological well-being among 207 immigrant Muslims living in Italy. First and second-generation Muslim immigrants participated to the research and a multigroup path analysis model was conducted using MPLUS. While for first-generation Muslim the impact of discrimination on psychological well-being is modest, for second-generation ones perceived discrimination resulted to be directly associated with psychological well-being (higher depression and lower satisfaction with migration decision), and indirectly associated with satisfaction with migration through the mediation of national identity and religious identification.

***

The Impact of War on Securitization of Refugees in Postwar Countries
(978) Ivana Katic (Fudan University Shanghai)

The goal of this research is to discover construction of security discourses on refugees in postwar Balkan countries. How countries that have faced tragedies of war, were framing other refugees as a threat. How war experience and having citizens who were running away from bullets, influences discourses, especially the security one, on refugee crisis. The focus is on two states – Croatia and Serbia. Both were significant Balkan route actors and share recent war history. It is still part of a daily political discourses, and often used as a valid argument in political decision-making. The main assumption is that war experience and remaining antagonisms between these two countries affected the way their leaders were framing refugees, and the way they were dealing with the crisis. The main theoretical framework is built on Securitization theory, introduced by Copenhagen School of Critical Security Studies (see, e.g., Buzan, Barry 1991; Buzan, Barry and Ole Wæver 1997; Bigo, Didier 2002; Baldwin, 1997; Williams 2003, Watson 2013) Taking constructivist stand that there is no objective definition of security, it rather explores the methods by which security threats are created. Securitization theory is mostly focusing on discursive level of security and the words that were used in process of moving "regular politics into the area of security by employing a discursive rhetoric of emergency, threat and danger aimed at justifying the adoption of extraordinary measures" (Campesi, 2011, p. 2). This research aims to expand the theory by focusing on postwar context and the role of war in either creating, or easing the "politics of unease" (Huysmans, 2006) towards refugees. It takes into consideration other variables such as domestic politics (political elections, change of government), big actor`s directives (EU, Germany) and negative events that happened in Europe (Paris attack, Koeln). However, all these factors were overshadowed by the postwar context. In order to answer this question, I used media analysis of mainstream Croatian (Večernji List, www.vecernjilist.hr) and Serbian media (Večernje Novosti, www.novosti.rs), focusing on dominant discourses (members of government and presidents) from September 2015 till February 2016, when the Balkan route was officially closed. The main criteria when choosing newspapers was scope, high circulation rates, online accessibility, reputability (although this research is not analyzing the way media reported about crisis, but government discourses). Postwar antagonisms between these two countries were shifted to formation of the refugee discourse. Refugees were often used as an argument in bickering which country was more humane, fed more people and gave them more sweaters. Both sides were invoking experience of having their own refugees (sometimes even exaggerating "kilometers long columns of our refugees"), condemning `inhuman behavior` of other countries in the region, especially between themselves. But in general, none of them wanted these people to stay. Even at the beginning, when refugees were "people in need", so-called "But discourse" was prevailing; "they are humans, but we won`t allow becoming a hot spot", "they are humans, but as long as they just pass by, it is fine" Within analyzed six months, from "people in trouble" and "humans" refugees were more often becoming "illegal immigrants". Change of Government, and growing influx of refugees were couple of the reasons that affected this transition. Although "Give us our country back" discourse wasn`t very popular as in other (non-postwar) countries, "once we fix our borders, everything will be fine" was usual assertion. However, leaders of these two countries were still very cautious with words; e.g. when they were considering the option of building a fence, they appealed "let`s call it an obstacle, not a razor-wire fence". Hence, even when "Border defense discourse" was dominating, in most cases it was endeavored to propagate it in "considerate" way. Striving to make border discourse more... humane.

***

SESSION 6D – Gender and Migration - 1

	Room: A5
Chair	**Paulette K. Schuster, Hebrew University Jerusalem, Israel**
1101	Shocks and Flows: How Conflicts and Other Grievances Affect the Gender and Age Composition of Asylum Seeker Flows Towards Europe- **Christian Bruss, Simona Gamba, Davide Azzolini, Federico Podestà**
1012	African Women in São Paulo's City, an Ethnography about New Aspect to Immigration in Brazil - **Alexandra Cristina Gomes De Almeida**
848	Social Mobility among the Bulgarian-Turkish Migrant Women in Turkey - **Özge Kaytan**
705	The Punishment of Poverty: A Transnational Problem for Immigrant Women - **Monica Valencia**

Shocks and Flows: How Conflicts and Other Grievances Affect the Gender and Age Composition of Asylum Seeker Flows Towards Europe
(1101) Christian Bruss (Research Institute for the Evaluation of Public Policies of Fondazione Bruno Kessler), Simona Gamba (University of Milan), Davide Azzolini (Research Institute for the Evaluation of Public Policies of Fondazione Bruno Kessle), Federico Podestà (Research Institute for the Evaluation of Public Policies of Fondazione Bruno Kessler)

This paper assesses the impact of different political, economic and environmental shocks on the size but also on the age and gender composition of asylum-related migration flows to Europe. Several studies have recently examined the determinants of forced migration towards Europe (Neumayer 2004, Neumayer 2005a, Neumayer 2005b, Schmeidl 1997). However, to the author's best knowledge, no attempt has so far been made to understand how the nature of shocks in origin countries affects the gender and age composition of asylum seeker flows toward Europe. Conflicting theories predict different outcomes concerning the relationship between political and environmental shocks and the migration flows composition. For example, violent conflicts, such as civil wars, might create situations that are too dreadful for the weakest segments of the populations, leading to relatively more asylum seekers in Europe among women, children, and the elderly vis-à-vis economic migration. Conversely, young males could primarily be pushed to out-migrate to avoid being recruited in armed conflicts. On top of these considerations, it is difficult to distinguish between humanitarian and economic-motivated migration decisions; e.g. when a family flees to a refugee camp and then sends a family member to ask for asylum in Europe. The authors analyze the effect of different types of shocks on the number, gender and age composition of first time asylum seekers originating from 154 sending countries. Among the political shocks, the authors consider: violence between combatants, violence against civilians, infringement of political rights and civil liberties, and state terror. Concerning environmental shocks, natural disasters (such as droughts, floods, epidemics, etc.) have been included. Data on monthly asylum seekers applying to any of the 32 Schengen Area countries between 2008 and 2015 come from Eurostat (2017), while data on shocks are retrieved from various sources. In particular, georeferenced conflict data come from the Uppsala Conflict Data Program (Sundberg et al., 2013), data on natural disasters from the Centre for Research on the Epidemiology of Disasters (Guha-Sapir), data on civil liberties and political rights from Freedom House (Freedom House), data on state terror from the Political Terror Scale (Gibney, Cornett, Wood, Haschke, and Arnon, 2016), GDP and population data from the World Bank (2016), and georeferenced population data from the Socioeconomic Data and Applications Center (GPWv3, 2005). The identification strategy exploits the different timing across the sending countries of the different types of shocks. The highly skewed distribution of the dependent variable is taken into account by using count data models. In particular, a Zero Inflated Negative Binomial model is adopted. Preliminary results show that different shocks - such as armed conflict and epidemics - exert a weak immediate effect on asylum-related migration flows but almost no effect on the gender and age composition. However, this result is certainly affected by the fact that no time lags have been introduced so far. Indeed, the time lags depend on several variables, such as distance, and the identification of appropriate time lags is still in progress. Analyzing the relationship between the causes and the composition of migration flows could yield more insights into the mechanisms behind migration decisions. In addition, this research may contribute to better informing national authorities in charge of receiving and providing assistance to migrants, since women and children/the elderly may require different assistance than young men (Collins, 2011). To be prepared to offer the correct services, the relevant institutions have to be aware of changes in composition based on the shock in question.

***

African Women in São Paulo's City, an Ethnography about New Aspect to Immigration in Brazil
(1012) Alexandra Cristina Gomes de Almeida (Federal University of São Carlos)

This research aims to analyze the recent immigration to Brazil from asylum seekers, specifically women from the African continent, as the Democratic Republic of Congo, Angola, Nigeria, and others. The proposal is to do an ethnography to understand how women refugee access the Brazilian public policy and this research has been development yet. Brazilian law and order for immigrants has changed by federal government and São Paulo municipal government but hasn't yet been satisfactory to protect the refugee people and asylum-seekers. Thus women asylum-seekers and refugees in São Paulo have used other legal ways to obtains documents, visa and to access the Brazilian public policies, and this fact open academical discussion about refugee's theory. Therefore, propose is exploring ethnography African women's perspectives, this viewpoint can open issues to reconsider the categories refugees. Christian Williams (2014) and Liisa Mallki (1995) illustrate this point and suggest necessary to research subjectivities and particular social context the refugees because this groups can produce a new perspectives immigration politically. Therefore, the ethnography will be going to access experience's reports and observation the African women about public and private Brazilian's institutions work imigration issues.

***

Examining Ageing in Place Among Turkish Migrant Older Adults: A Case Study in Edinburgh, UK
(403) Melisa Yazdan Panahi(Heriot-Watt University)

An ageing population and international migration are two concurrent phenomena occurring at different levels of intensity in countries with various levels of development.

The UK is no exception to this rule as a country with an ageing population of whom ethnic minorities are the fastest growing segment of the population. An ageing population has raised significant challenges in terms of how societies can best support older adults to live at home and in their communities. Although there has been considerable research conducted into the ageing population, research on the experiences of ethnic minority older adults is still in its infancy. It is estimated that there is a Turkish population of 500,000 in the UK and that this number is growing, yet they remain an 'invisible minority' and are under-represented in policy discourse. Policy on age friendly cities and communities has furthered the research agenda, yet there is a significant gap in terms of understanding the experiences of different ethnic minority groups as regards ageing-in-place. This paper presents preliminary findings from qualitative research conducted with the older Turkish community in Edinburgh, UK including semi-structured, one-to-one interviews. The findings articulate the barriers and facilitators to ageing-in-place amongst the Turkish older community and identify potential implications for urban planning and the age-friendly community agenda. This research is important if we are to understand how experiences of ageing-in-place differ across groups and how these experiences can be articulated within community supports.

***

Social Mobility among the Bulgarian-Turkish Migrant Women in Turkey
(848) Özge Kaytan (Middle East Technical University)

Social mobility in the sociology literature is mostly associated with occupational mobility and then educational achievements (Van den Berg, 2011:503). In the study of social mobility of Moroccan women in the Netherlands, Van den Berg (2011:503) suggests that social mobility, which has alternative approaches can be found in qualitative research, that takes social mobility beyond the analysis of paid work and schooling by defining a broader sense of class and "social upgrading". Hence, a need for a gender-sensitive alternative approaches appears in order to go beyond 'the narrow definitions of class' (Bourdieu 1989 in Van den Berg, 2011:504), which considers occupation and education as the primary determinants for social mobility. Dominant research on social mobility is not able to reveal all of the expectations and perceptions of migrant women, because of the only focus of paid labor and education; while migrant women do not fit into the dominant conceptions of social mobility, their children's social mobility can be clearly associated with occupational and educational attainment (Van den Berg, 2011:505). In that sense, social mobility cannot be a clear-cut research between generations, although it has a significant association between parents and children. In the study of the social mobility among ethnic groups in Britain, Platt argues that life chances depend on social class background in some closed societies, however, "levels of intergenerational class stability among minority groups comparable to those of the majority can also be read as indicative of greater openness within society to ethnic minority achievement" (Platt, 2005:446). This paper underlines that, social mobility among the Bulgarian Turkish migrant women are visible and worth to examine. I try to analyze the perception of migration in terms of how it brings inequalities regarding women's gendered experiences. How these gendered experiences turn into strategies for social mobility among migrant women is the core problematic in this paper. Hence, this paper aims at demonstrating the gendered experiences of a group of migrant women, which share significant commonalities with migrant women in similar or different settings. The primary research technique used in this research was semi-structured in-depth interviews. Interviews were conducted with twelve Bulgarian Turkish migrants who migrated in 1989 and after 1989 in İzmir. Five of the migrant women are university graduates, five of them are high school graduates and two of them are secondary school

graduates. Seven of them are between 39-55 and five of them 55-68 years old. All women are still married and all of them have children. In the interviews, I asked about their migration stories, their preferences whether to live in Turkey or Bulgaria, the meanings of poverty and wealth, their perception of discrimination and the differences between the two societies in Turkey and Bulgaria. Although migration from Bulgaria to Turkey was an ethnic migration, it has implications on the basis of gender and social mobility. As Pedraza (1991:310) implies even if migrant women are from the working class, in their aspirations they assume to be the middle class. Migrant women do not see work as an opportunity for their self-actualization because they see work as a support for the family (Pedraza, 1991:310). It is difficult to determine whether the Bulgarian Turkish women were the middle class or the working class because of the nature of the communist system in Bulgaria back then. However, it should be noted that all of the women were employed in paid works in Bulgaria. Hence, their motivation to enter into the labor force in Turkey is because of their past experiences and work discipline that they brought from the communist system. The characteristics of middle class can be observed in the children of Bulgarian-Turkish migrant women. Children's occupations compared to the older generations are more professional and their lifestyles seem to indicate upward mobility. It is clear that Bulgarian Turkish migrant women have experienced social upgrading in Turkey, through different ways. One of the most important determinants of that they have never abandoned working in paid employment in order to hold on to their new lives in Turkey. Also, migrant women work hard in order to give a good education to their children. They seem very ambitious when it comes to children's education because women are aware of the fact that education is a significant opportunity to climb the social ladder in a new community. Climbing the social ladder through their children appears to be a significant strategy for migrant women.
***

The Punishment of Poverty: A Transnational Problem for Immigrant Women
(705) Monica Valencia (University of San Francisco)

This research examines the feminization of poverty as a social problem and as an aspect of American life. The poverty that women experience is vastly perpetuated by the lack of economic autonomy for women in the U.S. and all over the world. Pervasive inequality in the United States has shaped the way in which phenomenon like domestic violence, wage discrimination, lack of reproductive health, homelessness, incarceration and sexual violence help preserve female poverty at astounding levels. However, a much narrower look at how poverty affects immigrant women upon arriving in the U.S., shows us a doubly-disproportionate group of people that will most certainly be unable to leave poverty in their lifetime. My research takes a deeper look at the root causes of the feminization of poverty and the intersection of legal immigration status. There is a gap in the literature that is needed in order to understand the complexities of poverty as it relates to immigrant women in the U.S. It is difficult enough for women to navigate social, economic, and political arenas in the fight for equity and justice, and yet their ability to advocate for themselves diminishes if they lack legal immigration status. Women who migrate to the U.S. in search of jobs and a better life, are consistently subjugated and subjected to economic and domestic abuse. My research finds it becomes even more problematic for immigrant women to fight in the same sphere as other women with legal status, since they must battle in a sub-category of people differentiated by legal status. The methodology for this study includes 40 interviews of Mexican and Central American undocumented women who migrated to California, and toil in agricultural fields or homes as laborers and domestic workers. I also interviewed several legal scholars addressing the phenomenon of labor discrimination, domestic violence, and immigration law, as it relates to immigrant women to show the intersection of social norms that affect undocumented women. Beginning with a brief history of how women have been traditionally viewed, and thus treated throughout time, this research paper hopes to shed light on how undocumented women in the U.S. experience domestic and employment abuse in modern times. In understanding such abuses, we must first look at the transnational process of abuse for immigrant women stemming from their home countries. This includes looking at country conditions that delineate femicide rates, violence, and systematic poverty. In the U.S., poverty affects women differently than it affects men. The gender gap in our society informs us about the reality of equity between the genders and the factors that help perpetuate such a reality for immigrant women. Despite the differences in the gender gap, another stark reality is that the added factor of legal status for immigrant women residing in the U.S. only exacerbates this gap. Immigrant women face other consequences, the most important one of which is deportation. Deportation is the leading cause for fear amongst undocumented women and they fear returning to a country that they most certainly fled from. Aside from addressing economic abuses, we must also understand the effects of domestic violence on immigrant women. Domestic violence is the most prevalent type of abuse between spouses and partners and it also comes in many forms. Often, with the threat of deportation by a spouse or by an employer, undocumented women prefer to endure the abuse then return home after risking their lives in their migration to the United States. With such a vulnerable population living in the shadows, how can they navigate their place in society enough to feel safe and find a way out of poverty? This is what this paper seeks to find out. My research finds a trend in culture and attitude towards the "normalcy" of abuse, the need to endure the abuse out of fear of deporation, and the reluctance in seeking legal remedies that immigrant women actually have access too. Additionally, social and legal advocates recommend that social service and law enforcement providers adequately make it know to immigrant women that there are legal remedies available and that victims of violence not be afraid to leave their abusive environments. The Violence Against Women Act (VAWA) for example, serves as protection for immigrant women. When victims take a stand against abuse, they are more likely to become independent and make positive steps out of poverty.

***

SESSION 6E – Göç ve Etkileri

	Room: B1
Chair	**Erkan Perşembe, Ondokuz Mayıs University, Turkey**
781	On Immigrant Radicalism and Immigrant Nihilism -Thoughts on Migrations from the Middle East to Turkey -**Mehmet Evkuran**
791	Historically Migration Receiving Areas and Their Worldwide Effect- **Mehmet Azimli, Özden Kanter**
782	Kayıp Neslin Eğitimi: İstanbul'daki Okullarda Öğrenim Gören Suriyeli Öğrenciler Örneği- **Kamil Çoştu**
1265	Göçmenlik ve Yerinde Yaşlan(ama) ma- **Sevim Atila Demir**

On Immigrant Radicalism and Immigrant Nihilism -Thoughts on Migrations from the Middle East to Turkey
(781) Mehmet Evkuran (Hitit University)

No matter the reason, recent immigration from the Middle East to Turkey is not just a 'displacement'. It will have a deep and lasting impact on the people. Migrant individuals and groups are forced to rethink their perspectives on the world and their personal values deradicalizing themselves as a consequence. This radical position is usually a result of the strife affecting their peace and comfort at home. Migration, if it is caused by civil war, or other traumatic events, may lead to the reversal of values or increased radical returns to the values and beliefs. An immigrant who is deliberating between nihilism and radicalism has to try various ways to solve this dilemma. Whether an immigrant is running away from something or running towards something determines their behaviour in the country of residence. The first scenario causes an immigrant to take a conservative stance on protecting their identity and values; the second causes signifies that an immigrant is open to transformation of their soul comes to the forefront. Immigrant radicalism and immigrant nihilism are expressions of these two different positions. In voluntary migrations, the prevailing instinct is to meet the new and different ones try to understand it, and even integrate it. This integration can vary depending on the individulas' level of education, cultural flexibility, and location of networks of solidarity. In massive and painful compulsory migrations, the immigrant's world of emotion and thought sharpens. In cases in which the families are scattered and fragmented, an eternal traumatic interaction takes place that affects future generations. The Arab Spring turned into a very different picture in Syria. Contrary to expectations, the regime has not collapsed; rather it has survived with the support of its international allies and has fought against its people. This had theo-political consequences, and the sleepy sectarian fault lines soon took action. The Shiite-Nusayri elites, who held power, gathered around its sectarian social base. This situation transformed the political clash into a Shia-Sunni conflict. The meaning of this development for the Middle East is the dissemination of sectarian conflict. Because the sectarian identities in the Middle East are very strong and the borders are unreal and durable, on the contrary they are coercive and mannered. For this reason, it is inevitable that any problem in any Middle Eastern country will affect the region. It is necessary to add long-term chaos in Iraq. The reflection of these problems as they affect Turkey can be categorized under two headings. The first problem is refugees as a result of mass migration, and the second is the rising sectarian tension… Today Turkey has more than 4 million immigrants, most of whom are Syrians. In addition to Syrian refugees there are also refugees from Afghanistan and Iraq. In this case, Turkey has become the country with the highest number of refugees in the world. This is an intolerable amount for most European countries. Turkey sacrifices much for immigrants as both a state an da society. However, it is also true that there are some chakkenges. The war in Iraq and Syria is widespread and the negative, destructive effects of chaos has spread across the Middle East. Strengthening of Aalafism in the Sunni world is one of its signs. The radical Salafi movement which is based on the enmity of Shiism, is attempting to spread in Turkey but has not been very successful. Empathizing with the emigrate is not to submit to his theological conflicts. Helping one to immigrate does not call for looking at the spread of internal tension and anger around him. Turkey has its own democratic experience and understanding of religion, offering it a different and unique position as compared to other predominately Islamic countries. Therefore, when it resolves the immigration problems, it has to protect and strengthen its social order. In this study, the phenomenon of migration and refugees will be dealt with in the context of the problem of redefinition of religion and values. It will be argued how immigrants can prevent their tensions from being carried to Turkey, while their humanitarian problems are simultaneously resolved.

***

Historically Migration Receiving Areas and Their Worldwide Effect

(791) Mehmet Azimli (Hitit University), Özden Kanter (Hitit University)

In this presentation, we will approach various cities and regions which have become center of attention - virtually like a vacuum – throughout history. With this, we aim to discuss the global scale effects of these cities and regions. We will commence our topic by mentioning Mekke which was a center of attention in Central Arabia but then lost this attribute to Medine. The favorable and adverse effect of this migration on World History is of paramount importance. Medina is actually a cornerstone which has formed the start of civilization in terms of Islamic history. Due to the Prophet's deployment here, it became the center of attraction of whole Arabia. The Arabs which have left a lasting mark on World history from this town where they had migrated, has been found to be interesting as well as worth examining. From which paradigms this migration, which still has a worldwide influence, has formed around is significant. From our point of view, the unstoppable effect has been realized with the combination of Arab Bedouin stimulant aspect and the Jihad spirit in Islam. The dexterity of the aspects which have transformed the potential energy into kinetic energy have a separate importance. The effect of this migration story is still felt from the Chinese Wall to Spain. Later on, we will present Kufa and Baghdad regions which took the places of Cündüşapur which was an important medical center of Sasanian Iran and their capital Medain. Herewith we will examine the reasons and consequences of population shift. Especially the intellectual population formed around Baghdad's House of Wisdom lead to the boom of the Islamic Civilization. The migration of the information generated here to the West and the leap made by the West based on this information is remarkable. The direction and development provided by these immigrant communities gathered first in Kufa and then Baghdad, has revealed many different developments in terms of both technology and sociology. We will give special emphasis on shining cities such as Kufa, Baghdad, Kayravan, Samarra, Cordoba, Cairo, Istanbul, Ankara, Diyarbakır which transformed into metropolises from villages and while mentioning their stories of transformation, we will convey the reasons and consequences of migration that lead to this change. The above-mentioned expressions are also valid for the cities herewith. Previously having had no effect, them becoming cities which have shaped the World or left significant effects cannot be explained other than migration. We can state that our study will shed a light on migration movements of the last century and especially the last decade and will add value in the comprehension of the reasons and consequences of these movements. What we essentially argue is; the effect of the consequences which will be caused by radical discourse in the new areas where this immigration takes place on the new generation. It should definitely not be forgotten that; if migration is coherently categorized, it will result in very pleasant outcomes as per above. However, if maladministered it will be an aspect which destroys societies and throws them to the abyss of history.

***

Kayıp Neslin Eğitimi: İstanbul'daki Okullarda Öğrenim Gören Suriyeli Öğrenciler Örneği

(782) Kamil Çoştu (Bartın University)

2011 Mart ayından günümüze yaklaşık üç milyona yakın Suriyeli ülkelerindeki iç savaş sebebiyle Türkiye'ye sığınmıştır. Bunların yaklaşık 800 binini okul çağındaki çocuklar oluşturmaktadır. Çeşitli travmalar yaşayan bu çocukların ailesine, topluma kazandırılabilmesi için eğitim, hayatî önem arz etmektedir. Türkiye Cumhuriyeti Devleti, 1995 yılında Çocuk Hakları Sözleşmesi'ni kabul ederek ülke içerisindeki bütün çocukların eğitim-öğretim sorumluluğunu üzerine almıştır. Kabul edilen sözleşmenin 2. Maddesi'nde; "Taraf Devletler, bu Sözleşme'de yazılı olan hakları kendi yetkileri altında bulunan her çocuğa, kendilerinin, ana–babalarının veya yasal vasilerinin sahip oldukları, ırk, renk, cinsiyet, dil, siyasal ya da başka düşünceler, ulusal, etnik ve sosyal köken, mülkiyet, sakatlık, doğuş ve diğer statüler nedeniyle hiçbir ayrım gözetmeksizin tanır ve taahhüt ederler" ifadesi yer almaktadır. Bu bildiride, Millî Eğitim Bakanlığı'nın İstanbul'daki Suriyeli göçmenlere tahsis ettiği okullarda öğrenim gören çocukların eğitim durumları ve karşılaşılan problemler (öğrencilerin, öğretmenlerin ve kurumların/okulların) deskriptif bir yöntemle incelenecektir. MEB verilerine göre, İstanbul'da Suriyeli çocuklar için özel olarak tahsis edilen 10 civarında okul bulunmaktadır. Örneklem olarak İstanbul'un tercih edilmesinin nedeni de, eğitim verilen okulların sayısının ve buna bağlı olarak eğitim alan öğrencilerin fazla oluşudur. Araştırmada, nicel teknik kullanılacaktır. MEB'ten gerekli izinler alınmış olup, hazırlanan anket ve mülakat soruları ilgili okullarda tesadüfi örnekleme yöntemi ile seçilecek öğrencilere uygulanacaktır. Verilerin analizi SPSS paket programı ile değerlendirilecektir. Araştırmada, Suriyeli göçmen çocuklarının eğitim durumları, Türkçe dil yeterlilik durumları, kurumlarda görev yapan öğretmen ve idarecilerin konuya yönelik değerlendirmelerinden hareketle analizler yapılmak suretiyle, göçmenlere yönelik yürütülen eğitim politikasının iyileştirilmesine ve geliştirilmesine yönelik önerilerde bulunulması hedeflenmektedir.

***

Göçmenlik ve Yerinde Yaşlan(ama) ma
(1265) Sevim Atila Demir (Sakarya University)

Sanayileşme sonrası yaşanan gelişmeler ile birlikte ölüm ve doğum oranlarının düşmesi baş-ta Batılı gelişmiş ülkeler olmak üzere dünya çapında yaşlı nüfus oranının artmasına yol aç-mıştır. Bu nüfus değişimleri yaşlanma olgusunu bir kat daha önemli hale getirmiştir. 2015 yılı verilerine göre her 8 kişiden 1'si 60 yaş ve üzerindedir. 2030 yılında ise her 6 kişiden birinin 60 yaş ve üzerinde olacağı tahmin edilmektedir. 2000 yılında dünyada 80 yaş ve üzeri 71 milyon kişi bulunmakta iken bu sayı 2015 yılında 125 milyona çıkmıştır. 2050 yılında bu oranın 434 milyon olacağı öngörülmektedir (United Nations Report 2015). Türkiye'deki du-ruma bakıldığında, 1965 yılı yaşlı nüfus oranı %4 iken yaşlı nüfusun toplam nüfus içindeki oranı 2014 yılında %8 ve 2015 yılında %8,2 olmuştur (TUIK, 2016). Yaşlanan nüfus içinde yaş ilerledikçe yaşlanma hızı daha da artmaktadır. Dünya genelinde, 2011 yılından 2100 yılına kadar yaşlı nüfus (60+) 3 kat artarken, 80 yaş üzeri nüfusun 5 kat artması beklenmek-tedir. Yani dünya genelinde önümüzdeki 90 yılda ileri yaşlı (80+) sayısı, genç yaşlılara (60+) göre daha fazla artış gösterecektir. Bu süre zarfında, ileri yaşlı nüfusun Kanada'da 3 kat, Almanya'da 2 kat, İtalya'da 2 kat, Rusya federasyonunda 3 kat, İngiltere'de 3 kat ve ABD'de 3 kat artması beklenmektedir. Türkiye'de 80 yaş üstü nüfusun artış hızı da oldukça dikkat çekicidir. 2011 yılında binde 9 olan 80 yaş üstü nüfus, 2050 yılında 4 kat ve 2100 yı-lına gelindiğinde tam olarak 10 kat artış gösterecektir (United Nations Report 2015- Arun, 2014:4). "Yerinde yaşlanma", toplum içinde (kendi mekanında) bakım, yaşlılara alışkın oldukları kendi ev ortamında en az sorun yaşanması ve gerekli toplum kaynaklarının aktarılması esa-sına dayalı sistemi ifade eder. Aynı zamanda yaşlıların fiziksel, zihinsel, sosyal, duygusal ve manevi iyilik hallerini artırmaya yönelik görülmektedir. "Aktif yaşlanma" ise yaşlı bireyin zihinsel sağlığı yerinde, üretken, aktif sosyal hayatını sürdürerek ve pozitif yaşam sürme anlamına gelmektedir. Yerinde yaşlanma yaşlılar için hem fiziki hem de sembolik anlamı olan mekanlara bağlı eşitsizlikleri gidermeye yönelik bir düzenleme olarak anlaşılmıştır. Yaşlıların sosyal ilişkilerinin ve tecrübelerinin var olduğu mekanlarda yaşlanması, yaşlılık sürecinde yaşanabilecek problemleri azaltmakta ve yaşlıların aidiyet hissettikleri yer ile bağ-ların kurulmasına yardımcı olarak yaşlıların kendine has rutin pratikler geliştirmelerini sağ-lamaktadır. Bu yaşlıların çevre ile kontrollü güven duygusu oluşturmalarını mümkün kıl-maktadır. Mekânla güçlü bağı olan yaşlıların kontrolü/güveni daha iyi sağlayarak mutlu oldukları bilinmektedir. Bazı durumlarda ev yaşlılar için yalnızlaşmaya yol açsa da (Türkiye'de tek kişilik hanelerin %45,8'ini yalnız yaşayan yaşlılar oluşturmaktadır- TUIK, 2016) araştırmalar yaşlıların çoğunun bağımsızlıklarını ve sosyal ağlarını sürdürebilmek için yerinde kendi mekanlarında yaşlanmak istediklerini göstermiştir (Esendemir, 2016: 15-18). Gerontolojik çalışmalar (Bkz: I. Tufan: 2016- Ö. Arun-

A. Çakıroğlu-Çevik:2013- Seeds-man, 2014) aktif ve başarılı yaşlanmayı sağlama amacına odaklanmakta ve aktif yaşlanmada yaşlı bireyin kültürel alışkanlıklarına dikkat çekmektedir (Torres, 2001:334). Bu çalışma göç sürecine katılan yaşlıların hem göç yolunda hem de hedef mekanda yaşadık-ları deneyimleri ve sorunları tespit etme amacı ile gerçekleştirilmiştir. Çalışma hedef me-kanda yaşlanan göçmenleri değil, ileri yaşta göçe katılan kişileri ve bu kişileri problemlerini incelemeyi hedeflemektedir. Bu amaçla yaşlı göçmenlerin beklenti, ihtiyaç ve sorunları ikincil kaynaklardan ve gözlemlerden hareketle betimsel analiz yöntemi ile incelenmiştir. Çalışmada mekânsal analiz düzeyi kullanılarak göç ve yaşlılık ilişkisi sosyal ağlar, aktif yaş-lanma ve yerinde yaşlanma kavramları çerçevesinde incelenmiştir. Elde edilen bulgular ile yaşlı göçmenlerin göç yolunda ve hedef ülkede karşılaştıkları sorun-lar kategorilendirilmiştir. Buna göre; Göçmenlerin hedef ülkeye uyum sağlamalarına yönelik psikolojik sorunlar; kaygı, depresyon, güvensizlik (i) yeni yaşam tarzı ve pratiklerine uyum sağlamalarına yönelik sorunlar; günlük ihtiyaçları karşılama, resmi prosedürler, sağlık ile ilgili pratikler, çalışma şartlarına yönelik sorunlar (ii) Son olarak sosyal ağlar ve toplumsal statü ihtiyacını sağlamaya yönelik sorunlar (iii) olarak üç ayrı kategoride incelenmiştir. Çalışmanın kısaca sonuçlarına göre göç, yaşlılığa bağlı maddi ve ilişkisel ihtiyaçları derin-leştirmekte ve genellikle göç olgusu yaşlının sosyal bağlarını negatif yönde etkileyerek kıs-men bu bağların kopmasına neden olmaktadır. Göçe katılmayan yaşlıların –aile bağları çer-çevesinde- sosyal bağlarının ve mutluluk düzeylerinin daha yüksek olduğu görülmektedir (Arun, 2014:6). Göç biçimi isteğe bağlı olmadığında hem göç sürecinde hem de göç edilen mekanda karşılaşılan güçlükler (mekanın belirsizliğinden dolayı) daha fazladır. Yaşlılıkta göç sürecine katılma yaşlı bireyin yaşam pratiklerini toplumdan soyutlanmadan gerçekleş-tirmesine engel olabilmektedir. Yaşlı göçmenlerin çoğu günlük rutinlere daha az uyumlu, daha fazla dağınıklık yaşamakta ve resmi prosedürlerde daha fazla zorlanmaktadır (Warnes and Williams, 2007:1258). Göçmenlerin istedikleri zaman ülkelerine geri dönüş yapamıyor olmaları ise göç ile gelen uyum sorunlarının daha fazla yaşanmasına da etki etmektedir. Bu nedenle yaşlı göçmenler profesyonel desteğe ihtiyaç duyması açısından iki kat marjinal bir sosyal kesimi (Seedsman, 2014: 240) oluşturmaktadır.

***

SESSION 6F – Göç ve Nüfus

	Room: B2
Chair	**Tuncay Bilecen, Kocaeli University, Turkey**
912	Geride Kalanlar ve Yaşlılık: Bulgaristan Göçünden Geride Kalanların Bakım Beklentileri-**Nilufer Korkmaz Yaylagül, Özlem Özgür**
880	Şanlıurfa'da Yaşayan Suriyeli Mültecilerde Kronik Hastalık Prevalansı ve Sağlık Hizmetinden Yararlanma Durumu - **Yüksel Duygu Altıparmak, Mehmet Akman**
1359	Teorik Bir Anlama ve Yöntem Yaklaşımı Olarak Çok Katmanlı Çeşitlilik - **Savaş Çağlayan, Taylan Banguoğlu**
1141	Fransa'da Yaşayan Türkiyeli Erkek Göçmenlerin Aileye, Kadın-Erkek İlişkilerine ve Boşanmaya Dair Görüşleri ve Değişen Türk Aile Normları - **Ceylan Turtuk**

Geride Kalanlar ve Yaşlılık: Bulgaristan Göçünden Geride Kalanların Bakım Beklentileri

(912) Nilufer Korkmaz Yaylagül (Akdeniz University), Özlem Özgür (Akdeniz University)

Bulgaristan'dan Türkiye'ye zorunlu ilk göç kitlesel olarak 1950-1951 döneminde gerçekleşmiştir. Bu dönemden sonra Bulgaristan'dan 1969'daki Yakın Akraba Göçü Anlaşmasına kadar kitlesel bir göç yaşanmamıştır. 1984'ten itibaren Bulgaristan'ın homojen bir millet yaratma çabaları önemli bir nüfus büyüklüğüne sahip Türkleri de etkilemiş, devlet bir takım idari tedbirlerle kültürel yasaklar uygulamaya başlamıştır. Bunlardan en önemlileri, Türkçe konuşmanın yasaklanması, Türkçe isimlerin değiştirilmesi ve dinsel ibadetler üzerindeki baskılardır. 1989'da ise Türkleri göç etmeye yönlendirme kararı alınmıştır. Bu tarihte Türkiye'nin de göçmenleri kabulüyle Bulgaristan Türkleri kitlesel olarak Türkiye'ye göç etmiştir. Ancak aile bireyleri hepsi bir anda göç edememiş, teker teker göç etmek zorunda kalmışlardır. Aile büyükleri genellikle önceliği çocuklarına vererek çocuklarını yollamışlar, bazıları en son kendi de gitmiş, bazılarına da hiç sıra gelmemiştir. Bazı aileler ise Bulgaristan'da kalmayı tercih etmişlerdir. Türkiye'ye göç edenlerin içinden bazıları ise uyum sağlayamamış, aradığını bulamamış veya ailesi Bulgaristan'da kaldığı için Bulgaristan'a geri dönmüşlerdir. Hiç göç etmemiş veya geri dönmüş olanların büyük bir çoğunluğu halen yaşlılık dönemindedir ve genel olarak yaşlılık döneminin getirdiği sorunlara kendi başlarına çözüm yolları aramaktadırlar. Bu araştırmada zorunlu göç dönemine tanık olan ve çocuklarından ayrı yaşayan 60 yaş ve üzeri bireylerin yaşlılık ve bakım beklentileri ele alınmıştır. Araştırmada zorunlu göç sonrası çeşitli nedenlerle Bulgaristan'da Kırcaali'de yaşayan 60 yaş ve üzeri 10 bireyle yarı yapılandırılmış görüşmeler yapılmıştır. Bunun yanı sıra Türkiye'de yaşayan aile bireyleri ile informal görüşmeler gerçekleştirilmiştir. Göç deneyiminin ve sonrasında yaşam koşullarındaki değişmelerin bireylerin gelecek ve bakım beklentilerini nasıl etkilediği, yaşam seyri perspektifi bağlamında ele alınmış, görüşmeler betimleyici nitel analiz tekniği ile analiz edilmiştir. Araştırmanın bulgularına göre, katılımcıların çoğu, hastalık, kaza vb. acil durumlar söz konusu olduğu durumlarda çaresizlik ve korku hissetmektedir ve genel olarak yalnız olduklarını düşünmektedirler. Tüm katılımcılar bakıma muhtaçlık durumunda aile bireyleri tarafından bakılmayı istemektedirler. Ancak Türkiye'deki çocuklarıyla hala sık sık görüşen, aile ilişkileri iyi olan katılımcılar ileri yaşlarda Türkiye'ye gidebileceklerini belirtirken, çocukları ile ilişkileri iyi olmayan ya da sık görüşemeyen yaşlılar çocukları Türkiye'ye götürse bile Türkiye'ye gitmek istememekte, Bulgaristan'da evlerinde kalmayı tercih etmektedirler. İleri yaşlılık döneminde evlerinde kalmanın mümkün olmadığı durumda ise kurum bakımı kaçınılmaz olmaktadır. Ancak katılımcılar arasında Bulgaristan'da da bakımevlerine yönelik negatif bir algı bulunmaktadır. Sonuç olarak, göç sürecinde zorluklar deneyimleyen katılımcılar, yalnızlık hissetseler de evlerinde kalmaktan memnundurlar. Katılımcılar, Bulgaristan devletine vatandaşlık aidiyetini taşımaktadırlar ve devletin sağlık ve bakım ile ilgili hizmetlerinden haberdardırlar ve çoğunlukla yiyecek, ısınma gibi yardımlardan yararlanmaktadırlar. Aile bireylerinden destek görmediklerinde devletten destek göreceklerini düşünmektedirler.

***

Şanlıurfa'da Yaşayan Suriyeli Mültecilerde Kronik Hastalık Prevalansı ve Sağlık Hizmetinden Yararlanma Durumu

(880) Yüksel Duygu Altıparmak (Marmara University), Mehmet Akman (Marmara University)

Ani ve hızlı bir çevre değişimi yaratan, böylece sosyal, kültürel ve fiziksel olarak toplumu ve bireyleri etkileyen göç, sağlık ve sağlık değişkenleri üzerinde de çok önemli etkilere sahiptir. Çalışmamızın amacı, Suriyeli mültecilerde kronik hastalıkların görülme ve kronik hastalığı olanların mevcut sağlık hizmetlerinden faydalanabilme durumlarını tespit etmektir. İkincil amaç olarak kronik hastalıklar bağlamında sağlık hizmetine ulaşmada yaşadıkları zorlukları ve öncelikle ihtiyaç duydukları hizmetleri belirlemektir. Çalışmamız kesitsel bir çalışmadır. Urfa ilinde Suriyeli misafirler koordinasyon merkezinde bulunan kayıtlardan saptanan verilere göre, göçmenlerin en yoğun yaşadığı mahalle olarak belirlenen Kurtuluş mahallesi seçilmiştir. Bu mahalleden randomize olarak 30 sokak seçilmiş ve seçilen her bir sokaktan rasgele belirlenen 7 hanede yaşan 18 yaş üstü bireyler çalışmanın örneklemini oluşturmuştur. Seçilen her bir haneye ziyaret yapılarak, Arapça ve Kürtçe bilen tercüman eşliğinde tüm hane halkı hakkında kronik hastalıklara yönelik bilgi toplanmıştır. Bilgi toplama aracı olarak araştırmacılar tarafından literatür taraması sonucunda oluşturulan anket kullanılmıştır. Her bir hanede öncelikle aile reisi ile görüşülmesi planlanmış, bu koşulun sağlanamadığı durumlarda aile reisinin eşi veya o anda evde olan ve anketi yanıtlayabilecek durumdaki en yaşlı bireyle görüşme yapılmıştır. Toplamda 210 hanede yaşayan, 18 yaş üzeri 617 kişiye ulaşılmıştır. Katılımcıların %47,5'i kadın, %52,5'i erkek, %68,7'si ilkokul mezunu olup yaş ortalaması 35,6 yıldır. 40 yaş üzeri katılımcıların %27,8'inde, 65 yaş üzerinde ise %65,2'inde en az bir kronik hastalığın var olduğu, saptanmıştır. Bu rakam tüm katılımcılar arasında %15,2'dir. Görüşülen kişilerin %40'ı sağlık hizmeti alabildiğini, %13,8'i gereksinim duyduğunda aile hekimine ulaşabildiğini belirtmiştir. Kronik hastalığı nedeniyle sağlık hizmetine başvuranların %76,5'i devlet hastanesine, %15,3'ü özel sağlık merkezine başvurmuştur. Aile hekimine kronik hastalık nedeniyle başvurma oranı ise sadece %2,4'tür. Sağlık hizmeti arayan katılımcılar %82,9 oranla ücretsiz sağlık hizmetini seçmişlerdir. Görüşülen kişilerin %11,5'i sağlık hizmeti almak üzere sağlık merkezlerine başvurmaktan vazgeçtiklerini beyan etmişlerdir. Bu durumun nedeni olarak %87,3 ile maliyeti karşılayamama endişesi ilk sırada gelmektedir. Çalışmamızda kronik hastalık görülme prevalansı ülkemizde Türkiye vatandaşları arasında yapılan çalışmalara benzerdir. Suriyeli mültecilerin kronik hastalıkları nedeniyle neredeyse hiçbir zaman birinci basamak sağlık hizmetlerinden yararlanmadıkları, hizmet ihtiyaçlarını ağırlıklı hastanelerden karşıladıkları görülmektedir. Suriyeli mültecilerin kronik hastalıklarının yönetiminde birinci basamağının rolünü artıracak ve birinci basamak sağlık hizmetine ulaşımlarını kolaylaştıracak planlamalara ihtiyaç vardır.

***

Teorik Bir Anlama ve Yöntem Yaklaşımı Olarak Çok Katmanlı Çeşitlilik

(1359) Savaş Çağlayan (Muğla Sıtkı Koçman University), Taylan Banguoğlu (Muğla Sıtkı Koçman University)

Güncel gelişmeler, göç olgusuna yönelik sosyoloji disiplinindeki ilginin artmasına neden olmuştur. Geçmiş göç teorileri daha çok ekonomi temelli bir yaklaşıma sahipken, günümüzde göçün kültürel boyutu da hesaba katılmaya başlamıştır. Göçe maruz kalan hedef ülkelerde zaman içerisinde, asimilasyon, entegrasyon, çokkültürcülük gibi sosyal politikalar uygulamaya konmuş ve toplumda kültürel ve toplumsal bir uyum tesis edilmeye çalışılmıştır. Ancak etnisite ya da dine odaklanan ulus-devlet politikalarını, göçün ulusaşırı alanlar yaratması, iletişim ve ulaşım teknolojilerinde yaşanan gelişmeler, kültürel ve ekonomik alandaki güncel küresel reelpolitik gibi etkenler zora sokmaktadır. Bu durum, göç teorilerindeki kültürel vurgunun artışına ve çeşitliliğin teorik ve yöntemsel açıdan bir değişken olarak ele alınmasına neden olan unsurlardan biri olarak gösterilebilir. Artan kültürel çeşitliliğe yapılan vurgulardan biri Steven Vertovec tarafından gündeme getirilmiştir. Vertovec etnisiteye odaklanan konvansiyonel göç çalışmalarının günümüz toplumlarını açıklamakta teorik ve yöntemsel açıdan yetersiz olduğunu belirtmiş ve 2007 yılında yazdığı bir makaleyle birlikte çokkatmanlı-çeşitlilik (super-diversity) kavramını ortaya atmıştır. Çokkültürcülük yaklaşımının etnisiteye odaklanması nedeniyle, aynı etnik grup içerisindeki bireyler arasındaki çeşitliliği yakalamakta yetersiz kalmasından dolayı bu kavramı geliştirmiştir. Kaynak ülkelerden göç eden grupların kendi içlerinde etnisite, din, siyasi görüş, ekonomik durum, eğitim durumu gibi birçok etkene bağlı olarak çeşitlilik göstermekte olması, bu kişilerin yaşadıkları göç pratiğinin ve göç ettikleri ülkede gerek devletle gerekse buradaki toplumla kurdukları ilişkinin farklılaşmasına neden olmaktadır. Özellikle savaş durumu ve kıtlık gibi etkenlerden dolayı dünyanın çeşitli yerlerinde yaşanan büyük hareketliliğin önümüzdeki zamanda da devam edeceği göz önüne alındığında ve

Türkçe literatürde çokkatmanlı-çeşitlilik yaklaşımına dair çalışmaların oldukça sınırlı olması nedeniyle, bu yaklaşımın ele almaya değer bir yaklaşım olduğunu düşünmekteyiz. Bu çalışmada çokkatmanlı-çeşitlilik yaklaşımı, yöntemsel açıdan diğer göç teorileriyle karşılaştırılarak, Türkiye'de kullanılabilme imkanı üzerinde durulacaktır.

***

Fransa'da Yaşayan Türkiyeli Erkek Göçmenlerin Aileye, Kadın-Erkek İlişkilerine ve Boşanmaya Dair Görüşleri ve Değişen Türk Aile Normları
(1141) Ceylan Turtuk (EHESS)

1984 yılında yayınlanan International Migration Rewiew'in "Women in Migration" adlı özel sayısı göçte kadın araştırmalarının mihenk taşı olarak kabul edilir. 1980'lere kadar sadece göçü erkek olana dair gören anlayışa kritik bir açıdan yaklaşıp, kadını sadece özel alanda hapsolmayan ve göçe maruz kalmayan, aynı zamanda eyleyen bir aktör olarak çizmiştir. Günümüzde kadına dair bir çok göç araştırması vardır. Ama bu göç-kadın araştırmalarında önemli bir nokta vardır ve Nasima Moujoud da dikkatimizi bu konuya çeker: Göç araştırmalarındaki göç veren ülke-göç alan ülke, batılı ülkeler-batılı gibili olmayan ülkeler, kadın-erkek gibi ikilik durumları birçok problem oluşturabilir. Sadece kadın deneyimlerine odaklanmak, toplumsal cinsiyet ilişkilerindeki genel durumu ve değişmeleri göz ardı etmemize neden olabilir. Doktora tezimde Fransa'da ayrılmış Türkiyeli kadınların göç deneyime ve Türk ailesindeki norm değişimlerini anlamaya çalışıyorum. Kadınlarla yaptığım anketler bu değişmenin belli bir kısmını aydınlattığı inancındayım. Bu nedenle, göçmen Türk ailesindeki normların daha iyi anlamak ve kadın erkek ilişkinin nasıl bir yön alabildiğini görebilmek için bu sene Fransadaki Türkiyeli göçmen erkeklerle "aileye, kadına, evliliğe ve boşanmaya dair görüşlerini" araştıran bir anket yapmaya karar verdim. Görüşmecilerim 20-65 yaş yaşında, Fransa'da doğmuş veya uzun yıllar Fransa'da yaşamış erkeklerden oluşacaktır. Yarı yapılandırılmış görüşme anketimizle bireysel mülakatlarını yanı sıra yeterli kadar görüşmecinin rızası olursa odak grup çalışması yapmayı planlıyoruz. Anket sorularımızla, erkeklerin ailedeki ilk sosyalizasyonda edindikleri "aileye, erkekliğe, kadınlığa ve kadın-erkek ilişkilerine dair görüşlerinin", göçmenlik sırasında Fransandaki aile modelleri (birliktelik, belediyelerce tanınan evlilik kadar yükümlükleri olmayan PACS, eşcinsel aileler, vb.) ve kadın-erkek ilişkileriyle karşılaşınca hangi yönde ve nasıl evrildiğini analiz etmeye çalışacağız. Türk ve Fransız ailesini nasıl gördükleri, Türk kadınına ve boşanmaya dair yaklaşımları bize toplumsal cinsiyet ilişkilerindeki farklı bir dinamiği okumamıza imkan verecektir.

***

SESSION 6G – Göç ve Edebiyat - 5

	Room: B3
Chair	**Hülya Bayrak Akyıldız, Anadolu University, Turkey**
1003	Türk Şiirinde Almanya'ya İşçi Göçü Olgusu - **Efnan Dervişoğlu**
1302	Divan Şiirinde Göç Eksenli Söyleyiş Kalıpları -**İlyas Yazar**
1044	Yakın Dönem Mübadele Romanlarındaki "Türk" ve "Rum" Algısına Dâir Mukayeseli Bir İnceleme -**Atıf Akgün, İsmail Alper Kumsar**
1324	Bir Âşığın Göç Serüveni: Âşik Reyhani - **Meltem Şimşek**

Türk Şiirinde Almanya'ya İşçi Göçü Olgusu
(1003) Efnan Dervişoğlu (Kocaeli University)

Toplumsal olayların bir tür tutanağı olan edebiyat, işçi göçüne de duyarsız kalmamış; 1960'larla birlikte başta Almanya olmak üzere çalışma amacıyla Batı Avrupa ülkelerine giden Türkiye göçmenlerinin yurt dışındaki yaşamlarına odaklanmaktan geri durmamıştır. Türkiye

göçmeni işçilerin en yoğun olarak çalıştıkları ülkenin Almanya oluşu, edebiyat ürünlerine de yansımış; Almanya gözlem ve deneyimlerinden yararlanan pek çok şair ve yazar, ülkedeki göçmen yaşamının sosyal ve psikolojik yönlerini ortaya koyan romanlar, şiir ve öyküler yazmıştır. Bu yapıtlarda; göçün nedenleri, Almanya'daki çalışma ve barınma koşulları, II. kuşağın eğitim sorunları, uyum güçlüğü ve kültürel çatışmalar gibi konular ele alınmış; edebiyat aracılığıyla Türkiye göçmenlerinin Almanya yaşamı anlatılmıştır. Bu yapıtların Türk edebiyatında önemli bir yer tuttuğu da bilinmektedir. Bu çalışmada, Yüksel Pazarkaya'dan Aras Ören'e, Refik Durbaş'tan Yaşar Miraç'a uzanan bir seyirde Almanya göçü ve sonrasında yaşananların Türk şiirine yansıması irdelenecek; şiirlerin sunduğu veriler ışığında yorum ve değerlendirmelerde bulunulacaktır.
***

Divan Şiirinde Göç Eksenli Söyleyiş Kalıpları
(1302) İlyas Yazar (Dokuz Eylül University)

Göç kelimesi sözlükte ekonomik, toplumsal ve siyasi sebeplerle bireylerin ya da toplulukların bir ülkeden başka bir ülkeye veya bir yerleşim yerinden başka bir yerleşim yerine gitmesi şeklinde tanımlanan bir kelime olup Osmanlı dönemine hicret, muhaceret gibi kelimelerle karşılanmıştır. Göç konusu özü itibarıyla bakıldığında modern dönemlere münhasır bir durum değildir. İnsanlık tarihi kadar köklü bir maziye sahip olan göç ve göçe dair yaklaşımlar, çağımızda çok farklı boyutlarıyla insanlığın yüzleştiği, ülkelerin ikili düzeyinden ziyade bölgesel ve küresel düzlemde tartışmaya açtığı trajik ve dramatik sahneleriyle hafızalarda keskin çizgileriyle yer almaktadır. Beşeriyetin hayatında derin izler bırakan ve toplumların sosyo-kültürel değerlerinde sıklıkla yansımaları görülen göç ve göçle ilgili birikimlere dayalı yaşantılar ulusların sanat ve edebiyat hayatında yüzyıllardan beri esin kaynağı olmaya devam etmiştir ve etmektedir. Türk tarihi açısından XI. asırdan bu yana üzerinde egemenlik mücadelelerinin aralıksız sürdüğü Anadolu coğrafyası da gerek doğudan gerek batıdan gelen tahakkümlerle göç ve göç ekseninde gelişen birçok buruk tecrübeye ziyadesiyle tanık olmuştur. Bu bağlamda Türk edebiyatının belirli bir dönemini ihtiva eden Divan şiirinin hüküm sürdüğü süreçte de göç ve göçe dayalı yaşantıların şairin dünyasında yer bulmaması düşünülemez. XIII. Yüzyılda ilk örnekleri görülen Divan Şirinin XIX. Yüzyıla kadar devam eden yapısı içinde hüküm sürdüğü coğrafyanın her noktasında birçok kesimde ve meslek grubunda kendisine yer bulması, bu edebi hareketin toplumun algısı, beklentisi ve yaşantısına dair kültürel birikimi malzeme olarak kullanması kültür tarihimiz açısından ciddi bir kazanç sayılmalıdır. Bu özelliği ile Osmanlı coğrafyasının asırları aşan sürekli değişen ve gelişen sınırları içinde yaşanan göç hareketliliği klasik şairin gözünde "göç, hicret, muhaceret… vb" söyleyiş kalıpları içinde sanatçı hassasiyeti ile bir üslup oluşmasına zemin hazırlamıştır. Bildirimizde Divan şairinin gözünden göç ve göçle ilgili imgelerin kullanım formları ve bu bağlamdaki söyleyiş kalıpları devirlere göre metinlerden hareketle değerlendirilecektir.
***

Yakın Dönem Mübadele Romanlarındaki "Türk" ve "Rum" Algısına Dâir Mukayeseli Bir İnceleme
(1044) Atıf Akgün (Ege University), İsmail Alper Kumsar (Duzce University)

1923 yılında gerçekleşen Lozan Antlaşması'na ek olarak yapılan sözleşme uyarınca yeni kurulan Türk ve Yunan devletleri arasındaki zorunlu göç kararı, Türklerin 'mübadele', Rumların ise 'andalayı' olarak adlandırdıkları trajik göç olayına sebep olur. Andalayı ya da mübadele komşu milletlerin sosyal hafızasında büyük yer etmiştir. Söz konusu göç hareketleri Yunan Edebiyatına, gerçekleştiği tarihten itibaren önemli oranda yansımış ve tematik düzlemde işlenmiş olsa da Türkiye'de konunun edebiyatımızda yakın dönemlerde ilgi gördüğü açıktır. Çağdaş Türk Edebiyatında özellikle yakın dönemde sayıları artan mübadele romanları aşk ve savaş izlekleri etrafında gelişen kurguları ile benzerlik gösterirler. Bu bağlamda söz konusu romanların çeşitli özelliklerini ortaya koyan birçok akademik çalışma yakın dönemde yapılmış ve yapılmaya devam etmektedir. Çalışmamızda ele aldığımız romanlarda iki millet, iki mekân, iki kültür ve iki dil başta olmak üzere ikili yapı çok belirgin olup; yazarların bu ikiliği romanda gerilim unsuru olarak kullandıkları görülür. Söz konusu düalite, bu romanların mukayeseli edebiyat çalışmaları açısından taşıdığı önemi artırmaktadır. Bu hususta komşu milletler olmalarına rağmen edebî münasebetleri son derece sınırlı olan Türk ve Yunan edebiyatlarının geçmişte paylaştıkları ortak bir kaderi günümüzde edebî alanda ortak bir tema etrafında tekrar ediyor olmaları önemlidir. Bu konuda yapılacak çalışmalarda mübadele romanları önemli oranda veri sağlayacak bir birikim oluşturmuştur. Özellikle iki milletin edebî eserlerinde yer alan 'Türk' ve 'Rum' imgesi, sosyolojik açıdan kayda değerdir. Bu çalışmada Türkiye'de yayımlanan ve mübadeleyi konu edinen 8 romandan hareketle, söz konusu romanlardaki Türk ve Rum imajına odaklanılmıştır. Romanın değişmeyen aslî unsuru olan varlık kadrosundan hareketle, örneklem romanlardaki kişilerin Türk ve Rum etnisitesi bağlamında genel karakteristiği, ruhsal yapıları, kimlik ve göç problemleri bu çalışmada metin merkezli bir yaklaşımla ve mukayeseli olarak ortaya konulmuştur.

***

Bir Âşığın Göç Serüveni: Âşik Reyhani
(1324) Meltem Şimşek (Karamanoğlu Mehmetbey Universty)

Âşıklar yaşamlarını ve sanatlarını devam ettirebilmek amacıyla başta Türkiye sınırları içinde, daha sonra Avrupa'da olmak üzere sanayileşmiş ve ekonomik olanakları gelişmiş büyük şehirlere göçler gerçekleştirmişlerdir. Geçim sıkıntısı çeken âşıkların göç etme sebebi, göç eden diğer topluluklar gibi öncelikle ekonomik sıkıntılarını gidermek, yaşamlarını devam ettirmek olmuştur. Başka memleketlerde hayata tutunmak âşıklar için kolay bir süreç olmamıştır. Bu yüzden göç ve gurbet âşıkların şiirlerinde birincil temalardan biri hâline gelmiştir. Göçün temel nedenini maddi sebepler teşkil etse de bir âşığın başka sebeplerle de memleketinden diğer diyarlara göç edebileceği görülmüştür. Âşık Reyhani de bu âşıklardan birisidir. Memleketini çok sevmesine rağmen yöresinden çok acı bir şekilde ayrılmak zorunda kalmıştır. Bu acıyı şiirlerinde de çok etkili bir şekilde dile getirmiştir. Bu çalışmada öncelikle âşık göçleri ve sebeplerine değinilerek daha sonra Âşık Reyhani'nin göçü ve bunun şiirlerine yansımaları üzerinde durulacak, böylece bir âşığın neden göç edebileceği irdelenmeye çalışılacaktır.

***

SESSION 7A – High-skilled Movers

	Room: A1
Chair	**Nirmala Devi Arunasalam, University of Plymouth, UK**
1096	Recognition and Improvement of Immigrants' Professional Competences - **Kari Lehtonen, Birgitta Nenonen-Andersson, Ari Koistinen, Heidi Stenberg**
1277	Contemporary Greek Emigration: Professional Groups' Resilience to Crisis - **Sokratis Koniordos**
1289	Brain Migration: Factors and Models - **Andrej Privara, O. Tolstoguzo, Maria Pitukhina, Magdalena Privarova**
1235	Why Local Programmes Are Better Than Transnational Higher Education: Malaysian Nurses' Views - **Nirmala Devi Arunasalam**

Recognition and Improvement of Immigrants' Professional Competences

(1096) Kari Lehtonen (Helsinki Metropolia University of Applied Sciences), Birgitta Nenonen-Andersson (Helsinki Metropolia University of Applied Sciences), Ari Koistinen, Heidi Stenberg

The first mapping of immigrants' and asylum seekers' competences in Finland was arranged in the Finnish reception centers during the winter 2015-2016. The purpose of the mapping of competences was to evaluate reading, writing, and language skills as well as education and work experiences. Two projects for recognizing immigrants' competences and for the support of higher education and career paths have been launched in 2016. The pilot projects are coordinated by the Finnish University Partnership for International Development (UniPID) -network in Jyväskylä and Metropolia University of Applied Sciences in Helsinki. The projects are based on the proposal for action by the Ministry of Education and Cultures (Publications of the Ministry of Education and Culture, Finland, 2016). Metropolia University of Applied Sciences has launched Supporting Immigrants in Higher Education (SIMHE) project for recognizing prior learning and competence of highly educated immigrants. Guidance and counseling services are offered to immigrants with eligibility for higher education, and immigrants with studies or a degree in higher education. The project is aimed at immigrants who have engineering or business background. We try to guide the immigrants along appropriate educational and career paths, in order to help them to integrate better into the Finnish society. Our services include personal guidance and monthly Guidance generalia sessions. We also offer them testing and training services in basic engineering. Immigrants can have their skills and competence evaluated through in-depth professional discussion, participating in a suitable Metropolia engineering project course, and demonstration of their abilities. Immigrants who intend to apply to engineering degree studies are offered a refresher course in mathematics (SIMHE, 2017). A pilot competence assessment was offered to recent asylum seekers who had some engineering background. We tried to assess professional competences valued by employers and we also wanted to evaluate what prior learning could be identified and recognized as a part of possible future studies. The test in engineering consisted of analysing a case in some engineering field. The mathematical competence was assessed using a test comprising 30 mathematics problems. The competence assessment took place in April 2016 at Metropolia. The mathematics test scores were generally very low. The engineering analyses were also substandard. Many asylum seekers had completed or given up their studies several years ago. They had experienced stress during the months before and after arriving in Finland. There were also a few unexpected cultural differences in understanding the problems (Author et al., 2016). The evidence from the pilot tests led to a new design for the recognition and improvement of competences, namely a preparation course in mathematics and an extended process for the mapping and demonstrating of professional competences. Metropolia University of Applied Sciences (UAS) has arranged several courses to prepare students with immigrant background for engineering entrance examination and studies in UAS. The five-credit Mathematics course offers weekly lectures and on-line study material. The course lasts from November 2016, to April 2017. The participants did mathematics skills test similar to the test given in April 2016. This time automatic STACK-based test series in Moodle were used. STACK is a system for computer-aided assessment in mathematics and related disciplines (STACK, 2017, Sangwin, 2013). Comparison between the pilot tests and the preparation course reveals that it is important to settle the cultural obstacles, language barriers, and methodological ambiguities. It would be helpful to arrange personal meetings in advance to deal with personal special problems. Advance study material and pre-tests could also be useful. The learning management system Moodle and the STACK problems support also asynchronous learning. In the future, blended learning could combine naturally face-to-face instruction with computer mediated instruction (Bonk & Graham, 2006). Mapping of competences comprises of two phases, self-evaluation and in-depth professional discussion with an expert in the relevant field of study. The participant will receive a document that describes what kind of competences could be identified and what kind of studies are recommended. Demonstrating of competences includes a 10 ECTS work-based project together with Metropolia students. The project can include lectures, self-study, team work, and meetings with a company and meetings with the lecturer. The participant will receive an assessment of his/her skills and competences in relation to the objectives of the project and an evaluation of general working life and project work skills (Guidance Services and Recognition of Prior Learning and Competence for Immigrants, 2017).

***

Contemporary Greek Emigration: Professional Groups' Resilience to Crisis
(1277) Sokratis Koniordos (University of Crete)

The focus of this paper presentation is on emigration from Greece, which forms a part of the new European migration. This migratory wave entails emigration from countries suffering from economic crisis, has largely been triggered by it and is primarily oriented towards western/northern European countries. The paper draws from a set of 230 face-to-face interviews with persons, most of which are highly educated professionals that have emigrated since the eruption of economic crisis in Greece. From this material, it emerges that this migratory movement although individualized, nevertheless is patterned too. These patterns are presented and discussed. This migration may be seen to operate in defusing some of the hardship-related tension and to alleviate economic strain that actors and their families experience. In addition, the particular migratory movement may be seen to play a rather significant role in achieving a modicum of resilience for particular categories of migrants and for their families too, both in the home country and in the host country so that they might, at a later stage, attempt to return. However, such resilience does not conform to a universal pattern. Instead, it correlates with specific social class backgrounds and levels of education/training and orientations.

***

Brain Migration: Factors and Models
(1289) Andrej Privara (University of Economics in Bratislava), O. Tolstoguzo (Russian Science Academy), Maria Pitukhina (Petrozavodsk State University), Magdalena Privarova (University of Economics in Bratislava)

State development in terms of innovative economy is of a great challenge. At the same time, innovative economy development is possible only with both human resources development and hu-man capital quality upgrading. It is important both to develop and improve human capital assets in order to achieve necessary results. Not only human capital assets advancing relate to skills enhanc-ing, but also brain migration policy regulating, scientific schools' development as well as state poli-cies aimed at market participants' discrimination elimination. There are listed a number of factors affecting brain migration and innovative development which are closely interconnected. As a result, a gravity model of contemporary brain migration is developed.

***

Why Local Programmes Are Better Than Transnational Higher Education: Malaysian Nurses' Views
(1235) Nirmala Devi Arunasalam (University of Plymouth)

In Malaysia, full-time and part-time post-registration top-up nursing degree programmes are provided to enable registered nurses to convert their diploma qualifications to a degree level. The demand for these part-time compared to full-time bridging programmes is higher as nurses are able to continue to work whilst undertaking their professional development. However, there is very limited provision of part-time programmes in Malaysia. In an attempt to meet the high demand, the Malaysian Higher Education and Malaysian Nursing Board collaborated and accepted part-time Transnational Higher Education (TNHE) programmes from certain UK and Australian Nurse Education universities. This paper presents the views of Malaysian nurses who chose to study on a local part-time programme compared to a TNHE programme. This has not been sufficiently examined in the literature. An interpretive approach with hermeneutic phenomenology was used. Six Malaysian nurses selected via snowball sampling method were interviewed in English and Bahasa Malaysia (Malaysian language. It was to enable them to describe and evaluate their experiences on a local programme and their views of TNHE nurses in their practice settings. Thematic analysis was used to analyse the interview data. Findings indicated that the main reasons nurses enrolled on a local programme was because a practice component was part of the programme. This was despite the cost of the programme was high. These nurses emphasised that as nursing is a practice based profession, it is key for the nursing knowledge taught to be grasped and applied in the practice setting. Their views highlighted that studying on a local programme with the theory-practice connection enabled them to provide quality and culturally competent patient care in comparison to the nurses who had studied on TNHE programmes.

***

SESSION 7B – Migration and Place

	Room: A2
Chair	**Didem Kılıçkıran, Kadir Has University, Turkey**
1115	Discussing Milan as a Sanctuary City: the case of the migrants in transit - **Maurizio Artero**
1219	Geo-Cultures and Aesthetics. The Contribution of the Syrian Diaspora in London - **Carmen Caruso**
737	The Grounded Theory of Control-tuning: How migration actors control Place-coping in migration movements - **Saija Niemi**
1124	Spaces of Gentrification and Migration - **Marina Gaboleiro Carreiras**

Discussing Milan as a Sanctuary City: the case of the migrants in transit
(1115) Maurizio Artero (Gran Sasso Science Institute)

Far from being a completely new phenomenon, transit migration – defined for the first time by the UN in 1993 as the 'migration in one country with the intention of seeking the possibility there to emigrate to another country as the country of final destination'- is a concept that has recently emerged due to the sheer number of the newly arrived migrants during the 'refugee crisis' and as a consequence of the harder line on migration policy from the countries of the Schengen zone. While attention has been put initially on transit migration in the external 'fringe' (e.g. Turkey), later this phenomenon has hit the headlines for the passage of migrants inside the 'European space', culminating in 2015, during the so-called 'Long Summer of Migration' (Kasparek, 2016). Italy represents one of most important 'transit country' within Europe: according to the UNHCR, only in 2015, 150,000 people set foot in Europe via Italy (UNHCR, 2016), in view of about 80,000 applications for asylum in Italy in the same year (Consiglio Italiano per i Rifugiati, 2016). This noticeable mismatch highlighting the presence of a high number of migrants that decide not to solicit

any form of subsidy from the state, mostly in order to reach other countries inside 'Schengen'. This passage brings about two different challenges: the irregularity of migrants that don't want to leave fingerprints and apply for asylum in Italy, and their temporary settlement. Italy has long perpetuated mostly a policy of 'tolerance' towards this dynamic, meaning the retraction of its sovereign "duties" on firm land (notably the unwillingness to fingerprint and assist rescued migrants, thereby enabling their further movement across EU space) in order to get rid of as many people entitled to international protection as possible (Heller & Pezzani, 2016). In this context, Milan has emerged as one of the main nodes of migrants' transit in Italy since it lays at the crossroad of the 'migration road' spanning from the Italian coast to Central and Northern Europe. The status of Milan as a 'transit city' has emerged and reached national reputation in the spring of 2014 with the surge of Syrians overlapping the long-standing influx of people in transit from other areas (e.g. Eritreans). The paper explores the city's institutional reaction in the last years, looking at the reasons, the changes and the conditions. In particular, it is based on a qualitative research making use of interviews with policy-makers and social workers operating within the network of assistance. Indeed, the municipality has been giving the opportunity to unregistered international migrants to receive assistance and a shelter for the night, apparently operating in defiance of the regulations, especially the controversial 'Dublin regulation' that also Italy signed up. From October2013 this system has added together institutions and organizations involved in the assistance of this population 'on the move' in an increasingly structured manner. In particular, the role of these organizations has to be highlighted, both in designing and in operating activities. Thus, according to the Municipality, as of 2016, in this period of time, Milan has offered assistance to 84,500 people circa, all of them have subsequently left for other European countries, except for 656 asylum-seekers. However, despite all this, it has to be stressed some problems and critical issues: - The Municipality was late to react; - The reaction (in particular a more structural response) was mostly the result of concern over public order and the visibility of the 'problem' in public spaces ; - The risk to bind this action on the basis of 'benevolence', thus the precariousness of this system; - The lack of willingness and ability to position Milan inside a network of cities sharing similar problems and to advocate at national and supra-national level; - The prevalence of a response through the provision of camp-like night shelters, spatially segregated, and the lack of other types of assistance. Therefore, comparing Milan's policy with the literature looking at the city as a 'sanctuary' and the DADT (don't ask don't tell) policy implemented by some cities in United States (e.g. Ehrkamp & Nagel, 2014; Marrow, 2012; Nail, 2010), it is discussed and disputed if we should consider Milan's local institution reaction as a real 'dissident' response or rather as an action in complicity with the broader Italian reaction towards the 'irregular' migrants.
***

Geo-Cultures and Aesthetics. The Contribution of the Syrian Diaspora in London
(1219) Carmen Caruso (University of Westminster)

Migration is not a novel phenomenon. People have moved from their home for centuries and for a variety of reasons: it might be said, Abraham was the first migrant (Levitt 2003). If migration is a constant and not an occasional phenomenon throughout history, what led scholars to talk about the age of migration is the acknowledgment that international migration "has never been as pervasive, or as socio-economic and politically significant as it is today" (Castles et al. 2014: 317). One key element of this work responds to the widespread recognition that contemporary life increasingly transcends national borders and cultures, and that individuals create culture using elements from various settings. Therefore, this research endeavours to investigate how migrants help shape the material and symbolic cultures of places and what is, if any, their contribution. More specifically, an intersectional empirical inquiry will be conducted as a means to focus on a specific case of migration, that is, the Syrian diaspora in London. Firstly, this will allow us to address a significant scientific lacuna on an urgent focus of study albeit through a different critical angle. Secondly, as the study of migratory phenomena has been for a long time dominated by positivist approaches, a growing interest in aspects such as processes of migration, decision making, identity formation through migratory experiences has risen (De Haas 2014). These dimensions of migratory phenomena are characterised by the centrality of meaning-making processes thus calling for more sophisticated theories that could account for the complexities of the relation between structure, culture and migrants' agency. This study will thus examine what is the contribution, if any, of the Syrian diaspora to London's geo-culture (Rogoff 2006; Berardi Bifo 2015). Eventually, we will try to raise more general epistemological questions concerning how to frame the relationship between migrants' agency and places.

***

The Grounded Theory of Control-tuning: How migration actors control Place-coping in migration movements
(737) Saija Niemi (University of Helsinki)

In migration research, there has been a long discussion in relation to the forced/voluntary nature of migration movements, labelling of migrants and the division of rural/urban and international/internal migration. There has been a call for finding theoretical ways to combine different types of migration movements, people with various statuses as well as migration movements within national borders and those crossing international borders (see for example King et al. 2008). The Control-tuning Theory, which I have developed by using the classic grounded theory method, responds to these requests and combines different sectors of migration under one theory. The objective of this paper is to introduce through the Control-tuning Theory how migration actors cope with spaces and places during migration movements. I will first shortly explain how I developed the new theory by using southern Sudanese migration data and the classic grounded theory method. Then I will introduce the Control-tuning Theory. After this, I will show how controlling processes occur through Place-coping. For my research, I collected qualitative data on southern Sudanese migration in Finland, Egypt, Uganda and Sudan (at the time of the fieldwork South Sudan was part of the state of Sudan). For data collection, I used qualitative methods such as interviewing and participant observation. The method I used during gathering and analyzing the data, and building the new theory, was the classic grounded theory method. Barney Glaser and Anselm Strauss (1965, 1967, 1968) developed the grounded theory method in the 1960s. Later, Glaser (1978, 1998, 2001, 2003, 2005) and Strauss (1998) continued to develop the method from different perspectives. In addition, other researchers, including Kathy Charmaz (2006), have further developed the method in their own research. The Glaserian or classic grounded theory method follows Glaser's way of doing grounded theory. This is the perspective I adopted in my research. During developing the new theory, it became obvious that the main concern for various migration actors was controlling. The Control-tuning Theory explains how controlling is the main pattern of behaviour of various migration actors in relation to migration movements and to dealing with variety of situations. Control-tuning as a concept refers to the action of modifying controlling in different stages of migration in order to deal with different events, things and actors during migration movements. The theory shows how migration actors solve controlling in relation to specific dimensions of migration movements like coping in place. Controlling processes include controlling causes, strategies, outcomes as well as intervening factors. Control-tuning takes place during being on the move in various environments and while staying put in places of origin, asylum, transit, resettlement, destination and/or return. Controlling occurs in relation to four subcategories: Place-coping, Knowledge Dealing, Authority Encountering and Link-keeping. Controlling Place-coping appears through six dimensions: Multi-routing, Place-sensing, Spatial Maneuvering, Establishing New Normal, Re-rooting Home and Problem Confronting. Only when controlling as a core category and its four subcategories with their various dimensions and properties are in connection with each other through controlling processes, the Control-tuning Theory forms. The Control-tuning Theory combines several migration actors such as asylum seekers, recognized refugees, education- and employment-induced migrants, local residents and authorities under one theory. It also unites migration movements between and within different types of areas and environments like rural and urban as well as internal and international. The Control-tuning Theory shows that it is possible to link different sectors of migration research in one theory. In migration research, controlling is usually explained from the state or alliance viewpoint, as for example states controlling documented or undocumented migration. The Control-tuning Theory shows controlling from another perspective – that of individuals and groups who participate in migration movements in various ways.

***

Spaces of Gentrification and Migration
(1124) Marina Gaboleiro Carreiras (University of Lisbon)

Migrations are a key issue for the understanding of contemporary societies as well as urban transformations. International flows (causes, characteristics and directions) shape and change societies, in terms of demography, cultural diversity, economy and urban dynamics. Within complex and flexible mobility patterns, the presence of migrants acquires special relevance in the context of valuing the rental market and the real estate business. This study is part of a research project that focuses on the Portuguese context and studies both the way immigrants are affected by gentrification and their role in the emergence and development of such process. Some of the territories undergoing gentrification or potentially subject to this process in the future are recognized as entrance gates and/or as meeting places for immigrant populations. At the same time, these gentrified neighbourhoods may be attracting new groups of immigrants. The association of these two processes is the focus of this research. An overview of contemporary international migration patterns shows a significant number of classical economic and political migrants, but also international students, sun-seekers or retired foreigners and residential tourists as well as foreigner investors and entrepreneurs in sectors such as retail or real estate. The ethnic diversification of cities and the reconfiguration of urban landscape is evidenced by the presence of immigrants, their housing needs, their entrepreneurship and the institutional discourses and policies that sustained the capture of capital gains associated with migration. The occurrence of gentrification has been observed in a large number of neighbourhoods contributing to the growing number of studies. Gentrification is a process of socio-spatial transformation which relates to the functioning of the housing market, cultural consumption and social interactions (Mendes, 2011; Savage & Warde, 2003). While gentrification and urban integration of immigrants have been researched autonomously by several researchers, their combined analysis remains relatively scarce, and has been poorly explored despite several works on the subject (Ascensão, 2015; Malheiros, Carvalho, & Mendes, 2013; Murdie & Teixeira, 2011; Sargatal, 2011). Nevertheless, some researchers describe the simultaneous occurrence of the two phenomena (Hall, 2015; Simon, 2010) although not confronting migration and gentrification. Also, immigrant protagonism in the

processes of gentrification has gained relevance in media and in research about transnational gentrification (Sigler & Wachsmuth, 2015) and internationalization of the real estate market (Bernardos, Martínez-Rigol, Frago, & Carreras, 2014). Drawing from extensive analyses of quantitative data and migration and housing policy documents we seek to identify the interrelation and the overlaps between the processes of gentrification and migration. This combined approach leads to a discussion around the main follow topics: i) The description of the different types of actors, namely, immigrants, foreign investors, city-users considering their housing needs, presence in the territory and the legal framework; ii) Scenarios of gentrification in Portuguese urban centres including elements about turistification that has been observed. This phase uses census data, adapting the work of Walks and Maaranen (2008) to trace occurrence and evolution of gentrification in the Lisbon Metropolitan Area; iii) Finally, the results of the previous two components are considered together. We aim to conceptualize contemporary migration patterns as a key to understand such urban transformation and place the changing categories of immigration within the recent debates on gentrification. Multi-level analyses is carried out, considering several territorial scales and some immigrant population groups, namely Chinese, Russians and French, who appear as some of the most advantaged and representative immigrants in the access to "Golden visa" and in the status associated with "Non Residual Residents" (SEF, 2015). The research results contribute to a less fragmented view of migration and gentrification. To treat this intertwined complex process as a research topic will allows us to explore urban transformation under the lens of migration and confront various issues such as rehabilitation of historical centres or lifestyle migration. It also allows debates on the limitations and scarcity of migration data as well as on different conceptualizations of migration categories, For Portugal, this is a relevant subject. On the one hand, Portugal authorities advocate the attraction and integration of immigrants, considering housing and habitat as a fundamental right for all residents. On the other hand, housing is recognized as a sector with deficits, inequalities, mismatches between discourses, policies and practices and potentially generator of tensions between Portuguese and foreign citizens.
    ***

SESSION 7C – Integration and Education

	Room: A4
Chair	**Marie Godin, University of Oxford, UK**
1026	Inclusion of Syrian Refugee Children in Education in Turkey - **Ulaş Sunata, Amal Abdulla**
1087	Schooling Time among Migrant and Non-migrant Adolescents - **Paula Alonso**
1089	Barriers and Facilitators to Parental Involvement in Education: Perceptions and Experiences of Turkish Mothers in Berlin - **Hande Erdem**
722	"Thank You Crisis" – The Integration of Refugee Children into Public Education in Greece - **Zsofia Nagy**

Inclusion of Syrian Refugee Children in Education in Turkey
(1026) Ulaş Sunata (Bahçeşehir University), Amal Abdulla (Paris School of International Affairs)

Being a key factor in the inclusion of refugees in their host societies, education systems within existing national education structures that accommodate for the needs of refugee students have for long been developed in countries that offer protection to asylum seeking communities. This is the case of many States that are party to the international conventions and agreements related to refugee protection. The right to education is indeed one of the most essential rights to be given to asylum seekers once they are granted the status of a refugee. Not only does access to national education structures offer a sense of stability to the lives of these populations in distress, but they are essential in their inclusion and integration in the society in which they become a part of. Turkey is historically a target land where populations seeking protection head, and where people from around the world receive various protection statuses. The process by which refugees in Turkey are integrated in the national education system differs, however, from that of the European experiences in refugee education for example. In studying the case of refugee education in Turkey, particularly the situation of Syrian refugee education, we may notice that there is a lack of a consistent structure that adapts for the educational needs of refugees. Today, with around 3 million Syrian refugees in Turkey, one may observe a sense of "shock" in the way that Turkey arranges for the stay of refugees on its territory. This shock reflects greatly on how solutions of refugee education are constantly being rethought and developed not only by the Turkish Ministry of National Education but also by a very active civil society on this matter. This paper studies this very development of Syrian refugee education in Turkey through the case study of various schooling experiences in the Turkish city of Istanbul, where Syrian refugees are offered a number of options to continue their learning. The study looks at the activity of various NGOs that work on the matter of education, the existence of Syrian Arabic Temporary Education Centers and the developing practice of the State in terms of the integration of refugees in Turkish schools. This leads us to take note of the distraught nature with which the mass influx of Syrian refugees across the borders was met and the remedies to this sense of shock by the attempts to find solutions for the increasingly complex situation.

***

Schooling Time among Migrant and Non-migrant Adolescents
(1087) Paula Alonso (Universidade da Coruña)

This article compares the use of time in migrant and non-migrant adolescents within the school framework. By applying the survey technique to 3,600 students of ESO (Spanish Compulsory Secondary Education) throughout the Spanish territory, we analyse from a compared and descriptive approach, how that time is managed between these both group of students in this important context, as the school is. We think that time is an important and non-common used factor to study the socialization processes and curriculum development. First of all, as the article focus on how the scholar time fits in the whole life, we start from a demographic and social profile of the families (household composition): members of the family who are living together, educational skills, labour market, origin and nationality. Knowing this, we analyse three main aspects of schooling times that are good to understand the objective and subjective realities of the students: meanings, relationships, school performance what education provides them. First, we focus on the perceptions that students have about curricular activities which are developed by them every day (classic, innovative and personalised activities). Second, we consider the school performances in two ways: "objective" qualifications and their self-perception about the specific dynamics. Third, we introduce the important of relationships during the recess. Describing these main dimensions, we get a general knowledge about the students' behaviour based in a particular use of time according to their origin. This article reveals the opportunity for researches on migration to use the time as a valuable resource, through which we corroborate our hypothesis about the existence of a differential management uses of time. Results validate the differential use that students make of their time according to their origin, shaping individual stories about their socialization patterns.

***

Barriers and Facilitators to Parental Involvement in Education: Perceptions and Experiences of Turkish Mothers in Berlin
(1089) Hande Erdem (Free University of Berlin)

Parental involvement is seen as an important aspect of children´s success in education; however, especially regarding immigrant families this issue has to be further studied and a research from a gender perspective could provide a deeper insight into it. Experience of motherhood predominantly has a relation with sociocultural concerns during migration experience. Women of Turkish background and their social integration hold a particular place in public discourses in Germany. These discourses are reproduced during the education of their children with linking to the school failure and parental involvement. This study aims at understanding the characteristics of barriers and facilitators to parental involvement in education through the perceptions and experiences of Turkish mothers with focusing on their gendered, classed and racialized positions in the context of Germany. To achieve this objective, qualitative methodology is applied and semi-structured in-depth interviews are conducted with Turkish mothers in different neighborhoods in Berlin. When the first part of the study focuses on barriers and facilitators at the individual level with linking to the aspect of social integration, the second part concentrates on pre-school and school environment at the institutional level and provides advices for inclusive education.
***

"Thank You Crisis" – The Integration of Refugee Children into Public Education in Greece
(722) Zsofia Nagy (Eötvös Lorand University)

The paper is based on a 3-week ethnographic fieldwork in Greece and focuses on the government's attempt at partially integrating refugee children living in Athens' hospitality camps into public education, and the actors involved in this effort, interrogating the problematic phenomena and interconnectedness of 'crisis' and 'hospitality'. At the center of this movement – from the refugee camps to the schools – stands the bus that transports the children every afternoon from one place to another. The logic of the paper follows the bus's route and movement and the actors participating in it. Among numerous other issues, the double crisis – the financial breakdown beginning around 2009 and the so-called „refugee crisis" of the recent years - has brought to the fore the issue and role of social movements in western societies during times of abrupt social change. In this context during the past decade Greece has become the center of international media attention in connection with two crises that are both also local variations of wider global problems. First, being hit hard by the financial crisis and following, yet unsuccessful austerity measures, present day Greece can be taken as the case of a country in chronicity where crisis has become normalized. Second, as a consequence of interrelated international phenomena, Greece has been witnessing the increase of migratory flows recently, while the EU-Turkey deal of 2016 created a bottlenecked country where presently about 65 thousand refugees wait in what Bauman describes as „frozen transience". Neither crisis can be understood solely on economical and/or political terms and needs to be situated in the broader cultural context as well. The rather complicated issue of filaksenia (hospitality) which serves as a stereotype, a political communication tool, and a target of criticism at the same time in Greece is briefly discussed in the paper. The paper takes the case of the semi-integratation of refugee children into public education initiated by the Greek government in October 2016 and currently underway in Greece. The so-called preparatory classes for refugee children take place in public schools in Athens with the participation of 1,000 children aged 6-15 at the time of writing. These are not forms of integrated education as students are taught in these classes separately. Neither do they target every refugee group as it focuses specifically on children living in hospitality camps. Between October 2016 and January 2017 5 primary schools entered the program with plans for 9 more primary schools to join in the following weeks. The highly publicised case of Perama – a working class neighborhood of Athens – where members of the far-right party, Golden Dawn threatened the school that would accept refugee children calls attention to the conflicts and interactions between actors – parents, teachers, organizations, the state, politicians, etc. - involved in the process. Part of the research are therefore field visits at research camps and schools; and interviews with teachers, parents, members of the solidarity network, representatives of NGOs and employees of the Ministry of Education. Finally, the research also interrogates abstainers from the programme: refugee families and solidarians who do not participate in the effort. Crisis narratives, the emic conceptualization of refugees either as guests or as „fellow sufferers" of the crisis, regressive and progressive approaches to broader political and societal issues, apathy and mobilization are the central patterns that emerge in these discussions. As its theoretical contribution, the research poses two interrelated claims. First, regarding the concept of crisis - applying the approach of crisiology - it argues that rather than taking crisis as an event to be endured, one needs to look at the crisis as a process that reveals on the one hand and that leads to an incentive to invent on the other. It follows from this that the chronic conditions of the Greek crisis have led to the emergence of new types of social movements, usually labeled as „solidarian" in the literature. While academic discourse is replete with the comparison of these non-hierarchical initiatives with more formal types of volunteering, associations and NGOs, the second claim that the paper makes is that instead of this dichotomised view one needs to „scale up" and look at the interaction of these actors and the state and international actors in their responses to the crisis.

***

SESSION 7D – Gender and Migration - 2

	Room: A5
Chair	**Paulette K. Schuster, Hebrew University Jerusalem, Israel**
758	Gender, Religion, and Migration: Perceptions of Gender Relations among Immigrant Muslim Women in London, Ontario - **Wei-Wei Da**
898	The Rocketing Raise of Bride Price in the Rural China: Intimacy and Family Changes Brought by Rural Urban Migration - **Liu Lei**
1043	The Gender Performance and Mobility of Transpinay Entertainers in Japan - **Tricia Okada**

Gender, Religion, and Migration: Perceptions of Gender Relations among Immigrant Muslim Women in London, Ontario

(758) Wei-Wei Da (Brescia University College)

This paper examines perceptions and attitudes toward gender relations among recently arrived Muslim women living in London, Ontario. There were over one million of Canadians who identified themselves as Muslims (Statistics Canada 2012). This population has been doubled since the 1990s, representing 3.2% of the total population in 2011 Canadian census. Despite the rapid growth of this population, research on how Muslims settled in the new country is scarce. Gender relations among Muslims have been widely perceived and publically circulated as hierarchical and patriarchal, and Muslim women are assumed occupied a subordinated position in the family and various socio-economic relations in society. However, we do not know how Muslim women themselves view gender roles and gender relations and the kind of lives they have in the family. These issues have not been explored systematically. The objective of the study is to gain first-hand information from Muslim women to contribute to the existing knowledge concerning gender relations from the perspective of gender, religion and migration. This study has been informed by a set of literature on gender attitudes among Muslims immigrants in the diaspora. Comparative studies of values of gender equality have showed that immigrant Muslim women are less likely to perceive gender equality in the family than native women, such as Kulik's (2007) study of Arabic women living in Israel, and Dielh and associates' (2009) study of migrant Muslims living in Germany. Hyhagen Predelli's (2008) study of Muslim women in Oslo found that heightened levels of religious participation of immigrant women in Mosques helped empower women in the domestic sphere. Hyhagen Predelli (2004) also pointed out that attitudes towards gender relations are differentiated by social and economic status and education. Muslim women's subordinated position is often associated with the hijab, and religious beliefs. Several prominent Muslim feminists have argued that gender inequality is not associated with Islamic teachings but patriarchal culture (Ahmed, 1992; Barlas 2002; Moghissi 2003). Scholars also argued that Muslim women wearing Hijab is not a sign of subordination but the resistance of western hegemony (Bartkowshi and Read 2003). Several theoretical frameworks were used to guide this study. Symbolic interactionist theory provides canon to fieldwork with an emphasis on research participants' perspective. Gender and power structure framework proposed by Connell (1987) offers an analytical tool to gain insights into gender relations in the family as well as the society at large. The study must also consider the impact of intersectionality of gender, religion and migration on gender relations among immigrants (Denis 2008). Data were collected in two formats: semi-structured face-to-face interviews and participant observation. A total of 44 Muslim women with diverse countries of origin were recruited and interviewed between 2011 and 2013. Drawing on part of data from a main project on childrearing experience among Muslim women, this study focuses on three major inquiries, including: 1) cultural values and attitudes towards gender role and gender relations; 2) decision making process in the family; 3) division of household work. Demographic data were also gathered from each research participant, including types of immigration, marriages, and information about their husbands, and types of marriage and marriage satisfaction. All data are incorporated into analysis. English is the main language used for all interviews. The study followed institutional research ethical guidelines based on voluntary participation, and ensured confidentiality and anonymity to research participants. The demographic data revealed several patterns: 1) a majority of these women reported marriage satisfaction; 2) cross-country marriages are common; 3) most women perceived their marriages as semi-arranged; 4) identity is complex due to family migration. Muslims are not a homogenous population. Interview data revealed that most women believed and supported gender equality, which is in consistency with Islamic teachings. Most of them reported they had egalitarian-oriented gender relations in the domestic sphere. Most women involved in decision-making process in the family, but women tended to make more decisions over domestic issues and financial management. Most women reported fathers' participation in domestic work but varied by employment status of women. There was a mix of traditional and modern gender role performances. Muslim women's perceptions of gender relations in the family are associated a wide range of factors including education, social class, pre-migration experience, immigration and economic status, cultural values, and social transformation in their home countries and the cultural context in Canada.

***

The Rocketing Raise of Bride Price in the Rural China: Intimacy and Family Changes Brought by Rural Urban Migration

(898) Liu Lei (University of Trento Italy)

This paper concerns on a special phenomenon of rocketing of bride's price in rural China after the rural-urban labor migration nowadays. It provides a brief overview of three major prospective on marriage exchange, especially impose the local marriage market due to the post-migration economic environments. Then the author highlights on several factors that influence the rocketing raise of rural marriage gifts using both the primary data from census 2010 and the interviews from the field study, such as one-child policy and the unbalanced sex ratio with the familiar context parents used different strategies in raising their sons and daughters so as to best hold their own interests, causing inequality between females and males. Then this was broken by the independence of rural women and the phenomenon of cross-regional marriage after the free mobility of labor resource between rural areas and urban areas which gives women equal rights to choose their spouses together with some publicly policies that accelerate the decline of patriarchy. In the end, the author spells out a framework of migration influence on rural marriage for some theoretical and policy implications of the findings.

***

The Gender Performance and Mobility of Transpinay Entertainers in Japan
(1043) Tricia Okada (Tamagawa University, Waseda University)

This research examines the gender performance[5] in the mobility of transpinay[6], also known as male-to-female (M2F or MTF) Filipino transgender or transwomen entertainers in Japan, a unique Filipino subgroup of entertainment workers. This paper aims to contribute to understanding the ways in which transpinays engage in gender performance by analyzing the intersectionality of gender, mobility, and work in their lives. It looks into their performance of gender by explaining the changes and discrepancy between how being a transgender is in the Philippines and in Japan. It illustrates how transpinay entertainers "perform"[7] their gender as self-empowerment which is valued in the host society through nurturing personal relationships with the Japanese---as clients, business partners, and lovers. In addition, this study also discusses how work experience in Japan facilitates flows of social remittances in the Philippines in the form of social capital, performing skills, ideas and styles that transgender returnees are able to pass onto younger, aspiring performers. Mapping the journey of entertainers in the 80s, 90s, and 2000s through their narratives, I evaluate how their social mobility to and from Japan influences their gender affirmation and whether years of engaging in entertainment work has intensified or declined both their sense of belonging to the Philippines. Transpinay entertainers provide a significant case for differentiating the meaning of work over space that links Japan and the Philippines and in which their commitment toward entertainment work transforms over time.

***

SESSION 7E – "Burden" of Migration

	Room: B1
Chair	**Fethiye Tilbe, Namık Kemal University, Turkey**
965	Put the Burden on Whom? Transit or Destination Countries: The Cases of Greece and Croatia – **Rukiye Deniz**
835	The Effect of Humanitarian Aid on Host Community-Refugee Relations: Evidence from Turkey - **Ümit Seven**

[5] Judith Butler, Gender Trouble: Feminism and the Subversion of Identity, UK: Routledge, 1990.
[6] The term, a portmanteau of "transsexual" and "Pinay" (Filipino woman), was created by the Society of Transsexual Women of the Philippines (STRAP). http://en.wikipilipinas.org/index.php/Transpinay accessed 14 July 2016.
[7] Erving Goffman, The Presentation of Self in Everyday Life, Random House, 1959.

Put the Burden on Whom? Transit or Destination Countries: The Cases of Greece and Croatia

(965) Rukiye Deniz (Istanbul Medeniyet University)

Europe has been experiencing an influx of migrants since mid-2015. Several people try to reach Europe in search of a better life away from their war-devastated homelands. Their first entry into Europe is mainly the countries close to their homelands. Greece, therefore, has been the focus of the international community due to vast numbers of persons reaching its shores every single day, especially since the escalation of the Syrian civil war. Selected as a hotspot, it received assistance from the European Union. On the other hand, Croatia has been unexpectedly subjected to thousands of migrants within a short period of time. Eventually, it was awarded financial support from the Union. Upon migrant crisis, the EU introduced new mechanisms to support the states facing migrant influx. In this article, measures and attempts by the European Union to support Greece and Croatia in handling the migrant crisis are reviewed. The article tries to answer to what extent such attempts have been successful in assisting Greece and Croatia.

***

The Effect of Humanitarian Aid on Host Community-Refugee Relations: Evidence from Turkey

(835) Ümit Seven (Université libre de Bruxelles)

Although humanitarian aid for refugees is intended to alleviate human suffering and to maintain human dignity by providing relief to vulnerable populations in the aftermath of an emergency, it does not necessarily aim to address the needs of vulnerable hosts as the main concern. As is epitomized in Syrian refugee crisis, refugees fleeing to neighboring countries such as Turkey, which have an already fragile context, have posed a new and diverse challenge to national authorities, humanitarian actors and host communities, leading to a potential tipping point for conflict between the two communities. To this end, the objective of this paper is to identify negative impact of humanitarian aid, as a driver of tension, on host community-refugee relations in Turkey, particularly in the restive Southeastern Turkey, which has become a region that has hosted people internally displaced by the conflict between Turkish Security Forces and Kurdistan Workers' Party (PKK). This empirical research argues that in-kind humanitarian assistance targeting vulnerable refugees in conflict-ridden poor host societies have a potential to increase social tensions between host communities and refugees, and if not designed well, it can be a source of conflict. There exists a vast literature that aims to assess the impact of a rapid influx of refugees on the host communities living in areas where refugees eventually settle down, focusing on destabilizing factors. In parallel to previous research, this paper offers a new insight in understanding the impact of humanitarian aid to refugees in terms of promoting social cohesion and reducing social tensions in the unique context of Turkey. This article relies on fieldwork observations, focusing on formal and informal meetings with the NGOs, Head of Social Assistance and Solidarity Foundation (SASF) offices and members of the host communities in the SASF offices as well as personal experiences mainly in Gaziantep and Diyarbakir. Despite the lack of a reliable data concerning Turkey's internal displacement figures, the Internal Displacement Monitoring Centre (IDMC) estimates that there are at least 954'000 IDPs in Turkey as of December 2015 (IDMC,

2016). Accordingly, Humanitarian Implementation Plan (HIP) for Turkey, which sets out the humanitarian strategy under the Facility for Refugees in Turkey by the European Commission, stresses that due to the resumption of hostilities between Turkish security forces and PKK, 350,000 Turkish citizens (as well as Syrian, Iraqi and other refugees) have been internally displaced in the provinces of Batman, Siirt, Urfa, Gaziantep, Van, and Mersin (EC, 2016). In this context, evaluating the effects of different transfer modalities (i.e. cash transfers, vouchers, and in- kind transfers) on the host community-refugee relations, the paper pays specific attention to the Emergency Social Safety Net (ESSN), a multi-purpose cash assistance scheme for more than one million of the most vulnerable refugees living in Turkey, and traditional in-kind assistance such as food rations, shelter materials and kits of household. As the largest EU humanitarian aid programme, ESSN has been launched nationwide by the World Food Programme (WFP) in partnership with the national authorities on 28 November 2016. ESSN applications are being taken in 276 SASF offices and 14 Service Centers in 73 provinces. Although a spirit of hospitality still persists in the community that welcomes refugees, vulnerable hosting communities, particularly those who have been affected by the recent violence between Turkish security forces and PKK, express their resentment against refugees due to their exclusion from the humanitarian assistance. Believing that they receive no attention from the aid organization, members of the host communities tend to highlight disadvantages and vulnerabilities in their communities. Accordingly, rather than having separate offices that only accept ESSN applications from refugees, as is the case in Service Centers, SASF offices serve for both vulnerable Turkish citizens and refugees, and consequently, these offices become a site in which host communities and refugees confront each other. Some minor incidents between the members of host communities and refugees in these offices have been reported. Herein, I aimed to investigate an aspect of the potential negative externalities associated with humanitarian aid. There is evidence for an increase in social tensions as a result of humanitarian aid excluding vulnerable host communities. However, cash-based intervention appears to reduce many of the risks associated with in–kind assistance, and is therefore, when designed well, an effective modality for assisting people in need in vulnerable and conflict-ridden communities hosting refugees.
***

Support or Obstacle?: Effects of Immigrants on Domestic Labor Force in Turkey
(831) Atakan Durmaz (Bayburt University), Özge Korkmaz (Bayburt University)

The phenomenon of migration, as old as human history, is one of the most interested subjects of countries in the 21st century, especially in the last 10 years. Undoubtedly, one of the important reasons for this is the fact that migration has significant influences on from economic to social life almost every subject in terms of both emigrating countries and receiving countries. The fact that economic factors and security problems are the main causes of migration movements also laid the groundwork for the work done in the field of economy to concentrate on this subject. At this point, there are also studies of the impact of receiving countries on labor market, although the impact of migrant movements on emigrating countries' economy is largely a matter of focus. However, there is no consensus on the work done in this regard. As a matter of fact, some studies have found that immigrants have a negative effect on the labor market because they are willing to work at lower wages, while in some studies they have found that immigrants have a positive influence on the labor market by increasing labor supply in areas where the local labor does not want to work. At this point, Turkey has taken its place in studies in the literature as a country that both emigrating (especially from the early 1960s to the 1990s) and receiving country (especially in the last 10 years as a result of events happening in neighboring countries). Although the vast majorities are refugee status, a growing number of immigrants are involved in the labor market and this affects the position of the domestic labor force on the labor market. From this point of view, the effect of immigrants on the labor force participation rate of the local labor force has been examined by means of regression analysis, using immigrant data from 26 provinces in Turkey between 2011 and 2015. According to the study results; Migrants allowed to work in Turkey have a positive effect on the participation rate even if just a bit. From a gender perspective, it has been found that immigrants have positive effects on women's labor force participation rates. But, there has been no significant impact on the male labor force participation rate of migrants. In the study, there has been also found that the increase in the level of education of men has a positive effect on the labor force participation rate, while in women, it has been found to be a negative effect of the higher education graduation although the primary and high school graduation has a positive effect on the labor force participation rates.

***

The Impact of the Syrian Refugee Crisis on The Civil Society Sector in Lebanon
(708) Laura El Chemali (Université Libre de Bruxelles)

This article is driven by an interest to explore the role of local non-governmental organizations (NGOs) and community-based organizations (CBOs) that deal with Syrian refugees in Lebanon seeing the void left by the Lebanese failing state to cope with this situation. I will have a look at how the Syrian conflict has affected the NGO landscape in Lebanon and how the inflow of international aid has affected the work of this local NGOs, as well as, their relationship with Lebanese state authorities on the national and local levels. To this extent, the ways in which the management of Syrian refugees by local NGOs and CBOs has been affected by external factors, including the Lebanese government policies and the role of international organizations (EU, UN) in managing the crisis in Lebanon will be examined. Since the beginning of the Syrian conflict and the influx of millions of refugees into Lebanon, the civil society sector in Lebanon has undergone significant transformations. To cope with the overwhelming number of Syrians living in Lebanon, Lebanese civil society has expanded with the creation of new NGOs as well as the introduction of additional programs and projects in existing NGOs to assist refugees. These civil society organizations fill a void created by the Lebanese government in its unwillingness or inability to assist with the refugee response in the areas of healthcare, education and vocational training.

***

SESSION 7F – Göç ve Uyum

	Room: B2
Chair	**Cumhur Aslan, Canakkale 18 Mart University, Turkey**
1031	Uygulayıcıların ve Sivil Toplum Örgütü Temsilcilerinin Gözünden Mülteci ve Sığınmacılarda Eğitim: Eskişehir Örneği – **Filiz Goktuna Yaylacı, Harun Serpil**
1266	Sosyal Ağların Evlilik Yolu ile Toplumsal Cinsiyet Rollerini Dönüştürme Etkisi – **Sevim Atila Demir ve Pınar Yazgan**
1172	Stuttgart Eğitim Fakültesi Göç ve Çokkültürlülük Yüksek Lisans Programı Türkçe Öğretiminde Karşılaşılan Sorunlar ve Çözüm Önerileri – **Günay Kayhan**
1360	Suriyelilerin İstihdamı ve Şanlıurfa'da Göçmen Emeğine Dayalı Kalkınma – **Ayşe Cebeci**

Uygulayıcıların ve Sivil Toplum Örgütü Temsilcilerinin Gözünden Mülteci ve Sığınmacılarda Eğitim: Eskişehir Örneği

(1031) Filiz Goktuna Yaylacı (Anadolu University), Harun Serpil (Anadolu University)

Altı yıldır devam eden Suriye İç Savaşı milyonlarca Suriyelinin zorunlu kitlesel göçlerle ülke dışına gitmesine yol açmıştır. Söz konusu kitlesel göç akınlarından en fazla etkilenen ülkelerden birisi de Türkiye olmuştur. 29 Nisan 2011'de 252 kişilik ilk Suriyeli kafilenin Hatay'ın Cilvegözü sınır kapısından girişiyle birlikte Türkiye'de mülteciler ve sığınmacılar açısından yeni ve önemli bir sayfanın açıldığı söylenebilir. Altı yıllık sürecin ardından sayıları bugün 3 milyonu aşmış olan Suriyeliye ev sahipliği yapmakta olan Türkiye'nin göç alan hedef ülke konumu daha da belirginleşmiştir. Bunun yanı sıra Cenevre Sözleşmesi uyarınca üçüncü bir ülkeye yerleştirilmek üzere Türkiye'de bulunan şartlı mültecilerin varlığı da dikkat çekici boyutlara ulaşmıştır. Gerek Suriyelilerin gerek mültecilerin varlığı açısından özellikle uydu kentler hedef ülke Türkiye'nin görece kalıcı misafirlerini ağırlayan hedef kentler olarak önem kazanmaktadır. Suriyelilerin ve diğer mültecilerin giderek daha görünür ve kalıcı olmalarıyla birlikte Türkiye'deki tüm mülteci ve sığınmacıları merkeze alan çalışmalar da yoğunluk kazanmıştır. Özellikle zorunlu kitlesel göç sonucunda Türkiye'ye gelen Suriyelilerin acil ve temel gereksinimlerinin karşılanması için çeşitli önlemler alınmaya çalışılmıştır. Genellikle zorunlu kitlesel göç durumunda acil ve temel gereksinimlere verilen önem nedeniyle arka planda kalmış gibi görünse de eğitim gereksinimleri söz konusu göçmen gruplar açısından büyük önem taşımaktadır. Belirsiz bir geleceğe, yabancısı bulundukları bir kültürün içinde hazırlanmak durumunda olan yetişkinler ve özellikle çocuklar için eğitim, güvende hissetmenin, geleceğe hazırlanmanın ve yaşamaya devam etmenin başka bir ifadesi niteliğindedir. Dolayısıyla Suriyelilerin ve diğer mültecilerin eğitim sorunlarının irdelenmesi, çözüm yollarının araştırılması ve yürütülmekte olan eğitim hizmetlerinin etkililiğinin artırılmasına yönelik çalışmaların bu noktada yaşamsal öneme sahip olduğu söylenebilir. Bu bağlamda bu çalışmada en fazla şartlı mülteciye ev sahipliği yapan uydu kentlerden birisi olan ve aynı zamanda Suriyelilere de ev sahipliği yapan Eskişehir özelinde mülteci ve sığınmacılara yönelik eğitim etkinlikleri konu edilmiştir. Çalışmanın temel amacı uygulayıcıların ve STK temsilcilerin görüşlerine dayalı olarak Eskişehir'de özellikle mülteci ve sığınmacı çocuklara yönelik olarak yürütülen eğitim etkinliklerine ilişkin genel bir değerlendirme yapabilmektir. Bu doğrultuda mülteci ve sığınmacı çocukların eğitim süreci ile ilgili olarak yapılmakta olanlar saha da birinci derece ilgili ve yetkili kişilerle görüşmeler yapılarak saptanmaya çalışılmıştır. Bu çerçevede Göç İdaresi Genel Müdürlüğü, Eskişehir İl Milli Eğitim Müdürlüğü ve Halk Eğitim Merkezi yetkilileri, öğretmenler ve STK temsilcileri ile görüşmeler yapılmıştır. Saha çalışmasında elde edilen bulgulara göre Eskişehir'de Suriyeli sayısı diğer kentlere göre daha az olduğu için Suriyelilerin eğitimi ile ilgili bir takım projelerde pilot şehir arasına girmemektedir. Bunun yanı sıra Suriyelilerin yaklaşık beş katı büyük bir nüfusa sahip şartlı mültecilerin de görünür kılınması gerektiği dikkat çekmektedir. Mülteci ve sığınmacılarla ilgili yapılan iyi niyetli çabalar dikkat çekmekte ancak daha sistemli ve sürdürülebilir kesin programların varlığına da gereksinim duyulmaktadır.

***

Sosyal Ağların Evlilik Yolu ile Toplumsal Cinsiyet Rollerini Dönüştürme Etkisi

(1266) Sevim Atila Demir (Sakarya University), Pınar Yazgan (Sakarya University)

Günümüzde göç olgusu küreselleşme ve hareketlilik bağlamında karmaşık bir süreç olarak incelenmektedir (eg. Cohen & Sirkeci; Sirkeci, 2009; Yazgan, 2016). Bir yerden başka bir yere hareketliliği ifade eden göç olgusunu açıklamaya yönelik birçok kuram bulunmaktadır. Göç kuramlarının bireyci ve ekonomi-merkezli boyuttan çoğulcu ve sosyo-kültürel boyuta kaydığı ve göçmenin kendi seçiminin ön plana geçtiği görülmektedir. Burada seçim, bireylerin gelirlerini daha üst seviyeye çıkarmak için yaptıkları bir tercihtir. Sosyal sermaye göç ile gerçekleşen evliliklerde belirleyici rol oynayabilmektedir. Evliliğin gerçekleşmesinde etkili olan ağlar bağlayıcı sosyal sermaye içerir ve zaman içerisinde baskı aracına dönüşebilmektedir. Böylelikle cinsiyet rolleri daha da belirginleşebilir ve göçle gelinen kentlerde toplumsal cinsiyette dönüşüm yaşanabilmektedir. Türkiye kökenli göçmenlerin bir arada hakim kültürden farklı bir yaşam tarzı oluşturmaları evlilik ve aile biçimini de etkilemiştir. Evlilik göçleri de bu bağlamda değerlendirilebilir. Özellikle ithal evliliklerin ikinci kuşakta yoğunluk kazandığı dikkate alındığında, birinci ve ikinci kuşağın kendi kültürlerini yaşatma, sürdürebilme ve Türkiye ile bağları güçlendirebilme yolu olarak çocuklarının Türkiye'den biri ile evlenmelerini teşvik ettiği görülmüştür. Almanya örneğinden yola çıkıldığında evlilik göçü işgücü göçünün bir uzantısı olarak görülmektedir. Yoğunluk derecelerine göre göç etme nedenlerine bakıldığında; üniversite eğitimi (1.398), çalışma (1.256), dil öğrenimi ve üniversite dışındaki eğitim (103), diğer (83), insani nedenler (81) olarak sıralanabilir (Migrationsbericht, 2006:111). Göç yoluyla gerçekleşen evliliklerde göç edilen bölgenin yapısına ve yaşam standartlarına uyum sağlayamama sınırlandırmanın daha keskin yaşanmasına yol açabilmektedir. Göçmenlerin sahip olduğu ağlar sosyal sermayeyi güçlendirmekle beraber, anavatan temelli ilişkilerin göç alan ülkeye taşınması sebebiyle bir sosyal kontrol ağını da beraberinde getirmiştir (Yazgan, 2010: 234). Özellikle ithal evliliklerin ikinci kuşakta yoğunluk kazandığı dikkate alındığında, birinci ve ikinci kuşağın kendi kültürlerini yaşatma, sürdürebilme ve Türkiye ile bağları güçlendirebilme yolu olarak çocuklarının Türkiye'den biri ile evlenmelerini teşvik ettiği görülmektedir (Atila Demir, 2011:910). Bu çalışma ilk olarak Almanya'da yaşayan ve evliliklerini sosyal sermaye ve sosyal ilişki ağları aracılığı ile gerçekleştiren bireylerin evliliklerindeki durumların nasıl sosyal sermayenin olumsuzluklarını üretip çatışmaya sebep olduğunu göstermektedir. İkinci olarak ise göç yoluyla gerçekleşen evliliklerde sosyal kontrolün iç grup açısından artışına ve dış grup açısından azalmasına paralel olarak toplumsal cinsiyete etkisine ve dönüşüm potansiyelimi tartışmaktadır. Çalışmada nitel araştırma yöntemleri uygulanmıştır ve 8 boşanmış kadın ile yapılan derinlemesine mülakatlar "sosyal ağlar", 'sosyal sermaye" "baskı/sınırlandırma", "sosyal ilişkiler", "aile baskısı", "akrabalık ilişkileri" kavramları çerçevesinde analiz edilmiştir. Boşanmış 8 kişi üzerinde gerçekleşen mülakatlar iki boyutta incelenmiştir. Birincisi, evlilik öncesi sosyal ağların ve sosyal sermayenin etkisi, ikincisi ise boşanma sürecinde ve boşanma sonrası sosyal ağların ve sosyal sermayenin etkisi. Bu kısım "hemşerilik", "baskı/sınırlandırma", "sosyal ilişkiler", "aile baskısı", "akrabalık ilişkileri" kavramları çerçevesinde analiz edilmiştir. Başlangıçta ifadelendirilen bu tür ilişki durumlarının dönüştürücü etkisine odaklanılmıştır. Bu iki süreçte sosyal sermayenin etki biçimindeki değişim ele alınmıştır. Evlilik şekli ister göç yolu ile isterse göç ağları kullanılmadan olsun sosyal ağlar bağlayıcı bir boyuta sahiptir. Evlilik göçü ile sosyal ilişki ağları arasında güçlü bir ilişki vardır. Bu anlamda tanıdık olma bireyin özellikle göç sürecinde ihtiyaç duyduğu bir özelliktir. Güveni içerisinde barındırır. Göçmenlik kişiye sahip olduğu sosyal ağlardan mahrum olmanın verdiği umutsuzluğa yol açar ve bu süreç yeni tanıdıklar ve ağlar ile giderilmeye çalışılır. Bunun yanısıra bu ağlar bazı durumlarda zorlayıcı ve korku verici biçimlere bürünmektedir. Çalışmanın sonuçlarına göre bağlayıcı ağlar aktörlerin davranışlarını yönlendirici boyuta geçtiğinde çatışma doğar ve varolan sosyal sermaye negatif yönü ile tanımlanır. Aynı zamanda toplumsal cinsiyet rolleri sosyal ağlar yolu ile gerçekleştirilen bu evliliklerde daha keskin biçimleri ile ayrışmakta ve sosyal ağların bağlayıcılığını belirginleştirmektedir. Kadınların evlilik aracılığı ile göç ettikleri mekanların dış grupta sosyal kontrolü düşük ancak iç grupta, evlilikler sosyal ağlar ile gerçekleştiği için, sosyal kontrol yüksektir. Bu çelişki hem sosyal sermayenin negatif bağlayıcılığını güçlendirmekte hem de kadınların bilinç düzeyini etkilemekte ve toplumsal cinsiyet kalıplarında dönüşüme neden olmaktadır. Mülakatların analizi neticesinde sosyal sermaye aracılığı ile kurulan evliliklerin belirli bir zaman sonra nasıl biçim değiştirmekte olduğu ve yeniden sosyal sermayenin negatif bir biçimde üretilmesine sebep olduğu görülmüştür. Kurulan bağların çözülmesine neden olan negatif yönde bu etki bireylerin davranışlarındaki yönlendirme/baskı ve sınırlandırma şeklinde kendini göstermiştir.

***

Stuttgart Eğitim Fakültesi Göç ve Çokkültürlülük Yüksek Lisans Programı Türkçe Öğretiminde Karşılaşılan Sorunlar ve Çözüm Önerileri
(1172) Günay Kayhan (Ondokuz Mayıs University)

Bu calisma Stuttgart/Almanya Eğitim Fakültesi Çokkültürlülük ve Uyum Yüksek Lisans Programı Türkçe Öğretimi çalışmalarındaki deneyim ve gözlemlere dayanarak gerçekleştirildi. Almanya uzun yıllardan beri çok kültürlü bir ülke olduğu için, göçmen kökenli çocuk ve gençlere yönelik sosyal pedagoji çalışmalarına büyük önem vermektedir. Almanya'dakı bir çok Eğitim Fakültesi Göçmen Bürolarında çalışanlar için Master programları ve bu programlarda göçmen dillerinin öğretimi fırsatı sunmaktadır. Eğitim Fakültesi Çokkültürlülük ve Uyum Master Programı kapsamında Türkçe kursları düzenlemektedir. Burada Yüksek Lisans yapanlar, meslek sahibi yetişkinlerdir ve Türkçe öğrenmede problem yaşamaktadırlar. Özellikle, dil öğreniminde sürekli iki dili karşılaştırmalı olarak öğrenme ve ikidilli ders materyalleri kullanma eğilimdedirler. Bu çalışmanın amacı, göçmenlere yardım etmekle görevli yetişkinlere yönelik bu programlarda Türkçe'nin nasıl en etkin ve en hızlı bir şekilde öğretileceği sorusuna yanıt aramak ve İkidilli Ders Kitaplarının önemini vurgulamaktır.

***

Suriyelilerin İstihdamı ve Şanlıurfa'da Göçmen Emeğine Dayalı Kalkınma
(1360) Ayşe Cebeci (Harran University)

2011 itibariyle Suriye'de yaşanan çatışma ve savaştan ötürü -Birleşmiş Milletler 2016 verilerine göre- 5 milyon Suriyeli çeşitli ülkelere göç etmiştir. Türkiye'nin hem sınır ülkesi hem de Avrupa'ya geçiş ülkesi olması nedeniyle önemli ölçüde sığınmacı Türkiye'ye gelmiştir. Zira çeşitli yayınlar sadece Türkiye'de kayıtlı ve katılı olmayan toplamda 4 milyon sığınmacının bulunduğunu belirtmektedir. Günümüz itibariyle altıncı yılına girmekte olan çatışmalı sürecin devam etmesi ve Suriyeli sığınmacıların, hukuki statülerinden -"geçici koruma"dan- öte kalıcı olması ve kalıcı olmalarının etkileri, uyum süreci ve vatandaşlık tartışmalarını gündeme getirmiştir. Bu tartışma aynı zamanda Türkiye vatandaşları ile Suriyeli sığınmacıların toplumsal alanda yaşadıkları çatışmaların incelenmesini ve çözüm önerilerinin oluşturulmasını gerektirmektedir. Bu çalışmanın amacı ise Suriyeli sığınmacıların yoğun olarak yaşadığı Şanlıurfa'da istihdam süreçlerinde ve çalışma ilişkilerinde nasıl bir dönüşümün gerçekleştiğini analiz etmek ve sürecin sermaye birikimine etkilerini tartışmaktır. Bu amaçla, Şanlıurfa'da Sanayi sektöründe, Şanlıurfa Evren Sanayi ve organize sanayi bölgelerinde 66 işyerinde 157 Suriyeli ile 155 yerel işçiye ana dillerinde anket uygulanmıştır. Hizmet sektöründe, faaliyet gösteren 19 işyerinde 42 Suriyeli ile 27 yerel işçiye anket uygulanmıştır. Gene inşaat sektöründe 3 şirkette ve şantiyelerinde anketler uygulanmıştır. Aynı işyerinde çalışan Türkiye vatandaşı işçilere, Suriyeli işçilere ve işverenlere olmak üzere üç farklı soru seti uygulanmıştır. Gene ilde faaliyet gösteren sivil toplum kuruluşları ve bir nevi işçi kiralama bürosu olarak çalışan Suriyeli STK'lar ile de mülakatlar gerçekleştirilmiştir. Resmi rakamların çok daha üzerinde kayıt dışı çalışmanın olduğu ilde Suriyelilerin istihdamının artması bazı sektörlerde çalışma ilişkilerinin dönüşümüne, artı-değer ve rekabet gücüne de etkileri olmuştur. Çalışma göç sonucu Şanlıurfa işgücü piyasasındaki ve çalışma ilişkilerindeki dönüşümün ildeki sektörlere ve sermaye birikimine etkilerini tartışmaktadır.

***

SESSION 7G – Göç ve Edebiyat - 6

	Room: B3
Chair	**Gülnihal Gülmez, Anadolu University, Turkey**
1017	Cengiz Dağcı'nın Romanlarında Sürgün Teması - **Hülya Bayrak Akyıldız**
1268	Farklı Kültürlerin İç İçe Geçtiği Bir Göç Romanı Olarak Elveda Selanik ve Çeviri Stratejileri Üzerine Karşılaştırmalı Bir İnceleme – **Seda Taş**
1300	Memet Baydur'un Kamyon'unda Köy-Kent İnsanı ve İletişimsizlik – **Şengül Kocaman**
1329	Güney Dal'ın Romanlarında Göç, Kimlik ve Farklılık - **Fatih Özdemir**

Cengiz Dağcı'nın Romanlarında Sürgün Teması
(1017) Hülya Bayrak Akyıldız (Anadolu University)

Kırım Tatar edebiyatının önemli yazarı Cengiz Dağcı, kendi deneyimlerinden yola çıkarak, Kırım Tatarlarının sürgününü ve yurtsuzlaştırılmasını romanlaştırır. Korkunç Yıllar, O Topraklar Bizimdi, Badem Dalına Asılı Bebekler ve Anneme Mektuplar, sürgünün ve izlerinin gözlendiği eserlerinden birkaçıdır. Bu eserlerde çocukluktan yetişkinliğe uzanan anlatıcıların gözünden toprak ve toprakla kurulan bağlar, yurt kavramı, bu bağların kimlik açısından önemi, sürgünün kimlik algısı üzerindeki etkileri anlatılır. Bu bildiri sürgünün koşulları, sebepleri ve sonuçlarının nasıl yansıtıldığını, romancının bakış açısını ve sürgünü nasıl kavramsallaştırdığını konu eder. Sosyolojik ve tarihsel eleştiri yöntemlerini kullanarak romanlarda tarihsel arka planın nasıl kurgusallaştırıldığını; bu bağlamda sürgünün yurt, kimlik, benlik algısı, yabancılık gibi kavramlarla ilişkisini inceler. Çalışmanın bulgularına göre Dağcı'nın toprak/yurt kavramını kimlik kavramının temeline oturttuğu görülür. Yazarın bu önceliği, Kırım Tatarları açısından sürgünün yarattığı travmayı ve sürgünün/yurtsuzlaştırmanın ne ölçüde dramatik bir olay olduğunu daha iyi açıklar. Yazar bu temaların işlenmesini kendi kimliğine ve halkına karşı bir ödev olarak görür.
***

Farklı Kültürlerin İç İçe Geçtiği Bir Göç Romanı Olarak Elveda Selanik ve Çeviri Stratejileri Üzerine Karşılaştırmalı Bir İnceleme
(1268) Seda Taş (Trakya University)

Çeviri bir dilden bir dile gerçekleştirilen basit aktarım, yalnızca sözcüklerin dönüşümü veya bir bilgi taşıma yolu değildir. Farklı toplumların birbirini tanımasına ve kültürlerarası diyaloğu arttırmaya hizmet eden bir etkinliktir. Fakat diller ve kültürler arasındaki farklılıklar kültürel unsurlarla yoğun olarak bezeli metinlerin çevirisinde çevirmen için çeşitli sorunlar doğurabilmekte ve çevirmenin çeviri stratejilerinde belirleyici bir rol oynayabilmektedir. Bu çalışmada Leon Sciaky'nin Farewell to Salonica adlı romanı ve Elveda Selanik adlı Türkçe çevirisi karşılaştırmalı olarak ele alınarak kültürel unsurların çevirisinde çevirmenin kullandığı stratejiler saptanmaya çalışılacaktır. Çalışmaya bütünce olarak seçilen roman, yüzyılın başlarında Balkanlar'da yaşananlarla birlikte değişen ve dönüşen hayatların gölgesinde bir Selanik betimlemesi sunarken aynı zamanda göçe mecbur kalan bir ailenin yaşam öyküsü aracılığıyla okurun tarihe tanıklık etmesini de sağlar. Yirminci yüzyılın başlarında Doğu ile Batı'nın buluştuğu yer olan Selanik, caddelerinde Türkçe, Arapça, Yunanca, Bulgarca, Fransızca, İspanyolca ve İbranice konuşulan zengin bir dünyayı resmeder ve muazzam bir kültürel çeşitlilik sunar. Bu kültürel zenginliğin çevirisi, çevirmenin belli kararlar almasını gerektirir. Çevirmenin stratejisi kültürel mesafeyi yansıtmaya veya kaynak kültürün dilsel ve kültürel farklılığını ortaya koymaya mı yönelik olacaktır, yoksa kültürler arasındaki farklılığı gözetmeyen ve erek kültürde okunabilirliği amaç edinen bir çeviri stratejisine mi yönelik olacaktır? Çalışmada bu soruya cevap aramak için kuramsal çerçevede çeviribilim araştırmacısı Venuti'nin "yabancılaştırma" ve "yerlileştirme" olarak ortaya koyduğu çeviri stratejilerinden yararlanılacaktır. Hangi stratejinin çeviride ağırlıklı olarak etkili olduğuna ilişkin yapılacak incelemede hem kültürel unsurların yer aldığı metin içi hem de kapak, sözlük, dipnot gibi metin dışı unsurlar göz önünde bulundurulacaktır. Bu doğrultuda farklı kültürlerin erek kültüre nasıl yansıdığına/tıldığına ışık tutulmaya çalışılacaktır.

***

Memet Baydur'un Kamyon'unda Köy-Kent İnsanı ve İletişimsizlik –
(1300) Şengül Kocaman (Dicle University)

Türk yazın dünyasında özellikle Almanya üzerinde odaklaşan göç ve göçmenlik konusu, toplumsal sorunlarla tiyatro aracılığı ile hesaplaşan bir anlayışın doğmasını sağlayan Melih Cevdet Anday, Haldun Taner, Vasıf Öngören ve nihayet Memet Baydur gibi yazarlar tarafından da ele alınmış, ülke ve toplum gerçeklerine olan duyarlılıklarını tiyatrolarıyla göstermişlerdir.

Oyunlarının merkezine insanı ve insana dair sorunları koyan ve göç olgusuna kayıtsız kalmayarak bazı oyunlarında birincil bazı oyunlarında da ikincil tema olmak üzere yer veren Memet Baydur, Özellikle, Kamyon oyununu "yerinden yurdundan edilmiş, köylerinden kasabalarından çeşitli yöntemlerle sürülmüş, büyük kente doğru itilmiş olanlara" ithaf eder. 1960 yılında yazılan oyun, İstanbul'a mal taşıyan bir kamyonun Ege bölgesinde ıssız bir yerde bozulması ve tamirci gelecek diye bekleyen ve her biri Türkiye'nin farklı yörelerinden olan göçmen köylülerin hikâyesidir. Doğduğu köylerde yaşama tutunamamış şansını kentlerde denemek isteyenlerin hikâyesi... Kamyon, Baydur'un diğer oyunları gibi yazarın yaşadığı döneme tanıklık eden, arka planda kalan asıl gerçekleri yansıtmayı amaçlayan, sorgulayan ve seyircisini sorgulamaya davet eden bir oyundur. Çalışmamızda, göç teması etrafında Kamyon oyununu metne dayalı eleştiri yöntemi ile incelemeyi hedefliyoruz. Ancak bunu yaparken, Çağdaş Türk Tiyatrosuna büyük bir katkı sunduğuna inandığımız Baydur tiyatrosunun belli başlı özelliklerinden de söz etmeyi ihmal etmeyeceğiz. Dil kullanımından, trajik ile komiğin sentezine, dekordan kostüme, kısaca tiyatroya değin her özellik inceleme konumuz olacaktır.

***

Güney Dal'ın Romanlarında Göç, Kimlik ve Farklılık
(1329) Fatih Özdemir (Karamanoğlu Mehmetbey University)

Almanya'da yaşayıp Türkçe yazan Güney Dal, romanlarında kurguya önem vermesi ve kendine özgü anlatım yollarıyla öne çıkar. Edebiyata Toplumcu Gerçekçilik anlayışıyla başlamış, Almanya'daki ilk kuşak yazarlardan biri olarak tanıklık ettiği işçi göçünü ele almıştır. Kapitalist Batı toplumuyla karşılaşan göçmenlerin yaşadığı değişimleri ve yabancılaşmayı İş Sürgünleri ve E-5'te konu edinir. 1980'li yıllardan sonra ise Türk edebiyatında postmodernist teknikleri uygulayan ilk romancılardan biri olarak öne çıkar. Bu dönemde de genellikle göçmen karakterler üzerinden Doğu-Batı arasında kalmışlık, kimlik ve kişilik sorunları gibi konuları ironik bir dille ele alır. Kılları Yolunmuş Maymun, Fabrikada Bir Saraylı, Gelibolu'ya Kısa Bir Yolculuk, Aşk ve Boks gibi romanlarında hem roman dili ve tekniğinde yeni arayışlara girişir hem de roman kişilerini genellikle göçmenlerin içinden seçer. Bu yazıda Avangard metinler üreten Güney Dal'ın romanlarındaki göç olgusu ve bu doğrultuda öne çıkan kimlik-yabancılaşma-dil-kültür gibi meseleler ele alınacaktır.

***

Inside Perspectives of Refugees on the Process of Smuggling
(867) Alexandra Koptyaeva (Linköping University)

The impossibility to continue the way to Europe because of the closed borders is the sorrowful reality the thousands of refugees are faced with in Greece now, being trapped in a country that currently serves as a 'precarious transit zone' as a result of the recent migration policies. Smuggling as an 'illegal' form of assistance is seen as an alternative for those who happen to be on the 'wrong side' of the border and need to flee from the place of origin for the purpose of own safety. The literature on this topic is mostly one-sided with a high attention devoted to the criminalization of smugglers as those who "make a fortune from people's desperation", the notion of borders constructions and motives for migration, lacking the accounts of those who has an experience of crossing borders by being smuggled or by arranging it. Current research project is based on the results of the ethnographic fieldwork that was conducted in a Refugee Accommodation and Solidarity Space 'City Plaza' in the center of Athens in 2017 and aimed to explore the personal stories of its residents by focusing on the following questions: how refugees experienced border crossings through smugglers, how they were found and chosen, how the payment methods were conducted, and can the negotiation of price take place?
***

Capabilities and Integration of Refugees
(845) Lilija Wiebe (University of South Africa)

The Capabilities Approach by Martha Nussbaum is a well-known philosophical concept. The main question of her approach is: "What is each person able to do and to be?" (Nussbaum, 2013, p.18). The final purpose of the Capabilities Approach is, through combining the individual capabilities of a person, to enable him/her to live a life worthy of human dignity (:32). Nussbaum proposes ten central capabilities, which every government should make available to all of its citizens (:32–34). Interlinking the Capabilities Approach with an integration theory, follows the goal to generate a combined theory, which focuses on the capabilities of the individual refugees to enlarge his/her choices for integration. The chosen integration theory "Theory of Successful Integration" is authored by Friedrich Heckmann (Heckmann, 2015, p.289). In his opinion, the individual integration of refugees takes place in four dimensions which are: structural, cultural, social and identificational integration (:72). The combination of both concepts could enhance Heckmann´s theory in two ways. Firstly, it would set the focus on the individual migrant and on his/her capabilities. This would secondly lead to the question: Which of the refugee´s capabilities need to be combined for integration to be successful? The aim of the study is to make a contribution to the integration discourse with a focus on the capabilities of the refugees. The central problem statement is: "Which advantages does the Capabilities Approach bring to the integration discourse in Germany? How would this change the integration theory and praxis?" Based on comparative analysis I will be relating the Theory of Successful Integration by Heckmann with the Capabilities Approach by Nussbaum via interlinking both theories. The aim is to find out in which way(s) the Capabilities Approach can complement the Theory of Successful Integration. As method, the "Coordinated Theory Analysis" according to Schneider is indicated (Schneider, 1999, p.290). The Coordinated Theory Analysis is, in contrast to the conventional way of theory comparison, not about comparing main concepts of theories to interrelate them (Greshoff, 1999, p.16), instead its focus is about trying to identify problem areas in the theories, to which they may contain complementary solutions. Because this method assumes that the problem context and the terms are known, the strengths and weaknesses of the two theories will be displayed at the beginning. Then the interpretation and explanation potential and possibilities of supplementation of the Capabilities Approach to the Theory of Successful Integration will be elaborated. This way of comparing two theories makes it possible to fill in any gaps in either one or both of the two comparative theories (Schneider, 1999, p.290). National and provincial governments have recognised that refugees and emigrants do have capabilities and that it would be wise for the integration process to unlock these potentials (Bundesregierung Deutschland, 2016, p.1). But there is still no integration theory existing, which incorporates them. Since the Capabilities Approach and the Human Development Approach are well-known and valid concepts, they will build a reliable and accepted basis for a new theory. By combining the Capabilities Approach with a familiar theory of integration, which is already accepted in Germany, this new theory will gain credibility. This study will bring a topic to the integration discourse which is not unfamiliar to it, but nevertheless not adequately recognised. It is well known that refugees do have capabilities and that the recognition of them falls short. Besides that, the German integration discourse does not have an integration theory with the emphasis on the capabilities of the immigrants. This is why the consolidation of the Capabilities Approach with an integration theory has the potential to add to an enhanced view of successful integration. The result may give NGOs and government agencies in Germany an orientation or direction for their future integration assistances.

***

Host State Responses to Refugees: A Case Study of India
(1203) Madhusmita Jena (JNU)

Committed to the doctrine of peaceful co-existence and brotherhood of humankind, historically India has provided space to thousands of refugees for centuries. These assimilating cultures notwithstanding refugees in India neither have any legal status, nor any clear protection regime to turn for help. In the absence of any national law for refugees, India deals with them at the political and administrative level. The refugees are, therefore, dependent on the benevolence of the state rather than on the regime of rights to reconstruct their lives in dignity. Nevertheless, protection and assistance is offered to the refugees, void of any legal sanction. A close and perceptive look at India's responses to diverse refugee groups that have entered the Indian territory and given refuge brings bare the facts that in the absence of a national refugee legislation, India's responses are characterized by inconsistency, ad hoc approaches and idiosyncrasies. Against this backdrop, the present paper endeavours to explore, what premises the provision of assistance and protection to these refugee groups (Tibetans, Sri Lankan, Burmese etc) in India in the absence of national refugee protection legislation; and whether this protection and assistance is devoid of discrimination and differential treatment towards different refugee groups. Against   this backdrop, the present paper endeavours to explore, what premises the provision of assistance and protection to these refugee groups in India in the absence of national refugee protection legislation; and whether this protection and assistance is devoid of discrimination and differential treatment towards different refugee groups.

***

Migration Flows in Southern Europe: Comparing migrant labour populations in Greece and Italy with the use of the census data
(1245) Stergiani Liakou (Harokopio University)

Migration flows have excessively increased during the last decades in Europe. The economic development of countries, the social exclusion and the demand for cheap labour have contributed to the increase of migration flows. In the last few years has been a growing interest in study of socioeconomic integration of migrants in southern European countries because of the crisis debt. The purpose of this abstract is to describe the distribution and comparison of migrant labour populations in regions of Greece and Italy. With reference to the relevant sources of literature, integration of migrants is based on their demographic and socioeconomic characteristics. The size of migrant flows is co-related to other socioeconomic phenomena such as demographic evolution. Therefore, it is important to look at both the quantitative and qualitative aspects of migration. First of all, migration has been increased rapidly after 1990s in Greece. Migrant inflows were favored by the domestic demand for cheap labour and the affordable cost of living. Regardless of their expertise in the country of origin, the majority of immigrants choose to be settled in Greece in order to find a job. Rural regions are in demand for workers in agriculture sector and women for domestic services. On the contrary, urban regions are in demand for highly educated migrant labor force for working as employees in a wide variety of services. The synthesis of immigrant population has changed impressively in the 1980s and 1990s because of numerous inflows in Italy. Italy is characterized by large regional and social disparities, too. Although labour market conditions are more favorable in the North, including for immigrants, in comparison with the native-born, immigrants fare much better in the South. The foreigners with regular permits tend to concentrate in regions which offer the greatest working opportunities. For instance, developed northern regions are in demand for qualified labor force in manufacturing and business sector, whereas in southern regions non-qualified and manual workers are in demand for domestic services and agricultural sector respectively. Regions in Greece and Italy appear many similarities and differences about migrant labour markets from 2001 to 2011. The overall population growth is the common point in both countries but there are a lot of native-born residents and immigrants in Italy, who correspond to millions of people. In 2011, migrant labour populations are increased, especially in urban regions. The majority of employees dominate in tertiary sector in both countries of Greece and Italy. There are many self-employed immigrants in urban districts because of the creation of new businesses in Italy. Many enterprises are closed but informal sector has developed in rural regions because immigrant cheap labor force is in great demand in Greece. Moreover, the most of employees are working in public administration, tourism and scientific activities in urban centers of Greece. In conclusion, the results indicate that migrant labour population increases more and more in Greece and Italy. Despite the fact that migrant flows could not be determined accurately, crisis debt in Southern Europe has strongly influenced the magnitude of inflows and outflows of migrants.

***

Human Trafficking: Is the law of the Western societies effective or not?
(1258) Alexia Kapsampeli

The human trafficking is widely thought to be the modern form of slavery. It started before many years and still exists. Nowadays a great number of people, especially women and children, are trafficked, mainly from poor to developed states, in order to be exploited either for sex or for labor. The Western societies, including the international organizations and institutions, have taken measures, as they have tried to eliminate it. The most characteristic attempt is the Palermo Protocol. However, the legislation has been proved ineffective, therefore the states in collaboration with the organizations should realize the basic dimensions of this phenomenon and legislate based on them.

***

Diaspora Bonds as a New Foreign Capital Tools A Research on the Countries Applying and Potential of the Turkish Diaspora
(817) Atakan Durmaz (Bayburt University), Adem Kalça (Karadeniz Technical University)

Developing countries that want to sustain their economic development and close the economic gap between developed countries need foreign capital, especially because of insufficient domestic savings. In this context, there are many ways in which countries resort to attracting foreign capital. However, since the early 1990s, some countries have seen diaspora as a source of foreign capital they need and have developed methods for this source. One of these methods is the diaspora bond, which emerges as a new generation financial borrowing instrument and which has different advantages in terms of both the issuing country and the buyer compared to other financial instruments and is generally presented only to diaspora members. From this point of view, the aim of this study is to present the effectiveness of these diaspora bonds used as a new generation borrowing instrument and to provide an alternative source of foreign capital that Turkey needs in line with its economic objectives. It is also to raise awareness of this issue.

***

Resources for Asylum Seekers and Migrants in Terms of Current Conditions in Turkey
(963) Melek Zubaroğlu Yanardağ (Mehmet Akif Ersoy University), Umut Yanardağ (Hacettepe University)

By entering into a different country, a great majorityof migrants and refugees lose their support systems. A tough process waits them until they develop new support strategies in the host country. There are a lot of national and international documents and codes/laws which determine the rights of the migrants' and the asylum seekers. Recently it has become clear that with the increasing migration movements, legal regulations on migrants' and refugees' human rights have been handled more comprehensively. Particularly after the 6458 numbered "Law on Foreigners and International Protection" which, camed into force in 2014, the statutes of foreigners started to become clearer. By the authority granted by the law, a public institution called the "Directorate General of Migration Management" was established under the Ministry of Interior, and came into operation in the same year. This institution is one of the legal authorities that deal with the migrants' problems in Turkey. The main purpose of this presentation to discuss the needs and the resources of the individuals (generally asylum seekers and temporary protection beneficiaries) who were enforced to migrate to Turkey. The psycho-social needs arise among the population who has come to Turkey through the irregular migration flow to the country., such as the needs of "housing, nourishment, health, psychological, educational and employment" These needs are met by public institutions within the framework of legal regulations and by non-governmental organisations within the bounds of their capacities. On the other hand, a lot of migrants work in registered or unregistered jobs in order to effort their expenses. In Turkey, the individuals, who come from non-European countries like Afghanistan, Iraq, Iran and demand "international protection" have to be registered first by the national Migration Management Office and then by the UNHCR (United Nations High Commissioner for Refugees) Office. After the registration process, these individuals, whose applications are in the evaluation process, are directed to one of the 62 satellite cities decided by the Directorate General of Migration Management. For the Syrian people who entered the country through a mass influx and are called "temporary protection beneficiaries", the process is not the same and as a resultthey are not supposed to follow the international protection procedure. For the Syrian population who is within the frame of international law, "open door politics, non refoulement principle and meeting the basic needs" criterias are in operation at all times. Within this context, the group that needs Turkey more to meet their needs (especially the needs of housing and nourishment), is the group settled in the camps with a temporary protection status Among all the temporary protection beneficiaries there are a huge amount of people who prefer to live outside the camps and they comprise about 90% (more than two and half million people) of all the Syrians in Turkey. These people generally meet their needs by working as an unregistered worker or by their self savings which they have brought from their country. For both of the groups which has the "international protection" status and the temporary protection status Syrians) the process of benefiting from other rights such as access to health services, working, access to education services, and available resources are common and the processes are similar. It is seen that the asylum seekers and the migrants in Turkey have several rights and resources in order to maintain their life and social functioning. Particularly for the Syrian with the temporary protection there are many supplementary resources provided. Especially the social workers who work in the migration field should endeavor in order to ensure a better protection and a better development of these rights and resources. At this stage, communication both with the public institutions and the NGOs is essential. Additionally, the involvement of the asylum seekers and migrants to the advocacy activities is equally important.

***

SESSION 8A – Work and Migration - 1

	Room: A1
Chair	**Ana Isabel López García, El Colegio de la Frontera Norte, Mexico**
1183	How Much Migrant Agency Matters in an Era of Precarity? Looking into the 'Resilience Repertoires' of African Migrants in Greece – **Apostolos G Papadopoulos, Loukia-Maria Fratsea**
1113	"United We Stand, Divided We Fall! We Could Rise Together but I Ain't Need Any Associations, I'm Better Alone!" Precarious, Low-Status Work Repercussions on Community Networks of Solidarity of Pakistanis, Ethiopians and Filipinos in Greece in Hard Times – **Theodoros Fouskas, Fotini-Maria Mine**
1143	Diaspora or Diasporas: The Divisions among Economically Active Female Emigrants from Serbia - **Dunja Poleti Cosic**
1361	Chinese Labour Migration during World War I–**Jonathan Liu, Ibrahim Sirkeci, Brian Hook, Chungwen Li**

How Much Migrant Agency Matters in an Era of Precarity? Looking into the 'Resilience Repertoires' of African Migrants in Greece
(1183) Apostolos G Papadopoulos (Harokopio University), Loukia-Maria Fratsea (Harokopio University)

Greece has been one of the main arenas of economic crisis in Europe. Due to this unprecedented financial and socioeconomic crisis, which has severely affected the indigenous populations, migrants have seen their social position worsen further while their vulnerability increased considerably. Rising unemployment, income insecurity, labour precarity and rising anxiety about future employment opportunities and livelihoods have been particularly acute for migrants. Recent migrant populations originating mainly from Africa and Asia face much harder economic conditions than their predecessors who came largely from the Balkans and Eastern Europe. At the same time, migration policies designed by the European Commission and implemented at the national level by the different member states reflect the securitization concerns of the European nations. The persistent austerity measures - which had a negative impact on employment opportunities and standard of living - intensified the precariousness of migrant populations who elaborated various 'repertoires of resilience' in their attempt to cope with amidst a rapidly changing socioeconomic and political environment. African migration in Greece is presented as an exemplary case of how migrant agency is created in form of multiple responses to changing social and economic structures. The paper delves into the various individual and family strategies developed by African migrants in their struggle to alleviate their precarity in the labour market and living insecurity. The analysis is based on empirical material collected amidst Greece's economic recession (2010-2014) and includes both survey data and qualitative material (interviews, focus groups). Our main argument is that African migrants have devised a number of 'resilience repertoires', which include coping practices, recurrent actions and mobility trajectories that interact with structural and institutional factors.

***

"United We Stand, Divided We Fall! We Could Rise Together but I Ain't Need Any Associations, I'm Better Alone!" Precarious, Low-Status Work Repercussions on Community Networks of Solidarity of Pakistanis, Ethiopians and Filipinos in Greece in Hard Times
(1113) Theodoros Fouskas (Hellenic Association of Political Scientists), Fotini-Maria Mine (Lund University)

How does precarious, low-status/low-wage jobs affect the participation and representation of migrants in community associations, collective organizations and trade unions? Has the recession increased their interest in membership in collective networks of solidarity and organized labor claims? What perceptions and practices have migrants developed towards community, labor and workplace solidarity and collective forms of organization and protection? In Greece, immigrants and refugees have become part of a cheap workforce reserve that is continually renewed while the division of labor prompts and entraps migrants into wage labor and low-status/low-wage jobs, distinguishing them by class, gender, race-nationality (Psimmenos 2011). The jobs in which migrants are largely employed are paid or not paid occupations outside the margins of formal employment and unregistered. They are considered non-attractive, without social prestige and inferior by the workforce of the reception society, however they do provide economic profits and social status attainment to the customer or employer (Portes, Castells and Benton, 1989, Parreñas, 2000; Anderson, 2000). The labor that migrants are exposed to is not only characterized by precarity, low-status and low-wages, exploitation, flexibility and instability, isolation and individualization, but also by decollectivization (Author, year, year), or in other words by alienation from familial, community, collective, networks of solidarity and labor rights. Precarious work is employment that lacks all the standard forms of labor security (Vosko, 2006) and creates enormous and complex barriers to labor organization strategies due to the isolated, atomized and non-unionized nature of immigrant employment (Choudry and Thomas, 2012). Greece comes first among the 21 OECD country-members where 24% of Greek GDP is formed by the underground/shadow economy (Williams and Schneider, 2013). Moreover, the percentage of uninsured workers is among the world's highest (37.3%) and so is the percentage of irregular immigrants working (4.4%) (Williams and Schneider, 2013). This presentation focuses on the cases of Pakistanis Ethiopian and Filipino workers and how the frame of their work and employment in precarious, low-status/low-wage jobs affect their participation in secondary groups of solidarity and workers and their representation in them, i.e. community, migrant labor associations and trade unions, during the economic crisis in Greece. According to the results of in-depth interviews migrants are entrapped in a frame of isolative and exploitative working conditions, i.e. street-vending, unskilled textile and manual labor, personal services and care and domestic work. In this working context, most of the interviewed migrants appear to have developed individualistic perceptions, they act in an atomistic manner, form materialistic beliefs, are indifferent to collectivity and solidarity and are isolated from their compatriots and other workers. They have low self-perceptions and expectations for social advancement and deal with their social and labour related problems individually, or completely resign from claiming them.

***

Diaspora or Diasporas: The Divisions among Economically Active Female Emigrants from Serbia
(1143) Dunja Poleti Cosic (University of Belgrade)

The main focus of this paper will be on the migration practices of economically active female emigrants from Serbia, who emigrated after 2000 and live in France and Germany. International emigration from semi-periphery countries has been very important issue for the past several decades. In that sense, Serbia makes a good case study: since the fall of the Milosevic's regime, in 2000, the country has started with endless processes of "transition", which led to the political opening and the increase of the unemployment rate at the same time. Consequently, the emigration of labour force became burning question. Unfortunately, empirical studies on emigration are relatively rare in Serbia, as researchers face great organizational and material obstacles. By and large, the incentives for international migration of labour force have been sought in the economic reasons, such as differences in expected wages or living standards. But for a long time, the influence of gender regimes on mobility was neglected. In recent years, feminist-inspired studies have confirmed that migration process is not gender neutral, that gender affects motivation, conditions of mobility and its outcomes, sometimes being more important than the country of origin or destination, age, class, race, ethnicity, or culture. The paper aims to enlighten the intersection of gender regimes and migration practices of economically active women, as well as to mark the main structural differences within this group, through the reconstruction of migration experiences. Gender regimes could be defined as "relatively structured relationships between men and women, masculinity and femininity, in the institutional and non-institutional environment, on the level of discourse and the practice. This structuring is embodied in different gender roles, different identities and different gender representations" (Blagojevic Hjuson, 2012). They also concern gender ideologies and unequal distribution of power. Gender regimes are at the same time the products and the producers of society, although their second role is much less obvious and explored. France and Germany are both traditional destination country for labour force from Serbia. Certain characteristics of the two countries are very similar – the size, the welfare state type, both are founders of the EU, both have a long immigration tradition – but they differ according to work-family reconciliation regimes, among themselves and in comparison, to Serbia. The given regimes refer to the institutional (family policy), cultural (value), labour (the structure of the labour market) and economic (living standards) structures at national level (Kotowska et al, 2010.). Three sets of research questions were imposed. Firstly, could the interdependence between gender regimes and migration practices be found in different phases of migration (before migration, during migration and after settling in the destination country)? In which way internalized micro and macro gender regimes determine migration practices: how do they influence the decision-making process, transfer across borders, adaptation and integration processes or work activity? Additionally, does the act of migration recurrently affect gender regimes after moving to the country of destination and how? Secondly, are there important changes in gender regime-migration patterns interdependence across various institutional environments? How different are the experiences of women who have moved to France comparing to Germany? And finally, how much social and structural position that woman holds mediate above-mentioned interdependence? Does the relationship between migration and gender regime change along the lines of social division? How do gender and migration practices intersect with other social features, like education, class, labour market position and family/marital status? Is there one diaspora or we can talk about various diasporas that do not have too much in common? Data are collected through 60 semi-structured in-depth interviews with the reconstruction of the life trajectory with female emigrants in France and Germany. Two social features have been recognized as essential regarding the work chances for women – level of education and family/marital status. In contrast to the most common way of defining migrants through their formal status, the study included economically active women, regardless of how the legal system classifies them.

***

Chinese Labour Migration during World War I
(1361) Jonathan Liu (Regent's University London), Ibrahim Sirkeci (Regent's University London), Brian Hook (Regent's University London), Chungwen Li (Ming Ai Institute)

In this paper, we focus on the motivations, incentives and patterns of mobility among the Chinese Labour Corps who worked for the British Army in the First World War. The data comes from secondary literature and qualitative interviews conducted with the veterans and/or their families who served in the Corps. In this paper, we aim to bring this special case of international human mobility into the migration debate. These labourers carefully selected in China and transported through a dangerous and equally difficult route to work behind the front line in France. There are questions about the motivations as well as mechanisms and patterns of their movement. Their journeys from rural China to the port of Wei Wei, a British dominion at the time, and experiences at selection as well as through and after the journey warrants a systematic investigation. Our analysis draws upon the limited literature on this historic case of migration and the qualitative data collected by Ming Ai Institute London in 2015-2016. The field research was generously supported by Lottery Heritage Foundation and Regent's University London.

***

SESSION 8B – Spatial Patterns in Human Mobility - 2

	Room: A2
Chair	**Filiz Künüroğlu, Tilburg University, Netherlands**
1321	Migration Pathways in Turbulent Times: Delineating the Social and Spatial Mobility of Immigrants in Greece – **Loukia - Maria Fratsea**
1024	Perception and Appropriation of Territory. Bissau-Guineans in Lisbon: Two Generations in Comparison – **Anna Ludovici**
1033	The Trade-Off in 'Relocation': A Comparative Understanding of Vulnerabilities of Disadvantaged Migrants Moving from Rural Origins to Urban Areas in the Context of Bangladesh - **Mohammad Ehsanul Kabir, Peter Davey**
1216	Renegotiating Sovereignty and Governance through the Reconfiguration of the European Border Regime: The Case of Greece - **Dimitris Parsanoglou**

Migration Pathways in Turbulent Times: Delineating the Social and Spatial Mobility of Immigrants in Greece
(1321) Loukia - Maria Fratsea (Harokopio University of Athens)

The concept of social mobility lies at the heart of social sciences as it is directly related to the social reproduction and change over time. Especially, during the last two decades much attention was directed towards the degree in which migrants' social mobility is enabled or hindered in European societies. In this context however, migration studies in Greece has mainly focused on migrants' integration challenges and prospects in which their social trajectories are examined in view of their participation to the labor market. Since the early 1990s migration towards Greece has changed considerably as it was rapidly transformed to new destination country. Albanian migration was followed by new migrant flows originating mainly from Africa and Asia. The recent economic crisis and the Syrian refugee flows have induced new challenges for migrants themselves living in Greece, the national authorities and policymakers in Greece. The paper critically discusses the relevant literature of immigrants' social mobility and analyses the social and spatial aspects of their mobility in Greece. The paper elaborates statistical data from various sources (e.g. Population Census, Labour Force Survey) in order to explore the socio- economic characteristics and the occupational patterns of migration flows. The quantitative analysis is enriched by qualitative material based on preliminary interviews conducted during the economic downturn in order to shed light on the ways migrants themselves assess their social pathways.

Perception and Appropriation of Territory. Bissau-Guineans in Lisbon: Two Generations in Comparison
(1024) Anna Ludovici (University of Lisbon)

The notion of public space is associated with the modern age. The nation-state's own territorial conception involves the idea of a public space generated and controlled by the central power (of the State), and whose property is not exclusive of a single individual or group. However, the use of public space and its access maintains endogenous inequalities and spatial injustice (Soja, 2010). At the same time, we believe that the way as a territory socially produced influence the behaviour of social actors in the space, is one of the fundamental components of the processes of appropriation and representation of space (Lefebvre, 1991). Paraphrasing Habermas (1984), we can measure the level of democracy of a state, through the observation of his space (in its political "extension"), which has to be conceived also as a space of participation (Martins, 2007). The production of space, therefore, remains a central theme in studies concerning the correlation between social dynamics and urban planning. Neoliberal agendas, which determine the "success" and competitiveness of contemporary cities, impose public policies for the management and organization of territories. This process has impact on urban landscapes and affects the ways of experiencing public space at different scales. In this glocal context (Swyngedouw, 2004), cities play a determining role in delineating new instruments of reading, decoding, interpreting and reconstructing space. The high concentration of economic, social, financial resources makes global cities attractive for a growing number of diverse interests and stakeholders. On the one hand, it is possible to affirm, therefore, a general tendency towards multiculturalism and multi-ethnicity, which questions about our relationship with "the others" and about the strategies of inclusion adopted. On the other hand, the use of space and its transformation, both at the individual private level, and in terms of public policies, determine new forms of "being in the cities", conditioning the daily practices and the behaviours of its residents. The increasing inequality and the socio-spatial exclusion generate specific dynamics that raise questions regarding the effective right of access to the city (Lefebvre, 2012; Harvey, 2012) and challenge innovative and alternative forms of planning. In the last decades, migration studies have progressively included questions related to the process of settlement and social segregation in urban spaces of destination.

In this perspective, we analysed the constitutive process of the rehousing neighbourhood of Quinta do Mocho, in the Metropolitan Area of Lisbon, whose history gave us important clues regarding the spatial evolution of the city in the critical years of the post-revolution, underlining the role of its suburbs, the needs and orientations of its housing policy and the importance of the presence of migrants in the current territorial configuration. With this aim, we focused our attention on the specific group of Bissau-Guinean immigrants in Lisbon, considering the rich cultural and ethnic background of the transnational Bissau-Guinean community, particularly related to symbolic and sacred meaning of the territory, and considering the time of arrival in Portugal and the gender of the first and the second generation of immigrants. However, the progressive marginalization of the "undesirable areas", allows in some cases the peripheries to gain a greater connotation in terms of specificity and self-representation, i.e., the production of a greater sense of belonging to the neighbourhood. In fact, if in the city (understood as centrality) the social behaviour is conditioned and pushed by the logics of consumption, the public space of the neighbourhood still allows a no-economic-conditioned way of living the space, through the production of informal and spontaneous practices, and a quite direct use of the space. Comparing the two generations of migrants, it was possible to analyse their different behaviour in public and private space, the adoption (or not) of informal practices, and the prevalent use of the neighbourhood's space instead of the city's one. This showed how the national/local policies of urban planning condition social behaviours in the space, as well as the immigrants' spatial practices, their ethnicities and fragilities influence urban settlement. This research was developed between 2015 and 2016 in a master dissertation (Ludovici, 2016). It was based on a qualitative reflection, favouring a theoretical approach, applied experimentally through the conduction of semi-structured interviews and participant observation. Based on a geographical approach, we tried to contribute, even from a small database, to question the traditional conceptual categories used in social and spatial analysis of residential areas of immigrants, and also to develop an alternative thinking about the relevance of the inclusion of different perspectives in the epistemological validation process.

***

The Trade-Off in 'Relocation': A Comparative Understanding of Vulnerabilities of Disadvantaged Migrants Moving from Rural Origins to Urban Areas in the Context of Bangladesh

(1033) Mohammad Ehsanul Kabir (Griffith University Australia), Peter Davey (Griffith University Australi)

Background: It has been widely recognized by academics and policy makers that people across the world are moving from their habitual residence driven by poverty, war, political insurgency, environmental degradation and the climate change impacts amongst others (Salauddin, 2010; Lilleor & van den Broeck, 2011; IPCC, 2014). Until recently the issue received comparatively little attention within mainstream debates that the majority of this mobility will take place within the geographical boundaries of affected countries than across borders; referred to as internal migration (International Organization for Migration, 2009). By this century, the number of internal migrants may increase from approximately 25 million to over 200 million worldwide (see projections in IOM, 2009; IDMC, 2016; Biermann & Boas, 2010). For many low incomecountries, most of the internal migrants from rural areas are attracted to cities. Cities of many low-income countries like Bangladesh have limited infrastructural and governance capacity to response to the high number of disadvantaged migrants coming every year in search of livelihood (IDMC, 2016; Black, Bennett, Thomas & Beddington, 2011). Hence the increasing influx of rural-urban migrant increases densification of slum population that leads to further deteriorating living condition and widening intra-urban inequalities (Greiner und Sakdapolrak, 2013). Traditionally, policy-making has viewed the vulnerabilities of such disadvantaged groups from a static geospatial point of view i.e. either from geographic origin or from geographic destinations (Zimmerman, Kiss and Hossain, 2011). Yet the vulnerabilities of contemporary mobility are more complex often involving multistage exposure to various risks including environmental, economic and social components (Gray et al, 2014). Such exposures may occur several times considering what the migrants may experience throughout the process of mobility involving various issues in travel and destination phases. This study makes a comparative assessment of general vulnerabilities of disadvantaged migrants at their place of geographic origins and present geographic destinations. The paper tests whether the migrants' vulnerabilities reduce after migrating from rural areas to slums in larger cities in Bangladesh. Grounded on recent theoretical development in vulnerability and migration scholarship, the study fieldwork involved interviewing household members of migrants both at geographic origins and at destinations. The drivers of vulnerability that are affecting their livelihood in both geographic origins and geographic destinations have been compared. Objectives: This study aims compare the drivers of vulnerability of the disadvantaged rural-urban migrants at two different locations – before migration at geographic origins and after migration at geographic destinations in the context of Bangladesh. Methodology: This study identified two Northern districts of the country as geographic origins which are (natural hazard) hotspots for seasonal drought, crop failure and riverbank erosion. Secondly, four urban locations have been identified which largely recognized as usual geographic destinations of the migrant population are coming from the identified geographic origins. Data was obtained at two stages, firstly at the geographic origins and then at geographic destinations. In total 115 in-depth interviews (75 interviews at geographic origins and 40 at geographic destinations) have been conducted. Additionally, 10 Focus Group Discussions with local participants and 20 Key Informant Interviews involving different government and non-government stakeholders and policy makers across the country have been considered as the primary method for data collection. Results: The drivers of vulnerabilities have been classified into some broader categories involving financial, infrastructural, environmental, governance, political, health and social components. Result compared the drivers of vulnerabilities identified at geographic origins and geographical destinations. While at origins, most of the households stressed financial drivers including poverty and credit burden as top drivers negatively influencing their livelihood stability at destinations, the most frequently appearing drivers of vulnerabilities include infrastructural issues like risk of eviction at slums, followed by social issues. In contrary with geographic origins, higher frequency of social issues like drug abuse, child labour and sexual harassment appeared at geographic destinations as key drivers of vulnerabilities affecting disadvantaged rural-urban migrants. Conclusion: From the perspective of vulnerabilities this study will argue that understanding vulnerabilities at the geographic origins are important policy information for planning any intervention at both geographic origins and destinations, such as knowing about communicable diseases at geographic origins is helpful to design health activities and vaccination for short term migrants roaming over geographic destinations. Again, some of the pre-migration vulnerabilities from geographic origins like stress may escalate new vulnerabilities such as high blood pressure and heart disease at geographic destinations. Policies to protect such disadvantaged migrant in cities and manage vulnerabilities will be most effective if they consider issues involved at both locations, not only at geographic destinations.

***

Renegotiating Sovereignty and Governance through the Reconfiguration of the European Border Regime: The Case of Greece
(1216) Dimitris Parsanoglou (Panteion University)

The current 'refugee crisis' has sparked off a series of shifts in several aspects of the European border regime. In this paper, I will focus on a case study, where one can find all these shifts in a hybrid but also paradigmatic form: we will focus on Greece, and more specifically on the ways in which both state sovereignty and governance have been challenged in unprecedented intensity. Since the beginning of the 'refugee crisis', and particularly since the spring of 2015, multiple actors, local and international, governmental, intergovernmental and non-governmental, technical and humanitarian, have thrived throughout the country wherever emergency conditions occurred. In this paper, I will attempt a two-fold approach: on the one hand, we will propose a typology of actors that have been and still are present in the broad field of the 'management of refugee crisis'; on the other hand, we will try to analyse the repercussions of the 'intrusion' of supranational and non-state actors into services, activities and interventions that belong to the hard sphere of State sovereignty.

***

SESSION 8C – Migration as Journey

	Room: A4
Chair	**Anastasia Christou, Middlesex University, UK**
1008	Journey as Method: Unpacking Transnational Journey of Refugees to Canada via Turkey - **Uğur Yıldız**
1279	Of Crocodiles, Magumaguma, Hyenas, and Malayitsha: Zimbabweans Crossing the Limpopo in Search of a Better Life in South Africa – **Chipo Hungwe**
959	Two Different Sections on History: The Sea Peoples and Syrian Migrants – **Barış Gür**
1197	(Re)making Boundaries: Migration, Classifications and Otherness – **Joana Sousa Ribeiro**

Journey as Method: Unpacking Transnational Journey of Refugees to Canada via Turkey
(1008) Uğur Yıldız (Carleton University)

This paper is about transnational journeys of non-European asylum travellers to Canada via Turkey. The paper aims to demonstrate multi-dimensional and multi-layered aspect of asylum journey of refugees by empirically focusing on asylum seeking practices in Turkey and Turkey's geographical limitation and resettlement practices to Canada and Canada's government-assisted refugee resettlement program in accordance with UNHCR's global refugee protection regime. In other words, the paper explores the asylum journey of non-European asylum applicants towards Canada by seeking asylum in Turkey where they wait for UNHCR's refugee status determination; where they temporarily and uncertain times stay due to the country's geographical limitation; and, where they hope for resettlement to Canada as the country of resettlement through Canada's government-assisted, blended, and privately sponsored refugee resettlement programs. This asylum journey to Canada via Turkey actualizes in accordance with UNHCR's coordination and cooperation with Turkey, Canada, and asylum applicants from non-European countries of origin. The main research question I focused in this research is "What is a journey?" According to Brigden and Mainwaring (2016: 244), journey is "an experience with indeterminate beginnings and ends." The aim of this question is to unpack the asylum journey of migrants in order to transcend easy conceptual borders, labels and journeys by empirically concentrating upon the asylum journey to Canada via Turkey and practices of asylum travellers en route to Canada via Turkey. To answer this research, I employ qualitative research design founded upon semi-structured interviews conducted with asylum applicants in Turkey and resettled refugees in Canada. And, I conducted field trips to Istanbul, Ottawa, and Tehran between April 2014 and October 2015. In line with this ethnographic journey and the central research question, the paper devises journey as method formula by following Mezzadra and Neilson's (2013: viii) border as method notion which "provides productive insights on the tensions and conflicts that blur the line between inclusion and exclusion." Journey as method is important to approach the journey as an experience itself and to see the journey of migrants "a living, micro-cultural and micro-political system in motion" (Gilroy, 1993: 4). The asylum journey is a micro-political image since it illustrates the fluidity and relativity of attributed identities and labels by the state's migration system. By adopting journey as method formula, the asylum journey at stake involves multiple border-crossings and several journeys of asylum travellers within the journey, and both mobility and stasis in the course of asylum journey towards Canada. In other words, the journey is not only about physical mobility. It also contains immobility, stops and waiting in the course of the journey of refugees. Immobility or stasis in this asylum journey is a natural part of the ongoing mobility towards the country of resettlement. The research suggests that the asylum journey is a multi-layered, multi-dimensional, relational, and processual assemblage in which both states, non-state actors, institutions, and refugees and networks of refugees interact, encounter and negotiate each other. Therefore, it is important to disassemble the assembled asylum journey for detailed analysis of experiences of migrants. Disassembling the asylum journey is a challenge to binary conceptions of a forced/vulnerable versus voluntary migrant by demonstrating the calculated decision-making process. Furthermore, the paper argues that asylum journey is, first of all, an encounter between practices of asylum travellers and policies/regulations of institutions and states. Second, it is based on negotiations between states such as Turkey and Canada, between institutions and states like UNHCR, IOM, Turkey and Canada. Third, it is based on interaction among past, present, and future asylum travellers. This interaction occurs through the production, reproduction and diffusion of knowledge among past, present, and future asylum travellers. More importantly, the reproduced and diffused knowledge forms an asylum version of habitus (Bourdieu, 1977), an asylum habitus, among migrants through their transnational networks, social and familial ties in the country of asylum and resettlement.

***

Of Crocodiles, Magumaguma, Hyenas, and Malayitsha: Zimbabweans Crossing the Limpopo in Search of a Better Life in South Africa
(1279) Chipo Hungwe (Midlands State University)

Many stories have been told of how 'hyenas' facilitate undocumented migration and in the process, negotiate and protect migrants from the much feared magumaguma who prey on the 'innocent lives' of would-be migrants desiring a better life in South Africa. The paper relies on first hand accounts of individuals who have crossed the Limpopo River and Zimbabwe-South Africa border as undocumented migrants. It utilises qualitative in-depth interviews of Zimbabwean migrants in Johannesburg. These individuals have had to deal with some, if not all, of the following: 'hyenas', crocodiles, magumaguma and the malayitsha. This paper demonstrates the central role of human smugglers such as the malayitsha and hyenas/impisi and the precarious nature of undocumented Zimbabwean migration showing the sheer will to survive against all odds; migrating to a perceived better life. Death will not deter migration or the aspiration to change one's life by migrating. The paper creates a good case for the need for further research targeting the magumaguma and the malayitsha so that a critical mass of literature can be created on these human smugglers. This paper is important as it comes up with a conceptual framework on understanding undocumented Zimbabwean migration to South Africa.

***

Two Different Sections on History: The Sea Peoples and Syrian Migrants
(959) Barış Gür (Dokuz Eylul University)

Significant changes have been observed in the late Bronze Age throughout Greece, Aegean Islands and Anatolia. According to the Egyptian documents, there is a great famine in Anatolia. Meanwhile the Late Bronze Age palaces in Greece were destroyed and also archaeological evidences indicate that traces of destruction in different settlements in this period extend from Anatolia to the coasts of northern Syria. Written documents in the Near East, give an information about a mass migration movement from west to east. The Egyptians call them sea peoples and they did not want them in their lands. After 3200 years from these events, this time in opposite direction an immigration movement is experienced from east to west. Causes are similar: Due to civil war, people are in an environment of insecurity and unrest. There is nothing to provide for their livelihood. So, they have to migrate from the land they were born. There are similar facts in both periods: Chaos, insecurity, famine, and being persona non-grata... The Egyptians fought and killed the Sea Peoples in the mouth of the Nile river under the leadership of Ramses III in 1176 B.C. because they did not want them to enter lands of Egypt, in 2010's A.D. For the same reason, some European countries have closed their borders to Syrian migrants. In this presentation, the similarities between two different periods and two different groups of people will be discussed.

***

(Re)making Boundaries: Migration, Classifications and Otherness
(1197) Joana Sousa Ribeiro (Center for Social Studies)

The regimes of population´ classification are one of the dimensions of bio-politics (Foucault, 1979). The social construction of the category of `skilled migrant` results from the intertwined of admission and inclusion selectivity policies (Kofman and Kraler, 2006). The `skilled migrant` tend to be defined either by the level of education, corresponding to the ones who attended tertiary education (Borjas, 2003); either by the occupation (Bouvier and Simcox, 1994). Depending on the used definition, the spec-trum of migrants that could be named `skilled` varies accordingly. The aim of this article is to analyse the production, appropriation and (self)-representation of the following migrant categories, tacking the healthcare sector as a case-study: the `international postgraduate student under emergency assistance`, the `Eurozone migrant` and the `overstayed and overqualified migrant`. For that, this paper considers the displacement of populations due to socio-economic (`labour migrants`) and humanitarian reasons (`asylum seekers`) (Fassin, 2011) to (and from) a postcoloni-al, semi-peripheral and e-/ immigration country, like Portugal. This paper contributes to debate how the process of production and classification of `otherness` are embedded on wider social, political and economic transformations. In this vein, it also turns visible the process of categories´ detachment (in this case, from Refugee, Emigrant and Undocumented Migrant´ categories) as a process of inclusion through exclusion.

***

SESSION 8D – Gender and Migration - 3

	Room: A5
Chair	**Elif Uyar Mura, Çanakkale Onsekiz Mart University, Turkey**
796	Gender Identity and Performance of Filipino Female Student Migrants in Korea - **Cathe Ryne Denice Basco Sarmiento**
1294	Gender Identity, Social Class and Conflict based Perception of Mobility: Case of LGBTTI-Q individuals from and in Turkey – **Pınar Yazgan, Oğuzhan Uzun, M. Murat. Yüceşahin, Deniz Eroğlu-Utku**
872	Migration and Gender: The Case of Domestic Workers in Europe - **Aneta Tyc**
954	Women's Social Rights and Migration in Turkey: A Legal Analysis from Gender Perspective – **Altın Aslı Şimşek Öner**

Gender Identity and Performance of Filipino Female Student Migrants in Korea
(796) Cathe Ryne Denice Basco Sarmiento (Korea University)

Korea is one of the countries in the Asia-Pacific region with the highest student net migration. An increasing number of international students, specifically from neighbouring Asian countries, have been moving to the country to pursue higher education. As one of such countries, the Philippines has a greater number of female students engaging in Korean study abroad programmes compared to their male counterparts. Recognizing the differences in educational principles and socio-cultural relations between the two countries, this research aims to explore the academic experiences and examine the gender identity and performance of Filipino female student migrants in Korea. This qualitative study was carried out by conducting in-depth interviews of five (5) Filipino female students enrolled in a graduate school programme in Korea at the time of study. As high-skilled women from a developing country, Filipino female students construct an understanding of the society they are in based on observations and experiences from both home and host cultures. In some cases, they choose to reconstruct their gender identity and performance to align them with Korean gender norms. The results of this study provide supplementary insights on educational migration and how this process affects gender relations.
***

Gender Identity, Social Class and Conflict based Perception of Mobility: Case of LGBTTI-Q individuals from and in Turkey
(1294) Pınar Yazgan (Sakarya University), Oğuzhan Uzun (Sakarya University), M. Murat. Yüceşahin (Ankara University), Deniz Eroğlu-Utku (Trakya University)

The rapid political and social changes in today's world are having a serious effect on human mobility and, consequently, migration is becoming an increasingly important subject in different areas. One of these, which should not be ignored, is the position of LGBTTI-Q (lesbian, gay, bisexual, trans, and/or intersex) individuals in the migratory process. On the one hand, migration can effect change in gender norms which may enable the migrant to gain access to education and economic opportunities to which access was previously limited. These more equitable social norms can also improve LGBTTI-Q rights and access to resources. Either LGBTTI-Q individuals keep staying home or settle in a new country or they construct their own space and bring and perform new norms. On the other hand, migration can also result in gender discrimination, violence and in the proliferation of sex-segregated legal or illegal markets, for example, in the case of undeclared house workers and illicit trafficking of people. Furthermore, gender roles in the contemporary world are at the heart of understanding migration studies. From this point forth recent developments in human mobility have heightened the need for bringing the gendered approaches to all aspects of the issues of conflict and movement regarding states, societies, and families from broadening perspectives to the accurate understanding of the whole process (Sirkeci et al., 2012; Brettell, 2016). Analysis of the gendered effects involved in migration both internally and internationally was first carried out by E. G. Ravenstein (1885), LGBTTI-Q mobility, however, has also been an issue for many years now. Alas, however, not much progressed in the literature and policy making process in this regard and there is still a long way to go. The beginnings of LGBTTI-Q analysis dates back to the beginning of the 1970s. In 1984, Thadani and Todaro's produced a paper in which they point out Gender-related differences in migration and the need for an analysis of female migration. They offer a gender-specific framework and a model. We claim that our case study uncovers to the expanding stream of LGBTTI-Q migration and the problem of analysing LGBTTI-Q migration and its causes, results and difficulties. Caroline Sweetman (1998) argues that gender analysis is a fundamental tool in studying migration and claims that migration is part of a livelihood strategy, of a family that human existence depends not only on production but reproduction. In 2006, Manalansan's case study entitled "Queer intersections: Sexuality and gender in migration studies" analyses the Filipina migrant workers and the historical and theoretical development of sexuality in migration research. The study discusses the central role of sexuality in the future of gender and migration research. Recent developments in the field of LGBTTI-Q studies have led to a renewed interest in gender studies; nevertheless, these changes are having an effect and express a need for different theoretical and analytical tools other than sex as a dichotomous variable. There is an increasing concern about using theoretical approaches of gender relationally, spatially and contextually (Jolly and et al., 2005: 1). Therefore, gender is an increasingly important concept in different areas as an analytical tool and as a research lens to understand how societies function. Gender studies do not only include women's studies but also cover men's and LGBTTI-Q studies. The literature on gender has highlighted several issues specifically: gender identity, gendered representations, gender roles, gender politics, femininity and masculinity, and gender identities. West and Zimmerman (1987: 126) state that "doing gender involves a complex of socially guided perceptual, interactional, and micro political activities that cast particular pursuits as expressions of masculine and feminine "natures"". The aim of the research is to answer the questions on how LGBTTI-Q people perceive their gender identity? (i) If they have any tendency to migrate for any reason connected to their gender identity related to conflict? (ii), what are key reasons for changing their perception of mobility? (iii) Migration has been identified as a significant contributing factor for the rising of gender role awareness and building human capital. Generally, migrants are coming from conflict areas, and this forced mobility provides them access to resources such as health, legal, and financial services for gender- specific vulnerable people (Fleury, 2016). When it comes to specific levels of disadvantages, LGBTTI-Q is of particular importance. This case study from phenomenological approach and conflict based migration (see Sirkeci, 2003) focuses on LGBTTI-Q migration from Turkey and potential mobility of LGBTTI-Q individuals those who still living in the country. Specifically, we argue how social status and gender identity effect the perception of mobility in terms of from those who feeling sense of belonging that community. 20 participants were selected and classic and online face-to-face interviews were carried out. Both snowball sampling and purposive sampling methods were employed; 5 of them had already migrated and 15 are living in Turkey. Our main results show that there are strong connections between gender identity and the motivation which resulted in a decision of migration. Furthermore, social status is a key determinant of how they percept their life and how change their perception of discrimination and mobility.

***

Migration and Gender: The Case of Domestic Workers in Europe
(872) Aneta Tyc (University of Lodz)

According to ILO, migrant domestic workers are estimated at approximately 11.5 million persons worldwide, and "women comprise the majority of domestic workers, accounting for 80 per cent of all workers in the sector globally" (ILO, 2016, p. ix-x). Moreover, gender is fundamental in relation to migration. European women are being replaced in their household tasks by immigrant women from Africa, Asia and Eastern Europe (Triandafyllidou, 2013, p. 6). Firstly, my intention is to analyse international legal instruments relating to the protection of migrants: The United Nations', the ILO's and the Council of Europe's instruments. Secondly, using evidence from secondary sources, I will look at the effectiveness of human labour rights of migrant domestic workers residing in Europe. I will take as a starting point Drzewicki's typology which divides international standards concerning labour as a matter of human rights into four groups: rights relating to employment (e.g. the prohibition of slavery and forced labour); rights deriving from employment (e.g. the right to social security, the right to just and favourable conditions of work); rights concerning equal treatment and non-discrimination, and instrumental rights (e.g. the right to organise, the right to strike, and the right to collective bargaining) (Drzewicki, 2012, p. 75-77). There is evidence (eg. provided by recent high-profile UK court cases) of migrants being kept 'like slaves' in their employers' homes. It constitutes a proof of the existence and "possible prevalence of forced labour experiences among migrants in the UK" (Lewis et al., 2015, p. 589). According to the report of the non-governmental organisation Kalayaan from London, in 2010, 60% of migrant domestic workers registered with Kalayaan were not allowed out unaccompanied, 65% had their passport withheld, 54% suffered from psychological abuse, 18% physical abuse/assault, 3% sexual abuse/harassment, 26% did not receive regular/sufficient food, 49% did not have own room, 67% worked seven days a week with no time off, 48% worked at least 16 hours a day, 58% had to be available 'on call' 24 hours, 56% received a salary of 50 GBP or less per week (Lalani, 2011, p. 12 and 35). Such abusive working conditions have been qualified as 'modern slavery', not only in the literature, documents of governmental and non-governmental organisations, but also in case law (Mantouvalou, 2012, p. 165). Even if international instruments provide a broad protection of human labour rights of migrant workers, I will show – providing evidence of so-called modern slavery, hyper-precariat and discrimination – that some of them exist only in writing. I will prove insufficient effectiveness of the first three groups of rights according to Drzewicki's typology. Action should be taken to encourage countries to take responsibility for those pathologies. In particular, we should look at their approach to the ratification of international instruments, e.g. the lack of ratification or even signing (by any of the EU countries) of the International Convention on the Protection of the Rights of All Migrant Workers and Members of their Families, certainly does not provide the answer to the challenges of migration processes. In addition, the demands contained in the ILO's Fair Migration Agenda should be considered, e.g. with regard to increasing the effectiveness of laws on equal treatment and non-discrimination (ILO, 2014, p. 7). It is also to emphasise that host countries should improve domestic law and migration policies, ensuring decent working conditions and freedom from exploitation. As highlighted by ILO, law is to be drafted in an accessible way and should be accompanied by instruments and strategies for its communication and dissemination. Workers will benefit equally from such measures, as in many cases, they will be unfamiliar with applicable laws and protective provisions. The tools and methodologies available to ensure compliance with the applicable law should be adapted to the specific circumstances of domestic work. Protection of victims, prevention of transgression, accessible assistance, and complaints procedures are important from the point of view of all domestic workers, especially live-in migrant domestic workers (ILO, 2012, p. 4). Additionally, a system that pushes migrant workers to report abuses of their rights should be created, and employers should be prosecuted as a result of the complaints (Sivakumaran, p. 151). The situation of migrant domestic workers could be also improved by implementing programs analogous to the Irish pilot scheme of labour inspections of private homes (Murphy, 2013, p. 611-613; Daly, 2013, p. 119-120). The aim should be to establish monitoring and inspection systems to cover unregulated work in the informal economy, especially domestic work (Lean Lim et al., 2003, p. 44).

***

Women's Social Rights and Migration in Turkey: A Legal Analysis from Gender Perspective
(954) Altın Aslı Şimşek Öner (Atılım University)

Legal gaps are considered as a weakness on protecting and promoting human rights for everyone, especially for migrants and refugees. Thus, legal systems lack of gender perspective causes an on-going discrimination and violence against women. In this regard, the subject of this study is gender stereotypes constructed, reproduced or contested in legal texts and practice about immigrant or refugee women's social rights in Turkey. There are three main arguments in Turkey about the obligations of the state on immigrant/refugee women's social rights. First of all women's experience in the context of migration or asylum is not visible enough in migration law, refugee law and practice. Secondly there are criticisms against social rights about their justiciability. These criticisms make the migrants and refugees human rights weak and vulnerable against violations. For example, liberal, legal theory claims that social rights are abstract and unspecific, not justiciable. They do not have the characteristics of a subjective right. Third argument is feminist critics about the efforts on finding solutions to immigration issue and refugee crisis without correlating them with social rights and feminism.Within this scope the analysis of legal texts and case law is made by using feminist legal theory. This theoritical framework is used for examining the reasons why immigrant or refugee women's experiences are not visible in social law. Understanding these reasons is going to help us to see injustice and discrimination caused by gender stereotypes. Therefore, the main research questions of the study are as following: What are immigrant or refugee women's social rights in Turkey? Is there an effective legal infrastructure for enjoying these rights equally both with male migrants/refugees and Turkish citizens? Looking through a gender perspective, does the Turkish constitutional principle about welfare state have enough mechanisms to protect, respect, promote and fulfill migrant/refugee women's social rights. Thus, the aim of this paper is to explore how gender stereotypes in legal system construct margianalised and disadvantaged groups in hierarchies among genders and citizens. The study shows that the relationship between migration and women's social rights should be understood beyond an anti-migration politics or safety concerns of modern nation states. Rethinking this relationship and findig solutions to migration/asylum issue from a gender perspective provide women's human rights. By taking into account that legislation and jurisdiction are not gender neutral, the focus is on the legislations regulating social rights and migration and the case law about these regulations. The legal instruments available under the United Nations Women's Convention (CEDAW) and The Council of Europe Convention on Preventing and Combating Violence Against Women and Domestic Violence (Istanbul Convention) are used for naming gender stereotypes in Turkish legal system and exposing their harms to women's human rights. Different forms of gender stereotyping in domestic law (i.e.

Turkey's Constitiution of 1982, Law On Foreigners and International Protection, Law No. 6284), and jurisprudence as well as international conventions (i.e. the International Covenant on Economic, Social and Cultural Rights (ICESCR), The Convention Relating to the Status of Refugees, International Convention on the Protection of the Rights of All Migrant Workers and Members of Their Families), legal repertoire of the European regional human rights regime (i.e. European Social Charter, European Convention on Human Rights) and the case law and the decisions of the comissions are analysed. Thus, cases from Turkish Constitutional Court feature heavily in the discussions as examples of whether judges reproduce and continue to underwrite gender stereotypes or eliminate them, and contest and seek to transform gender stereotypes about immigrant/refugee women.
***

SESSION 8E – Migration and Governance

	Room: B1
Chair	**Ülkü Sezgi Sozen, University of Hamburg, Germany**
766	The evolution of the legalization of illegal migrants in Greece: A note on the new legislative framework – **Anna Katsari**
1056	Stakeholder's collaboration into the Registration and Procedure Centres in Switzerland - **Marwan Alkhouli, Rémi Baudoui**
887	Asylum Under Pressure: International Deterrence and Access to Asylum - **Vasiliki Kakosimou**

The evolution of the legalization of illegal migrants in Greece: A note on the new legislative framework
(766) Anna Katsari (Secretary General of Decentralized Administration of Peloponisos, Western Greece & Ionion Directorate of Foreigners & Immigration Department of Residence Permissions of Laconia)

During the 1990s, Greece experienced a significant flow of migrants originating from the neighboring Balkan countries (Albania, Romania, Boulgaria) and also from the former USSR (Russia, Ukraine, Moldova, etc.), a fact that transformed Greece to a receiving country from a sending one, a fact attributed to the improvement of the quality of life and the economic conditions of the country, making it susceptible to migration flows (Fakiolas, 2003). The mass inflow of migration proved that the country was not well prepared to face the numerous migrants entering the state and this is supported by the fact that the first legislation on this issue was implemented in 1997 and 1998 (Presidential Decrees 358 and 359). The actual implementation of an efficient migration policy in order to deal with the issue of legalization of illegal migrants began in 2001 with the law 2910/2011 (Tsitselikis, 2013). This law gave the opportunity to native employers to legally call migrants for employment (on certain jobs with relative skills and abilities) and also included provisions for green card issuances on specific groups of illegal migrants who were provided temporary visas according to the previous legislative frameworks (Triandafyllidou, 2014, 2015). Only in 2005 and after the passage of law 3386/2005, the Greek state started to deal with this issue on a more permanent basis (following relative EU legislation) allowing the legalization of illegal migrants who were residing in the Greek territory until the 31st of December 2004 (Psychogiopoulou, 2015). Nevertheless, all of the above legislative attempts did not have a long-term focus and were mainly temporary in nature, indicating that the central government considered migratory flows as rather temporary (Triandafyllidou, 2009, 2014, 2015). The scope of this study is to analyze the contribution of the new legislative framework (laws 4251/2014, 4332/2015 and the ministerial decision 58114/2016) which refers to the legalization of illegal migrants who reside and work in the country. Due to the particular characteristics of the Greek terrain and in conjunction with the lack of efficient monitoring mechanisms (border control and policing) the inflow of illegal migrants is constantly increasing during the last two years. The new legislative framework deals with the issue of illegal migration in a more permanent manner, allowing illegal migrants who live and worked until now in the country to obtain a work permit with all prerogatives and obligations abiding to it. Being more specific, the new framework allows migrants who: a) had entered the country legally three years before the submission of their application, b) provide proper documentation indicating that they have stayed in the country and have created family, social and economic relations (bonds) during the last seven years thus their stay will be deemed necessary and c) had a residence permit which has expired during the last decade before the submission of their application. Moreover, the new framework takes into consideration the second-generation migrants who were born or concluded at least six years of schooling and were not allowed a permit so far and until the submission of their application were still residing in the country. In conclusion, the new legislative framework has a more permanent character relative to the previous ones and provides the opportunity to a large number of migrants who live, work and have created social and family bonds in the country to be granted a legal residence permit. Nevertheless, one issue that has to be considered by the central government is that Greece may be transformed to a friendly destination for illegal migrants and this is justified by the lack of efficient border monitoring mechanisms making very difficult to control for illegal inflows and in conjunction with the provisions of legalization of the new legislative framework.

***

Stakeholder's collaboration into the Registration and Procedure Centres in Switzerland[8]

(1056) Marwan Alkhouli (Geneva University), Rémi Baudoui (Geneva University)

Our paper aims to explore the administration and accommodation process of asylum seekers in Registration and Procedure Centres (CEPs) of Swiss Confederation, which are managed by the State Secretariat for Migrations (SEM). It is the result of an unprecedented survey we have conducted in two federal Centres. By exploring the various stakeholders and service providers' work tasks and spaces, we highlight the interactions between SEM administrative staff, management and accommodation employees (ORS Service) and asylum seekers who are received in the CEPs for a temporary period at the beginning of the asylum procedure. We will be confronted with the hypothesis that despite the integrated reception process implemented by the SEM in these centres, tensions persist between the various stakeholders and are due to several factors such as the limits and the monitoring of space, the cohabitation between people of different ethnic origins, the background and personal history of each asylum seeker as well as the different interpretation of the integration concept.

***

Asylum Under Pressure: International Deterrence and Access to Asylum

(887) Vasiliki Kakosimou (Greek Asylum Service)

International Deterrence is on the rise putting forward complex migration control arrangements. It implies extraterritorial measures undertaken by a developed state in

---

[8]With an excellence scholarship from Swiss Confederation, this paper is part of a research work on the Integration Process of Syrian Refugees in Switzerland. We would like to thank the Swiss Confederation for the funding of this research, as well as the State Secretary of Migration and ORS Society for their close cooperation and the data provided in this purpose.

cooperation with a developing state to prevent access to asylum in the first state, and has unilateral aspects, such as visa controls, interdiction on the high seas etc, alongside with international ones, such as financial incentives, gifting and equipment, training and capacity building etc. Since non-entrée has evolved, different approaches have been mapped: US States, Australia and EU are the main exponents of international deterrence. Non-refoulement is a principle in international refugee law which prohibits states from returning a person to any territory where there is a risk that his or her life or freedom would be threatened on account of race, religion, nationality, membership of a particular social group or political opinion. The prohibition of refoulement must be respected in any type of forcible removal, including deportation, expulsion, extradition, informal transfer or 'renditions' and return of refugees to countries of origin or unsafe third countries. It also implies that refugees or asylum seekers cannot be prevented from requesting protection, even if they enter unlawfully, or if they are at the border. It encompasses non-admission of stowaway asylum seekers and push-backs of boat arrivals or interdictions on the high seas and in general the non-rejection at the frontier, if rejection would result in an individual being forcibly returned to a country of persecution. It may also concern fences, as the construction of border fences may limit the ability of persons in need of international protection to seek and access protection. If there are no places along the border that asylum seekers can reasonably reach to request asylum, the presence of a fence might violate the obligation of Member States to comply with obligations related to access to international protection. While the ECHR is not an international instrument concerned with the protection of refugees per se, Article 3 has been interpreted by the ECtHR as providing an effective means of protection against all forms of return to places where there is a risk that an individual would be subjected to torture, or to inhuman or degrading treatment or punishment. Article 19 of the EU Charter not only provides the principle of non-refoulement, but its first paragraph prohibits collective expulsions. The provision applies to everyone and it is not limited to third-country nationals or to people claiming international protection. The source of this provision is Article 4 in Protocol No 4 of the ECHR. Its purpose is to guarantee that every decision is based on a specific examination and that no single measure can be taken to expel all persons having the nationality of a particular state. The Refugee Convention also prevents expulsions and refoulement of persons who have already been determined to be refugees, safe for a few exceptions. These exceptions to the fundamental prohibition against expulsion and refoulement of refugees are grave in their consequences and the threshold for their application is uniformly recognized to be high. The absolute prohibition of torture- a form of added protection- is a principle in international human rights law applicable at all stages of the asylum-seeking process. Any state under whose jurisdiction a person falls, by being on its territory or under its effective control, has a corresponding duty to meet its obligations under the international prohibition of torture. Some member states have sought to limit the extraterritorial nature of the prohibition of torture and ill-treatment to minimize its impact on expulsion cases. Mass refugee influxes have led to numerous arguments about the need to adapt, limit or exempt from the fundamental principles relating to non-refoulement. States have turned to restrictive migration policies by pursuing a series of measures to prevent refugees and other migrants from entering their territory. Borders closures and barriers, pushbacks, interdictions on the High Seas and off-shore processing arrangements, are deterrence strategies applied by states to avoid their international obligations, instead of burden sharing as a response to mass influxes.

***

SESSION 8FGöç, Eğitim, Kültür

	Room: B2
Chair	**Abulfaz Suleymanov, Uskudar University, Turkey**
1120	Yabancı Uyruklu Yükseköğretim Elemanlarının Beyin Göçü: Erzurum Atatürk Üniversitesi Örneği – **İsmail Öz, Pınar Laloğlu**
1208	Türkşeker Fabrikalarında Güvencesizliğin ve Ayrımcılığın Çerçeveleri: İşgücünün Market Entegrasyonunu ortadan kaldıran Taşeronluk Sistemi – **Bahadir Nurol, Bayram Unal**
856	Fransa'da Yaşayan II. Nesil Türklerde Görülen Kültür Değişikliği ve Kimlik Tanımı - **Nurcan Aksoy**
1200	Bulgaristan Türkiye Bağlamında Roman (Çingene) Dilbilimi Çalışmalarına Karşılaştırmalı Bir Yaklaşım - **Talat Şafak**

Yabancı Uyruklu Yükseköğretim Elemanlarının Beyin Göçü: Erzurum Atatürk Üniversitesi Örneği

(1120) İsmail Öz (Atatürk University), Pınar Laloğlu (Atatürk University)

Modernleşme çabalarının bir sonucu olarak 19. yy'ın ilk yarısında Osmanlı devletinde batı tarzında kurulmaya başlanan ve yeniden gözden geçirilen yüksek eğitim kurumları, batılı eğitmenleri ve uzmanları da beraberinde getirir. Özellikle ordunun ihtiyaçları doğrultusunda açılmış olan Tıbbiye ve yenilenen Mühendishane ve Harbiye gibi kurumlar, eksikliği duyulan modern pozitif ilmin öğretimini batılı hocalar aracılığıyla ilk elden sağlamaya çalışır. Bu modern kurumlardan mezun olmuş pek çok aydın subay, Osmanlı devletinin yıkılışının ardından ön sıralar içinde yer alacakları kurtuluş mücadelesiyle yeni devletin temellerini atarken, sivil kimlikleriyle yarıda kalan modernleşme uğraşının devam etmesi yolunda kararlılık gösterir. İnkılap ve devrimlerin merkezinde yer alan eğitim, yükseköğretim anlamında da uygulamalara sahne olur. Yeni ulus-devletin Osmanlı öncesi bir tarihsel köke yönelik vurgusu, bu köklerin tarihsel yazımına kaynaklık edecek, iyi eğitimli pek çok sürgün Rusya Türkünün (Yusuf Akçura, Sadri Maksudi Arsal, Zeki Velidi Togan gibi) yanı sıra alanında uzman yabancı bilim adamlarının (çoğunlukla tarihçi ve antropolog) da yurda davet edilmesinin yolunu açacaktır. Söz konusu tarih yazımı kadar yurt dışında cereyan eden gelişmeler de yeni bir beyin göçünün ülkemiz topraklarına yönelmesine vesile olur. Avrupa'daki faşist hareketler ve özellikle nasyonel-sosyalizmin tırmandırdığı Yahudi düşmanlığı, Türk üniversiteleri için dünyaca ünlü pek çok önemli ismin kazanılmasına imkân sağlar. Günümüze gelindiğinde ise üniversitelerin uluslararasılaşma çabaları içinde ikili anlaşmalarla öğretim elemanı değişimi yapılırken, beyin kazanımı ve beyin dolaşımı aracılığıyla da pek çok alanda üniversitelerde yabancı öğretim elemanı istihdam edilebilmektedir. Bu üniversitelerden biri olarak Atatürk Üniversitesinin uluslararasılaşması bağlamında yabancı öğretim elemanları tarafından tercih edilirliği, çalışmanın temel sorgulamasını oluşturur. Nitel araştırma yöntemine dayalı olarak yabancı öğretim elemanlarıyla gerçekleştirilecek yüz yüze görüşmelerle elde edilen veriler, üniversitenin ileriye yönelik gelişimci ruhuna vizyon oluşturacak şekilde yorumlanacaktır.

***

Türkşeker Fabrikalarında Güvencesizliğin ve Ayrımcılığın Çerçeveleri: İşgücünün Market Entegrasyonunu ortadan kaldıran Taşeronluk Sistemi[9]

(1208) Bahadir Nurol (Ömer Halisdemir University), Bayram Unal (Ömer Halisdemir University)

---

[9] Bu çalışma Ömer Halisdemir Üniversitesi Bilimsel Araştırma Projeleri desteği kapsamında SOB2015-10 BAGEP proje numarası ile yürütülmüştür.

Taşeronluk sistemi işgücü maliyetlerini düşürür iken aynı zamanda görünür bir şekilde, geçici, çocuk, genç, kadın ve yaşlı işgücü gibi dezavantajlı grupların iş ilişkilerinde ayrımcılığa maruz kalmasına neden olmaktadır. Bu ayrımcılık göçmenlik gibi genel bir şemsiye altında tanımlanan geçici, çocuk, genç, kadın vb. işgücü açısından son derece daha fazla öne çıkmaktadır. Bunun nedeni, işçilerin çoklu ayrımcılığa maruz kalmasına ek olarak göçmenlerin çok daha karmaşık bir ayrımcılığa maruz kalmasıdır. Zira bir işçi, hem göçmenliğinden hem de kadın olmasından dolayı ayrımcı pratiklerin nesnesi haline gelebilmektedir. Çoklu-Ayrımcılık kavramı, göçmenlik, işçilik ve ayrımcılık üçlemesindeki negatif ilişkiyi ölçülebilir bir kavramlaştırmaya dönüştüren önemli bir kavramdır. Ayrıca, çalışma ortamında ve ilişkilerinde ırk, dinsel farklılıklar, yaş, toplumsal cinsiyet ve göçmenlik üzerinden olası tüm ayrımların kesişimini ifade ettiğinden de kullanışlı bir kavramdır. Bu çalışmada, çoklu ayrımcılığı normal ve göçmen işçiler üzerinden uygulayan taşeronluk sisteminin işgücünün market entegrasyonunu ne derece güvencesizlik sınırına getirdiği tartışılmaktadır. Bu çoklu ayrımcılık, işyerinde işçilerin güvencesizlik dereceleri, toplumsal cinsiyetleri ve doğum yerleri üzerinden tartışılmakta olup, Bor Şeker Fabrikasında işçiler, usta başları ve taşeronlar ile derinlemesine ikili görüşmeler yapılmıştır.
***

Fransa'da Yaşayan II. Nesil Türklerde Görülen Kültür Değişikliği ve Kimlik Tanımı
(856) Nurcan Aksoy (Namık Kemal University)

Genel anlamda, göç olgusu ile birlikte ele alınan kültürleşme, kimlik tanımı, uyum, asimilasyon gibi konular, sosyal bilimler alanında ve özellikle de toplumbilim çalışmalarında genellikle karşımıza çıkmaktadır. Avrupa'da Türklerin sosyal entegrasyonu, son yıllarda önemli politik ve sosyolojik konular arasında yer almaktadır. Biz çalışmamızda Fransa'da yaşayan, özellikle II. nesil Türk göçmenlerin bu ülkeye sosyal uyumlarını ele aldık. Çalışmanın temel amacını Fransız kültürünü benimseyen, bu kültüre uyum sağlayan veya Türk kültürünü devam ettiren/ettirmeyen düzeyin kuşaklararasındaki farklılıkları ve bu farklılıklar üzerinde etkili olan faktörlerin incelenmesi oluşturmaktadır. Demografik değişkenler ve sosyal uyum boyutları olan kimlik, etkileşim ve sosyal-ekonomik-politik konum değişkenleri birlikte ele alındığında yapılan analiz sonucunda kuşak değişkeninin Türk kültürünü devam ettirme ile negatif yönde ve Fransız kültürünü benimseme ile de pozitif yönde ilişkili olduğu fark edilmiştir. 1960lı yıllarda iş bulma ümidi ile Avrupa'ya göç eden Türkler bu göç dalgasını başlatan nesildi. Yeni bir ülkeye giden Türkler için bu fırsat zamanla ekonomiye dönüşerek artık yeni bir yaşam alanı halini almıştır. Kastoryano'ya göre, 1980li yıllarda Türkler göç gerçeğinde artık bir dönüm noktasına ulaşılmıştır. Bu dönüm noktası kimi zaman göçün kendisini ilgilendiren toplumsal deneyim konuları olmuştur veya vatandaşlık ve entegrasyon sorunları üzerine siyasi içerik olarak düşünülmüştür. (2003: 4). Bu bağlamda Fransa'da yaşayan Türk asıllı Fransızlara 50 soruluk bir anket hazırladık ve bulundukları ülkede günlük davranışları, tutumlarını, tarzlarını, her iki kültürde türdeş ve ayrışık fikirlerini kültürel ve psikolojik faktörlerin etkisiyle tarif etmelerini istedik. Sonunda tüm verileri topladığımızda varılan sonuç ise iş bulma ümidiyle giden nesilden farklı olarak II. nesil, değerlerlerini korumuş, uyum sağlamış veya asimile olmuştur. Bu çoklu kavramı araştırmacı Berry, genel anlamda dört farklı sınıfa ayırmıştır: Yeni kültüre uyumun baskın olduğu durum 'asimilasyon', her iki kültüre de uyumun olduğu durum 'çoklu entegrasyon' etnik kültüre uyumun baskın olduğu durum 'ayrılma' ile her iki kültürün de reddedildiği durum 'marjinalleşme'dir. (2003: 23). Araştırmacının bu yorumlaması göç olgusunda 'Kültürleşme Ölçeği' olarak kullanılabilmektedir.
***

Bulgaristan Türkiye Bağlamında Roman (Çingene) Dilbilimi Çalışmalarına Karşılaştırmalı Bir Yaklaşım
(1200) Talat Şafak (Trakya University)

Avrupa Konseyinin "Number of Roma and Travelers in Europe" 2007 raporuna göre Bulgaristan'da 650 000 civarında, Türkiye'de ise 1 900 000 civarında Roman yaşamaktadır. Bu rapora göre Türkiye Avrupa'da en fazla Roman bulunduran ülkeyken, Bulgaristan Avrupa dördüncüsüdür, kendisinden önce Romanya ve İspanya vardır. Sorunsal olarak, Bulgaristan ve Türkiye'de Roman dilbilimi çalışmalarının durumu karşılaştırmalı olarak tespit edilmeye çalışılmıştır. Çalışmamızda Bulgaristan Ulusal Kütüphanesindeki kitap koleksiyonları ve Ulusal Dokumentasyon ve Enformasyon Tez Sorgulama Merkezi (НАЦИД) teki tezler ve makaleler, aynı şekilde Türkiye'de Milli Kütüphanenin katalogları, Ulusal Tez Merkezindeki tez koleksiyonları ve makale sorgulama siteleri tarandı, buradan elde edilen veriler Romanların (Çingenelerin) konuştuğu anadillerle ilgili (Bulgarca, Romanes, Türkçe, Ulahça,) gerek kültür dilbilimi, budun dilbilimi, toplum dilbilimi, ruh dilbilimi, genel dilbilimi, derlem dilbilimi, uygulamalı dilbilimi çalışmaları sınıflandırılarak sayısal veriler elde edildi. Ayrıca her iki ülkede makale, bildiri, kitap, tez, sınıflandırılmasına da gidilerek yıllara göre Romanların konuştuğu diller ile ilgi bir sınıflandırma daha yapıldı. Romanları çalışan kurumlar tespit edildi ve her iki ülkedeki sayıları karşılaştırıldı. Ayrıca Bulgaristan ve Türkiye'de Romanların dilini çalışan bilim insanların sayıları da karşılaştırıldı. Son olarak, bildiride her iki ülkede çalışılan ve çalışılmayan alanlar tespit edildi ve sunuldu.
***

SESSION 8G – Göç ve Edebiyat - 7

	Room: B3
Chair	**Yıldız Aydın, Namık Kemal University, Turkey**
1237	'Göç Kültürü ve Çatışma Modeli' Temelli Bir Göç Romanı İncelemesi: Yüksel Pazarkaya'nın Savrulanlar'ı -**Ali Tilbe, Kamil Civelek**
833	İvan Alekseyeviç Bunin'in "Lanetli Günler" Eserinde Ekim Devrimi ve Vatan Savaşının Halk ve Entelektüel Kesim Üzerindeki Etkisi– **Nuray Şahinkaya**
855	Göç Yazınında Bir Kimlik Üretimi Olarak Dil – **Semran Cengiz**
1323	Sürgünlüğün Yazar Üstündeki Etkileri: Refik Halit Karay Örneği - **Mert Öksüz**

'Göç Kültürü ve Çatışma Modeli' Temelli Bir Göç Romanı İncelemesi: Yüksel Pazarkaya'nın Savrulanlar'ı[10]
(1237) Ali Tilbe (Namık Kemal University), Kamil Civelek (Atatürk University)

Göç olgusu genel bir bakışla; insanların ekonomik, toplumsal, siyasal ya da ekinsel çok değişik nedenlerle yerleşik uzamlarından başka bir uzama yerleşmek için yaptıkları devinimler olarak tanımlanabilir. Bu tanıma en uygun devinimlerden biriside altmışlı yıllarda başlayan ve günümüzde de karşılıklı olarak süreğen ekinsel bir nitelik kazanan Türklerin Almanya'ya ulusötesi göçüdür. Bu bildiride İbrahim Sirkeci ve Jeffrey H. Cohen'in Çatışma ve Göç Kültürü Modeli temelli geliştirdiğimiz göç yazını inceleme yöntembilimi yaklaşımıyla çağdaş Türk-Alman yazarlardan Yüksel Pazarkaya'nın Savrulanlar adlı romanını incelemeyi erek ediniyoruz. Roman, iki ülke arasında arafta kalan insanların ekinsel ve toplumsal uyum ve yeni bir kimlik edinmek için vermiş olduğu savaşımı, yıllar sonra gurbette bir trende karşılaşan iki askerlik arkadaşının yeniden kurulan dostluklarını ve aile öykülerini çarpıcı bir biçimde betimlemektedir.

---
[10] Bu çalışma, Namık Kemal Üniversitesi Bilimsel Etkinliklere Katılım Destek Programı kapsamında desteklenmiştir.

İvan Alekseyeviç Bunin'in "Lanetli Günler" Eserinde Ekim Devrimi ve Vatan Savaşının Halk ve Entelektüel Kesim Üzerindeki Etkisi
(833) Nuray Şahinkaya (Trakya University)

Rus göçmen yazarların önde gelen isimlerinden olan ve Rus yazarlar arasında ilk olarak Nobel Ödülü'ne layık görülen İvan Alekseyeviç Bunin, Rusya tarihinde büyük bir öneme sahip olan 1917 Ekim Devrimi, I. Dünya Savaşı ve Vatan Savaşı yıllarına tanıklık etmiş bir yazardır. Bu çalışmada; Rus halkının hayat çizgisini değişime uğratan Ekim Devrimi ve Vatan Savaşı yıllarında, ülke bütünlüğünün bozulduğu, "Tek Rusya" kavramının yok olduğu bir dönemde, halkın ve entelektüel kesimin çektiği sıkıntılar İ. A. Bunin'in Окаянные Дни (Lanetli Günler) eseri üzerinden aktarılacaktır. Bu çalışmanın amacı henüz Türkçeye çevrilmemiş ve Türkiye'de üzerinde bir çalışma yapılmamış olan "Lanetli Günler" eserinde, yazarın tanıklık ettiği ve kronolojik olarak anlattığı 1918-1920 yıllarının halk ve entelektüel kesim üzerinde bıraktığı izleri yansıtmaktır.

***

Göç Yazınında Bir Kimlik Üretimi Olarak Dil
(855) Semran Cengiz (Bartın University)

Bu çalışmada, göçle gelen kimlik yitimi/inşası sürecinde dilin etkinliği, oynadığı ideolojik rol, Türk-Alman Edebiyatı örnekleminde ve yazın dünyasının gerçekliğinde ele alınmaktadır. Küreselleşmeyle birlikte ivme kazanan bir sosyal fenomen olarak göçün, toplumsal yaşamın her alanına olduğu gibi kültürel çalışmalara da etkisi tartışmasız ki çok büyük. Göç, bir kültürden başka bir kültüre geçişe zemin hazırlayan, çoğu zaman kişide ya da gruplarda travmatik semptomlar oluşturan bir olgudur; çünkü göç her anlamda yeni karşılaşmaların oluşmasına sebep olur. Dillerin karşılaşması da bunlardan biridir. Göçün hem bireysel hem de ortak kimlik alanlarına etkisi iki yönlüdür. Kişi ya da grup göç nedeniyle ortak kimlik alanından uzaklaşıp "öteki" nin kimlik alanına dahil olduğunda, geriye ve ileriye dönük olarak çatışmalı bir durum yaşar. Sahip olunan kimliğin korunması ya da karşılaşılan kimliğin yadsınması ekseninde gelişen bu çelişkili durum, hem bireysel hem de ortak kimlikte gediklere yol açar. Ortak kimlik, öteki karşısında çoğu zaman sinmeyi tercih ederken, bireysel kimlik psiko-somatik sendromlar halinde seyreden bir buhranlı süreç geçirir. Göç, önce kimlik yitimi ardından yeni kimlik inşası sarkacında kişiye/gruba gidiş-gelişler yaşatır. Bu süreçte dil belirlenmiş bir kültürel kimliğin en işlevsel sembolü vasfıyla, "öteki" yle kurulacak köprünün ilk ayağı olarak bir yandan değişimi hızlandırırken, bir yandan da değişimin önündeki en büyük engelleyici olabilir. Kültürel kimliğin içinde dilin belki de en fazla görünür olduğu an, bu andır. Dil, kültürel kodları bireysel ya da sosyal anlamda aktarırken, göçün bellekte yarattığı gedikleri, yadsıma ya da inşa etme biçiminde doldurarak kişiye/gruba bir koruma alanı oluşturur. Böylelikle kültürel özdeşleşmenin bağı çözülür ya da güçlenir. İşte göç yazınının da sorunsalı olarak beliren bu durum, üç kuşaktır Almanya'da gelişen edebiyatın yazarlarınca hangi bakış açısıyla ele alınmakta ve kimlik-dil özdeşliği yazın dünyasının gerçekliğinde ne kadar yer bulmaktadır soruları etrafında irdelenmektedir.

***

Sürgünlüğün Yazar Üstündeki Etkileri: Refik Halit Karay Örneği
(1323) Mert Öksüz (Karamanoğlu Mehmetbey University)

Refik Halit Karay, yaşamı boyunca farklı siyasi iktidarlar tarafından iki kez sürgüne gönderilmiştir. (1. 1913/1918-2. 1922/1938) Bu sürgünlerin izleri onun yaşamında ve edebî metinlerinde görülmekle beraber özellikle kurmaca yapıtları Memleket Hikâyeleri, Gurbet

Hikâyeleri ve Sürgün'ün içeriği yazarın sürgünlük hayatında yaşadıklarından oluşmaktadır. Karay'ın kurmaca metinlerini merkeze alarak onu sürgün edebiyatı bağlamında değerlendirmiş farklı hacimde incelemeler yapılmıştır. Bu yazıda ise Karay'ın sürgünlüğü ve bu süreçte geçirdiği entelektüel değişim, yazarın gündelik yaşamı düzleminde değerlendirilecektir. Bu doğrultuda Karay'ın sürgünlüğüne dair basın dünyasındaki yaklaşımlardan, yazarın kendi yayımladığı anılarından ve bir diğer sürgün entelektüel Rıza Tevfik'e gönderdiği mektuplardan yararlanılacaktır.

***

SESSION 9A – Work and Migration - 2

	Room: A1
Chair	**Benedicte Brahic, Manchester Metropolitan University, UK**
1346	Local Food Production and the Role of Migrant Labour: A Tentative Analysis of their Interrelationship in the case of Western Peloponnese (Greece) - **Apostolos G. Papadopoulos, Panagiota Kogiannou**
745	Migration: A Triangle of Aspiration, Opportunity or Exploitation? A Migrant's Perspective - **Shweta Sinha Deshpande, Aashna Banerjee**
774	Engaging the Albanian Communities Abroad: One on One Mentoring – **Joniada Barjaba, Arben Malaj**
1209	A Review of International Volunteers as a Transnational Consumer Type and a Case Study – **Nevin Karabıyık Yerden, Ebru Bilgen Kocatürk, Ferahnur Özgören Şen**

Local Food Production and the Role of Migrant Labour: A Tentative Analysis of their Interrelationship in the case of Western Peloponnese (Greece)
(1346) Apostolos G. Papadopoulos (Harokopio University), Panagiota Kogiannou (Harokopio University)

Migrant employment has been prevalent in rural areas of Greece and southern Europe in general for over two decades. The contribution of migrant labour in agriculture and food production is often mentioned in terms of providing unskilled labour and responding to seasonal labour demands. However, depending on the local production systems migrants fulfill different roles. Promoting quality food in Europe allows for less known localities into the world economic map. Consumers favour local food due to the fact that the 'local' is identified with a sense of trust, authenticity and security. The indigenous population who were traditionally employed in food production has aged and is less able to work in the fields. Migrants fill in a significant void in rural areas and food production in particular by responding to various labour demands. This paper aims at analyzing the interrelationship between migrant labour and local food production in an emblematic rural area of Greece. The research was carried out in the prefecture of Ileia and focused on two local products: a) wine grapes and b) watermelons. Both are vital food products for economic growth in the area. Migrant populations include in their majority Albanians, Bulgarians and Romanians, but recently there are Asian migrants, from countries such as India, Pakistan and Bangladesh. A number of interviews were carried out with farmers (10 interviews) who produce watermelons and wine producers (4 interviews). The paper is structured around the following axes: Firstly, the need of rural economies to shift towards local food production in order to achieve the target of local development. Secondly, the variation of migrant integration into local labour markets is related to migrants' origins and their socio-cultural background. Thirdly, the particularities of migrant contribution to local food production are seen through the eyes of farmers/ producers. Finally, the qualitative focus of research allows for a better understanding of migrant labour role in local food production. The analysis reveals that local food production is a significant factor for the economic development of rural areas. Moreover, migrants have boosted agricultural production, but they are introduced into local economies in form of specific migrant/ethnic groups with their own comparative advantages for farmers/ producers. It seems that Albanians are more accepted as semi-/un-skilled migrant labour in watermelon production, while on the other hand wine producers do not value migrant labour as an important input for their local food production process. Therefore, migrant labour is not necessarily valued in equal terms when considering different local food production systems. Their role in local food production is rather determined by the perceived capacity of the various migrant groups to integrate and contribute in the labour market.

***

Migration: A Triangle of Aspiration, Opportunity or Exploitation? A Migrant's Perspective

(745) Shweta Sinha Deshpande (Symbiosis School for Liberal Arts), Aashna Banerjee

In recent years, migration theory has accounted for the concept of agency in the phenomenon of human migration. However, migration theory even today does not account for lived experiences of migrants. These experiences stem from human agency in interaction with the home and the host spaces, and hence it appears that there is a need to relook at migration theory. The primary objective of this research study is to gain an understanding of the lived experiences of migrants, and evaluate the phenomenon of migration through the lens of the former in relation to the triangle of aspiration, opportunity and exploitation. Ethnographic data was collected in the form of case studies from 24 random migrants in Pune, India. The sample population is diverse in caste, gender (female n = 9; male n = 15), class, socio-economic backgrounds and the experience of mobility in terms of rural-urban, within urban and international geography (international n = 13 and internal n = 11). This data was collected by students in a Migration Studies course over a period of 12 months from August 2015 to May 2016. An analysis of the data collected led the researchers to develop the triangle of aspiration, opportunity and exploitation. This triangle is built on the foundation that all migrants possess and display agency to overcome the challenges posed by hostile and structurally mitigating home space. Migration both internal and international is used as an effective tool to restructure their lived experiences, motivated primarily by their agency and aspiration for a better life. The mobility from a home space to a host space leads to diverse experiences, positive to negative in nature. However, regardless of the negative nature of their experiences, migrants view their experiences of migration as primarily opportunistic, embedded in the idea of a better future while subduing the exploitative lived experiences. Therefore, the triangle of aspiration, opportunity and exploitation asserts that fuelled by their agency and motivation to overcome structural challenges in their home space, migrants perceive their lived experiences in the host space through a positive lens. By extension, regardless of the negative nature of their lived experiences, migrants perceive their experience of migration with opportunities which will lead to a higher level of well-being in the future. This leads to a negation of experiences which can be construed as exploitative in nature by external organizations and individuals. However, this does not take away from the exploitative socio-cultural conditions that are an inherent component of most migrant realities. Therefore, this triangle emphasizes the importance of migrant agency and provides a unique perspective in understanding the way in which migrants perceive their reality; as opposed to structural and functional perspectives, fuelling the increasing migration across the globe. In addition to developing the triangle of aspiration, opportunity and exploitation, the researchers found that there is a dynamic interplay of meso-level and macro-level factors, along with the micro element of the phenomena - the migrants themselves. This interplay leads to shaping of migrant agency and consequently determines the perceived nature of the lived experiences of migrants. In conclusion, the researchers assert that migration is primarily viewed as a positive and opportunistic experience by migrants. The experience of migration leads migrants to the path of the hedonic treadmill. Subsequently, the continued experience of migration by individuals due to the hedonic treadmill has led to the twenty first century being labelled as the 'Age of Migration'. Overall, the findings of this research have two-fold ramifications. First, it has ramifications for academia to relook theories of migration keeping in sight the lived experiences of migrant. Second, the research findings have ramifications for policy makers to include migrant friendly policies since the migrant perceives mobility as a tool for development and their future wellbeing.

***

Engaging the Albanian Communities Abroad: One on One Mentoring
(774) Joniada Barjaba (University of Sussex), Arben Malaj (Luarasi University)

Currently, the Western Balkans is facing the challenge of reinforcing peace and prosperity. While peace establishment is taking place, prosperity remains a challenge. Prosperity can be achieved through integration and economic cooperation. Peace establishment through prosperity is an important task, taking into account that the EU integration process has not been at its full potential. Successful development of economic integration requires sustained economic growth. Good social capital is a potential determinant that contributes to economic growth in the region. Social capital resources are diverse, but in this paper, we only focus on diaspora's potential role. We focus on Albania's diaspora because of several unique factors such as high migration flows, highly educated professionals, and effective cooperation with diaspora. There is an agreement that migration and development are linked. However, the impact of migration on development in the origin countries continues to be an open debate. Scholars are divided between migration optimists and migration pessimists. The optimists see migration as a positive phenomenon, having a beneficial impact on the development of countries (Lewis, 1954; Todaro, 1969). On the other hand, pessimists consider migration as a negative phenomenon undermining the sustained development of migrant sending countries (Frank, 1969; Papademetriou, 1985). In this paper, we examine the argument that Albanian communities abroad have the potential to assist in the development of Albania. One way for communities abroad to contribute is through promoting research and development and innovation. Studies show that these areas are important for the country's development (Afza & Nazir, 2007; Khan, 2015). Hence, Albania should focus on the advancement of scientific research and innovation through Diaspora's engagement. For this paper both qualitative and quantitative data were used. For gathering qualitative data, I used document review and analysis that involved examination of a variety of policies and literature in order to develop the theoretical framework of the research. Although my research was mainly based on qualitative approach, quantitative data were also collected. With the quantitative data, I was able to identify Albanian populations abroad and get country-specific information. The data mainly come from census and immigration sources available online. This paper focuses on engaging the Albanian communities abroad in the development of the country and having a clear approach to diaspora engagement. The term "Albanian communities abroad" refers to Albanian citizens abroad and any other individual that has ancestral or affinity based linkages with Albania. Albanian communities abroad are becoming important for Albania's development. While some scholars see Albanians abroad as a loss, the engagement of ACA can also be an asset for Albania. Brain drain can become brain gain and brain exchange (Ite, 2002). The Global Talent Competitiveness Index (2015–

16) ranks Albania 85 out of 109 countries. The Index shows that Albania needs a sustainable platform for cultivating and attracting talented Albanians from abroad. Based on Albania's context, we suggest that knowledge transfer through diaspora may be an important approach. Albanian communities abroad can enhance development through the outflow of knowledge and skills. Kosmo and Nedelkoska (2015) confirm that Albanian-American communities have a qualification advantage when compared to non-Albanian counterparts. Also, data shows that the most popular approaches of engaging communities abroad in the country's development are education (81%) and professional exchange (76%). The majority of Albanians abroad are well educated and overqualified (Barjaba, 2015). ACA possess valuable skills, experiences, and contacts that they can transfer to individuals in Albania through mentoring and coaching. Additionally, ACA can offer career guidance and study abroad counseling. Albania has an increasing number of students leaving to study abroad every year. Mentoring is an effective and powerful way to help different individuals progress. Many professionals from ACA can share their knowledge with the individuals living in Albania through temporary return in the country. However, a mentoring web platform can also be built, which does not require physical presence. Establishing professional networks that would connect Albanians abroad with professionals in the homeland is an important step. Networks provide information regarding job positions, facilitate mentoring, and highlight the scientific and professional achievements of overseas fellows. Also, statistical profiling of Albanian communities abroad is limited and remains a key task to be completed before trying to engage these communities. The government should consider building and implementing mechanisms to strengthen the country's ties with Albanians abroad, specifically Albanians coming from academia and business communities. Albanian universities and enterprises should lead this process.

***

A Review of International Volunteers as a Transnational Consumer Type and a Case Study
(1209) Nevin Karabıyık Yerden (Marmara University), Ebru Bilgen Kocatürk (Kırklareli University), Ferahnur Özgören Şen (Kırklareli University)

In this study, transnational consumers are researched. Transnational consumers are classified by some properties. One of them is high skill profesionals. High skill profesionals include employees of organizations operating in various countries. These organizations include profit-oriented organizations as well as non-profit organizations. Employees who are active on the voluntary basis of non-profit organizations are mobilized to take part in the international activities of their organizations in a short or long time in various countries. Today, the activities of both transnational organizations and transnational volunteers are increasing all over the world. However, the literature on transnational volunteer seems to be insufficient. This is an initial study aiming to conceptualize the subject of transnational volunteer. In addition, the study of transnational volunteering activities of Habitat, an international voluntary organization, is being studied. This study is a conceptual study based on literature review and a case study.

***

SESSION 9B – Movers and Non-movers

	Room: A2
Chair	**Jeffrey H. Cohen, Ohio State University, US**
971	Somali Non-Migrants and The Role of Transnational Family– **Marja Tiilikainen**
1193	Separated Families: To Stay or to Go - **Megan Passey**

Somali Non-migrants and the Role of Transnational Family
(971) Marja Tiilikainen (University of Helsinki)

An extensive body of research focuses on migrants and their transnational practices, transnational relationships and transnational family life. Much less is known, however, about the experiences of those family members in transnational families who, for one reason or another, are not mobile internationally but stay in the country of origin. For example, in the case of Somalis, much attention has been paid to asylum-seekers and refugees who resettled in Western countries following the civil war. Furthermore, research has focused on the role of Somali diaspora in the development, peace and conflict in Somalia as well as family connections of the Somali migrants and their children to the country of origin. This presentation will explore the experiences and views of those members of transnational Somali families, who have chosen to stay in Somalia or who have not had a chance to join the Somali diaspora. The aim of the presentation is to analyse, on one hand, reasons for their immobility, and on the other hand, the role of family members in the diaspora in the lives of non-movers in Somalia. The presentation draws on qualitative interview data that I have collected in Somalia (Somaliland and Puntland) as part of my research project "Islam and security revisited: Transnational Somali families in Finland, Canada and Somalia", funded by the Academy of Finland. In particular, I will analyse interviews of ten individuals, belonging to nine different families, whose transnational families in Finland and Canada are part of my larger research project. Furthermore, I will use as additional data 24 interviews collected in collaboration with some students of Puntland State University. Tentative results show that in addition to material security, family members abroad mean also other assets and opportunities. However, interviewed individuals and families in Somalia, as well as their family members in the diaspora, differed in terms of societal position, which further impacted the opportunities, strategies and relationships in transnational families.
***

Separated Families: To Stay or to Go
(1193) Megan Passey (Mixed Migration Platform)

The decision to move from the Middle East to Europe is made for a variety of reasons, and not only by those who make the journey. A significant body of research has been gathered on refugees and other migrants arriving in Europe in recent years, but comparatively little is known about how decisions to move or stay are made within families, nor about how irregular migration affects those left behind. This qualitative study sought to understand the different influences on decision-making within families across the Middle East, specifically how gender, cultural and socio-economic factors play a role. Focusing on the experience of 90 Syrian, Afghan and Iraqi families across five countries, the research examines how families negotiated the decision to migrate; how migration has affected the everyday lives of those left behind, as well as their aspirations and future intentions.
***

Children or Immigrants? Disputing Un-Accompanied Migrant Minors
(973) Olivia Teresa Ruiz (El Colegio de la Frontera Norte)

Children and adolescents have been migrating to the United States since the 19th century. While they have generally arrived in the company of family, most recently many have crossed the border on their own. According to USCBP* reports, 68,541 unaccompanied children (UAC) were apprehended in FY 2014. The numbers dipped to 39, 970 in FY2015, but climbed again the following year to 59,692, the majority arriving from Central America and Mexico. Their presence has been accompanied by a wide range of reactions at all levels of United States society and government, from calls to step up their deportation, to pleas to provide asylum, thus revamping the debate about who has the right to stay in the country and who should be expelled. In an effort to shed light on the reception and treatment of child and adolescent undocumented migrants to the United States, this paper examines two cases of civic mobilizations in response to federal mandates to temporarily house young undocumented migrants in the cities of Escondido and Murrieta, California, in the summer 2014. At first glance, the mobilizations in both cities appeared to adhere to protectionist and humanitarian discourses that have defined much recent debate concerning international migration. On closer examination, however, it becomes clear that the dispute reflected conflicting narratives regarding the young migrants' identity—on the one hand, as children, on the other, as immigrants, and the corresponding burden of responsibility of each. Protesters contended that the minors should be seen and treated as another potential threat of "illegal" immigration; as such, their plight was of their own making and their responsibility. Counter-protesters, in contrast, argued that the migrants were children, first and foremost, and thus vulnerable and deserving of support and protection. In short, to a large degree the conflict centered around disputing claims as to whether or not the minors were indeed vulnerable children, or, as I propose in more analytical terms, whether they embodied the narrative of child authenticity and innocence. As I conclude, the children's "failure" to live up to the narrative's premise and expectations made the young migrants appear unchild-like and suspect, which placed them squarely in the category of "illegal alien" and undeserving of humanitarian aid and protection, thus leading to their rejection in both cities. To identify dominant narratives and record events in both cities, I turned to on-line news accounts at the local, state, national and international levels. Methodologically, the paper employs a modified content analysis of narratives of immigration, one that, following Newton's suggestion, focuses on dominant themes. Sources used to contextualize both the young Central American and Mexicans' migrations as well as the forces driving the mobilizations in both cities include: USCBP statistics, census reports, results of the EMIF, records of local legislative proposals regarding immigration, and voting records, among other secondary sources. Conceptually, the paper draws on Schneider and Ingram's work on negatively-constructed social representations and Newton's study of the importance of narrative in configuring social problems related to immigration and placing blame. For narratives of children, I turn to the reflections of Arneil, Wall and Pasquerella on the moral construction of childhood. Borrowing from Boyer's and Santa Ana's work, I understand media as a form of mediation that plays a role in modern social subjectivity, that is, a medium of documentation that reflects and shapes social and political views and wider societal narratives.

***

Motives of Social Identity, Boundary Definitions, and Attitudes towards Syrian Refugees in Turkey

(816) Nagihan Taşdemir (Anadolu University)

The present study examined how the motives attributed to having a Turkish identity predict the attitudes toward Syrian refugees in Turkey. The study also examined how the in-group identification and definitions of Turkish identity boundaries mediate the relationships between the motives and inter-group attitudes. Social identity theory (Tajfel & Turner, 1979) proposed that in order to enhance their self-esteem individuals tend to evaluate their in-groups more positively compared to the out-groups. According to optimal distinctiveness theory (Brewer, 1991, 1993, 2007), the needs for belonging and distinctiveness shape the individuals' in-and out-group attitudes. More recently, researchers suggested that perception of in-group continuity (Smeekes & Verkuyten, 2014) and in-group efficacy (Fritsche et al., 2013) have an important influence in individuals' inter-group attitudes. Vignoles (2011) argued that all the motives for self-esteem, distinctiveness, belonging, continuity, and efficacy (and meaning) underlie the construction of social identities and it is crucial to explore which is/are stronger predictor(s) in a given context of social identity and inter-group relations. In the Netherlands, for example, researchers showed that among the others, the motive for continuity constitute stronger predictor for the national identification (Smeekes & Verkuyten, 2013) and perception of in-group continutiy increases the likelihood of negative atttiudes towards the immigrants (Smeekes & Verkuyten, 2014). However, there seems still scarce research examining the motives altogether in one study in the prediction of in-group identification and inter-group attitudes. The motives of social identity are also likely to affect how people define the boundaries of their in-group, which have often been shown as predicting the inter-group attitudes (Taşdemir & Öner-Özkan, 2016). Brewer (2001) argued that people tend to satisfy their need for belonging (and distinctiveness) in groups defined in exclusive ways than groups defined in inclusive ways. However, there seems no research examining these relationships empirically. Definitions of Turkish identity boundaries have been suggested as National Participation and National Essentialism. According to the former, "citizens of Republic of Turkey", "people who adopt and advocate Turkish culture", "people who live in Turkey", "people who contribute to Turkey", "people who speak Turkish" and "people who adhere to Atatürk's doctrine" can have a Turkish identity. According to the latter, "people who are willing to feel Turkish" (the reverse), "people who are Muslim", "people who have a Turkish father" and "people who have a Turkish mother" can have a Turkish identity (Taşdemir & Öner-Özkan, 2016). In a later study, however, the criteria about being a Muslim changed a dimension and loaded on National participation as considered in the present study. Researchers showed that different from the Western countries, in Turkey, the more inclusive definition (National participation) predict more negative inter-group attitudes than the more exclusive one (National essentialism), which have been associated with the construction of national identity in Turkey. The present study examined the mediating role of these definitions and in-group identification to predict the attitudes toward Syrian refugees considered in terms of perception of threat, social distance, and in-group favoritism. 157 university students participated in the study. They completed the measures of motives attributed to having a Turkish identity (15 items) (e.g., "To have a Turkish identity means to be proud of being Turk", "To have a Turkish identity feels oneself a part of wholeness", "Turkish identity is an identity that makes Turks distinctive from others", "Turkish identity is an identity that will exist forever"), definitions of Turkish identity boundaries (12 items), social distance (7 items), perception of threat (7 items), in-and out-group evaluation (2 items) and in-group identification (2 items). A series of multiple regression analyses were conducted to predict the in-group identification, boundary definitions, and attitudes toward Syrian refugees. Independent variables were the five motives attributed to having a Turkish identity. According to the results, in-group identification was predicted by the belonging motive, National participation by the self-esteem and belonging motives, and National Essentialism by the efficacy motive. In-group favoritism was predicted by the self-esteem and belonging motives, the perception of threat by the distinctiveness motive, and social distance by the self-esteem and distinctiveness motives. Among mediators, in-group identification predicted the in-group favoritism, National participation did the in-group favoritism and perception of threat, and National essentialism predicted the social distance. A model is tested suggesting the in-group identification, National participation and National essentialism as mediators in the relevant relationships, and also, National participation predicting the perception of threat and social distance and the distinctiveness motive predicting the perception of threat.

***

SESSION 9C – Mobility, Education, Culture

	Room: A4
Chair	**K. Onur Unutulmaz, Ankara Social Sciences University, Turkey**
946	The ERASMUS Experience as a Source of Motivation for Mobility: Understanding Education as Emigrational Capital in the Case of Turkey - **Besim Can Zırh, Eren Çalışkan**
1198	Inter-Generational Educational Mobility in Children of Migrant Sending Households and Its Impact on Human Capital Development in the Source Region - **Anu Abraham**
1137	Mobile People- Mobile Ethnographer: Thinking about Cultural Mobilities - **Maria Panteleou**
906	Social Determinants of International Students' Mobility: 'A Case of PhD Students from Turkey' - **Setenay Dilek Fidler**

The ERASMUS Experience as a Source of Motivation for Mobility: Understanding Education as Emigrational Capital in the Case of Turkey
(946) Besim Can Zırh (Middle East Technical University), Eren Çalışkan (Middle East Technical University)

The forms and strategies of border crossings have significantly changed during the last two decades in parallel to a series of dramatic transformations in the global system. On the one hand, political instability surrounding peripheral centres has triggered multi-layered and gradual population movements from the failed peripheral towards the countries of the centre. On the other hand, culturally and economically successful sections of peripheral societies have begun searching for more secure living conditions in the very same central countries. In the midst of these new global population movements, participation in international higher education programs can be turned into very valuable cultural capital, increasing the potential for emigration to countries of the centre. Needless to mention, as part of a larger politico-economic project, the ERASMUS Programme provides a very specific example of this phenomenon, as the program bridges young students from both the peripheral and central countries in the specific regional context of Europe. This study aims to understand how the decision to participate in the ERASMUS Programme is taken by higher education students in Turkey and what narratives have developed surrounding this decision in the case of Middle East Technical University (METU). METU is a Turkish higher education institution which has been involved in the ERASMUS Programme since the first ERASMUS pilot schemes in 2003. The number of student applications to the programme by METU students is steadily rising each year, from 37 beneficiaries in 2004 to 576 in 2016. As one of the leading universities in the country in terms of depth and breadth of international ties and as an institution using English as the language of instruction, students at METU are more open to international experience and developing significant capital towards emigration, facilitating their decision to leave the country in future. Within this framework, a comprehensive online survey will be applied to the cohort of 2016-2017 academic year METU applicants, which is expected to comprise more than 1,000 students. The survey will be specifically directed at the approximately 250 students who will be accepted to the programme. Among this participant group, 25 students will be selected according to their gender and socio-economic background and in-depth interviews will be conducted with these students and their parents before and after their ERASMUS experience. In the framework of this study, we aim to understand if the ERASMUS experience can be seen as a source of motivation for mobility in later years and if higher educational experiences can be studied as a form of capital facilitating emigration.

***

Inter-Generational Educational Mobility in Children of Migrant Sending Households and Its Impact on Human Capital Development in the Source Region
(1198) Anu Abraham (Indian Institute of Technology Madras India)

Any social phenomenon affects the society in which it takes place by changing its social fabric. Various studies have looked at the impacts of migration on the source region through multiple channels and multiples areas. These are mainly developmental impacts through the inflow of remittances, knowledge and skills, which had led to the accumulation of physical, social and human capital of the migrant sending households. Studies have analyzed the impact of migration on unemployment, poverty, income inequality, health and educational outcomes and other socio-economic aspects in the sending regions. The paper is an exploration of the impact of voluntary (?) economic migration originating in developing countries/regions, specifically those that are of a temporary/ cyclical nature, on the development of the source region with a focus on Human Capital. We frame migration of an individual as a household's joint decision to diversify income and reduce risk based on Stark's household model of migration and examines its role as a driver for development. The impact of migration on the source region is focused specifically on human capital development. It is analysed on the basis of educational attainment of children and human resource re-allocation of left behind women, in the household. The study analyses these queries not just as migrant – non-migrant differentials but also compares between households that have internal and international migrants. The southern Indian State of Kerala, India is the area of study as it has a unique feature of high social development and large temporary out-migration. We examine the impact of out-migration from Kerala on the educational attainment of children using the intergenerational educational mobility (IEM) Approach. The study hypothesis a positive causative relationship between the migration status of the household and the educational attainment of the child. The study also intends to analyse how much of this impact comes from the 'migrant status of the household' and how much of it due to the income effect arising from the remmitance received. Further, the sample of male and female children are analysed separately to explore possible gender specific differences in the IEM.

***

Mobile People- Mobile Ethnographer: Thinking about Cultural Mobilities
(1137) Maria Panteleou (University of the Aegean)

In current fluid and uncertain political, economic and social conditions are experienced by the most countries in the world, many people choose to emigrate in search of better living conditions. Anthropological studies claim that the movement of people in modern globalized world is an ongoing, continuous and complex process in which migrants establish relations, create networks and connect many places beyond local and national boundaries (Schrooten, Salazar, & Dias, 2015, p.24-25). The possible routes of immigrants

are often involuntary, unpredictable and are influenced by the global political system of states that regulate and control the parameters of their transnational movements (Salazar & Smart, 2011, p.iii). Thus, we should consider the transnational context of their lives in order to understand the immigrants' experiences, which are constantly changing and are influenced by historical and structural factors and perceptions prevailing in both the country of origin and the host country (Glick Schiller et al., 1992, p.8). The aim of this presentation is to propose the approach of cultural mobilities as an analytical lens for understanding contemporary forms of movement, highlighting the multiple ways in which people and their cultural practices are not limited to a fixed ground, but constitute a part of multiple spatial networks and interconnections (Glick Schiller & Salazar, 2013, p.185-186). The establishment of a unified approach to mobility, which will examine the general category of the movement in all its range, is problematic because all forms and types of mobility are deeply impregnated with the cultural meanings of each society and should be studied within the specific cultural, economic and social conditions which are created (Glick Schiller & Salazar, 2013, p.196). The instability and fluidity that characterize the cultural mobilities of immigrants' routes lead us to search for new methodological tools, far removed from the traditional fieldwork that predominantly performed in stable environments. The fieldwork among the mobile groups is a practice that unfolds, according to Kurotani, into scenes and spaces and not in sites or places, which exist only through active participation and presence of the informants (Kurotani, 2004, p.210). The ethnographer is asked to follow their temporary lives and to put himself within the global system where the multiple aspects of their experiences unfold and to interpret their experiences living with them and not looking at them and interpreting them "from above» (Marcus, 1995). As aptly pointed out by Wulff, if she was not able to follow the Irish dancers who studied on their trips to Japan and Washington, she would be the only one that would be left behind in the field. Think of a field researcher without field (Wulff, 2002, p.119). Concerns on particularism of knowledge in multi-sited research which results in this context should be sidelined because even if we succeed we are constantly present in the movements of our informants, paraphrasing Geertz, we will always hear a discussion that has started before we have arrived to the field and which will continue after we have gone (Kurotani, 2004, p.211). Adopting the approach of cultural mobilities in migration studies, we highlight the subjective migratory experiences, which reflect on culturally defined reasons for mobility. The latter in turn affect other factors such as the sense of belonging, power relations, nationalism and transnationalism (Salazar, 2010, p.64). Looking mobility "from below" in conjunction with the policies adopted by the states for her - "from above" – can be given sustainable solutions to the immigration issues that afflict the global world.
***

Social Determinants of International Students' Mobility: 'A Case of PhD Students from Turkey'
(906) Setenay Dilek Fidler (University of Westminster)

Studying abroad was described in literature, "a stepping-stone to permanent residency" (Gribble, 2008, p25) or as "the first step toward settling in a foreign country" (Gungor and Tansel, 2003, p15). Furthermore, non-return PhDs are defined either as "la crème de la crème' (Docquier and Rapoport, 2009) or 'elite brain drain' by emphasizing the fact that they are the best and brightest ones amongst highly qualified mobile groups. Nevertheless, despite being recognized as an issue the mobility of PhD students has received scant attention, particularly PhD students from Turkey in the UK. Additionally, earlier studies have failed to explain how development (both at national and individual level) affects mobility and have overlooked capabilities and aspirations of individuals in the mobility

process. Therefore, in order to fill the theoretical and knowledge gap in contemporary mobility studies, this study focuses upon PhD students from Turkey (Sending Country) in the UK (Receiving Country), drawing upon the Theory of Structuration by Giddens and the Capability Approach by Sen. The main motivation behind choosing these two countries is that the UK is the second most popular destination for international students in the world (UKCISA, 2016) and international students comprise the second highest proportion of UK migrants (Jena and Reilly, 2013). Turkey is one of top international student sending countries in the world and one of the target markets for international students of late for the UK (HM Government, 2013). In the last decade, non-returning students have become an important issue for Turkey (Gungor and Tansel, 2014). The purposes of this study are to: (1) identify the factors impacting on the mobility of international students. (2) evaluate how far the capabilities and functioning of international students influence their mobility. Accordingly, in-depth semi structural interviews were conducted with 40 PhD students, 4 professors and 4 experts at micro, meso and macro levels between January and April 2017. Findings suggested that firstly; although, there are different factors at macro, micro and meso levels that play a role in students' return or non-return plans, politic factors in the form of such as the anti-democratic practices, the current conflict between the Turkish and the Kurdish population together with freedom of speech in and out of academia were considered as the main factors influencing return to Turkey. Secondly, capability has a significant role in future mobility plans and studying abroad expands students' capabilities and choices, regarding their mobility plans. This paper will extend the debate on international mobility beyond an economic perspective and it will provide an insight into political, social and cultural aspects behind the mobility by considering both the diversity of individuals (e.g. gender) and the multiple motivation factors (from instrumental to intrinsic values) behind mobility. This study's findings could be significant for those countries that have similar experiences to Turkey and the UK in terms of tackling the loss of highly qualified people or attracting them, in order to expand the highly qualified proportion of their population. It would also be helpful to both the UK government and its related bodies, for instance, the British Council, the Home Office and future research on international student flows and highly qualified mobility e.g. OECD, the World Bank.
***

SESSION 9D – Gender and Migration - 4

	Room: A5
Chair	**Kim Kwok, Caritas Institute of Higher Education, Hong Kong**
790	Deconstructing Gender-Migration Relationship: Performativity and Representation - **Mustafa Murat Yüceşahin**
1182	Intersectional Approaches to Gender and Mobility - **Anitta Kynsilehto, Elina Penttinen**
1362	Between War and Europe: Humanitarian and Political Aspects of Refugee Crisis - **Ali Askerov**
767	Family Capital, Education and Cross Border Mobility-Evidence from China Family Panel Study – **Xiaochen Zhou, Jia Li**

Deconstructing Gender-Migration Relationship: Performativity and Representation
(790) Mustafa Murat Yüceşahin (Ankara University)

A rainbow-variety of theories has been debated upon to explore the underlying dynamics and reasons behind migration. Majority of the research made in the field confirmed that main motivation behind migration is the will to attain a dignified life standard with an elevated economic, social and environmental status. Not being limited down to an economic event only, migration presents its obvious aspect, that it is 'culturally produced, culturally expressed and cultural in effect'. A close look into the nature of migration will immediately reveal its selective nature. 'Migration selectivity' manifests itself as the migration tendency that is determined only in accordance with various factors such as diverse characteristics of the individual's socio-demographic, socio-economic, and socio-cultural statuses. Therefore, it is obvious that this diversity in these characteristics such as age, education, financial wealth, and other factors may or may not trigger migration, and on various levels of intensity, even if it does. Migration's highly selective nature further encourages us, the researchers, to take one step further into the depths, perhaps review gender-aspect of this social phenomenon. A closer look into migrants' social, economic strategies and practices in transnational social spaces will walk us through some objective comparisons: While an overall comparison of men and women in terms of international migration will reveal almost no difference in developed countries, the difference is much more distinct in less developed countries where men portray higher rates of migration in search of employment. Women, on the other hand, with much less mobility, were identified as the care provider within the well-defined boundaries of households. Other comparisons on a scale of other socio-demographic indicators also play role in migration selectivity. That is, factors such as marital status, parental status, gender relations and practices will significantly shape migration process, migrant selectivity and the (re)production of transnational spaces. Although there is no chronological time line to pinpoint exactly when the gender-focused approach in migration perhaps first began, the first steps of this particular approach to migration studies were heard towards the end of 19th century, thanks to E. G. Ravenstein, well-known geographer, who referred to the presence of some gender-perspective related differences in migration patterns. The fact that these differences lacked in-depth analysis and were undocumented, caused gender-approach in migration studies to remain invisible until 1970s, the years of feminism-based analyses first blooming with a focus shift on women issues in social research. In line with the gradual growth of awareness and of the importance of studying migration-gender relations also in a multi-disciplinary perspective, feminist migration scholars shifted their focus from studying women towards studying 'gender, as a system of relations which was influenced by migration' in the mid- and late-1980s. Since 1990, there is an obvious increase in the academic interest focusing on 'feminization of migration', a concept to correspond to the dynamics of women's increasing participation in international migration in recent years. The post-modern era then unfolds its most important characteristics, which are formation of new stress field, a new pull-push polarity - between localization and the increased globalism; and self-manifestation of the neoliberal policies in urban areas. Rise in international mobility of populations in this new era triggered and is currently further increasing the interaction between the gender practices, norms, cultural routines performed by such variety of new identities in the recently migrated areas. This is exactly why; it is gaining further significance to focus on gender-migration relations in the context of post-modern dynamism. And it is through this dynamism that transnational social and all spaces are reconstructed or reproduced. The relation migration has with movement, mobility-gender stands as important as not to be underestimated solely down to being addressed as gender inequality in migration/movement. Studying in the field of gender-migration relation certainly is not easy either, due to the complexity inherent due to multi-façade nature and many other inputs inherent in this subject relation. Upsurge in globalization and technological developments not only facilitated mobility of populations in the world but also created a new human capital, which led to the reconstruction of cosmopolitan geographies. In the meantime, boundaries and patterns of the cities densely populated with international immigrants have been undergoing certain changes as triggered by international mobility of populations. This triggering affect, along with how it is interwoven with gender-migration texture, causes the cultural acts in the region of origin and total human capital to be transferred to the destination. What is actually transferred to the destination is far more than what is immediately visible: These are all set of experience and accumulated culture back in the immigrant's country of origin, such as all cumulative understanding of gender roles, gender practices; ways, perhaps routines to cope with life challenges; what confirms and maintains the immigrant's identity, especially through gender roles and practices; and thus inequalities as possibly formed by and as reflection of their social strata, age, language, religion, ethnicity, level of education, demographic features etc. This is what turns transnational spaces into increasingly cosmopolite and complex structures from migration-gender relation perspective. In fact, what cannot possibly be overemphasized at this point is that not even the push-pull polarity of the economic activities between the country of origin and the destination is exempt from gender-issues or from migration-gender aspect being part of the subject pull-push polarity. Indeed, as Jarvis et al. stated: "The starting point of any gender analysis of migration has to be that economic push and pull factors are not gender neutral" (2009: 177). As clearly seen, many receiving countries already present cultural textures in the neoliberal order to which the immigrant is generously welcomed to the existing gender inequality weaved into the country's economy and market conditions. With some help from neo and/or post-liberal influences, economies and market conditions of these countries are reconstructed as to neglect gender inequality. In fact, they reproduce gender-based division of labour; segregation of private-public spaces and inequalities. This is why, it is crucial to ensure that the gender-based approaches towards migration take into account the inequality patterns both in sending and receiving country. This is especially important as the dominant gender-regime from the sending countries, - although with some possible variations from individual to household levels-, is transferred to and therefore is likely to affect that of the receiving country, or vice-versa. The dominant gender-regime of the receiving country, in response, may potentially grow hybrid with the influence from immigrants' gender practices in its diaspora/transnational spaces. This potential formation and process of a hybrid is then almost a result of the two colliding gender regimes (partly subject to be shaped by individual or household strategies, practices) and is therefore focal interest of gender analysis of migration. This is why; migration is an inclusive process; and therefore, deserves a comprehensive study, where complex relations in terms of gender practices and how they mutually interact and weave one another are analysed. Thus, gender analysis of the migration process addresses a set of complex relations of factors no longer limited down to families, households or women's lives, but expanded to a larger perspective as to include immigrants' lives and employment processes for both sexes, the politics and governance of migration, neoliberal or welfare state policies toward migration or foreign-born populations in diasporas.In this paper, I aim at introducing a theoretical spatial approach in order to reach a resolution in gender-migration relation dynamics. While doing so, I bring together gender relations and practices of the country of origin and destination. My paper centres on performativity and representation of migration-gender relations in terms of establishing transnational spaces. First, I review gender practices of the migrating households in the scope of performative patriarchal power relations. Secondly, I address the relations among gender, migration and economic reconstruction in transnational spaces. Finally, discuss the interactive transformation of gender, international migration and urbanization process within the scope of reproduction of transnational social spaces.

   ***

Intersectional Approaches to Gender and Mobility

(1182) Anitta Kynsilehto (University of Tampere), Elina Penttinen (University of Helsinki)

Our world is characterized by mobility. The number of refugees on the global scale has increased considerably. Meanwhile border control measures and legal avenues for mobility have been severely curbed, and the political climate has become all the more violent against racialized and gendered "Others". Business elites traverse the fast-track lines to financial hubs and tourists discover new destinations. Ageing societies need people from abroad to perform care work. Domestic workers carve out nearer and further paths to reach employment, often leaving their family members behind in need of care. This paper examines global mobilities from gendered perspectives, asking how gender together with race/ethnicity, social class, nationality and sexuality shape globally mobile lives. Drawing on postcolonial feminist scholarship, critical disability studies and queer studies, we develop analysis that cuts through economic structures, policies and individuals enacting agency and demonstrate how intersectional feminist analysis helps to comprehend uneven mobilities. We argue that engaged ethnographic analyses of various different forms of mobility and immobility are fundamental for understanding, imagining and relating to the world in manifold ways.

***

Between War and Europe: Humanitarian and Political Aspects of Refugee Crisis
(1362) Ali Askerov (University of North Carolina)

The new wave of the violent conflict in the Middle East has caused a grave humanitarian crisis which, in turn, created political, social, and economic problems for many nations in the West and some Middle Eastern countries, such as Jordan, Lebanon, and Turkey. As the crisis grew, it became more apparent that most European countries were reluctant to accept refugees from the Middle East, and subsequently, the humanitarian crisis shifted to a political form, at least partially; and the issue became a topic for negotiations between the European Union (EU) and Turkey. The latter is the largest receiver of refugees and perhaps the best host country that has offered estimable opportunities for its refugees. This paper will discuss the basic policies of the Turkish government to address refugee problems in the country and examine the details of the negotiation between the EU and Turkey. The methods used to collect data for this project are interviewing and content analysis.

***

Family Capital, Education and Cross Border Mobility-Evidence from China Family Panel Study
(767) Xiaochen Zhou (University of Hong Kong & King's College London), Jia Li (University of Hong Kong)

China has been the largest source country for international students. From 1978 to 2014, there have been accumulatively 3.5 million international students. In this background of educational internationalization, there is emerging number of Chinese parents having the intention to send their children study abroad. International education can accumulate cultural capital and reproduce social advantages in the long term, and for those international students, their international credentials are rewarded over local graduates back home, which trigger another round of privilege reproduction in the long run. In this context, international educational decision-making becomes an important issue to be studied. However, what is the situation of Chinese parents' intention of children's international education, and what are the possible familial factors that may affect the decision-making of the Chinese parents still remain uncovered. The study explores a set of hypotheses regarding the relationships among parental intention of sending children studying abroad and parental educational expectation, family capitals, including economic, social, and cultural capital. Data from the China Family Panel Study (CFPS) (2014 wave) was adopted.

The dataset contains adequate information on the community and household background, as well as self-reported questions that assess parental intention of sending children studying abroad. The analytical sample size was 5124 and the study tested whether parental intention of sending children studying abroad can be delineated by family background and further investigated the distinctive dispositions towards the relationship parental educational expectation in China. Two main theoretical perspectives are adopted in this study to understand the overall picture of the Chinese parents' intention to send children study abroad, which are reproduction theory built by Bourdieu (1986) and the family educational decision-making model first developed by Breen and Goldthorpe (1997). While reproduction theory tends to provide explanation on the role of education in class reproduction and social mobility on a macro level, family educational decision-making model assists to underline the importance of rational decision-making within a family in children's educational attainment. Based on Bourdieu's reproduction theory, social capital and cultural capital are crucial elements in the reproduction of multiple opportunities including the access to educational resources, with important implications on educational outcomes, labor market differentials and social mobility. In this study, family cultural capital was generated from parents' education, economic capital was generated from family income, assets and educational expense, and social capital was generated from the families' network. The dependent variable is measured by the question that directly asking parents whether they have ever thought about sending their children to study abroad. In addition, according to the "model of educational decisions" built on rational action theory by Breen and Goldthorpe (1997), the upper class is indicated to have high abilities and educational expectations, which also affect the intention of making educational decisions. The variable of educational expectation in this study is measured by parents' expectation regarding the lowest level of education the child should achieve. The relationship between parental educational expectation and their intention of sending children to study abroad, the correlation between family capital and parental educational expectations are examined under the guideline of family educational decision-making model. Descriptive and logistic regression analysis methods have been adopted. The preliminary findings are: 1) In line with Bourdieu's reproduction theory, the three forms of family capitals that been tested in this study are positively associated with the parents' intention to send children studying abroad; 2) As suggested by the family educational decision-making model, the educational expectation of the Chinese parents has a strong positive correlation with their intention of children's international education. 3) Parental educational expectation plays a mediating role in affecting the relationship between family capitals and parents' intention to send children study abroad. The findings indicated that the situation of Chinese parents' intention of international education is consistent with the western theories predictions, and besides the objective family capitals, the subjective educational expectation plays a crucial role in family educational decision making. The potential contribution of this study is to build the scholarship to uncover the national situation of parental intention of sending children to study abroad, and also to figure out the affecting familial factors in educational decision-making. In addition, it also attempts to test the western educational theories in the modern Chinese context. The limitation of this study firstly lies in cross-sectional design. Besides, only associations but not causal relationships can be summarized based on the model of this study.

***

SESSION 9E – Political Participation and Migration

	Room: B1
Chair	**Elli Heikkilä, MigrationInstitute of Finland**

Political Refugees Who Migrated to the UK from Turkey after September 12, 1980 Coup D'état: Processes, Social Integration and Political Reactions
(1105) Barış Mutluay (Hacettepe University)

The main aim of this study is to investigate the changes in 37 years period of different political identities and strata (socialists, Kurds, Alevies) of Turkish origion migrants who migrated from Turkey to the UK as political refugees following the military coup d'etat on September 12, 1980, and to compare the differences between the various perceptions of them concerning the time of migration and today situations. The data of the study are collected with 375 household surveys, 75 structured and semi-structured interviews done with the related residents of Cambridge, Cardiff, Bournemouth, Coventry, and particularly in London where the Turkish population resides in England at most in 2016. To achieve the aim, firstly, the reasons of migration from Turkey to the UK are searched. Secondly, a comparison made on their political views, economic standarts and life expectations between the time they arrived UK and today. It is found that there are important changes in their political views, political insprations, political thoughts and behavioral conducts from beginning to today time.
***

Turkey's External Voting Experience: The Case of Germany and France -
(810) İnci Öykü Yener-Roderburg (University of Duisburg-Essen University of Stasbourg)

Across the world, the majority of constitutions enshrine the right of their citizens to vote. However, citizens living outside their home countries come across difficulties while exercising their voting rights. The situation generally stems from restrictive election procedures or the lack of voting regulations for the citizens living abroad. The increase in the number of migrants heightened the interest of the overseas electorates and accordingly policy makers of their home countries. Countries like Turkey with a sizable overseas voting population started extending right to vote to external voters for a better state of democracy. This study examines the changes to Turkish election law in 2012 that enabled external voting for Turkish nationals living abroad since August 2014 Presidential Election. It has been observed that starting from 2014 election, the two general elections that took place in June and November 2015, and the referendum in April 2017 had different procedures while electorates were casting their votes. Despite every change that has been put into effect positively influenced the voter turnout, analysis of these procedures is necessary to have a better approach in minimizing the future challenges. Due to its focal area, this work will be empirical research that would be analysed both qualitatively and quantitatively. Having the two largest Turkish populations outside of Turkey, Germany and France will be the case countries. Therefore, the primary sources will be the detailed results of the elections that took place in August 2014, June and November 2016, and lastly in April 2017. In addition to the election results, in-depth interviews will be conducted to 30 people from each country. Samples will be equally distributed across the levels of demographic variables.

International Immigration and Election Results in Dutch Municipalities
(908) Panagiotis Chasapopoulos (Tilburg University)

The literature distinguishes between economic and non-economic factors that determine individual attitudes towards immigrants. In particular, public opinions on immigration appear to be shaped by labour market conditions, welfare system concerns and by social or cultural considerations of the local population (Scheve and Slaughter, 2001; Mayda, 2006; Hanson et al. 2007; Dustmann and Preston, 2007; Facchini and Mayda, 2009). Economic theory suggests that immigration has a significant impact on the labour market by affecting the potential wages and the employment opportunities of natives (Card, 2001; Borjas, 2003; Ottaviano and Peri, 2012; Dustman et al., 2013; Docquier et al., 2013). In addition, there are also important fiscal consequences of immigration in receiving countries due to redistributive benefits and taxes. The participation of immigrants in the social security and welfare programs may have serious fiscal spillovers through the contributions that foreigners pay and the public benefits they receive (Lee and Miller, 2000; Dustmann et al., 2010; De la Rica et al., 2013). Consequently, natives who benefit from the presence of immigrants in the country are likely to encourage further immigration while the part of local population which is negatively influenced might prefer limiting immigration inflows. Beside the economic determinants the literature underlines also the importance of other social and cultural factors that shape public opinion on immigrants. Actually, immigration changes the composition of the host country's population imposing non-economic externalities on the local society. Natives' attitudes on immigration are likely to be influenced by concerns over 'compositional amenities' associated with common language, customs and religion in their neighborhoods or workplaces (Card et al., 2012). Furthermore, cultural differences between natives and immigrants could be perceived as a treat to ethnic composition and traditions of the local population and thus they strongly affect people's attitudes toward foreigners (O'Rourke and Sinnott, 2006; Dustmann and Preston, 2007). Moreover, racial prejudices that immigrants are more prone to be involved in criminal activities than locals have been a cause for additional security concerns (Mayda, 2006). As stated by Dustmann and Preston (2001), increasing immigration inflows can determine individual attitudes toward foreigners by two different ways. On the one hand, according to the authors, social interaction and frequent communication with immigrants could eliminate the existing racial prejudices of natives (contact hypothesis). On the other hand, the intense participation of immigrants in the society is likely to spread a fear of loss of ethnic identity and culture of local population. Therefore, immigration issue plays an important role in determination of natives' attitudes toward foreigners which in turn can affect their political opinion and voting behavior. Previous research reveals that the number of immigrants and the negative public opinion on them have a profound impact on election outcomes and support for parties with anti-immigration views and agenda (Lubbers et al., 2002). Indeed, recent empirical studies find a significantly positive effect of immigration on the success of extreme right parties in Europe. Otto and Steinhardt (2014), show that an increase in the share of foreigners enhances the electoral success of radical right parties, using data on the city districts of Hamburg. In addition, Hamon (2012) argues that increases in local ethnic diversity in Danish municipalities lead to electoral support for anti-immigrant nationalist parties. Similarly, Halla et al. (2012) find a positive effect of the residential proximity of immigrants on votes for the extreme right party in Austria. The purpose of this paper is to empirically investigate the relationship between international immigration and political ideology in The Netherlands. More specifically, we aim to study how immigration inflows and stock of foreigners affect the electoral success of radical right-wing parties in Dutch municipalities. Furthermore, in order to understand whether differences do exist between different municipalities we also examine the role of crucial socioeconomic, political and cultural factors. Therefore, additional variables such as the economic prosperity and urbanization level of municipalities as well as composition and educational level of the local population are taken into account in our model. Moreover, previous restrictive immigration climate which enhances the support for ethnic exclusion and cultural differences among natives and immigrants are included as moderators in the relationship above. Consequently, by this way the current study intends to complement previous research on individual attitudes towards immigrants and contribute to the growing literature on international immigration and political outcomes providing empirical findings from Dutch municipalities. With regard to the dataset of this study, we draw our data from two different sources. First, we use information on our dependent variable political ideology, which is measured by the outcomes of national elections in Dutch municipalities, from Electoral Council (Kiesraad). Moreover, data on immigration inflows and stock of foreigners are provided by Statistics Netherlands (CBS). CBS provides also information about the rest of explanatory and control variables in our model such as composition of population, educational levels, crime rates etc. Finally, our dataset consists of 338 Dutch municipalities and it covers the last five national elections (2003-2017) in The Netherlands. Our preliminary empirical findings indicate that the stock of foreigners in Dutch municipalities does not have a significant effect on the support of extreme right parties in the national elections of the Netherlands.

***

Role of Argentina's State Policies and Civil Society Activism in Refugee Integration
(1009) Asya Pisarevskaya (University of Milan)

This paper is exploring the discourse of state policies and civil society activism addressing the integration of forced migrants in contemporary Argentina. Argentina was a popular destination for European forced migrants in the first half of the XXth century, and increasingly for Latin Americans – in the second half. Nowadays, asylum seekers originate from Africa, Syria, Eastern Europe and Latin America. These groups are quite diverse in their socio-demographic and cultural characteristics (Dirección Nacional de Población, 2014) what results in the different needs and different level of support required in the process of adaptation and integration to life in the host country. According to previous research conducted, integration is a complex, two-way process, involving receiving society and immigrants (Ager & Strang, 2004; Castles, Korac, Vasta, & Vertovec, 2002; Da Lomba, 2010; Mestheneos & Ioannidi, 2002). On the receiving side, there are at least two types of actors: the governing institutions and local individuals. The state regulates the legal framework of integration and through policy, it can support civil society activism in welcoming the newly arrived populations. Civil society may take action, where the support is needed, but the state's intervention is absent or inefficient. As Ager and Strang (2008) highlight in their theoretical framework of integration, there are multiple domains in which this process happens: socio-economic markers of wellbeing; social connections; linguistic, cultural and security facilitators; and foundation of integration – access to equal rights and formal acceptance of a migrant as a member of the host society (citizenship). In each of these domains, the roles of state, of the host civil society and of the integrating individuals vary. For example, some aspects are regulated largely by laws, others influenced by the informal connections and community support, yet others by individual capacities and aspirations of immigrants. Of cause, it is important to remember that none of these elements act in isolation - they interact and conjointly shape the course of integration and its results. The study conducted in November-December 2016, consisted of the review of the legal texts and policy documents and 10 semi-structured interviews with practitioners of NGOs and representatives of the National Commission for Refugees in Buenos Aires, Argentina. The City and Province of Buenos Aires host the vast majority of forced migrants. Based on this material, I analyse how the regulatory framework, on the one hand, and the activities and projects of civil society organizations, on the other hand, support or hinder integration of refugees and humanitarian migrants. The results of this research show that asylum and refugee laws – as the product of the state's regulation – create strong "foundation for integration" (Ager & Strang, 2008). Asylum seekers have right to participate in the economic life of Argentina almost immediately after arrival. The law allows recognized refugees and humanitarian migrants to undertake official employment, become self-employed or start their enterprise. Access to public medical care and education is also guaranteed. After two years of residence all migrants become eligible to apply for citizenship. The difference in the social and economic rights between Argentine citizens and these categories of forced migrants is, thus, rather small. However, there are more problems with the ability of the forced migrants to exercise these rights dues to lack of language skills, prejudices or lack of knowledge from the side of the locals and bad economic situation in the country. The government hardly takes any active measures to battle this, neither in the form of funding. That is where some civil society groups come to help. Frustrated by inaction of the state agencies, they try to create and run programmes of livelihood and integration support on their own. Especially the Syrian crisis drew much attention and triggered mobilisation of new humanitarian initiatives. While there are few established organizations with trained professionals providing language support, job search advice and legal consultations, many new initiatives conduct their integration efforts on the basis of informal community networks. Current support of NGOs and civil society groups is available for small number of beneficiaries and, according to the practitioners, is usually targeted to the most vulnerable individuals. The integration of refugees does not seem to be high on the Argentine government's agenda, thus the role of the state is mostly in the creation of the legal conditions favourable for integration. And then, it is the task of humanitarian migrants and sympathetic local community organizations to make use of these legal freedoms in practice.

***

SESSION 9F – Access to Services

	Room: B2
Chair	**Nirmala Devi Arunasalam, University of Plymouth, UK**
928	How "Universal" Are Decentralized Health Care Systems in Spain and Sweden? An Exploration of Asylum Seekers and Undocumented Immigrants' Access to Health Care - **Daniela Cepeda Cuadrado, Camila Rodrigues-Vieira**
1163	Spaces and Social Services for Refugees in the Destination City: Mapping to Re-Think Reception – **Gisella Calcagno, Carolina Russo**
1184	Access to Health Services for Asylum Seekers and Refugees in Turkey: Comparison between Metropol and a Satellite City -**Faize Deniz Mardin, Nuray Özgülnar**
937	Barriers to Professional Help Seeking for Mental Health Problems among Thai Immigrant Women – **Melanie Lindsay Straiton, Tone Jersin Ansnes**

How "Universal" Are Decentralized Health Care Systems in Spain and Sweden? An Exploration of Asylum Seekers and Undocumented Immigrants' Access to Health Care

(928) Daniela Cepeda Cuadrado (Hertie School of Governance), Camila Rodrigues-Vieira (Hertie School of Governance)

As part of the challenges brought upon by recent immigration flows, European countries need to fulfill the international and regional obligations to secure the health of all. Within this context, many European governments claim that welfare systems can act as magnets of poorer immigrant populations, thus justifying their little willingness to attend their needs (Hagen-Zanker & Mallett, 2016). Questions arise on the kind of approaches taken by European countries, especially those with "universal" health care systems: are they providing asylum seekers and undocumented immigrants with equal health care access? Or is the universality principle only applied to serve their citizens' rights to health care? Based on the Spanish and Swedish health care policies between 2011 and 2015, this research project responds to the question: to what extent has the decentralization of universal health care systems limited or fostered asylum seekers and undocumented immigrants' access to health care? This abstract firstly explains the objectives of this research project. Secondly, it provides literature reviews on the nexus between immigration and health care access, and the decentralization of health care systems. Thirdly, it explains its methodology. To conclude, it provides preliminary findings. This research has normative, practical and theoretical implications. First, it provides an overall picture on whether Spain and Sweden fulfill their human rights obligations on health, according to the international and EU legal frameworks subscribed. Second, its findings can assist Spanish and Swedish governments in understanding the gaps in their approaches to immigrants' health care. Finally, it fulfills literature gaps and connects two theoretical strands: the nexus between immigration and health care access; and the effects of decentralization on equal health care access. With regard to the former, there is very little public health research on how different groups fare in health care systems (Bambra, 2007; Kawiorska, 2015). Some scholars analyze policy approaches on immigrants' health care rights, focusing on barriers shaping their access (Cuadra, 2012; European Migration Network, 2014; Mladovsky, 2009; Norredam & Krasnik, 2011; Norredam, 2008; PICUM, 2007). Others identify the type of immigration (Huber et al., 2008; Mladovsky, 2007) and incorporation regimes in place (Cuadra, 2012; Ingleby, 2009; Ingleby et al., 2005; Messina, 2011; Mladovsky, 2009) as shapers of immigrants' inclusion/exclusion in/from health care systems. However, they do not offer clear analytical frameworks that link these causes to the outcome (immigrants' health care access). This research identifies decentralization as a factor shaping immigrants' exclusion/inclusion to the health care system. With regard to the latter, a common concern is the effects of decentralization on health care access. Those proponents argue that local decision makers have more knowledge than national policymakers in capturing locals' health needs (Jiménez-Rubio & Smith, 2005). Critics say that decentralization could lead to a non-optimal health system structure, increasing territorial inequalities in health care access (Antón, et al., 2014). What is lacking is a consideration of how decentralization can influence immigrants' access to public services. To this date, there is no sufficient empirical evidence suggesting that decentralization actually hinders or facilitates health care access. This research follows a method of agreement (Hancké, 2009; Heijden, 2014) to compare the Spanish and Swedish health care systems. It also conducts within-case studies at the regional level in both countries. The analysis is based on assessing the latest policy documents and government programs that address the issue of asylum seekers and undocumented immigrants' right to health care between 2011 and 2015. Spain and Sweden have similar health systems, but differ in immigration histories, numbers of asylum seekers intake, treatment towards asylum seekers and undocumented immigrants, and public opinion on immigration. Ultimately, this research highlights how undocumented immigrants and asylum seekers experience different regional institutional environments (Beckfield, Olafsdottir, & Sosnaud, 2013) within similar national structures of health care systems. Sweden and Spain provided limited health care access for asylum seekers and undocumented immigrants between 2011 and 2015. This suggests an infringement upon international and regional commitments to protect the right to health care for all. Decentralization, however, allowed some regional authorities to act differently: while Västra Götaland and Comunidad de Madrid followed the national standards, Stockholm and Catalunya expanded health care rights for asylum seekers and undocumented immigrants beyond national guarantees. With no homogenous strategies across Spain and Sweden, the main consequence for asylum seekers and undocumented immigrants is that their health care access depends very much on where they are located.

***

Spaces and Social Services for Refugees in the Destination City: Mapping to Re-Think Reception
(1163) Gisella Calcagno (University of Florence), Carolina Russo (University of Naples Federico II)

Recent mass arrivals of migrants and asylum seekers at European borders are stressing the capacity of reception systems to guarantee adequate standards of living to needy, and vulnerable, applicants, according to international rights, European directives (2013/33/EU) and national laws. The dimension of the phenomenon, and its impact at urban level, is calling for a real monitoring and contingency planning (COM (2016) 465 final), and urban innovative actions (Urban European Agenda, 2016), to escape emergency and segregation, prospecting resilient communities and cities. Considering the Italian case study, reception system is managed by a multi-level governance (Ministero degli Interni, 2015), resulting in its complexity as a controversy, a shared uncertainty. Looking at the social and spatial dimension of welcoming asylum seekers and refugees, the study uses the Actor Network Theory (Latour, 2005), and its codification in the Mapping Controversies method (MACOSPOL, 2012), to investigate the relationships of humans and no-humans actors in reception systems, mediator of the service and the space of reception. To understand actors' spheres of activity, we develop a documental analysis of sector regulations and deriving administrative acts, which regulate the reception demand (Ministero degli Interni, 2016), and matched them with inquiries (Camera dei Deputati, 2014) and reports on reception conditions (Iniziative Civiche, 2016), which testify the effective reception supply. Results show the general emergency management (ECRE, 2016), origin of the lack, differentiation and inadequacy of reception spaces to ensure human rights and enhance social integration: the un-ordinary and top-down approaches obstruct the attention to the receiving local context and impact, and so its planning (as the settlement options and long-term solutions). The diffuse, dispersal, and sometimes hidden de-institutionalization of reception is suggesting to re-negotiate and share the actors'agency as precondition to re-think services and spaces. Reading the phenomenon through these lens, we can evaluate real reception needs, generating an information space as shared basis for strategic assessments, decision-making and participative planning. The proposed mapping should be used as an operative tool for policies at urban level, to measure its reception capability and analyse its reception potentiality: it is both a monitoring and planning tool, as required by forthcoming directions. Such capability and potentiality need to be known, systematised and connected, looking at existing or under-estimated resources, with the scope to regenerate reception systems. Opening the concept of reception centre in social infrastructure, we can escape critical spaces and segregation designing a urban network with communities-hubs of social innovation (Manzini, 2015), which should overlap and improve arrival cities in resilient and inclusive (HABITAT, 2016).

***

Access to Health Services for Asylum Seekers and Refugees in Turkey: Comparison between Metropol and a Satellite City

(1184) Faize Deniz Mardin (Istanbul University), Nuray Özgülnar (Istanbul University)

During the last decades Turkey became a country of immigration after a long emigration history. In Turkey by January 2017, there were 295.401 refugees and asylum seekers registered by United Nations High Commissionaire of Refugees and up to that 2.910.281 Syrian refugees registered by the Prime Ministry Disaster and Emergency Management Authority. The new law which has been published in April 2013, titled "The Law for Foreigners and International Protection" provides national health insurance also to asylum seekers while previously it was only available for refugees. This study aims to define the barriers to access to healthcare for refugees and asylum seekers in a metropolis as Istanbul and in a satellite city as Eskişehir after the establishment of the new law. Differences on access to health services between these two cities can be explained thanks to the description of rights in Migration and Health in Nowhereland report. Istanbul is a metropol where it is difficult to have a residency permit except some health conditions. This make Istanbul a "minimum rights" for access to healthcare compared to Eskişehir where almost everyone has a residency permit which defines Eskişehir as a "more than minimum rights" regarding to access to healthcare for refugees and asylum seekers. This is a descriptive study based on semi-structured interviews with refugees and asylum seekers in Istanbul and in Eskişehir at the Human Resources Development Foundation. This foundation has been working with refugees and asylum seekers since 2001 and gives legal consultations and psycho-social support. Interviews with refugees and asylum seekers took place at the Human Resources Development Foundation in Istanbul's office between 06.11.2015 and 08.01.2016 and in Eskişehir's office between 22.09.2016 and 14.10.2016. These interviews include questions about demographic data, UNCHR status, health problems and their experiences related to access to health services followed by their suggestions on how to improve the access to healthcare in Turkey. There has been 30 refugees and asylum seekers interviewed both in Istanbul and Eskişehir. Interviews were conducted with the help of translators of the Human Resources Development Foundation and participants' consents were taken. Among 30 people interviewed in Istanbul 14 (46,67%) were from Iraq, 12 (40,00%) from Iran, others were from Somali, Sudan, Central African Republic and Ethiopia. Regarding their UNHCR status 11 (36,67%) among them got the "Refugee" status and mean time was 24,18 ± 9,96 months to get this status. In Eskişehir among the people interviewed 12 (40.00%) were from Iraq, 7 (23,33%) from Iran, 5 (16,66%) from Democratic Republic of Congo, 4 (13,33%) from Afghanistan and others from Cameroon and Jordan. Regarding the UNHCR status 15 (% 50) of them got the "Refugee" status and mean time to get the status was 27,73 ± 22,18 months. Access to health services is analyzed on organizational, professional and community based barriers. The most common barrier in both cities was not knowing the rights to access to health services. In Istanbul one of the important barriers was difficulty to get residence permit and consequently to access to health services which is not a common barrier in Eskişehir. In Turkey, there has been done big steps regarding access to health services and health insurance coverage but still most of the refugees and asylum seekers do not know their rights. The society in Turkey is changing and the health problems are going to be much more diversified, therefore health services has to attune to this evolution.

***

Barriers to Professional Help Seeking for Mental Health Problems among Thai Immigrant Women

(937) Melanie Lindsay Straiton (Norwegian Institute of Public Health), Tone Jersin Ansnes (Oppdal Immigrant Services)

Thai migration to Norway has increased in recent years, with almost six times as many women as there are men (Sandnes & Henriksen, 2014). Family establishment is the most common reason for moving, with many women marrying Norwegian men (Sandnes & Henriksen, 2014). Research suggests that immigrants, especially women, experience more social disadvantage than non-immigrants (Statistics Norway, 2014; 2016). They are also at greater risk of social isolation, abuse and exploitation (Kotecha, 2009). These factors may be associated with mental health problems. Yet, Thai women are underrepresented in primary health care services for mental health problems (Straiton, Powell, Reneflot & Diaz, 2016). The purpose of the study is to explore the factors that influence Thai immigrant women`s willingness to seek professional help for common mental health problems. We conducted semi- structured interviews with fifteen Thai immigrant women living in Norway (31-55 years old). They had been living in Norway an average of 8 years. The women were asked about health care experiences in Norway, perceptions of mental health problems and the experience of stress / depression. The transcribed data were analysed using thematic analysis. Many of the women viewed common mental health problems as something manageable without professional help. Help-seeking was often associated with stigma. The women gained strength from their religious and spiritual beliefs and social support networks. Lack of familiarity, and negative experiences, with health care services in Norway may contribute to reluctance to seek help. Informants also experienced a number of structural barriers related to their position as immigrant women. Beliefs and values, experiences with the doctor and alternative coping strategies influenced Thai immigrant women's willingness to seek help for mental health problems. There are a number of barriers that need to be addressed in order to increase the propensity of help seeking, including improved accessibility of health information and awareness of available mental health services. This may also help reduce stigma. Health care providers should be trained in cultural competence in order to better understand immigrant women's challenges and needs.

***

SESSION 9G – Göç ve Edebiyat - 8

	Room: B3
Chair	**Füsun Bilir Ataseven, Yıldız Teknik University, Turkey**
749	İçsel Göç – Lena, Leyla ve Diğerleri - **Sevim Akten**
750	Yalnızlık Dolambacında Issız Bir Göçmen İncegül Bayram – **Tuğrul İnal**
748	Bilimin Mucizevi Göçü -Kanadı Kırık Kuşlar- Ayşe Kulin –**Tanju İnal**
866	E. Auerbach'ın İstanbul Yılları: Mimesis'in Yazarı ve Türkiye'nin Hümanist Reformu - **Gülnihal Gülmez**

İçsel Göç – Lena, Leyla ve Diğerleri

(749) Sevim Akten (Atatürk University)

Zehra İpşiroğlu toplumsal cinsiyet araştırmaları kapsamında farklı toplumsal kesimlerden kadınlarla şiddet üzerine yaptığı röportajlardan birinin kahramanını kurmaca evrenine taşımış. Lena, Leyla ve Diğerleri adlı tiyatro oyunu yabancı ve eril bir toplumun kadına bakışı ve davranışı karşısında hırpalanan kadınlık durumunu eleştirel bir bakışla anlatan yaşanmış bir öykü. Oyunun metni Toplu Oyunlar, Lena, Leyla ve Diğerleri ile Pinokyo Kral Übü'nün Ülkesinde, Mitos/Boyut da 2014 yılında yayınlanmış. Yazar, kadın, aile, özgürlük, toplumsal değişim, din, başkaldırı, yabancılaşma ve göç gibi alışılagelmiş izlekler üzerinden GÖÇ olgusunu kendi içinde yaşayan bir kadında somutluyor. Yaşanmış bir olayın kahramanı olan Lena / Leyla göçün benliğinde bıraktığı izleri önce anlamaya çalışıyor, sonra bir varoluş sorgulamasıyla ve içsel hesaplaşmayla yeni bir kimlik arayışına girerek silmeye çalışıyor. Yaşadığı içsel göç her ne kadar akıl hastanesinde sonlansa da umut her zaman var. Adı ne olursa olsun özbenliğinden kopamayacağını anlayan kadının yaşadığı içsel göçü bu çalışmada, izleksel bir yaklaşımla irdelemeyi amaçlıyoruz.

***

Yalnızlık Dolambacında Issız Bir Göçmen İncegül Bayram
(750) Tuğrul İnal (Hacettepe University)

Adalet Ağaoğlu Fikrimin İnce Gülü başlıklı romanında toplumbilim ve insanbilim sorunlarıyla göç sorununa düşünsel bir düzlemde bireyselden evrensele evrilen bir çizgide olağanüstü duyarlılıkla odaklanıyor. Ekonomik, toplumsal ve kültürel yapılarıyla insani ilişkilerin ve insan psikolojisinin diyalektik olarak değiştiğini, bunun sonucunda da gelişmiş ya da varsıl ülkelerin insanlarıyla ve sahip olmuş oldukları olanaklarıyla, geri kalmış ülkelerin yoksul insanları arasında ne denli büyük boyutlu çelişkiler ve çatışmalar oluştuğunu, ortaya çıkan çelişkiler yumağının insan ruhunda ve bilinçaltında türlü kompleksler gibi sonuçları son derece ağır, dahası traji-komik duygular ve durumlar uyandırdığını altı diziden oluşan bir film boyutunda sahneliyor. Filmin başoyuncusu aslında bir Don Kişot- bir Don Hiçkimse olan, bal renkli Mersedes'li, Franz Lehar gömlekli, tutkulu, o kadar da saf göçmen işçi Ballıhisar'lı Bayram'dır. Romancı, Kapıkule'den başlayan, anayoldan yirmi kilometre içerde, eski uygarlıkların kalıntılarında dış dünyaya kapalı, kuş uçmaz kervan geçmez Ballıhisar'da dramatik bir biçimde sonlanan bir kaç saatlik yolculuk boyunca, aşırı duyguların, doyumsuzlukların nasıl dışa vurulduğunu ve nasıl bir yalnızlık duygusu uyandırdığını hüzünlü bir film öyküsü biçiminde kurguluyor. Toplumbilimini ve insanbilimini romanına ustalıkla sokan Ağaoğlu'nun açık seçik kalıcı başarısı, yoksul, kompleksli, kapalı, suskun ve hülyalı Bayram'ın içsel yapısını çözümlerken ve onu ışık oyunlarıyla sahnenin orta yerine odaklarken, belirleyici özellik ve öncülleriyle koşutluk gösteren, ezik öteki mazlum ulusların insanı arasında benzerlik kurmasından ve evrensel bir tip yaratmasından kaynaklanıyor. Ağaoğlu bir çıkmaza dönüşen yalnızlık sorunsalının evrensele dönük gizlerini gösterirken bunun doyumsuzluklarla iç içe girmiş bir varolma sorunu olduğunu acı acı çalan çanlar eşliğinde okura duyuruyor.

***

Bilimin Mucizevi Göçü -Kanadı Kırık Kuşlar- Ayşe Kulin
(748) Tanju İnal (Bilkent University)

Kanadı Kırık Kuşlar adlı romanında ailelesiyle genç Türkiye Cumhuriyeti'ne sığınan, Yahudi kökenli bir bilim insanının öyküsünü kurgulayan Ayşe Kulin'in odak noktasında çarpıcı ve anlamlı iki tarih bulunuyor. İlki 1930: Almanya'da Hitler'in iktidara gelmesiyle, soyağacında Yahudi kökenli olduğu saptanan kişilere uygulanan türlü zulüm, baskı ve kötülüklerin başlangıcı. İkincisi 1933: Atatürk Türkiye'sinin Üniversite Reformu: İstanbul Üniversitesi'nin kurulmasıyla başlatılan, "rönesans hareketi" ve ülkelerinde "persona non-grata" ilan edilen Yahudi kökenli bilim insanlarına Türk Üniversite kapılarının açılması. Bu tarihten başlayarak, işlerini, kürsülerini kaybeden bilim, kültür ve sanat insanlarına Türkiye'nin yardım eli uzatmasıyla, İstanbul ve Ankara'ya gelen uzmanların İstanbul ve Ankara Üniversiteleri'nin bölüm ve enstitülerinde, konservatuvar ve tiyatro bölümlerinde coşkuyla çalışmaya başlamaları; Cumhuriyeti kurma ve geliştirme tutkusunu, heyecanını derinden paylaşmaları. Ayşe Kulin'in romanında Türkiye'ye iltica eden pataloji profesörü Gerhard Schlimann'ın, karısı ve iki çocuğu ile Türkiye'de zaman zaman mutlu, zaman zaman gergin ve güçlüklerle geçen yaşamına tanık olurken, ailenin dört kuşağınının - kızları ve torunlarının - "lento" başlayıp, "rapido" bir ritimle 2016 yılı Ocak ayına dek yayılan yaşam savaşımlarını ve yazgılarını belirleyen "sürekli yer değiştirme" olgusunu bir film şeridi gibi izliyoruz. 1933 yılından 2016 yılına dek yayılan zaman diliminde akademisyen ve aydınların bilimi geliştirmek ve yaygınlaştırmak için girişikleri kutsal, anlamlı çalışmalarına, Türk ulusuna "müteşekkir" göçmen bilim insanlarının Türkiye'de yaşadıkları olaylara, karşılaştıkları güçlüklere, engellere, çekişmelere, kimlik arayışlarına Ayşe Kulin 'in ilgi çekici, duyarlı anlatımıyla tanık ve ortak oluyoruz. Elsa, Suzan, Sude ve Esra, sıradışı ve inançlı "kadın kuşları" kimlikleriyle romanda ön sırada yerlerini alırlarken, Kulin, yurt sevgisi, yurtsuzluk acısı, insanın değeri, yüzyılların belası etnik ayrıştırma ve ötekileştirme sorunsalları üzerine okuru çok boyutlu biçimde düşünme ve tartışmaya çağırıyor.

***

E. Auerbach'ın İstanbul Yılları: Mimesis'in Yazarı ve Türkiye'nin Hümanist Reformu
(866) Gülnihal Gülmez (Anadolu University)

Hitler hükümetinin 1933'de ilki kabul edilen ırkçı yasalarının bir sonucu olarak, çok sayıda bilim ve sanat insanı, Ari ırktan olmadıkları ya da rejim muhalifi oldukları için üniversitelerdeki kürsülerinden kovulmuş ve Nazi Almanya'sını terk etmek zorunda kalmıştır. Sürgün entelektüellerin önemli bir kısmı, tam da aynı yıl bir eğitim reformu başlatmış olan genç Türkiye Cumhuriyetine sığınarak Türk üniversitelerinde çalışma imkânı bulmuştur. Bu göçmen bilim adamları için, 1933-1945 yılları arasında İstanbul'da ya da Ankara'da olmak, öncelikle hayatta kalmak demekti. Kaldı ki, mektuplar, anılar ve arşivler gibi çok çeşitli kaynaklar, Türkiye'deki görevlendirmelerin sığınmacı profesörlere maddi açıdan çok elverişli koşullar sunduğunu doğrulamaktadır. Ama bu sürgün yıllarının göçmen bilim adamlarına sağladığı bir diğer büyük fırsat da, birbirine yakın ilişkilerle bağlı bir Alman akademisyenler ortamında mesleklerini yapabilmek ve Alman bilim adamı kimliklerini sürdürebilmekti. Nitekim döneminin en önemli filolog ve dilbilimcileri biri olan Léo Spitzer'den 1936 yılında devraldığı görevle, İstanbul Üniversitesi Edebiyat Fakültesinde yeni kurulmuş olan Romanistik Kürsüsünde çalışmaya başlayan Erich Auerbach için de, Türkiye'deki 11 yıllık sürgün dönemi entelektüel üretkenlik açısından oldukça verimli geçmiştir. Öyle ki, karşılaştırmalı edebiyat tarihinde çığır açtığı kabul edilen baş eseri Mimesis'i yazmayı İstanbul'da tamamlamıştır. Kimilerine göre, Batı Edebiyatında Gerçekliğin Temsili alt başlıklı bu eser, özgünlüğünü Batı kültüründen uzakta, kitabın kıt, entelektüel diyaloğun zayıf olduğu bir kopuş ortamında yazılmış olmasına, bu koşullarda yoğunlaşan eleştirel düşünceye borçludur. Kimilerine göre ise tam tersine, filoloji geleneğinin büyük ismi Auerbach, İstanbul yıllarında, hümanist bilime çok önem verilen, oldukça canlı ve dostluk ilişkileriyle beslenen bir entelektüel çevre ve çeşitli kütüphanelerden yararlanarak çalışmış, Türk Hümanizminin parlak isimlerinin yetişmesine de değerli katkılarda bulunmuştur. Çalışmamızda, Erich Auerbac'ın İstanbul günleri bu iki görüşün farkında olarak incelenmiş ve Mimesis'in yazarının Türkiye'nin hümanist reform hareketine bakışı ve katkısı tartışılmıştır.

***

SESSION 9H –Poster Session - 2

Refugee, Settlement and Labor Market Integration Dynamics: A Case of Syrians in Istanbul in Comparison with Non-Syrian Migrants
(901) Ulaş Sunata (Bahcesehir University), Ezgi Araç (Bahcesehir University), Esra Yıldız (Bahcesehir University)

The number of internally displaced persons and refugees is expressed by millions in the beginning of 21st century, Syrian refugee is almost certainly a substantial topic. Turkey is one of the most refugee-receiving countries in this remarkable process in history of humanity. The number of Syrians in Turkey has reached 2,8 million in Turkey in the first month of 2017(UNHCR). Furthermore, Turkey receives migration not only from Syria but also from other countries such as Afghanistan, Iran, Iraq, and Somalia. The great Syrian emigration has been increased in the last two years in excessive ratio. However, statistics shows that in 2016 the increase substantially started to decelerate which means that it is time to focus on settled Syrian migrants. Thus, in our study the aim is to display the integration process of Syrians in comparison to migrants from different country of origin. To reach the aim 33 in-depth interviews have been conducted with migrants from different regions in the most migrant-receiving city in Turkey, Istanbul. In this qualitative analysis, all interviewees are presented in six criteria as gender, age, marital status, city of origin, time since they came to Turkey and current district of residence. The refugee route and build network have been excavated. Subsequently, labor market participation is determined as the primary subject in terms of the essential outcome of the integration process of immigration. It has been deducted that relations with co-workers and work-related problems are significant part of migrants' integration phase by providing a life.

***

The View of Turkish Families Who Have Immigration Experience Toward Syrian Immigrants

(1086) Yakup Azak (Istanbul University), Rümeysa Biçer, Nihan Özant (Istanbul University), Şule Kara

Turkey is constantly receiving immigration from various regions in different time frames because of its geographical location (Koçak & Terzi, 2012). These migrations sometimes originated in Turkish ethnic groups and sometimes in different ethnic groups from Afghanistan, Uzbekistan, Sub-Saharan region, Syria, Iraq, Balkans etc. (Arslan, 2008). When Turkey's recent history is examined, it has been seen that it has welcomed much more refugees from many countries for last 5 years due to the ongoing issues in the region of Middle East. When we gaze at the list of countries receiving immigration we can see Turkey on top (Erdis, 2016). The uprisings in Syria, which began 6 years ago with the influence of Arab Spring, turned into civil war as a result of the Assad regime choosing to suppress the uprisings with violence. It was then turned into a crisis that involved many actors from outside Syria. 6 million people took refuge in Syria to leave the country to another. Turkey, which implements the open-door policy towards the Syrians who flee the war, welcomes a large majority of the Syrians who have left their countries. Along with the migration, many changes occur in the life of the individuals who enter a different socio-cultural and socio-economic environment (Özer, 2015). Social identity theory which is based on struggle against the threats and the need to have positive perceptions about the group that an individual may have (Mummendey & Kessler, 1999). In general, the theory of social identities has assumptions that explain intergroup relations, in particular social conflicts. The first of these assumptions is that people tend to protect and develop positive self esteem. Second one is perception of self-esteem that is a group of individuals resulting from the identification. Lastly people establish positive social identity perception as going on social comparisons with external groups in a biased relation to their own internal groups (Tajfel & Turner, 1986). This study used social psychological approaches to investigate the question of migration from Syria and how to be categorized Syrian immigrants by the host groups who used to migrate from Bulgaria, Georgia, Caucasus and Greece. Starting from this point, study aimed to describe how these host groups interpret groups of Syrian immigrants in Turkey using the knowledge of their own group identities Thematic content analysis method was used in the research. Participant group was reached with snowball sample approach; Interviews consist of two groups from İzmir, two groups from Hatay with three participants and one group from Ankara with three participants. After the results of pilot studies, focus group interview technique and semi-structured approach were decided to use for the research. Each group were asked to tell interpretation on their own migration history and Syrian immigrants. The study was conducted with 13 participants aged between 40-60 from October 2016 to February 2017. All transcribed interviews were analyzed line by line by the four researchers using qualitative analysis program called Maxqda 12 at all stages of the research. Open coding approach was used during analysis. The meaning units and the themes of the data were formed as the result of continuous updating with the cooperation of the four researchers. Three themes were reached from results: comparison of immigration experiences, perception of group characteristics of Syrian immigrants and expectations from them. While participants perceive to their inner group dynamics positively they made a negative reference for Syrian refugees. This situation showed us that these findings support the theory of social identity.

***

A Qualitative Exploration of the Psychological Impact of Emigration on the Identity, Development, and Wellbeing of Young Irish Males
(1079) Thomas Conway (National University of Ireland), Pádraig Mac Neela (National University of Ireland)

Evaluating recent emigrants' adjustment to new cultures in terms of increased opportunity, adult development, future outlook, and identification with Ireland. Young Irish males will be the sole analytic focus in order to also understand how masculine gender roles and young male mental health are affected by such life-altering occurrences. A qualitative interview design is employed using a semi-structured interview schedule to explore emigrants' experiences. 15 Irish emigrants, who left between the ages of 18 to 25-years-old as a result of the recession, were interviewed. Participants completed an online interview through Internet communication. Intepretative Phenomonological Analysis is being used to develop individualised themes and integrate these into an overall account. Preliminary findings reveal that proactive cultural integration is key to succesful transition. Openness to experience and navigating settling-in difficulties is important for adaption to a new culture. All interpreted the experience as being beneficial regarding their resilience and wellbeing. The recent wave of Irish emigration is distinctive due to the relative ease with which on-going contact can be maintained with home and the increasing accessibility of cheaper travel. Nevertheless, it is still a potentially threatening move, requiring significant adjustment, but with equal potential for personal development.

***

Identity in-Between
(801) Jasmin Donlic (Alpen-Adria-University of Klagenfur)

This research project addresses the identity formation process of young people, for whom this process may prove a particular challenge. Though the study does not restrict itself to this aspect, these particular adolescents are very specifically situated in terms of their life-worlds, as they are: of Bosnian origin, thus they feature a so-called "migration background", of Muslim faith, which means they do not match the country's traditional "pattern of religion", and, what is more, they live in regions which have always exhibited autochthonous and/or allochthonous minorities, which can add further complexity to discursively co-determined identity formation processes. Furthermore, alongside the religious-denominational aspects, the study also aims to incorporate further individual and life-world aspects –including factors that may prove relevant for identity: value conceptions, socio-economic circumstances, access to education, and social participation. The research question is guided by the assumption that the particular situation of the selected cases studied exerts a significant influence on the process of identity formation: Which processes of hybrid, transcultural and transnational identity formation can be determined when considering the life designs and the life-world configurations of Muslim adolescents in the Alps-Adriatic regions Carinthia/Koroška, Slovenia/Slovenija and Italy/Italija? Guided by the central idea of the construction of identity, the scientific interest lies in the exploration of the life-worlds and daily routines of adolescents, who – due to their biographical peculiarities – may potentially find themselves caught between the conflicting priorities of the possibility of developing hybrid, transnational or transcultural variations of identity (Welsch 1995, 2004, Peterlini 2011), and a process of ethnicizing either by the self, or by others (Wakounig 2008, Ha 2004). The research design provides for a collection of the pertinent data using qualitative guided interviews with a subsequent evaluation of the raw material, which will follow the methodological approach of the Grounded Theory (cf. Kaufmann 1999, Glaser/Strauss 1998).

***

Research Notes on Refugee Women's' Everyday Life Self-Strategies: Preserving Self-Culture or Local Integration?
(1291) Merve Ayşe Köseoğlu (Hacettepe University)

In general, migration is human act. This move is interspatial and intertemporal. That's why it has so many different factors in it. And it has to be dealt in a multidimensional and interdisciplinary manner. Migration has different categorizations, obviously an immigrant is most of the time included in more than one category (Güllüpınar, 2012: 57). But this research paper is about migrating people who are forced to do so. There are concepts like migrant, refugee and asylum seeker. There is no sharp contrast between them so they are interchangeably in use. In fact, they are similar in a sociological perspective but they are different in the case of law. The sample of the research paper is refugees. According to 1951 Geneva Convention, the one that is being used in international law, a refugee is someone who has been forced to flee his or her country because of persecution, war, or violence. A refugee has a well-founded fear of persecution for reasons of race, religion, nationality, political opinion or membership in a particular social group. Most likely, they cannot return home or are afraid to do so. War and ethnic, tribal and religious violence are leading causes of refugees fleeing their countries. The people I worked with are the ones who left their countries because of war, internal conflict or political pressure. Those people live some changes called integration to the new country (Toğluk, 2009:3). Integration is a term on which there is no consensus but overall it refers to parity of life chances with members of the host society and being recognised as part of the receiving society. Hence it refers to economic, political, social and cultural spheres. Integration is a supported fact for immigrants. Those people also have to develop some protection mechanisms to realize themselves. Daily life is a space in which we can see power and those protection mechanisms together. Little tiny unimportant technical details in our everyday lives are power itself. But on the other hand, people distort that running of power with their little tiny unimportant creative tactics and can survive out discourse of power (De Certeau, 2008:47). At the end, power of practice and transformation power of everyday life is the core of the research. According to Castles and Miller (2008:14) migrations becoming feminized, means more women involve migrations. So, it needs a feminist view to handle the topic properly. Gender means femininity and masculinity are historical, cultural and political constructions. Connell says gender is a social practice (1995:65) that depends on space/time and changes. In the research, we are looking in the women's everyday livings who became refugees because of various causes. In detail, those women are taking a position between their own culture and the culture they came in. According to this, their strategies about local integration and preserving their own culture will be examined. Because they are supported for integration with education assistance, language courses, etc., but on the other hand the culture they have brought in is also an important fact for them to be themselves. And also, the position of governments and NGO's with the situation is important to handle the fact. We decided women refugees living in Çanakkale province to be as the sample of the research. Women from different nationalities, their behaviours in household, in government sphere and in their own communities and their survival strategies are subtopics of the paper.

***

Seasonal Workers at Lleida's Crop Season (Catalonia, Spain): The Case of Romanians Workers
(969) Juan Agustín González (University of Lleida)

Currently, agricultural and agroindustry activities are the main economic motors of Lleida's southern region. Every year, there are a large number of people who come to the Segrià, la Noguera, Garrigues and Pla d'Urgell (Catalonia, Spain) searching for a job in the crop season. This phenomenon takes place from the time of cherry's harvest in June to the apple's output in September (Achón, 2013). The vast majority of this group are immigrants and they are called seasonal workers. Some experts estimate they could reach the amount of 25.000 people (Gordo Márquez, Allepuz, Márquez Domínguez and Torres, 2015). The crop season is a very specific moment of the year which only lasts a few months. Then, this period requires an extra effort to organize the arrival of new workers. This group of newcomers is characterized by being extremely diverse. Within the different nationalities, the most numerous is the Romanian one (Achón, 2011). This situation to ask us how their situation is. For this reason, we propose to know the composition of this group and how their jobs at Lleida's crop season are. •   To identify the composition of Romanian seasonal workers at Lleida's crop season (gender, age and legal situation). •To detect what kind of jobs they do at Lleida (with or without a contract and typology of job). •   To know the characteristics of theirs jobs (wages, working hours and the way they used to find a job). This text came up from the project "Los temporeros en las comarcas de la llanura de Lleida" ("The seasonal workers in the region of Lleida's plain"). The project was founded by Diputació de Lleida and executed by members of the Observatorio Permanente de la Inmigración and research group GR-ASE. Thus, from mid-2015 to mid-2016, the research group made 900 surveys to seasonal workers and 150 surveys to employers in the regions of Segrià, Pla d'Urgell and La Noguera. Furthermore, the group made 40 in-depth interviews to agriculture business representatives, regional public institutions and some third sector organizations linked to seasonal workers. This research allowed us to know the reality of the collective of Romanian immigrants in Lleida's agriculture. Through the surveys, we have detected that the majority of this groups are women, young adults (between 25-45 years old) and almost all of them are in a legal situation. At the same way, the majority of them have a legal work contract. Surprisingly, we have discovered that just over half of them work in agribusiness. The means they used to find their job is very varied. However, the most common response was contracting at their own country. Furthermore, we have detected that the average salary of the Romanian immigrants doesn't reaches the 5 euros per hour. Finally, they claim to work more hours per week than the allowed legal limit.

***

SESSION 10A– Economics of Migration - 3

	Room: A1
Chair	**Anu Yijälä, City of Helsinki, Finland**
711	Exploring the Roles of Ethnic and Class Resources in South Asian Immigrant Economy in Hong Kong – **Kim Kwok**
902	Status and Stigma. Careers of Self-employed of Turkish Origin in Salzburg - **Heiko Berner**
1122	Labor Market Effects of Migration: An extension of the Ricardian Model – **Karen Jacqueline Contreras Lisperguer**
862	International Degree Students and Their Socio-Economic Integration into Turku, Finland - **Elli Heikkilä, Tytti-Maaria Laine**

Exploring the Roles of Ethnic and Class Resources in South Asian Immigrant Economy in Hong Kong
(711) Kim Kwok (Caritas Institute of Higher Education, Hong Kong)

The purpose of this paper is to explore the roles of class and ethnic resources in small immigrant businesses in the South Asian communities (Indian, Pakistani, Nepalese and Bangladesh) in Hong Kong. This paper relies on qualitative data collected from participant observation and 32 face-to-face semi-structured interviews with small South Asian entrepreneurs. Interview guidelines are designed according to the concept of mixed embeddedness, which investigates both the internal cultural factors and the opportunities and limitations shaped by the structural environmental factors. This paper identifies three groups of South Asian petit entrepreneurs with different earning opportunities and life experiences in Hong Kong. They are: successful, stable and survival entrepreneurs. Findings show that, first, while all South Asian petit entrepreneurs rely strongly on their group ethnic resources, stable and survival entrepreneurs are less endowed with individual class resources, and thus less privileged to act freely and on favorable terms. Second, although ethnic resources offer inexpensive solutions to costly problems, they fail to replace the roles of class resources in overcoming some structural barriers in the South Asian immigrant economy in Hong Kong. Third, ethnic and class resources are intertwined; they also interact with some environmental factors in the mainstream society in exerting impacts on immigrant economy. This paper contributes to the debate of immigrant business, in that it challenges the overestimation of cultural factors and ethnicity in the current literature. It argues that collective ethnic resources are important in immigrant economy. But highlighting their salient role should not obscure or neglect other individual factors and the larger structural context.

Status and Stigma. Careers of Self-employed of Turkish Origin in Salzburg
(902) Heiko Berner (Salzburg University of Applied Sciences)

The number of migrant enterprises in Austria rises continuously and there is a wide research on this subject. Research often focuses on the economic relevance or on effects of migrant businesses on society. In contrast, there exists less knowledge about the perspective of the entrepreneurs themselves and about changes in their lives. The paper is based on a doctoral thesis, that soon will be completed and submitted to the Pedagogic Faculty of the University of Innsbruck in Austria. Twelve semistructured interviews were conducted with self-employed persons of Turkish origin. The analysis followed a mixed design consisting of a content analysis of the whole interview corpus (Mayring 2010) and a more interpretative textual analysis of single cases (Koller 2012). The research questions concern educational processes on the way to self-employment and changes of living conditions of the self-employed. Educational processes here are understood as transformations of self-relations and of the relationship to the world. They are influenced by turning points or crises in ones live. Education in this sense is situated in daily live and does not exclusively take place in institutional contexts. The theoretical frameworks that inform this paper are the educational theory of Dewey (2008) and Honneth's theory (1994, engl. 1996) that understands social change as a result of fights for regognition. The results show that the reasons for getting self-employed very often correspond to structural disadvantages of persons of Turkish origin in Salzburg, for example unemployment, economical uncertainty or dequalification (Berner 2016). They are accompanied by intrinsic motivation and by support of role models or family. Entrepreneurs are changing social reality by influencing daily scripts (Bukow, Llaryora 1988), because as self-employed they dominate communicational rules in their business premises and in commercial negotiations. On the other hand, they mention experiences of discrimination in other spheres of life that they have only realized in the course of self-employment. At the same time, new forms of discrimination arise due to self-employment itself. Two kinds of status coexist for these entrepreneurs interviewed here. (1.) Status as increasing prestige. It rises gradually through social upward mobility: the interviewees in most cases now have more money than in the past or they feel more secure than in former employment. (2.) They perceive their membership to a status group of entrepreneurs. Yet, the majority of autochthonous categorically denies them this membership: The self-employed are not recognized as business people of a higher social position. Finally, they therefore develop a higher degree of sensitivity against stigmatization and discrimination, on grounds of their Turkish origin. The consciousness of the stigma rises with a higher social appreciation (more money, more job security) and with feeling part of a reputable status group: as a result of learning processes in the course of self-employment, discrimination is now felt more clearly. And: even new experiences of discrimination appear as a result of self-employment.

***

Labor Market Effects of Migration: An extension of the Ricardian Model

(1122) Karen Jacqueline Contreras Lisperguer (University of Agder)

One important discussion today is the possible negative effects that immigrants have on the wages of natives. In accordance with the theory of labor demand and supply, people believe that new immigrants could take the jobs of the existing workers. Many researchers have showed that there is little impact of immigration on wages and employment of existing workers as for example for the U.S. and the UK. The model fails to explain job polarization and wage inequality between natives and immigrants. Is it possible to model the effects of migration on wages in a different way that has the potential to be more tractable? Many of the shortcomings of the model can be addressed by using a task-based approach to the effects of migration in the labor market. This paper presents such extension following the Ricardian Skill Model (Autor, Levy, & Murnane, 2003). An analysis, without solving for the equilibrium and keeping capital and technology constants in the short run, gives us the following results: In the presence of migration, there will be a re-assignation of tasks. The wages of local workers will not be necessarily affected, but wage inequality within the labor market should increase.

***

International Degree Students and Their Socio-Economic Integration into Turku, Finland

(862) Elli Heikkilä (Migration Institute of Finland), Tytti-Maaria Laine (Migration Institute of Finland)

International migration has increased, and people are in growing numbers receiving their education or a part of it outside their home countries. When looking at international degree students, their stay can become permanent if, upon graduation, they do not return to their home countries but stay in the new countries of residence. Transitions to other countries' labour markets further expand the international migration flow of skilled persons for whom countries often compete (Heikkilä 2013). Most international students studying in Finland are keen to stay in the country after graduation and make a life there (Heikkilä & Pikkarainen 2008; CIMO 2016; Laine 2016). Finland's demography is changing; the population is aging and labor shortage is believed to be a great problem in the near future. Staying there after graduation, international students could become employees, tax-payers, consumers, even employers in the country that needs all of these. The threat is that these students will leave, because they cannot find work. Further, the benefits that the international students can bring to the host country cannot be measured only in monetary terms. The amount of knowledge, experience and international contacts, i.e. cultural and social capital, they possess are a valuable asset to any country (Mellors-Bourne et al. 2013; Naphy 2013). The aim of the Finnish Government is to triple the number of international students by 2020 (Opetus- ja kulttuuriministeriö 2013). This paper is analyzing international degree students as a part of international mobility using a case-study from the Higher Education Institutions in Turku, Finland. It brings new knowledge of what attracts international students to Turku, how they are integrating in socio-economic life and what are their plans after their graduation. Turku has been an international city attracting foreign-background people during its long history and present time. It is also one of the main regions where the immigrants have been concentrated in Finland. International students are one important segment of immigrants who enrich the life in the Finnish society. The study data has been gathered by the questionnaire which consisted of 303 respondents in 2015. 135 of them announced to be willing to take part in the follow-up survey a year later. Totally, 48 of them answered to the survey in 2016. Study data was gathered by Surveypal. Answers were analyzed both quantitatively and qualitatively. This research is part of the International talents as resource for expanding companies (PATH) -project funded by the European Social Fund and coordinated by Åbo Akademi University in Turku. The other partners, together with the Migration Institute of Finland, taking part in the project, are the University of Turku, Turku University of Applied Sciences, and the City of Turku. The results show that although international students seem to be very happy with their studies in Turku, many students needed more help with career planning, finding internships and learning Finnish. Most of the international students graduating in 2015/2016 had either completed an internship in Finland or had been employed in Turku. A third of the respondents had done both. Internships were found to be a very efficient stepping stone towards employment. Two thirds of the respondents stated that they would prefer staying in Finland after graduation if work was available. Also, two thirds of the respondents were interested or possibly interested in becoming self-employed in Turku. The follow-up survey's results showed that 44 percent of the international students and 90 percent of the graduates who had stayed in Turku worked. Most had Finnish friends and had at least some Finnish language skills. Three quarters felt at home while the rest did not.

SESSION 10B – Space and Identity

	Room: A2
Chair	**Tahire Erman, Bilkent University, Turkey**
1175	Indebted Identities, Fettered Subjects, and Reconstructed Indigeneity: Staying behind as a Formative Agent of Belongings in the Experience of Mardin Syriacs in Turkey- **Ozgur Bal**

Indebted Identities, Fettered Subjects, and Reconstructed Indigeneity: Staying behind as a Formative Agent of Belongings in the Experience of Mardin Syriacs in Turkey
(1175) Ozgur Bal (Middle East Technical University)

Basing its arguments in the findings of a qualitative research constructed in 2011, whereby in-depth and informed person interviews as well as focus groups were conducted and analyzed through grounded theory, this paper focuses on Syriacs in Mardin, Turkey, as a non-mover category, who were left behind of waves of e/migration of community members. I deem it important to understand the experience of staying behind for a people for whom not only personal experiences and memories, but also the collective memory inherited is interwoven into stories and influence of others' movement in various forms - forced and voluntary, across the borders and internal. Turning the lens on the experience of having not e/migrated, I argue that such experience itself becomes a vital element of the processes of present be-long-ings and identity construction for Syriacs of Mardin. Within a context elaborating on reasons for their not e/migrating or failing to do so; their relations with those who e/migrated in all economic, social, political terms; and how they conceive those e/migrants with symbolic meanings they attribute to having gone from or stay on living in the historical homeland Tur Abdin, I identify two patterns in which those processes of construction are revealed. One is the reconstruction and solidification of identity whereby memory becomes a 'blessing'; while the other is a formation of indebted identities acting on the motivation to realize the duty to the past, whereby memory becomes a 'burden' through the tensioned relation between loss and survival. Individuals turn to be fettered subjects, bound not only by their 'responsibility' to the past, but also by the forcing conditions of the present. The paper consequently, relates these processes with the experiences of miscellaneous forms of violence, social capital holding and economic integration of Syriacs in Mardin and Turkey.

***

"The Little Aleppo": Exploring the Sense of Belonging of Local Syrians in the Önder Neighborhood of Siteler, Ankara
(924) Tahire Erman (Bilkent University)

This paper aims to go beyond the simplistic view that Syrian refugees are creating their own places by re-appropriating spaces in poor neighborhoods in the big cities of Turkey. The Önder neighborhood is a good example to explore this issue. It is one of the early squatter/ gecekondu areas in Ankara, and, with its deteriorating housing stock mostly rented by poor families, it has turned into a slum area; with the incoming Syrians in large numbers, it is now called "the little Aleppo." As those Syrians with limited economic resources are clustering in Önder, they have been transforming it into their locality. Attracted by the furniture district Siteler in its proximity as well as its cheap rents, they have rented houses as well as stores, establishing their businesses ranging from small restaurants and bakeries to furniture stores and to even a fashionable clothing store opened recently. They have their open markets (Suriyeli pazarı) set up informally every morning. Their visibility in the neighborhood inscribed particularly by Arabic writings on store fronts, as well as the attention Syrians have received which was materialized in the aid coming from various groups, both formal and informal, have created a negative reaction from the majority of Turkish local population. In this paper, I ask to what extent Syrian residents feel belonging to the neighborhood, which is to be understood in the context of the perception held by the local Turkish people about their unruly re-appropriation of the locality that once belonged to them. It is based upon interviews conducted with both Syrian families (focusing more on women) and Syrian storeowners.

***

Stories of Being Invisible: Survival Strategies of "non-Syrian Immigrants" in Istanbul
(925) Oğuz Can Ok (Bilkent University)

Since 2011, millions of Syrians have fled to Turkey due to civil war. This wave of refugee seeking has increased the visibility of "international migration" in Turkey. But sadly, this visibility is generally limited to the Syrians. Even the legislative work on the international immigration in Turkey is carried out by defining the Syrians as the center. But only in 2016, 104.711 "irregular immigrants," excluding Syrians, were identified in Turkey. When we think together with the number of people who cannot be detected, this number becomes even more serious. The main question at this point is how the "Other of the Other," that is, different immigrant groups other than the Syrians, survive. Specifically, how do they meet their basic needs? How do they access to basic services such as the health care? This study examines these problems that "non-Syrian immigrants" have been experiencing in Turkey. This study, based on qualitative field research in Istanbul, conducted in Zafer neighborhood (Bahçelievler), Kumkapı (Fatih) and Sultanbeyli between September 2015 and March 2016, tells stories compiled from various actors involved in the field. The aim is to understand the problems that the Other of the Other (namely, those from Africa such as from Somali, Senegal, and Ghana, those from the former Soviet Union such as from Ukraine and Moldova, Turkic Republics such as Uzbekistan and Turkmenistan as well as Iraqis and Afghans) are experiencing due to their uncertain statuses and the strategies they have developed to solve these problems. The focus is on the relationship they have established with space and social networks during the process of developing solutions to their everyday problems.

***

Rethinking Refugees in Urban Areas, Problems and Key Challenges: The Case of Gaziantep
(1109) Kübra Cihangir Çamur (Gazi University), Hatice Seda Kılıç (Gazi University)

The massive migration of the Syrians has become an inevitable result of the war in Syria since 2011. Civil people have been forced to leave their homes and tried to find safer and better places to live and work. But this has brought many new problems for the accepting countries. As it is in other branches of science, Migration of Syrians has become a new title also in urban studies. They have chosen urban areas for job opportunities and better living conditions. This has resulted in a transformation process in urban areas and of refugees who try to adapt to their new habitats. By accepting over 3 million registered refugees, Turkey plays a very important role in the process. However, when the mass migration started, cities in Turkey were not ready as in case of Gaziantep, which is among the first choices of refugees. This study covers two districts of the Great Gaziantep City with a total population of 1.635.798 and is currently hosting 325.014 registered Syrian refugees with 19,9 %. In this context, in-depth interviews were conducted with eight Syrian refugees from different ages and professions. Four women and four men from Aleppo, between the ages

of 20-60 represent 28 people. Within the framework of the interview relating to daily urban life and spatial perception of refugees, "current status, qualifications, levels of satisfaction, social opportunities, negativities, and expectations from central and local governments, willingness to live in Gaziantep in the long-term" were questioned. Three main difficulties that have emerged during the interviews are problems of housing, finding a job and the negative neighborhood perception. While they are experiencing an intense process of economic and social worsening, they also couldn't meet their expectations in job opportunities and better living conditions. The most common problem is difficulties in finding a suitable shelter nearby the city center due to the easier accessibility to informal job opportunities. Additionally, rental prices have increased steadily, and refugees have been forced to move cheaper sub zones of the city for affordability. These have led them to unfavorable living spaces such as workplaces and garages with toilets and bathrooms extensions. Although refugees mainly state that the biggest problem they face is physical and economic and they accept to work in informal jobs at very low wages, answers given during the interviews indicate that they have also serious social problems. Because affordable housing problems and low wages not only pushed refugees to urban parts with worse living conditions but also caused ghetto areas to form in the city. Their low-income level and dissimilar culture are causes of the main social and spatial problems in the city. Segregation and social separation are two of them. What could be the solution? If an effective and sustainable political will with multicultural content is aimed, the adaptation and integration of the refugees can be possible. It is aimed to shed light on these problems in a contextual, multicultural and sustainable framework with the results of this study.
    ***

SESSION 10C – Migrant Integration

	Room: A4
Chair	**Petra Bendel, University of Erlangen, Germany**
1256	'We Are Not a Country of Immigration': Germany's Difficulties in Integrating the Turkish Gastarbeiter into Society – **Elizabeth Todd**
970	Leaving or Staying? Migration Motifs of People of Turkish Origin with German Graduation – **Cemal Sarı, Nataschka Anne-Isabelle Marie Faure**
930	Developing the Understanding of Migrant and Refugee Integration in the EU: Implications for Housing Policies –**Maria Psoinos, Orna Rosenfeld**
1126	House as a Spatial Form in Diaspora through the Glance of Kurdish Literary Narratives - **Suat Baran**

'We Are Not a Country of Immigration': Germany's Difficulties in Integrating the Turkish Gastarbeiter into Society
(1256) Elizabeth Todd (University of Leeds)

In the shadow of World War II, much of western Europe was left lacking manpower and in need of workers to support its industries and assist in rebuilding economies. Germany in particular, called on help from several countries through the signing of recruitment agreements, but its Treaty with Turkey in 1961, proved most significant. For the past century and more, governments have invited different peoples into their countries to support their industries, and then asked them to leave. These people; these communities, have an effect on politics regardless of whether or not they are legally considered part of the voting public. The question is, whether identifying and recognising their political presence would create more harmony rather than dissent. This is a question more prevalent now than ever, with the move of Britain to leave the European Union. Germany, a country plagued with its historic past and keen to remove itself from that association, arguably played the most welcoming role in the 'refugee crisis' of last year, allowing more than a million refugees through its borders. Such a response is not necessarily characteristic however, and many refer back to the failures of the Turkish Gastarbeiter programme Germany embarked on until 1973. What was meant as a temporary rotation of workers: who would stay for two years and then be replaced by new groups, became Germany's largest minority population. No attempts to integrate these people were made, seeing them as purely temporary, and not requiring knowledge of the German language or to settle into society. When the 1973 halt to foreign recruitment plans saw the surprising increase of immigrants rather than the opposite, Germany was finally forced to face the topic of integration, after denying for so long that these communities would settle. This process continued for the next twenty-five years, while the Government continued to rehearse the phrase 'we are not a country of immigration'. The reunification of Germany saw an attempt to define what German identity was, and in so doing, public discourse and action left the Turkish community as 'outsiders' more than ever before. Though citizenship laws changed at the turn of the century to move away from their previous focus on blood-lines, the relations between Turks and Germans remain somewhat tense, while the recent actions of Turkey's President Erdogan have not eased the relationship. Some deem these tensions the fault of failed integration in the sixties and seventies, and Germany's denial that it was indeed becoming a country of immigration. This paper will discuss how Germany dealt with her Gastarbeiter population differently to other Western European countries, and in what ways this led to the failure to integrate the Turkish population into German society. It will focus on the Anwerbestop of 1973, when Germany halted her Gastarbeiter programme along with most others, and how this was seen by the government as an 'end', but which in fact became the 'beginning' to integration. Historiography on the question of the Turkish Gastarbeiter during the sixties and seventies was scarce, as historians and journalists often seemed to avoid mentioning the gastarbeiter or anything concerning them to ensure they did not become a permanent feature of German society. There was a sense that if they were not spoken of or addressed, they did not really exist. Yet all the while their presence; their invitation, was having a massive and, what would eventually become, long-term consequence on Germany's industrial cities, its culture and its people. Scholarship on the question of the guest worker did not really take shape until the eighties and nineties. The voice of the guest worker themselves took a while to surface, as people began to be speak the German language and were then able to express themselves to a German audience, rather than merely through letters and diaries. This began as Gastarbeiterliteratur and gave a platform to names that have become well-known such as Aras Ören. Writers like Stephen Castles provide a good critique to the Gastarbeiter system across Western Europe, while Rita Chin takes a specific look at how Germany was different. The voice of the press is certainly louder in the 21st century and makes numerous links between current tensions in Germany with its foreign migration past, and the fiftieth anniversary of the Turkish agreement in 2011 provided a fresh hype around history and research on the topic. It is however the voice of the German common man that is less often heard, and leaves a curious gap in this history, and an important one at that.

***

Leaving or Staying? Migration Motifs of People of Turkish Origin with German Graduation

(970) Cemal Sarı (Ruhr-University of Bochum), Nataschka Anne-Isabelle Marie Faure (Ruhr-University of Bochum)

The aim of this research project is to examine why highly skilled Turks propose to migrate from Germany to Turkey and whether there are gender-related disparities in migration intentions. The rising migration of highly skilled Turks of the second and third generation has recently paid attention in both, Germany as in Turkey in research, politics, and economy as well as in the media. These highly skilled academics were born and grew up in Germany, enjoyed the education here and leave the country towards Turkey, to reach their career goals there. Fourteen qualitative interviews with highly skilled individuals of Turkish origin of the second and third generation in the Ruhr area (Bochum, Duisburg, Essen and Dortmund) were the foundation of a qualitative study to examine their motives to leave Germany towards Turkey. The results of this research project show that for the majority of the interviewees principally exists an openness to imagine a future life in Turkey. While women predominantly intend to leave Germany for family and partnership reasons, men would primarily migrate to Turkey for professional reasons and for their career. The study comes to the result that not a particular motif, but only the compound of numerous reasons, leads to a motivation for a migration from Germany to Turkey.

***

Developing the Understanding of Migrant and Refugee Integration in the EU: Implications for Housing Policies

(930) Maria Psoinos (Canterbury Christ Church University), Orna Rosenfeld (United Nations Economic Commission for Europe)

This paper examines how the concept of migrant and refugee integration has been theoretically developing in the past decades in social sciences and suggests applying this new conceptualisation to improving EU housing policies. The large migrant and refugee populations who have been recently resettling in Europe emerge as much more different from those of previous decades because they are very diverse in terms of country of origin, profile and motivation (OECD, 2015). This means that the ways in which they integrate (or not) in the society where they resettle are new and dynamic. Housing situation is one of the key indicators of integration. However, the housing dimension of migrant integration is weakly developed in most integration strategies compared to other issues. It is critical to examine integration through the lens of housing policies. Recent studies on social housing and affordable housing highlighted increased difficulties with regards to accessing decent and affordable housing for a large share of local populations, including increasingly low and medium income households (UNECE, 2015; OECD, 2017). The inflow of refugees puts further pressure on housing sectors in many countries in the region (Dizioli et al., 2016) resulting in tensions over what is increasingly seen as a scarce resource for different populations in housing need. In this context where migrants' and refugees' profile is changing, their needs are pressing and host societies are faced with a set of new housing challenges, it is imperative to develop the understanding of migrant and refugee integration. The paper first systematically reviews the past two decades' changes in the concept of migrant/refugee integration in social sciences (sociology, psychology, human geography). It then focuses on and critically discusses John Berry's (1997, 2001) classic theory on migrants' psychological acculturation, which has been widely used for examining at the micro level migrants' adaptation to the host society and overall well-being. In most cases, the migration experience is accompanied by acculturation (Berry, 2005) which is defined as 'the process of cultural change and adaptation that occurs when individuals from different cultures come into contact' (Gibson, 2001:19). Berry (1997, 2001) described acculturation attitude as determined by the extent to which an individual is willing to retain an old culture and adopt a new one. This results in four types of attitudes: integration (accept both old and new culture); assimilation (reject old culture, accept new); separation (accept old culture, reject new); and marginalisation (reject both). This theory has been gradually moving from approaching integration as a static and one-sided phenomenon, to an increasingly dynamic and multi-level process, where risk and protective factors constantly interact at various levels (individual refugee, sending and receiving community, society) (Prilleltensky, 2008). By reviewing how the concept of migrant and refugee integration has been dynamically evolving and critically discussing one of the most widely-used approaches to integration, this paper suggests that a more sophisticated understanding of integration today can also trigger more well-informed housing policies to facilitate migrants' and refugees' integration in the best possible way in the time of the general affordable housing scarcity.

***

House as a Spatial Form in Diaspora through the Glance of Kurdish Literary Narratives

(1126) Suat Baran (Istanbul Bilgi University)

The representations of "house" and "home" in the literary narratives produced by first-generation Kurdish immigrant writers living in the diaspora tell us a lot about the connection between nation and house as a spatial form, which might be more apparent in diaspora. Because - speaking in general terms - not only house becomes shelter for its inhabitant, but also nation or (the stateless) national-land does function as a larger symbolic "house" for its members. From this viewpoint, they both substitute each other in the memory and narratives of their members. Thus, in this paper I will explore the complex set of relationships between the idea of "house" or "home" and that of "nation" in order to investigate spatial loss and recurrent appearance of national land in the form of "house". So, in that sense I am particularly interested in examining how diasporic writing establishes a strong connection between the house as a living space and as a literary motif and the experience of migration and displacement among Kurdish immigrant writers such as Fawaz Husên (France) and Firat Cewerî (Sweden). As argued frequently, writers in diaspora may either take a strong position against national identity after their departure to foreign lands or feel a deep nostalgia for the land and house they have left behind. At this point, I would suggest that these writers unconsciously resume the sense of national belonging wherever they are but only as long as they are immigrants and experience the loss of the national land strongly. In other words, I believe that the analogy between the nation and the notion of "home/house" as a form of living space experienced in diaspora is worth being scrutinized as a symbolic representation, and an allegory of the nation. In this way, my research investigates the modalities of the deconstruction and/or reconstruction of group identity, of national sentiment, and of homeland and house as spatial forms. As the methodological sources, I would benefit from the subaltern and postcolonial studies along with the works such as Diaspora, Memory and Identity by Vijay Agnew; Writing Diaspora by Rey Chow; and the Future of Nostalgia Svetlana Boym, Imagining the Turkish House: Collective Visions of Home by Carel Bertram. All in all, although sociology and history have looked at the displacement and also diasporic experience of Kurds in great detail, in this paper I will try to argue "house" representations in correlation with the national-identity and (the stateless) national-land left behind in literary narratives as products of migration.

***

SESSION 10D – Migrant Women

	Room: A5
Chair	**Ulaş Sunata, Bahcesehir University, Turkey**
1170	Integration of Refugee Women: A Tool for Opening New Doors to Refugee Women - **Hilal Keleş**

741	Migrant Women as the Villans: "Syrian Kuma" (Second Wives) versus "Soviet Natashas" in Turkey – **Dilek Cindoğlu, Armagan Teke Llyod**
1051	Women's Burden: A Study on Overnight Guests as a Part of Internal Migration Process in Turkey – **Elif Sabahat Uyar Mura**
1296	The Role of Gender in Different Stages of Migratory Movements: Analysis of Voluntary and Involuntary Migration - **Deniz Eroglu Utku, Mustafa Murat Yucesahin, Pınar Yazgan**

Integration of Refugee Women: A Tool for Opening New Doors to Refugee Women
(1170) Hilal Keleş (Social Sciences University of Ankara)

As Syria crisis enters its seventh year, civil war in the country still continues at dangerous level and it does not see to end in the near future. Due to the foreseeable future of Syrian refugees, 2.9 million registered Syrian refugees in Turkey (UNHCR,2017) who were accepted as 'guests' by authorities from the beginning of the conflicts to till, should be seen as permanent settlers. Accordingly, the issue of integration of Syrian refugees into Turkish society has become vital subject as durable solution to deal with social unrest arose from both refugee and host community. This paper proposes to examine different ways of integration of refugee women into society, more specifically integration into society through accessing main rights and services as education and labor opportunities. The only common platform for integration of women seen based on accessing rights and services in the first hand especially for increasingly diverse Syrian communities. Focusing on integration of refugee women is not arbitrary. For successful integration into society, women play significant role due to experiencing negative effects of migration differently than man, made great efforts to secure transition for themselves and their families, and create different coping mechanisms to adapt the society. (Drachman and Ryan 2001). Also, it's selected because field researches show that changing gender norms have huge impact on women's integration into host community. While men were expected to be the primary breadwinners and protectors, women remained more home-based in traditional lifestyle, but new living conditions in the host community started to changed women's sitatus both in the family and the society which give more opportunity to women to empower themselves with coping mechanism and integrate the society with new opening platforms. Integration became the significant tool to change negative effects of displacement into empowering women. Integration is multi-dimensional process which mainly includes active participation to education opportunities, social and cultural life, and labor markets. Practises in the field shows that while government and other non-governmental organisations are mostly building their activities upon integrating through social life and social/cultural activities, supporting women integration with education and labor opportunities were disregarded. There are two main question to be address in this research: First one; which type of integration process is more successfull and permanent in the presence of women. For instance, empowering women in their social life and integrate into culture of host community can address their problems in the society and for themselves and meet with their practical need or not. Either integration though accessing main rights and services is more practical and useful for their life or not. Moreover, is there any other practical ways for integration of women will be another subject to research further opportunities. Main aim behind this question to research for is there any direct link between integration of women into host community and accessing main rights and services. Secondly, will integration be a good tool to turn negative effects of displacement into an advantage that women can enjoy both their rights, integrate with society better, and empower themselves to cope with challenges in their lives for their families and themselves. Moreover, another significant finding will be discovering the change in stereotyped image of Syrian women thorugh integration channel. By addressing the many issues centred around two main questions can produce knowledge about integration process of Syrian refugee women in Turkey and shows the differences among integration policies and their effects which are increasingly visible in reality but invisible in statistics and literature yet. Secondly, making a contribution to literature based on women's real and practical need and have an opportunity to see how meeting with this demand effect their social acceptability in the presence of public. Lastly, it will be useful to come up with policy recommendations about how to increase social integration and inclusion of refugee women through education and labor opportunities and making a lasting impact on integration process. To address the questions and make contributions identified above, this research will employ a 3-month empirical research to be conducted in Turkey, specifically Hatay. At the same time, the research will include case studies from each different integration way as participating education, labor, and social/cultural life. Moreover, this research will include good practises from the Hatay field, current activities of governmental and non-governmental actors for women integration in Hatay. It shall be combine participant observation with oral histories and subjective narratives collected through semi-structured in-depth interviews.

***

Migrant Women as the Villans: "Syrian Kuma" (Second Wives) versus "Soviet Natashas" in Turkey

(741) Dilek Cindoğlu (Abdullah Gul University), Armagan Teke Llyod (Abdullah Gul University)

This paper presents a comparative gendered analysis of different depictions of two groups of migrants –namely, Eastern European and Syrian women - within the public discourses and media coverages in Turkey. Starting from the beginning of 1990s, Turkey has witnessed an inflow of migrant women from former Soviet Union countries, mainly into three different economic sectors (entertainment and sex work, care work and suitcase trading). Despite the different occupational niches these migrant women occupy, they were categorized under the generic term of "Natasha's" associated with sex work, triggering a moral panic about foreign women's hyper-sexuality and looseness. The second flow of migration examined here concerns with forced Syrian migration after the 2011 Syrian Civil War. As opposed to associations with sex work, in public and media discourse, Syrian women were highlighted as "Second Wives" ("Kumas") who are stealing the well-off husbands in the established families. In using the concept of ethno sexual frontiers used by Joanne Nagel, this analysis tries to understand the intersection of ethnic and sexual frames through which migrant women are perceived as different forms of threats. Notwithstanding the differences, however, we also note that migrant women's threatening sexuality always remain as a marker of difference, through which its 'Otherness' in the dominant ethnic group (Turkey) is construed.

***

Women's Burden: A Study on Overnight Guests as a Part of Internal Migration Process in Turkey

(1051) Elif Sabahat Uyar Mura (Çanakkale Onsekiz Mart University)

The paper attempts to discuss a common phenomenon of internally migrated households in Turkey called as "overnight guest" through the framework of women's labor. Women, particularly within the first generation of rural-urban migrant households, bear the burden of hosting and providing labor-intensive services to various types of guests who visit the city with various motivations such as migrating, studying, getting medical treatment, finding a job or working. Researches on urban women have frequently pointed

at 'social norms' limiting women's work and mobility outside the household as a major constraint on women's employment in the metropolises of Turkey (exp. Bora 2005; White 2004; Hoşgör & Smits 2008; Özyeğin 2010). This paper emphasizes women's increased solitary workloads within the household after migration as another major constraint for women's employment and public space appearance/mobility outside the house. Moreover, as this research intended to explore, overnight guests become a usual part of family life in many migrated households, which even affected the prominant furniture design in the country (Çelikoğlu 2011). In that sense, the process of internal migration is very much related to the leap of furniture industry in 1980s, when convertible sofa (çekyat) became a core product as an effective tool for converting the nature of rooms in space-limited households. In this context, migrated women are not only obliged to perform the housewife routine but also constantly obliged to convert spaces and put an extra effort for hosting endless guests. Embracing the nature and consequences of this "guest labor" in these women's lives necessitates a qualitative and comparative study on migrated households to see the contexts and processes, which restrain women's mobility outside the house. This paper is based on a pilot study to comprehend the phenomena of guest labor, which, on the one hand, constitutes an important part of internal migration processes; on the other, presents a form of invisible and unpaid labor of women in Turkey. The data of the study is provided through 20 semi-structured qualitative interviews with first and second generation urban women, which reveals regional differences and transformation of hosting practices in time and provide insights abou peculiar perceptions and strategies of women.
***

The Role of Gender in Different Stages of Migratory Movements: Analysis of Voluntary and Involuntary Migration

(1296) Deniz Eroglu Utku (Trakya University), M. Murat Yucesahin (Ankara University), Pınar Yazgan (Sakarya University)

Gender is defined as 'the meaning people give to the biological reality that there are two sexes' (Pessar, 2005, p. 2). Thinking of its effectual role in migration movements is a late coming concern in migration literature, since the 1970s considerable amount of notable works that focus on women immigrants and analysis of gender has appeared in the field. In other words, widespread attitude of approaching migrants as genderless or men yield its place to academic interest to study of immigration and gender issues together (Sinke, 2006, p. 85). These studies mainly approach the migration as dependent variable and take the role of gender in relation to socio-economic variables (Chattopadhyay, 2000). In other words, rather than approaching migration itself, these studies more focus on changing role of gender according to socio-economic background of migrants. Therefore, the existing literature mainly occupied with labour market conditions to explain gendered migration movements. As the involuntary migration movements have increased, vulnerable and desperate situation of women in these movements also become apparent. Several UN reports (e.g. UNHCR, 1991, 2002, 2016) as well remarkable academic studies (Boyle et al., 2009; Kronenberger, 1992; Murray, 1999; Pittaway & Bartolomei, 2001; Spijkerboer, 1994) started to indicate this issue and underlined double discrimination of refugees. Very recently Syrian refugee crisis greatly contributed to the tragedy of women. According to the United Nations Population and Fund (2016), 13.5 million affected by the Syrian crisis. As a result of civil war inside the country, 1,2 million refugee women and girls of reproductive age (15-49), 80.500 pregnant refugee women. What is also important to underline that UNPFA indicates these numbers based on registered Syrians. Therefore, it is possible to consider the possibility of higher numbers when thinking of irregular movements. In this picture, it is not enough to take gender just an independent variable on the process of migration. It is equally important to compare its role in different types of migration. Therefore, this paper critically analyses the role of gender from very early stage of migration to final settlement by taking economic migrant-refugee difference into consideration. By examining various case studies, this study offers an analytical frame and provides a new understanding for the future field works. The study adopts a comparative approach to the process of migration and the role of gender on it as it aims to explore differences in each steps of migration. Mainly the study tackle two types of migrant- refugee and economic migrant and examine them by taking Boyd and Grieko (2003)'s categorisation of migration stages: the pre-migration stage, transition across state borders and post migration stage: All in all, this paper aims to theoretically discuss the whole migration process while taking gender issue and migration type together. A review of the literature provides evidence supporting the claim of gender has changing role in each steps of migration as well in different types of migration experience. The reminder of the paper is organized in the following way. First, we clarify the conceptual difference between the refugee and the economic migrant. Then we analyse the role of gender by considering different stages of migration and type of migration. Finally, we offer a new path for researchers focusing on gender issue and migration.

***

SESSION 10E – Human mobility, conflict, insecurity

	Room: B1
Chair	**K. Onur Unutulmaz, Ankara Social Sciences University, Turkey**
1078	"We Don't Want Them Back": Balancing the Rights of Displaced, Returning, and Remaining Populations in the Aftermath of ISIS in Nineveh Plains, Iraq - **Roger Guiu, Nadia Siddiqui**
1010	Refugee Status Determination Policy and Practice: The Australian Experience – **Petra Madge Playfair, Adriana Mercado**
712	Building or Burning the Bridges? The Determinants of Return Migration Intentions of German-Turk Generations - **Tolga Tezcan**
1178	Crimmigration in Brazil and The Netherlands: How the Phenomenon of Securitization can be a Fuel to These Processes? - **Azeredo Alves**

"We Don't Want Them Back": Balancing the Rights of Displaced, Returning, and Remaining Populations in the Aftermath of ISIS in Nineveh Plains, Iraq
(1078) Roger Guiu (Social Inquiry), Nadia Siddiqui (Social Inquiry)

International guidelines for durable solutions to displacement highlight the need to protect the rights of the internally displaced. This includes their right to return to their places of origin, based on informed, voluntary choice and in safety and dignity. While this framing is important, particularly after conflict, it often overlooks the rights and needs of those who have already returned and/or those who have remained and that returning is a continuous process happening over time. It may also miss the fact that returning to the status quo ante is impossible in post-conflict settings in practical terms and not a solution in rights-based terms either as the context was likely unjust previously, contributing to forced displacement in the first place. Nowhere is this clearer than within the communities of Nineveh Plains in Iraq. Comprising the rural, ethnically diverse territory surrounding Mosul City, the Nineveh Plains bore the brunt of brutal ISIS attacks in 2014 –in some cases pitting neighbours and whole villages against one another. Much of this area was retaken from ISIS by Iraqi and Kurdish forces in 2015. The arrival of ISIS and their later expulsion both caused waves of displacement and return. Tensions and divisions remain both between those groups that stayed or were displaced for a short time and returned as well as between these populations and those still displaced. The current military operations to retake Mosul City coupled with the lack of a formal durable solutions policy on behalf of the government have left these communities in a temporary stalemate as to who can come home and who cannot. [Research Group]'s recent in-depth research into the communities within the Nineveh Plains focused on understanding current local dynamics and identities, local peacebuilding mechanisms, and wider views on peace within the whole of the governorate. The research reveals the complexity of return in such a context, where legacies of violations and demographic engineering mix with current anger and fear in relation to ISIS affiliation. In providing a detailed case study, focused on Zummar and Wana subdistricts made up of Kurds and Arabs, we elucidate challenges and opportunities for durable solutions to displacement in Iraq, providing the basis for programming and policy that is focused on understanding needs related to victimization and justice on all sides, preventing revenge, and working toward building compromise between groups, regardless of displacement status.

***

Refugee Status Determination Policy and Practice: The Australian Experience
(1010) Petra Madge Playfair (Playfair Visa and Migration Services), Adriana Mercado (Playfair Visa and Migration Services)

Forced migration refers to the coerced movement of people from their country of habitual residence or nationality, typically in response to war or conflict. The phenomenon presents challenges as it not only affects the individual and the receiving community, but also has become a highly politicized issue that transcends borders. The difficulty is based on the fact that there is no simple answer to this global issue. Australia is a country that has been built on migration flows. Being an island, the determination to control of the border has become part of the national psyche. This drives a very different attitude to the forced migration of people experienced by Europe, where flows of people have been a constant theme through history. This paper will explore Australia's approach to dealing with the influx of immigrants, particularly people who have arrived by boat without a valid visa (thus, "unauthorized maritime arrivals"), such as a) the impact of policies and law, b) the practical disorder that may follow when applying certain policies, c) the financial and human cost, d) the juxtaposition of the Australia's current policy, which aims to be a deterrence for "unauthorized maritime arrivals" while simultaneously, in response to acknowledged human crises, it is increasing the number of authorized refugee arrivals. In a country that is 59 times bigger than Greece, with just a little over double its population, we will explore the repercussions that arise when a human issue becomes a political tool.

***

Building or Burning the Bridges? The Determinants of Return Migration Intentions of German-Turk Generations
(712) Tolga Tezcan (University of Florida)

What drives German-Turks to return to Turkey? This study attempts to answer this question by investigating the determinants of return migration intention among German-Turks. While German-Turks, invited to work in the booming post-war economy, have always been defined as "guest workers" and expected to return to Turkey eventually, they have preferred to stay in Germany, enjoy increased wealth by earning high wages, and benefits from the German welfare system. But things have changed since 2006, and the net migration number of Turks has now fallen to below zero for the first time. This study aims to identify the factors that influence the multifaceted issue of return migration intentions. I use the most recent "Migration Sample (M1)" of the German Socio-Economic Panel

(SOEP), which includes 463 respondents who have a Turkish background, to estimate logistic regressions models for return intentions. This study focuses on testing the effects of four domains: (1) economic integration, (2) social and economic ties with Turkey, (3) discrimination, xenophobia, and multiple identities, and (4) generational status. The results indicate that all these domains make a contribution to return decisions.

***

Crimmigration in Brazil and The Netherlands: How the Phenomenon of Securitization can be a Fuel to These Processes?
(1178) Azeredo Alves (Sao Paulo State University)

The purpose of this research project is to verify the extent to which Brazilian Migration Policy has been influenced by the US War on Drugs and how, justified through a security discourse, it employs practices that violate human rights. A key objective is to determine if the combined effects of drug securitization and historical racism are resulting in the start of a "crimmigration" process. The fact that the federal police, the agency in charge of policing drug trafficking, is also the one that manages immigration, is a major factor in this assessment. This paper further analyses the immigration policy of the Netherlands, for two key reasons. Because a Crimmigration process is also apparent in the Netherlands (VAN DER LEUN; BARKER; VAN DER WOUDE, 2017) , comparison with the Brazilian context provides for an assessment of the relative degrees of Crimmigration. Secondly, because Dutch drugs policy is fundamentally different to Brazil's, it provides scope for valuable insights into how differing causal factors lead to the same results, such as the fact both countries treat migration policy with a security bias. The research sets out to develop the proposition that Migration Policy is influenced by exogenous and Endogenous factors. Among the key exogenous factors to consider for Brazil, is racism towards afrodescendents and the prevalent perception of this ethnic group as crimminals, linked to ethnic profiling practices. Similarities can be drawn with the Netherlands in this respect; there are indications according to Leun and van der Woude (2011), that some ethnic groups, notably people from Antillean or Moroccan background are subject to greater police suspicion and investigation compared to the rest of the population. Differently from the Dutch historical welcome policy for immigrants from distinct origins during periods of high economic demand, Brazilian migration policy has historically selected desired immigrants in a racial basis. The situation in Netherlands changed over the past decades, prevailing a security bias towards some immigrant groups, characterizing what could be called a "culture of control" (LEUN; VAN DER WOUDE, 2011). In Brazil, migration law dates from the military dictatorship (1980) and, though not strictly racist in its official content, identifies migration as a security risk. This needs to be borne in mind when recent practices by the government and its agencies need to be observed considering these aspects. Amongst the exogenous factors, it is necessary to consider the influence of the US on Brazilian policies since the XIX Century (Monroe Doctrine). Due to the Globalization process, the International System values have also proven important influencers of governing policies, this is clearly evident in the prevalence of a security approach towards two phenomenon: drug trafficking and irregular migration. The methodology applied in this research is based on Portuguese and English bibliographic materials and governmental documents related to the immigration process in Brazil and in the Netherlands. The International Political Sociology (IPS) Approach will be used, because it can offer a multiple and holistic understanding about the sociological context where the issues are based. The IPS framework understands the important role of agents, because of this, this research will also contain interviews with public agents that deal directly with immigration issues, which is the Federal Police and also

civil society organizations. The theorical perspectives related to the Crimmigration process will be based on the material produced by the CINETS specialists group.
***

SESSION 10F – Göç Akımları ve Göçmenler

	Room: B2
Chair	**Nuray Karaca, Atatürk University, Turkey**
1255	Amerikada'ki Ahıska Türklerinde Sosyal Değişme, Milli ve Dini Kimlik İnşası – **İsmail Güllü**
739	Suriye'de Unutulanlar: Tanıdık Bir Hikaye, Çerkesler ve Göç – **Onur Limon**
1314	Suriyeli Mültecilerin Dayanışma Ağlarının İbn Haldun'un Asabiyet Kuramı Bağlamında Değerlendirilmesi - **Abulfez Süleymanov**
1363	Üç Büyük Göç Dalgası ve Gaziantep'in Mekânsal Sürekli Yeniden İnşası – **Nevra Akdemir**
1038	Kırsal Mahremin Kente Göçü – **Nuray Karaca**

Amerikada'ki Ahıska Türklerinde Sosyal Değişme, Milli ve Dini Kimlik İnşası
(1255) İsmail Güllü (Karamanoğlu Mehmetbey University)

Amerika'daki Ahıska Türkleri, tarihleri boyunca İlk olarak 1944 yılında Stalin döneminde Gürcistan'dan Özbekistan'a, 1989 yılında Özbekistan'dan Krasnodar'a son olarak ise 2004 yılında ise Amerika'ya olmak üzere bir çok sürgün tecrübesi yaşamış bir topluluktur. Bu araştırma, Amerika Birleşik Devletleri'nin New York eyaleti'ne bağlı Rochester şehrinde yaşayan yaklaşık 50 ahıskalı aile ile 2016-2017 yılında yapılan bir saha çalışmasına dayanmaktadır. Araştırma derinlemesine görüşme ve gözlem teknikleri ile gerçekleştirilmiştir. Ahıska Türklerinin sosyal yaşantıları farklı bir çok boyutunda yer alınarak bu gözlemler yapılmıştır. Kimlik olgusunun kendi çok boyutlu kavramsal ve teorik karmaşıklığı yanında bir de çoklu göç tecrübesi yaşayan bireylerde bu kimlik olgusu iç içe geçmiş daha karmaşık bir hal almaktadır. Herşeyden önce, dil ve dünya görüşü farklı coğrafyalarda ve kültür alanlarında şekillenen Ahıska Türkleri, Amerika toplumuna geldiklerinde adeta bir kültür şoku ile karşı karşıya kalmışlardır. Gürcistan, Özbekistan ve Rusya'nın görece birbirine yakın ve kendine özgü tarihsel ve toplumsal dinamikleri bu insanların kimlik inşasında belirleyici olmuştur. Yeni gelinen Amerika'daki toplumsal yapının özellikleri ise buradaki Ahıska Türklerinde çok daha derin ve farklı kırılmalara yol açmıştır. Uzun yıllar Rusya'da Amerika karşıtı bir söylemden sonra kendilerini Amerika'nın bir parçası olarak bulmak onlarda önemli bir ikilem meydana getirmiştir. Rochester'daki Ahıska Türkleri genel anlamda kendi içlerine kapalı bir yaşam tarzını sürdürmekle birlikte, burada yaşayan, Ahıska Türklerine göre daha eskiden gelmiş ve daha kalabalık bir nüfusa sahip olan Türkler ile yakın ilişki içindedirler. Bu ilişki evlilik, dini törenler, milli kutlamalar ve sosyal etkinliklerde belirginleşmektedir. Bunun yanında Ahıska Türkleri'nin bir diğer güçlü ve ilginç ilişki biçimi ise Rusça ortak paydası ile Rochester'daki Ukraynalılar ile olan yakın ilişkileridir. Ahıska Türkleri dil anlamında Rusçayı Türkçe'den daha iyi bilmektedirler. Özellikle iş hayatı konusunda Ukrayna kökenli Amerikalılar ile güçlü bir ilişkileri bulunmakta, bu durum da onların arkadaşlık ilişkileri ve sosyal hayatlarında önemli bir belirleyicilik üstlenmektedir.
***

Suriye'de Unutulanlar: Tanıdık Bir Hikaye, Çerkesler ve Göç
(739) Onur Limon (Trakya University)

Çerkesler, Çarlık Rusyası'nın sürgün politikalarıyla önce Kafkasya'dan, Anadolu'ya ve Balkanlar'a ve daha sonra Ortadoğu'ya göç etmek zorunda kalmıştır. Çerkeslerin

Kafkasya'dan başlayan bu göçü, farklı coğrafyalarda ve tarihsel periyotlarda devamlılık göstermektedir. Suriye iç savaşı nedeniyle ülkelerini terk etmek zorunda kalan Suriyeli Çerkeslerden anavatanları Kuzey Kafkasya'ya dönmek isteyenler ise Rusya Federasyonu'nun engelleriyle karşılaşmaktadır. Bugüne kadar Çerkesler ve göç ilişkisi üzerine birçok çalışma yapılmıştır. Diğer çalışmaların aksine bu çalışma, Çerkeslerin Kafkasya'dan başlayan göç hareketlerinin farklı coğrafyalarda ve tarihsel periyotlarda devamlılık gösterdiğini tarihsel bir içerik analiziyle, literatürde yer alan çalışmalara dayanarak ortaya koymaktadır. Çalışmanın amacı, Suriye iç savaşı nedeniyle ülkelerini terk etmek zorunda kalan Suriyeli Çerkeslerden Kafkasya'ya dönmek isteyenlerin karşılaştıkları zorlukları açıklığa kavuşturmaktır. Bu çerçevede, Rusya Federasyonu'nun Kuzey Kafkasya'da Çerkes nüfusu lehine demografik bir değişikliğe izin vermediği, tarihsel nedenlerin yanı sıra, bürokratik engeller, coğrafi etkiler, iş olanakları ve sosyokültürel uyum sorunlarının Çerkeslerin Kuzey Kafkasya'ya dönüşlerine engel teşkil ettiği anlaşılmaktadır.
***

Suriyeli Mültecilerin Dayanışma Ağlarının İbn Haldun'un Asabiyet Kuramı Bağlamında Değerlendirilmesi
(1314) Abulfez Süleymanov (Uskudar University)

Bu çalışmada İstanbul Sultanbeyli ilçesinde 200 Suriyeli mülteci üzerinde yapılan alan araştırmasından elde edilen bulgularla Suriyelilerin kendi aralarında kurdukları dayanışma ağları İbn Haldun'un asabiyet kuramı üzerinden değerlendirmektedir. Araştırma sonuçlarına göre zorunlu göç sürecinde mülteciler beraberinde kültür, gelenek, görenek ve yaşam biçimlerini yeni yerleşim alanlarına taşıdıkları ve mültecilerin beraberlerinde getirdikleri birikimlerin yeni ilişkiler örüntüsü ortaya çıkarmakta olduğu gözlenmiştir. Aile ve aile etrafında odaklaşmış ilişkilerle, akrabalık ve göçmen kimliğinden hareketle sağlanan birliktelikle yeni dayanışma ağları ortaya çıkarmaktadır. Bu dayanışma ağları mültecilerin entegrasyonunda önemli bir misyon üstlenerek; sosyal hayata katılmalarında bir sosyal sermaye özelliği taşımaktadır. Sahip olunan ağlar ile kurulan ilişkiler mültecilere önemli yararlar sağlamakla birlikte bulundukları toplumun ekonomik, politik ve kültürel değerleriyle etkileşim sağlamalarına da neden olmaktadır. Böylece soydaş dayanışması, grup üyeliği, grup bilinci ve aile bağlarına dayalı bir tür sosyalleşme olarak tanımlanan asabiye olgusu mültecilerin yeni koşullar karşındaki en önemli dayanak noktası olarak belirmektedir.
***

Üç Büyük Göç Dalgası ve Gaziantep'in Mekânsal Sürekli Yeniden İnşası
(1363) Nevra Akdemir (Gaziantep University)

Gaziantep, geçmişte Halep'in hinterlandı olarak ticaret ve küçük çaplı imalat faaliyetinin toplaştığı bir bölgesel merkez iken; günümüzde yıkılan Halep'in canhıraş kaçan insanları üzerinden birikim potansiyelini genişleten bir sanayi kenti olarak göze çarpmaktadır. Bu çalışma 1950'ler sonrası dönemde Gaziantep'in üç büyük göç dalgası üzerinden yaşadığı dönüşümü anlamayı hedeflemektedir. Göçü sadece emek havuzunu artıran bir olgu olarak tanımlamamakta; göçün aynı zamanda sermaye ve güç ilişkileri ile birlikte gelişen birikim olanağı olduğunu iddia etmektedir. Zira sermaye birikimi, sanayileşme gibi kavramlarla ifade edilen kentsel ekonomik yapının dönüşümü mekân üzerinden eşitsizlikler üreten bir süreçtir; bu manada kentsel mekan bahsi geçen ilişkilerin göstergesidir; üst üste açılan katmanlar olarak tarihsel dönüşümlerin izini taşımaktadır. Bunun yanı sıra sürekli inşa edilen çok boyutlu bir yerellikle etkileşim halinde siyasal-ekonomik ve toplumsal dokunun dönüşümünü belirlenmektedir. Gaziantep özelinde kentsel yapının dönüşümü ve üretim ilişkileri aile, dinsel cemaat ve/veya hemşerilik temelli bir siyasal stratejinin de etkisiyle oluşmakta ve Gaziantep'in emek ve sanayi coğrafyasını belirlemektedir. Bu çalışmada nitel araştırma yöntemi kullanılmış; belirlenen göç dalgaları ile ilişkilendirilen zamansal ve mekânsal kategorilere uygun olarak seçilen farklı kuşak göçmenlerle ve yerlilerle yüzyüze derinlemesine görüşmeler yapılmış ve çeşitli göç dalgalarının belirleyiciliğinde yeniden inşa edilen yerellik tanımlanmaya çalışılmıştır.

***

Kırsal Mahremin Kente Göçü
(1038) Nuray Karaca (Atatürk University)

Toplumlar sürekli değişim halindedir. Cumhuriyet tarihimiz sürekli olumlu değişim olan ilerleme ile olumsuz değişim olan gerileme kavramları ekseninde dönmektedir. İlerlemenin şartı olan batılılaşma toplumumuzda aynı zamanda kültürel olarak yaşanan çatışmanın da kaynağını oluşturmaktadır. Toplumumuzda teknik değişimin kentten kırsala (merkezden-çevreye) doğru gerçekleşmesi söz konusudur. Tıpkı B. Boran'da olduğu pek çok sosyal bilimci için gibi kentleşme batılılaşma, batılılaşma sanayileşmedir. Buna paralel olarak değişen toplumda zihniyetinde değişmesi dönüşmesi gerekir. Ayrıca teknik değişim ve dönüşüm insanların yaşama daha kolay uyum sağlamasını mümkün hale getirerek cazibe merkezlerinin sadece kent olmasını engelleme çabasıdır. Bunun sonucu olarak kırsalın iticiliği ortadan kalkacak kentlerin çekiciliği karşısında göç etmek isteyen insanların kırsaldan kente doğru göçü engellenemese de göç eden insan sayısı azalacaktır. Bu nedenle Boran'dan hareketle köy davası aslında kent davasıdır. 1950 den itibaren kentlere başlayan hızlı göç olgusu zamanla toplumun en önemli sorunları arasına girmiştir. Öte yandan 1980 den itibaren hız kazanan liberalleşme politikaları ise toplumun tabakaları arasında önemli farklılıklar yaratırken göç olgusu da kırsalla kent arasında yeni geçişler oluşturarak kentte özellikle orta tabakada yeni bir sınıf oluşturmuştur. Kırsal mahremin kente göçü sonucu oluşan bu sınıf önceden göç etmiş kırsal insanın oluşturduğu ne kentli ne köylü görünümünden ve zihniyetinden farklılaşarak kentte kendi kültürünü ve farkındalığını yaratacak kırsal mahremi merkeze yerleştirmiştir. Ilımlı İslam politikaları veya liberal İslam politikaları bu sınıfın geçişlerini kolaylaştırırken, kentte bu sınıfın içinde yer alan insan kırsalın mahremiyetini kaybetmeden moderne uyum sağlama becerisini bünyede buluşturmayı başardı. Bu çalışma kırsaldan kente göç eden insanların oluşturduğu bu sınıfın kentte kendilerini dışarıda bırakılmış hisseden ve kırsal mahremi temsil eden öteki insanları da içine alarak genişlemesindeki yarattığı kimliği ve kültürel unsurlarını belli başlıklar altında (siyaset, eğitim vb.) analiz edecektir.

***

SESSION 10G – Göç ve Edebiyat - 9

	Room: B3
Chair	**Atıf Akgün, Ege University, Turkey**
787	Alfabeden Alfabeye Zorunlu Göç: Türk Edebiyatında Bir "Sözde Transkripsiyon" Vakası -**Fırat Caner**
769	Göç Sözvarlığı Üzerine Bir Kavram Alanı Denemesi – **Asiye Mevhibe Coşar**
980	Göç Nedeniyle Kaybolan Diller ve Çeviriyle Yaratıla(n)/(bilecek) Farkındalık – **Füsun Bilir Ataseven, Anıl Yenigül**
1297	Masallar Bağlamında Dil Göçü – **Serli Nişanyan**

Alfabeden Alfabeye Zorunlu Göç: Türk Edebiyatında Bir "Sözde Transkripsiyon" Vakası
(787) Fırat Caner (Karadeniz Technical University)

Bir tarihçi olan İsmail Hami Dânişmend, 1947 yılında vefat eden eşi Nazan Hanım'ın şiirlerini, 1948 yılında, bir Selçuklu ya da Osmanlı şairi olduğu dedikodusu kulaktan kulağa yayılan Rabia Hatun'un şiirleriymiş gibi yayımladı. Rivayete göre İsmail Hami Dânişmend, bu şiirleri tesadüfen eline geçen bazı yazmalarda bulmuştu. Ancak zamanla, söz konusu şiirlerin bir tarihi şahsiyete ait olmayıp yirminci yüzyılda kaleme alındıkları, üstelik onları yayımlayan tarihçinin merhum eşi Nazan Danişmend'e ait oldukları ortaya çıktı. Mevcudiyeti iddia edilen kaynak metnin yazıldığı dilin, bir yabancı dil değil Türklerin günlük yaşamda kullandığı dil olması sebebiyle bu vaka, literatürde var olan türden bir "sözde çeviri" vakası değildi. Şiirler, Latin alfabesiyle yayımlanan bir dergide, bir tarihçi tarafından, eline geçen bazı yazmalarda bulunduğu iddiası ile yayımlandıklarından, bu vaka bir "sözde transkripsiyon" hadisesi idi. Böylesi eşsiz bir vakayı mümkün kılan da yine eşsiz olan bir başka tarihsel vaka yani 1928'de gerçekleşen alfabe devrimi idi. Bu devrimle metaforik olarak bir ana vatan olan eski alfabe ve eski alfabeyle üretilmiş yazılı kültür milletçe terk edildi. Bu zorunlu göç, tarihinde görülmemiş bir "sözde transkripsiyon" vakasının ortaya çıkmasını mümkün kıldı.

***

Göç Sözvarlığı Üzerine Bir Kavram Alanı Denemesi
(769) Asiye Mevhibe Coşar (Karadeniz Technical University)

Ekonomik, toplumsal, siyasi sebeplerle bireylerin veya toplulukların bir ülkeden başka bir ülkeye, bir yerleşim yerinden başka bir yerleşim yerine gitme işi olarak tanımlanan göç; taşınma, hicret, muhaceret kelimeleri ile eş anlamlı olarak kullanılmaktadır. Türkçe, "göç" kavram alanında alınma kelimelerle birlikte çoğu zaman "acı ve hüzün" taşıyan bir söz varlığı içerir. Bu söz varlığı içinde eş ve yakın anlamlı olarak kullanılan hicret, göç, göçmen, göçebe, göçebelik, göçer, göçerlik, göçkün, ihlâl, iskân, iltica, işgal, kıyım, muhacir, muhaceret, tehcir, mülteci/sığınmacı, mübadil, sürgün, soykırım, savaş gibi kelimeler hep bir "yerinden olma, yer değiştirme" anlamı barındırır. Arapça bir kelime olan zulüm de "Ya bir noksan ya bir ilave yahut vaktini ve yerini değiştirmek suretiyle bir şeyi kendisine mahsus yerden başka bir yere koymak" (Ulutürk; 1990) şeklinde tanımlanmaktadır. Bu manada insanları vatan bildikleri topraklardan ayırmak, hicrete zorlayarak ayrılığa duçar etmek bir zulümdür. Muhacirlik, hicret, sürgün ya da rıza dışı göç, insandan insana yönelik ilk kıyımın kitlesel türevi; dünya üzerinde toplumların birbirine uyguladıkları büyük bir zulüm olarak nitelendirilebilir. Bir yandan "kayıplar manzumesi" şeklinde tanımlanan göç, türüne göre değişen oranda güvensizlik ve stres kaynağı (Sevinç; 2013) olarak da gösterilir. Bu bağlam, potansiyel tanımı dışında kullanımdan kaynaklanan tanımları ile göç olgusuna bakmayı zorunlu kılar. Uluslararası Göç Örgütü tarafından yayımlanan Uluslararası Göç Hukuku/ Göç Terimleri Sözlüğü (Ed.: Çiçekli; 2009), İngilizce-Türkçe karşılıkları ile göç kavramı çerçevesinde oluşan söz varlığını hukuk dilinin ihtiyaçları bağlamında ele almaktadır. Bu çalışmada ise göç kavram alanını belirleyen bağlam temelli bir sözlük oluşturulmaya çalışılacaktır. Böylece Türkçede göç kavram alanına dair zihinsel algı ve kabuller ortaya konulacaktır.
***

Göç Nedeniyle Kaybolan Diller ve Çeviriyle Yaratıla(n)/(bilecek) Farkındalık
(980) Füsun Bilir Ataseven (Yıldız Technical University), Anıl Yenigül (Yıldız Technical University)

Göç, son yıllarda üzerinde en çok araştırma yapılan, kavram olarak yeniden tanımlanan, yarattığı sonuçlar açısından çeşitli değerlendirmelere uğrayan bir olgu olarak ortaya çıkmaktadır. Göç sonunda toplumlar, oradan oraya çeşitli nedenlerle savrularak sürüklenen insanlar; alışkanlıklarını, gelenek, göreneklerini ve özellikle dillerini tehlikeye atmaktalar. Kullandıkları dil, anadilleri olmaktan çıkmakta, melezleşmekte, hatta hakim dilin baskısıyla kaybolma tehlikesiyle karşı karşıya kalmaktadır. Quebec'te 1992 yılında yapılan Uluslararası

Dilbilim Kongresi'nde dilbilimciler şu beyanatta bulunmuşlardır: Herhangi bir dilin yok oluşu insanoğlu için telafisiz bir kayıp olduğundan, şu ana dek çalışılmamış veya belgelere yeterince dökülememiş tehlikedeki veya ölmekte olan dillerin, sözlü edebiyatlarının kaydedilmesi desteklenmelidir, bu konu UNESCO'nun öncelikli görevlerindendir. (Crystal. 2007:7). 2003 yılındaysa UNESCO tarafından yapılan Uluslararası Uzman Toplantısı'nda dünyanın her yanından gelen uzmanlar, Tehlike Altındaki Dilleri belgelemek ve yeniden canlandırmak için izlenecek politikaya son şeklini vermişlerdir. (Crystal. 2007:5). Türkiye'de, günümüzde yaşayan diller olarak Türkçe, Arapça, Arnavutça, Boşnakça, Çerkezce, Abazaca, Ermenice, Gürcüce, Hemşince, Kürtçe, Lazca, Pomakça, Romanca, Rumca, Süryanice, Yahudice, Zazaca sayılmaktadır. (Buran, Çak. 2012:296). Ancak bu dillerden bir çoğu tehlike altında görülmekte git gide bu dilleri konuşanların sayısı azalmaktadır. Dil ölümü, o dili konuşan insan veya toplulukların biyolojik olarak ölmesine bağlı değildir. Diller kullanılmadıkları ve yeni nesillere aktarılmadıkları için ana dil olmaktan çıkarlar. Böylesi durumlarda da insanlar, anadillerinin katilleri konumuna düşerler. Çünkü toplum kendi eliyle kendi kimliğini yok etmiş olmaktadır. Dil ölümü nedir? Dil ölümü ile dil değişimi arasındaki ilişki nedir? Dil ölümü ile kültürel kimlik arasında bir bağ var mıdır? Dil bilimciler, bir dilin doğal konuşanı ölürse ortadan kalkar. veya herhangi bir sebeple bir dil, hiç kimse tarafından konuşulmuyorsa ölür demektedirler. (Crystal: 2000:1). Yani herhangi bir dilin ölmesi için iki şart gereklidir: ya o dili konuşan herkesin ölmesi, ya da insanların başka bir dili iletişim ve anlaşma aracı olarak tercih etmesidir. Bu araştırmada amaç, göç nedeniyle Türkiye'de tehlike altında görülen dilleri mercek altına alıp, çeviri yoluyla toplumda farkındalık yaratmaktır. Araştırma yöntemine gelince, araştırmacının, dışsal bir kişi olmasından çok, katılımcı gözlemci olarak araştırmaya dahil edilmesini öngörmektedir. Nitel araştırma yaklaşımı, katılımcı gözlemciler aracılığıyla, öz-düşünümsel bir bakışla gerçekleştirilen yöntem ve teknikleri içerdiğinden; araştırmada izlenecek bilimsel yol olarak seçilmiştir. Pierre Bourdieu fenomolojik yaklaşımla yapısal yaklaşımı, epistemolojik olarak tutarlı ve evrensel olarak geçerli, bütünleşmiş bir araştırma kipliğinde kaynaştıracaktır diye açıklar. (Bourdieu, 2003:14) Araştırmacı çalıştığı göçmen toplulukla nasıl ilişki kurar? Görüşmecilere nasıl ulaşır? Çalıştığı topluluğun mensubu olması araştırmayı nasıl etkiler? Soruların yanıtları araştırmanın kilit noktalarını oluşturmaktadır. (Körükmez &Südaş, 2015:201). Bilindiği üzere, bir araştırmada sorunsalın belirlenmesi kadar alan araştırması ve yazım aşamasında kullanılacak yöntemlerin seçilmesi de önemlidir. (Harmanşah & Nahya, 2016:38) Etnografi ve çevrimiçi etnografi tekniklerinin kullanılması öngörülen araştırma verilerin değerlendirilmesiyse eklektik alan çözümlemesi yoluyla gerçekleşecektir. (Binark, 2014:118). Bu doğrultuda çeviri, dillerin yok olma süreçlerinde kültürlerin de hayatta kalmasına katkıda bulunacak ve değişerek, gelişerek varlığını sürdürmesine yardımcı olacaktır. Araştırmanın evrenini Hemşin ve Laz dil ve kültürlerinin oluşturmaktadır. Yıllar boyu göçler sonucu bölgede bulunan halkların hareketliliği gibi dil ve kültürlerin dönüşümü çeviri olgusuyla açıklanmaya çalışılacaktır. Bölgedeki göç hareketleri sonucunda gerçekleşen sosyal, ekonomik ve mimari değişimler de çeviri faaliyeti olarak değerlendirilerek, kültürel evrim içerisinde çevirinin rolü saptanacaktır. Bu noktada, Hemşin'den Rusya ve Polonya başta olmak üzere yurtdışına göç eden ve orada öğrendikleri pastacılık zanaatını Türkiye'nin birçok yerinde uygulayan ve özellikle Anadolu'nun değişik yerlerinde fırınlar ve pastaneler açarak kültürel bir aktarım yapan gurbetçilerin memleketlerine döndüklerinde Hemşin'de inşa ettirdikleri Hemşin Konakları inceleme konusu yapılacaktır. Öte yandan, Hemşince ve Lazca dillerindeki çeviri faaliyetleri incelenerek, özellikle, Saint Exupéry'nin Küçük Prens adlı eserinin Hemşince ve Lazcaya (Ardeşen Lazcası ve Hopa Lazcası olmak üzere iki farklı çeviri mevcuttur) yapılan çevirileri değerlendirilecektir. Bu bağlamda dünyada en fazla dile çevrilen kitaplardan biri olma özelliğini taşıyan Küçük Prens'in Hemşince ve Lazcaya çevirileri bu iki dile evrensel edebiyat dizgesinde önemli bir eserin sesi olarak görünürlük ve tanınırlık sağladığı savunulacaktır. Çalışmanın araştırma boyutunda öncelikle bölgedeki tüm kaynaklar taranacak ve veriler toplanacaktır. Ayrıca, bu dillerin en saf haliyle konuşulduğu belli köylerde çeşitli ses ve video kayıtları, röportajlar ve anketler neticesinde dil ve kültür öğelerinin yanında, bu öğelerin her geçen gün nasıl daha fazla yok olmakla yüz yüze kaldığı vurgulanmaya çalışılacaktır. Çevrimiçi deneyimlerin de yer alacağı araştırmada kültürel doğasının anlaşılması için kişinin durduğu konumu anlaşılmaya çalışacaktır. (Binark, 2014:73).

***

Masallar Bağlamında Dil Göçü
(1297) Serli Nişanyan (BNI PPD)

Toplumsal olgular ve yaşanmışlıklar, toplumun öncelikle dilini etkilediği gibi toplumsal psikolojisini de etkilemektedir. Bu nedenle, yapılan araştırmalarda görülmektedir ki, en eski edebi türlerden biri olan masallar, toplumsal hafızanın yeni nesillere aktarılma yollarından en güçlü olanıdır. Bu çalışmada, dinamik olan ve sürekli etkileşime maruz kalan masalların, göç ile ilişkilendirilerek edebiyattaki etkisi irdelenmektedir. Böylelikle, masalların dil ve yaşanmışlıklar açısından gösterdikleri farklılık önemsenmekte ve kıyaslanmaktadır; dilin, göç ile birlikte nasıl evrim geçirdiğini ve aslında dil göçünün yaşandığını göstermek amaçlanmaktadır. Bu çalışma, Yunanca, Ermenice, Türkçe ve Farsça dilleri çerçevesinde etkilenmelerin ne şekilde yaşandığını masallar üzerinden değerlendirmektedir. Yapılan literatür taraması ve röportajlarla birlikte araştırmalar yapılmaktadır. Bu araştırmalar, Yunanca masallar alanında Apostolos Karderinis ile 2016 yılında Atina'da, Türkçe'de Türkan Oktay ile 2016'da İstanbul'da, Farsça'da Hüseyinzade Ailesi ile 2017 yılında İstanbul ve İran'da, Gohar Gurdikyan ile 2015 yılında Ermenistan'da ve yine Ermenice'de İstanbul'da Sultan Balıkçı ile 2014 yılında yapılan röportajlar ile desteklenmektedir. Kültürlerin tarihsel süreçlerinde yaşadıkları her durum, her toplu olay toplumsal dil belleğine kayıt olmakta ve bu nedenle kişilerin kullandıkları kelimeler, cümle yapıları da bu duruma göre değişmektedir. Masallar da bir sonraki nesillere (çocuklara) yaşanmışlıkları direk ya da dolaylı olarak anlatmaktan bir edebi türdür. Özellikle uykunun hemen öncesinde masalların anlatılması da, ailelerin gizli yönlendirmeleri ve mesajları ile yeni neslin bazı olguları, bilgileri, gelenekleri unutmaması için uygulandığı düşünülmektedir. Çünkü bu süreç, unutulmaması istenilen şeylerin beyinde normal zamana göre daha rahat kodlanmasını sağlamaktadır. Bu araştırma, toplumun etkilendiği ve geleceğe taşımak isteyeceği toplumsal duyguları göç neticesinde şekillenen dilin kullanımını incelemeyi amaçlamaktadır. Edebiyatta, masalın varoluşu ele alınmaktadır. Bu nedenle kişilerin hayatlarını etkileyen kelimelerin masallardaki kullanımları, toplumsal psikoloji, edebiyat kültürü, gelecek nesillere toplumsal tarihin ve duyguların aktarılması açısından önemi, masallar üzerinden vurgulanmakta ve değerlendirilerek çeşitli bulgulara ulaşılmaktadır.

***

SESSION 11A – Economics of Migration - 4

	Room: A1
Chair	**Brandon Lundy, Kennesaw University, USA**
1139	Neoliberal Governing through Economization and Ethnicization of the 'Ideal' Migrant Subject: Subjectivation Processes of Migrant Entrepreneurs from Turkey in Austria - **Alev Çakır**
1023	Economic Adaptation of English Speaking Skilled Iraqi Asylum Seekers in Finland – **Anu Yijälä**
1049	The Differentiation of Performances among Immigrant Entrepreneurs: a Biographical Approach - **Daniela Gnarini**

Neoliberal Governing through Economization and Ethnicization of the 'Ideal' Migrant Subject: Subjectivation Processes of Migrant Entrepreneurs from Turkey in Austria

(1139) Alev Çakır (University of Vienna)

This paper analyzes how subject formations promoted in policies and discourses on migration, in particular on migrant entrepreneurship, are negotiated by migrant entrepreneurs from Turkey. This research explores the question of how the subjectivation of work by entrepreneurs from Turkey in Vienna in the context of the post-guest worker era is connected to a neoliberal Leistungsverständnis (performance). It also examines the relationship between subject positions (i.e. identities, categorizations, characterizations of migrant entrepreneurs) promoted in policies and subjectivities of people by taking the example of entrepreneurs from Turkey. Therefore, it will be also analyzed how policies at the international and supranational level such as the European Union (EU) or the Organization for Economic Cooperation and Development (OECD) and national/local level such as various municipal authorities enhance the economization and ethnicization of the 'ideal' migrants. Thereby, this paper examines which continuities, overlaps but also breaks and resistances or disconnections occur in these subjectivation processes. This paper also explores which categories (i.e. gender and ethnicity) and their intersectionality structure these subjectivation processes. Migrant entrepreneurship has been increasingly emphasized in the political agenda of the EU, OECD, Austria and in policies and societal discourses. With respect to Austria, entrepreneurs from Turkey are a crucial group targeted within the respective policies and discourses. Their positioning has to be understood in a post-guest worker context which is characterized by discrimination experiences and exclusions and is linked with post-Fordist employment conditions which presuppose precarious working conditions. This paper assumes that neoliberal economization of the migrant subject is particularly effective due to experiences of discriminations and exclusions of people with migration histories who thus, have to proof, work and perform more than members of the majority society. Additionally, in the policy papers of the EU or OECD, migrants have been framed as having a particular 'migrant entrepreneurial spirit', meaning that they are more prone to start businesses and also more prepared to take risks. The respective policies, discourses but also migrant entrepreneurs themselves reproduce 'migrants' as ethnicized and economicized 'Others' or 'Selfs' and link entrepreneurship with social mobility, integration, economic development and the figure of the 'ideal migrant'. Hence, this analysis also demonstrates how ethnicity is also strategically used as a resource or becomes commodified i.e. in form of social capital by the migrant entrepreneurs. This paper is based on Frame Analysis of policies (i.e. policy documents of the EU, OECD) and 20 expert interviews with representatives of institutions promoting migrant entrepreneurship and 40 semi-structured interviews with migrant entrepreneurs from Turkey in Austria. Additionally, it is based on document analysis of policy papers and reports relevant for policy formulations for the institutions such as the EU, OECD and international as well as national intermediary actors such as the International Centre for Migration Policy Development (ICMPD) or Public Employment Service Austria (AMS). Additionally, the paper also analyzes brochures, booklets or policy papers of institutions promoting migrant entrepreneurs such as the Austrian Federal Economic Chamber (Wirtschaftskammer

Österreich, WKÖ) or Vienna Business Agency (Wirtschaftsagentur Wien). Firstly, this paper contributes to the debate on the relationship between subject position and subjectivation of people by integrating policies as important framework in subjectivation approaches. Secondly, this research includes into the debate on neoliberal subjectivation processes the subjectivities of people with migration histories from an intersectional perspective. Intersectional perspective means to examine subjectivities along social categories such as class, gender, ethnicity and political identity. Thirdly, it contributes to migration research by exploring issues of external governance and techniques of self-governance of people with migration histories. The preliminary findings are, on the one hand, a typology in which entrepreneurship has various meanings for the migrant entrepreneurs such as following: Entrepreneurship as a way of integration into the Austrian society; as social, economic and political participation; a way of emancipation and independence in terms of economic, social but even political independence; as resisting practice to proof that one is not depending on and is performing better than members of the majority society; a way out of financial difficulties and resistance against racist discriminations on the labour market and thus, to become one's own boss; and as a kind of status of prosperity with good reputation. On the other hand, the results emphasize in particular frictions and resistances of the migrant entrepreneurs that occurred in examining the relationship between subject positions in policies and the subjectivities of the entrepreneurs. A systematic and intersectional analysis of the relationship between subject formation and subjectivation of migrant entrepreneurs from Turkey offers contributions to the debate on forms of inequality and precarization in the context of migration and capitalist labour markets, ethnicization processes, integration and the role of policies in subjectivities of migrants.

***

Economic Adaptation of English Speaking Skilled Iraqi Asylum Seekers in Finland
(1023) Anu Yijälä (City of Helsinki)

The unprecedented number of forced migrants looking for peace and starting a new life within the European Union was also noted in Finland, as more asylum seekers than ever (32,476) entered the country in the autumn of 2015. Although the movement towards northern member states of the EU has thereafter decreased, more forced migrants can be expected to come to Europe in the years to come. Consequently, to be able to constructively discuss both the potential and the needs of the newcomers, it is important to gain an understanding of the phenomenon. This paper considers the factors potentially relevant for a successful acculturation process of the potential newcomers to the Finnish society, while taking into account their difficult background situation in their previous homeland. Since asylum seekers from an Iraqi background were over-represented when it comes to the asylum requests registered in Finland, this particular group was chosen to be interviewed for the study. More specifically, the paper builds on the findings of a qualitative study of English speaking skilled Iraqi asylum seekers (N = 22) who arrived in Finland during 2015–2016. This group could be expected to have a head start regarding integration into the Finnish society and the labour market in comparison to other, less educated asylum seekers with no English language proficiency. During the time of the first round of interviews, the participants were waiting for the decision about their asylum requests in Helsinki or Turku. In 2017, those participants that had received a permission to stay in Finland are being re-interviewed, and the data will be analysed before the conference dates in August, enabling presentation of the results of their longer-term adaptation in Finland. Berry's a acculturation framework (e.g. Berry 1997) was used as the main theoretical framework of the study, stressing the reciprocal nature of the acculturation process through

intercultural encounters (Berry 2005). The study builds on the social constructivist research approach, arguing that the reality is in constant evolution and change, where everybody's thoughts, words and actions form the reality that we live in (Patton 2001, pp. 96–103). The data is being gathered through semi-structured interviews, conducted both through personal and focus group interviews, and analysed using the Atlas.ti software. Iraq and Finland can be argued to be two countries with a vast cultural distance (Hofstede 1991): the strong influence of Islam that permeates all aspects of life in Iraq, from politics to the private life behind closed doors, is almost unimaginable for Finns used to freedom of expression, keeping religious beliefs to themselves as an extremely private matter. Moreover, adjusting to Finland's harsh climate as well as difficulties in making friendships have been reported to be major challenges even among the international professionals in Finland (Yijälä et al. 2009). Unfortunately, in Finland, also the economic adaptation (cf. Aycan 1997) of the newcomers may prove equally challenging, since especially the visible minority groups are more often unemployed than native Finns (Sarvimäki 2011). The presentation discusses the fulfillment of aspirations that this privileged group of Iraqi asylum seekers have had regarding their future work life. Furthermore, it considers the challenges that the differences in the Finnish and Iraqi working cultures might have posed to their future labour market integration. According to the results of the first stage of the study, while waiting for the decision that will have a huge impact on the rest of their lives, the asylum seekers find themselves in a tough, limbo-like stage of their migration process: On one hand, the difficult experiences in Iraq and the arduous trip have left their mark on those who managed to escape. On the other hand, being in a new country without knowing whether or not they can stay, poses severe challenges to their psychological well-being and integration process. Nevertheless, at that point in time, the future hopes and dreams of the participants reflected things that are very similar to those of Finns: finding work, getting married, raising a family and living a peaceful life. After the second round of interviews, it is possible to reflect on their situation after spending 1–1.5 years in a new country: Were they ready to meet the requirements of the Finnish labor markets? How did the (un)employment affect other facets of their adaptation to a new country? What kind of role have their networks played in their employment – or were they rather formed after finding work? Did (un)employment affect their well-being and what could be done in order to better support their adaptation in Finland?
***

The Differentiation of Performances among Immigrant Entrepreneurs: a Biographical Approach
(1049) Daniela Gnarini (University of Trento)

This paper aims to contribute to the field of immigrants' entrepreneurial performance. The debate on immigrant entrepreneurship has been dominated by cultural explanations, which argue that immigrants' entrepreneurial results are linked to groups' characteristics (e.g. Bonacich, 1975; Light, 1984; Altinay, 2008). However, cultural theories do not consider the huge differences in performances also within the same ethnic group. Furthermore, other important dimensions influence entrepreneurial performances, such as human and social capital (e.g. Sanders and Nee, 1996; Portes and Sensebrenner, 1993), and the context where immigrants are embedded in (e.g. Kloostermann and Rath, 2001). Moreover, the individual path of the immigrant entrepreneurs should be taken into account while analysing performances. Few studies have implemented a biographical approach, by analysing experiences and motivations of immigrant entrepreneurs at the starting phase of the business (e.g. Kontos, 2003). Hence, the current study adopts a biographical approach, both at theoretical and at methodological level, which can allow to understand the main

aspects that make the difference in immigrants' entrepreneurial performances, by exploring the narratives of immigrant entrepreneurs, who operate in the restaurant sector in two different Italian metropolitan areas: Milan and Rome. Through the qualitative method of biographical interviews, this study analyses four main dimensions and their combinations: a) individuals' migratory and entrepreneurial path: this aspect is particularly relevant to understand the biographical resources of immigrant entrepreneurs and their change and evolution during time; b) entrepreneurs' social capital, with a particular focus on their networks, through the adoption of a transnational perspective, that takes into account both the local level and the transnational connections. c) entrepreneurs' human capital, including both formal education and skills acquired through informal channels. The latter are particularly relevant, since in the interviews and data collected the role of informal transmission emerges. d) embeddedness within the social, political, and economic context, to understand the main constraints and opportunities both at local and at national level. The comparison between two different metropolitan areas within the same country helps to understand this dimension.
***

The Immigrant Native Wage Gap in Malaysia: The Preliminary Results
(763) Borhan Abdullah (University of Aberdeen), Alexandros Zangelidis, Ioannis Theodosiou

This paper focuses on the wage gap between native and immigrant workers in Malaysian labour market. This paper uses the Productivity and Investment Climate Survey (PICS) 2 for 2007 to explore the components of the immigrant-native wage gap. The Oaxaca decomposition analysis and quantile regression decomposition were applied in this study. By exploiting the PICS data, the result of this study shows that the immigrant has a lower human capital return on earnings compared to native. Another significant finding is that the wage gap between native and immigrant is mostly explained by the difference in the characteristics of the workers, while, the remaining were explained by the discriminatory effects.
***

"Working with and Employing Refugee Populations - Preventing Perpetuation of Violence and Oppression in the Workplace"
(1133) Jordan Elizabeth Fallow (Australian Institute of Business)

Organisations that serve refugee/forced migrant populations are staffed by a large percentage of former refugees themselves, and these staff are vulnerable to re-traumatization due to the nature of work they do;-   they   are   often   at   risk   of exploitation (both from their communities at large and from organisations), leading to burn-out, compassion fatigue and exhaustion; -   these risks are exacerbated by a lack of organisational awareness of how intersecting identities (race, class, gender, nation, ability etc) and power dynamics affect the workspace. Encourage an awareness of intersectionality principles in the workplace, so that diverse organisations in the sector do not risk perpetuating structural violence and retraumatization. This will draw on systems theory and intersectionality theory, as well as strategic human resource management and performance management texts. -   Organisations in the refugee health sector employ people from refugee backgrounds thus necessitating an increased awareness of intersectionality into their policies in order to; -   Increase employee satisfaction and performance, leading to better health outcomes for both employees and clients at large; -
      Decrease risks of re-traumatization, burn-out, poor performance, workplace bullying and harassment, ethical breaches etc; -   Indirectly   Increase   community

education around mental and physical health and self-care. A case study of one of the largest refugee and asylum seeker settlement organisations in Australia was conducted. The organisation services over 30,000 clients across Australia and employs large numbers of staff from former refugee backgrounds. This in depth investigation gathered qualitative and quantitative data from a variety of sources, including interviews and observation of key staff and policy changes. Issues of ethics were discussed with the Australian Institute of Business, the organisation and the staff themselves. Organisations need to ensure a number of steps are taken in management of refugee staff to reduce the increased risk of burn out, compassion fatigue and retraumatisation. These include: 1.　　Increased access to professional development and opportunity to pursue relevant qualifications. 2.　　Adequate compensation comparable to that of non-refugee staff. 3.　　Access to culturally competent reflective practice, supervision, and peer learning circles. 4.Communication mechanisms to ensure access to management to address concerns. 5.　　Adequate debriefing and supervision after critical or serious incidents. 6.　　Training for managers and organisations around cross cultural communication. 7.　　Education around related topics such as family violence, substance abuse, community engagement for all staff. 8.　　Principles of intersectionality should be drawn upon when managing and appraising staff performance.
　　***

SESSION 11B – Spatial Patterns in Human Mobility - 3

	Room: A2
Chair	**George Mavrommatis, Harokopio University, Greece**
1016	Migrants' Journey, Vulnerabilities, Access to Information and Endured Violence During the Journey and in Refugee Camps in Ioannina, Attica, Athens and Samos, Greece – **Jihane Ben Farhat, M Bouhenia, P.J Bjertrup, K Blanchet, P Mayaud, L Salumu, C Perrin, K Porten, S Cohuet**
850	A Short Ethnography at the Port of Piraeus Refugee Camp: Going Back in Time, Rethinking the Experience - **Alexandros Koutras**
1142	Mapping Shipwrecks of Refugees and Immigrants in the Mediterranean Sea Since 2015 - **Artemis Tsiopa**
1191	Inadmissible Person on the Border - **Bilge Erson Asar**

Migrants' Journey, Vulnerabilities, Access to Information and Endured Violence During the Journey and in Refugee Camps in Ioannina, Attica, Athens and Samos, Greece

(1016) Jihane Ben Farhat (Epicentre), M Bouhenia (Epicentre), P.J Bjertrup (Epicentre), K Blanchet (LSHTM), P Mayaud (LSHTM), L Salumu (MSF), C Perrin (MSF), K Porten (Epicentre), S Cohuet (Epicentre)

Since 2015, Europe has been facing an unprecedented arrival of refugees and migrants. More than one million people has entered Europe via land and sea routes. With the closure of the FYROM border and the EU/Turkey deal, around 60,000 refugees and migrants are stuck in Greece [1]. During their journey, refugees and migrants often face harsh conditions, forced detention and violence in transit countries. However, there is a lack of evidence on their experiences and their mental health status. The objective of the survey is to document the vulnerabilities and mental health difficulty of refugees and migrants in their home country, during their journey and in Greece. We conducted a cross-sectional population-based retrospective survey combined with an explanatory qualitative study from November 2016 and February 2017 in seven sites in Greece: 4 refugee camps,

1 hotspot et 2 hotels. We used exhaustive sampling on 3 sites and systematic sampling on 4 sites. The survey consisted of a questionnaire on experienced violence and an anxiety disorder screening tool. Furthermore, we collected data on demographics, crossed countries, health status, access to healthcare and legal aid, and life plans. For the qualitative part, in-depth interviews and focus group discussions were conducted. The in-depth interviews explored experienced violence and mental health difficulty in home country, during the journey and in Greece and the focus group discussions examined access to services and information in relation to asylum procedures. In total, 1293 individuals were included; 60.9% were aged ≥15 years and 7.8% were 0-5 years. Sixty percent were males and 64.4% were from Syria. Depending on sites, 48.7% (37.8-59.8) to 94.7% (90.1-97.2) reported fleeing from war. Twenty four percent (18.3-31.6) to 54.7% (46.6-62.6) reported having experienced at least one violent event, during the journey or in Greece. Access to an appropriate medicine for those who suffered from a chronic disease on sites varied from 38.1% (26.0-51.9) to 83.5%. Seventy three percent of the population have been screened positive to the anxiety disorder screening tool. Among them, 41.2% refused to be referred to a psychologist. Access to legal assistance and information about asylum procedures are considered as non-existent for the majority of the population. The qualitative interviews show the difficult and violent conditions of border crossings and the tense and stressful interactions with smugglers. These experiences together with experiences of war in home country stand out as traumatic experiences for the participants. Recent studies have emphasized daily stressors in relation to high rates of psychological distress often found in conflict driven migrants [2, 3, 4]. The study underlines various daily stressors as negatively affecting the mental wellbeing of migrants and refugees in Greece. Lastly, the qualitative part indicates barriers to accessing mental health care. This survey conducted among refugees in a European country provides important quantitative and qualitative data on refugees and migrants living in different camp contexts and describes their vulnerabilities during journeys and in Greece. Similar documentation should be repeated throughout Europe in order to better respond to the needs of this vulnerable population.

***

A Short Ethnography at the Port of Piraeus Refugee Camp: Going Back in Time, Rethinking the Experience
(850) Alexandros Koutras (Harokopio University)

The European refugee crisis changed the migration dynamics of many EU member states. As a result of this mass movement of refugees, the Western Balkan route was formed. Along this route, temporary settlement camps were created to cater to the needs of people on the move. This short paper is based on an ethnography that took place at the port of Piraeus (Athens, Greece) camp. Through insights from participant observation, it brings to the fore dreams of movement and inclusion in Central and Northern European societies along with desperate efforts of local integration on the ground. This paper is reflective on the ethnographic experience, but most importantly, it is reflective to what happened to these people one year after their coming to Greece. Are there populations integrated into society? Have they applied for asylum in Greece? How many of them have been relocated to other EU member states? In short, what can we learn from putting side by side the Piraeus informal camp experience to the current conditions of refugees in Greece? Can we talk about improvement or not?

***

Mapping Shipwrecks of Refugees and Immigrants in the Mediterranean Sea Since 2015
(1142) Artemis Tsiopa (Harokopio University), Stamatis Kalogirou (Harokopio University)

In the recent years, the continuous political tensions and the multiple civil wars, in the Middle East (mainly in Syria) and in Northern African countries, have caused a dramatic increase of people emigrating. Most of these people are trying to reach a European Union country where they become immigrants and refugees. Since 2015, the numbers are so high that this is considered a migration crisis in the EU. There are multiple challenges in this crisis. Examples include humanitarian aspects (provision of food and health care) as well as political aspects (internal political tensions, country relationships, respect of human rights). This crisis significantly affects Greece since the Eastern Mediterranean route has been used by hundreds of thousands of immigrants to reach Western Europe. Thus, since 2016 this route has been sealed in order to stop more people moving to Central and West European countries. Most immigrants enter the EU by sea. They use small boats to reach the shores of Greek islands in the Aegean Sea and big boats to reach the shores of Italy, Malta and Spain. It is evident that these boats very often sink due to a great variety of reasons, such as the dangerous weather conditions. These shipwrecks cause the death of thousands of immigrants and refugees in recent years. This paper aims to record and present the shipwrecks that have occurred during the period 2015-2017 in the Mediterranean Sea, as well as, the number of the dead, the missing and the rescued persons from each shipwreck. For this purpose, data from the International Organization for Migration (IOM) are being used. These data are presented in thematic maps that are created by using the Geographical Information Systems (GIS). From the produced maps there are evident certain outcomes. The majority of the shipwrecks occur in a short distance to the shores and often near the same areas. This observation could be associated with the existence of specific routes that lead to certain areas in the shores, as well as with their popularity. In addition, it is apparent from the produced maps that the shipwrecks with the highest number of dead, missing and rescued persons, also, occur near the shores. In the same context, the dead from the recorded shipwrecks appear to be more than the rescued and the missing.

***

Inadmissible Person on the Border
(1191) Bilge Erson Asar (Istanbul Kultur University)

Developments in international aviation law throughout the 20th Century has shortened journeys worldwide, and has allowed individuals to reach various parts of the world more easily. Therefore, air travel has become a widely preferred method of migration today. However, air travel is not immune to problems; far from it. When a migrant travel to a foreign country by air, the journey can end in two ways. The person can either be admitted into the country, or be declared as an inadmissible (INAD) person; this prevents entrance to the country. The circumstances and the rules governing an INAD person are laid out in international civil aviation law. The Convention on International Air Law (Chicago Convention), widely regarded as the constitution of the ICAO (International Civil Aviation Organization), and, more generally, of international civil aviation law, was adopted in 1944. Chicago Convention explicitly and implicitly establishes the rights, responsibilities, and obligations of states that intend to determine international principles and arrangements in order to ensure a safe and orderly system in international aviation law. These rights and obligations are also laid down as Standards in Annexes, which are an integral part of the Chicago Convention. Annex 9 imposes obligations on states and aircraft operators of INAD persons. As far as INAD is concerned, airline operators have increasingly been forced to take on the role of international immigration officers, since Annex 9 opens the door for states to impel them to assume this role. Annex 5.9 asserts that the state is responsible for the cost of custody and care of all other categories of inadmissible

persons—other than those holding improper documents—from the moment these persons are found to be inadmissible until they are returned to the aircraft operator for removal from the state. In practice, however, states pass this responsibility over to airline operators, and even fine them in the event of the arrival of an inadmissible person. At this juncture, the aircraft operator is obliged to remove the INAD person to the point where he is able to commence his journey, or continue to any place where he is admissible. Problems arise when the INAD in question reaches a destination where, again, he is regarded as inadmissible, and is forced to fend for herself. In a worst-case scenario, individuals are forced to wallow in airports, where recourse to the law is scarce, owing to the nature of the blurred lines of borders characteristic of international airports. On March 17, 2017, the European Court of Human Rights (ECHR) delivered a judgement on the Case of Z.A. and Others v. Russia, which evinced one of the most difficult scenarios that a person could experience. The verdict demonstrates the conditions which INAD people are exposed to in the transit hall of the country to where they are stranded, and the obligations of the states concerning their fundamental human rights and safety. The decision is also the first comprehensive decision the ECHR has made for INAD people so far. This decision is also important when reconciling the rules of international aviation law with the rules on human rights. In my presentation, first of all, I will summarize the civil aviation legal system which governs the rules of INAD. I will focus on the circumstances through which a person can be declared an INAD. After summarising the ruling of the ECHR, I will consider the situation in Turkey, and will focus on the problems that regulations concerning migration issues in Turkey unveil within the framework of ECHR decision. In the last part of my presentation, suggestions will be put forward to ensure that the responsibilities of states laid out in Annex 9 are fulfilled to international human rights law standards.
***

SESSION 11C – Conceptualising Migration

	Room: A4
Chair	**Deniz Eroğlu Utku, University of Thrace, Turkey**
1071	Power and Regulation in Migration Systems - Bring in Critical Theory – **Robert Westermann**
1135	Do Emigrants Self-Select Along Cultural Traits? Evidence from the MENA Countries - **Frédéric Docquier, Aysit Tansel, Riccardo Turati**
871	Rethinking Refugee Activism within and beyond the State: The Trajectory of Refugee Activism – **Birce Altıok Karşıyaka**
1150	Alfred Schütz's Theory of Foreignness of in the Context of Public Health – The Case of Family Caregivers of People with Dementia – **Hürrem Tezcan-Güntekin**

Power and Regulation in Migration Systems - Bring in Critical Theory
(1071) Robert Westermann (University of Hildesheim)

Until now 'World System' approaches, also known as 'Critical Theories', are mainly applied in IR Research. In the following I will illustrate on one example, the 'Neogramscian Approach' of Robert Cox, how global correlations of social forces, forms of state and global orders profoundly affect international migration processes and should be considered by theoretical debates in migration studies. Furthermore, I will show how the historical 'transformation' perspective in combination with the awareness of local agency of 'Critical Theories' can be a promising "Add-on" for research designs based on migration systems. The overall aim of this theoretical adaptation is to formulate a fixed structure of interrelating levels of action and categories of power within an international migration system. A second step would be to explain how this international migration system generates forms of transnational hegemony as a product of consensual social processes and how transformations build new forces of influence at different stages (world order, social forces and forms of state).

***

Do Emigrants Self-Select Along Cultural Traits? Evidence from the MENA Countries

(1135) Frédéric Docquier (UCLouvain, Belgium), Aysit Tansel (Middle East Technical University), Riccardo Turati (UCLouvain, Belgium)

Human capital and cultural traits are proximate drivers of modernization, economic growth, and democracy. Hence, factors that affect human capital accumulation and the distribution of cultural traits have persistent effects on economic and political outcomes. International migration is one of these factors, and the existing literature has long emphasized that migrants self-select by education (Belot and Hatton (2012)). On the contrary, migrants' selection by cultural traits, beliefs and practices has been largely understudied. Focusing on the MENA countries, this paper tackles this issue, and tests whether migration aspirations, plans to emigrate and preferred destination choices are influenced by cultural traits. We focus on religiosity and attitudes towards women's rights, two traits that are correlated with economic outcomes and for which MENA countries exhibit distinctive distributions.We use the Gallup World Poll microdata and extract 12 questions on opinions and beliefs, as well as question on migration aspirations, plan to emigrate within 12 months, and individual characteristics. Using a double principal component analysis, we identify four cultural indicators and normalize them between zero and one (zero being interpreted as the most conservative value and one being the most progressive or liberal value). Among them, religiosity and gender-egalitarian attitudes are the only ones being correlated with income per capita. We then investigate (i) whether cultural progressiveness affects the aspirations and plans to emigrate over the 2007-2011 period, (ii) whether selection on culture varies with country-specific characteristics, and (iii) whether the selection intensity has changed after the Arab Spring looking over the 2007-2016 period. We show that intended emigrants from the MENA and individuals with concrete emigration plans are culturally selected, and that this selection on cultural traits depends on the type of preferred destination. Intended migrants to OECD countries exhibit significantly lower levels of religiosity than intended non-migrants. As far as attitude towards women's rights are concerned, intended migrants to OECD countries are more progressive, but the results are driven by the composition of the Muslim population. We find an effect of the Arab Spring on the intensity of cultural selection with respect to a subsample of countries that were highly affected by this historical event. Our results thus indicate that emigration to OECD countries potentially impacts the distribution of cultural traits among those left behind. It is worth stressing that our analysis does not make any value judgment about specific cultural traits, and does not argue that cultural differences should be combated or that a set of traits dominates others. Culture shapes the utility function of people, implying that comparisons of economic outcomes do not reflect comparisons in welfare. This is evidenced in Campante and Yanagizawa-Drott (2015), who show that religious practices in Muslims' countries (as measured by the length of the Ramadan fasting period) have negative implications for economic performance, but increase subjective wellbeing among followers. Nevertheless, there are several reasons that justify focusing on cultural selection in general, and on selection by religiosity and by views on gender inequalities in particular. First, cultural selection is one of the main mechanisms through which emigration affects the distribution of cultural traits in the population left behind. If not compensated by ex-post transfers of norms and beliefs from destination to origin countries, study such transfers of norms. Selection on gender-egalitarian attitudes is likely to impact effective gender inequality, which is repulsive in its own rights. In the same vein, the distribution of cultural traits may affect the openness to innovation and the modernization potential of the origin country. Second, cultural selection may increase the cultural distance between poor and rich countries, which has been seen as a brake on technology diffusion and on the transmission of democratic values. Third, cultural selection is a key determinant of the cultural distance between migrants and host-country citizens, therefore determining the level of cultural diversity at destination, opinions towards immigration, and migrants' capacity to assimilate. The literature on these potential channels has been growing rapidly for the last decade or so. Migrants' selection on culture determines the level of cultural diversity in the host country. Although multiculturalism induces beneficial effects on the host country (Alesina et al. (2016); Docquier et al. (2016)), a number of empirical studies show that immigrants' economic outcome depends on the distance between immigrants' identity and the dominant norms (e.g., Pendakur and Pendakur (2005); Battu and Zenou (2010); Casey and Dustmann (2010); Bisin et al. (2011); Islam and Raschky (2013)). The effect is usually negative and its size is uncertain. Perceived cultural distance is also the source of negative attitudes towards immigrants (Card et al. (2006)), leading to discrimination, marginalization and exclusion from the economic, social and political life.

***

Rethinking Refugee Activism within and beyond the State: The Trajectory of Refugee Activism
(871) Birce Altıok Karşıyaka (Koc University)

This paper aims to build a theoretical model on refugees' political struggle for human rights with connection to activism and social movement theories through adopting a trajectory of right-claim by the refugee/migrant and pro-migrant alliances. The research undertakes an interdependent theoretical approach to state sovereignty and autonomy of the refugee debates through categorizing forms of activism under the hierarchical model of migrants' access to rights by decomposing variance in refugee activism. Through such classification, it aims to find a middle ground for the discussions between refugee/migrant struggle within the citizenship debate and the critical approach challenging the autonomy of migrants by integrating the limits of right-based actions that are shaped by the sovereign state policies and practices. The literature on refugee and migrant activism conduct theoretical discussions within and beyond the realm(s) of citizenship (Turner, 2016, p.151). The latter, referred as critical citizenship studies, challenge traditional understanding of citizenship and broaden the meanings attached to it; whereas, the former, the autonomy of migration perspectives take citizenship as part of state instrument, and attentive to control and governance by the sovereign (Ataç, Rygiel and Stierl, 2016, p.532-3). Under the beyond citizenship debate, the struggles of migrants open up "new spaces of citizenship that potentially enable both new ways of being political and new visions for the type of politics" (Nyers and Rygiel, 2012, p.9). It is through the political acts of refugee/migrant subjects that they challenge and transform citizenships. Whereas, the autonomy of migration takes a critical stand on the widening scope of citizenship by incorporating the refugee/migrant struggle, instead, it argues that citizenship cannot be thought without the control and governance role attributed to the sovereign (Papadopoulos and Tsianos, 2013). Between these two approaches, the concept of citizen is subject to transformation and the limits cannot be reduced to state sovereignty (Nyers, 2015). In other words, it would be inaccurate to take citizenship as fully autonomous contra the state, or associate it completely with the sovereign. Rather, autonomy as well as sovereign state perspectives contribute to the emergence of new spaces of political action, and change the definition and practices of previously attached meanings to citizenship. Therefore, just like yin yang, two contrary forces pulling-pushing each other towards a more complementary form. Since the history of men is the history of struggle against the almighty and powerful, whether there emerges a global citizenship (Isin and Nyers, 2014), 'acts of citizenship' (Isin and Nielson, 2008) or 'abject cosmopolitanism' (Nyers, 2003), the fight for equaliberty (Gündoğdu, 2015, p.23) and the acts to right the wrong manifest itself in the form of varying voices that needs a much more detailed look. The trajectory perspective aims to decompose the refugee claims for rights from the initial act of refugee flight. I argue that activism is inherent in different dimensions of refugee acts. The initial act of flight is a political act in the sense of contesting against the real/perceived threat of persecution (Nyers and Rygiel, 2012, p.8). It is an 'act of resistance' to counter intolerable conditions (Lewis, 2006) or 'for many, [it is] simultaneously a strategy of resistance and an attempt to better one's life conditions through mobility' (Isin and Rygiel, 2007, p.187). However, as the flight continues and knocks on other countries doors, the political act takes different forms with varying characteristics. It is the main focus of this theoretical paper to stress on the continuance of acts of resistances followed by the act of 'taking a refuge.' Initial act of flight is categorized under inexplicit form of activism. It is inexplicit due to forced and involuntary nature of the act different than contentious politics adopted by the contemporary definitions of citizenship. The inexplicit transforms itself to explicit forms through change from involuntary to voluntary activism as the flight takes new forms. The hierarchical model, therefore, disintegrates rights making and claiming of refugees through the prism of 'acts of citizenship' and 'state sovereignty' by taking into account two factors' interdependency and interconnectedness. For example, an open-door policy of a state fulfilling the non-refoulement principle opens new avenues for state refugee policies to realize, for better or worse, and in return, refugees' levels of expectations and satisfactions in accordance with these policies, highlight the agenda of activism and create varying contentious political forms depending on the encampment policy and conditions, access to asylum procedures, access to work etc. The paper will present a theoretical model by categorizing forms of activism and empirically support it with evidences of refugee activism cases from different country settings and refugee groups.

***

Alfred Schütz's Theory of Foreignness of in the Context of Public Health – The Case of Family Caregivers of People with Dementia
(1150) Hürrem Tezcan-Güntekin (Bielefeld University)

Background: In line with demographic changes the number of elderly migrants in Germany is on the rise. Most of them came to Germany during the recruitment of workers and planned to stay only a few years, however they stayed for decades and became elder residents in Germany. The theory of foreignness of Alfred Schütz (1972) explains how migrants try to belong to the new community and how they organize their understanding of the new reference lines. Migrants perceive themselves as belonging to a community in different ways. The situation of being a family caregiver of a person with dementia can lead people feel as strangers in the life world they have gotten used to, again. In order to develop a new sense of belonging to their life world, they use different coping strategies to activate self-management competencies. Aim: The investigation scope of this study is to study the circumstances in which family caregivers can activate self-management competencies to implement the nursing care setting into their life setting. Addition to this empirical aim, the theoretical aim of the project is to reformulate the theory of foreignness of Alfred Schütz

(1972) in the context of public health. Method: A qualitative study is conducted with 10 semi-structured interviews with Turkish family caregivers of people with dementia. The data are analyzed by content analyses (Mayring 2006) and parts of the data with the reconstructive documentary method (Bohnsack 2003). Results: Family caregivers suffer from helplessness and only some of them can change their attitude in a paradigm shift to an attitude of constructive action. The moment of decision to leave the helplessness to act in a constructive active way is dependent on a paradigm shift, which can be triggered by different things like input from another person, accepting the symptoms as an illness and reflection of the own situation. The outcome of this paradigm shift in regard to Schütz's theory of strangeness gives rise for a reformulation as a theory of diversity in public health, because the life worlds of caregivers, regardless of whether they have a migration background or not, are already very heterogeneous and the starting reasons of the paradigm shifts as well. Conclusion: Foreignness in context of dementia concerns not only family caregivers with migration background, but family caregivers with different diversity characteristics and has to be considered as a wider social matter. Instruments to help family caregivers to achieve this paradigm shift have to be developed for a diverse community – with and without migration background – and different diversity characteristics living in different life worlds.

***

SESSION 11D – Data and Methods

	Room: A5
Chair	**Murat Yüceşahin, Ankara University, Turkey**
1063	Thinking about Data: Potentialities and Limitations of Administrative Records on Migration in Brazil – **Nayara Belle Nova da Costa, Helen da Costa Gurgel**
897	Data on refugees in Germany – gaps and ways to close the gaps - **Axel Kreienbrink**
1165	Transnational Migration and Methodological Discussion of Communication Studies set in the Internet from the Latin American bias - **Daiani Ludmila Barth**
1177	Ethics and Responsibility in Refugee/Migration Research and Artistic Expression - **Christina Akrivopoulou**
743	The Application of the Analytical Hierarchy Process (AHP) Model in the Process of Conflict Management - **Nena Nenovska Gjorgjievska**

Thinking about data: potentialities and limitations of administrative records on migration in Brazil
(1063) Nayara Belle Nova da Costa (University of Brasilia), Helen da Costa Gurgel (University of Brasilia)

This work intent to present the state of arts in terms of advances, limitations and potentialities of Brazilian administrative records related to migration flows to support public policies, exchange experiences and allow the worldwide academic community to also have access to this data. Proposing to analyse the data from an organizational perspective in which the legal and administrative structure of migration management is the support to demonstrate the control points in the process as well as its weakness, we will be presenting administrative records from the Ministry of Labour and Social Welfare, Ministry of Justice and from the Department of Federal Police systematised by the International Migration Observatory (OBMigra). Thus, this work will provide a wide understanding of the role of Brazilian government bodies involved with immigration process. Additional, to better illustrate the possibilities of usage and data crossing, we will present some examples of flows analysis and thematic cartography for the period from 2000 to 2014.

***

Data on refugees in Germany – gaps and ways to close the gaps
(897) Axel Kreienbrink (Research Centre of the Federal Office for Migration and Refugees)

The massive inflow of asylum seekers to Germany in 2015 and 2016 put the country under pressure and challenged all responsible levels of the state. One of the main challenges was to know how many refugees entered, who they were and where they stayed. Due to the high numbers of incoming persons in the border regions the previously used procedures of registration resulted ineffective as the refugees had to be transported to reception accommodations all over the country within the shortest time. As the different administrations involved (Border police, Federal Office for Migration and Refugees, etc.) all had their own data systems comparability and interoperability were not given. In this situation measures were taken to modernize the refugee data structure and fill the gaps. This paper gives an overview of the most pressing data problems in the wake of the refugee crisis and traces the way the gaps were closed through administrative innovation, especially by the Data Exchange Improvement Act. It also highlights the additional ways several administrative actors delivered information needed, especially though secondary analysis of existing data sets and innovative research projects.

***

Transnational Migration and Methodological Discussion of Communication Studies set in the Internet from the Latin American bias
(1165) Daiani Ludmila Barth (University of Rondônia, University of Brasília)

The significant increase of human displacement in all its expressions (emigration, immigration, refuge, return, traffic and smuggling of people, etc.) refer to the cultural diversity of dynamic and irregular migratory geography in urban environments, report on Migration in the World (2015), organized periodically by the International Organization for Migration (IOM). In this context, it is interesting to know the changes experienced in the study of these phenomena in multiple scenarios, from a classical perspective until analyses and reflections on multi-localized or transnational (Marcus, 1995; Goig, 2007). There are also works that take multi and interdisciplinary perspectives on the phenomenon of transnational migration and as regards research techniques, emerge the prevalent use of participant observation, as well as ethnography, beyond tools for data analysis, that provide the discussion about the potentialities and limits of the use of sources such as interviews, photographs, videos, documents, data and memories, as well as life stories and autobiographies. This work, however, specifically aims at the methodological discussion in the studies derived in the field of Communication by the epistemological bias of Latin America (Martin-Barbero, 2008) based on empirical approaches of research oriented to the study of the interactions and uses of Internet resources mediated by socio-cultural experience of transnational migration. Specifically, it is based on the experiences obtained in field work in the scope of research on media reception with Latin American migrants conducted in 2006 and 2009 (Barth, 2006, 2009, 2012), including recent work on border and citizen journalism (2016). In them, methodological definitions are based on empirical choices in the course of the research, that is, according to the findings of the field work in order to reconsider the basic principles of research, avoiding methodological certainties a priori attributed (Markham & Baym, 2008). Among the emerging considerations, it is important to highlight the methodological reflection derived from the experience of multiterritoriality related both to the increase of transnational migrations in the contemporary world, and to the intensification of access and use of resources provided by global communication networks and their repercussions (Sassen, 2006; Fragoso, S., Recuero, R., Barth, D. L., 2011). Thus, there is a discussion of the use of Internet as a field of study and in the perspective of digital method (Rogers, 2010) for the study of transnational migrations, the experimentation of ethnography on the internet (Hine, 2000; Markham & Baym, 2008) as an approach demanded by the dimensions of mobility and transnationalism (Portes, 2003; Mezzadra, 2005; Urry, 2007) that, after all, give rise to continuities and discontinuities both on the Internet and in migrations. In addition, the mediated and non-mediated dynamics of the Internet are included in the context of transnational migrations and, finally, the distinctions and convergences between migratory networks and social networks mediated and not mediated by the Internet. Therefore, the final reflection is made on the epistemological and methodological challenges that transnational migrations assume for social research practices, beyond the inertia and epistemological assumptions characteristic of modernity.

***

Ethics and Responsibility in Refugee/Migration Research and Artistic Expression
(1177) Christina Akrivopoulou (Aristotle University of Thessaloniki,)

During the Syrian refugee crisis from 2015 scientific field research has increased immensely as well as the artistic expression based on pictures from the life of refugees and migrants or even scenes from their dramatic arrivals. This development forces the researcher as well as the artist or the journalist to rethink basic principles of ethics and responsibility in the framework of the human rights protection of vulnerable population. The present paper intends to set out the basic principles that a truly ethical scientific research on migrants and refugees should obey in order to safeguard their dignity, personality, privacy and data protection, to avoid their stigmatization, marginalization or even their manipulation and treatment as research objects than subjects. Based on basic principles regarding the protection of human dignity as recognized in a different framework in the Oviedo convention, the present paper aims in setting out a number of perquisites that should lead a responsible researcher and an ethical research in migrants and refugees as far as prior consent, language barriers, respect to cultural difference and special protection of minors, women and elderly are concerned. Moreover, the role of the 'cultural insider' will be developed as of major significance for a truly culturally responsible research. On a similar framework, the present paper will aim in illustrating the limits of artistic freedom in picturing or narrating everyday life or dramatic scenes of refugees and migrants as well as the limits of their dissemination in the press and the network.

***

The Application of the Analytical Hierarchy Process (AHP) Model in the Process of Conflict Management
(743) Nena Nenovska Gjorgjievska (University of Sts)

The incitement and the occurrence of the conflicts, their escalation, ceasefire and de-escalation are processes which are continually appearing, lasting and resolving. The resolution of the conflicts is a subject of many debates which head towards the proper way of their resolution. There are different methods for conflicts de-escalation and therefore their resolution. The differentiation of the conflicts is directing us for using different methods, which in the concrete cases may be most appropriately applied. The application of the Analytical Hierarchy Process (AHP) as a method for conflict resolution has proven as successful in couple of cases of conflict resolution in the Middle East countries. In the scientific paper, this AHP method will be presented to show its productive effect for

resolving particular conflicts. A short overview will be given of the main elements of the AHP method and how it is applied in the conflict resolution.
***

SESSION 11E – European Migration Policy

	Room: B1
Chair	**Emilia Castro, University of Hamburg, Germany**
1107	When Third Countries Matters: The European Union Politics Management of Refuges through Agreements with Third Countries – **Ingrid Berns Pavezi**
756	Narratives of (Non) Deservingness and the Normalization of Borders in European Migration Policies - **Sara Marino**
1138	Integrated Border Management: A Challenge for the EU? - **Ebru Dalğakıran**
1108	European Migration Policy and Cooperation with Third Countries: The Creation of "Buffer Zones" - **Foteini Asderaki, Eleftheria Markozani**

When Third Countries Matters: The European Union Politics Management of Refuges through Agreements with Third Countries
(1107) Ingrid Berns Pavezi (Albert Ludwig University of Freiburg)

The departure point is the political deployments of the current politics between the European Union and third countries, as i.e. Turkey and Libya, for the management of refugees towards the European continent. This topic will be analysed through the following developments: (1) the contextualization of the politics between European Union and third countries in a broader context, from a sociological-historical analysis and applying the methodological cosmopolitanism; (2) the policies, speeches and developments of the political relations and agreements between European Union and third countries on the topic of migration, asylum and visa policies and (3) the dynamics that the actors involved have been assuming, related to the topic in its plural aspects. The methodology employed will be encompassing the methodological cosmopolitanism and the historical-comparative perspective of the objects of research. As methods of research, this thesis will use textual analysis; subdivided as content analysis and discourse analysis. This paper aims to contribute to the theoretical and methodological developments of the refugee and migration studies, the world-system theory, the studies of inequalities, and the sociological-historical analysis of politics. Additionally, this investigation has as objective to improve the methodologies of research, especially through the post and de-colonial perspectives.
***

Narratives of (Non) Deservingness and the Normalization of Borders in European Migration Policies
(756) Sara Marino (King's College London)

Confronted with the images that have been reaching us since the influx of refugees entered new dimensions last year in Europe, the term 'Fortress Europe' has been increasingly used to identify the continent's heightened concerns about security. What are we going to do with them? What do we know about them? A generalised state of moral panic and anxiety over the porosity and vulnerability of our nation state's borders demanded responses and actions: close the border, build the fence, stop the unwanted and unwelcome guests. At the same time, while all European governments seemed to agree that a crisis of enormous proportions was threatening the 'soul' and 'authentic spirit' of Europe, the hardening of borders and their transformation into instruments of exclusion and

segregation emerged as the only effective response to citizens' safety and security (Carr, 2015; Mouffe, 2013). I argue that what we are facing today is the normalization and moralization of borders as a result of the need to exclude certain categories of people to protect our legitimate citizens on the one hand, and Europe's interpretations of borders as a morally necessary act on the other (Vollmer, 2016). Behind such practices of normalization, narratives of (non) deservingness feed the us vs. them populist rhetoric (Wodak, 2015). Exclusion creates citizenship, legitimates the good citizen, and protects the community from the fear of the unknown (Bauman, 2016). My contribution will follow two areas of inquiry. First, I intend to address – from a philosophical point of view – what lies behind Europe's moral panic and the widespread fears that specific categories of people are threatening the well-being of our societies, contaminating the order and putting our safety at risk. In order to do so, I will use two theoretical frameworks, Elias Canetti's theory of power and persecution (1962), and Rene Girard's analysis of scapegoating (1982). The reason why I think it is important to explore the roots, characteristics and impact of today's politics of fear and security obsession is a very practical one. Very often it is said that the economic and political crises that Western societies are facing are responsible for the widespread belief that immigrants will steal our jobs, weaken our national identity, put pressures to our welfare and health systems, and more generally threaten the well-being of our societies. Indeed, both Canetti and Girard recognise how every time there is a crisis and control is lost, there seems to be an exacerbation of feelings of suspicion and mistrust against those perceived as "strangers". That said, this explanation is only partial and demands a different type of analysis that looks at our ancestral relationship with diversity, a relationship that has always been filled with violence since the development of the very first human community. In simple terms, my personal contribution precisely lies in the belief that what we are experiencing today along European borders is not merely related to the current economic crisis, but is consequence of humans' intrinsic inability to embrace otherness and to accept what is considered as "different". By going back to the origins of human culture and society, Girard and Canetti will help to explain why no modern society is entirely free from the scapegoating tendency; in fact, persecutionary strategies have always operated on the fantasy that the enemy is contaminating the body politic, corrupting the youth, eroding the economy, and sabotaging peace. The second part of my contribution will specifically address the material consequences of the migration crisis, and the centrality of the borders within the current political agenda. Borders will be examined as institutions of power, as processes of identity formation, and as performances (Marino, 2016). The focus on borders is deemed as crucial as in this age of neoliberal globalization, mobility - 'the most basic understanding of human freedom', 'the ability to traverse space to make place for oneself in the world', has become a right that is accorded to some and denied to others on the basis of citizenship (Walters 2010, p. 74). Behind the construction of borders and fences, narratives of (non)-deservingness and the consideration of migrants as 'bare lives' that do not deserve a humanitarian treatment are becoming normalised and legitimised political strategies that serve to protect the community of good and hard-working citizens (Agamben, 1998; 2000; 2005). My presentation seeks to evaluate the philosophical and symbolical mechanisms behind the moralisation of borders and their role within the construction of the other, the disenfranchised, and the re-negotiated stranger.
***

Integrated Border Management: A Challenge for the EU?
(1138) Ebru Dalğakıran (Marmara University)

It is known that one of the most successful acquisitions of the European Union (EU) in its history is the abolition of the internal borders. However, especially following the civil war in Syria, the EU is faced with the most severe migration flows into its borders since the WWII. Therefore, to guarantee peace and stability in its internal borders, the EU's attempts to externalize its immigration policy beyond third countries and cooperation on border issues have gained importance. Given this context, the fundamental aim of this study is to understand the evolution of the external dimension of the EU's immigration policy with particular reference to Integrated Border Management (IBM). The study focuses on the questions of why the EU have launched IBM and how it influences the border policies of the third countries. In this framework, firstly, it will be identified the reasons for the EU's need for third country cooperation on borders to handle migration flows into Europe. Secondly, by using externalization approach as the theoretical framework, how the EU exports IBM will be conceptualized. Finally, Turkey will be examined to clarify whether the EU successfully exports its IBM strategy beyond its borders.

***

European Migration Policy and Cooperation with Third Countries: The Creation of "Buffer Zones"

(1108) Foteini Asderaki (University of Piraeus), Eleftheria Markozani (University of Piraeus)

Cooperation with third countries of origin and transit of migration flows has been a significant method for the creation of security buffer zones around EU, preventing irregular access to the member states (Lindström, 2005). Since the European Programs of Tampere (1999) and The Hague (2005), EU has been engaged in the fight against irregular migration with the means of external policy and diplomacy. EU has developed a variety of instruments in order to enhance the external dimension of AJFS such as multilateral or bilateral agreements, ministerial meetings, assistance programs, bilateral dialogues and specific tools under the Global Approach to Migration and Mobility framework adopted by the European council in December 2005 (European Commission 2011). The underlying ideas of European external policy on migration has been the cooperation with key-third countries, the support of their migration management systems (such as border controls), and the targeted development aid against the roots of migration. However, this paper argues that the current refugee crisis and the subsequent securitization of irregular immigrants has led EU decision makers to focus on security concerns undermining, at the same time, humanitarian and development considerations. Indeed, the concentration of EU on the aversion of the entrance of irregular immigrants of current migration crisis has provoked the subversion of the fight against the roots of migration such as poverty, violence and human rights violations. 1. Readmission Agreements and European Policy towards irregular migration: EU implements Readmission Agreements on the voluntary or compulsory return of irregular immigrants to the state of their origin, which includes the organization of common flights for the departure of illegal immigrants from EU soil. Readmission agreements are funded by the European Migration Fund (AMIF) and their application is based on the Charter of Fundamental Rights. Though EU has signed seventeen Readmission Agreements, the current crisis underscored the weaknesses of the European readmission system and the restricted area that the agreements cover (European Commission 2015c). Moreover, readmission agreements have usually been a precondition for granting development aid towards selected countries (Concord Report, 2015). 2. Migration flows management and European Development Policy: EU has also established circular migration and mobility partnerships which aim at the allocation of responsibilities of the migration flows management (European Commission 2011) and several regional protection programs which focus on the development of tools for the just allocation of

refugees and migrants (such as the AENEAS program 2004-06). Recently, EU organized the Valletta Summit, in November 2015, between the European and African Presidents and Prime Ministers, who decided on the implementation on specific measures to uproot the primary causes of irregular migration. Nevertheless, the resources from the Emergency Trust Fund for Africa including Libya, Tunisia, Algeria, Morocco and Egypt, are extremely poor, reaching almost up to 1,8 billion euros. Thus, as the Concord Policy Report outlines "European development aid to developing countries continues to be instrumentalised to serve 'migration management' objectives" (Concord, 2015: 2). 3. The Agreement with Turkey and European Security policy: Diplomatic pressure has also been exerted on Turkey, with which EU has signed an agreement in November 2015, aiming at coordinating the necessary actions for the management of the refugee crisis. Within the framework of the European Agreement with Turkey, Greece and Turkey have enabled the readmission process with the direct return of irregular migrants from the Greek islands to Turkey. Nevertheless, the EU-Turkey Joint Action Plan has stimulated several considerations on the legal issue of which country is considered by EU a "safe country" for refugees. Indeed, the Asylum Procedures Directive requires that an immigrant should be readmitted in a country which can provide him international protection in accordance with the provisions of Geneva Convention. However, the protection of human rights in Turkey is a rather questionable issue since several legal cases have been reported on violation of refugees' and immigrants' rights (Ulusoy 2016). Thus, the external security measures of EU lie on the creation of external buffer zones capable of interrupting migration flows before entering the European soil (Gabrielli 2011).
***

SESSION 11F – Cumhuriyet'in Başlangıcında Göç

	Room: B2
Chair	**Gökçe Bayındır Goularas, Yeditepe University, Turkey**
1116	94. Yılında Türk-Yunan Nüfus Mübadelesi – **Gökçe Bayındır Goularas**
1186	Selanik Efsanesi ya da Göçebeliğin Çingene Halleri (1856-1923)- **Sinan Şanlıer**
772	Cumhuriyetin İlk Yıllarında Balkanlardan Türkiye'ye Gelen Göçmenlerde Sosyal ve Kültürel Uyum - **Hikmet Öksüz**
1128	İstanbul Basınında 1964 Zorunlu Rum Göçü - **Gülten Madendağ**
746	İşgal Yıllarında İstanbul'dan Ankara'ya Aydın Göçü - **Yaşar Şenler**

94. Yılında Türk-Yunan Nüfus Mübadelesi
(1116) Gökçe Bayındır Goularas (Yeditepe University)

Cumhuriyet Dönemi'nde Türkiye'ye doğru yapılan en önemli göçlerden biri 1923 Türk-Yunan Nüfus Mübadelesidir. Mübadele sözleşmesiyle İstanbul, Gökçeada ve Bozcaada'da ikamet eden Ortodoks Rumların dışında Anadolu ve Doğu Trakya'da ikamet eden tüm Ortodoks Rumlar Yunanistan'a, Batı Trakya dışında Yunanistan topraklarında yaşayan tüm Müslümanlar Türkiye'ye gönderilmiştir. Mübadele sonucu Yunanistan'dan Türkiye'ye 450.000'den fazla Müslüman gelmiş ve çoğunluğu Ekim 1923'te kurulan Mübadele İskan ve İmar Vekaleti tarafından belirlenmiş olan köy ve şehirlere yerleştirilmiştir. Bu zorunlu göç, sadece her iki ülkenin tarihini etkilemekle kalmamış, aynı zamanda yüzbinlerce kişinin ve ailelerinin yaşamlarını derinden etkilemiş, kültürel kimlik ve toplumsal hafızaları üzerinde son derece etkili olmuştur. Yeni toplumlarına uyum sağlama sürecinde mübadiller, bir yandan farklılıklarını en aza indirmeye çalışmışlar, diğer bir yandan ise kimliklerinin ve kültürlerinin devamlılığını sağlamak için uğraşmışlardır. İskanı takiben kısa zaman içinde doğulan toprakları zorunlu olarak terk edişin yarattığı travma, yeni topraklarda eskiyi yaşatmak için kurulan düzenlerle giderilmeye çalışılmıştır. Kuşaktan kuşağa aktarılan kültürel kimlikler ve ortak hafıza, oldukça özel bir örnek olan bu göçmen grubunun, grup içi farklılıklarına rağmen yerel kimliklerinin günümüze kadar koruması ve yaşatmasındaki etkisi bakımından özellikle dikkat çekmektedir. Diğer taraftan, mübadele ve mübadiller ile ilgili çalışmalar ülkemizde geç dönemde karşımıza çıkmaktadır. Yunanistan'da gerek bilimsel gerek sanatsal gerekse dernekleşme anlamda bu konuya verilen önemin aksine Türkiye'de mübadil derneklerinin ortaya çıkışı bile 2000li yıllara denk gelmiştir. Aynı dönemden itibaren mübadele ve mübadiller üzerine yapılan çalışmaların sayısı da hızlıca artış göstermiştir. Bu çalışma, Mübadele Anlaşmasının imzalanmasının 94. yılında mübadeleyi, gerek Türkiye ve Yunanistan gerekse mübadeleye tabi tutulan kişiler açısından sebep ve sonuçları ile tartışmayı amaçlamaktadır.

***

Selanik Efsanesi ya da Göçebeliğin Çingene Halleri (1856-1923)
(1186) Sinan Şanlıer (Independent researcher)

Çingenelerin tarih yazımında göçlerden söz edildiğinde genellikle doğudan batıya doğru bir hareketlilikten söz edilmekte, kayıtlar da bunu kanıtlamaktadır. Ancak, Çingenelerin tarihinde öyle bir dönem var ki, Balkanlar'da göç tersine dönmüş, özellikle 1856 yılında köleliğin kaldırılmasıyla birlikte bütün Avrupa ve balkanlar etkilendiği gibi Türkiye toprakları da bu tersine göçten etkilenmeye başlamıştır. Türkiye'deki Çingene nüfusunun oluşumunu ve coğrafi dağılımı belirleyen faktörlerin başında, Türkiye-Yunanistan arasında 1923'te imzalanan nüfus mübadelesi ve bu anlaşmadan daha öncelerine dayanan göçler gelmektedir. Osmanlı-Rus Savaşları, Balkan Savaşları ve I. Dünya Savaşı bu hareketliliğin öneli nedenleridir. Bu denli bir hareketliliğin olmasına rağmen göç edenlerin etnik aidiyetleri konusunda çok şey yazılmış değildir. Rivayetler üzerinden hareket edilmiş, mübadele ile önemi bir kat daha artan Selanik kentinin konumu, haklı olarak bir efsane gibi anlatılmış ve günümüze kadar ulaşmıştır. Bu anlatılarda Selanik'le birlikte, Türklerin ulusal kahramanı Mustafa Kemal de zikredilmekte, "bizi Atatürk getirtti" denilmektedir. Belli ki bu ifade toplumun çoğunluğu ile bir bütünleşme çabasıdır. Gerek arşiv kayıtları ve gerekse Osmanlı belgeleri, bu nüfusun oluşumunun belirlenmesinde sadece 1923 yılındaki Mübadele anlaşmansın olmadığını, daha önceki yıllarda da ciddi ve düzensiz göçlerin bulunduğunu göstermektedir. Mübadele dönemindeki kayıtlarda her ne kadar etnik bir aidiyet belirtilmese de, daha önceki kayıtlarda gerek Çingene ve gerekse Kıpti lafızların rastlanmakta, Mübadele ile ilgisi olmamasına rağmen Bulgaristan ve Romanya bu kayıtlarda defalarca yer almaktadır.

***

Cumhuriyetin İlk Yıllarında Balkanlardan Türkiye'ye Gelen Göçmenlerde Sosyal ve Kültürel Uyum
(772) Hikmet Öksüz (Karadeniz Technical University)

Türk dünyası içinde Balkan coğrafyası için göç, bir kader olarak nitelendirilebilir. Balkanlar söz konusu olduğunda Türk tarihinin en eski dönemleri bir yana Osmanlı döneminden neredeyse günümüze gelinceye kadar devam eden Türk göç hareketlerinin tarihsel arka planı birçok siyasi gelişmeye yaslanır. Bu siyasi gelişmelerin bir yüzü sosyal ve kültürel niteliği ile ayrıca incelenmeye değerdir. Balkan Savaşlarındaki yenilgileri takiben Türk nüfusun Osmanlı topraklarına göçlerini I. Dünya Savaşı dönemindeki göçler takip etmiştir. Kurtuluş Savaşı'nın ardından Lozan Antlaşması ile kurulan yeni Türkiye Cumhuriyetine göçler devam etmiş; nüfus mübadelesi, siyasi yaptırımların yol açtığı zorunluluklar, savaşlar gibi nedenler bu göç sürecini belirlemiştir. 1989'da Bulgaristan'dan sürülen yüz binlerce Türk'e, 90'lı yıllarda Bosna Hersek'ten gelen Boşnaklar, Kosova'dan gelen Arnavutlar eklenmiştir. Bireyin bir yandan kendi köken kültür ve kimliğini korurken öte yandan göç ettiği ülkenin kültürüne uyum sağlama süreci bir bütünleşme sürecidir. Bu süreç ise insanların mazilerini, miraslarını ve gelecek hayallerini yerleştirdikleri mekândan kopmanın acı tecrübesine dayanır. Arkada bırakılan toprakla birlikte bir değerler manzumesinin yeni yaşama taşınması ve yeni mekânda yeni ekonomik ve sosyal şartlara eklemlenme, bu sebeple travmatik de olabilir. Bu durumun aşılması, göç edenin gittiği coğrafyada getirdiği kültürü kısmen terk etmesi, yeni kültüre uyumu ve katkısına bağlıdır. Göç eden; geleneklerini, yeme-içme, giyim-kuşam alışkanlıklarını, dilini, müziğini kısaca kültürel değerlerini korumak endişesi ile kabul görme korkusunu bir arada yaşar. Balkanlardan Türkiye'ye göçlerin coğrafya değişikliğinden ayrı olarak aslında çoğu zaman bir geri dönüş hikâyesi olması da önemlidir. Bu anlamda Cumhuriyet'in ilk yıllarına tekabül eden Balkan göçlerinde göçmenlerin sosyalleşme süreci ve kültürel uyum sorunları kendine has özellikleri bakımından irdelenmeye değer görülmüş ve bu çalışmanın konusunu oluşturmuştur.

***

İstanbul Basınında 1964 Zorunlu Rum Göçü
(1128) Gülten Madendağ (Sakarya University)

1964'te Rumların Türkiye'den zorunlu olarak göç ettirilmesi, Cumhuriyet dönemi süresince gayr-ı Müslimlere uygulanan göç politikalarının devamı ve sonuncusu niteliğindedir. İnönü Hükümeti, Kıbrıs meselesinde Yunanistan'la anlaşamayınca 1930'da imzalanan "İkamet, Ticaret ve Seyrüsefain Antlaşması" nı iptal ettiğini açıklamıştı. Antlaşmanın tek taraflı iptaliyle Rumlar, yanlarına yalnızca 20 kilo valiz ve 200 Türk lirası para almalarına izin verilerek sınır dışı edildiler. Bu süreçte yazılı basın, Kıbrıs'ta yaşananları katliam haberleri ve fotoğraflarıyla kamuoyuna duyurarak Rumlara karşı öfke duygusunu körüklemiştir. Böylelikle kamuoyu zorunlu göçe hazırlanmış, Rum göçünün son dalgası gerçekleşmiştir. Bu çalışmada, Rumlar'ın Türkiye'den zorunlu göçüne İstanbul yerel basınının yaklaşımı ele alınacaktır. 1964 yılında İstanbul'da yayınlanmakta olan Dünya, Ekspres, Yeni İstiklal, Son Baskı gazetelerinde adı geçen konunun ele alınış şekli Young ve Cohen tarafından geliştirilen "ahlâki panik" (moral panic) kavramı üzerinden değerlendirilecektir. Cohen'e göre toplumlar ahlâki panik dönemleriyle karşı karşıya kaldıklarında, bir olay, kişi ya da grup toplumsal değerlere ve çıkarlara karşı bir tehdit olarak tanımlanmaya başlar. Bu bildirinin iddiası, adı geçen gazetelerin Türkiye'deki Rumları ötekileştirmeye, onlara karşı öfke ve sosyal tepki oluşturmaya katkı sağladıkları yönündedir.

***

İşgal Yıllarında İstanbul'dan Ankara'ya Aydın Göçü
(746) Yaşar Şenler (Namık Kemal University)

Birinci Dünya Harbi, Osmanlı İmparatorluğu için yıkımı ve ardından işgali getirir. Başkentteki bazı aydınlar ve bayrak adamlar tutuklanarak sürgüne gönderilir. Bu durum bir direnişin, özgürlük hareketinin başlatılmasını zorunlu kılar. Esaret altındaki İstanbul'dan Anadolu'ya geçen Mustafa Kemal, Samsun'dan başlamak üzere Amasya, Tokat, Erzincan, Sivas ve Erzurum gibi Anadolu şehirlerinde halkı özgürlük mücadelesi ideali doğrultusunda bilinçlendirir. Çeşitli şehirlerde birbirinden bağımsız ve habersiz kurulmuş olan küçük milli direnişleri ve milis hareketlerini organize ederek bir amaç doğrultusunda birleştirir. Anadolu'nun bağrında, stratejik bir nokta olan Ankara, genç Türk devletinin çekirdeğini oluşturacak yeni bir merkez olur. İstanbul'daki subay ve aydınlar yavaş yavaş Ankara'ya, bu cazibe merkezine geçerek milli mücadeleye katılırlar. Bu aydınlardan biri olan Halide Edib'in Üsküdar'daki Özbekler Tekkesi'nden başlayarak Ankara'da sona eren meşakkatli yolculuğu esnasında yol boyunca ona başta eşi Adnan Adıvar olmak üzere pek çok şahsiyet katılır. Bunların arasında Câmi Bey'i, Çerkez Ethem'in kardeşi Binbaşı Reşit'i, Keskin mebusu Rıza

Bey'i, Manavoğlu Nevres Bey'i, Yenibahçeli Şükrü Bey'i, Ahmet Halim'i, Teğmen Bekir'i, Trabzon Mebusu Yarbay Hüsrev'i, Ankara Genelkurmay İkinci Reisi Albay Kâzım'ı, Albay Seyfi'yi, İstanbul'dan silah kaçıranlardan biri olan Yarbay Naim Cevat'ı, Hüsrev Bey'in kardeşi Yarbay Besalet'i, İstanbul'da Yeni Gün Gazetesi'ni çıkaran ve gruba Geyve'de katılan Yunus Nadi Bey' sayabiliriz.

***

SESSION 11G – Göç ve Edebiyat - 10

	Room: B3
Chair	**Asiye Mevhibe Coşar, Karadeniz Teknik University, Turkey**
1249	Kristevacı Bir İğrençlik Olarak Anneyi Kusmak: Sevim Burak'ın *İşte Baş İşte Gövde İşte Kanatlar* Adlı Oyununda Göçün Dili – **Duygu Toksoy Çeber**
1250	Roland Topor'un 'Masanın Altında' Oyunundaki Göç Olgusunun Sahne Plastiğine Yansımaları - **Elif Özhancı**
1234	Göç Olgusunun Yarattığı Toplumsal Kriz Bağlamında "Keşanlı Ali Destanı" Oyunu - **Tamer Temel**
1248	Plastik Sanatlardaki Üretimlerde Ele Alınış Biçimiyle Göç Olgusu - **Tansel Ceber**
1238	Bir Göç Tarihinin Romanlaştırılması ya da Tarihsel Göç Romanı: Önce Annelerini Vur - **İrfan Atalay**

Kristevacı Bir İğrençlik Olarak Anneyi Kusmak: Sevim Burak'ın *İşte Baş İşte Gövde İşte Kanatlar* Adlı Oyununda Göçün Dili
(1249) Duygu Toksoy Çeber (Atatürk University)

Sevim Burak, Bulgaristan'dan İstanbul'a göç etmek zorunda kalmış Yahudi bir annenin kızıdır. Burak, annesi Maria Mandil'in evlendikten sonra adını değiştirmesine rağmen, bozuk Türkçesiyle çevresinde hep bir alay konusu olduğundan bahseder. Sevim Burak, annesinin gizlemeye çalıştığı Yahudiliğinden o yıllarda nefretle karışık bir utanç duyduğunu dile getirir. Daha sonra Sevim Burak'a bir dil farkındalığı kazandıracak olan bozuk Türkçe ve anneyle olan çatışması, bizi zorunlu göçün doğurduğu kültürel etkileşimler konusunda düşünmeye sevk eder. Julia Kristeva iğrençlik çözümlemesinde bir şeyi iğrenç kılanın kirlilik ya da hastalık olmadığını, iğrenç olanın bir kimliği, bir sistemi, bir düzeni rahatsız eden bir şey olduğunu; iğrencin arada, muğlak ve karışmış olan olduğunu söyler. Kristeva, iğrençlik çözümlemesinin merkezine anneyi ve anne ile yemek arasındaki ilişkiyi alır. Kristeva'ya göre, yemek, insanın diğerleriyle ve annesiyle kurduğu arkaik ilişkileri düzenleyen oral nesne (iğrenç)'dir ve hem diğerleriyle hem de anneyle olan çatışmalı aynılık ve farklılık ilişkisinin de bir metaforudur. Bu anlamda göçün getirdiği zorunlu karşılaşmalar açısından dilin ve yemeğin merkezi bir konumda yer aldığı söylenebilir. Sevim Burak edebiyatını, minör bir ses olarak ortaya çıkaran anne dili, İşte Baş İşte Gövde İşte Kanatlar adlı oyunda aynı zamanda bir yemek yeme ritüeli biçiminde karşımıza çıkar. Bu yazı, Kristevacı iğrençlik üzerinden Sevim Burak'ın İşte Baş İşte Gövde İşte Kanatlar adlı oyununda göçün doğurduğu kimlik ve dil sorununu, yemek metaforu ve anne dili bağlamında incelemeyi amaçlamaktadır.

***

Roland Topor'un 'Masanın Altında' Oyunundaki Göç Olgusunun Sahne Plastiğine Yansımaları
(1250) Elif Özhancı, (Atatürk University)

1938 yılında Fransa'da Polonyalı Yahudi göçmen bir ailenin çocuğu olarak dünyaya gelen Roland Topor, Masanın Altında adlı oyununda göçmen insanların hayatlarını mizahi bir üslupla ele almıştır. Topor bu oyununda göç olgusunu, özgürlüğü, zorbalığı, şiddeti, umudu, aşkı günlük yaşamın dinamikleriyle birlikte harmanlayarak kendi göçmen kimliğine eylemci bir özellik kazandırmıştır. Topor'un "Göçmenler insanlık düzeyinin altında muamele gördüklerine göre, masanın altında yaşamaları da anormal görülmemelidir" dediği Masanın Altında adlı oyunu ile göçün sorunsallaştırdığı bireylerin sıradan yaşamlarının görmezden gelindiğini vurgular. Masanın Altında, çevirmenlik yaparak geçimini sağlayan genç kadın Florence Michalon'un, çalışma masasının altını, ayakkabı tamirciliği yapan düşük gelirli bir göçmen olan Dragomir'e kiralaması ve bu komşuluktan doğan olaylar üzerine kuruludur. Bu iki kişi arasında paylaşılan deneyimler, göçmen yaşantısına getirilen kara komedi vurgusudur. Bu çalışma, Roland Topor'un Masanın Altında adlı oyununun sahne plastiğine yönelerek sahnede göçmen kimliğinin görselleştirilmesine odaklanacaktır.

***

Göç Olgusunun Yarattığı Toplumsal Kriz Bağlamında "Keşanlı Ali Destanı" Oyunu
(1234) Tamer Temel (Atatürk University)

1950'lerde Türkiye'de tarım alanında makineleşmenin artmaya başlaması; iş gücünün makineye kaymasına neden olmuş ve kırsal alanda toprağa bağlı çalışan köylülerin işsizlik sorunu ortaya çıkmıştır. Bu durum, zorunlu olarak iç göçleri doğurmuş ve köylerden büyük kentlere büyük ölçülerde göçler başlamıştır. Kentlere yapılan bu göç, "gecekondulaşma", "sınıf farklılıkları" ve "çarpık düzen" gibi toplumsal sorunları da beraberinde getirmiştir. Haldun Taner'in 1964 yılında yazdığı ve Çağdaş Türk Tiyatrosu'nun en iyi örnekleri arasında yer alan "Keşanlı Ali Destanı" adlı oyunu, Anadolu'nun çeşitli bölgelerinden göçen ve Sineklidağ adındaki bir gecekondu mahallesinde yaşayan insanların karşılaştığı sorunlara odaklanır. Oyunda Sineklidağ mahallesi özelinden yola çıkılarak dönemin göç sorunsalına, göçün oluşturduğu çarpık yapılaşmaya ve sömürü düzeninin işleyiş mekanizmalarına ironik bir toplumsal eleştiri getirilir. Bu çalışma da, "Keşanlı Ali Destanı" oyunundan hareket ederek, ülkemizde 1950'lerden itibaren başlayarak zamanla artan "göç sorunsalına" ve bu sorunsalın tetiklediği pek çok toplumsal soruna odaklanılacak ve halen devam etmekte olan "göç sorunu"na çözüm önerileri sunulmaya çalışılacaktır.

***

Plastik Sanatlardaki Üretimlerde Ele Alınış Biçimiyle Göç Olgusu
(1248) Tansel Ceber (University College Dublin)

Göç olgusu tarih boyunca toplumların oluşumunda ve kültürel değişimlerinde başat bir rol oynamıştır. Sanat ise hayata dair her türlü veriyi içinde barındıran ve yansıtan bir olgudur. Sanat her ne kadar öznel bir tavrın yansıması olsa da o öznel tavrın oluşmasında toplumsal oluşumların etkisi yadsınamaz bir gerçektir. Dolayısıyla, toplum içinde yaşayan ve toplum yapısından doğrudan etkilenen sanatçının üretimi de göç ile beslenen toplumun da yansıması olacaktır. Toplum ve kültür yapısının biçimlenmesinde önemli bir yeri olan göç olgusunun sanat üretimi üzerindeki etkisi, özellikle az gelişmiş ülkelerden gelişmiş ülkelere göç eden sanatçıların çalışmalarında belirgindir. Göç konusunu ele alan sanatçıların yeni coğrafyalarda kimliksizleşme ve kimlik çatışmalarını ele aldıkları görülür. Bu bildiri, farklı kültürlerden göç etmiş sanatçılar ve onların göç konusunu ele alan plastik sanatlar alanındaki çalışmaları üzerine odaklanarak sanatçıların çalışmalarındaki göç sorununu örneklerle incelemeyi amaçlamaktadır. Bu kapsamda Fas asıllı Fransız sanatçı Leila Alaoui, Türk asıllı Alman sanatçı Nasan Tur, Afrikalı-Amerikalı sanatçı Gleen Ligon, İranlı sanatçı Faig Ahmed, Doğu-Batı çatışmasını ele alan Türk sanatçılar Halil Altındere ve Şener Özmen'in çalışmaları üzerinden göç olgusunun sanattaki yeri irdelenecektir.

***

Bir Göç Tarihinin Romanlaştırılması ya da Tarihsel Göç Romanı: Önce Annelerini Vur

(1238) İrfan Atalay (Namık Kemal University)

Âşık Veysel, "Sazım ben gidersem, sen kal dünyada/ (…)" derken, sürekli ölümsüzlük ve kalıcı olma arayışı içinde olan ölümlü dünyalının temsilcisi olma işlevini üstlenerek söyler bu sözleri. Bir anlamda ozan Veysel, döneminin ve toplumunun bilincini yansıtan temsilci aydın niteliğindedir. Benzer bir temsilci işlevini Önce Annelerini Vur adlı romanıyla Hasan Kalyoncu üstlenir. Kalyoncu, '93 Harbi' diye bilinen 1877-1878 Osmanlı-Rus savaşlarının belleklerde bıraktığı acılar, ölümler, açlık ve yokluklar daha silinmeden, Birinci Dünya Savaşı yıllarında yeniden körüklenen anlaşmazlıklar sonucu Temmuz 1916'da Rusya'nın ülkemizin Doğu ve Karadeniz Bölgesinde başlattığı işgali, işgale karşı başlatılan cılız direnişi ve bunların insanlara yansıyan olumsuz etkileri sonucu Batı Anadolu'ya doğru yönelen göçün her aşamasında yer alan, ancak günümüzde neredeyse canlı tanıkları kalmayan, insanların yaşanmışlıklarını, sıkıntılarını, kısacası savaş ve göç tanıklıklarını kurmaca bir evrene yerleştirerek 'roman' diye sunar bizlere. Tarihin derinliklerine gömülmekte olan gerçeklikler hep yaşasın, "ölümsüz insan"la kalıcı olsun diye aktarır bunları romana. Bir yandan tarihi romanlaştırırken, bir yandan tarihsel roman yazar. Roman, adı okurun imgeleminde farklı senaryo ve içerikleri çağrıştırmış olsa da, tarihsel niteliklidir. Bu bağlamda Önce Annelerini Vur romanı da, Trabzon iline bağlı Tonya yöresi özelindeki Rus işgalinde etkin rol üstlenen ya da bu işgali ve onun neden olduğu göçü yaşayanların öykülerini aktarır. Yazar, kişilerini simgesel kişiliklerden seçer, tarihsel olguya bağlı olarak kişilerinin kimileri etkin, kimileri edilgen karakterlidir. Anlatı yapısına ve olay örgüsüne bağlı olarak, yazmaları ve konuşmaları için kişilerine yerine göre kalem, yerine göre söz vererek onları canlı bir kimliğe büründürür. Çalışmamız, tarihsel roman perspektifi içinde ve göç kuramları ışığında, hakkında çok şey yazılmamış bir göç öyküsünün geçmişteki ve günümüze yansıyan sonuçlarını; toplum bilincinin zorlamasıyla yazarın yaşayan tarihe katkısını ortaya koymayı hedeflemektedir.

***

SESSION 11H –Poster Session - 3

Health Communication in Refugees: A Study on Teachers

(859) Salih Gürbüz (Ministry of National Education), Özlem Duğan (Uşak University)

Communication means to have a healthy communication with others. There are a lot of factors in order to make healthy and correct contact. Especially language problem prevents the communication. Using the same language in communication and the similarity of the cultures make the communication easy. While taking health service to make the prognosis and treatment easier, the communication process between healthcare personnels and patients should be healthy. The refugees who left their countries and have settled different countries have many problems. One of these problems is communication problem because of language difference while they take health service. The refugees, who don't communicate with the healhtcare personnels, have to live with their health problems. The aim of this study is to determine the views of the Syrian refugee teachers about the communication problems that they take healthcare service. The qualitative research design was used and 16 Syrian refugee teachers, who have settled in Konya and have been working in Temporary Learning Centres (TLC), participated in this study. The data of the study were collected open coding technique and analyzed by the program of SPSS and descriptive analysis technique. As a result of this study it can be said that because of the language problem Syrian refugees have difficulty in taking healthcare service, have to delay their treatment, don't communicate with the healthcare personnels healthfully and try to solve the language problems through translators.

***

Why Study Medicine? Study Motivation of Medical Students Considering Migration and Gender

(1227) Gloria Tauber (Medical University of Innsbruck), Heidi Siller (Medical University of Innsbruck), Margarethe Hochleitner (Medical University of Innsbruck)

Social science research explores which motivations are decisive that students choose their studies, especially under the gender aspect. Surveys in France (Lefevre et al. 2010), Netherlands (Kusurkar et al. 2011) and Austria (Hochleitner 2003) have consistently reported a high importance of person oriented motives and the desire to care for and help others as prime motivation to study medicine, for female students even more so than for male students. The considerations of financial rewards and prestige were of low importance. The objective of our study was to investigate whether migrant medical students had different motivations for studying medicine than non-migrant students. Further gender comparisons in these motivations were sought. In the study 350 medical students (197 women, 153 men; 208 born in Austria, 142 not born in Austria) participated. The questionnaire included sociodemographic questions and questions about study motivations. Spearman-correlations were used. As expected the analysis showed women were more motivated for entering medicine by helping others ($r=-.17$, $p=.002$) and working with people ($r=-.13$, $p=.022$) than were men. Migrant students were more likely to study medicine because of prestige ($r=.16$, $p=.003$) than non-migrant students. The prospect of high earnings motivated more migrants than non-migrants ($r=.12$, $p=.027$) and more male ($r=.16$, $p = .003$) than female students. Also, men stated more that they study medicine because of the prestige ($r=.13$, $p = .018$) than did women. The variables helping others, working with people and family-work-compatibility did not correlate with the descent (rs $<.086$, ps $>.108$). The question arises why prestige and high earnings are higher motivations for entering medicine for migrant and also for male students than for non-migrant and female students. Perhaps it is a social phenomenon that in other countries than Austria medicine is seen as more prestigious and is connected to good job positions thus students believe that a medical study is the best option for prestigious life and high earnings (Hummrich 2009).

***

The Views and Voices of Migrant Minors in Contexts of Risk. Lessons Learned from Two Studies Based on Photovoice

(1121) Rocío Garrido (University of Seville), Angelina Delgado (Ayuntamiento de Camas)

Migrant youth people sometimes live in contexts of risks that put them in a vicious circle where they suffer the consequences of inequity. In this work, we presented the lessons learned from two studies that used photovoice as research-intervention tool so as to explore the views and voices of migrant minors who suffer oppression in different enclaves of Europe: (1) a vulnerable multicultural neighborhood in Seville (Spain) and (2) a refugee camp in Ritsona (Greece). Photovoice is a strategy that implies a process based on taking photographs and developing associated narratives in order to elicit reflection on the challenges and the strengths of a community (Nicotera, 2007). It encourages the involvement of participants in their contexts and in processes of change (Wang and Burris, 1997). Study 1: Framework: It was carried out with teenagers with different cultural roots who live in "Su Eminencia", a multicultural neighborhood on the outskirts of Seville (Spain). It epitomizes the vulnerable communities that were created when a periphery grew in a rapid and disorganized manner to offer cheapest houses to migrants, cultural minorities (like gypsies) and other excluded people. Objective: Increase their neighborhood activism and their empowerment. Participants: Eight young women between 13 and 18 years old from a low socioeconomic status and different countries of origin. Furthermore, we form a comparison group composed by other eight young women whit similar characteristics. All participants attended a grassroots youth organization called "El Escalón Salesiano" in their neighborhood. Process: participants took photographs in order to reflect upon the strengths and challenges of the neighborhood. The images of strengths were related to nature, friendship and spirituality and the images of challenges were about racism, poverty, unemployment, drugs and trash. Additionally, we developed an artistic intervention on photographs to express the desired changes and then the group discussed how to make these changes effectively. Lastly, the photographs were exposed to the whole community, involving them as a reflection. Narratives which emerged during the meetings were analyzed. Complementary, the measurement of the intervention impact was accomplished by using a pre-post questionnaire and the comparison of the participant group vs. the comparison group. Results: Quantitative results showed that participants increased their level of psychological sense of community and their participation desires, but continued with the same level of empowerment. Nevertheless, qualitative results indicated the photovoice sessions as a process of acquiring power within their community. Study 2: Framework: It was held with young people who live in the Ritsona Refugee Camp, Greece (UNHCR, 2017). It epitomizes the extreme situation that stranded minors suffering in reception places at the Mediterranean borders of Europe. Objective: Provide a tool for self-expression and building resilience and empowerment. Participants: Seven people aged between 14 and 23 years. Five were from Syria, and two came from Iraq. Their participation was voluntary and we explained them that their photos would be shown in Europe making visible their situation. Procedure: With the slogan "take pictures of what you see, what you think and what you feel", they captured and created narratives about their living conditions in the Camp, advocating their rights. The photos and their comments were exposed to the rest of the residents, arousing their interest and community awareness on such issues. Results: Photos were classified in five thematic areas: (1) discouragement and hopelessness, (2) complaint and interpellation, (3) vulnerable people in the Camp, (4) hope and strength and (5) advocacy and empowerment. Photovoice has allowed young refugees to express themselves freely, initiating a liberation process that breaks the circle of oppression in which they are immersed, denouncing the humanitarian crisis of refugee in Europe from its own participants. Lessons learned: - Photovoice is a strategy that allows collecting data of young people in a participatory way, and also stimulates their critical thinking and their capacity to act within their community. - Photovoice is useful to explore opinions of people from different cultures, due to its design based on artistic and emotional processes in which language is in the background. - Photovoice is a powerful tool denouncing oppression in the voice of victims. - Photovoice is a competent tool of opening up new opportunities for increasing community participation, resilience and empowerment, among young populations and thus, breaking the vicious cycle of vulnerability. - Photovoice should be evaluated though the combination of qualitative and quantitative methodology to assure the intervention's effects. Nevertheless, a complete evaluation in contexts of risks is sometimes almost considered impossible. - New technologies facilitate use and possibilities of this methodology.

***

Belgo-turcs et Belgo-marocains: quelle différence entre ses enfants d'immigrés?
(1213) Rukiye Tınas (Eskişehir Osmangazi University)

Parmi la population belge forte de 10 827 519 habitants (2010), 2 738 486 sont d'origines étrangères. Les Marocains et les Turcs, respectivement 412 310 et 218 852 personnes, constituent les deux plus grandes communautés étrangères en Belgique. Ils y sont arrivés dans la même période pour être recrutés massivement dans l'industrie minière, le secteur du bâtiment, du textile, et de la construction automobile dans le cadre de conventions bilatérales signées par la Belgique avec la Turquie (16 février 1964) puis avec le Maroc (17 février 1964). Entre 1961 et 1967 plus de 130 000 premiers permis de travail à l'immigration sont accordés. La demande de main d'œuvre est tellement forte que la législation exigeant un permis de travail comme préalable à la délivrance d'un permis de séjour n'est plus appliquée à la lettre. Parallèlement au recrutement officiel, de nombreux travailleurs immigrés arriveront comme « touristes » en Belgique et ne régulariseront leur séjour sur le territoire qu'après avoir trouvé un travail. En raison de la crise économique de 1974, les frontières sont bloquées, ainsi l'objectif notamment des travailleurs marocains change. Au départ, comme tout immigré, les Marocains souhaitaient résider temporairement dans les « pays d'accueil », en l'occurrence en Belgique. Il s'agit alors d'une intégration à long terme. Dès 1975, des regroupements familiaux, à savoir l' « immigration familiale », se produisent en vue aussi d'augmenter la natalité dans le pays d'accueil. Dans cette même période, la Turquie souffre d'une instabilité politique. Les conflits sanglants entre les militants de l'extrême gauche et de l'extrême droite ont mené vers deux interventions militaires, en 1971 et 1980. Les militants de l'extrême gauche, droite et également kurdes se sont par conséquent rendus en Europe. Il est donc question d'immigration dite « politique ». Du début des années 90 jusqu'à nos jours, l'immigration turque à destination entre autres de Belgique se fait dans un but de regroupement familial. Bien qu'ils soient arrivés dans la même période en Belgique, les immigrés d'origine turque et marocaine – tous majoritairement de confession musulmane – présentent des profils bien différents. Ceci a bien été constaté ces derniers mois dans le cadre de la question du terrorisme djihadiste. Les attentats terroristes perpétrés par de jeunes kamikazes belgo-marocains nés en Belgique entre autres à Paris (novembre 2015) et à Bruxelles (22 mars 2016) ont tous été revendiqués par Daesch. Depuis novembre 2015, la question de l'intégration en Europe en général, et en Belgique en particulier, se pose alors. A la lumière de ce qui précède, je propose une étude sur les communautés belgo-turque et belgo-marocaine afin de mieux comprendre leurs réactions face à toutes difficultés, dont les principales sont la discrimination, le racisme et le chômage. La question est de savoir « pourquoi la première est encadrée de toutes déviances alors que la seconde, prétendument mieux intégrée dans la société belge est devenue un foyer de djihadistes dans la capitale européenne? ».

***

Absconding from Shelter Accommodation Facilities: A Qualitative Study of Unaccompanied and Separated Children in Athens, Greece
(1021) Maria Gkioka (Faros), Dan Biswas

The last years an increased number of unaccompanied and separated children (UASC) entered Greece. According to National Center of Social Solidarity in Greece from January 2016 to February 2017 5.685 UASC have been referred to national services in order to be placed1. Before March 2016 when the agreement between Greece and Turkey was signed and the close of the boarders the children used to leave shelter accommodation facilities 48 hours after entering. Europol has reported more than 10.000 children have disappeared from authorities through the last year. The purpose of this study is to understand drivers behind absconding of UASC from shelter accommodation facilities and present helpful recommendations for organizations that run shelters to prevent absconding. The study draws upon data from three sources using a mixed-methods approach. Firstly, semi-structured interviews were conducted with ten unaccompanied minors that have absconded from a shelter in the past. As the part of the interviews, the participants made a drawing related to the absconding situation, which were analyzed. In addition, were conducted eight semi-structured interviews with care-givers working in shelters in Athens. Finally, eight guardians for UASC responded in a questionnaire about absconding. The qualitative data were analyzed using content analysis as described by Graneheim and Lundman. This study explored drivers for why children abscond from shelter accommodation facilities. A number of factors were identified as part of the study. Firstly, we found that there is need for improvement of the conditions inside the shelters and the proper age assessments are conducted prior to placements. Moreover, children reported a need for knowledge about rules, procedures and the policies in the shelter. Secondly, children reported the need for enhanced psychosocial support. Trauma and the loss of their daily routine has led to mental health challenges, and minors expressed stress expressed and other symptoms related to trauma and grief. Some children expressed a lacked a feeling of security in their shelter. Thirdly, unaccompanied migrant and refugee children came to the decision to leave their countries not only due to war, but also because a better future for themselves. Their hopes were to find a work and to be able to live independently, as well as to support their families. Children in the study expressed pressure from their families to continue their journey towards the destination country in Northern Europe. The long procedures regarding family reunification and relocation was also a factor that influenced UASC to leave from shelters.There is need for a holistic approach that addresses the needs of UASC in shelter accommodation facilities, which include the provision of psychological, educational, and recreational activities and support. Through integrated activities and basic education, children will have the opportunity to start building and organizing their lives. A recommendation from the study is that shelters organize interactive workshops about basic reasons and consequences of absconding. This will empower children to seek appropriate information, increase awareness about the major dangers of absconding, how to manage unpleasant emotions, and use support of peers and their caregivers.

***

Suriyeli Mülteci Göçü Bağlamında Risk Grupları: Çalışan Çocuklar
(1290) Gülay Acar Yurtman (Uskudar University)

Suriye'deki savaştan kaçıp Türkiye'ye sığınan ve sayıları üç milyonu aşan Suriyeli mültecilerin önemli bir kısmını 18 yaşından küçük çocuklar oluşturmaktadır. Bu çocuklar beslenme, barınma, sağlık, eğitim gibi sorunların yanında çocuk işgücünün istismarına maruz kalmakta ve ve erken yaşta çalışmak zorunda bırakılmaktadırlar. Bu bağlamda "çocuk emeğinin sömürülmesi" de önemli bir sosyal sorun olarak öne çıkmıştır Nitekim bu çocuklar çalıştıkları/çalıştırıldıkları için eğitimleri aksamakta veya yarıda kalmaktadır. Böylece, çalışmayla beraber diğer akranlarıyla aralarındaki mesafe kapanmayacak bir hal almakta ve kayıp nesil riski artmaktadır. Aynı zamanda mülteci çocukların çalışması/çalıştırılması beraberinde; çocuk suçluluğu, madde kullanma, sokakta yaşama alışkanlığı, şiddete maruz kalma, ihmal ve istismarı getirmektedir. Bu çalışmayla, çalışan mülteci çocuklar olgusuna sebep olan nedenler ile çocukların erken yaşta çalışma hayatına girmeleri durumunda karşı karşıya oldukları riskleri sosyal değişkenler çerçevesinde ortaya koymaktır. Araştırmada; İstanbul'un Bağcılar, Zeytinburnu, Fatih ve Sultanbeyli ilçelerinde çalışan/çalıştırılan mülteci çocukların bazı sosyo-demografik ve ekonomik özellikleri, çocukların çalışmalarında etkili olan etmenler, çocukların çalışma esnasında karşı karşıya kaldıkları ihmal/istismar ve çalışma koşullarının yarattığı bazı olumsuzluklar gibi konular irdelenmiştir. Veriler, yaşları 6 ile 15 yaşında değişen, farklı iş kollarında çalışan 70 Suriyeli çocukla araştırmacı tarafından geliştirilen anket formu ve yerinde gözlem yapılarak toplanmıştır. Araştırma bulgularına bakıldığında, mülteci çocukların çalışmalarında etkili olan unsurlar içerisinde özellikle yoksulluk faktörleri dikkat çekmektedir. Ayrıca bu çalışmada; çalışmaya başlayan mülteci çocukların cinsel, fiziksel ve duygusal şiddete maruz kaldıkları ve aynı şekilde çocukların giderek suça eğilimli hale geldikleri yönünde bulgular saptanmıştır. Çalışan çocukların iş türlerine göre yaptıkları faaliyetlere ve çalışma koşullarına bakıldığında, çocukların çok sayıda risklerle karşı karşıya oldukları gözlenmektedir. Öte yandan bazı çocukların, çalışmaya başlamalarıyla birlikte bazı risklerle karşı karşıya kalabilmelerinin yanı sıra aynı zamanda giderek suça eğilimli hale de gelebilmektedirler. Bu çerçevede mülteci çocukların ailelerine yeterli maddi ve manevi yardımlar yapılmalı, çocukların okulla olan bağları güçlendirilmeli, göç sürecinde oluşan sosyo-psikolojik sorunları bertaraf etmek için rehabilite edici çalışmalar yapılmalıdır.

***

Intergenerational Transmission of Parenthood and Parenting Values and Practices among Romanian Immigrants

(792) Anca M. Bejenaru (Lucian Blaga University of Sibiu)

The transition to parenthood is often perceived as a natural event and as a milestone of the adult life cycle. However, it is well known that human parenting, although is influenced by biological factors is not even predominantly their outcome, but the result of the developmental history of the parents and of their interaction with different socio-cultural backgrounds. In traditional communities where people mobility was reduced, parental models were limited, and they were transmitted as such or with little variation from one generation to another. Currently, the increased access to information and the mobility of parents allow them to make contact with a wide variety of models of parenting. International literature presents four hypotheses explaining migrants transition to parenthood and parental values and practices. The socialisation hypothesis is based on the premise that migrants keep in the private, familial environment, the cultural norms and values of the country of origin. In their care, the transition to parenthood reflects the models of origin country (Rundquist & Brown, 1989, Singley & Landale, 1998, Kulu, 2005, Kulu & Milewski, 2007). The accommodation and assimilation hypothesis assumes that families tend to assimilate the norms and values of the country in which they migrate and adapt sooner or later to them (Rundquist & Brown, 1989, Singley & Landale, 1998, Kulu, 2005, Kulu & Milewski, 2007). The adjustment is not a linear process but involves learning, negotiation, and accommodation (Hernandez & McGoldrick, 1999). Regarding youth migrants, was formulated the disruption hypotheses. It suggests that immediately after migration, they adopt an adaptation strategy. In their case, economic accommodation becomes a priority for them and they tend to postpone the transition to parenthood and keep a low level of fertility (Kulu & Milewski, 2007). Besides the age factor, selection hypothesis leads us to consider other characteristics that influence fertility behaviour and parenting models. Among these, economic and social status and migration motivation seem to be particularly important (Singley & Landale, 1998). Thus, young people who possess the economic and social resources allowing them to take risks, perhaps even a temporary loss, anticipating future professional achievement and gains, show a preference for fewer children and significant investment in them. On the other hand, if immigrants are part of disadvantaged groups they can manifest an increase in fertility behaviours in the destination country, children often representing a source of income and not of the investment (Rundquist & Brown, 1989, Singley & Landale, 1998, Kulu, 2005, Kulu & Milewski, 2007). In this context, our paper aims to answer a series of research questions such as: How migration affects the timing of the transition from childlessness to parenthood? How is the transition to parenting perceived in the context of migration? How immigrant parents' child-rearing values and practices are maintained, contested, or renegotiated under the influence of the new culture? Research data were gathered in the MIGLIFE project, using a narrative interview approach. For the purpose of this paper were selected 11 women with

low and medium levels of education, from rural or small urban areas. All these women have migrated at least five years in countries such as Spain or Italy. All of them became mothers during migration. The main goal of migrant women was to secure their economic prosperity. The results indicate their tendency to the transition to motherhood after starting a family and ensuring economic security. When unplanned pregnancy occurred, it was seen as a threat to the initial goal. These last ones either had an abortion or requested psychological support for acceptance of pregnancy. Regarding parental values and practices, it has been identified a transition from a traditional "model of interdependence" in which they were socialized at home, to "a model of autonomous relatedness" (see Kâğıtçıbaşı 1996, Keller et al. 2006). Most talked about economic and emotionally difficult childhood they had. They associate these difficulties with their mistrust, lack of vision and aspiration, which most have left the country. For most, migration meant personal development and overcoming limits. They believe that changes in their parenting values and practices are the result of personal change. In conclusion, the disruption hypothesis, followed by assimilation and adaptation to new cultural values appear to be suitable for explaining the transition to parenthood and parenting models adopted by the Romanian migrant women. Mothers who experienced many risks in their own childhood, placed in a favourable environment, tend rather to change values and behaviour than to proliferate those learned.
***

SESSION 12A – Economics of Migration - 5

	Room: A1
Chair	**Fethiye Tilbe, Namık Kemal University, Turkey**
837	Deciding to Stay: Bissau-Guinean Labour Migrants in Cabo Verde, West Africa – **Brandon D. Lundy, Kezia Lartey**
1102	Nature and Consequences of Migration to Gulf Countries: A Study of Inayat Patti Village of India - **Mohammed Taukeer**
1190	Migration: The Solution to Europe - **Minos Fylaktos**
1282	Migration-Induced Women's Empowerment - **Şule Akkoyunlu**
1330	Economic Behavior of Albanians Immigrants in Economic Crisis - **Dorina Kalemi**

Deciding to Stay: Bissau-Guinean Labour Migrants in Cabo Verde, West Africa
(837) Brandon D. Lundy (Kennesaw State University), Kezia Lartey (Kennesaw State University)

Cabo Verde, once serving as a migration transit country into Europe and the Unites States, is becoming a final destination for some immigrants. Many regional immigrants can enter Cabo Verde under the Economic Community of West African States' open borders agreement, eventually overstaying and potentially contributing to increased conflict over resources. The aim of this research was to discover why and how Cabo Verde is becoming a destination point for labour migrants and the effects these changes are having on immigrant/host community relations. The research questions asked in this study are: how do regional immigrants integrate into host communities in the face of resource pressures, and what is convincing them to stay? We found that a majority of immigrants had stable, fulltime work, began families, and joined community organizations. Additionally, what friction was observed stemmed from disenfranchised domestic youth, which seemed to lessen as integration improved. This study has implications for realizing successful community integration of labour migrants, especially within the Global South.
***

Nature and Consequences of Migration to Gulf Countries: A Study of Inayat Patti Village of India
(1102) Mohammed Taukeer (Govind Ballabh Pant Social Science Institute)

This paper attempt identified the facts about international migration from Inayat Patti village in Allahabad District of State Uttar Pradesh in India through primary data. In India, Uttar Pradesh is ranked first in low skilled labour migration to abroad particularly to Gulf countries. Therefore, Uttar Pradesh is selected as purposively. The Village is selected through pilot visit. Hence, it is observed that people migrated within India and Gulf countries for the purpose of the employment. The primary data is collected by mixed method approach for better understanding of the nature of the study. Main purpose of the paper was to explore the nature causes and consequences of Gulf migration but paper explored how internal migration leads the international migration. The economic and non-economic factors stimulated the migration to Gulf countries. Indian economic capital Mumbai and Saudi Arabia was the major destinations. The socio-economic status of the migrant households improved post-Gulf migration relative to pre-Gulf migration. Following the inflow and utilisation of remittances created culture of migration to Gulf countries.
     ***

Migration: The Solution to Europe
(1190) Minos Fylaktos (Harokopio University of Athens)

Demographic ageing is at hand. Europe is ageing every year, and this phenomenon has widespread impact to almost every country of said region. This impact affects social and economic policies. The European Commission stated in 2015 that currently as high as 17% of the total EU population is over 65 years old. This is the result of healthcare development, life standards etc. The retirement rates are also high, because of the growing elderly/pensioners' percentage, the extending life expectancy, the unemployment rates and the cadent percentage of the active population combined. The obvious solution is to increase the taxes to secure the pensions' monthly budget. Having already an economic crisis here in Europe it is not impossible in the nigh future all these would escalate to a social and/or financial crisis. For that matter, the EU has a response for the demographic ageing, called "Active Ageing". This is a concept deployed by the European Commission in the past decade and evokes the idea of longer activity to postpone the retirement age. Although it seems well planned has yet to show its potential, plus not all countries apply this policy. In our time, a refugee crisis has also emerged, with millions of refugees crossing the EU borders. The policy of many countries is to make things difficult for the refugees to avoid having them. By legitimizing the force of the army at national borders, building walls to separate refugees from locals, we only make things worse. But what if the EU accepted the refugees and solve this unprecedented demographic ageing? What if the solution of the economic crisis and the demographic ageing is lying in the refugees? We could avoid an ominous future. In the past, there are several occasions of countries that avoided financial crisis by bringing new populations. By the end of the second world war, the US accepted thousands of refugees and since then the economy has enormously evolved. In the 1960's Germany also accepted a massive wave of refugees and strengthened the local economy. Today we are once more at siege of the migrant crisis. Refugees could help to the much-desired economic growth. A population that would shuffle the demographic allocation, reform the labor market and mutually refugees and Europeans share an economic development. In a world of racism, and religious diversity, we could merge populations and with the proper education of both European and refugee parties, we could find a solution for many issues. Economic, demographic, politics', and even financial problems of less rich countries such as Greece, Slovakia and Hungary could be deliberated. Let's build bridges amongst nations, not walls.

***

Migration-Induced Women's Empowerment
(1282) Şule Akkoyunlu (Migration Policy Centre (MPC), Robert Schuman Centre for Advanced Studies (EUI))

Migration not only contributes to development through financial remittances, but also through flows of knowledge and through the diffusion of social, cultural and political norms and values. In fact, contributions through flows of knowledge and the diffusion of social, cultural and political norms and values are more appreciated during economic and financial crises, as financial remittances become unstable or decrease during economic downturns. This paper, therefore, addresses the effect of migration on women's empowerment in Turkey. The number of women in parliament in Turkey is chosen as women's empowerment and is explained by the emigration rate, the relative education of women to men, and a measure of democracy. Utilization of data over six decades from 1960 until 2011 gives the possibility that these series can be spuriously correlated. Therefore, the paper addresses the issue of spurious correlation in an analytical way. Spurious correlation entails the risk of linking the share of women in parliament, for example, to the emigration rate when in fact there is no association. This study adopts the bounds testing procedure as a method to determine and thwart spurious correlation. The results of bounds testing give clear-cut evidence that women's empowerment, the share of women in parliament in the present context, is related to the emigration rate, the relative education of women and to a measure of democracy. The bounds-testing procedure is replicated for emigration flows by destination country groups such as European and other core OECD countries, Arab countries, and Russia and CIS (Commonwealth Independent States) countries. Again, it is found that the share of women in parliament is related to the country groups with the largest effect in European and core OECD countries. The results are robust to the inclusion of asylum seekers and refugees in the emigration data. These results have important policy implications for the sending as well as for the destination countries, which are discussed in the paper.

***

Economic Behavior of Albanians Immigrants in Economic Crisis
(1330) Dorina Kalemi (Harokopio University)

This paper develops an empirical model to investigate the main determinants of economic behavior of Albanian's immigrants in Greece. The aim of this study is to investigate Albanian's immigrants rate of monthly private income and savings in economic crisis. In addition, the results analyze the remittances that sent in their home country from 2008 to 2011. Also, the results show the expected income of immigrants. The study is based on 371 survey responses from the area of Attica, in Greece and they are analysed econometrically using regression techniques. In particular, the empirical results, based on the estimation of regression analysis suggest that economic and consumer variables are statistics significant factors of the possibility to return to their home country. Finally, the empirical analysis showed that the factors affecting the probability of return to their home country because of the economic crisis are the participants who believe that they are still paid less than the natives, the participants who have said that their income in the host country is being reduced and the participants who own assets in their home country.

***

SESSION 12B – Citizenship

	Room: A2
Chair	**Deniz Eroğlu Utku, University of Thrace, Turkey**
1210	Greek Citizenship Tradition and Parliamentary Discourses of Differentiated Nationality – **George Mavrommatis**
1005	New Times, Old Dilemmas? Mobilising 'Law' and 'Nature' in Negotiations of Citizenship in Greece - **Maria Xenitidou, Irini Kadianaki, Antonis Sapountzis, Eleni Andreouli, Lia Figgou**
905	The Heirs of Spanish Citizenship - **Montserrat Golías Pérez**
904	In Searching Law on The Indonesian Diaspora: Lesson Learnt from South Korea and India Experiences - **Susi Dwi Harijanti, Bilal Dewansyah, Ali Abdurahman, Wicaksana Dramanda**

Greek Citizenship Tradition and Parliamentary Discourses of Differentiated Nationality

(1210) George Mavrommatis (Harokopio University)

Greek citizenship tradition, up until recently, has been on the ethnocultural path with the acquisition of citizenship strictly depended on jus sanguinis or the law of blood. Since 2010, this strict ethnocultural character of Greek citizenship tradition became openly antagonized by a civic conception of nationality mostly through Law 3838/2010 and the introduction of jus solis elements. More concretely, what this paper will try to do is to shed some light on parliamentary discourses on citizenship that became verbalized during the discussion of Law 3838/2010 and the acquisition of Greek citizenship by migrant children born or schooled in the country. To be more specific, this paper will bring to the fore a particular discursive construction of differentiated citizenship, which emerged from certain political actors and 'talked' about a clear dichotomy between ethnic and civic elements of nationhood. Furthermore, this discursive dichotomy was built upon a strict linguistic distinction between the terms of 'ithageneia' and 'ypikootita' that in Greek language both stand for citizenship. Last but not least, this differentiated narrative of citizenship should be understood as a way of defending the long-standing ethnocultural character of Greek nationhood against civic views. As it appears traditions die hard especially when they are ingrained in language, too.

***

New Times, Old Dilemmas? Mobilising 'Law' and 'Nature' in Negotiations of Citizenship in Greece

(1005) Maria Xenitidou (University of Surrey), Irini Kadianaki (University of Cyprus), Antonis Sapountzis (Democritus University of Thrace), Eleni Andreouli (Open University), Lia Figgou (Aristotle University of Thessaloniki)

This paper draws on public deliberation discourses on a new citizenship law in Greece and discusses the lines of argument identified in the ways in which (Greek) citizenship is negotiated in the context of 'the current situation in Greece' – the financial situation and ensuing political consequences internally and in the EU, and the refugee and migration issues, heightened since the beginning of 2015. The law, which included for the first-time provisions for jus soli access to Greek citizenship, was introduced in 2010, withdrawn in 2012, revised in 2015 and uploaded for public deliberation on the online platform www.opengov.gr. We analysed the posts submitted to the platform (N=712) focusing on the ones addressed to the article which concerned citizenship provisions for the children of immigrants (N=602), as this seemed to be the apple of discord. These were analysed based on the premises of rhetorical and critical discursive social psychology. The analysis indicates that commentators mobilise 'law' and 'nature' in contradictory ways in negotiating citizenship. For example, nature may be constructed as above 'human' laws while at the same time drawing on legal rhetoric in constructing the citizenship law as unconstitutional or the natural law as sediment in universal laws, and immigrants as accountable to the law or as illegal. In other arguments, appeals were made to the legal system to protect the natural law or to holding a referendum, distinguishing between the state and the people. In these negotiations, we interrogate who the 'other' is in each case and, by implication, how commentators position themselves, how the in-group is constructed and what its composition is. Finally, we discuss the ways in which these arguments are implicated in processes of othering and inclusion in the context of current immigration debates.

***

The Heirs of Spanish Citizenship [11]
(905) Montserrat Golías Pérez (Universidade da Coruña)

On October the 31st, 2007, the Spanish Parliament passed the Law for the Recovery of the Historical Memory. For many Spaniards, the coming into effect of this Law meant correcting the absences of the transitional period, in the shape of a legal and symbolic reparation for the victims of the Civil War and Franco's dictatorship. For those not familiar with its contents, the actual text of the Law had little to do with the "acquisition of the Spanish nationality of children and grandchildren of emigrants", given that in a legislation of this kind this granting would only affect the descendants of those who had lost their status as Spaniards as a consequence of exile, and members of the International Brigades in a very symbolic way. It was the contact with the applicants themselves and the allusions in the media to queues of grandchildren in the Buenos Aires and Havana's consulates that invited us to take a deeper look into the seventh additional provision of the Law, which extended this granting to all children and grandchildren of labour emigration. Focusing deeper in my chosen subject matter, I found out that the inclusion of the option to the nationality in the text of the Law, responded to a claim, if not contrary, certainly different from the one brought up by descendants of Civil War and dictatorship victims. It was about the children and grandchildren of Spaniards abroad who wished to recover the so far denied 'right of blood' by which they would receive the Spanish nationality of origin. This observation raised the first question of this study: Why do the grandchildren of Spaniards wish to acquire the nationality of their grandparents? In other words, the aim was to know the motivations of those applying for the Spanish nationality by means of the Law for the Recovery of the Historical Memory. The initial hypothesis lay on a dual answer: • It was a matter of identity- the inheritance of a family legacy; • Or, on the contrary, a pragmatic use of the status as a Spanish national and citizen of the EU was desired. In the light of this approach, a 'real time' investigation began both in Cuba and Argentina, the two countries with the highest number of applicants for the Spanish nationality via this law. And by means of the qualitative methodology I approached its protagonists, observing a range of responses through which these born Cubans and Argentinians pursued to become Spaniards. Two motivations which are not mutually exclusive- memory and utility with a multitude of uses for this nationality depending on the applicants' profiles and their contexts of origin.

***

---

[11]This proposal presents part of the results of the research carried out by the author and published in the book: Golías Pérez, M. (2016) Los herederos de la ciudadanía. Barcelona: Icaria

In Searching Law on The Indonesian Diaspora: Lesson Learnt from South Korea and India Experiences

(904) Susi Dwi Harijanti (Padjadjaran University), Bilal Dewansyah (Padjadjaran University), Ali Abdurahman (Padjadjaran University), Wicaksana Dramanda (Padjadjaran University)

The existence and movement of diaspora across the world significantly challenge the existing legal norms on citizenship and migration. The responses from the law-makers from origin countries vary. Most of European, Latin America and African countries adopt dual citizenship law to their diaspora for the different reasons, including immigrant integration, maintenance of loyalty to ex-citizen or the closeness ethnic relation (author, 2016a, p. 4). However, most of countries in Asia-Pacific region - which gain their independence through decolonization process - do not favor dual citizenship towards their diaspora, including Indonesia. This is mostly because of the ideological perception of citizenship (Hassall, 1999, p.49). In this sense, many countries grant the special status or scheme to their diaspora (neither citizens nor residents of the country) as an external quasi-citizenship based on ethnic descent as argued by Bauböck (2007, p. 2396) as "ethnizenship." In Indonesia case, academically, dual citizenship proposal can be justified as a qualified exceptionally legal policy to natural born Indonesia's citizen that acquired other citizenship status, not applicable to all aliens (author, 2016b, p.13). However, the rejection of dual citizenship proposal is unavoidable in practice and leads the issues of nationalism and security (author, 2017, p.2). Thus, the rejection leads to the idea to adopt a kind of ethnizenship status as an alternative regulatory model for Indonesia diaspora, which is supported by a number of proponents. In this regard, the President of Global Indonesia Diaspora Network/IDN (Global Network of Indonesian Diaspora), Al Arief strongly proposes that Indonesia might adopt Indian's model in a way that India does not formally apply dual citizenship status (author, 2016a, p. 7). Similarly, M. Iman Santoso, Indonesian immigration law professor, also suggests that the Indonesian government might officially provides a Person of Indonesia Descendent's Card (Kartu Keturunan Orang Indonesia) for ex- Indonesia's citizens and their descendents. This proposed Card would ensure that ex-Indonesian citizens and their descendents would not require visa to enter Indonesian territory and they would be entitled to have some legal rights, except political rights (M. Iman Santoso, 2014, p. 118). The discourse itself is not merely academic because it has political relevance in the context of Citizenship Law amendment plan as stated in National Legislation Plan 2014 – 2015. In order to search the suitable and realistic regulatory scheme for Indonesian diaspora, this paper - which based on the ongoing research - will compare experience from others countries which adopt a quasi-citizenship for their descendants overseas. India and South Korea have been chosen for comparative object since both countries have particular statutes that recognize and regulate diaspora status. Moreover, they have been considered as two countries which have similar stage of development with Indonesia as post-colonial Asian states that gain independence in nearly period. India creates the Person of Indian Origin (PIO) card scheme since 1998 and Overseas Citizens of India (OCI) card scheme in 2003 (Naujoks, 2015, pp. 21 -24). These two schemes merged in 2015 in to Overseas Citizens of India Card Holder (OCC) scheme through Citizenship (Amendment) Act 2015. These schemes give benefit to Indian diaspora more than visa exemption to visit and stay in India, but also guarantee some legal rights with exception in political and participation rights (Xavier, 2011, p. 46). While India adopts regulatory model of diaspora through citizenship law regime, South Korean experience show the different path toward their diaspora. The Korean government refuses the Korean diaspora's proposal for dual citizenship, and it creates a semi-citizenship called 'Overseas Korean' status through the immigration law regime as regulated in the Act on the Immigration and Legal Status of

Overseas Koreans (the Overseas Koreans Act/OKA) in 1999 with F-4 visa scheme with its amendment in 2004 which include Korean-Chinese diaspora (Lee, 2012, pp. 93 – 94).This law gives the benefit for the Korean diaspora, including some fundamental rights, such as freedom in employment and economic activity, and national treatment with regard to real property rights and transactions, foreign exchange transactions, and health insurance and pensions (Lee, 2003, p. 109). This paper will discuss both India and South Korea's experiences dealing with diaspora in order to propose suitable regulatory model for Indonesia's diaspora.

***

SESSION 12C – Migration and Family

	Room: A4
Chair	**Fuat Güllüpınar, Anadolu University, Turkey**
939	The Effect of Male Out-Migration on the 'Women-Left-Behind': Evidence from a Case Study in Far Western Nepal – **Jeeyon Janet Kim**
1230	Female Movers and Mothers in Brexit Britain: Narratives of Transformations, Privileges and the Quite Everyday - **Benedicte Alexina Melanie Brahic**
1243	To Be Wife in the Absence of Husband: Transnational Family Experiences among Turkish Women Immigrants in Italy - **Gül İnce Beqo**
994	Reshaping Identity Through Family and Work: The Case of Highly Skilled Korean Migrant Women in Urban Japan - **Dukin Lim**

The Effect of Male Out-Migration on the 'Women-Left-Behind': Evidence from a Case Study in Far Western Nepal
(939) Jeeyon Janet Kim (Tufts University)

International migration remains a highly gendered phenomenon in Nepal. Compared to global figures where women make up about half of the world's migrant population, 90% of Nepalese migrants are men (1). Many of these men migrate alone, leaving behind their families as they earn wages abroad. In Nepal, women have limited decision-making power and their social discrimination is further bolstered by discriminatory legal policies and cultural norms. For example, women's access to land and property is derived through her marriage and their access to property and resources (e.g. farmland, houses, livestock) are mediated by men (2). The majority of empirical studies examining the effect of migration focus on the monetary aspect of migration; comparatively, less attention has been paid to the social and cultural effects of migration on the 'left-behind' (3). Moreover, studies examining the effect of male out-migration on women-left-behind (WLB) in Nepal have been limited in scope and have thus far been conducted only in the Hills and Terai (plains) Ecological Zones (1,4,5). In a country where nearly one third of the male population have left behind their families to earn wages, the limited research on the relationship between male out-migration and WLB's workload and decision-making role in Nepal is a major knowledge gap. The objective of this study was to understand the effect of male out-migration on WLB's workload and their household decision-making role in Maulali, a Village Development Committee (VDC) in the Mountain Ecological Zone of Far Western Nepal. Nearly all households in the VDC are engaged in agriculture and male labor out-migration is a major livelihood strategy. The vast majority of migrants are male (81.9%) who leave behind their families to migrate for unskilled wage labor, almost exclusively in India. Over the course of a year, the study conducted 24 focus group discussions and 46 iterative in-depth interviews in Maulali; respondents were recruited through stratified purposeful sampling. Focus groups were stratified by caste and gender while interviews were stratified by the same criteria in addition to households' migration status. Repeated

field visits as well as the iterative interview design enabled the researcher and her translator to build rapport with the respondents in order to gain a more in-depth understanding of the research topics. Almost all interview respondents had a current or former migrant household member (husband and other male household members). Unanimously, respondents noted that migration was necessitated by poor production and a lack of employment opportunities. Migration to India, destination of all of interviews' household members, was a compulsion, never a choice. Respondents reported that women's workload increased when their husband migrated. With the exception of plowing the field with oxen and going on the roof which were considered to be male responsibilities, women shared that in their husbands' absence, all household responsibilities fell to them. From early morning to evening, women reported that they had to work, often leaving their children home alone. Many women noted feeling spread very thin and stressed about taking on multiple responsibilities without their husbands' help. Child care and discipline were noted as major challenges. It appears that even in their absence, men retain household decision-making powers. While some respondents noted that women were free to make decisions about daily activities and food consumptions, others shared that they had to call their husbands to get their advice on basic interactions, such which seeds and grains to buy from the market. The use of mobile phones appears to have changed the nature of migration and intra-household dynamics. Women explained that they are expected to call their husbands to ask when and where to plant, to seek permission to sell an animal, and to ask if they can leave the village to visit relatives. Respondents - both men and women - felt that women were largely powerless without a man, noting that people did not listen to women. Women who had to take on additional household decision-making role in their husbands' absence shared that the experience was burdensome and anxiety-inducing. Citing economic dependence on male breadwinners, patriarchal gender norms, and lack of education, respondents – especially women – shared that WLB lack the self-confidence, experience, and skills to make decisions on their own. This is the first study to qualitatively explore the effect of male out-migration on WLB in Nepal's Mountain Ecological Zone. Results from this study will help to fill a knowledge gap about the effect of migration on those left-behind, particularly women, and provide a more nuanced understanding of the intra-household dynamics of labor out-migration in Far Western Nepal.
  ***

Female Movers and Mothers in Brexit Britain: Narratives of Transformations, Privileges and the Quite Everyday
(1230) Benedicte Alexina Melanie Brahic (Manchester Metropolitan University)

Up until the 23rd June 2016, European movers and their (often bi-national) families living in the UK were relatively invisible. They have gained prominence almost overnight in the aftermath of the Brexit vote to leave the UK. An estimated three million European nationals living in the UK are now caught - some observers prefer to say 'held hostage' - in the Brexit negotiations. Many of them have started relationships and families in the UK and now feel the lives they had built are under threat. This paper explores how the recent decision of Britain to leave the European Union impacts on female European movers and their families of procreation living in the UK. Brexit is deemed to be a catalyst for change; are European female movers (and their families) 'bargaining chips' caught in the Brexit negotiations or can new opportunities arise alongside the challenges brought by this historical change? Using Manchester as a base, this paper draws on two series of thirty-two and forty-two semi-structured movers (living in Manchester with their family of procreation), an online survey answered by 167 parents of bilingual (English with Finnish, French or Polish) children and the author's auto-ethnographic reflections. The paper first explores the construction of the (sometimes-jumbled) continuum of identities of female movers, wives (female partners) and mothers in times of unprecedented change in modern Britain. It then examines aspects of European female movers' lives concerned with cultural and linguistic maintenance and migrant community building focusing on how the Brexit process affects them.

***

To Be Wife in the Absence of Husband: Transnational Family Experiences among Turkish Women Immigrants in Italy
(1243) Gül İnce Beqo (Catholic University of Milan)

This paper is a preliminary study and a part of my doctoral thesis which seeks to analyse the transformation of family practices among Turkish immigrants in Italy through qualitative and exploratory interviews with first generation Turkish migrants identified by snowball sampling (N.30, two interviews for each family) who are currently residing in North Italy. Men and women are interviewed, as much as possible, separately and their migration experience is analyzed through their family relations. Turkish migration from Turkey to Italy is a typical example of male migration where men migrate first and later occurs the family reunification. Among those interviewed there is a high presence of consanguineous marriage (especially between first-cousins) and the traditional arranged marriages are very common. In generally, male migrant's mother chooses her best nephew as her future daughter in-law. In some cases, men, can not leave the host country while their asylum application are processed and for that reason they can't participate in their own engagement or wedding ceremony. Thus, women get married alone and meet their husband only when men are allowed to invite their spouses for family reunification. So, this paper, in the light of the recent literature on transnational families, examines, through in-depth interviews, the transnational experiences of migrant women and their family formation.

***

Reshaping Identity Through Family and Work: The Case of Highly Skilled Korean Migrant Women in Urban Japan
(994) Dukin Lim (University of Tokyo)

Since the mid-1980's, Japan has been experiencing the effect of globalization on its national economy with the influx of foreign migrant workers (Yamasaki 2003: 38). At the same time, Korea has been transformed through rapid democratization and subsequent globalization, thus promoting international travel and exchange. These contemporary changes stimulated Korean women migration to Japan. Unlike the migration of Korean oldcomer women who were born and raised in Japan, those working in the sex industry and marriage migrants, newcomer Korean women make their own migration decisions and migrate alone. Various individual aspirations shape their mobility: education, tourism and business. They enter Japan as transient visitors and then decide to stay in Japan permanently by settling in the country through marriage with a Japanese man or continuing their career. Despite the rise of this recent migration pattern, existing literature has focused solely on Korean women who migrated to Japan through previous channels, highlighting their struggles and vulnerabilities as women and as migrants. What remains to be underexplored are the challenges, limitation and possibilities (potential) of female migrants in Japan. This qualitative study is about highly- skilled Korean female migrants who came to Japan on their own. It investigates the socio-economic adaptation and settlement processes. It also documents their life narratives, focusing on the ways in which migration and social integration to Japanese society has been reshaping their social identities. This research

examines how they negotiate work and family life, seek a sense of belonging to family and workplace, and pursue economic integration in Japan. In order to explore women's agency through their transnational migration and identity, this qualitative study undertook several research methods in data collection: two focus group discussions with (11) Korean migrant women, individual in-depth interviews with (48) Korean female respondents and (9) children, and migrant support groups. This research explains how highly skilled Korean migrant women have gained greater agency in globalized spaces, and autonomy in terms of making personal life choices. It aims to analyze the degree to which newcomer Korean women have been transforming the identity and social position of Korean migrants in contemporary Japan. While they have obtained mobility and agency in modern times, there is a need to recognize both their struggles as they adapt to host society, and their agentic position in terms of making decisions, utilizing their resources and skills in order in to manage their transnational lives. This paper highlights that highly-skilled Korean women's agency is influenced by structural factors in the context of Japan. Despite the gradually changing gendered views and expectations on female migrants, Japanese society continues to be heavily influenced by media, politics, and public discourse Patriarchal norms and ideologies are still prevalent in globalized city of Tokyo. Nevertheless, highly-skilled Korean women are able to opportunities to move out of Japanese traditional social spaces and challenge to evade rigid norms through advancing their education and career experiences as well as Japanese language ability. Therefore, this paper mainly argues that Korean migrant women fully realize their agency following migration to Japan through active social and economic participation to attain, work-family balance, social mobility and egalitarian position with local Japanese men and women. Despite facing significant lifestyle challenges due to cultural differences and language barriers, some highly-skilled Korean women's socio-economic success and adaptability in Japanese society indicate that female migrants' agency can enable them to have a sense of security and better prospects for the future.
***

SESSION 12D – Mevsimlik Göç

	Room: A5
Chair	**Saniye Dedeoğlu, Muğla University, Turkey**
988	Bereketli Topraklar, Zehir Gibi Yaşamlar: Türkiye'deki Suriyeli Göçmen Tarım İşçileri – **Saniye Dedeoğlu, Ertan Karabıyık**
917	Adana Ovası'nda Mevsimlik Tarım İşçiliği Genel Durumu ve Çocuk İşçiliğini Önlemeye Yönelik Yerel Politika ve Programların Tarihsel Süreci - **Ertan Karabıyık**
1039	Mevsimlik Tarım İşçiliğinin Feminizasyonu - **Sidar Çınar**
824	Türkiye'de İller Arası Göç Ağının Mekânsal Görünümü: Doğum Yeri Verisine Göre Sosyal Ağ Analizi (1950-2015) - **Mustafa Yakar, Fatma Sert Eteman**

Bereketli Topraklar, Zehir Gibi Yaşamlar: Türkiye'deki Suriyeli Göçmen Tarım İşçileri[12]
(988) Saniye Dedeoğlu (Muğla Sıtkı Koçman University), Ertan Karabıyık (Kalkinma Atolyesi)

---

[12] Bu çalışma, Adana Ovası'ndaki çadır yerleşiminde yaşayan 266 Suriyeli göçmen hanehalkının temsilcilerine uygulanan ve 1662 kişi hakkında bilgi veren ve işveren, tarım aracıları, STK'lar ve kamu kurumları ve diğer ilgili kuruluşlarla derinlemesine görüşme sonuçlarını kapsamaktadır.

Orman Kemal'in, meşhur "Bereketli Topraklar Üzerinde" romanında Çukurova Bölgesi'ndeki tarım işçilerinin bir lokma ekmek için yaşadığı acımasız yaşam ve çalışma koşullarını anlatmaktadır. İşçilerin zehir gibi yaşamla devam eden hayatta kalma koşulları, toprak sahipleri için zenginlik ve refah kaynağı olmuştur. Kemal'in romanında anlattığı 1940'ların ve 1950'lerin yıllarında Çukurova'nın tarım işçileri çoğunluğu topraksız köylülerdir. Kemal'in romanında anlattığı günden beri verimli toprakların kazananları ve kaybedenlerin durumu pek değişmedi, ancak topraksız yerel tarım işçilerinin yerini Güneydoğu'dan Çukurova Bölgesi'ne çalışmak için gelen mevsimlik tarım işçileri aldı. Urfa, Adıyaman ve Mardin illerinden gelen Kürt ve Arap işçiler, 1990'lı yılların başından bu yana mevsimlik tarım işlerinde önde gelen emek grupları haline geldi. Güneydoğudaki Kürt ve Arap işçilerinin yerini ise, 2011 başından beri Suriyeli sığınmacılar tarafından sunulan emek almaya başladı. İşgücü arzındaki bu tipolojik değişim, Türkiye'de mevsimlik tarım işlerinin doğasında ve Türkiye'de işgücü piyasasında uluslararası göçmenlerin varlığı konusunda radikal bir değişime işaret etmektedir. Tarım sektörü hem farklı işçi grupları arasında Suriyeli göçmenlerin gelişi ile bir rekabet ortamı yaratırken hem de Suriyeli göçmenlere sunduğu çalışma imkanları ile onların enformel bile olsa Türkiye toplumuna entegrasyon imkânı sunmaktadır. Tarım sadece geniş bir kayıt dışı sektör olarak ekonomik krizin derinleştiği bir ortamda, Suriyeli göçmenlerin işgücü piyasası faaliyetlerinin ve hayatta kalma stratejilerinin ön koşullarını hazırlamaktadır. Türkiye'deki emek piyasasının yeni ön koşulu, Suriyeli göçmenlerin asgari ücretten daha düşük ücretlerle işgücü piyasasına katılımını öngörmektedir. Tarım, tekstil, inşaat ve hizmetlerin dışında Suriyeli göçmen işçi çalıştıran en önemli sektörlerden biridir. Bu bildiri, Adana ilinde mevsimlik tarımsal üretimde Suriyeli göçmenlerin çalışmasını değerlendirmektedir. Bildirinin amacı, Suriyeli göçmenlerin tarım sektöründe çalışma biçimlerini, aynı işler için rekabet eden yerel işçi gruplarıyla anlaşmazlıkların yanında resmi olmayan bir entegrasyon stratejisinin bir biçimi olabileceğini göstermektir. Adana'da 2016 yaz aylarında gerçekleştirilen bir araştırmanın bulgularına odaklanarak, Suriyeli göçmen tarım işçilerinin ve ailelerinin çalışma ve yaşam koşullarına genel bir bakış sunmaktadır. Göç örüntüleri, mevsimlik tarım iş piyasasının işleyişi ve tarım aracıları ile işçiler arasındaki ilişkiler ve çadır yerleşimlerinin koşulları ele alınmaktadır.

***

Adana Ovası'nda Mevsimlik Tarım İşçiliği Genel Durumu ve Çocuk İşçiliğini Önlemeye Yönelik Yerel Politika ve Programların Tarihsel Süreci
(917) Ertan Karabıyık (Kalkinma Atolyesi)

Adana Ovası yakın tarihinin hemen hemen her döneminde, uluslararası ticaretle de ilişkilenen yoğun bir tarımsal üretime konu olmuştur. Yaygın ve yoğun tarımsal üretim ise her zaman mevsimlik tarım işçiliğini ve farklı ücretli emek kullanım biçimlerini ortaya çıkarmış, tarımsal ücretli işçiliğin en yaygın gerçekleştiği coğrafyalardan biri olagelmiştir. Bu yörede mevsimlik tarım işçiliğinin ilk kayıtlı izlerine 1800'lü yıllardan itibaren ulaşmak mümkündür. Tarihin farklı dönemlerinde tarım işçiliği bağlamında farklı politika ve programların odağına alınan bölge, son yıllarda ise sayıları hızla artan mevsimlik tarım işçiliği ve onların çocuklarına yönelik uygulanan eğitim, sağlık, çocuk koruma, yaşam ve çalışma ortamı iyileştirme program ve projeleri bağlamında araştırma ve uygulamaya programları için adeta bir laboratuvar niteliğini almıştır. Bu araştırma, uygulama ve programları daha iyi değerlendirmek ve inceleme konusu edindiği sosyal grupların hayatlarında ortaya çıkarmayı hedefledikleri iyileştirmeyi anlamak için, bu çalışma Adana Ovası'nda tarımsal üretime odaklı çalışmaların tarihsel seyrini ortaya koymak amacıyla arşiv ve diğer dokümanları içeren bir masa başı çalışmasının bulguları sunulmaktadır. Buna ek olarak, Çukurova'nın tarımsal üretim tarihi hakkında araştırma yapmış kişilerle yüz yüze görüşmeler ve bu konuda makale, yüksek lisans, doktora tezleri hazırlamış kişilerin dokümanlarına da erişilmiştir. Ayrıca, bu çalışma için özel olarak geliştirilen bir form aracılığıyla da Adana Ovası'nda uygulanan rutin faaliyetler, program ve projeler; program ve/veya projenin uygulandığı yıl(lar), uygulayan kuruluşlar veya kişiler, program (proje adı, tema ve sonuçları) şeklinde derlenmiştir. Adana Ovası'nda istihdam edilen mevsimlik tarım işçileri ve onların çocuklarına yönelik eğitim, sağlık, çocuk koruma, yaşam ve çalışma ortamını iyileştirme çalışmaları bağlamında son 200 yıllık döneme bakıldığında bu çalışmadan elde edilen bulgular; a. Kapsamlı faaliyetlerin son 30 yılda ortaya çıktığı görülmektedir. Yalnızca çocuklara odaklı ilk araştırma ise bundan 25 yıl önce gerçekleştirilmiştir. Çocuklar ailenin bir parçası olarak ele alınmış ve değerlendirmeler buna göre yapılmıştır. b. Mevsimlik tarım işçilerine ve çocuklarına yönelik uygulanan program ve projeler genellikle yöre dışından, hatta uluslararası kurumların etkisiyle gerçekleştirilmiş, ulusal ve yerel kurumlar harekete geçirilerek müdahale sağlanmaya çalışılmıştır. Elçilikler, yurtdışı sendikaları, yurtdışı vakıflar, BM kuruluşları fon, teknik destek ve eğitim olanakları sağlayan başlıca kuruluşlardır. c. Program ve projeler kapsamında ulusal ve yerel kurumsal kapasite geliştirme çalışmaları gerçekleştirilmiş, ancak kurumsal kapasitenin bir süre sonra ortadan kalktığı, kalıcı olmadığı görülmektedir. Örneğin METİP kapsamında istihdam edilen bütün kişiler farklı kurumlarda ve işlerde çalışmaktadırlar. Ayrıca geçmişte uygulanan program ev projelerle ilgili dokümanlara erişilememektedir. d. 1990'lı yılların başına kadar mevsimlik tarım işçilerine odaklı faaliyetler ağırlıklı olarak sağlık sorunlarına, özellikle sıtma ile mücadeleye yoğunlaşmış, bu yıllardan sonra eğitim, çocuk koruma, çalışma ve yaşam ortamının iyileştirilmesi faaliyetleri gündeme gelmiştir. Mevsimlik tarım işçilerine yönelik rutin faaliyetlerin, program ve projelerin sürdürülebilirliği ve kalıcılığı gerçekleşmemiş; sürekli program ve proje bazlı çalışma yaklaşımı benimsenmiştir. Program ve projelerin çıktıları kamusal politikaya dönüşmemiştir.

***

Mevsimlik Tarım İşçiliğinin Feminizasyonu
(1039) Sidar Çınar (Mardin Artuklu University)

Neo-liberal dönüşüm sürecinin tarımda üretim ilişkileri üzerindeki en önemli etkilerinden birisi kadınların tarımsal işgücünde görünürlüğünü artırması olmuştur. Tarımsal üretimde her dönemde önemli bir yere sahip olan kadın emeği, bir yandan ihracata dayalı tarımsal üretimde yaşanan artış diğer taraftan aile işletmelerinde emek gücünün yeniden organizasyonu ile birlikte tarımsal üretimin sürdürülebilirliği açısından daha hayati bir konuma sahip olmuştur. Bu bakımdan işgücünün feminizasyonunu tartışırken iki önemli konu ortaya çıkmaktadır. Birincisi özellikle ihracata dayalı tarımsal üretimin emek yoğun ve mevsimlik/geçici işlerinde kadınlar daha fazla istihdam edilmesidir (Deere, 2005; ILO, 2003: 14; Katz, 2003; Lastarria-Cornhiel, 2006: 17; Raynolds, 1998: 6). İkincisi Erkeklerin kentsel istihdama doğru hareketlilikleri ile birlikte kadınların emek güçlerinin hem aile işletmelerinde hem de tarımsal işgücünde daha önemli olmaya başlamasıdır. Bu bildiride yukarıda bahsedilen iki konu ekseninde Türkiye'de mevsimlik tarım işçiliğinde feminizasyonu saha araştırması bulguları etrafında tartışılacaktır. Bir yandan Türkiye'de mevsimlik tarım işçisi ailelerin geçinme stratejilerinin bir sonucu olarak erkekler tarım dışı sektörlere geçerken mevsimlik tarım işçiliğinin giderek feminize olması üzerinde durulacaktır. Bu konu mevsimlik tarım işçiliğinde çalışma ilişkilerinin örgütlenme biçiminin feminizasyon sürecinin yolunu nasıl açtığı ile birlikte ele alınacaktır. Sonrasında işverenlerin üzerindeki maliyet baskısı ve talep ettikleri işgücünün nitelikleri ile yine çalışma ilişkilerinin kurulma biçiminin bu alanda feminizasyonu nasıl karşılıklı olarak desteklediğinden bahsedilecektir. Saha çalışmasının mevsimlik tarım işçisi kadınlarla ve onların işverenleri ile yapılması planlanmaktadır. Araştırmada mevsimlik tarım işçiliğine kadınların daha fazla katılmasına neden olan ataerkil değerler çerçevesinde geçinme stratejileri, diğer taraftan işverenlerinin talep ettikleri işgücünün niteliklerinin nasıl feminizasyon sürecini açtığı anlaşılmaya çalışılacaktır.

***

Türkiye'de İller Arası Göç Ağının Mekânsal Görünümü: Doğum Yeri Verisine Göre Sosyal Ağ Analizi (1950-2015)

(824) Mustafa Yakar (Süleyman Demirel University), Fatma Sert Eteman (Munzur University)

Türkiye'de 20. yy'ın ortasından itibaren başlayan iç göçler, zamanla kurulan göçmen ilişki ağları ile süreklilik kazanmış ve ülke içinde nüfusun yeniden dağılışında belirleyici olmuştur. Kaynak ve hedef saha arasındaki akışın oluşturduğu göçmen ağlarının mekânsal olarak kuruluşu, boyutları ve zamanla gösterdiği gelişimin ağ analizleri ile incelenmesi iç göç araştırmalarına önemli katkılar sağlayabilir gözükmektedir. Türkiye'de iç göç araştırmaları göçün nedenleri veya sonuçları üzerine yoğunlaşırken, göç hala neden devam ediyor sorunsalı ise genellikle kaynak sahanın iticilikleri üzerinden açıklanmaya çalışılmıştır. Oysa göçün devamlılığında çok daha belirleyici olan kaynak ile hedef sahalar arasındaki göçmenlerin oluşturduğu ilişki ağları yeterince incelenmiş değildir. Bu araştırmanın amacı; Türkiye'de iç göçün, doğum yeri verisinden hareketle sayılan/ikamet edilen yerdeki nüfus miktarına göre alınan ve verilen göç akışının büyüklüğünü iller ölçeğinde yönlü ağlar kullanılarak 1950'den günümüze gelişiminin analiz edilmesidir. Veri ve Yöntem: Araştırmada, TÜİK (DİE) tarafından yayınlanmış olan 1950-2015 dönemine ait, iller ölçeğinde doğum yerine göre sayılan/ikamet edilen yer verisi kullanılmıştır. Veriler, doğum yerine göre iller nüfusunun sayılan/ikamet edilen illere göre olan dağılımını gösteren dönemlere göre değişen (67x67, 73x73 veya 81x81) boyutlarda matris şeklindedir. Veriler, Microsoft Excel'in sosyal ağ analizi yapan NodeXL modülüne uygun bir şekilde dönüştürülerek görsel ağ grafikleri ve ağ ölçütleri kullanılarak analiz edilmiştir. Ayrıca; her bir ilin toplam nüfusun içindeki kendi ili doğumlu olup yine aynı ilde yaşayan nüfus oranı (göç etmeyen yerli nüfus), her bir ilin kendi ili dışı diğer iller doğumlu nüfus oranı (içeriye/alınan göçler), her bir ilin kendi ili doğumlu olup fakat diğer illerde yaşayanlar oranı (dışarıya/verilen göçler), yurtdışı doğumlular oranı (yurtdışından gelen göçler) gibi verilerden de yararlanılmıştır. İllerin diğer illerden aldığı ve diğer illere verdiği göçün ağ haritaları çizdirilmiştir. NodeXL ile oluşturulan ağ grafikleri ve istatistiksel göstergeleriyle göçün kaynak ve hedef sahaları arasındaki akışın ortaya çıkardığı ağ görünümü, Türkiye'de iç göçün 1950'den itibaren geçirdiği dönüşümün çeşitli yönlerini ortaya koymaktadır. Nitekim, Türkiye nüfusunun 1950'de % 8.1'i doğduğu il dışında sayılırken, bu oranın 2015'de % 31'e erişmiş olması, ağ yapısının giderek karmaşıklaşmasına ve zamanla tam bir ağ yapısına sahip olmasıyla sonuçlanmıştır. İstanbul'un zamanla ülkenin tamamına hâkim olan ağdaki merkezi konumunun oluşumu yanı sıra yeni göç merkezlerinin ortaya çıkışı ve gelişimi ağlar üzerinden izlenebilmektedir. İller arası göçlerin bir sonucu olarak ortaya çıkan bu durum, illere ve bölgelere göre önemli farklılıklar gösterdiği gibi, nüfusun mekânsal olarak farklı köken sahalardan meydana gelmesine ve böylece giderek de heterojenleşmesine yol açmıştır. Türkiye nüfusunun geçen yüzyılın ortasından itibaren geçirdiği iç göç süreçleriyle birlikte ülke içinde kurulmuş ve zamanla gelişerek oldukça karmaşık bir görünüme sahip ağ yapısının olduğu ileri sürülebilir. Kurulan ağlar göçlerin devamını sağladığı gibi, göçün yöneldiği merkezlerde daha heterojen nüfus yapılarının ortaya çıkmasına yol açmıştır. Dolayısıyla göçün hedef sahalarında giderek belirginleşen hetorojenleşme eğilimi kentsel mekanlarda sosyo-mekansal ayrışmalar şeklinde gözlenmeye başlanmıştır.

***

SESSION 13A – Economics of Migration - 6

	Room: A1
Chair	**Şule Akkoyunlu, Rimini Centre, Wilfrid Laurier University, Canada**
984	Pacific Seasonal workers in Australia agriculture: Voices from the field – **Branka Krivokapic-Skoko**
1169	The Exploitation of Migrant Labour in the Countryside of Northern Puglia - **Giorgia Cantarale**
736	Importing a Labor Force for Catalonian Agriculture. Sustainability and Successes - **Olga Achón Rodríguez**
1090	Welcoming Communities: The Resettlement and Integration of Syrian Refugees in Rural Canada - **Stacey Haugen**
1029	Re(presentation) of Refugees in Integration Programs and their Transition in Times of Crisis - **Ameera Masoud**

Pacific Seasonal workers in Australia agriculture: Voices from the field
(984) Branka Krivokapic-Skoko (Charles Sturt University)

Australia has a very large temporary immigration program, but unlike most other immigration nations in North America, and New Zealand - Australia has not had a large scale seasonal worker program of temporary agricultural workers. Due to lobbying from growers and the industry, a Pacific Seasonal Worker Pilot Scheme was introduced in Australia in 2008 for three years. According to the scheme, Pacific Islanders will work in low-skilled jobs in the horticulture industry across Australia. The program allows seasonal workers from East Timor, Nauru, Kiribati, Papua New Guinea, Samoa, Solomon Islands, Tonga, Tuvalu, Vanuatu and Timor Leste to work in low-skilled jobs for up to seven months in a 12-month period. The Australia government renewed the Pacific Seasonal Worker Program in the horticulture industry across Australia and extended the range of occupations to include tourism (accommodation); agriculture (sugar cane, cotton); and fisheries (aquaculture) industries in limited locations. The program is demand driven with 12 000 visa places available over the 2012-16 period (DIBP, 2013). Pacific Island Seasonal Workers will likely become increasingly important to the Australian agricultural sector in coming decades. After a successful pilot programme in the horticultural sector, the Pacific Seasonal Workers Programme is now an uncapped demand-driven source of labour supply for the agricultural sector (Brickenstein, 2015; Doyle and Howes, 2015; Underhill and Rimmer, 2016, World Bank, 2006). The Pacific Seasonal Worker Program is also one component of the broader commitment that the Australian Government is prepared to make as part of Australia's Regional Aid Program. It should be mentioned that 'Australia's Regional Aid Program has its roots in the historical nature of setting class agendas particularly by the white ruling class in the 1800s. The Australian ruling classes owned acreages, however trying to find cheap labor was almost non-existent. Relations with local Indigenous populations remained tensed over the harsh colonial practices of the white settler. Therefore, the Pacific Island labor filled that gap. The history of the use of Pacific Islanders - Kanakas' –as forced or indentured labor for Queensland cane fields in the late nineteenth century was one of clear exploration of Pacific Islander labor in Australia (Markus 1979). While on a broader scale this type of the schemes may reinforce a sense of neocolonialism, the everyday realities for Pacific Seasonal workers in Australian horticulture is defined by middleman labor contractors as well as by plentiful and sustained exploitation, where examples of co-ethnic exploitation are very common. This presentation is based on the preliminary field work and focus group discussions organized with seasonal workers from the Papua New Guinea and Kiribati in the regional Victoria, Australai. The focus was on getting in-depth insights into a settlement process, working and living condition and their relationship with the community. The recurring themes gathered from the field work were challenging landscape, poverty, community morality issues and exclusion, as well as the potential for exploitation. Apart from three major dimension of vulnerability common for all migrant workers – pay, working time and work intensity- (Sargeant and Tucker, 2009) the field research identified two other aspects of the lived experience of Pacific Seasonal Workers is 'place/landscape', and 'community'. This disconnect between aspiration and reality of income-earning in Australia is not a rare phenomenon migrant worker, but in the case of PSWs they are in debt the moment they arrive in Australia. They are expected to pay off all the costs the labour hire companies have incurred to give them work and bring them to Australia. The workers were aware that they had to pay off their debts, but the realization that the wages were not enough to cover the costs was a rather late one. Landscape and rurality of the places PSWs have been sent to has been perceived as rather harsh, and that ruggedness of the place combined with isolation made their work on the farms even more challenging. Finally, community connectedness, which is ingrained in the cultural milieu of Pacific Island, was evidently missing in the context of settlement of PSWs in Australian rural communities.

***

The Exploitation of Migrant Labour in the Countryside of Northern Puglia
(1169) Giorgia Cantarale (Sapienza University of Rome)

As of the first half of the eighties, the Italian agriculture – as well as that of many southern European countries – was completely transformed because of socio-economic changes of a larger scale: the progressive abandonment of rural areas by the "natives", less and less inclined to carry out difficult and unprofitable jobs; the change in consumption patterns as a result of the birth of the so-called Big Organised distribution; the defined a new agri-food system, that of large transnational corporations; the reorganization of work based on ethnicity; the adaptation of national policies in a neoliberal production system, based on the ideology of an organized global growth (Corrado & Colloca, 2013, pp. 14-15). The countryside became global and reorganized its production intensively, generating increasingly specialized and industrialized agriculture (Sassen, 2013). The organization of labour in agriculture in southern Italy is strictly associated with the modalities of daily labour reproduction. Residential segregation is a central element in the management of the market and the labour force. Many workers, mostly from the countries of the former Soviet bloc, and many African migrants contribute to the construction of large "ghettos", i.e. concentrations of hundreds of workers housed in self-constructed barracks or in agglomerates of empty dwellings away from towns: this is the case of the "Great Ghetto", the largest African slum in southern Italy, or the "Ghana House", located in the territories of the city of Foggia, in northern Puglia (Hazard, 2002; 2010). The Great Ghetto is in open country and it differs profoundly from US rural ghettos, approaching the residential forms found in the suburbs of major African cities. It is a clear form of "heterocentered territorialisation", where there is «a rational regionalization that expresses and supports a social rationality gained elsewhere, namely out of the cultural and spatial context of the society that we're watching» (Turco, 1988, p. 145). In all phases of the creation of that territory, in the symbolic deployment, material and structural, residents show membership in other identity, the sharing of social rules that end up creating a place as heterotopia space (to resume a concept dear to Foucault). The physical isolation, the division of space, is one of the strategies that allows to have nothing in common with these communities (Cristaldi, 2012). Moreover, urban studies, since the Chicago tradition with Park and Wirth, have often described the strong social ties that are set up within ghettoized ethnic spaces by the same

situation of segregation. However, the Mezzogiorno ghettos have at least two specific elements that differentiate them from other situations of segregation. In the first place, these are rural ghettos where spatial distance accentuates segregation. Secondly, these establishments are directly linked to a productive activity and have a seasonal character. The concept of "seclusion", conceived as «a placement in space that reinforces the superposition between work, leisure, rest and more generally the reproduction of the daily life of an individual or a group in a single place, where they are formally free to go out at given times of the day or, more often, of the week» (Gambino, 2003, pp. 104-105), makes it possible to better characterize this mode of placement of the labour force. It is an organization of daily life and work which differs from the internment and the form of the camp (Agamben, 1998), since, at least on the formal level, it does not deprive the right to spatial freedom. The caporalato is a form of clientelism that characterizes politics, society, and economy of southern Italy and which has been defined as «mediating capitalism» (Schneider & Schneider, 2013). « [...] migration makes it possible to maintain the flexibility of the labour market» (Castles, de Haas & Miller, 2014, p. 275), but «the management of labour on the part of criminal organizations generate an outrageous human degradation framework for our state of civil law» (Cicerchia & Pallara, 2009, p. 35). The availability of occupied labour force with just-in-time mode and low-cost is the answer to an economic system in which the temporal logic that prevails is that of immediacy and short-term, where the successful model is that of the slave uses disposable (Bales, 1999). Migrant workers represent a "surplus humanity", in the balance between state laws and criminal powers, constantly bridled by a slow and controversial bureaucracy that produces their illegal status, forcing them to fit into working networks and informal economies, potential victims of exploitation and abuse (Settineri, 2013, p. 100). The agricultural sector is a safety net within which migrants, with or without proper documents, they can find shelter and cover: it becomes a place of transit awaiting payment or a better job, or the first space in entering the Italian labour market (Reyneri, 1998, pp. 6-7).
    ***

Importing a Labor Force for Catalonian Agriculture. Sustainability and Successes
(736) Olga Achón Rodríguez (Universidad de Barcelona)

Once the family farming model was replaced by an industrial agricultural system of production based on hired labor, the Catalonian (Spanish) agricultural organization Unió de Pagesos, with the consent of the State, reinvented itself as a provider of services related to the acquisition of manpower through a "recruitment and supply" system – referring to the set of practices to recruit foreign workers abroad and their placement by the Union. The State's migration polity is responsible for the emergence of such a system, and we can trace its origin in the symbiotic relation between the State and the Union, whose interests – the social control of the foreign worker and the just in time delivery of labor – run parallel to those of the State. In the dormitories, a transformation is envisioned through different devices - regulations for accommodation, the presence of personnel to monitor the facilities, a visit regime and exit permissions, among others – similar to other institutions such as labor camps, where individuality is tamed through subordination to a dominating power in order to create a new subject, whose value is exteriorized through obedience to those who manage the institutions. In the history of the development of production systems, labor placement strategies have constituted a solution to the basic problem of workers' freedoms, which is an indicator of possible desertion of work. It appears that societies constructed along closed social divisions, such as caste systems or feudal estates, are to a lesser degree dependent on such institutions - for they, as a whole, are configured as prisons where the individual has no freedom to alter his position on the social ladder.

On the other hand, societies which allow certain porosity along social boundaries and where individuals are free to initiate mobility processes - be they structural or topographical - usually require the presence of institutions to confine manpower, for such autonomy implies a problem for the development, consolidation or survival of some specific economic activities. The existence of places to accommodate labor which are created under the rule of law is a paradox for these societies. The dormitories for foreign workers recruited in their homeland established by the agricultural union Unió de Pagesos are no exception to this rule. The form of the dormitories - which also resembles, in a way, that of jails and military barracks - helps deliver, place and distribute workers spatially, classify them in order to gain their maximum time and power, educate their body and codify their behavior, to keep them visible to the power that subjects them. This is achieved not only by architectonically configuring a suitable space for their creation, but also by trapping workers in a web of registers and annotations containing accumulated and centralized information. The dormitory is the place to observe the consequences of the foreign workers' recruitment system which is the subject of this study. Our hypothesis is that such a system of recruitment, importation, concentration and supply of labor implemented by Unió de Pagesos prevents the exercise of personal freedoms considered basic by the political order, producing a subject deprived of fundamental rights: mainly freedom of work and, consequently, of circulation and residence. The study was focused on the so-called "collective" dormitories. The main characteristic of the collective dormitories is that in them we can see a permanent control over and supervision of the workers, which is fundamental for their transformation into subjects' ready to deliver. Most of the collective lodgings are concentrated in the district of the Segrià, l'Urgell and the Plà d'Urgell, so fieldwork was primarily carried out in these locations (from 2003 to 2010). This methodological decision is supported by the fact that there is a higher density of collective lodgings found in the district of Segrià (Catalonia, Spain). This work aims to expose a system that produces a subject whose rights and liberties – which must be protected not only because they are workers, but also because they are human beings – are severely limited.

***

Welcoming Communities: The Resettlement and Integration of Syrian Refugees in Rural Canada
(1090) Stacey Haugen (International Development Research Centre (Canada))

Since January 29, 2017, more than 40,081 Syrian refugees have been resettled across Canada at the invitation of the federal government (Government of Canada 2017). While the majority have been resettled in major urban centers, there is a growing number of refugees being resettled outside of major Canadian cities. Despite this reality, much of the current literature focuses on urban refugee resettlement and integration policies. This research addresses this gap in the literature and studies resettlement and integration processes and policies in rural regions and small communities in Canada. The knowledge produced from this research informs policies which will address the challenges and enhance the benefits of resettlement for both refugees and rural communities. It points to new ways in which Canada, and other developed countries, can continue to share the responsibility of refugee resettlement globally. The limited body of work that has been completed on the topic of rural resettlement focuses on specific issues such as the integration of refugees into Canadian communities in general (Canadian Council for Refugees 2011; Hyndman 2011), dispersal policies in Europe (Andersson 2003), the fear of ethnic concentration in cities (Aroche, Coello, Momartin 2012, 134-5), and the ability of refugees to access services in regional Australia (Sypek, Clugston, and Phillips 2008; Schech 2013; McDonald-Wilmsen et al. 2009). Comprehensive research that specifically explores the benefits and challenges of rural refugee resettlement and addresses the resettlement and integration policies in rural regions and smaller communities is lacking both in Canada, and globally. Addressing this knowledge gap using a qualitative, multiple case study approach, this research project examines the community-level challenges and benefits of rural resettlement and integration, so as to inform Canadian resettlement policies. This research asks: what are the benefits of rural refugee resettlement for both refugees and rural communities, and how can best practices regarding resettlement and integration inform Canadian policies so that more refugees can be successfully resettled and integrated into rural communities? There is also a strong gender component to this research which seeks to understand the gendered realities of refugee resettlement in rural Canada and how previous cultural norms and assumptions of gender are evolving throughout the integration process. The research consists of a comprehensive literature review, interviews with Canadian immigration officials and experts, and in-depth case studies in Canadian rural communities which involve local community stakeholders, refugee families, service providers and sponsoring groups. Refugee resettlement is beneficial for smaller communities, who benefit from a boost in population and increased diversity, refugees, who benefit from the enhanced social capital and housing/living affordability options that such places offer, and the Canadian government, who, with the necessary policy changes, could successfully resettle and integrate more refugees within their borders at a lower cost. Evidence suggests that, because of smaller populations and distance from urban areas, small communities generally have enhanced social capital, understood as the "relationships between people characterized by trust and norms of reciprocity that can be used to achieve individual and collective goals," when compared to metropolitan areas (Deller and Halstead 2015, 174). Strengthening social capital is essential for the sustainability of small communities and the successful integration of refugees into host societies. Building social capital is an important way that smaller communities can improve their resiliency in the face of increasing challenges and stressors, which include declining populations, diminishing services, environmental degradation and various international pressures. When a community increases its connections and interactions with diverse groups on a local, national and global scale it builds "enduring social capital" through strengthened relationships and knowledge sharing and increases "community initiative, responsibility, and adaptability" which is needed to ensure sustainable communities (C. B. Flora and Flora 2013, 118-9). Refugees in particular can have a lot to offer smaller communities looking to build social capital as "refugees are for the most part resilient and resourceful, and often come from societies that place a higher value on interpersonal relationships...making them quite adept at developing effective social networks" (Aroche, Coello, Momartin 2012, 149). Importantly, research suggests that refugees are an asset to host communities and do not represent a burden on economic and social resources. Betts et al. found that in many cases refugees "create sustainable livelihood opportunities for themselves" and "often make a positive contribution to the host state economy" (Betts et al. 2014, 5). Communities with a high degree of social capital have a lot to offer refugees including the creation of social bonds and maintenance of community support (Hyndman 2011, 21). Specifically, social capital can improve the confidence of refugees, encourage a sense of belonging, diminish feelings of isolation and improve language skills and local knowledge (Strang 2010, 599). This research seeks to understand the dynamics of refugee resettlement and integration in a local context, and determine if rural communities, in Canada and across the developed world, are being under-utilized as sites for refugee resettlement.

***

Re(presentation) of Refugees in Integration Programs and their Transition in Times of Crisis

(1029) Ameera Masoud (University of Helsinki)

Refugees and migrants transition into the new society has become a topical issue nowadays across Europe. Integration into the society is merely seen successful when migrants manage to find a job. Programs designed for vulnerable youth have failed to address their needs and their inclusion remains a challenge (Brunila et. al in press; Kurki, Masoud, Niemi, re-submitted). In Finland, integration programs designed for refugees and migrants in general, have become projects that do not fulfil their initial objectives as much as they are fulfilling political and market-oriented interests (Kurki & Brunila, 2014). This paper aims to analyse the influence of integration policies, practices and discourses on young refugees (aged between 18 and 30), as they are usually in a transition phase towards gaining new forms of skills and practices enforced by the neoliberal logic as well as the integration requirements (Olssen, 2008; Brine, 2006). The transition of young refugees in integration programs, have shown that in most cases education struggles to meet their expectations and it influences their identity formation as well as their integration into the labour market (e.g. Rogers, 2006). I argue that integration and transition to find a job is highly individual and integration policies promote the perception that individuals have the autonomy towards their self-realization, achievements and actions. The result of such governing makes the individual accountable and responsible for whatever misfortune they may encounter (Rose, 1999; Gorman, 2002; Brunila et. al in press). Failure is usually blamed on the individual, and as a result remains in a cycle of education programs under the cover of integration, which impedes refugees' transition, while it disregards and masks other problems in the society that are the reason. For example, in a study published by the Ministry of Employment and the Economy in Finland it stated that "employers displayed a preference for hiring a young person without vocational training or a long-term unemployed rather than someone with an immigrant background" (Larja et. al, 2012 p.60). Hence, how could we expect vulnerable individuals to find a decent job that matches their skills and their educational background? Therefore, we need to disrupt current practices of discrimination and work with employers and businesses in order to promote acceptance, tolerance and cultural knowledge of the other, as a valuable other and not as a threat. When looking at the refugee integration as a crisis, the result of that are policies and practices as an intervention to solve the crisis (De Genova et. al 2016). It disregards that refugees are individuals with previous knowledge, identity, and agency (Brun, 2001; Grove & Zwi, 2006). Youth refugees that I interviewed have always shown how desperately eager they are to find work, to learn (even if they have to learn again and again) in order to prove they are willing to do anything to build new stable lives, and challenge the dominant thoughts about them that they are in Europe to live on the social security and welfare (Keskinen, 2016). While other types of migration is welcomed, refugees and non-western migrants are still perceived as a burden and a threat. The global discourse regarding refugees and certain categories of migrants is framed on a "rhetoric of exclusion" (Wodak & Boukala, 2015; Caponio & Cappiali, 2016). This perpetuates policies, media, and governments to strategize mechanisms that emphasize refugees as a burden, a crisis, a threat; creating negative implications, thus focusing on finding solutions to the negativity that might already be a non-existing exaggeration. Instead of steering the policies and integration programs into establishing common grounds for integration not as the threatening vulnerable 'other' but as a person with skills, valuable perspectives and enriching new experiences to the society. It is important to study discursive practices and what is taken for granted (Bacchi & Bonham, 2014), especially that discourses allow for certain forms of power to govern integration programs towards a collective pathway, creating inequities. The issue of

refugees' representation in discursive practices and its impact on integration programs as well as the refugees' integration, has not been studied adequately (Huot et. al, 2015). This paper utilizes the concept of othering, to examine discursive practices which are embedded in and are a force of shaping refugees' transition as well as influencing integration programs. Othering becomes and is a result of a discursive process. The term othering which stems from the postcolonial theory, is seen as process that allows categorization to occur, producing Western hegemonic power that promote exclusion and disempower vulnerable groups in general and those from the so called Third World in specific (Spivak, 1988; Said 1979). While one might argue that postcolonialism is limited to studying the colony, the colonizer and colonialism; this paper tends to build on one of the fields of postcolonial studies as presented by Dirlik (1994): "as a description of a discourse ... that is informed by the epistemological and psychic orientations". In this sense "the identity of the postcolonial is no longer structural but discursive" (p. 332).
***

SESSION 13B – Transnationals, living and working in Saudi Arabia

	Room: A2
Chair	**Simeon S. Magliveras, King Fadh University of Petroleum and Minerals, KSA**
982	Indonesian Intellectual Migrants in Saudi Arabia – **Sumanto Al-Qurtuby**
1041	Migration in Saudi Arabia: Some Political and Policy Implications- **Muhammad A. Z. Mughal**
885	Migration, Employment and Work Prestige in Saudi Arabia - **Muhammad Saeed**
1134	Alienation and Nostalgia of Algerian Scholars in Saudi Arabia - **Ahmed Bendania**
1127	Overseas Filipino Workers (OFW's) in the Kingdom of Saudi Arabia - **Simeon S. Magliveras**

Indonesian Intellectual Migrants in Saudi Arabia
(982) Sumanto Al-Qurtuby (King Fahd University of Petroleum and Minerals)

Interactions between Arabia (especially Yemen and Hijaz) and Southeast Asia (particularly the Malay-Indonesian archipelago) have existed long before European colonial times. Historically, Arabs, particularly Hadramis (from South Yemen), journeyed to the archipelago mainly for trade, residing, or spreading Islam. Indonesians, on the other hand, voyaged to Hijaz in northern Arabia due to two main factors: (1) to perform hajj pilgrimage and other religious activities in the Holy Cities of Mecca and Medina (Haramain), and (2) to learn Islamic knowledge and sciences in the birthplace of Islam and Prophet Muhammad. After performing hajj, the vast majority of Indonesians returned to their country, while a small minority chose to stay in Mecca and Medina to learn about Islam and Arabic. Whereas some stayed on for months or several years to study before returning to their home countries, others continued to reside there until they deceased. By the early 17th to mid 20th centuries, some of these initial educational travellers who then resided in the Haramain, became respected imams of Haram Mosque (Masjid al-Haram), fine teachers of Islam, and noted Islamic scholars (ulama). This tradition of "educational travel" continues till today. Saudi Arabia is now home to thousands of Indonesian Muslim students pursuing diverse studies from Islamic disciplines to hard sciences and engineering. In the past, a great number of Indonesian scholars taught purely Islamic sciences in madrasah, mosques, and informal centers of learning in the Haramain. However, in the recent decades, some Indonesians have begun to teach "secular sciences" at universities and colleges across Saudi Arabia. This talk will discuss the history, changes, and contemporary developments of these intellectual sojourners.

***

Migration in Saudi Arabia: Some Political and Policy Implications
(1041) Muhammad A. Z. Mughal (King Fahd University of Petroleum and Minerals)

A good deal of literature has emerged on the issues related to economic migration in Saudi Arabia. Temporary economic workers in Saudi Arabia come from various countries like Pakistan, India, Bangladesh, Philippines, Egypt, and Sudan. The economic remittances sent by these migrant workers back home is the major sources of income for a significant number of families in these countries. Therefore, the issues regarding these diaspora communities remain pivotal in the diplomatic relations between these countries and Saudi Arabia. Recently, Saudi Arab's government proposed Vision 2030 which seeks to diversify its native workforce and encourages the local population to be actively involved in national economic growth. However, the capacity building of Saudi citizens for certain jobs which are being performed by migrant workers, education quality, and post-industrial economic challenges in a globalized economy, women's role in the new economic scenario are some of the pressing concerns. This study maps out the existing body of literature to find out various political and policy implications with regard to migration in Saudi Arabia. It problematizes the cultural, economic, political, and policy aspects of migration in Saudi Arabia from national and international perspectives.

***

Migration, Employment and Work Prestige in Saudi Arabia
(885) Muhammad Saeed (King Fahd University of Petroleum and Minerals)

This paper examines the relationship between migration and employment or work prestige in the Kingdom of Saudi Arabia. The oil boom in Saudi Arabia in the 1970s created an attitude relating to employment and work prestige as respectable and unrespectable or preferable and least preferable jobs. The notion of employment prestige gap further widened when reflected in the labor policy of the Kingdom. Subsequently, all the managerial and authority driven positions were reserved for the Saudi nationals while the blue collar, labor intensive and hard jobs—considered as low status and unrespectable or less preferable jobs— were offered to foreign workers. This encouraged mass migration of foreign skilled and unskilled workers to Saudi Arabia. In this regard, Saudi Arabia became one of the top migrants' destination and source of remittances in the world. However, Saudi Arabia has been under much criticism from the international community for its unjust labor laws, abuse of the migrant workers and national-centric mercantilist policies. This paper argues that the Saudiazation policy, a decrease in the oil prices and Vision 2030 of the Kingdom have resulted in the de/reconstruction of the employment or work prestige. Thus, the fissure between respectable and unrespectable jobs are now squeezed. This paper concludes that new policies are influencing the pattern of economic migration to Saudi Arabia because Saudi nationals are now encouraged to gradually replace expats by taking on the blue-collar and physically demanding jobs. However, religious factor such as Saudi Arabia being the birthplace of Islam, and being custodian of the two holy mosques still drives people to travel and work in Saudi Arabia.

***

Alienation and Nostalgia of Algerian Scholars in Saudi Arabia
(1134) Ahmed Bendania (King Fahd University of Petroleum and Mines)

The songs «alghorba Saeeba" alienation is difficult are types songs many Algerians in France and Europe sing. The tunes are usually songs of nostalgia, the passage of time and the hope of travel to escape into the unknown. The songs were written when some disenchanted or hopeful Algerians took distant voyages to settle in places like Europe, Americas or Gulf. It was composed at the time when Algeria was in great political turmoil after Independence and during the Civil War in the nineties. People fled unrest and economic uncertainty. This paper examines a new migration in the context of this old tune. The Algerian migrants of today differ from those of the early 20th Century. Many of the migrants are highly educated professionals who are looking for a better life and to escape the burdens of the post nineties-crisis Algeria. This paper explores how these new migrants place themselves in the new global world and envisage themselves as subjects of nostalgia. Finally, this paper will examine the meaning contemporary Algerian migrants in Saudi Arabia understand the classic tunes.

***

Overseas Filipino Workers (OFW's) in the Kingdom of Saudi Arabia
(1127) Simeon S. Magliveras (King Fadh University of Petroleum and Minerals)

This paper's focus on the everyday life of Filipinos in Saudi Arabia. A few unique aspects of living in Saudi Arabia: As is commonly known, the genders are completely segregate in the public realm; in contrast with the United States and Europe immigration to KSA cannot be permanent; once a foreign worker finishes his work in KSA he/she is obligated to leave shortly after his/her work is done; in addition foreign workers are sponsored under the Kafala laws which limit the workers' rights; and salaries are primarily determined by national origin and only partially on professional qualifications. This paper examines the situation of living in Saudi Arabia and how Filipinos deal with their obligations in KSA and their obligation to home. Transnational Filipinos are thrusted from one socio-cultural system into another. Filipino nationals must navigate personal and family needs, their emotions, and their identity resulting from the act of migration. This talk explores the reasons why Filipino people immigrate and how they deal with the needs of the family left in their home country, the obligations they have in their new country of residence and if there is any gain in social, or economic capital. I conclude that though the obligations seem to be overwhelming, the majority of people I talked felt obligated to better their families' situations at home hoping their status would be elevated. This paper concludes that indeed for some OFW's it was the case, however, most OFW's still were very ambivalent about their sojourn. I would suggest this ambivalence is because migration is a permanent temporal / spatially displacement

***

SESSION 13C – Integration - 3

	Room: A4
Chair	**Gül İnce Beqo, Catholic University of Milan, Italy**
717	Acculturation Processes of Syrian University Students in Turkey – **Ayşe Şafak Ayvazoğlu, Filiz Künüroğlu**
1180	Acculturation in Multicultural Australia: The Experience of Second Generation Greek-Australians - **Paul Kalfadellis**
765	From "Haponesa" to "Issei": Ethnicized Identities of Okinawan War Brides in Post-War Philippines - **Johanna Orgiles Zulueta**
962	School Adaptation of Second Generation Return Albanian migrants - **Kalie Kerpaci, Martin Kuka, Teuta Bajo**

Acculturation Processes of Syrian University Students in Turkey

(717) Ayşe Şafak Ayvazoğlu (İzmir Katip Çelebi University), Filiz Künüroğlu (İzmir Katip Çelebi University)

The study aims to explore the acculturation experiences of Syrian university students in Izmir, Turkey, using semi-structured oral interviews among 17 informants. The study uses a qualitative approach and inductive content analysis to shed light on the factors influencing adaptation of Syrian refugees. The research uses Berry's theoretical framework and is geared towards understanding the three facets of acculturation in the case of Syrian students: acculturation conditions, orientations and outcomes as described in Berry (1997). The study adopts qualitative methods design in which in-depth semi-structured interviews is the main method of data collection. Seventeen students have participated in the 1.5-hour long interviews, which have been digitally recorded and transcribed verbatim. Transcripts were analyzed thoroughly and rigorously using inductive content analysis procedure. On the basis of the informants' self-reports we found that language barrier with the mainstream Turks, perceived discrimination, the differences in the educational systems, political and religious issues experienced emerged as major themes in refugees' narratives. The research revealed that adaptation difficulties varied substantially across socio-economic status of the informants and by the degree of in-group social support. The results are discussed within the framework of Berry's acculturation model. The findings of the study will also be invaluable for the counselors and professionals assisting in the process of cross cultural adaptation of refugees and the scholars seeking to deepen the understanding of acculturation. The implications of the study will be valuable to the policy makers in anticipating the acculturation-related concerns for the refugees, creating preventative measures and implementing durable long-term solutions.

***

Acculturation in Multicultural Australia: The Experience of Second Generation Greek-Australians

(1180) Paul Kalfadellis (Monash University)

Australia is one of the most culturally diverse countries in the world. Since 1945, more than 7 million people have migrated to Australia, resulting approximately one in four Australians being born overseas and 46 % of the population having a parent born overseas and nearly 20% of the population speaking a language other than English at home (ABS 2013). As part of this immigration program a large wave of Greek migrants came to Australia between the late 1950s and early 1970s, making Greeks one of the largest community groups in Australia (ABS 2004). A strong need on the part of the Greek migrants to maintain and impart the home country's cultural heritage to their children, resulted in second generation Greek-Australians (SGGAs) born in Australia or having moved to Australia at a young age, having to negotiate and integrate both their ethnic Greek culture and the mainstream Anglo-Australian culture in their daily lives. As Benet-Martinez & Haritatos, (2005) point out migration results in individuals having to inhabit and internalise dual cultural worlds. According to Berry (2005) migrants find themselves adopting different strategies in acculturating in their adopted homeland. Acculturation is a process that involves the maintenance of one's cultural heritage and the adoption of the practices and behaviours of the host culture (Berry, 2005). Berry (2005) suggests that acculturation strategies adopted by migrants include assimilation, separation, marginalization and integration. Integration suggests that individuals identify with both the mainstream and their ethnic culture, resulting in a bi-cultural identity. However, Berry (2005) also points out the dominant culture, in this case the Anglo-Australian culture depending upon the strategy it adopts helps create the environment which enables an acculturation strategy to be pursued by the minority group. Australia provided such an environment by adopting a policy framework of multiculturalism as part of its immigrant nation-building project post the 1970s. A regulated and well-ordered immigration program meant that in general Australians' have accepted cultural diversity (Soutphommasane, 2016) and multiculturalism, with 86% of the population agreeing that multiculturalism has been good for Australia (Markus 2015). Through an analysis of the literature, policy documentation and commentary surrounding multiculturalism and acculturation in Australia, this paper will argue that for Greek Australians and especially SGGAs, integration best described their acculturative process in Australia. Integration was encouraged and enabled in an amenable Australia, underpinned by a bi-partisan political embrace of multiculturalism from the early 1970s. Multiculturalism as a policy framework in Australia not only sought to deal with the integration of immigrant minorities and the growing ethno-cultural diversity of the country but also over time became part of the narrative both in terms of Australian nation building and identity (Koleth, 2010). Multiculturalism in the Australian context has been a very different experience from that often purported to be and passed off as multiculturalism in the European context. Characterized by a cultural plurality, multiculturalism in Australia unlike the European experience afforded its migrants and their offspring political/civil, social and cultural rights based on equality with the dominant Anglo-Celtic culture of the majority. At the same time the right to express one's cultural identity and heritage is coupled with rights and obligations to respect the democratic values of Australia such as democracy, the rule of law, equality of the sexes, and freedom of speech (Australian Government, 2011). Such an inclusive environment allowed SGGAs and other ethnic minorities to revel, partake and grow in a bi-cultural identity integrating both their cultural heritage and being Australian and in the main not having to suffer negative social consequences for doing so.

***

From "Haponesa" to "Issei": Ethnicized Identities of Okinawan War Brides in Post-War Philippines
(765) Johanna Orgiles Zulueta (Soka University)

This paper looks at these so-called "war brides" (Sensou hanayome) in the post-war Philippines, and their experiences upon migration to the Philippines in the 1950s to the 1960s. More specifically, I examine how ethnicity has become stigmatized in Philippine society of that time due mainly to wartime experiences. I also explore their how they lived their lives in varied degrees of discrimination, inclusion and exclusion. I particularly use the ascribed ethnic marker "Haponesa" or Japanese woman, in the Filipino vernacular, to illustrate how ethnicity has been stigmatized. I utilize life stories of those women who lived decades of their lives in the Philippines. While several of them choose to go back to Okinawa, many of them made the Philippines their home. Semi-structured interviews were done in 2009 and 2012, both in Okinawa and in the Philippines. I also use data I gathered in late 2011 to 2013, when I was doing on-and-off fieldwork in Okinawa.

***

School Adaptation of Second Generation Return Albanian migrants
(962) Kalie Kerpaci (Harokopio Panepistimio), Martin Kuka (Harokopio Panepistimio), Teuta Bajo (Arsakeio College)

There is an increasing interest on the issue of return migration, especially on the complexities of the return process (Cassarino, 2004). In this paper, we deal with the case of second generation Albanian migrants returning from Greece. More specifically, our focus is on those who attend the Arsakeio College, a bilingual Greek elementary and high school in Tirana, Albania. This is an ongoing research. So far, we have conducted interviews with 10 teenagers between the ages of 15 to 17. This age was chosen because it is easier for them to express themselves and reflect on their experiences before and after returning to their country of origin. We also intend to interview second generation return migrants, who go to public schools, for the purpose of comparing the role of school in the adaptation process of the teenagers. In our paper, we give emphasis on the process of their integration. We examine their attitude towards their parents' decision to return, the way they dealt with the challenges of their adaptation at school, their relations with their teachers and peers, and whether school facilitated in any way their integration. The data is collected through semi-structured interviews. We preferred this method because it gives the researcher the necessary flexibility in order to approach the issues at hand from all angles, with follow-up open-ended questions. Two rounds of interviews were made at Arsakeio in Tirana, an environment familiar to the students. At the same time, however, this environment could make the student reluctant of expressing their real views, especially any critical stance towards their institution. Thus, after introducing ourselves, stating our purpose, and inviting them to participate in this research, we made it clear that everything they would say would remain confidential, and used only for the purpose of the research. Then we waited at an empty classroom for those who decided to be interviewed. For the analysis of the interviews we used the thematic analysis according to the model of Brown & Clark (2006). Using thematic analysis, the researcher can actively choose a particular form of organizing, describing and interpreting the collected data (Brown, Clark & Rance, 2014). In this early stage of interviews analysis, it appears that the students initially disagreed with their parents' decision to return to Albania. Although they have visited Albania for holidays, and know the country mainly through their parents' narratives, they didn't like the idea of returning permanently, because of fear of losing their friends, as well as any other connection with Greece. In Greece, they grew up. Some of the students have accepted the decision to return, under the condition that they study at the Greek college in Tirana, and later return to Greece to continue their undergraduate studies. The Greek college functions as a bridge between the Albanian reality and the idealized Greek society, for which they express nostalgia. It is obvious to us that Greece is their home, while Albania simply their country of origin.

***

Immigrants' Integration Experience in seven EU Countries
(803) Emina Osmandzikovic (New York University Abu Dhabi)

The approach of academic literature on integration predominantly segregates objective integration outcomes from immigrants' integration experience and stands in stark contrast to the paucity of studies that jointly examine both. I bridge the two approaches by quantifying immigrants' integration experience via both subjective indicators: (i) overall life satisfaction and (ii) ease of applying for citizenship or permanent residence, and an objective indicator: (iii) employment status. By analyzing survey responses of 7 407 immigrants in seven European Union member states, I assess the factors that correlate with more positive integration experience of immigrants and the magnitude of their relationship. The background factors I examine are (i) the historical ties between immigrants' countries of origin and residence, and (ii) the level of development of country of origin. The immigrant-specific factor I examine is (iii) the reason for migration. The results show positive and statistically significant correlation between background factors and all three indicators of immigrants' integration experience. However, the correlation between the humanitarian reason for migration, an immigrant-specific factor, and immigrants' integration experience is negative, with the exception of ease of applying for citizenship. This paper, thereby, contributes to the literature by examining subjective and objective indicators of immigrants' integration in conjunction. Further, I demonstrate that integration is a complex process that is correlated with a heterogeneity of factors, both background and immigrant-specific ones, that need to be examined jointly.

***

SESSION 13D – Türkiye'de Suriyeli Çocuklar

	Room: A5
Chair	**İsmail Öz, Atatürk University, Turkey**
1092	Türkiye'deki Suriyeli Çocukların Eğitimi: Güçlükler ve Öneriler – **Coşkun Taştan, Zafer Çelik**
1057	Suriyelilerin Eğitimine Suriyelilerin Gözünden Bakmak: Eskişehir'de Suriyelilerin Toplumla Bütünleşme Perspektifleri Üzerine Değerlendirmeler - **Fuat Güllüpınar**
1027	Türkiye'deki Suriyeliler ve Eğitim: Gazetelerin Perspektiflerine Dayalı Bir Analiz - **Ali Faruk Yaylacı, Filiz Göktuna Yaylacı**
1365	Türkiye'de Sivil Toplum ve Göçmen Çocuğun Değeri - **Mehtap Erdoğan**

Türkiye'deki Suriyeli Çocukların Eğitimi: Güçlükler ve Öneriler

(1092) Coşkun Taştan (Ankara Yıldırım Beyazıt University), Zafer Çelik (Ankara Yıldırım Beyazıt University)

Şubat 2017 verilerine göre yaklaşık 3 milyon Suriyeli geçici koruma statüsü altında Türkiye'de yaşamaktadır. Türkiye'deki Suriyelilerin yaklaşık 1 milyonu 5-18 yaş arasındadır. Başka bir ifade ile yaklaşık 1 milyon çocuk okul çağındadır. 2011 yılından itibaren 200 binden fazla Suriyeli bebek Türkiye'de doğmuştur ve 340 bin civarında 0-4 yaş arasında çocuk bulunmaktadır. Bu veriler, oldukça geniş bir kitlenin eğitim çağında bulunduğunu ve dolayısıyla Suriyeli çocukların eğitiminin, Türkiye için büyük bir önem arz ettiğini göstermektedir. Milli Eğitim Bakanlığının verilerine göre, 2011'den bu yana ülkemizde bulunan Suriyeli mültecilerde yaklaşık 480 bin çocuk okullaşabilmiştir. Bu durum, Suriyeli çocukların en az yarısının eğitim imkânından mahrum olduğunu göstermektedir. Okullaşamamış 400 bine yakın Suriyeli çocuğun gelecekleri, kayıp bir nesil olmamaları, topluma kazandırılmaları eğitim almalarına bağlıdır. Buna ilaveten, okullaşamamış ve Türkiye toplumu ile uyum sağlayamamış Suriyeli çocukların gettolaşma ve marjinalleşme riski vardır. Türkiye, özellikle son bir yıldır Suriyeli çocukları okullaştırma konusunda yoğun bir çaba göstermektedir. Geçmişte Suriyeli çocukların ağırlıklı olarak geçici eğitim merkezlerinde öğrenim görmekteyken, artık Suriyeli çocuklar artan bir şekilde kamu okullarında öğrenim görmeye başlamıştır. Bu çalışmada, Türkiye'nin Suriyeli çocukların eğitimi konusunda yürüttüğü çalışmalar ve politikalar bu süreçte karşılaşılan güçlüklerin neler olduğu tartışılacak, daha fazla Suriyeli çocuğun okullaşması için öneriler sunulacaktır. Bu bağlamda araştırma verileri, bir yandan Milli Eğitim Bakanlığının Suriyelilere ilişkin resmi verileri ve dokümanları diğer yandan da Milli Eğitim Bakanlığı'nda Suriyeliler ile ilgilenen üst düzey yöneticiler ile Suriyelilerin çoğunlukta olduğu il yöneticileri ile yapılan görüşmeler ile elde edilecektir.

***

Suriyelilerin Eğitimine Suriyelilerin Gözünden Bakmak: Eskişehir'de Suriyelilerin Toplumla Bütünleşme Perspektifleri Üzerine Değerlendirmeler

(1057) Fuat Güllüpınar (Anadolu University)

Ülkelerindeki iç savaştan dolayı Türkiye'ye sığınan 3 milyona yakın Suriyeli için Türkiye, gerek kamplarda gerekse kamp dışında sağlanan imkânlarla önemli bir geçiş süreci fırsatı sunmuştur. Artık Suriyelilerin evine dönebileceği bir ortam tümüyle ortadan kalktığından dolayı, Türkiye acilen uzun vadeli bir çözüm ve bütünleşme stratejisini uygulamaya koymak durumundadır. Bu çalışma, Eskişehir'de yaşayan Suriyelilerin toplumla bütünleşmesinin temel araçlarından en önemlisi olan eğitim açısından acil ihtiyaçları ve uzun vadede ortaya çıkabilecek sorunları analiz etmeyi amaçlamaktadır. Suriyeli çocukların eğitiminin Türkiye'de hem müfredatın içeriği açısından hem de mevcut fiziki kapasite açısından milli eğitim sisteminin işleyişine ek yükler ve yeni düzenleme ihtiyacı yaratacağı öngörülebilir. Suriyelilerin eğitiminin, milli eğitimde çok-dilli ve çok kültürlü yeni düzenlemeler etrafında çelişkili ve tartışmalı bir gündem yaratacak görünmektedir. Suriyeli çocukların eğitime erişimlerini engelleyen faktörlerin başında çocuk işçiliği ve küçük yaşta evlendirilme gibi sorunların yanı sıra dil problemi, resmi kayıt prosedürleri vb. olgular bulunmaktadır. Suriyeli çocukların eğitime erişimlerinin önündeki kültürel, ekonomik ve toplumsal nedenler analiz edilirken toplumdaki imkânlar ve fırsatlar kadar, Suriyeli ebeveynlerin çocuklarının eğitimine yönelik kültürel eğilim ve tutumunun da analize dahil edilmesi ihtiyaç olarak görünmektedir. Bu amaçla bu çalışma kapsamında, Eskişehir'de yaşayan Suriyeli çocukların eğitimdeki temel ihtiyaçlarının ve Suriyeli mültecilerin toplumla bütünleşme konusundaki temel sorunlarının ayrıntılı bir bilançosunun çıkarılması hedefiyle Eskişehir'de Suriyeli öğrencilerin yoğunlukta olduğu bir ilköğretim okulu ve bir lisede okul yöneticileri, değişik branştan öğretmenlerin yanı sıra, Suriyeli veliler ve öğrencilerle toplam 20 adet derinlemesine mülakat yapılmıştır. Çalışmada yürütülecek saha araştırmasının verileri, konu hakkındaki raporlarla da desteklenerek, Suriyelilerin eğitim ve toplumla bütünleşme perspektifleri üzerine politika önerileri geliştirmek için kullanılacaktır.

***

Türkiye'deki Suriyeliler ve Eğitim: Gazetelerin Perspektiflerine Dayalı Bir Analiz

(1027) Ali Faruk Yaylacı (Recep Tayyip Erdoğan University), Filiz Göktuna Yaylacı (Anadolu University)

Suriye'deki iç savaşın yaratmış olduğu koşullar milyonlarca insanın komşu ülkelere göç etmesine yol açarken Türkiye de son birkaç yılda Suriye kaynaklı kitlesel sığınmacı akınlarına muhatap olmuştur. Sayıları üç milyonu aşan Suriyeliler giderek Türkiye'de daha kalıcı ve yerleşik hale gelmektedir. Suriyelilerin Türkiye'deki varlıkları çeşitli tartışmaların da konusu niteliğindedir. Toplumsal, siyasi ya da ekonomik gerekçelerin yön verdiği bu tartışmalar Suriyelilere ilişkin akademik ilgiyi de artırmıştır. Aynı zamanda Suriyelilerin medyadaki temsilleri de gerek kamuoyundaki tartışmalar gerek akademik ilgi bakımından önemli bir çalışma alanı olarak belirginleşmektedir. Medyada yer alan Suriyelilere ilişkin haberler kamuoyunu bilgilendirme ya da kamuoyundaki tartışmaları yansıtma işlevinin yanında Suriyelilere ilişkin algıları etkileyerek biçimlendirebilmektedir. Suriyelilerin Türkiye'deki yaşadıkları ya da yol açtıkları sorunlar ve bu sorunların çözümü için geliştirilen politika ve uygulamaların başarısı açısından güçlü bir kamuoyu desteği önem taşımaktadır. Söz konusu desteğin sağlanmasında gazetelerde yer alan haberlerin ve haberleştirme tarzlarının ciddi bir etkisi olacağı söylenebilir. Suriyelerin yaşadıkları sorunlar ve Türkiye toplumu ile karşılıklı etkileşimleri ve uyum süreçleri bakımından en önemli alanlardan birisinin de eğitim olduğu açıktır. Zorunlu göçün yol açtığı kitlesel sığınmacı hareketlerinin ardından barınma, beslenme ve güvenlik gibi temel ve acil ihtiyaçların giderilmesi yaşamsal öneme sahiptir. Bununla birlikte yerinden edilmiş sığınmacıların belirsiz gelecek algıları, uyum sorunları ve göçün yol açtığı travmaların aşılması sürecinde eğitim hizmetlerinin önemli katkılar sağlayacağı alanyazında sıklıkla vurgulanmaktadır. Türkiye'de bulunan Suriyelilere ve özellikle çocuklara yönelik çeşitli eğitim hizmetleri yürütülmektedir. Milli Eğitim Bakanlığı Suriyelilerin eğitim sorunlarını çözmek üzere çeşitli uygulamalar geliştirmiştir. Kamplarda yaşayan çocukların bu hizmetlerden daha yüksek düzeyde yararlandığı bilinmektedir. 15 bine yakın Suriyeli yükseköğrenim görürken 500 bine yakın Suriyeli çocuk da eğitim görmektedir bu bağlamda son yıllarda Suriyelilere ve onların eğitim sorunlarına ilişkin çalışmalar artış göstermiştir. Ancak Suriyelilerin eğitim sorunlarının ve Türkiye'de sunulan eğitim hizmetlerinin medyadaki yansımaları konusunda araştırmaların eksikliği söz konusudur. Bu doğrultuda bu çalışmanın Suriyeliler ve eğitim konusunu gazete haberleri temelinde tartışılması açısından alana ve politika belirleyicilere katkı sağlayacağı düşünülebilir. Nitel bir çalışma olarak desenlenen bu araştırmanın temel amacı Suriyeliler ve eğitim bağlamında incelenecek gazetelerin temel perspektiflerini belirlemek ve bu doğrultuda haberleri irdeleyerek genel bir değerlendirme yapabilmektir. Ulusal gazetelerde yayınlanan Suriyeliler ve eğitim konulu haberler inceleme kapsamına alınmış, haberlerin incelenmesinde içerik analizi ve eleştirel söylem analizinden yararlanılmıştır.

***

Türkiye'de Sivil Toplum ve Göçmen Çocuğun Değeri
(1365) Mehtap Erdoğan (Karadeniz Technical University)

Göçmen çocuk birilerine bağımlı olarak yaşayan, kendi hak ve özgürlüklerinin tam bilgisine sahip olmayan ve dolayısıyla bunları kullanamayan gruplardır. Hem çocuk hem de göçmen olmaları onların dezavantajlı durumunu derinleştirmektedir. Eğitim, dil, din, beslenme, sosyalleşememe, yasal statü, aile içi şiddet gibi konular Türkiye'de sayısı 1,5 milyonu bulan refakatli veya refakatsiz çocuk problemlerinden sadece birkaçıdır. Onların ekonomik, psikolojik ve toplumsal, sağlık ve eğitim dâhil ihtiyaçlarını karşılayabilmek için sivil toplum kuruluşlarına daha fazla rol düşmektedir. Sivil toplum ise bilgisi ve kapasitesi dâhilinde devlet sektörü ve özel sektör yanında üçüncü bir sektör olarak faaliyet göstermektedir. Sivil toplumların, göçmen çocuklara yükledikleri değerler, aile ve toplum içinde çocuğun yeri ve rolüne bir anlayış sağlaması, ayrıca insan gelişimine ışık tutması bakımından önemlidir. Bu araştırma, Türkiye'de göçmen çocuklar üzerine çalışmalar yürüten sivil toplum örgütlerinin çocuğa yükledikleri ekonomik, sosyal ve psikolojik değeri ölçme amaçlamaktadır. Göçmen çocuk ile ilgili çalışmalar yürüten sivil toplum kuruluşlarının mevcut potansiyellerinin tespiti ile bugüne kadar yapılan ve yapılması planlanan çalışmaların öğrenilmesi göçmen çocuğun sivil toplum bazında değeri hakkında tespitlerde bulunma imkânı sağlayacaktır. Araştırmada temelde, göçmen çocuk ile ilgili çalışma yapanların vakıf ve dernek ile gerçekleştirilecek alan araştırmasına dayanmaktadır. Bu kapsamda Dernekler Bilgi Sistemi (DERBİS)'e ve Entegre Vakıf Otomasyon Sistemi (EVOS)'a kayıtlı dernek ve vâkıfa anket uygulanacaktır. Ayrıca bu dernek ve vakıflardan ulusal ve/veya uluslararası destekle göçmen çocuk ile daha önce proje yürütmüş veya yürütmekte olan 20 sivil toplum kuruluşlarla derinlemesine mülakat gerçekleştirilecektir.

Araştırma sonunda elde edilen veriler bu çalışmayı yapan araştırmacının doktora tezinin geliştirilmesinde kullanılacaktır.

Author Index

272

274

www.migrationcenter.org
www.gocdergisi.com
www.migrationletters.com
www.tplondon.com/bordercrossing
www.tplondon.com/rem
www.tplondon.com/jgs
www.tplondon.com
www.turkishmigration.com

www.ingramcontent.com/pod-product-compliance
Lightning Source LLC
Chambersburg PA
CBHW071845270326
41929CB00013B/2104